Thieves & Kings
Volume One

Thieves and Kings: Volume One
Copyright © 2015 One Peace Books, Inc.
Individual issues first published by I Box Publishing in 1996

ISBN 13: 978-1-935548-97-3

Corrections to this work should be forwarded to the publisher for consideration upon the next printing.

Cover design by Tsukuru Anderson

One Peace Books
43-32 22nd Street #204 Long Island City, NY 11101 USA
http://www.onepeacebooks.com

Printed in China
1234546789

Mark Oakley

Thieves & Kings

Volume One

Introduction...

Never Never Land is a real place. I used to live there.

Well, I *lived* in Toronto. *Never Never Land* was in my backyard.

You could walk into it, completely leave the real world, experience adventure and derring-do, move invisibly across space and time and exit -this is the best part- to appear anywhere in the whole city. For real. It was great! You could probably work it into a bank heist plan if you wanted, though I never did. Money isn't terribly important in *Never Never Land*.

I didn't call it *Never Never Land*, of course. That's a childish name. Not that childish is a bad thing. Not a bit! After all, *Thieves & Kings* is mostly about being a kid. But *Never Never Land* is for those children who aren't quite old enough to read on their own just yet (Peter Pan could read a bit, I believe, but he would probably have found this book slow going). My version of *Never Never Land* was for kids a little older. Not much, but enough.

I was once a boy who once stood at the bottom of a wild ravine. A ravine is like a small valley, maybe about as deep as a tall house and filled with trees and bushes and such. This particular ravine was ripe with cricket song and peaty smells in the shade. Running shoes got muddy and burrs lit into socks, gnarled there to be discovered upon return. All right in the middle of a sprawling suburban metropolis. Glaciers had milled the land long ago with their blue ice tonnage and left a sprawling network of wrinkles in the terrain. Dutiful cartographers recorded all of this, filling maps with thousands of veiny lines, cross-sections of a giant's lungs. But who looks at such maps today? Property developers and serious people, perhaps.

The significance has been lost.

Each miniature valley had a little stream or creak at the bottom, or sometimes just a muddy crease in the shallower examples, but if you followed any of them they would lead one to the next, finally opening into enormous V-shaped gorges with Big Rivers that sometimes drowned careless explorers. Hundreds of these ravines criss-crossed the city! Houses and streets and city things were built on the high ground between them.

So you see, you could splash and traipse and bushwhack your way through the ravine system clear across civilization without once being spotted topside; a commuter system of root and stone. Hulks of half-digested shopping carts and other unlucky pieces swallowed whole from the world above quietly moldered along the path, consumed by vines and bracken. This other world was superimposed upon our clattering modern one (or rather, the other way around), its mysterious negative spaces in contrast to the hard corners of technology and cement. Its entrances dark and thorny, beckoned from the far end of ten thousand back yards.

Rear ends of houses squatted in rows along the edges of these natural trenches, backs turned, preferring instead to gaze at neighborhood streets and family cars and ordered civic planning. The world above was made of tidy squares of mowed lawn, of road hockey and banana seat-peddle-backwards-to-brake bicycles, and yellow pencils and pocket change lost on sidewalks outside grade school playgrounds. That was the real world; with swimming pools and barbecues. It wasn't a bad world to grow up in.

But that Other world... it skulked at the bottom of public parks, behind shopping malls, forcibly bridged over and walled off by the city's custodians—and guarded in kind behind brambles and fans of rag weed by that Something Else. Always present. Cloaked in shade. Patient.

The Summers were libraries and model rocket clubs and 8-bit video games in basements. They were music videos and subway rides to the comic store and movie theaters. Commercial treasures delighted in at the corner shops. There were potato chips by the bag puffed in brights salts to make your mouth run wet, slushies made from cola drinks, and trading cards packaged with pink planks of chewing gum, even French fries boiled in lard. When school let out there was a world sparkling with the wonders of civilization. But also, without fail...

That Old World from the age of glaciers would put out its call, throaty and deep and moist, summoning for fealty, inhaling deep in the thick of the hot season. And the children would be overcome with a certain mood, ducking some undefined guilt, unspoken rules warily ignored. Drawn by ones and twos, sometimes in whole pirate gangs, away from bicycles and street games, they cut across private property to descend into the wild, to become savages and explorers. Twisting ankles and bleeding from thorns, yes, but also to yell and hide and throw stones and splash and breathe hard in exertion and triumph. Eyes sharp, fingers raw, fitting easily among the trees and stones and moss. The Lost Boys were never lost. They knew exactly where they were, *what* they were. In their hearts they did, feeling it. Words and distinct definitions were for the world above, not *this* place. A different knowledge stirs far down within; and if you pay attention, you *know*.

And so there are two provinces of human existence—always have been. In Toronto, they just happen to be plainly divided, almost too obviously for a serious reality (you can see the borders; the fourth wall is right there!), one always a mere sidestep from the other. Trip, and you're gone. Except nobody enters by accident. You have to *choose*. You have to pay *attention*. Rarely discussed, often ignored or forgotten, but *there*, a reclining giant, it's body the whole crust and root of the land, murmuring and seeping with rot and life. Supplying a kind of food, the sort we grow pale without, calling those who step sideways and enter to remember themselves; to remember the Old from which we all emerged.

Phew! Can you imagine? Growing up with all *that* in your backyard? Trying to sleep with *that* breathing just beyond the window?

Thieves & Kings came from that place. You will recognize it instantly, those of you who came marching home with mud and scratches when you were small. This whole book is made of it! When a certain mood came blowing for me again, I found myself laughing, "Me? I am far too grown up to climb the neighborhood fences and hurl stones, you foolish thing! But watch me now! You call when I am no longer a pirate and a thief? Ha! Today I have a pencil, and you will see!"

I hope you enjoy the story.

Mark Oakley,
Wolfville, 2015

Chapter 1

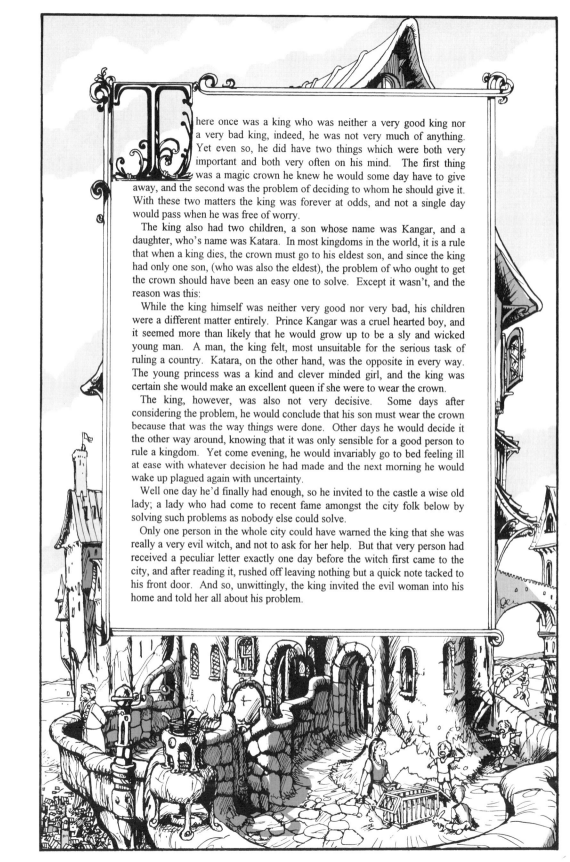

here once was a king who was neither a very good king nor a very bad king, indeed, he was not very much of anything. Yet even so, he did have two things which were both very important and both very often on his mind. The first thing was a magic crown he knew he would some day have to give away, and the second was the problem of deciding to whom he should give it. With these two matters the king was forever at odds, and not a single day would pass when he was free of worry.

The king also had two children, a son whose name was Kangar, and a daughter, who's name was Katara. In most kingdoms in the world, it is a rule that when a king dies, the crown must go to his eldest son, and since the king had only one son, (who was also the eldest), the problem of who ought to get the crown should have been an easy one to solve. Except it wasn't, and the reason was this:

While the king himself was neither very good nor very bad, his children were a different matter entirely. Prince Kangar was a cruel hearted boy, and it seemed more than likely that he would grow up to be a sly and wicked young man. A man, the king felt, most unsuitable for the serious task of ruling a country. Katara, on the other hand, was the opposite in every way. The young princess was a kind and clever minded girl, and the king was certain she would make an excellent queen if she were to wear the crown.

The king, however, was also not very decisive. Some days after considering the problem, he would conclude that his son must wear the crown because that was the way things were done. Other days he would decide it the other way around, knowing that it was only sensible for a good person to rule a kingdom. Yet come evening, he would invariably go to bed feeling ill at ease with whatever decision he had made and the next morning he would wake up plagued again with uncertainty.

Well one day he'd finally had enough, so he invited to the castle a wise old lady; a lady who had come to recent fame amongst the city folk below by solving such problems as nobody else could solve.

Only one person in the whole city could have warned the king that she was really a very evil witch, and not to ask for her help. But that very person had received a peculiar letter exactly one day before the witch first came to the city, and after reading it, rushed off leaving nothing but a quick note tacked to his front door. And so, unwittingly, the king invited the evil woman into his home and told her all about his problem.

The witch listened to him very carefully, clucking her tongue and saying things which made her sound sympathetic and wise. Once the king had finished with his tale, the witch nodded in thought and then told him what she thought he ought to do. The king's face lit up; the things she told him seemed very wise indeed. He thanked her grandly and immediately set out to follow the advice he had been given.

As soon as it was dark, the king stole off into the woods with the crown tucked beneath his cloak, and there in the forest, he hid it in a place where it would be difficult to find. What he did not know, however, was that the witch had followed him to see where that hiding place would be, for she meant to come back the next day and take it for herself.

What the *witch* did not know, however, was that wicked young Kangar, had crept up to the key hole to hear all the things she and his father spoke that afternoon, and he had guessed what she was up to. So when the witch secretly followed the king into the woods, the wicked young prince secretly followed the witch. After his father had hidden the crown and gone off back home, and after the witch had seen where he had hidden it and crept away as well, prince Kangar took the crown and put it in a different place entirely so that only *he* would know where it was. Then he went back home as well, feeling very wicked and very clever indeed!

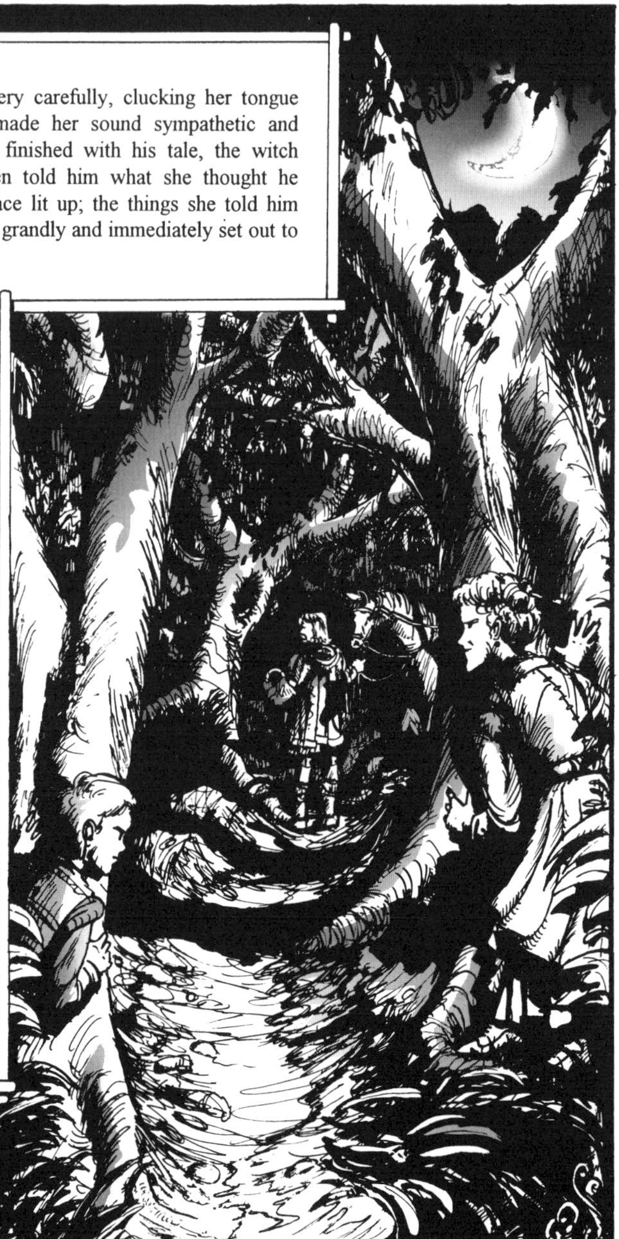

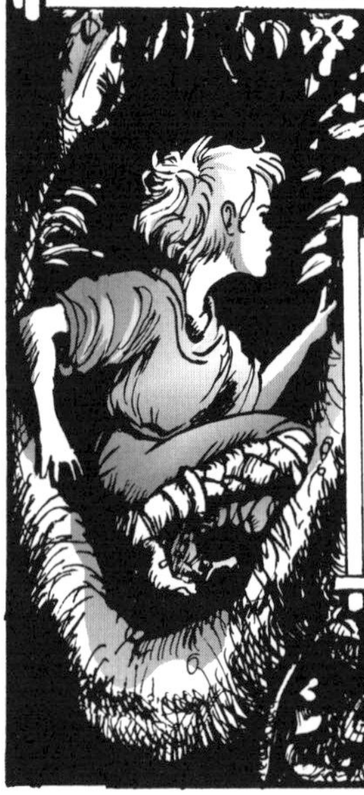

What *none* of them knew, however, was that a young thief, being rather surprised to see so many people creeping about in the woods, had decided to follow along as well. When he saw that a golden crown was the cause of all the fuss, he too became interested. And so, after the young prince had gone off back home, the thief took up the crown from where it had been hidden and skipped away with a whistle, singing, "Oh what a find I've found!"

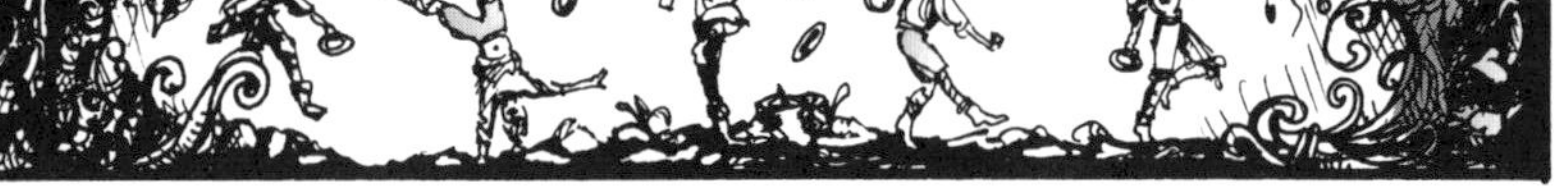

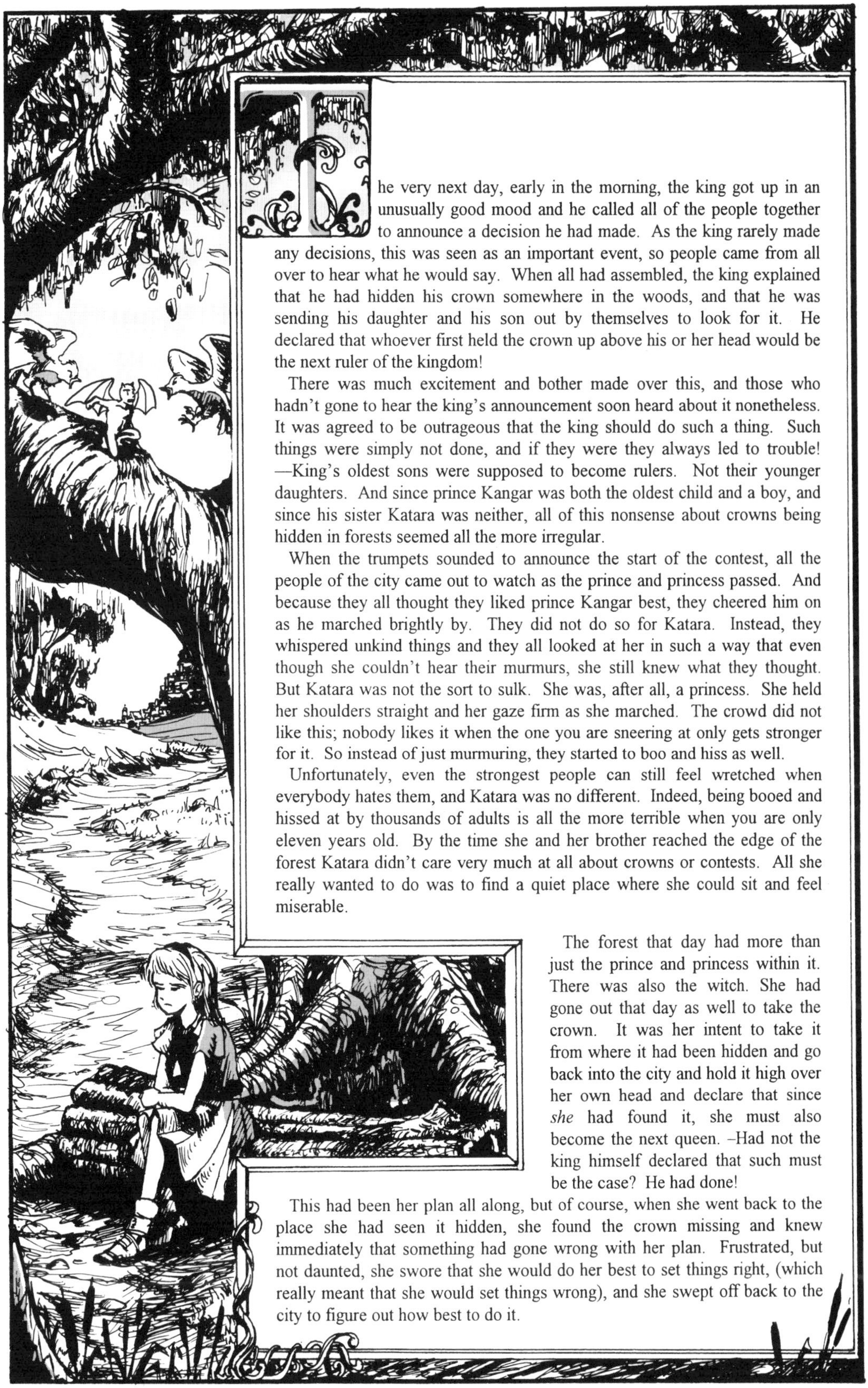

The very next day, early in the morning, the king got up in an unusually good mood and he called all of the people together to announce a decision he had made. As the king rarely made any decisions, this was seen as an important event, so people came from all over to hear what he would say. When all had assembled, the king explained that he had hidden his crown somewhere in the woods, and that he was sending his daughter and his son out by themselves to look for it. He declared that whoever first held the crown up above his or her head would be the next ruler of the kingdom!

There was much excitement and bother made over this, and those who hadn't gone to hear the king's announcement soon heard about it nonetheless. It was agreed to be outrageous that the king should do such a thing. Such things were simply not done, and if they were they always led to trouble! —King's oldest sons were supposed to become rulers. Not their younger daughters. And since prince Kangar was both the oldest child and a boy, and since his sister Katara was neither, all of this nonsense about crowns being hidden in forests seemed all the more irregular.

When the trumpets sounded to announce the start of the contest, all the people of the city came out to watch as the prince and princess passed. And because they all thought they liked prince Kangar best, they cheered him on as he marched brightly by. They did not do so for Katara. Instead, they whispered unkind things and they all looked at her in such a way that even though she couldn't hear their murmurs, she still knew what they thought. But Katara was not the sort to sulk. She was, after all, a princess. She held her shoulders straight and her gaze firm as she marched. The crowd did not like this; nobody likes it when the one you are sneering at only gets stronger for it. So instead of just murmuring, they started to boo and hiss as well.

Unfortunately, even the strongest people can still feel wretched when everybody hates them, and Katara was no different. Indeed, being booed and hissed at by thousands of adults is all the more terrible when you are only eleven years old. By the time she and her brother reached the edge of the forest Katara didn't care very much at all about crowns or contests. All she really wanted to do was to find a quiet place where she could sit and feel miserable.

The forest that day had more than just the prince and princess within it. There was also the witch. She had gone out that day as well to take the crown. It was her intent to take it from where it had been hidden and go back into the city and hold it high over her own head and declare that since *she* had found it, she must also become the next queen. –Had not the king himself declared that such must be the case? He had done!

This had been her plan all along, but of course, when she went back to the place she had seen it hidden, she found the crown missing and knew immediately that something had gone wrong with her plan. Frustrated, but not daunted, she swore that she would do her best to set things right, (which really meant that she would set things wrong), and she swept off back to the city to figure out how best to do it.

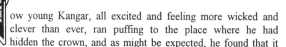

ow young Kangar, all excited and feeling more wicked and clever than ever, ran puffing to the place where he had hidden the crown, and as might be expected, he found that it was missing as well. When he discovered this he flew into a worry, and then into a panic! All about he searched, looking here and there, digging under leaves and poking into holes and thinking all the while that he had made some mistake in the dark. –That he had hidden the crown in a place which had looked differently by the moon's light, but of course, this was not the case, for the crown was in the young thief's sack!

And that very thief was also in the forest that day. After discovering the crown the previous evening he had not gone home, but instead had skipped on through the night, whistling and singing and feeling very pleased with himself. And because he'd been in the forest all night, he had heard nothing of the all commotion in the city. It was, however, getting late in the morning, which often for a thief was the same as getting late at night, so he was heading now back to the city to sleep. It was only natural that he should meet the princess who was still sitting at the forest's mouth. This surprised him. Princesses were hardly ever to be found outside the city, and if they were, then never all alone, without even so much as a single horse or servant.

With his curiosity piqued, he stepped from the trees and asked her what she was all about, which was a very bold thing for him to do. People are supposed to kneel before princesses, or at least lower their heads in respect, neither of which he did. Worse still, common folk are never supposed to speak to royalty unless they are spoken to first. Thieves, however, do not have to worry about things like that, and so he didn't.

But Katara saw that his eyes were kind, and since she was feeling lonely for kindness, she told him all about what had happened to her; about how the crown was hidden in the forest, and how she and her brother had been sent to find it. She told him also, (with narrowed eyes), that she had a very strong feeling that her brother was somehow cheating. –Except it didn't really matter, because nobody wanted her to find the crown anyway. Nobody liked *her* very much.

The young thief's heart was wrung by her words, and he was so happy to have the chance to do a good deed for a princess that he immediately took the crown from his sack and held it up high into the sunlight for her to see. She gasped when she saw it, and he bowed deeply and laid it at her feet.

Katara gasped, partly from the surprise of seeing the crown, but mainly because she saw that he was the first to hold it up above his head, and knew by her father's own words that this boy must now become the next king. But when she explained this to him, he only laughed. –Who had ever heard of a thief becoming a king? And why should he want such a thing when everything in the world was already his to take?

Why indeed? Still, Katara knew that there was no getting around it. Such matters involving king's decisions and royal crowns were not to be taken lightly. And since they both felt that Katara's father, (as well as all the people), would be most perplexed to discover that the crown was to go to somebody who wasn't even related to the royal family, the princess and the thief both sat down in thought.

As Katara was a clever girl, and as a good thief is never short of a good idea, between them a solution was quickly found. With the thief's knife, Katara cut forth from her tresses a lock of strawberry hair, and upon it the thief swore himself to her in all matters great and small using the very strongest oaths he knew. And Katara, thinking it only fair, swore that he would have all her blessings with which to face all the perils he should ever come to meet.

Once done with that, the thief pressed the crown into her hands, and he told her that because he was sworn to her, 'Now, Before and Forever more,' that he had found the crown for her and not for himself at all. He declared that a thief's oath was stronger than any king's decision, and he swore that no king would ever make him wear a crown or sit on any throne, no matter what royal decisions might have been made. (Though they both agreed it would probably be best if Katara didn't tell her father, just in case).

So then they parted, each well pleased. The thief now had a princess and a lock of pretty hair, and Katara had a thief's oath and the crown's warm metal firmly in her hands. With it, she marched back into the city, her eyes flashing and her chin held high before all the people who caught their breathes as she stepped up before her father.

The king was overjoyed, and he kissed his daughter upon her forehead and told her quietly that he was *very* pleased, which was something for a man who had never been very much of anything. The people, however, were outraged and they all felt as though they had been greatly wronged in some way, and they complained and griped all the way back to their homes and they swore that this was but the beginning of all the troubles doomed to come.

And they were right.

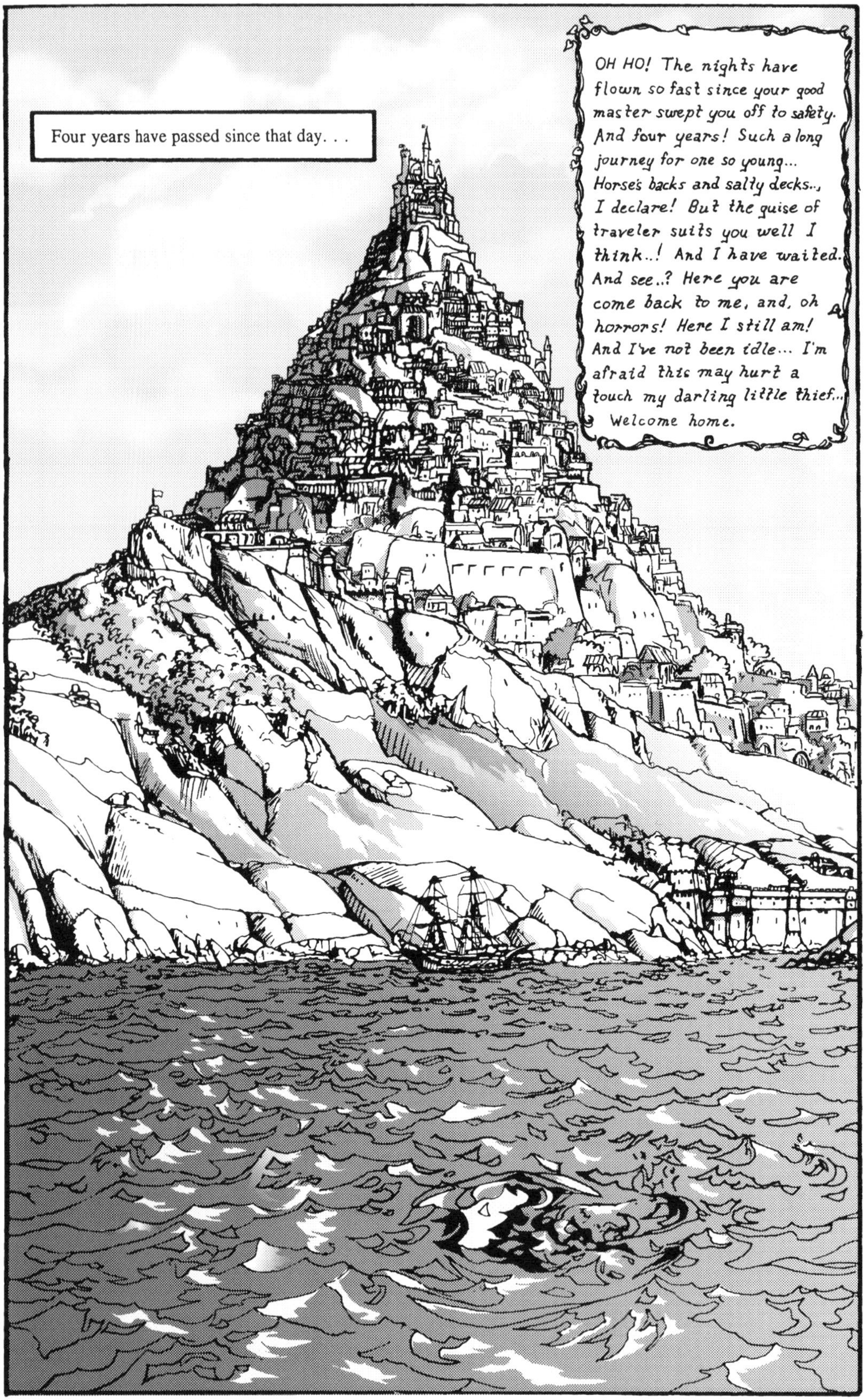
Four years have passed since that day. . .
OH HO! The nights have flown so fast since your good master swept you off to safety. And four years! Such a long journey for one so young... Horse's backs and salty decks.., I declare! But the guise of traveler suits you well I think..! And I have waited. And see..? Here you are come back to me, and, oh horrors! Here I still am! And I've not been idle... I'm afraid this may hurt a touch my darling little thief... Welcome home.

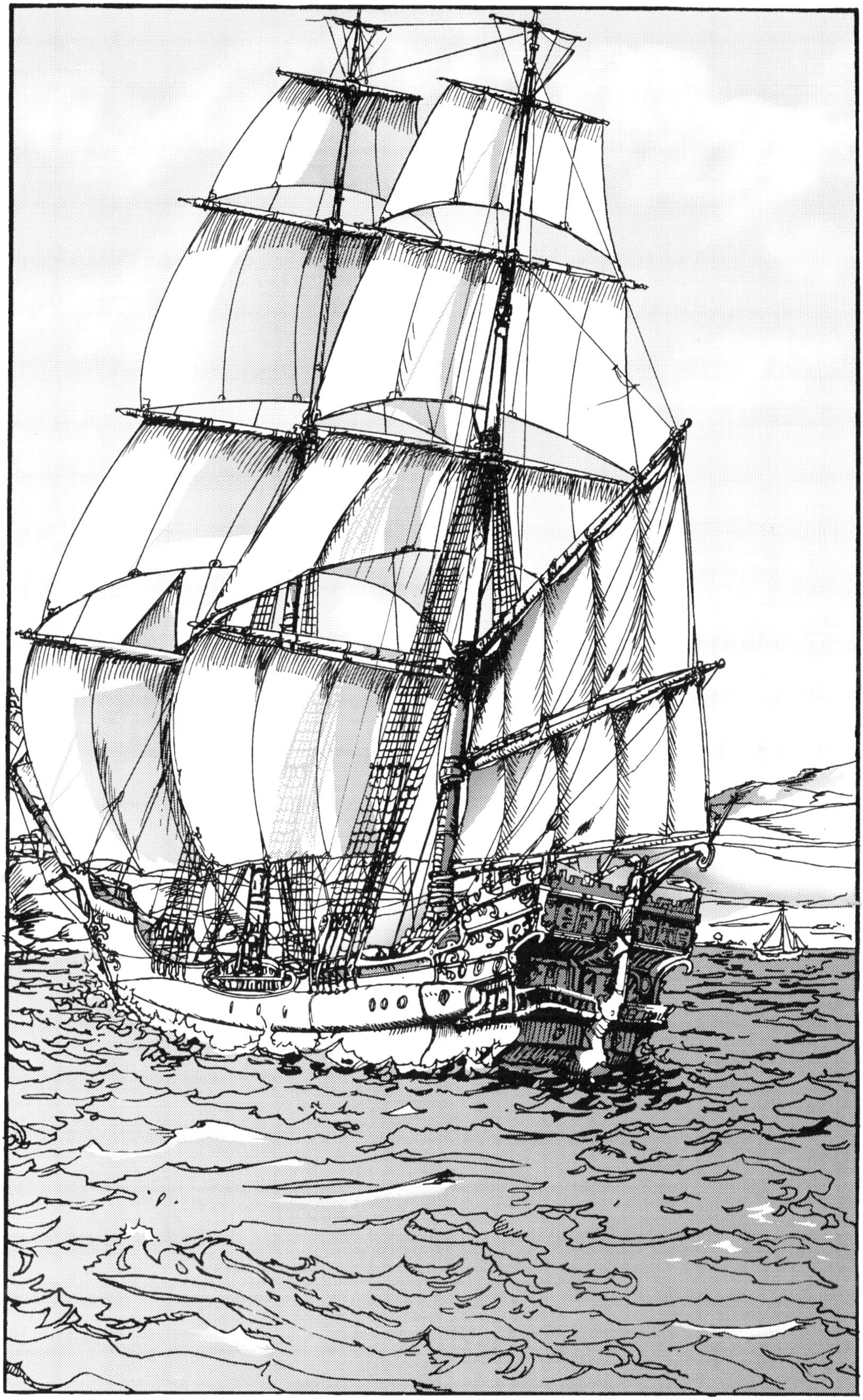

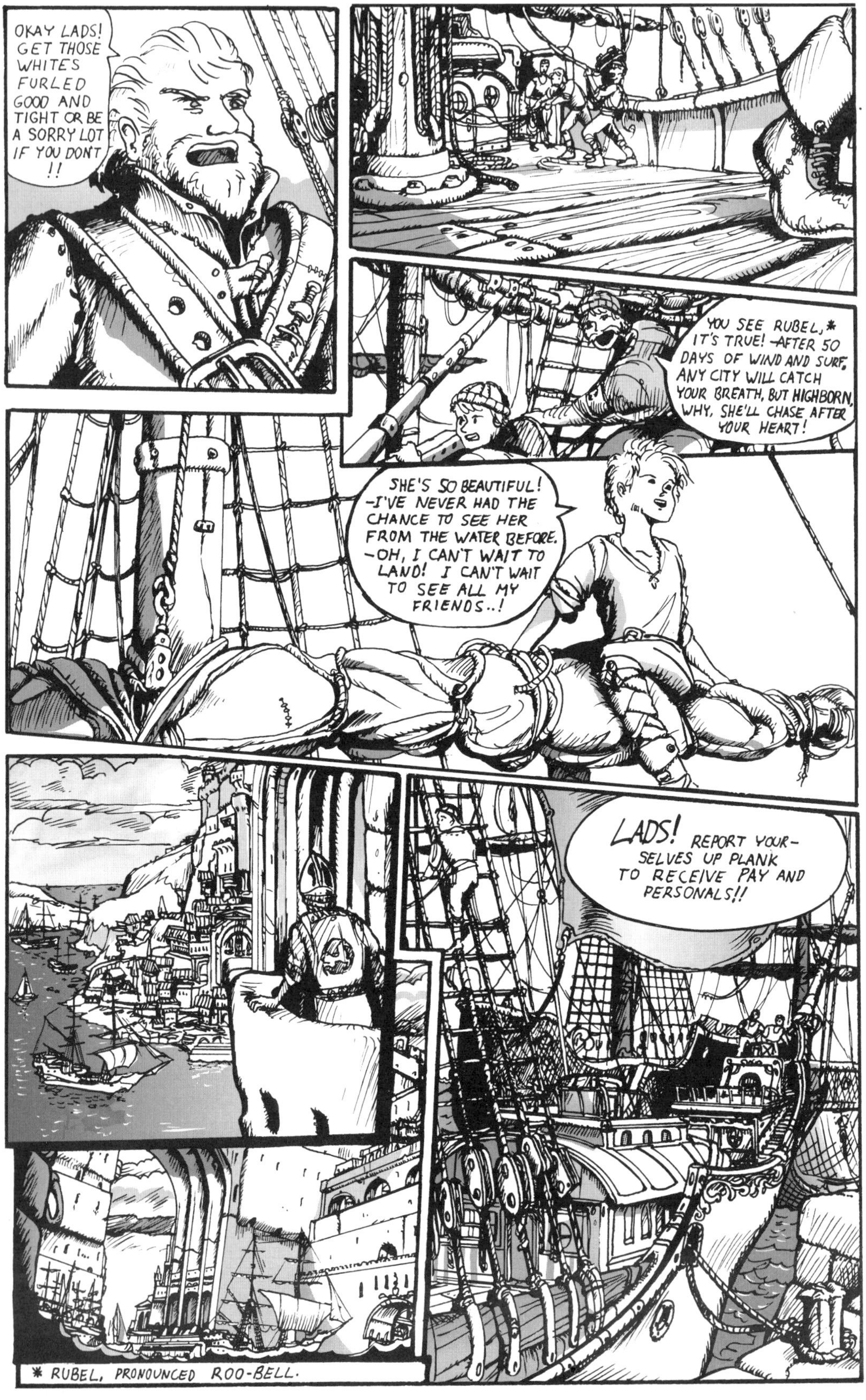
OKAY LADS! GET THOSE WHITES FURLED GOOD AND TIGHT OR BE A SORRY LOT IF YOU DON'T!!
YOU SEE RUBEL,* IT'S TRUE! -AFTER 50 DAYS OF WIND AND SURF, ANY CITY WILL CATCH YOUR BREATH, BUT HIGHBORN, WHY, SHE'LL CHASE AFTER YOUR HEART!
SHE'S SO BEAUTIFUL! -I'VE NEVER HAD THE CHANCE TO SEE HER FROM THE WATER BEFORE. -OH, I CAN'T WAIT TO LAND! I CAN'T WAIT TO SEE ALL MY FRIENDS..!
LADS! REPORT YOURSELVES UP PLANK TO RECEIVE PAY AND PERSONALS!!
* RUBEL, PRONOUNCED ROO-BELL.

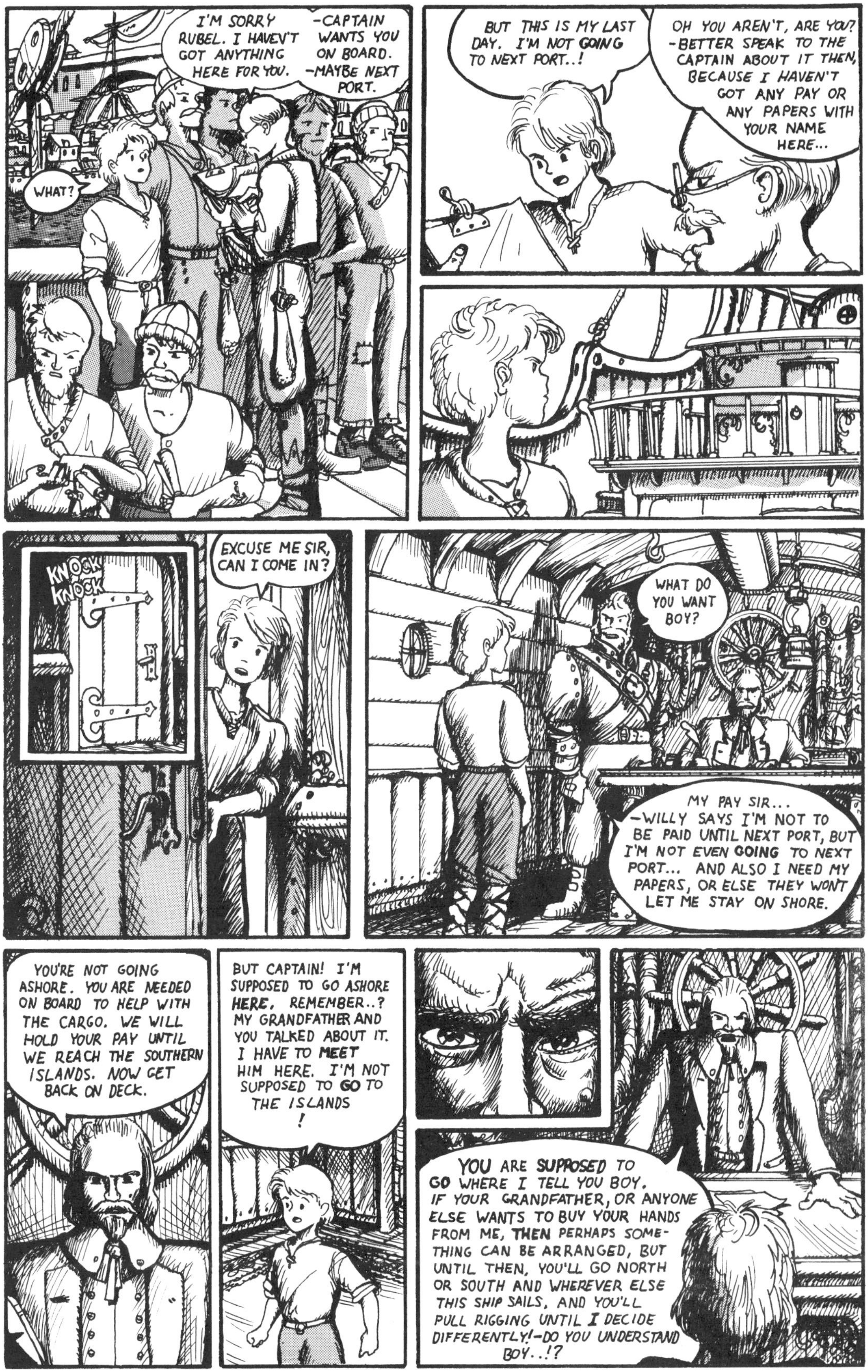
I'M SORRY RUBEL. I HAVEN'T GOT ANYTHING HERE FOR YOU.
-CAPTAIN WANTS YOU ON BOARD. -MAYBE NEXT PORT.
WHAT?
BUT THIS IS MY LAST DAY. I'M NOT GOING TO NEXT PORT..!
OH YOU AREN'T, ARE YOU? -BETTER SPEAK TO THE CAPTAIN ABOUT IT THEN, BECAUSE I HAVEN'T GOT ANY PAY OR ANY PAPERS WITH YOUR NAME HERE...
KNOCK KNOCK
EXCUSE ME SIR, CAN I COME IN?
WHAT DO YOU WANT BOY?
MY PAY SIR... -WILLY SAYS I'M NOT TO BE PAID UNTIL NEXT PORT, BUT I'M NOT EVEN GOING TO NEXT PORT... AND ALSO I NEED MY PAPERS, OR ELSE THEY WONT LET ME STAY ON SHORE.
YOU'RE NOT GOING ASHORE. YOU ARE NEEDED ON BOARD TO HELP WITH THE CARGO. WE WILL HOLD YOUR PAY UNTIL WE REACH THE SOUTHERN ISLANDS. NOW GET BACK ON DECK.
BUT CAPTAIN! I'M SUPPOSED TO GO ASHORE HERE, REMEMBER..? MY GRANDFATHER AND YOU TALKED ABOUT IT. I HAVE TO MEET HIM HERE. I'M NOT SUPPOSED TO GO TO THE ISLANDS !
YOU ARE SUPPOSED TO GO WHERE I TELL YOU BOY. IF YOUR GRANDFATHER, OR ANYONE ELSE WANTS TO BUY YOUR HANDS FROM ME, THEN PERHAPS SOMETHING CAN BE ARRANGED, BUT UNTIL THEN, YOU'LL GO NORTH OR SOUTH AND WHEREVER ELSE THIS SHIP SAILS, AND YOU'LL PULL RIGGING UNTIL I DECIDE DIFFERENTLY!-DO YOU UNDERSTAND BOY..!?

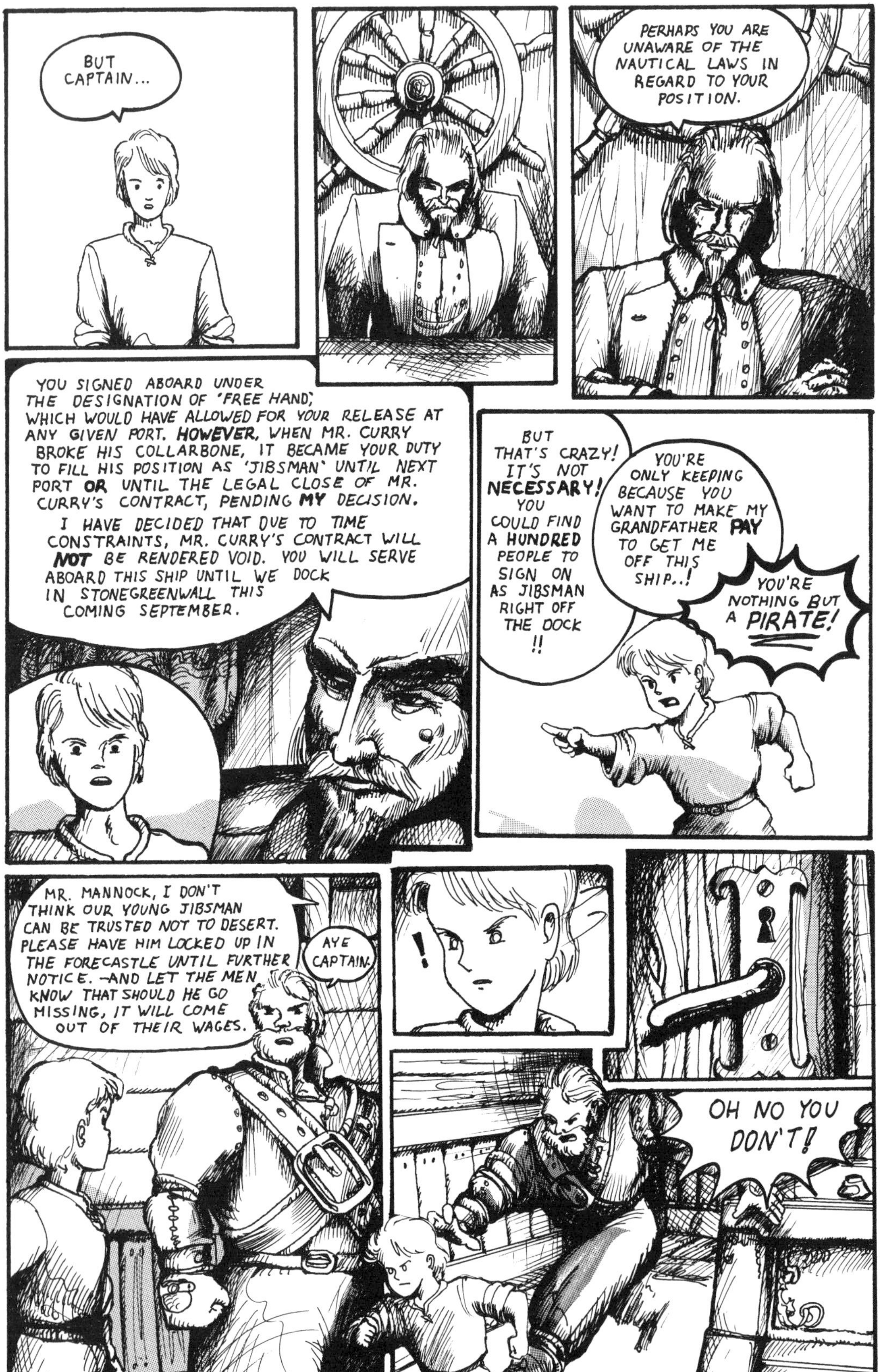
BUT CAPTAIN...
PERHAPS YOU ARE UNAWARE OF THE NAUTICAL LAWS IN REGARD TO YOUR POSITION.
YOU SIGNED ABOARD UNDER THE DESIGNATION OF 'FREE HAND', WHICH WOULD HAVE ALLOWED FOR YOUR RELEASE AT ANY GIVEN PORT. HOWEVER, WHEN MR. CURRY BROKE HIS COLLARBONE, IT BECAME YOUR DUTY TO FILL HIS POSITION AS 'JIBSMAN' UNTIL NEXT PORT OR UNTIL THE LEGAL CLOSE OF MR. CURRY'S CONTRACT, PENDING MY DECISION.
I HAVE DECIDED THAT DUE TO TIME CONSTRAINTS, MR. CURRY'S CONTRACT WILL NOT BE RENDERED VOID. YOU WILL SERVE ABOARD THIS SHIP UNTIL WE DOCK IN STONEGREENWALL THIS COMING SEPTEMBER.
BUT THAT'S CRAZY! IT'S NOT NECESSARY! YOU COULD FIND A HUNDRED PEOPLE TO SIGN ON AS JIBSMAN RIGHT OFF THE DOCK !!
YOU'RE ONLY KEEPING BECAUSE YOU WANT TO MAKE MY GRANDFATHER PAY TO GET ME OFF THIS SHIP..!
YOU'RE NOTHING BUT A PIRATE!
MR. MANNOCK, I DON'T THINK OUR YOUNG JIBSMAN CAN BE TRUSTED NOT TO DESERT. PLEASE HAVE HIM LOCKED UP IN THE FORECASTLE UNTIL FURTHER NOTICE. —AND LET THE MEN KNOW THAT SHOULD HE GO MISSING, IT WILL COME OUT OF THEIR WAGES.
AYE CAPTAIN.
!
OH NO YOU DON'T!

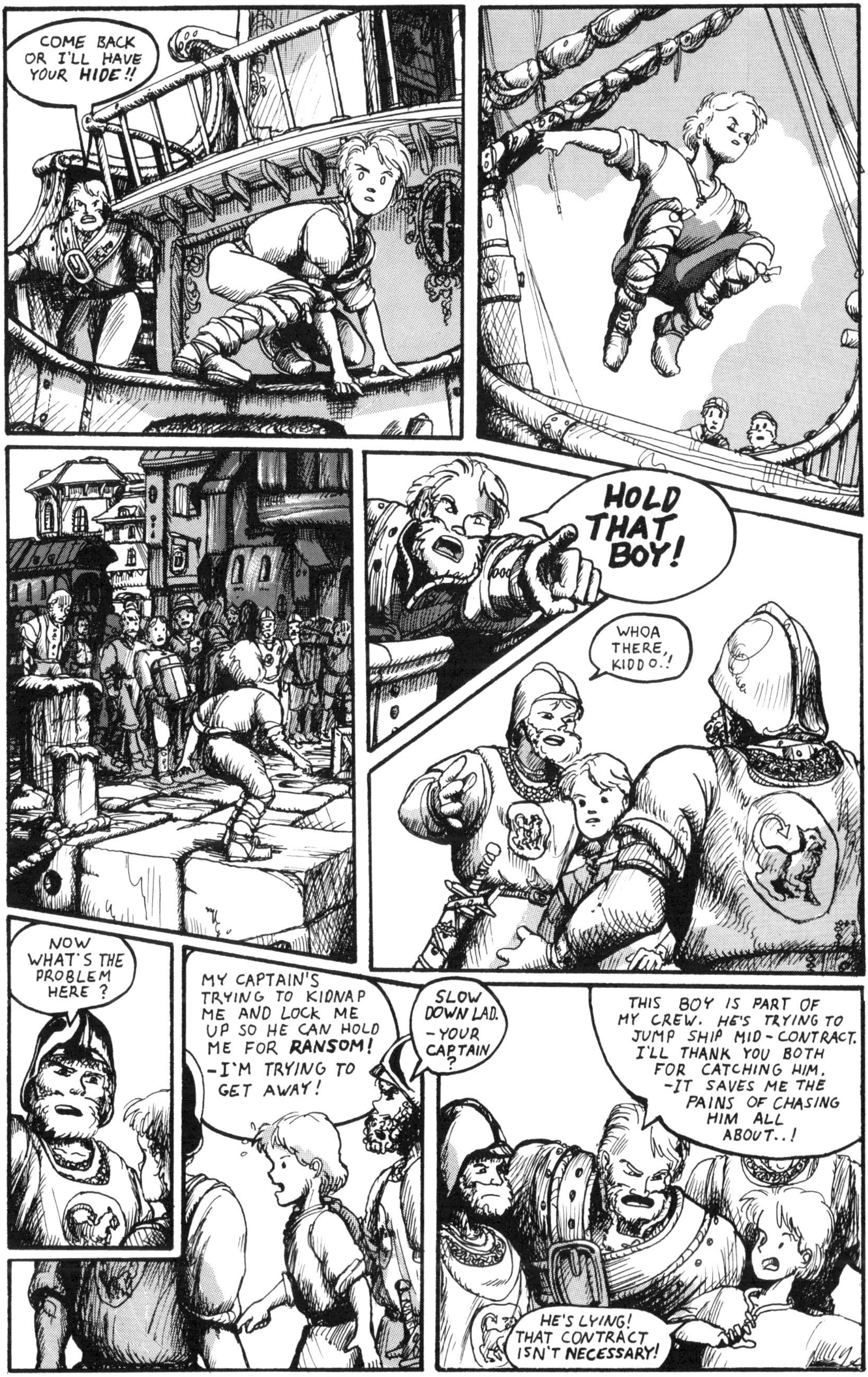
COME BACK OR I'LL HAVE YOUR HIDE!!
HOLD THAT BOY!
WHOA THERE, KIDDO..!
NOW WHAT'S THE PROBLEM HERE?
MY CAPTAIN'S TRYING TO KIDNAP ME AND LOCK ME UP SO HE CAN HOLD ME FOR RANSOM! -I'M TRYING TO GET AWAY!
SLOW DOWN LAD. -YOUR CAPTAIN?
THIS BOY IS PART OF MY CREW. HE'S TRYING TO JUMP SHIP MID-CONTRACT. I'LL THANK YOU BOTH FOR CATCHING HIM. -IT SAVES ME THE PAINS OF CHASING HIM ALL ABOUT..!
HE'S LYING! THAT CONTRACT ISN'T NECESSARY!

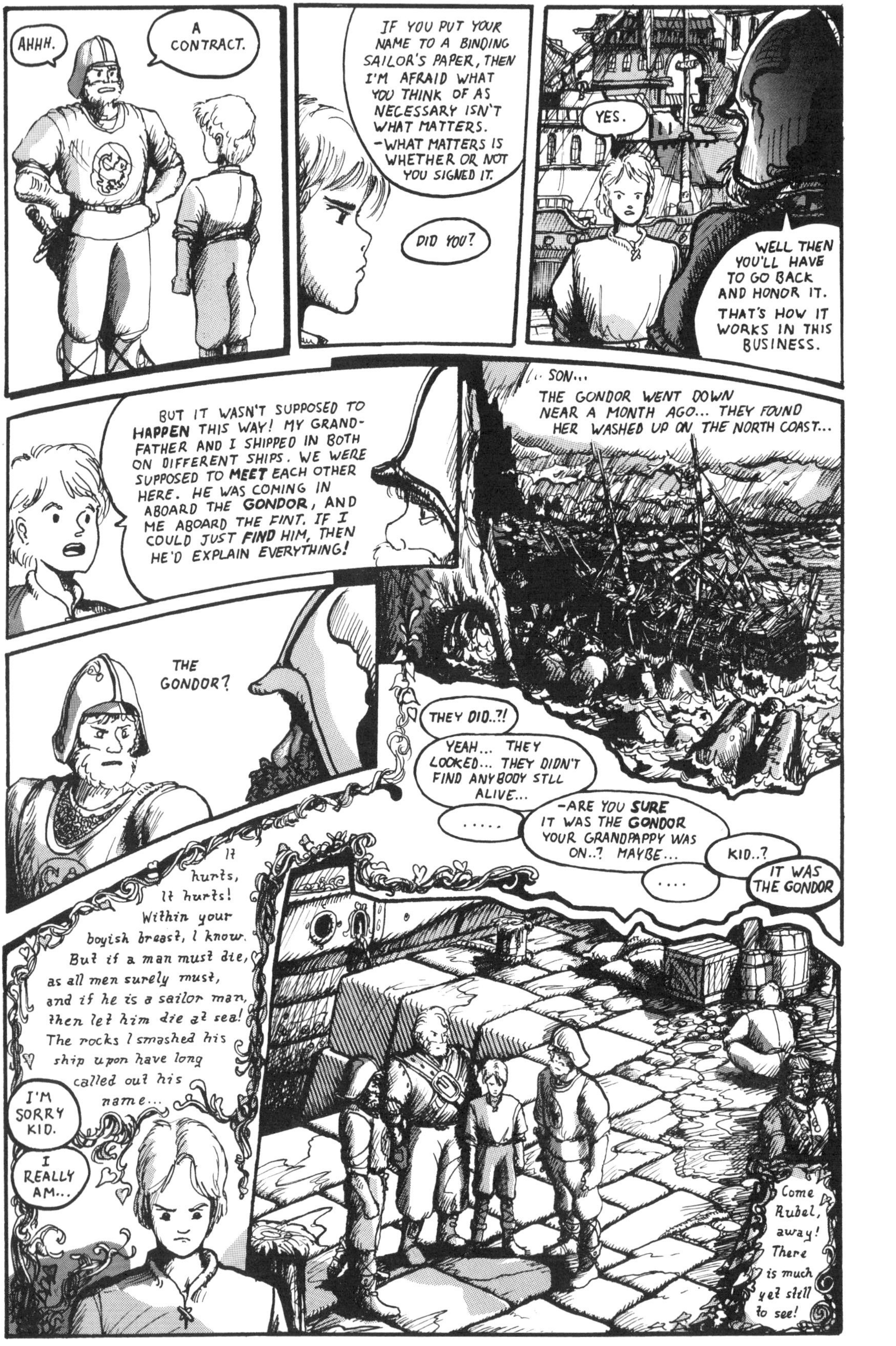

AHHH.
A CONTRACT.
IF YOU PUT YOUR NAME TO A BINDING SAILOR'S PAPER, THEN I'M AFRAID WHAT YOU THINK OF AS NECESSARY ISN'T WHAT MATTERS. -WHAT MATTERS IS WHETHER OR NOT YOU SIGNED IT.
DID YOU?
YES.
WELL THEN YOU'LL HAVE TO GO BACK AND HONOR IT.
THAT'S HOW IT WORKS IN THIS BUSINESS.
BUT IT WASN'T SUPPOSED TO HAPPEN THIS WAY! MY GRAND-FATHER AND I SHIPPED IN BOTH ON DIFFERENT SHIPS. WE WERE SUPPOSED TO MEET EACH OTHER HERE. HE WAS COMING IN ABOARD THE GONDOR, AND ME ABOARD THE FINT. IF I COULD JUST FIND HIM, THEN HE'D EXPLAIN EVERYTHING!
THE GONDOR?
.. SON...
THE GONDOR WENT DOWN NEAR A MONTH AGO... THEY FOUND HER WASHED UP ON THE NORTH COAST...
THEY DID..?!
YEAH... THEY LOOKED... THEY DIDN'T FIND ANYBODY STILL ALIVE...
.....
-ARE YOU SURE IT WAS THE GONDOR YOUR GRANDPAPPY WAS ON..? MAYBE...
KID..?
....
IT WAS THE GONDOR
It hurts, It hurts! Within your boyish breast, I know. But if a man must die, as all men surely must, and if he is a sailor man, then let him die at sea! The rocks I smashed his ship upon have long called out his name...
I'M SORRY KID.
I REALLY AM...
Come Rubel, away! There is much yet still to see!

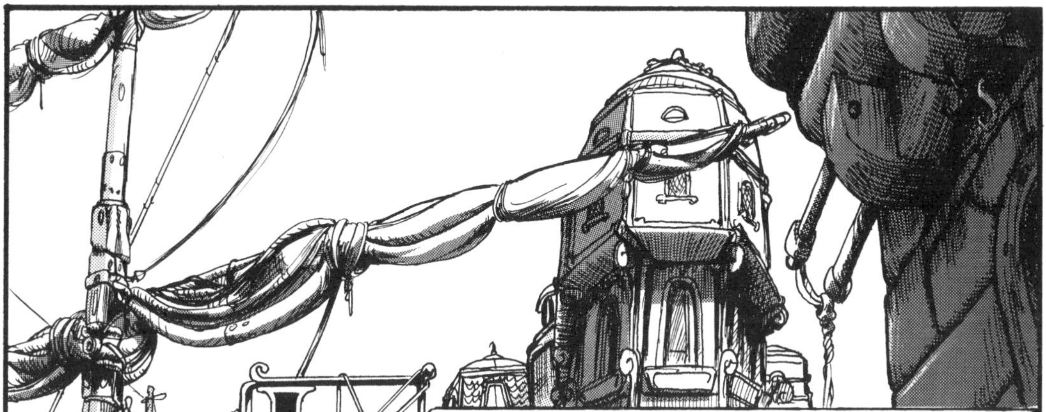

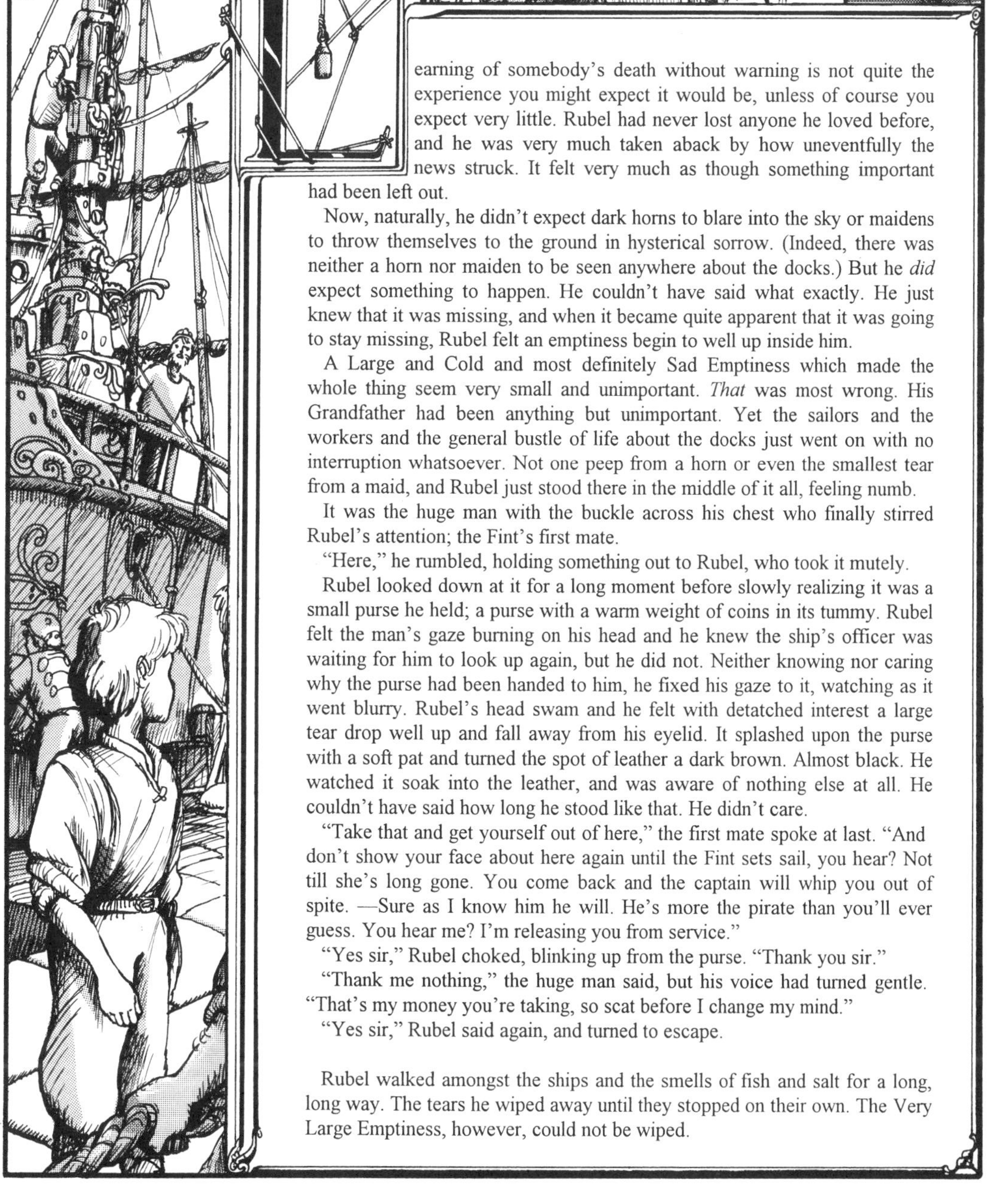

Learning of somebody's death without warning is not quite the experience you might expect it would be, unless of course you expect very little. Rubel had never lost anyone he loved before, and he was very much taken aback by how uneventfully the news struck. It felt very much as though something important had been left out.

Now, naturally, he didn't expect dark horns to blare into the sky or maidens to throw themselves to the ground in hysterical sorrow. (Indeed, there was neither a horn nor maiden to be seen anywhere about the docks.) But he *did* expect something to happen. He couldn't have said what exactly. He just knew that it was missing, and when it became quite apparent that it was going to stay missing, Rubel felt an emptiness begin to well up inside him.

A Large and Cold and most definitely Sad Emptiness which made the whole thing seem very small and unimportant. *That* was most wrong. His Grandfather had been anything but unimportant. Yet the sailors and the workers and the general bustle of life about the docks just went on with no interruption whatsoever. Not one peep from a horn or even the smallest tear from a maid, and Rubel just stood there in the middle of it all, feeling numb.

It was the huge man with the buckle across his chest who finally stirred Rubel's attention; the Fint's first mate.

"Here," he rumbled, holding something out to Rubel, who took it mutely.

Rubel looked down at it for a long moment before slowly realizing it was a small purse he held; a purse with a warm weight of coins in its tummy. Rubel felt the man's gaze burning on his head and he knew the ship's officer was waiting for him to look up again, but he did not. Neither knowing nor caring why the purse had been handed to him, he fixed his gaze to it, watching as it went blurry. Rubel's head swam and he felt with detatched interest a large tear drop well up and fall away from his eyelid. It splashed upon the purse with a soft pat and turned the spot of leather a dark brown. Almost black. He watched it soak into the leather, and was aware of nothing else at all. He couldn't have said how long he stood like that. He didn't care.

"Take that and get yourself out of here," the first mate spoke at last. "And don't show your face about here again until the Fint sets sail, you hear? Not till she's long gone. You come back and the captain will whip you out of spite. —Sure as I know him he will. He's more the pirate than you'll ever guess. You hear me? I'm releasing you from service."

"Yes sir," Rubel choked, blinking up from the purse. "Thank you sir."

"Thank me nothing," the huge man said, but his voice had turned gentle. "That's my money you're taking, so scat before I change my mind."

"Yes sir," Rubel said again, and turned to escape.

Rubel walked amongst the ships and the smells of fish and salt for a long, long way. The tears he wiped away until they stopped on their own. The Very Large Emptiness, however, could not be wiped.

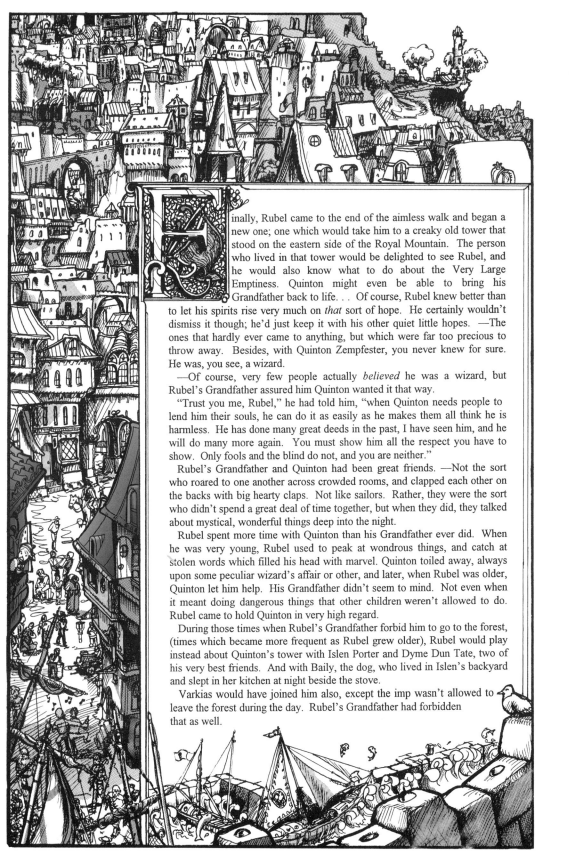

inally, Rubel came to the end of the aimless walk and began a new one; one which would take him to a creaky old tower that stood on the eastern side of the Royal Mountain. The person who lived in that tower would be delighted to see Rubel, and he would also know what to do about the Very Large Emptiness. Quinton might even be able to bring his Grandfather back to life. . . Of course, Rubel knew better than to let his spirits rise very much on *that* sort of hope. He certainly wouldn't dismiss it though; he'd just keep it with his other quiet little hopes. —The ones that hardly ever came to anything, but which were far too precious to throw away. Besides, with Quinton Zempfester, you never knew for sure. He was, you see, a wizard.

—Of course, very few people actually *believed* he was a wizard, but Rubel's Grandfather assured him Quinton wanted it that way.

"Trust you me, Rubel," he had told him, "when Quinton needs people to lend him their souls, he can do it as easily as he makes them all think he is harmless. He has done many great deeds in the past, I have seen him, and he will do many more again. You must show him all the respect you have to show. Only fools and the blind do not, and you are neither."

Rubel's Grandfather and Quinton had been great friends. —Not the sort who roared to one another across crowded rooms, and clapped each other on the backs with big hearty claps. Not like sailors. Rather, they were the sort who didn't spend a great deal of time together, but when they did, they talked about mystical, wonderful things deep into the night.

Rubel spent more time with Quinton than his Grandfather ever did. When he was very young, Rubel used to peak at wondrous things, and catch at stolen words which filled his head with marvel. Quinton toiled away, always upon some peculiar wizard's affair or other, and later, when Rubel was older, Quinton let him help. His Grandfather didn't seem to mind. Not even when it meant doing dangerous things that other children weren't allowed to do. Rubel came to hold Quinton in very high regard.

During those times when Rubel's Grandfather forbid him to go to the forest, (times which became more frequent as Rubel grew older), Rubel would play instead about Quinton's tower with Islen Porter and Dyme Dun Tate, two of his very best friends. And with Baily, the dog, who lived in Islen's backyard and slept in her kitchen at night beside the stove.

Varkias would have joined him also, except the imp wasn't allowed to leave the forest during the day. Rubel's Grandfather had forbidden that as well.

When Rubel was young, he figured that the reason for not allowing little Varkias to the city was so people wouldn't try to catch him and kill him. And though it made Varkias grumpy and irritable, it was a good enough reason for Rubel. Yet even so, he felt there was something more to it than just that. Something important.

He tried to ask Quinton about it, but found it difficult to explain exactly what his question was. Rubel was only eight years old then, and words for eight year olds are not as easy to fit around complicated ideas as they are for older people. He didn't bother with it again. There were more distracting concerns at hand. That day he was helping Quinton build a device which would let them speak with birds.

When it was done, the device worked for Quinton and Islen and even for Dyme Dun, who hardly ever got Quinton's things to work. It even worked for Baily, and he was a dog. In fact, it worked for all of them except Rubel, and he tried the hardest. Islen, (who was feeling mean that afternoon), teased him and stuck out her tongue and they got into a fight which ended with Rubel stomping away saying angry things. He said he hoped the stupid thing broke.

The very next day, they found it shattered on the floor, and they all thought he had done it. Rubel insisted he had seen in the moonlight, a shadow person climb out of the tower window, but he was sure they didn't believe him. —Baily did, and he would have said angrily that Rubel would never lie about such a thing, but all Baily could do was growl.

Quinton believed. And he believed it enough to frown and look troubled by the news. Rubel was eternally grateful to him for that.

But that was all long ago. Now Quinton had vanished as well.

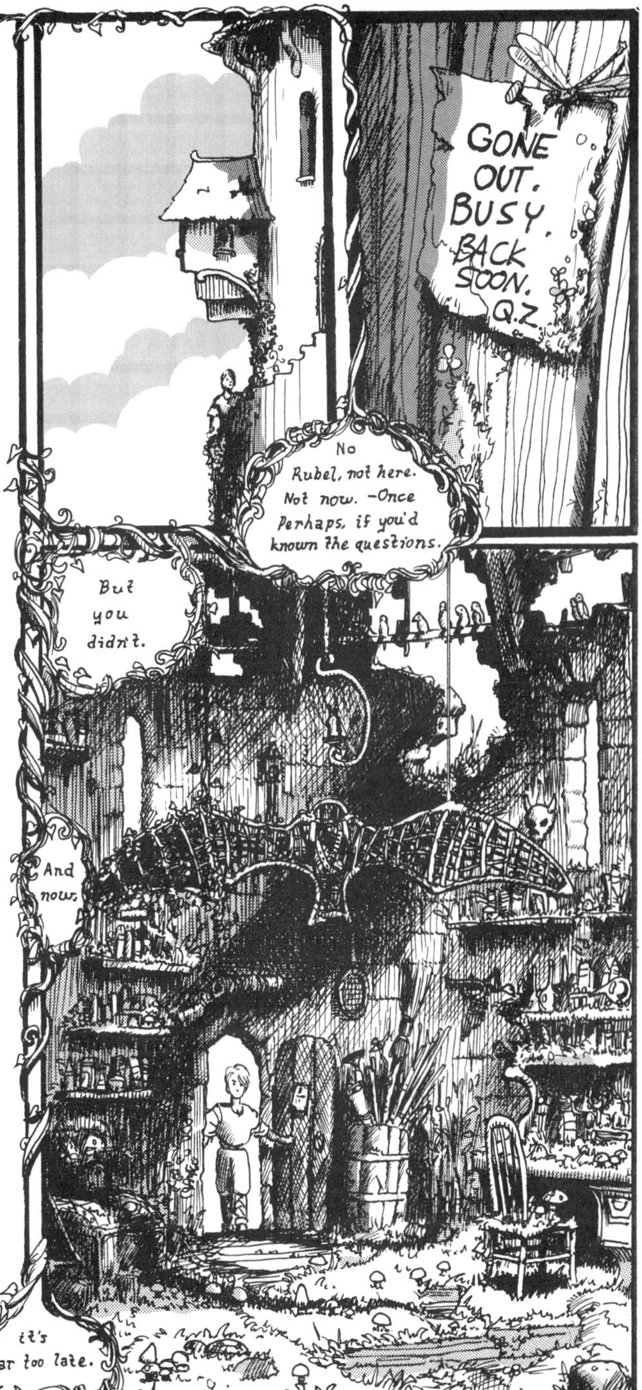
GONE OUT. BUSY. BACK SOON. Q.Z.
No Rubel, not here. Not now. —Once Perhaps, if you'd known the questions.
But you didn't.
And now,
it's far too late.

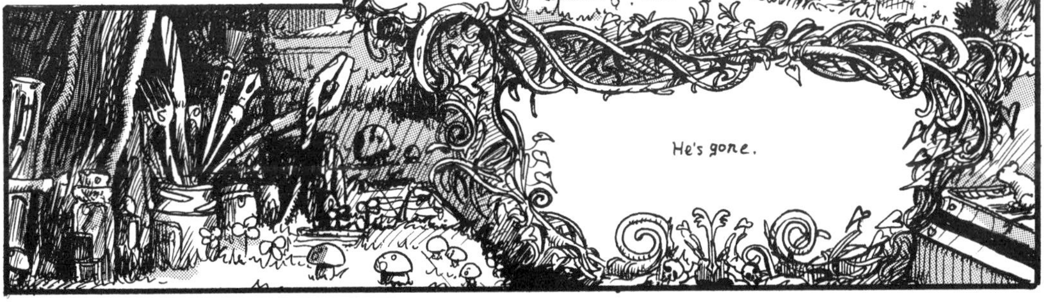
He's gone.

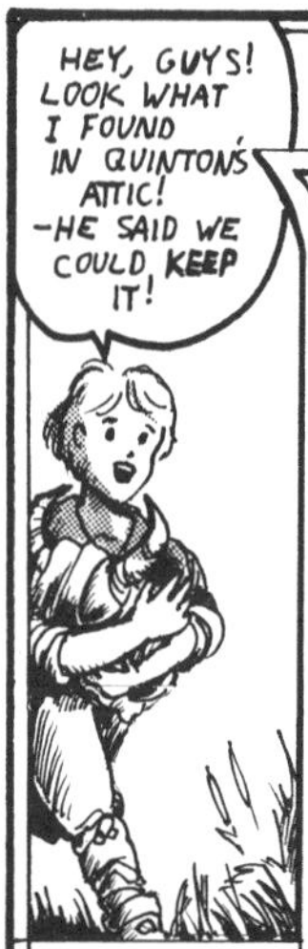
HEY, GUYS! LOOK WHAT I FOUND IN QUINTON'S ATTIC! -HE SAID WE COULD KEEP IT!

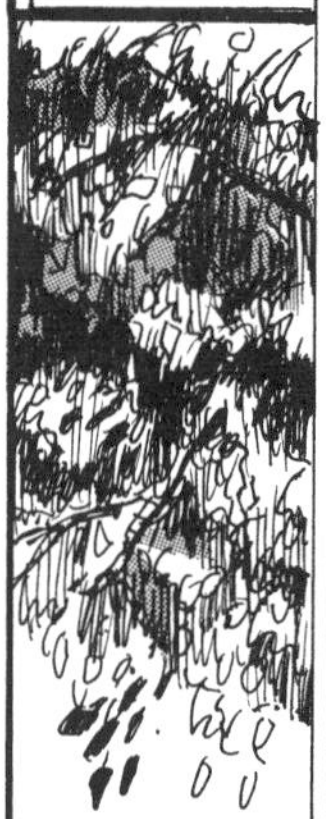

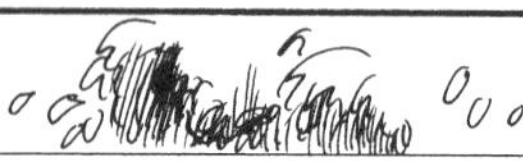

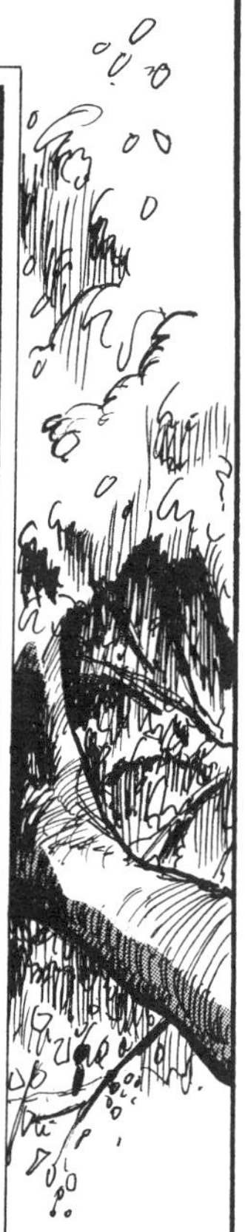

Rubel descended half way down the outside tower stairs, and there sat down. He was anxious not to reach the bottom just yet. Once he did, he knew that he would have to think of somewhere else to go.

Quinton *and* his Grandfather were gone, so now there was nobody to take care of him. —That wasn't really the frightening thing though; he'd been on his own before, and he was good at it. He rather liked it even. It made him feel adventurous. The frightening part about it was that before, if he got tired of it or if something bad happened, he could always just go home. It wasn't like that now.

This was a most unsettling feeling, and it did nothing to help with the Very Large Emptiness inside him. Indeed, it helped to make it grow. But rather than give into such hopeless feelings, he concentrated instead on trying to work out a way of fixing things. It came upon him all at once.

It was a very good idea; the sort of idea which made him sparkle with that wild sort of happiness which always accompanies Big, Wonderful, Exciting ideas which are absolutely Perfect. Rubel sat up straight on the steps with delightful shivers running down his spine and he sat frozen like that for a long moment and he went over everything in his head to make double sure it really was perfect. Then he leaped up with an energy and bounded down the rest of the stairs two and three at a time. When he came to the bottom, he gave a happy hoot which echoed back and forth across the yard.

Finding Quinton wouldn't just be a regular journey. A search for a lost wizard was the sort of thing more properly called a quest, and quests needed adventurers. That meant the Monster Slayers.

The Monster Slayers were a secret society Rubel and his friends had formed after listening to one of Quinton's more stirring tales about fighting evil things. Rubel was the thief, and Islen was the sorceress. Dyme Dun was the knight, Baily, was their hound, and Varkias, naturally, was their Demon.

Though, of course, Varkias was only with them the times Islen and Dyme were allowed to stay out late, which wasn't very often. —Or during those very few times they sneaked out to the forest where all the real monsters lived.

For three years, the Monster Slayers reigned over the city and lands of Asaria, keeping her safe and pure from the wicked who sought to make her ill. Together, they fought and killed many terrible beasts, and swore many deep and terrible oaths.

Oh, he thought, What a grand way to be reunited with his friends! How surprised and excited they would be when he marched up before them, as if from nowhere, and announced that they must all dash off at once on an important quest to rescue a wizard!

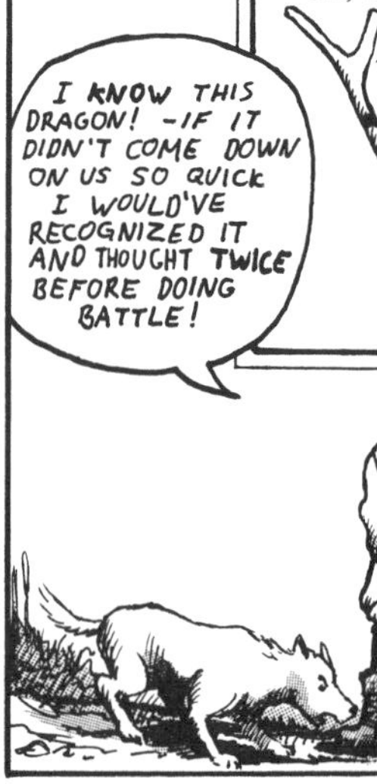
I KNOW THIS DRAGON! -IF IT DIDN'T COME DOWN ON US SO QUICK I WOULD'VE RECOGNIZED IT AND THOUGHT TWICE BEFORE DOING BATTLE!
I RECOGNIZE HIM TOO! -IT'S CESPINARVE ROGUE! -RIGHT?
NO WONDER HE WAS SO HARD TO KILL!

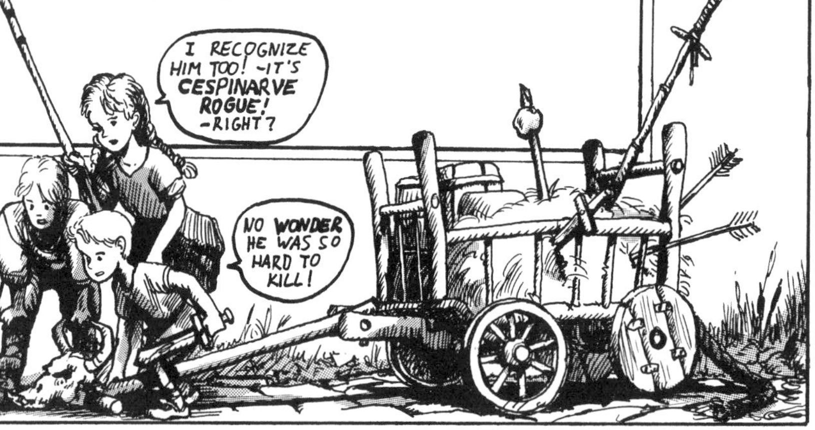

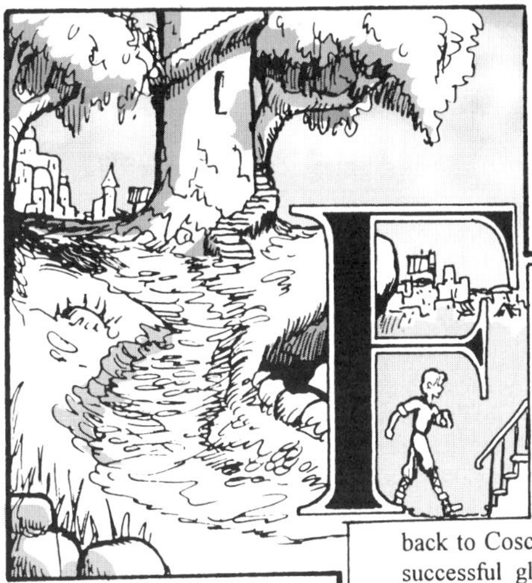

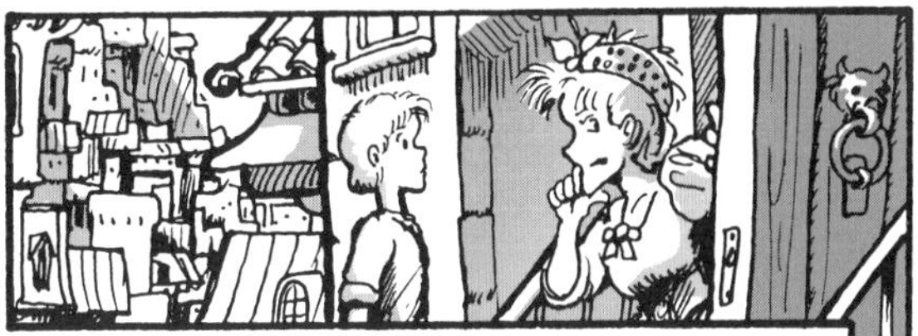

First he went to the house where Dyme Dun Tate lived. He stepped right up to the front door and rapped the knocker three solid times. A woman answered who was not Dyme's mother, and she told him that the whole Tate family had moved back to Coscove Gates where Dyme's uncle had started a very successful glasswares business and needed Dyme's father to help him if he would. Dyme's father said it was an exciting idea with good prospects, so he packed up his whole family, sold the house and moved to Coscove Gates. And that was the end of that. Rubel's knight was gone.

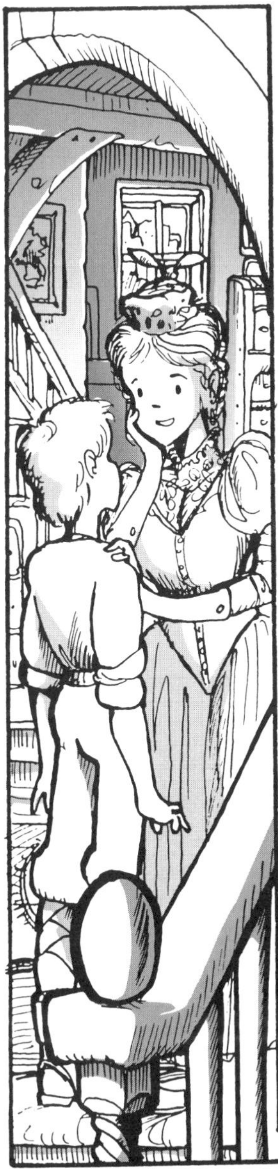

Undaunted, Rubel went next to the house where Islen Porter lived and knocked on her door. Islen's mother answered and told him that her daughter had married the baker's boy who she now lived upstairs with, and that they were both out working in the bread store down the street, and did he want to come inside and wait until dinner time when they would be back and could sit together with him? Rubel said No, but was persuaded nonetheless. Mrs. Porter had always rather liked him and was delighted to see him again.

She wanted to know where he had gone in the world, and what had become of his handsome Grandfather and she gave Rubel a cup of tea and a small frosted cake and a seat on the nice sofa chair, all of which he accepted miserably but as politely as he could. He didn't want to tell her about his Grandfather, or about Quinton, and certainly not about his plan to go on a quest with her daughter. He didn't want to tell her, partly because he felt somehow certain that his Big Wonderful plan would sound both silly and awkward there in Mrs. Porter's stuffy living room, but mostly because he knew that Mrs. Porter would immediately feel sorry for him. She would want to take care of him and give him the small cot in their attic to sleep on, and eggs and bacon every morning for breakfast, and for a variety of reasons the mere thought of this was unbearable to him. The purse of coins Mr. Mannock had given to him was already weighing like so many cakes of poison in his mind.

Proper thieves didn't need sympathy. A proper thief would have gone and spoken strong words with his captain and made him pay his rightful wage. —A proper thief would have struck him down if he had not, but Rubel had done neither of these things. Instead he had cried.

So he didn't tell Mrs. Porter all about the troubles he had inside him, and she didn't hug him to her breast and promise to make everything okay. Instead he asked where his dog was.

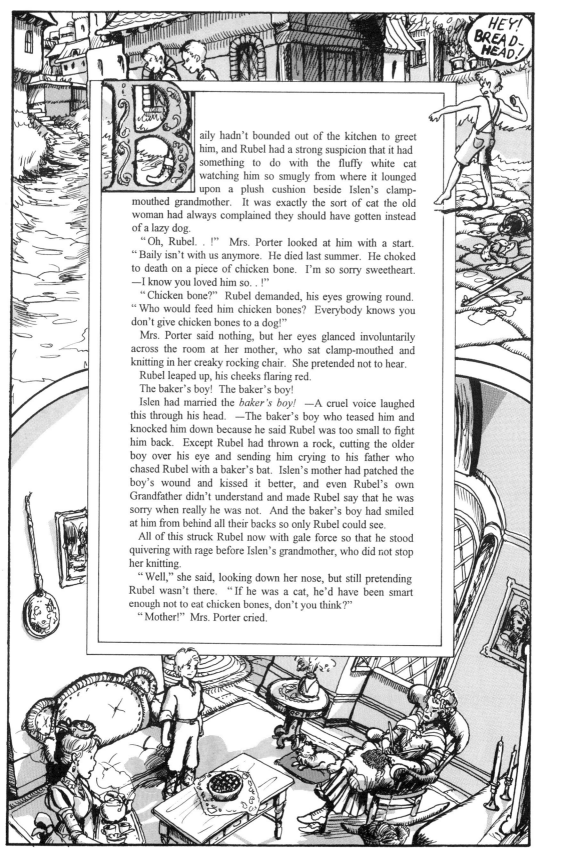

HEY! BREAD-HEAD!

Baily hadn't bounded out of the kitchen to greet him, and Rubel had a strong suspicion that it had something to do with the fluffy white cat watching him so smugly from where it lounged upon a plush cushion beside Islen's clamp-mouthed grandmother. It was exactly the sort of cat the old woman had always complained they should have gotten instead of a lazy dog.

"Oh, Rubel. . !" Mrs. Porter looked at him with a start. "Baily isn't with us anymore. He died last summer. He choked to death on a piece of chicken bone. I'm so sorry sweetheart. —I know you loved him so. . !"

"Chicken bone?" Rubel demanded, his eyes growing round. "Who would feed him chicken bones? Everybody knows you don't give chicken bones to a dog!"

Mrs. Porter said nothing, but her eyes glanced involuntarily across the room at her mother, who sat clamp-mouthed and knitting in her creaky rocking chair. She pretended not to hear.

Rubel leaped up, his cheeks flaring red.

The baker's boy! The baker's boy!

Islen had married the *baker's boy!* —A cruel voice laughed this through his head. —The baker's boy who teased him and knocked him down because he said Rubel was too small to fight him back. Except Rubel had thrown a rock, cutting the older boy over his eye and sending him crying to his father who chased Rubel with a baker's bat. Islen's mother had patched the boy's wound and kissed it better, and even Rubel's own Grandfather didn't understand and made Rubel say that he was sorry when really he was not. And the baker's boy had smiled at him from behind all their backs so only Rubel could see.

All of this struck Rubel now with gale force so that he stood quivering with rage before Islen's grandmother, who did not stop her knitting.

"Well," she said, looking down her nose, but still pretending Rubel wasn't there. "If he was a cat, he'd have been smart enough not to eat chicken bones, don't you think?"

"Mother!" Mrs. Porter cried.

Rubel said nothing but turned and left the house. He tried his best out of respect for Mrs. Porter not to storm and bang the door, but when he was outside everything ran free.

And he sang within his mind. . .

The Angel's Tree!
The Angel's Tree!
I'm going to see the Angel's Tree!

No Knight
No Sorceress, nor Dog have I,

But Varkias, Varkias!
Away up in the Angel's Tree!
Oh let him still be there for me. . !

Rubel sped like wind towards the forest where his very last friend in all the world would be, —his last friend besides Islen, who he was frightened now to see, and besides Mrs. Porter who could not understand magic things.

Mrs. Porter hadn't believed in the wishing key, and she thought Islen had found it and not won it as she had. She took it away from her and gave it to a city guardsmen who she said would know best what to do with it. She told them wisely, "Children shouldn't have things made from gold," and sent them all off home, and her daughter to a bath where she said Islen's ears and knees needed a good scrubbing.

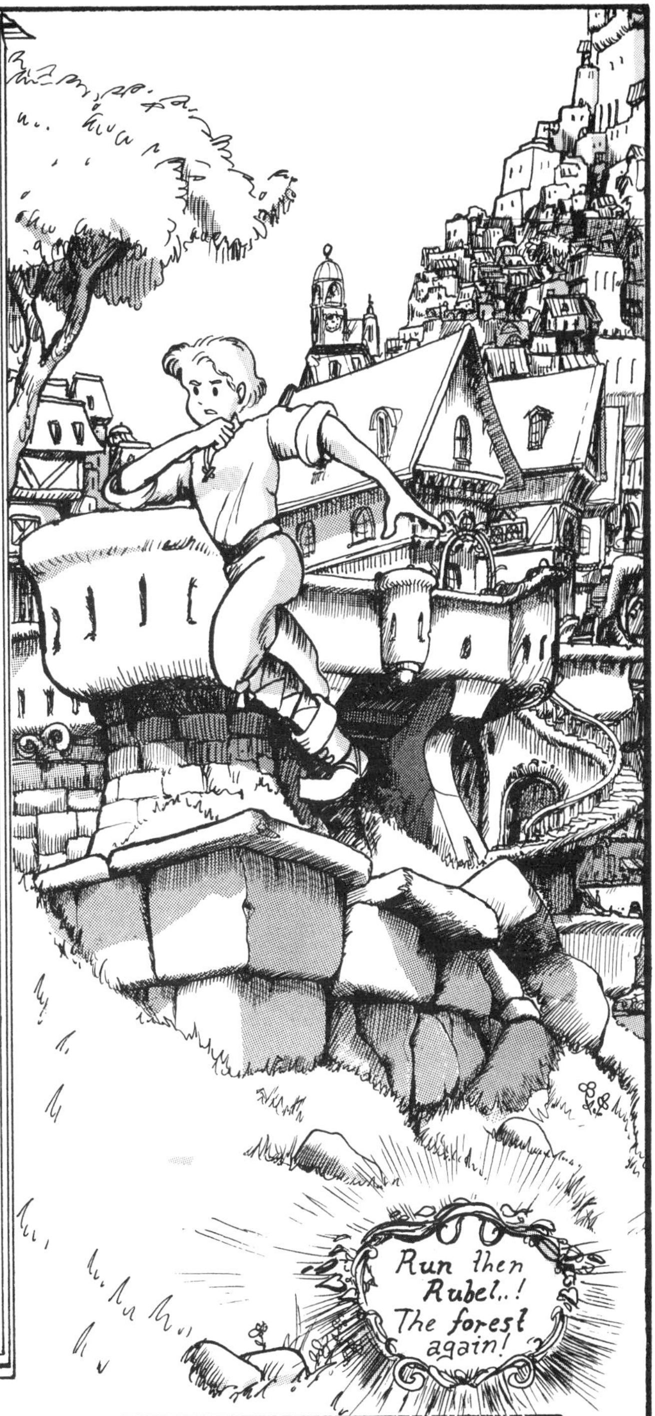
Run then Rubel..! The forest again!

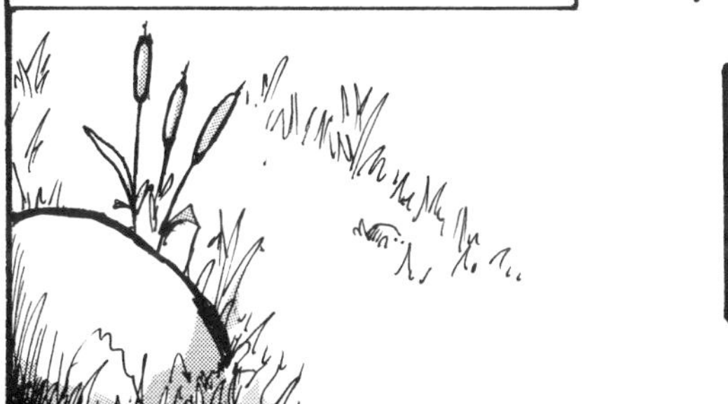

Varkias! Varkias!

It chanted it through his mind. But something, he felt certain now, was very, very wrong.

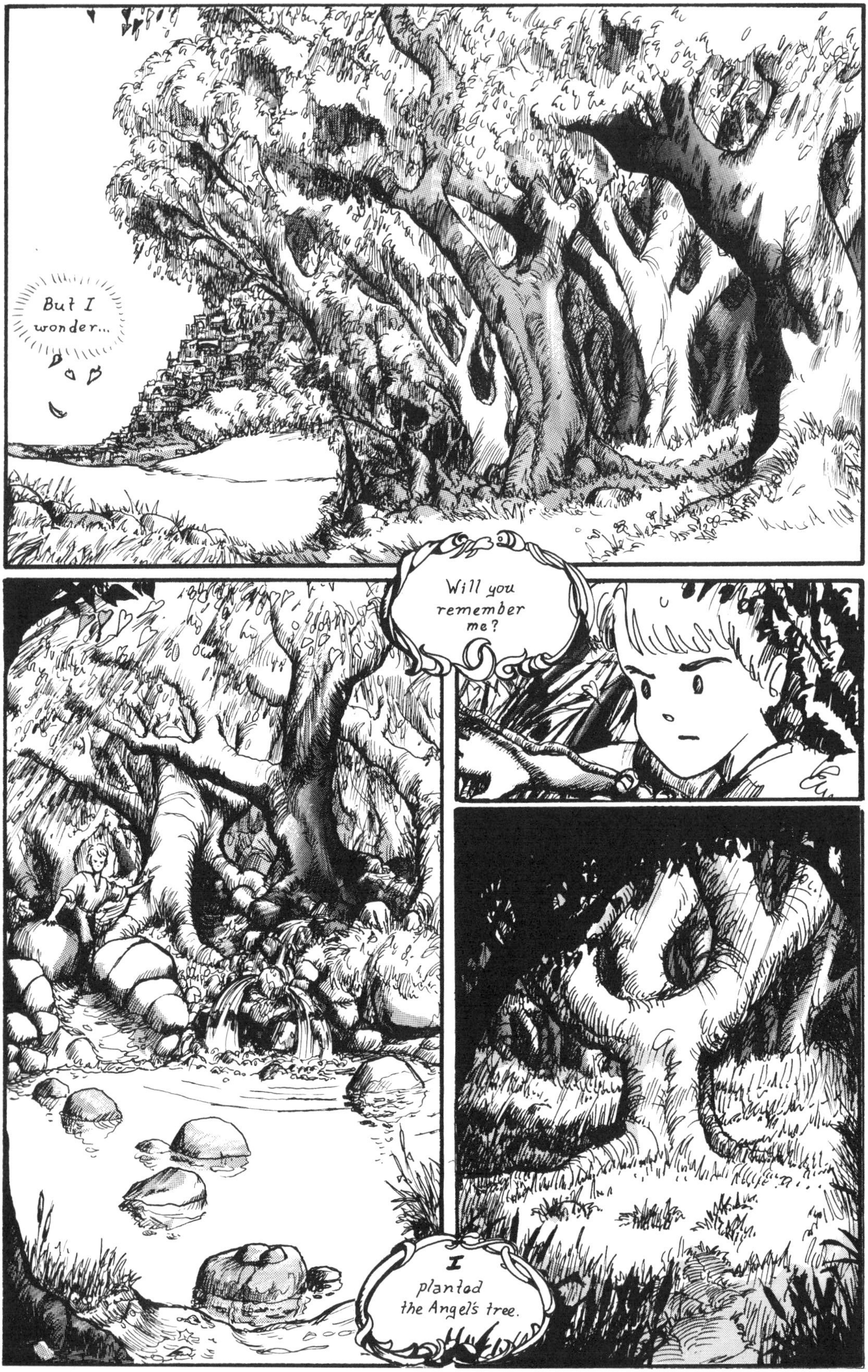
But I wonder...
Will you remember me?
I planted the Angel's tree.

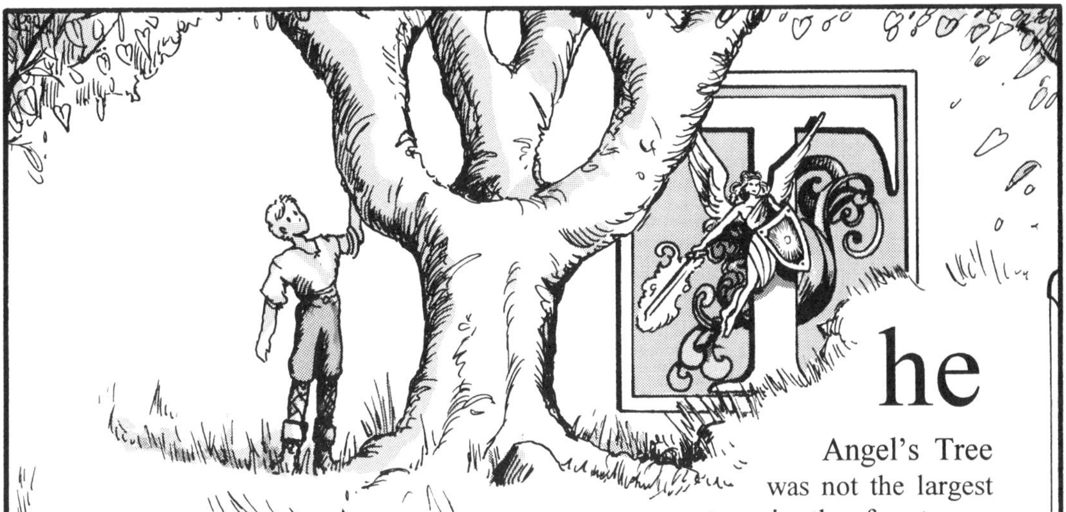

The Angel's Tree was not the largest tree in the forest, nor was it the most magical, nor even the most beautiful; not to the eye at any rate. But you could crawl into the cup of its palm and there sit entirely apart from all the world and be as content as you could ever be. You could curl up and take a nap, or hum and sing out loud, or think of grand stories where you were the main character, while all about the brooding forest lay. —The Tree was like a desert island in the middle of a dangerous ocean; an island with palm trees and big warm rocks to lie on.

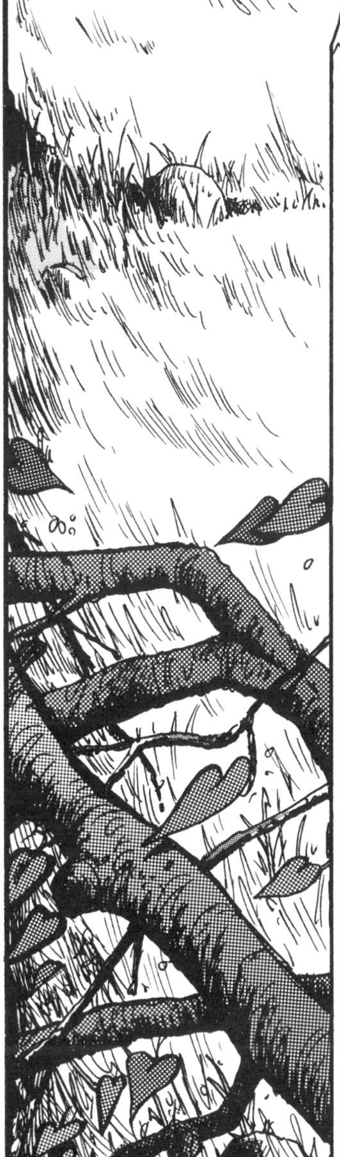

"Oh, Tree, oh Tree," Rubel breathed, "I am back," he said. "I forgot how much I missed you!"

It was true. Just seeing it again made everything seem much better. The Tree had always been there; ever since he could remember. And it could not vanish like Quinton, and it couldn't choke like Baily, nor could it grow up and forget him, or fall into the ocean and drown. The Tree stood as it always had, firmly rooted in the sleeping wood.

"Oh Tree!" Rubel said again, a big warm feeling of relief filling his entire being. "So!" he thought aloud. "I am not alone after all!"

He was wrong though, and when he realized it the warm feeling inside him shuddered and turned at once to ice. It was in the air. —Or rather, it was not.

The Tree's perfume was gone. No warm scent of green and flowered things; of *living* things. Now all he could smell was the leafy decay of the forest floor. —Dead smells, and nothing more.

His heart began to pound very fast and he swung his head up to look into the wreath of branches above. —The wreath of branches which should have been lush with summer foliage. All of them were dry; all bare, but for a scatter of crispy leaves which clung to the ends of kindling stalks and rattled like dead beetle shells. Rubel took a shaky step backwards, a soft lump rising to his throat and the Emptiness yawning wide. The Angel's Tree was dead.

In around clenched teeth Rubel drew a breath, his blood pounding in his ears.

"VARKIAS!" he yelled. He yelled it into the sky, spinning once about in the bright grass with his arms held out at his sides. "VARKIAS!" he cried, "WHERE ARE YOU!"

Nothing.

"VARKIAS!" He called again, his face going red and quivery for how hard he shouted. "IT'S RUBEL! *I'VE COME BACK! I'M BACK FROM THE OCEAN!*"

But the forest swallowed his words entirely, and gave him nothing in reply but the rustle of insects and leaves and the calls of wild birds, —all just mindless chatter above the deep and throaty silence which was the Ancient Wood.

He let his arms sink back to his sides, and he stood with the rawness of his yells sitting in the back of his throat like scraped knees. Then he saw.

Just in the elbow of a branch above him was a little dark shape, with little demon's horns and wings. But something was not quite. . .

Rubel leaped into the tree, both his fear and his hope frozen together by uncertainty. On tip toes he reached into the branch, and there he found the tiny wooden chest he'd hidden once before.

Upon it sat Varkias the imp.

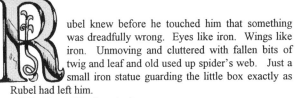ubel knew before he touched him that something was dreadfully wrong. Eyes like iron. Wings like iron. Unmoving and cluttered with fallen bits of twig and leaf and old used up spider's web. Just a small iron statue guarding the little box exactly as Rubel had left him.

"Varkias. . !" he breathed.

He had never heard of an imp turning into metal before, but it seemed like the sort of thing an imp might well do. —If something bad happened, perhaps. Like if you left him alone for too long, sitting by himself. . .

This thought stung Rubel so hard his hand seized and Varkias was knocked from his perch. Rubel held himself rigid as the imp tipped from view and a moment later thumped to the crunchy forest floor. Rubel moved to see the statue lying upon its back, gazing up past him with metal eyes, through the dead mesh of branches above, and far into the sky beyond.

A feeling of pure misery burst upon him, like a barrel side smashed in, sloshing out its contents, filling him up so that his head swam and everything in his world turned frothy and bitter. The Emptiness rose up now and this time not to merely chill his heart and weaken him, but to swallow him entirely. He did not try to stop it.

Sometimes when people feel this way, they want to kill themselves. They want to hang themselves or stab themselves, so that the Mrs. Porters in their lives will see them dead and clap their hands to their mouths in horror and utter, "Oh, how horrible!"

And so it was *this* specter the Emptiness chose to release. Rubel remained motionless as it swirled around inside him, laughing and snatching at all the tasty parts from which his mind was made.

Except people didn't just clap their hands to their mouths and say sympathetic things. Rubel knew this. Many people also say secretly within their minds, "Oh, how foolish and useless he must have been to not have had a single friend! How weak he must have been to lie down as such and die! We had no need of him! The very worst of us are better by leaps and bounds, and twice as brave to face our lives and not to wither up like he!"

At this thought, a cloud of flaming anger burst within his head. He pounded a fist upon the tree and yelled out a strangled, wordless cry, startling for a space even the ancient forest from its mammoth brood.

"I *shall* be a thief yet!" he shouted to the sky, "And a *madman* too, if that is what it takes! Let Islen be grown up and married! I don't care a bit! And let them think what they will of me! *I* shall live in the forest! I shall run with animals and I shall be their king! And the people of the land will only see me through the trees, and if they ever bother me, I will bite their necks like a dog! And I will steal a sword and cut off their scalps and wear them on a string around my neck! And the ones I let live will tell all the others until everybody in the land will wonder at me and tell stories about the Wild Thief of the Sleeping Wood!"

Nobody heard though, and nobody cared, so thief or no Rubel sat himself down in the palm of his dead tree and he cried. Properly, for everything he'd lost that day, and for anything else he could think of that was also bitter and sad just to make it feel worse. —Tears to wash the filth away and drown the Emptiness into something small and tired and weak. Except. . .

Before his cheeks got red and puffy with tear water salt. . , before he reached the bottom of his misery and ran out of things to feel sorry for so that he could begin to rise again and feel better; before any of these healthy things could happen, something very different happened to him instead.

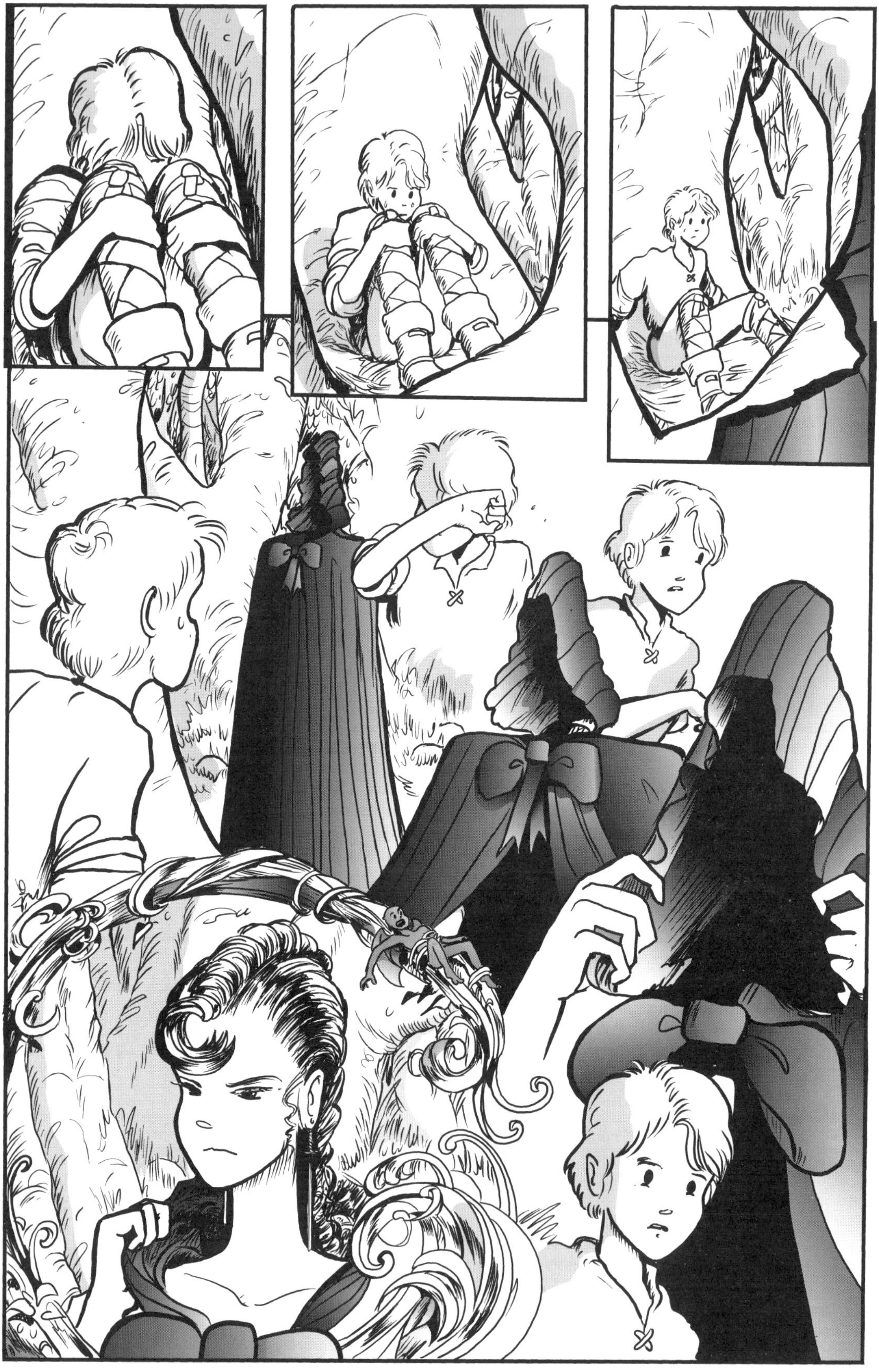

hrough the woods like smoke and shadow she came and into the clearing without a sound. Cloaked from head to toe in all her dark majesty, she rose before Rubel and bid him well the day, saying, "What is this now, my thief?" her words moving like the silk of her hood which she let fall back. She had soft black hair, and eyes like powdered ash, —eyes which twinkled nonetheless, like moonlight on melting ice, all unveiled before him so that he could see. "All in tears I find you," said she. "All in tears, Rubel! Tell me now, what is this?"

She was tall and she was beautiful and she smelled of old autumn leaves. Rubel's breath was taken quite away, and all at once he felt as though he were very small again. He dashed away his remaining tears with the crook of his sleeve and he wanted to stand up and face her like a proper thief ought, but he had been caught in the middle of his weeping and so his thoughts and senses were hopelessly mixed up.

"You are scared of me?" she asked. —She asked it in a curious way, moving forward with such a grace as only supernatural creatures are able.

"I am not scared of anything!" he told her.

"You are a liar."

"I am not! Who are you?"

"You are a liar twice," she said. "You know who I am, but you are afraid to tell me how."

"I am not afraid! I have never seen you before."

"Never?" she asked, raising up one eyebrow. Careful, now Rubel," she said. "Careful now! You have only three chances, and in half a breath you have used up two. If you spend as well the third as such, avoiding petty fears, then that is how you will spend the rest of your days. Your heart will go blind and you will live and die a common man and never know a magic thing again."

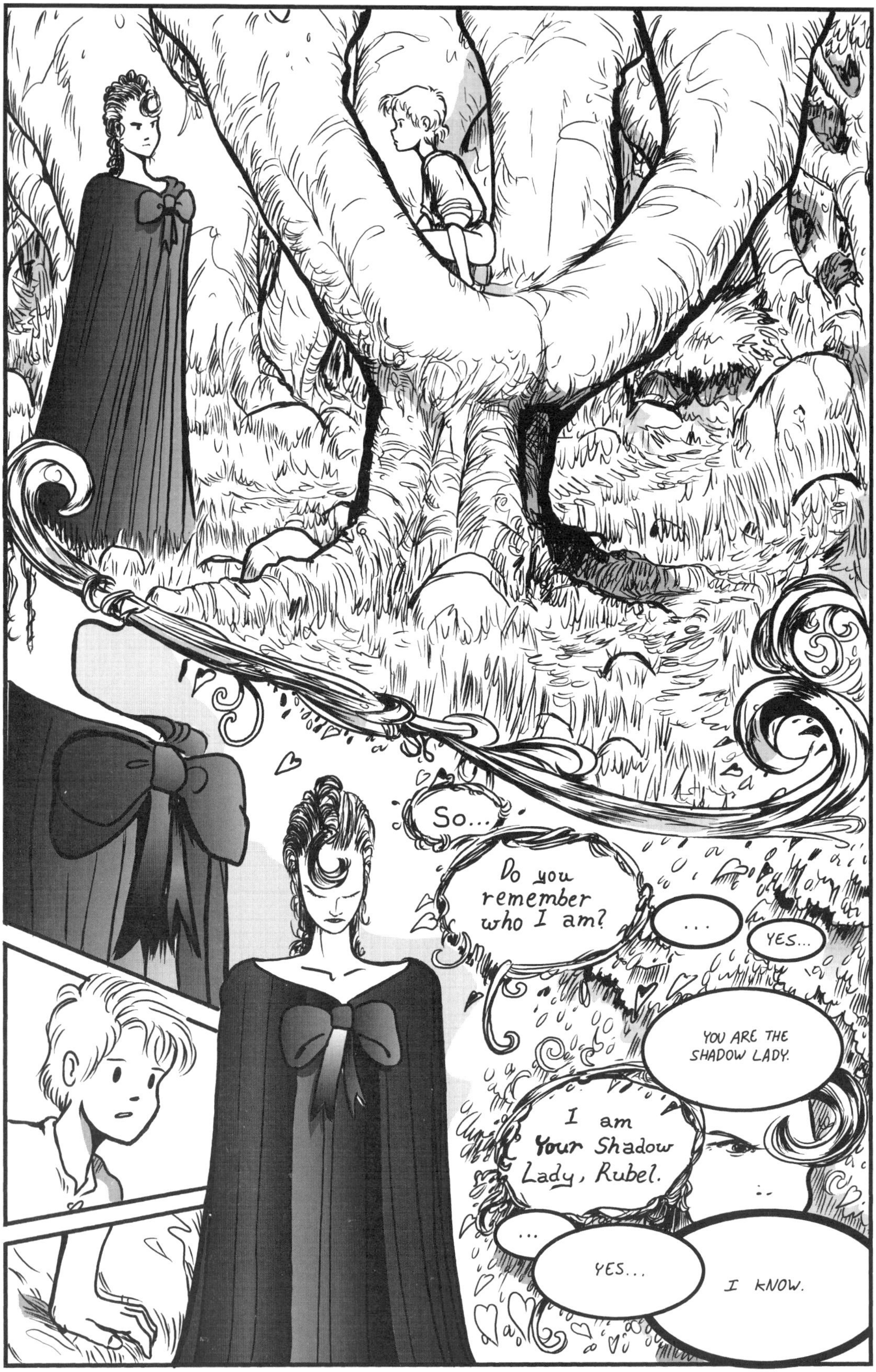
So...
Do you remember who I am?
...
YES...
YOU ARE THE SHADOW LADY.
I am Your Shadow Lady, Rubel.
...
YES...
I KNOW.

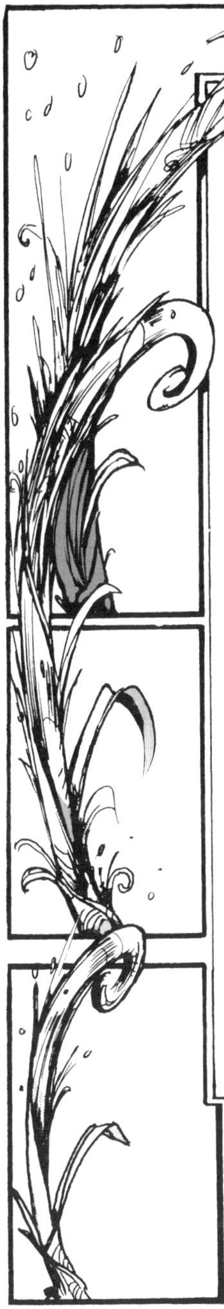

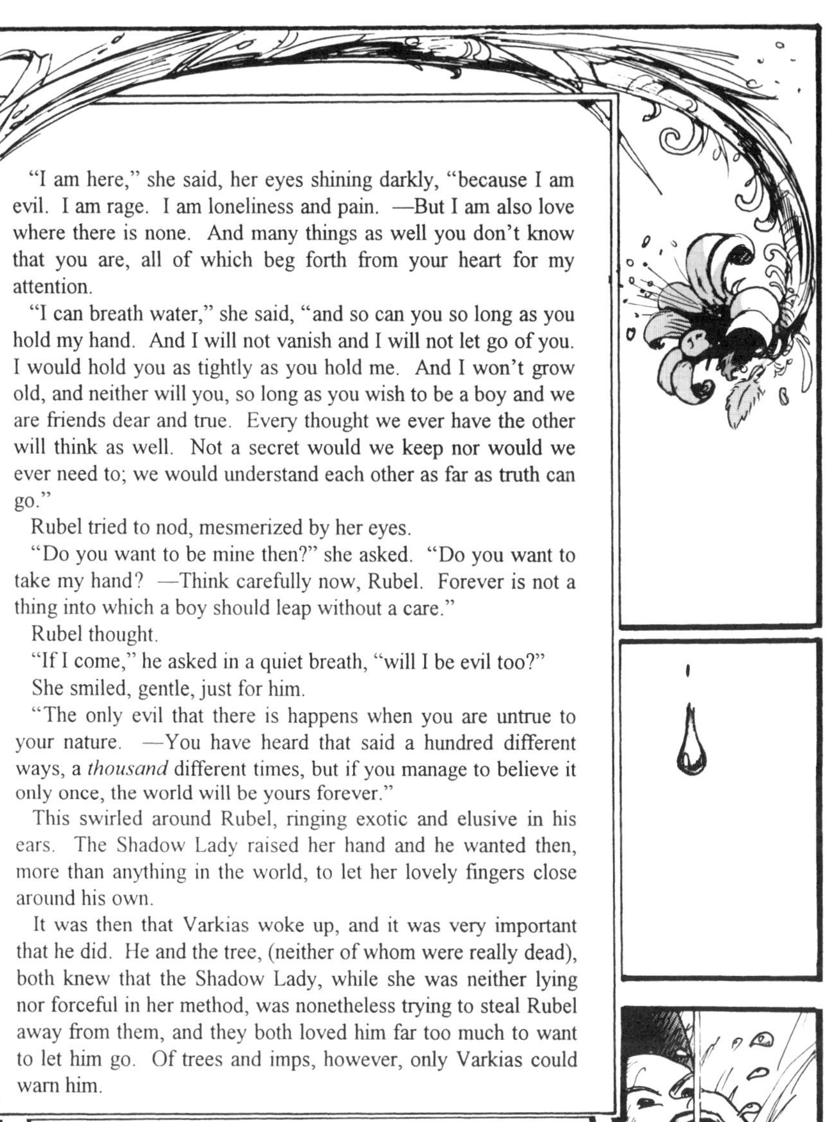

"I am here," she said, her eyes shining darkly, "because I am evil. I am rage. I am loneliness and pain. —But I am also love where there is none. And many things as well you don't know that you are, all of which beg forth from your heart for my attention.

"I can breath water," she said, "and so can you so long as you hold my hand. And I will not vanish and I will not let go of you. I would hold you as tightly as you hold me. And I won't grow old, and neither will you, so long as you wish to be a boy and we are friends dear and true. Every thought we ever have the other will think as well. Not a secret would we keep nor would we ever need to; we would understand each other as far as truth can go."

Rubel tried to nod, mesmerized by her eyes.

"Do you want to be mine then?" she asked. "Do you want to take my hand? —Think carefully now, Rubel. Forever is not a thing into which a boy should leap without a care."

Rubel thought.

"If I come," he asked in a quiet breath, "will I be evil too?"

She smiled, gentle, just for him.

"The only evil that there is happens when you are untrue to your nature. —You have heard that said a hundred different ways, a *thousand* different times, but if you manage to believe it only once, the world will be yours forever."

This swirled around Rubel, ringing exotic and elusive in his ears. The Shadow Lady raised her hand and he wanted then, more than anything in the world, to let her lovely fingers close around his own.

It was then that Varkias woke up, and it was very important that he did. He and the tree, (neither of whom were really dead), both knew that the Shadow Lady, while she was neither lying nor forceful in her method, was nonetheless trying to steal Rubel away from them, and they both loved him far too much to want to let him go. Of trees and imps, however, only Varkias could warn him.

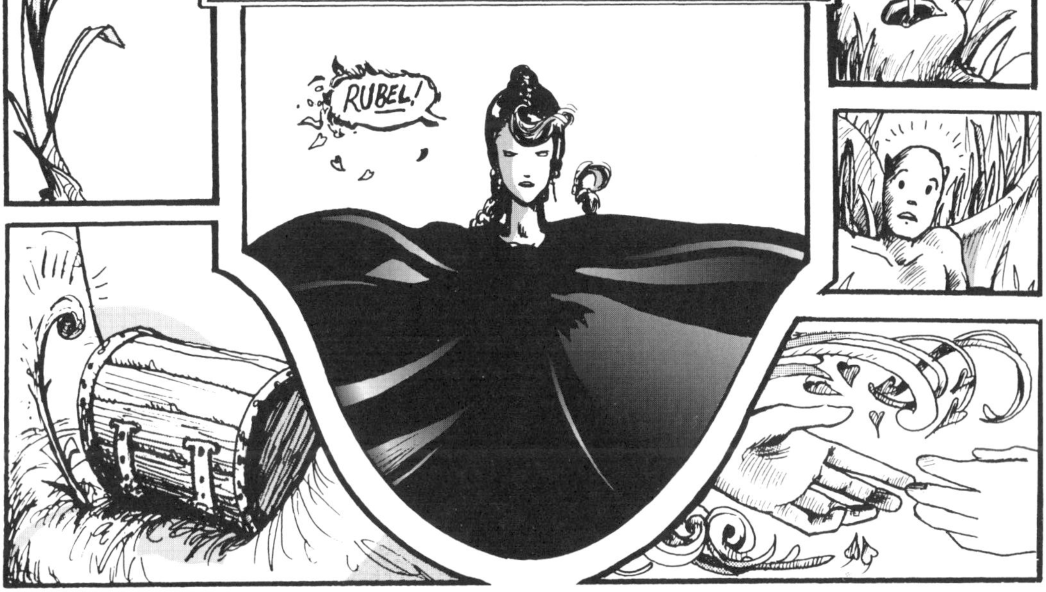
RUBEL!

She's trying to catch you!" he cried, "Don't let her touch you! Don't let her!"

Rubel's mind was swimming, the dark spell cloaking him now at the deepest swell of its power. But there was just enough still working properly inside his head, *just* enough, to hear the imp and pause before his fingers would have brushed into her palm. And though she might easily have done so, the Queen of Halves did not snatch his hand. A thief's hand might be caught, but never his heart. Not like that. Varkias flapped into the air, and in a flurried instant, stood upon Rubel's shoulder and yelled into his ear.

"Rubel, you mustn't touch her! She's only telling half the truth! She's more than what she says she is! She's something else instead!"

Rubel looked at the imp, his eyes slightly glazed.

"I saw her!" Varkias told him breathlessly. "I saw her the day you were a baby! She came through the trees and her eyes were on fire, and she took the blanket you were wrapped up inside and tried to fly away. And she fought with the Angel and she killed her! She slew her through her middle with a sword black as night! But her wings got cut and your Grandfather had a hammer with a head as big as an anvil, and he swung it back and forth and roared like a giant and frightened her away!"

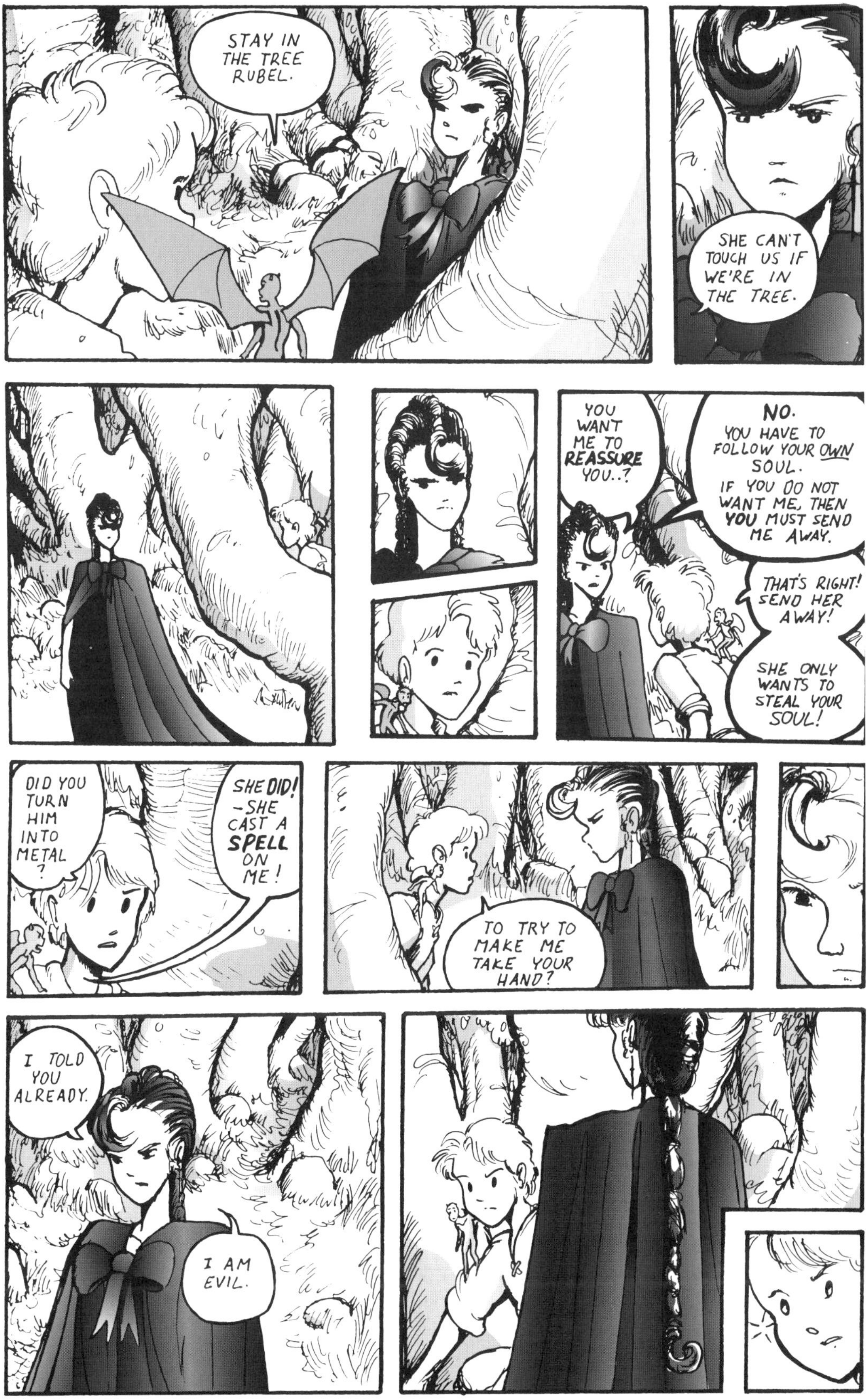
STAY IN THE TREE RUBEL.
SHE CAN'T TOUCH US IF WE'RE IN THE TREE.
YOU WANT ME TO REASSURE YOU..?
NO. YOU HAVE TO FOLLOW YOUR OWN SOUL.
IF YOU DO NOT WANT ME, THEN YOU MUST SEND ME AWAY.
THAT'S RIGHT! SEND HER AWAY!
SHE ONLY WANTS TO STEAL YOUR SOUL!
DID YOU TURN HIM INTO METAL?
SHE DID! -SHE CAST A SPELL ON ME!
TO TRY TO MAKE ME TAKE YOUR HAND?
I TOLD YOU ALREADY.
I AM EVIL.

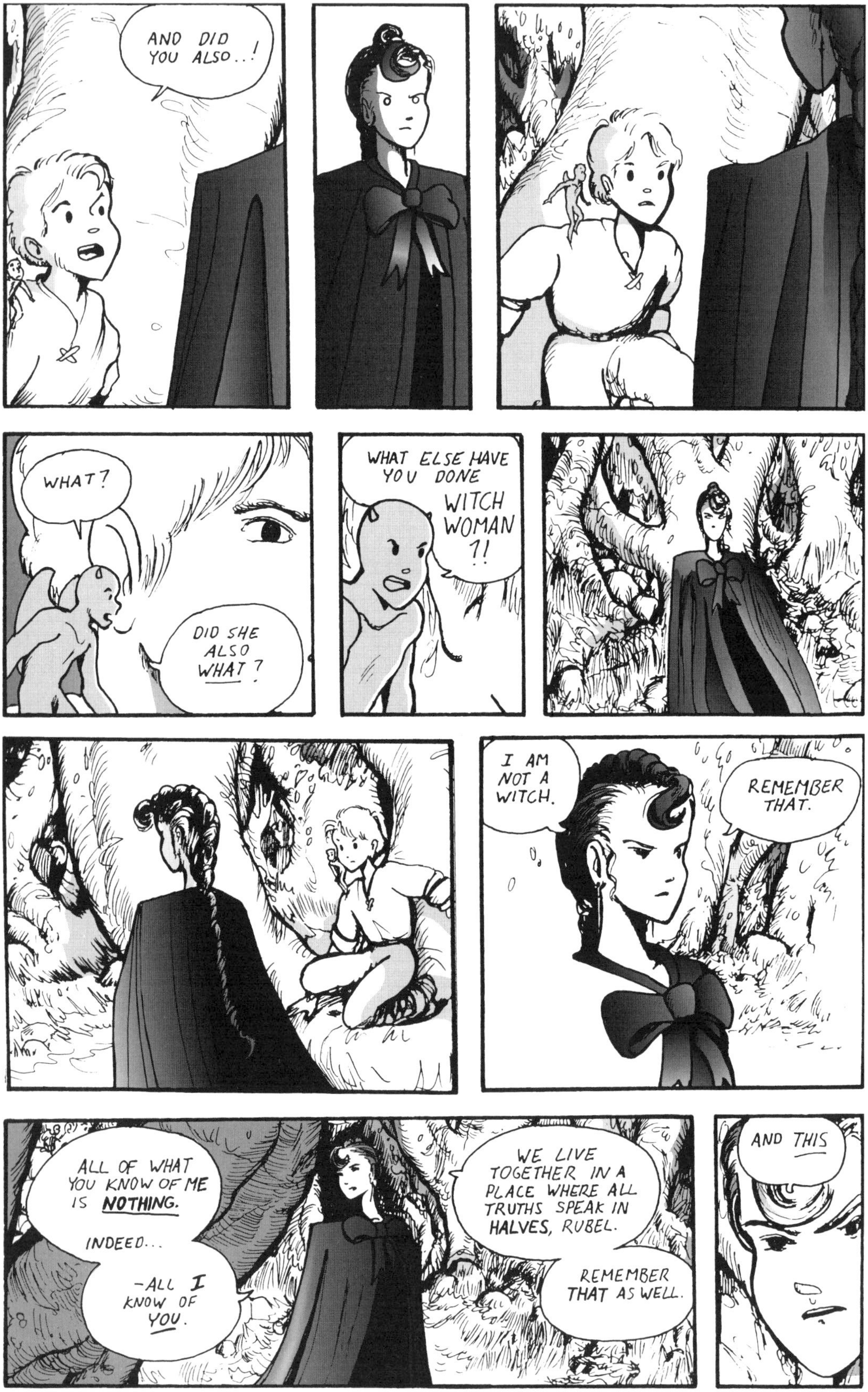
AND DID YOU ALSO..!
WHAT?
DID SHE ALSO WHAT?
WHAT ELSE HAVE YOU DONE WITCH WOMAN ?!
I AM NOT A WITCH.
REMEMBER THAT.
ALL OF WHAT YOU KNOW OF ME IS NOTHING.
INDEED...
-ALL I KNOW OF YOU.
WE LIVE TOGETHER IN A PLACE WHERE ALL TRUTHS SPEAK IN HALVES, RUBEL.
REMEMBER THAT AS WELL.
AND THIS

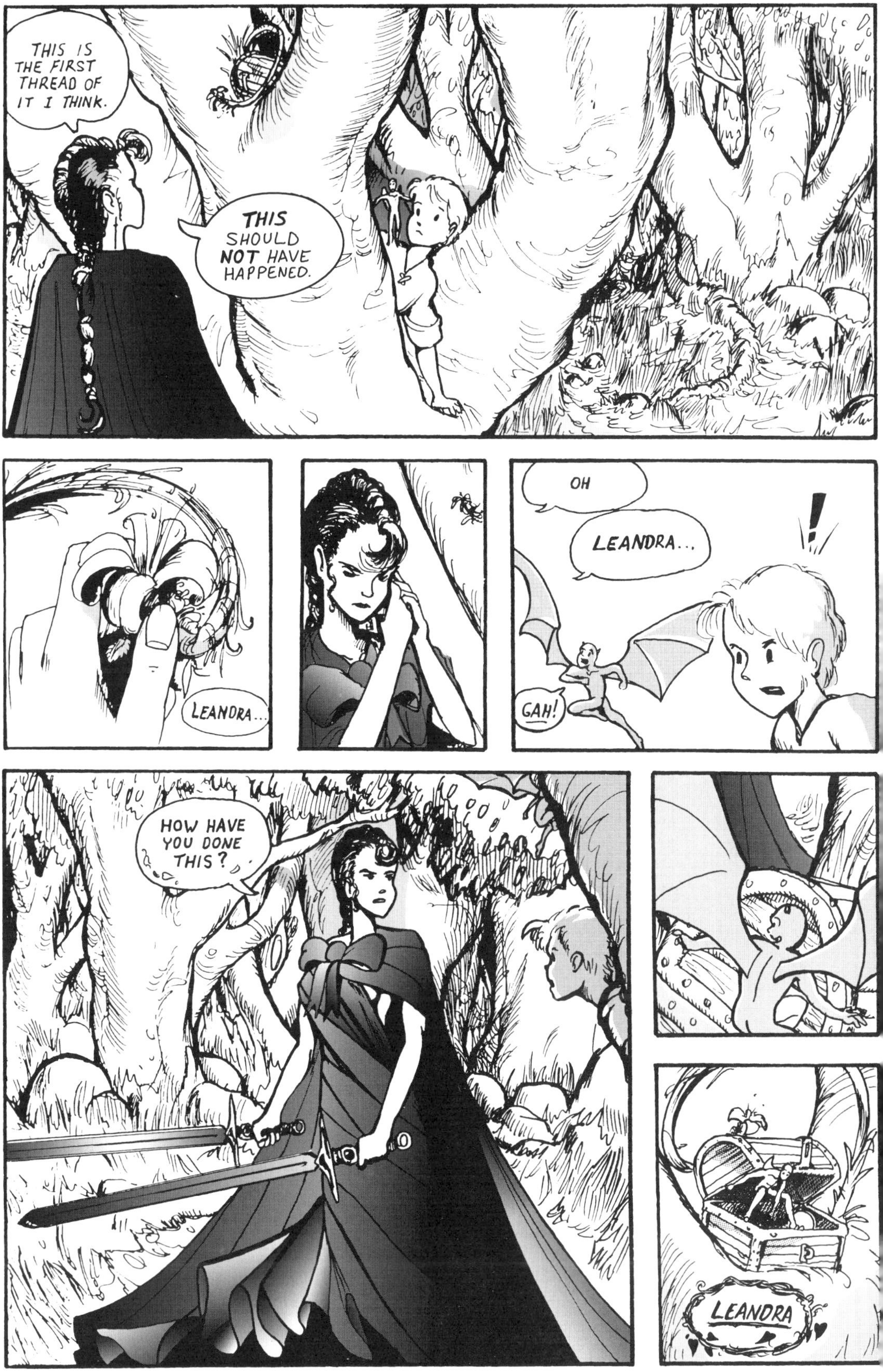
THIS IS THE FIRST THREAD OF IT I THINK.
THIS SHOULD NOT HAVE HAPPENED.
LEANDRA...
OH
LEANDRA...
!
GAH!
HOW HAVE YOU DONE THIS?
LEANDRA

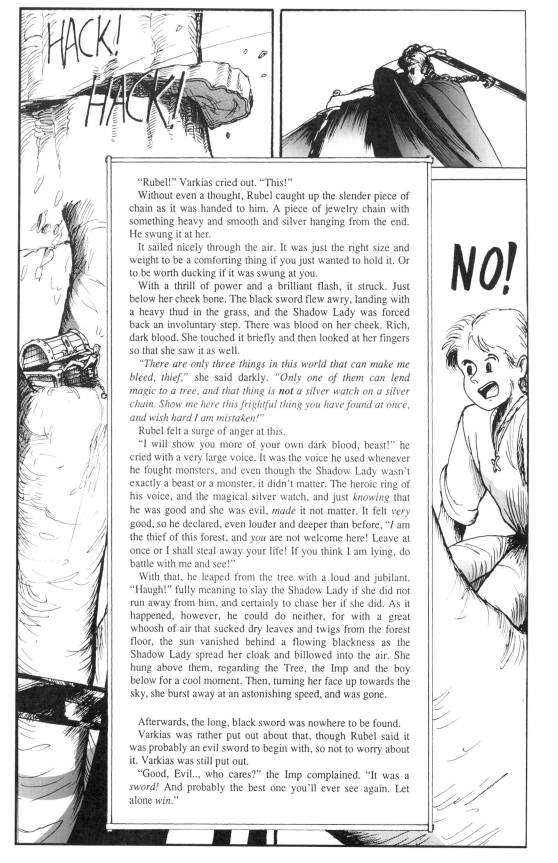

"Rubel!" Varkias cried out. "This!"

Without even a thought, Rubel caught up the slender piece of chain as it was handed to him. A piece of jewelry chain with something heavy and smooth and silver hanging from the end. He swung it at her.

It sailed nicely through the air. It was just the right size and weight to be a comforting thing if you just wanted to hold it. Or to be worth ducking if it was swung at you.

With a thrill of power and a brilliant flash, it struck. Just below her cheek bone. The black sword flew awry, landing with a heavy thud in the grass, and the Shadow Lady was forced back an involuntary step. There was blood on her cheek. Rich, dark blood. She touched it briefly and then looked at her fingers so that she saw it as well.

"There are only three things in this world that can make me bleed, thief," she said darkly. *"Only one of them can lend magic to a tree, and that thing is **not** a silver watch on a silver chain. Show me here this frightful thing you have found at once, and wish hard I am mistaken!"*

Rubel felt a surge of anger at this.

"I will show you more of your own dark blood, beast!" he cried with a very large voice. It was the voice he used whenever he fought monsters, and even though the Shadow Lady wasn't exactly a beast or a monster, it didn't matter. The heroic ring of his voice, and the magical silver watch, and just *knowing* that he was good and she was evil, *made* it not matter. It felt *very* good, so he declared, even louder and deeper than before, "*I* am the thief of this forest, and *you* are not welcome here! Leave at once or I shall steal away your life! If you think I am lying, do battle with me and see!"

With that, he leaped from the tree with a loud and jubilant, "Haugh!" fully meaning to slay the Shadow Lady if she did not run away from him, and certainly to chase her if she did. As it happened, however, he could do neither, for with a great whoosh of air that sucked dry leaves and twigs from the forest floor, the sun vanished behind a flowing blackness as the Shadow Lady spread her cloak and billowed into the air. She hung above them, regarding the Tree, the Imp and the boy below for a cool moment. Then, turning her face up towards the sky, she burst away at an astonishing speed, and was gone.

Afterwards, the long, black sword was nowhere to be found. Varkias was rather put out about that, though Rubel said it was probably an evil sword to begin with, so not to worry about it. Varkias was still put out.

"Good, Evil.., who cares?" the Imp complained. "It was a *sword!* And probably the best one you'll ever see again. Let alone *win.*"

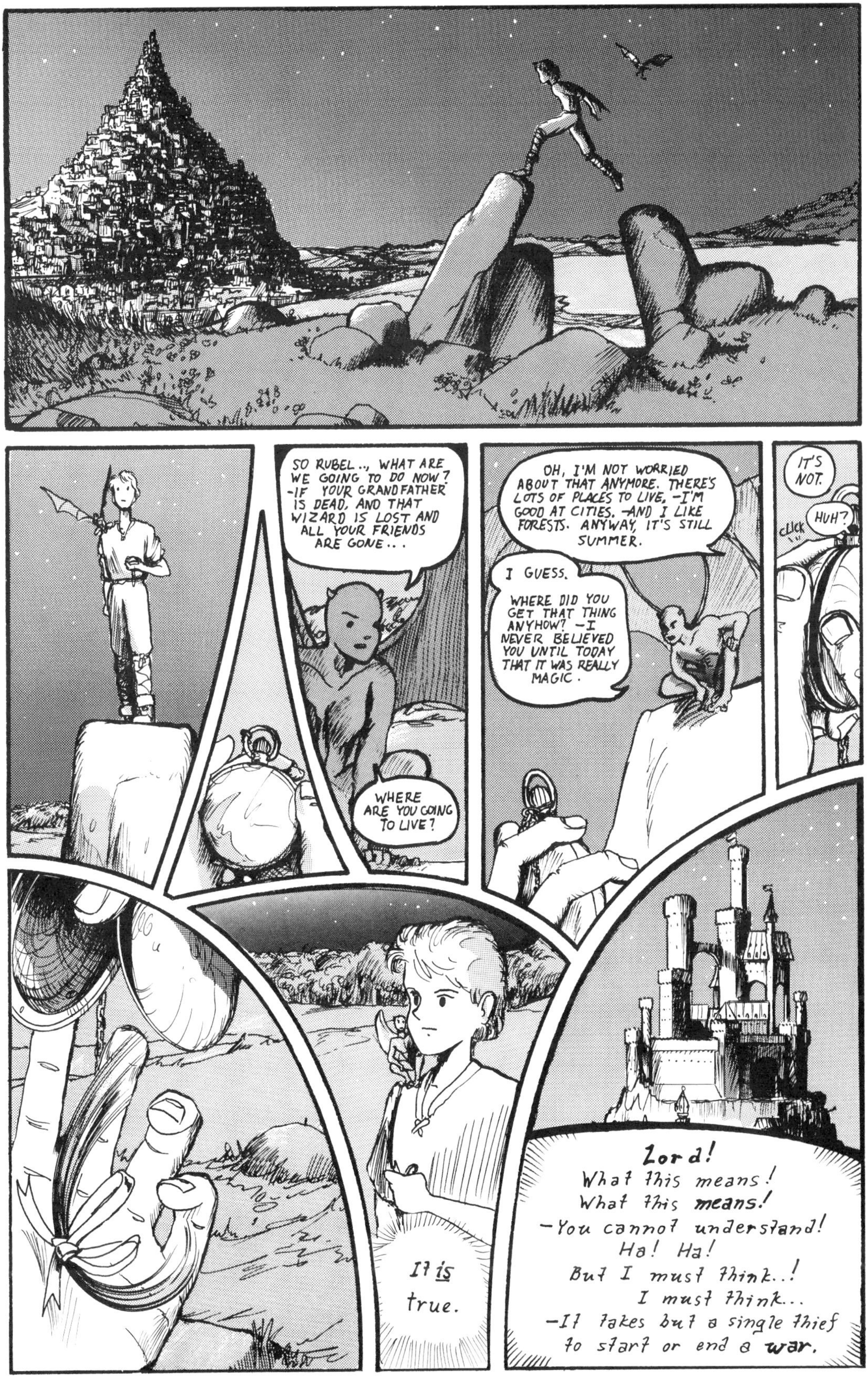
SO RUBEL.., WHAT ARE WE GOING TO DO NOW? -IF YOUR GRANDFATHER IS DEAD, AND THAT WIZARD IS LOST AND ALL YOUR FRIENDS ARE GONE...
WHERE ARE YOU GOING TO LIVE?
OH, I'M NOT WORRIED ABOUT THAT ANYMORE. THERE'S LOTS OF PLACES TO LIVE. -I'M GOOD AT CITIES. -AND I LIKE FORESTS. ANYWAY, IT'S STILL SUMMER.
I GUESS.
WHERE DID YOU GET THAT THING ANYHOW? -I NEVER BELIEVED YOU UNTIL TODAY THAT IT WAS REALLY MAGIC.
IT'S NOT.
HUH?
CLICK
It is true.
Lord!
What this means!
What this means!
-You cannot understand!
Ha! Ha!
But I must think..!
I must think...
-It takes but a single thief to start or end a war.

Chapter 2

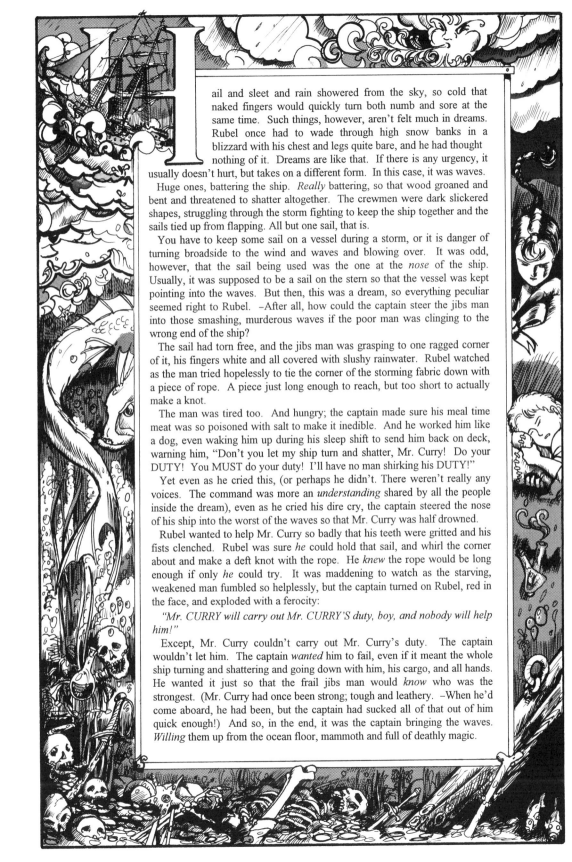

ail and sleet and rain showered from the sky, so cold that naked fingers would quickly turn both numb and sore at the same time. Such things, however, aren't felt much in dreams. Rubel once had to wade through high snow banks in a blizzard with his chest and legs quite bare, and he had thought nothing of it. Dreams are like that. If there is any urgency, it usually doesn't hurt, but takes on a different form. In this case, it was waves.

Huge ones, battering the ship. *Really* battering, so that wood groaned and bent and threatened to shatter altogether. The crewmen were dark slickered shapes, struggling through the storm fighting to keep the ship together and the sails tied up from flapping. All but one sail, that is.

You have to keep some sail on a vessel during a storm, or it is danger of turning broadside to the wind and waves and blowing over. It was odd, however, that the sail being used was the one at the *nose* of the ship. Usually, it was supposed to be a sail on the stern so that the vessel was kept pointing into the waves. But then, this was a dream, so everything peculiar seemed right to Rubel. –After all, how could the captain steer the jibs man into those smashing, murderous waves if the poor man was clinging to the wrong end of the ship?

The sail had torn free, and the jibs man was grasping to one ragged corner of it, his fingers white and all covered with slushy rainwater. Rubel watched as the man tried hopelessly to tie the corner of the storming fabric down with a piece of rope. A piece just long enough to reach, but too short to actually make a knot.

The man was tired too. And hungry; the captain made sure his meal time meat was so poisoned with salt to make it inedible. And he worked him like a dog, even waking him up during his sleep shift to send him back on deck, warning him, "Don't you let my ship turn and shatter, Mr. Curry! Do your DUTY! You MUST do your duty! I'll have no man shirking his DUTY!"

Yet even as he cried this, (or perhaps he didn't. There weren't really any voices. The command was more an *understanding* shared by all the people inside the dream), even as he cried his dire cry, the captain steered the nose of his ship into the worst of the waves so that Mr. Curry was half drowned.

Rubel wanted to help Mr. Curry so badly that his teeth were gritted and his fists clenched. Rubel was sure *he* could hold that sail, and whirl the corner about and make a deft knot with the rope. He *knew* the rope would be long enough if only *he* could try. It was maddening to watch as the starving, weakened man fumbled so helplessly, but the captain turned on Rubel, red in the face, and exploded with a ferocity:

"Mr. CURRY will carry out Mr. CURRY'S duty, boy, and nobody will help him!"

Except, Mr. Curry couldn't carry out Mr. Curry's duty. The captain wouldn't let him. The captain *wanted* him to fail, even if it meant the whole ship turning and shattering and going down with him, his cargo, and all hands. He wanted it just so that the frail jibs man would *know* who was the strongest. (Mr. Curry had once been strong; tough and leathery. –When he'd come aboard, he had been, but the captain had sucked all of that out of him quick enough!) And so, in the end, it was the captain bringing the waves. *Willing* them up from the ocean floor, mammoth and full of deathly magic.

Exhaustion finally closed its grip on Mr. Curry, and his face contorted with the expression people make when they *know* their disaster is an instant away. A stinging blast of sleety wind ripped the sail from the man's grip, taking one of his fingernails with it. He was flung; his arm went through an iron hard square of rope, right up to his shoulder where it twisted awkwardly, and broke with a resounding crack. Rubel gasped, and the night was eclipsed by the captain's roar, more terrible than the storm itself. All the sailors cowered with fear.

All but Rubel. He didn't cower. He *hated* the captain! With a growl, he leaped into the rigging and fought to catch the wild sail. He would *not* let the captain have his dark victory. He would not! But when the captain saw Rubel on his determined mission, he laughed. Rubel ground his teeth, and went on, catching the sail and tying it to the rope with such force that the knot squeezed as dry as a knob of bone. The captain only laughed.

He laughed because he knew something Rubel did not, and though Rubel couldn't remember what exactly it was, he *did* know he'd been made a fool. The captain's hair flew in the rain like a witch's. His eyes bulged. His skin was white and slick with sleet and his mouth somehow seemed too wide. In Rubel's vision, his captain, captain Lewis Tuck McGovern, seemed to transform into a demon. In revulsion and hate, Rubel's anger flared white hot. And now, the Shadow Lady smiled. She gave to him a sword, black and shiny, —as though fresh with oil.

Rubel seized the sword and leaped at the captain, ramming it through his chest. *Now,* the captain stopped laughing. He made a choking cry instead. Thick, horrid fluid belched from the wound and all the sailors cheered as their captain crumpled and died at Rubel's feet. They cheered, crying, 'Hero!', and even the first mate, who Rubel thought was a very great man, nodded at him with approval. . .

Rubel felt himself waking up.

The dream seeped away as dreams do, and he didn't try to stop it. His chest was sweaty and his stomach tight, but slowly he felt himself ease into the real world. He moved beneath the blanket and sighed as the morning sunlight and smell of fresh dew washed away the dream entirely from his mind. He sighed again and then sat up.

Rubel looked about and spied Varkias sitting high above him. The imp's wings and arms were stretched out in a leisurely yawn.

"Good morning, Varkias," Rubel called up to him, really meaning it.

"Yeah, it's not bad," the imp said, looking around at the misty country side with a speculative sort of look. "You were right, I guess. No bandits came and killed you. Didn't rain either."

"I told you this was a good place."

It was a good place, even when it *did* rain. He'd camped there on occasion when he was young, even going so far as to pack a blanket and pillow into a secret hiding spot. After four years they were still intact. Clean and dry, too.

"Yeah," the imp said vaguely. "–We going to the city today?"

"Uh huh." Rubel's stomach made an empty noise. "I'm starving. The last time I ate was yesterday morning on the ship, and that was just salt meat and biscuit. I'm going to get some real food for breakfast. Some bread and jam. And some oranges. And some eggs and bacon!" he added, smacking his lips.

"You going to steal it?" Varkias asked with an interest.

"No. I have money."

"Oh."

"And after, we're going to see the princess."

Varkias stopped. "We are?"

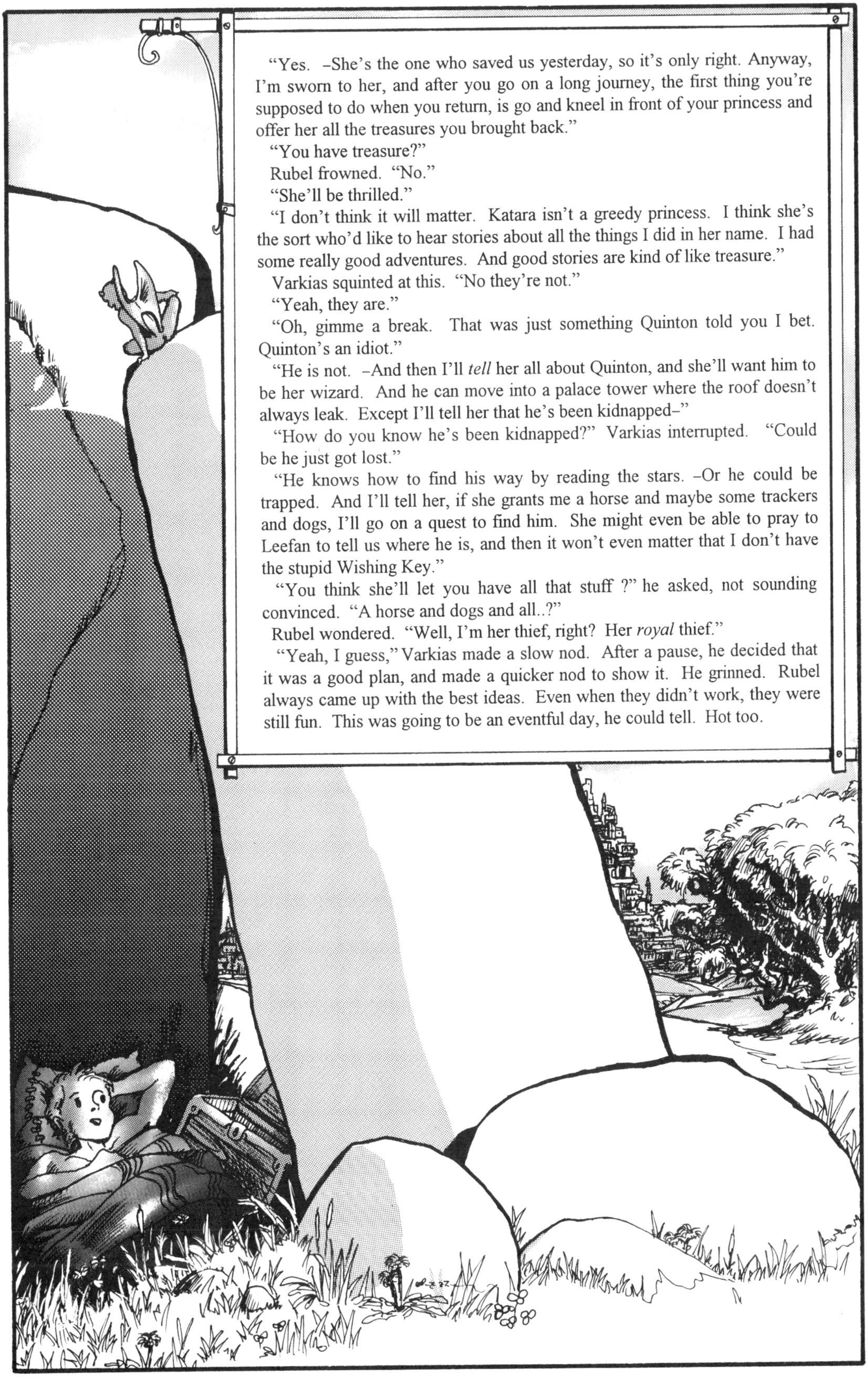

"Yes. –She's the one who saved us yesterday, so it's only right. Anyway, I'm sworn to her, and after you go on a long journey, the first thing you're supposed to do when you return, is go and kneel in front of your princess and offer her all the treasures you brought back."

"You have treasure?"

Rubel frowned. "No."

"She'll be thrilled."

"I don't think it will matter. Katara isn't a greedy princess. I think she's the sort who'd like to hear stories about all the things I did in her name. I had some really good adventures. And good stories are kind of like treasure."

Varkias squinted at this. "No they're not."

"Yeah, they are."

"Oh, gimme a break. That was just something Quinton told you I bet. Quinton's an idiot."

"He is not. –And then I'll *tell* her all about Quinton, and she'll want him to be her wizard. And he can move into a palace tower where the roof doesn't always leak. Except I'll tell her that he's been kidnapped–"

"How do you know he's been kidnapped?" Varkias interrupted. "Could be he just got lost."

"He knows how to find his way by reading the stars. –Or he could be trapped. And I'll tell her, if she grants me a horse and maybe some trackers and dogs, I'll go on a quest to find him. She might even be able to pray to Leefan to tell us where he is, and then it won't even matter that I don't have the stupid Wishing Key."

"You think she'll let you have all that stuff ?" he asked, not sounding convinced. "A horse and dogs and all..?"

Rubel wondered. "Well, I'm her thief, right? Her *royal* thief."

"Yeah, I guess," Varkias made a slow nod. After a pause, he decided that it was a good plan, and made a quicker nod to show it. He grinned. Rubel always came up with the best ideas. Even when they didn't work, they were still fun. This was going to be an eventful day, he could tell. Hot too.

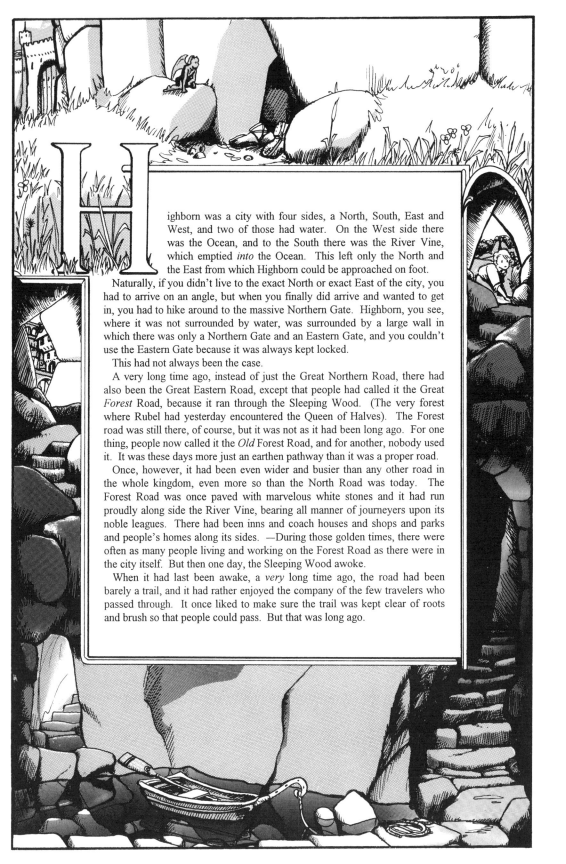

ighborn was a city with four sides, a North, South, East and West, and two of those had water. On the West side there was the Ocean, and to the South there was the River Vine, which emptied *into* the Ocean. This left only the North and the East from which Highborn could be approached on foot.

Naturally, if you didn't live to the exact North or exact East of the city, you had to arrive on an angle, but when you finally did arrive and wanted to get in, you had to hike around to the massive Northern Gate. Highborn, you see, where it was not surrounded by water, was surrounded by a large wall in which there was only a Northern Gate and an Eastern Gate, and you couldn't use the Eastern Gate because it was always kept locked.

This had not always been the case.

A very long time ago, instead of just the Great Northern Road, there had also been the Great Eastern Road, except that people had called it the Great *Forest* Road, because it ran through the Sleeping Wood. (The very forest where Rubel had yesterday encountered the Queen of Halves). The Forest road was still there, of course, but it was not as it had been long ago. For one thing, people now called it the *Old* Forest Road, and for another, nobody used it. It was these days more just an earthen pathway than it was a proper road.

Once, however, it had been even wider and busier than any other road in the whole kingdom, even more so than the North Road was today. The Forest Road was once paved with marvelous white stones and it had run proudly along side the River Vine, bearing all manner of journeyers upon its noble leagues. There had been inns and coach houses and shops and parks and people's homes along its sides. —During those golden times, there were often as many people living and working on the Forest Road as there were in the city itself. But then one day, the Sleeping Wood awoke.

When it had last been awake, a *very* long time ago, the road had been barely a trail, and it had rather enjoyed the company of the few travelers who passed through. It once liked to make sure the trail was kept clear of roots and brush so that people could pass. But that was long ago.

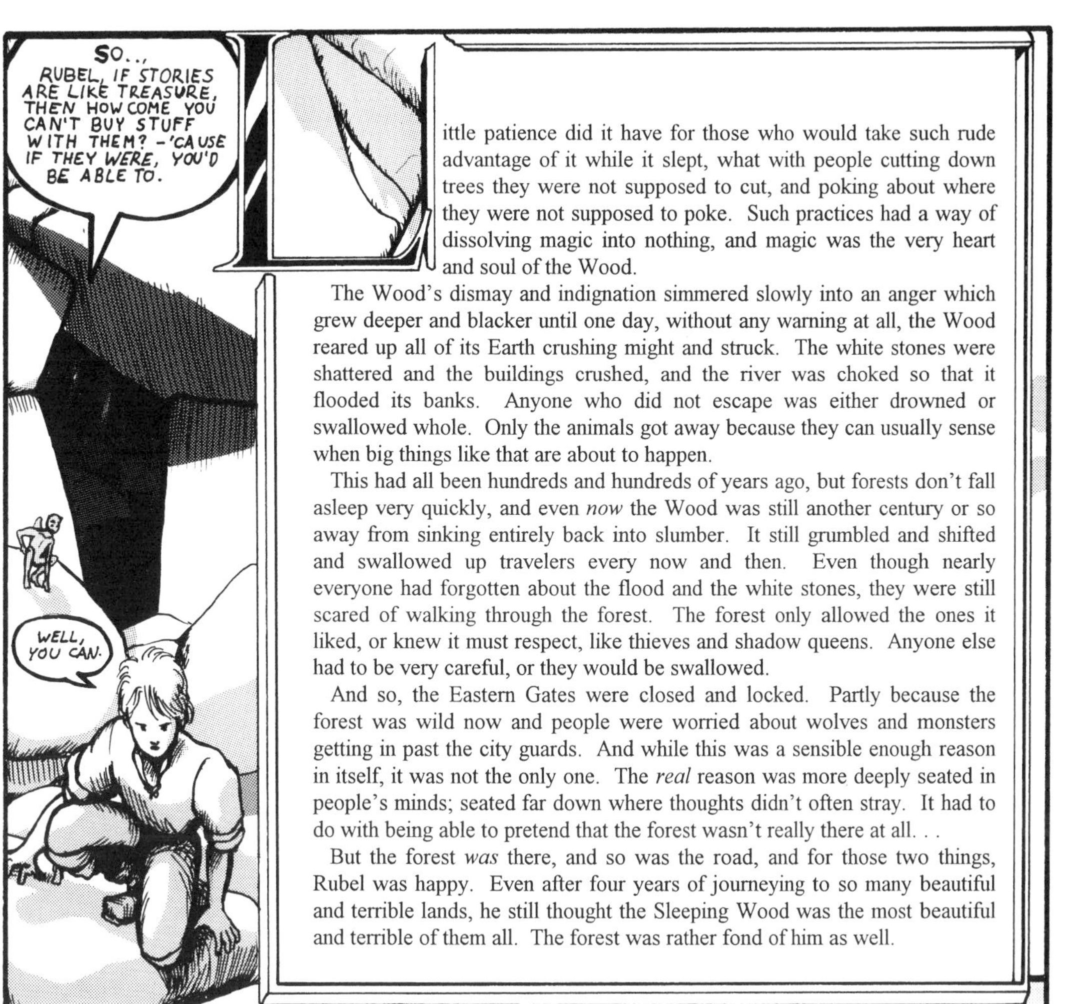
SO.. RUBEL, IF STORIES ARE LIKE TREASURE, THEN HOW COME YOU CAN'T BUY STUFF WITH THEM? -'CAUSE IF THEY WERE, YOU'D BE ABLE TO.
WELL, YOU CAN.

Little patience did it have for those who would take such rude advantage of it while it slept, what with people cutting down trees they were not supposed to cut, and poking about where they were not supposed to poke. Such practices had a way of dissolving magic into nothing, and magic was the very heart and soul of the Wood.

The Wood's dismay and indignation simmered slowly into an anger which grew deeper and blacker until one day, without any warning at all, the Wood reared up all of its Earth crushing might and struck. The white stones were shattered and the buildings crushed, and the river was choked so that it flooded its banks. Anyone who did not escape was either drowned or swallowed whole. Only the animals got away because they can usually sense when big things like that are about to happen.

This had all been hundreds and hundreds of years ago, but forests don't fall asleep very quickly, and even *now* the Wood was still another century or so away from sinking entirely back into slumber. It still grumbled and shifted and swallowed up travelers every now and then. Even though nearly everyone had forgotten about the flood and the white stones, they were still scared of walking through the forest. The forest only allowed the ones it liked, or knew it must respect, like thieves and shadow queens. Anyone else had to be very careful, or they would be swallowed.

And so, the Eastern Gates were closed and locked. Partly because the forest was wild now and people were worried about wolves and monsters getting in past the city guards. And while this was a sensible enough reason in itself, it was not the only one. The *real* reason was more deeply seated in people's minds; seated far down where thoughts didn't often stray. It had to do with being able to pretend that the forest wasn't really there at all. . .

But the forest *was* there, and so was the road, and for those two things, Rubel was happy. Even after four years of journeying to so many beautiful and terrible lands, he still thought the Sleeping Wood was the most beautiful and terrible of them all. The forest was rather fond of him as well.

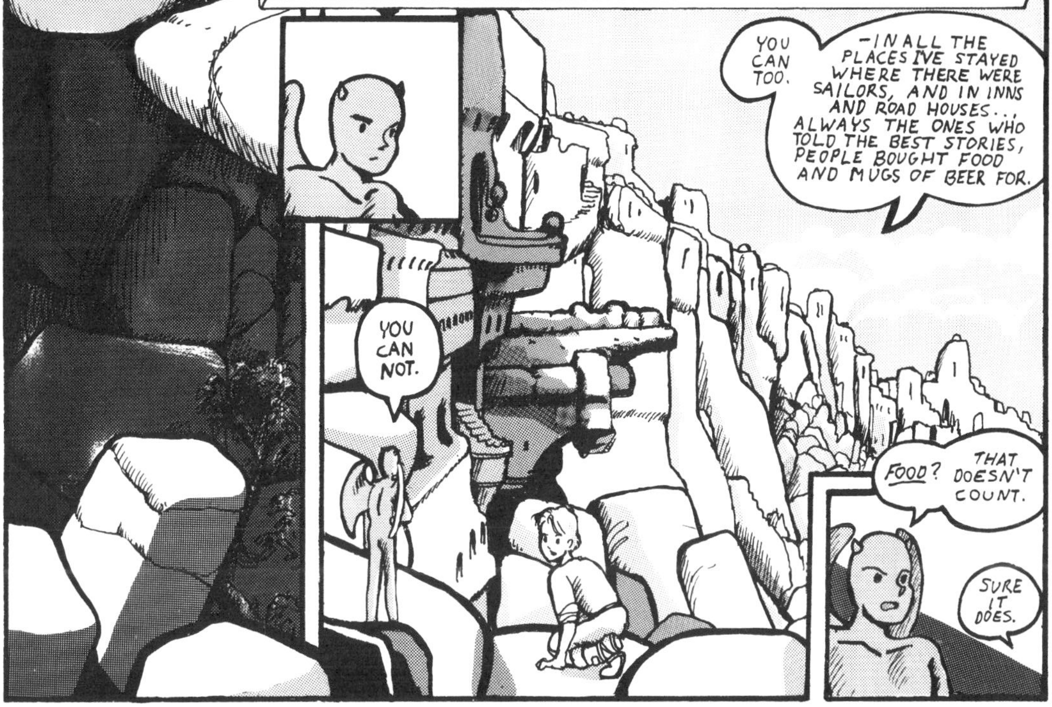
YOU CAN NOT.
YOU CAN TOO.
-IN ALL THE PLACES I'VE STAYED WHERE THERE WERE SAILORS, AND IN INNS AND ROAD HOUSES.. ALWAYS THE ONES WHO TOLD THE BEST STORIES, PEOPLE BOUGHT FOOD AND MUGS OF BEER FOR.
FOOD? THAT DOESN'T COUNT.
SURE IT DOES.

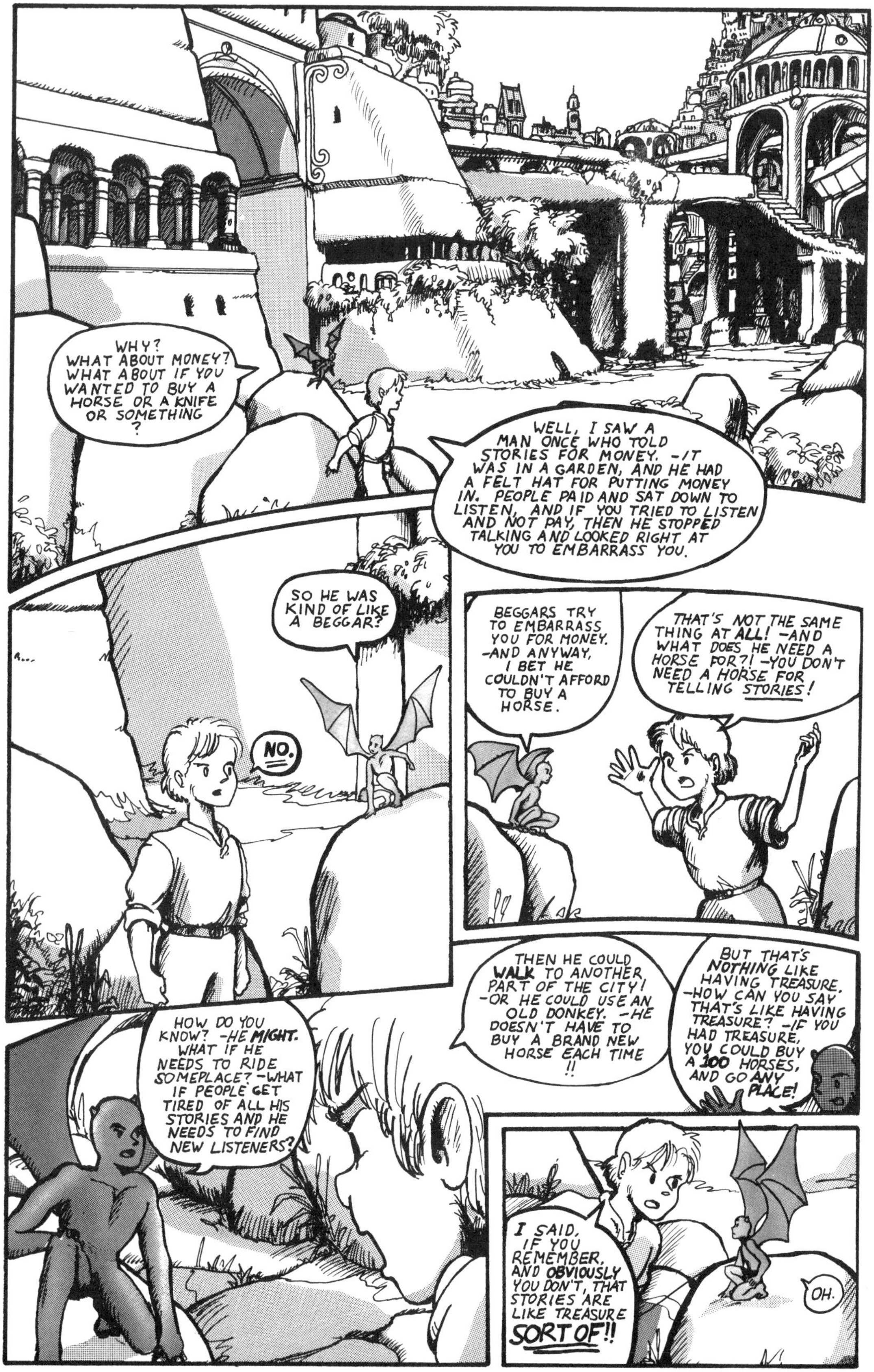
WHY? WHAT ABOUT MONEY? WHAT ABOUT IF YOU WANTED TO BUY A HORSE OR A KNIFE OR SOMETHING ?
WELL, I SAW A MAN ONCE WHO TOLD STORIES FOR MONEY. -IT WAS IN A GARDEN, AND HE HAD A FELT HAT FOR PUTTING MONEY IN. PEOPLE PAID AND SAT DOWN TO LISTEN, AND IF YOU TRIED TO LISTEN AND NOT PAY, THEN HE STOPPED TALKING AND LOOKED RIGHT AT YOU TO EMBARRASS YOU.
SO HE WAS KIND OF LIKE A BEGGAR?
NO.
BEGGARS TRY TO EMBARRASS YOU FOR MONEY. -AND ANYWAY, I BET HE COULDN'T AFFORD TO BUY A HORSE.
THAT'S NOT THE SAME THING AT ALL! -AND WHAT DOES HE NEED A HORSE FOR?! -YOU DON'T NEED A HORSE FOR TELLING STORIES!
HOW DO YOU KNOW? -HE MIGHT. WHAT IF HE NEEDS TO RIDE SOMEPLACE? -WHAT IF PEOPLE GET TIRED OF ALL HIS STORIES AND HE NEEDS TO FIND NEW LISTENERS?
THEN HE COULD WALK TO ANOTHER PART OF THE CITY! -OR HE COULD USE AN OLD DONKEY. -HE DOESN'T HAVE TO BUY A BRAND NEW HORSE EACH TIME !!
BUT THAT'S NOTHING LIKE HAVING TREASURE. -HOW CAN YOU SAY THAT'S LIKE HAVING TREASURE? -IF YOU HAD TREASURE, YOU COULD BUY A 100 HORSES, AND GO ANY PLACE!
I SAID, IF YOU REMEMBER, AND OBVIOUSLY YOU DON'T, THAT STORIES ARE LIKE TREASURE SORT OF!!
OH.

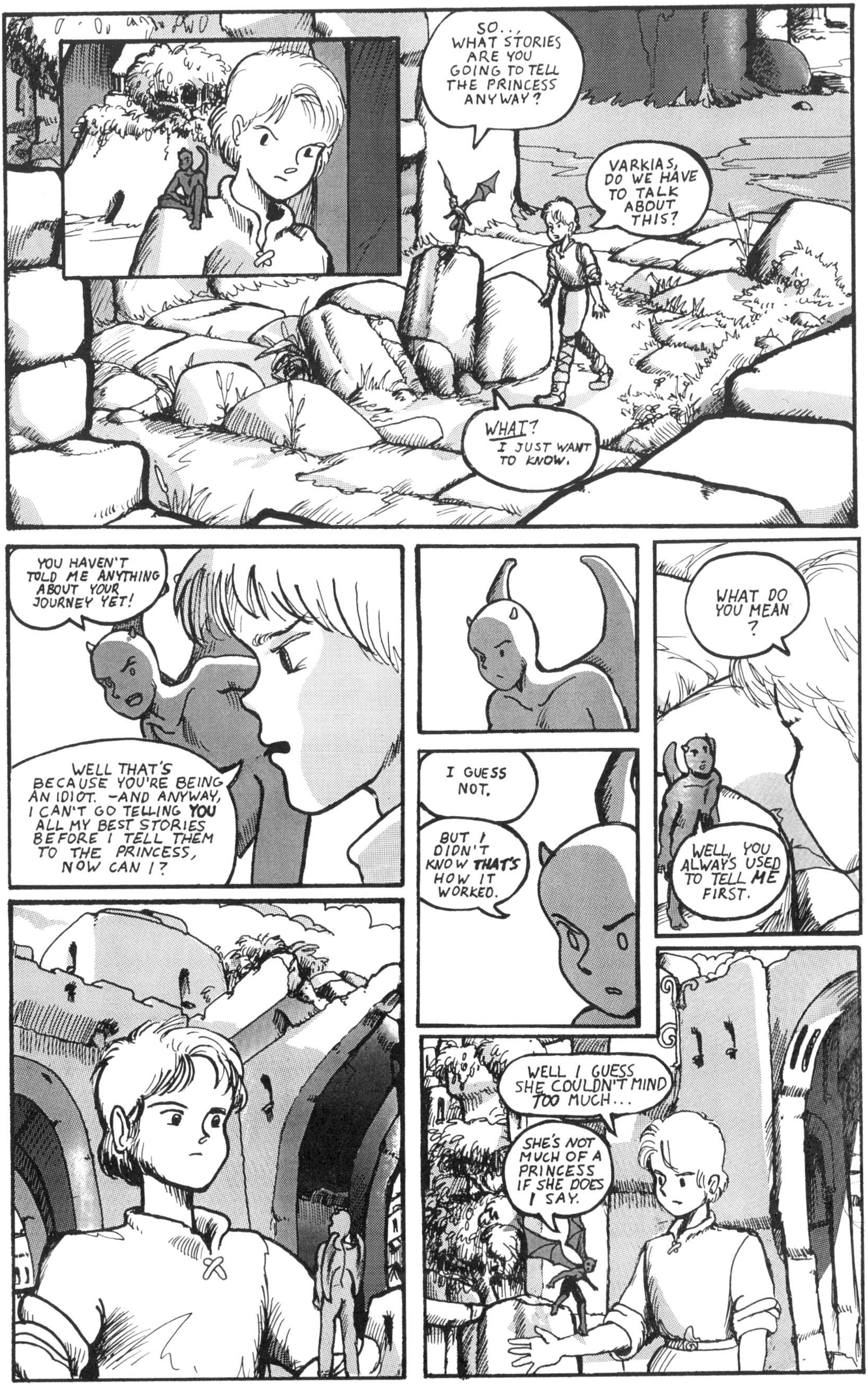
SO.., WHAT STORIES ARE YOU GOING TO TELL THE PRINCESS ANYWAY?
VARKIAS, DO WE HAVE TO TALK ABOUT THIS?
WHAT? I JUST WANT TO KNOW.
YOU HAVEN'T TOLD ME ANYTHING ABOUT YOUR JOURNEY YET!
WELL THAT'S BECAUSE YOU'RE BEING AN IDIOT. -AND ANYWAY, I CAN'T GO TELLING YOU ALL MY BEST STORIES BEFORE I TELL THEM TO THE PRINCESS, NOW CAN I?
WHAT DO YOU MEAN ?
WELL, YOU ALWAYS USED TO TELL ME FIRST.
I GUESS NOT.
BUT I DIDN'T KNOW THAT'S HOW IT WORKED.
WELL I GUESS SHE COULDN'T MIND TOO MUCH...
SHE'S NOT MUCH OF A PRINCESS IF SHE DOES I SAY.

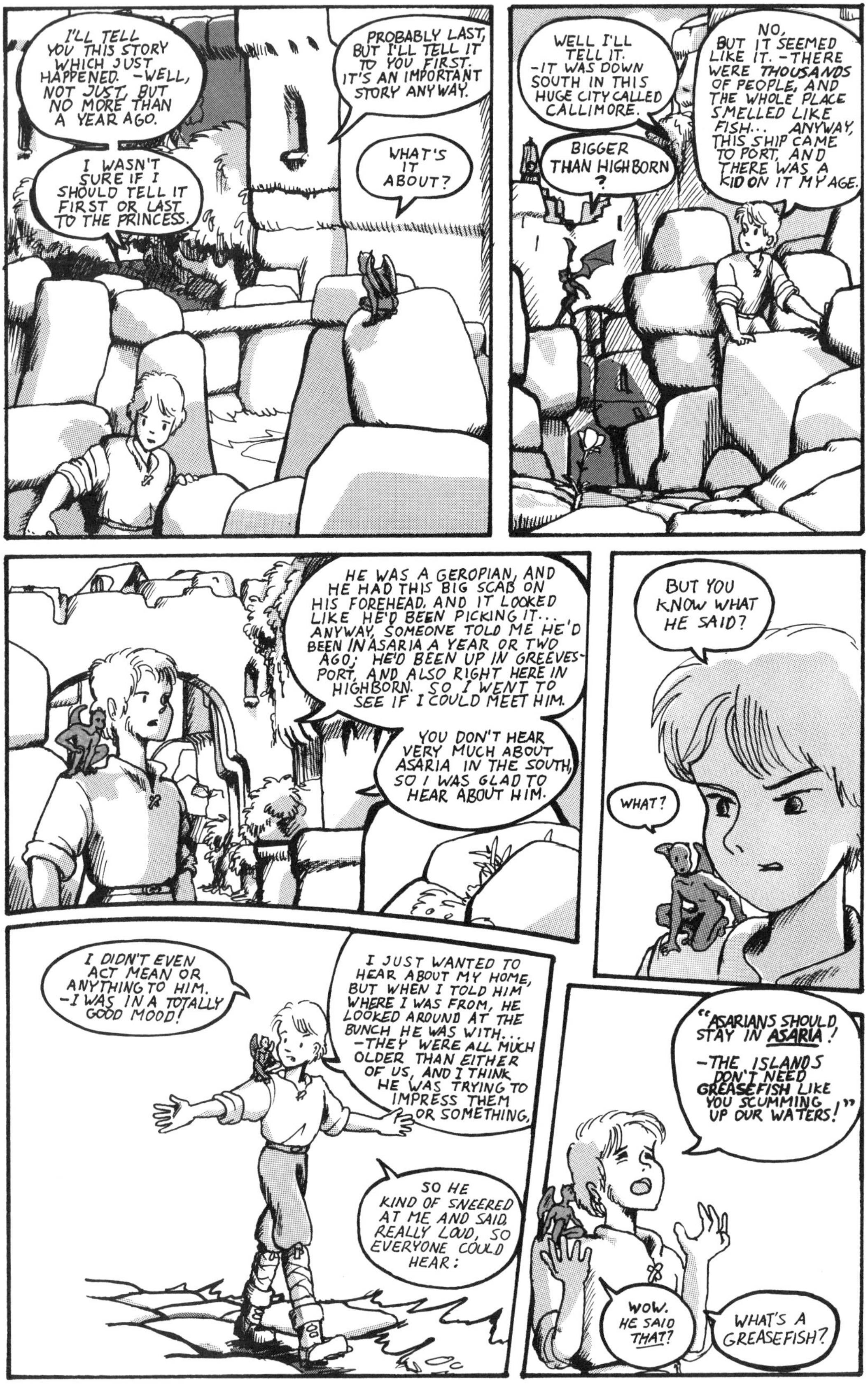
I'LL TELL YOU THIS STORY WHICH JUST HAPPENED. —WELL, NOT JUST, BUT NO MORE THAN A YEAR AGO.
I WASN'T SURE IF I SHOULD TELL IT FIRST OR LAST TO THE PRINCESS.
PROBABLY LAST, BUT I'LL TELL IT TO YOU FIRST. IT'S AN IMPORTANT STORY ANYWAY.
WHAT'S IT ABOUT?
WELL I'LL TELL IT. —IT WAS DOWN SOUTH IN THIS HUGE CITY CALLED CALLIMORE.
BIGGER THAN HIGHBORN?
NO, BUT IT SEEMED LIKE IT. —THERE WERE THOUSANDS OF PEOPLE, AND THE WHOLE PLACE SMELLED LIKE FISH... ANYWAY, THIS SHIP CAME TO PORT, AND THERE WAS A KID ON IT MY AGE.
HE WAS A GEROPIAN, AND HE HAD THIS BIG SCAB ON HIS FOREHEAD, AND IT LOOKED LIKE HE'D BEEN PICKING IT... ANYWAY, SOMEONE TOLD ME HE'D BEEN IN ASARIA A YEAR OR TWO AGO; HE'D BEEN UP IN GREEVES-PORT, AND ALSO RIGHT HERE IN HIGHBORN. SO I WENT TO SEE IF I COULD MEET HIM.
YOU DON'T HEAR VERY MUCH ABOUT ASARIA IN THE SOUTH, SO I WAS GLAD TO HEAR ABOUT HIM.
BUT YOU KNOW WHAT HE SAID?
WHAT?
I DIDN'T EVEN ACT MEAN OR ANYTHING TO HIM. —I WAS IN A TOTALLY GOOD MOOD!
I JUST WANTED TO HEAR ABOUT MY HOME, BUT WHEN I TOLD HIM WHERE I WAS FROM, HE LOOKED AROUND AT THE BUNCH HE WAS WITH... —THEY WERE ALL MUCH OLDER THAN EITHER OF US, AND I THINK HE WAS TRYING TO IMPRESS THEM OR SOMETHING,
SO HE KIND OF SNEERED AT ME AND SAID, REALLY LOUD, SO EVERYONE COULD HEAR:
"ASARIANS SHOULD STAY IN ASARIA! —THE ISLANDS DON'T NEED GREASEFISH LIKE YOU SCUMMING UP OUR WATERS!"
WOW. HE SAID THAT?
WHAT'S A GREASEFISH?

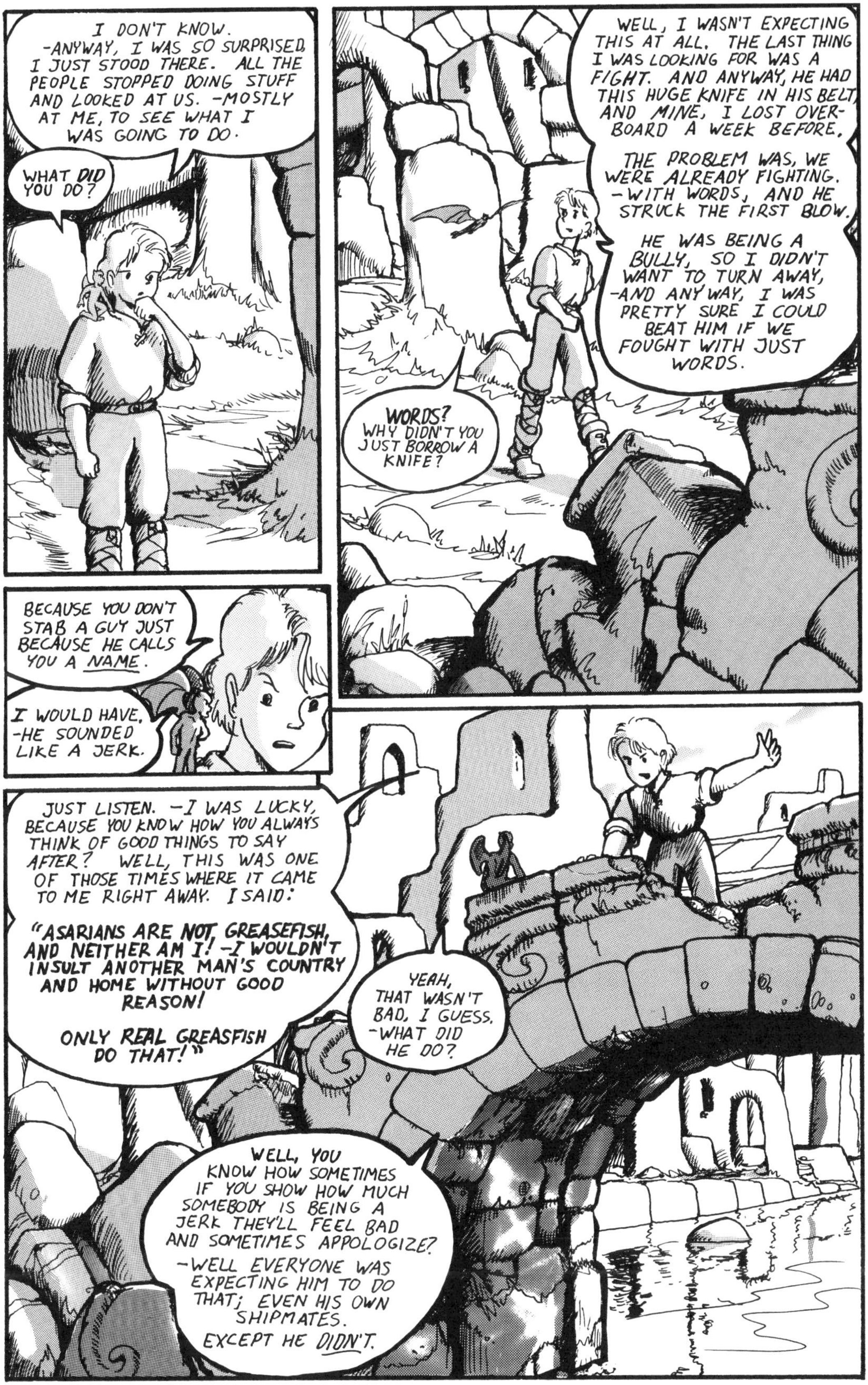
I DON'T KNOW. -ANYWAY, I WAS SO SURPRISED I JUST STOOD THERE. ALL THE PEOPLE STOPPED DOING STUFF AND LOOKED AT US. -MOSTLY AT ME, TO SEE WHAT I WAS GOING TO DO.
WHAT DID YOU DO?
WELL, I WASN'T EXPECTING THIS AT ALL. THE LAST THING I WAS LOOKING FOR WAS A FIGHT. AND ANYWAY, HE HAD THIS HUGE KNIFE IN HIS BELT, AND MINE, I LOST OVER-BOARD A WEEK BEFORE.
THE PROBLEM WAS, WE WERE ALREADY FIGHTING. -WITH WORDS, AND HE STRUCK THE FIRST BLOW.
HE WAS BEING A BULLY, SO I DIDN'T WANT TO TURN AWAY, -AND ANYWAY, I WAS PRETTY SURE I COULD BEAT HIM IF WE FOUGHT WITH JUST WORDS.
WORDS? WHY DIDN'T YOU JUST BORROW A KNIFE?
BECAUSE YOU DON'T STAB A GUY JUST BECAUSE HE CALLS YOU A NAME.
I WOULD HAVE. -HE SOUNDED LIKE A JERK.
JUST LISTEN. -I WAS LUCKY, BECAUSE YOU KNOW HOW YOU ALWAYS THINK OF GOOD THINGS TO SAY AFTER? WELL, THIS WAS ONE OF THOSE TIMES WHERE IT CAME TO ME RIGHT AWAY. I SAID:
"ASARIANS ARE NOT GREASEFISH, AND NEITHER AM I! -I WOULDN'T INSULT ANOTHER MAN'S COUNTRY AND HOME WITHOUT GOOD REASON!
ONLY REAL GREASFISH DO THAT!"
YEAH, THAT WASN'T BAD, I GUESS. -WHAT DID HE DO?
WELL, YOU KNOW HOW SOMETIMES IF YOU SHOW HOW MUCH SOMEBODY IS BEING A JERK THEY'LL FEEL BAD AND SOMETIMES APPOLOGIZE?
-WELL EVERYONE WAS EXPECTING HIM TO DO THAT; EVEN HIS OWN SHIPMATES.
EXCEPT HE DIDN'T.

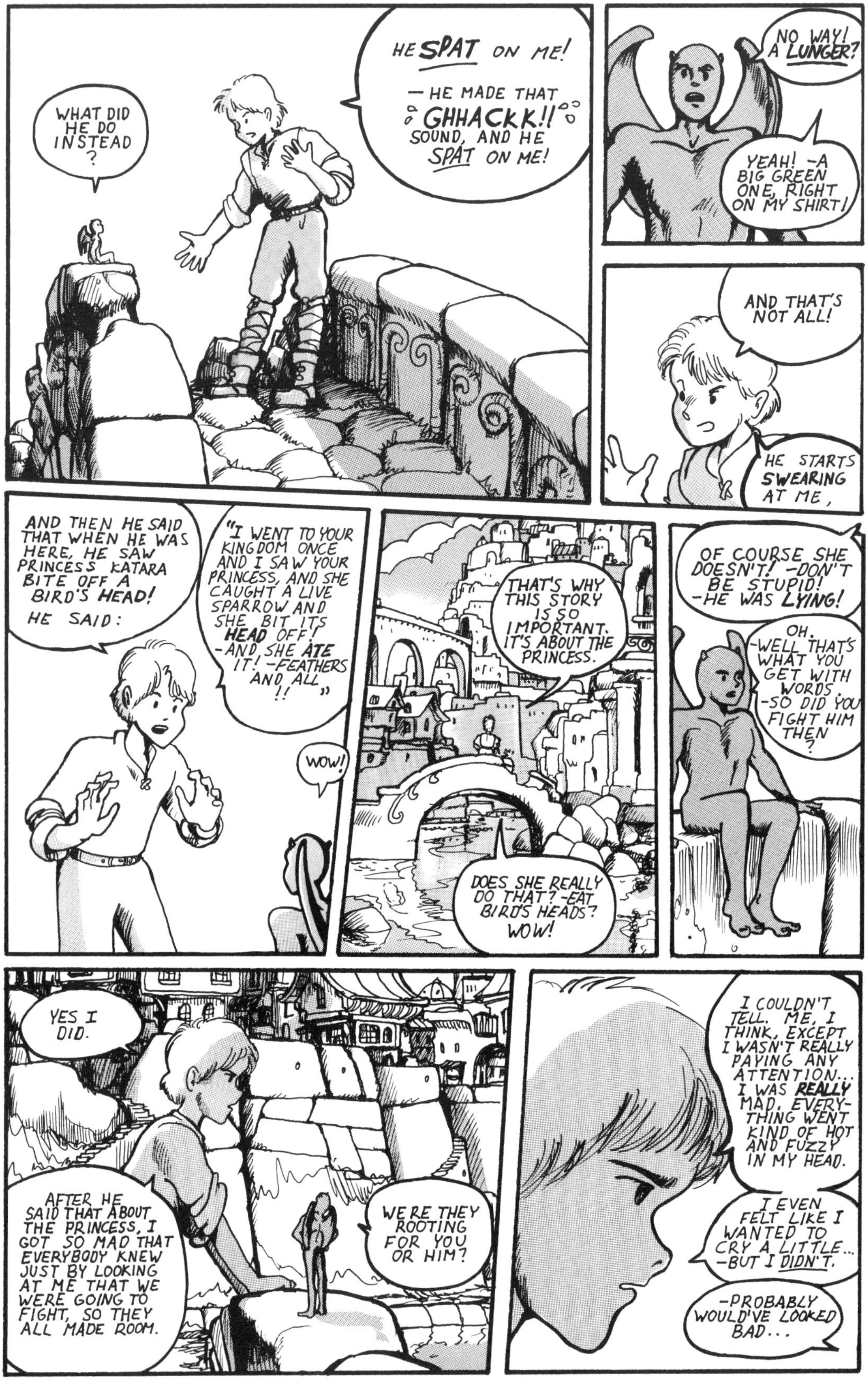
WHAT DID HE DO INSTEAD ?
HE SPAT ON ME!
—HE MADE THAT GHHACKK!! SOUND, AND HE SPAT ON ME!
NO WAY! A LUNGER?
YEAH! —A BIG GREEN ONE, RIGHT ON MY SHIRT!
AND THAT'S NOT ALL!
HE STARTS SWEARING AT ME,
AND THEN HE SAID THAT WHEN HE WAS HERE, HE SAW PRINCESS KATARA BITE OFF A BIRD'S HEAD!
HE SAID:
"I WENT TO YOUR KINGDOM ONCE AND I SAW YOUR PRINCESS, AND SHE CAUGHT A LIVE SPARROW AND SHE BIT ITS HEAD OFF! —AND SHE ATE IT! —FEATHERS AND ALL !!"
WOW!
THAT'S WHY THIS STORY IS SO IMPORTANT. IT'S ABOUT THE PRINCESS.
DOES SHE REALLY DO THAT? —EAT BIRD'S HEADS? WOW!
OF COURSE SHE DOESN'T! —DON'T BE STUPID! —HE WAS LYING!
OH. —WELL THAT'S WHAT YOU GET WITH WORDS —SO DID YOU FIGHT HIM THEN ?
YES I DID.
AFTER HE SAID THAT ABOUT THE PRINCESS, I GOT SO MAD THAT EVERYBODY KNEW JUST BY LOOKING AT ME THAT WE WERE GOING TO FIGHT, SO THEY ALL MADE ROOM.
WERE THEY ROOTING FOR YOU OR HIM?
I COULDN'T TELL. ME, I THINK, EXCEPT I WASN'T REALLY PAYING ANY ATTENTION... I WAS REALLY MAD. EVERYTHING WENT KIND OF HOT AND FUZZY IN MY HEAD.
I EVEN FELT LIKE I WANTED TO CRY A LITTLE... —BUT I DIDN'T.
—PROBABLY WOULD'VE LOOKED BAD...

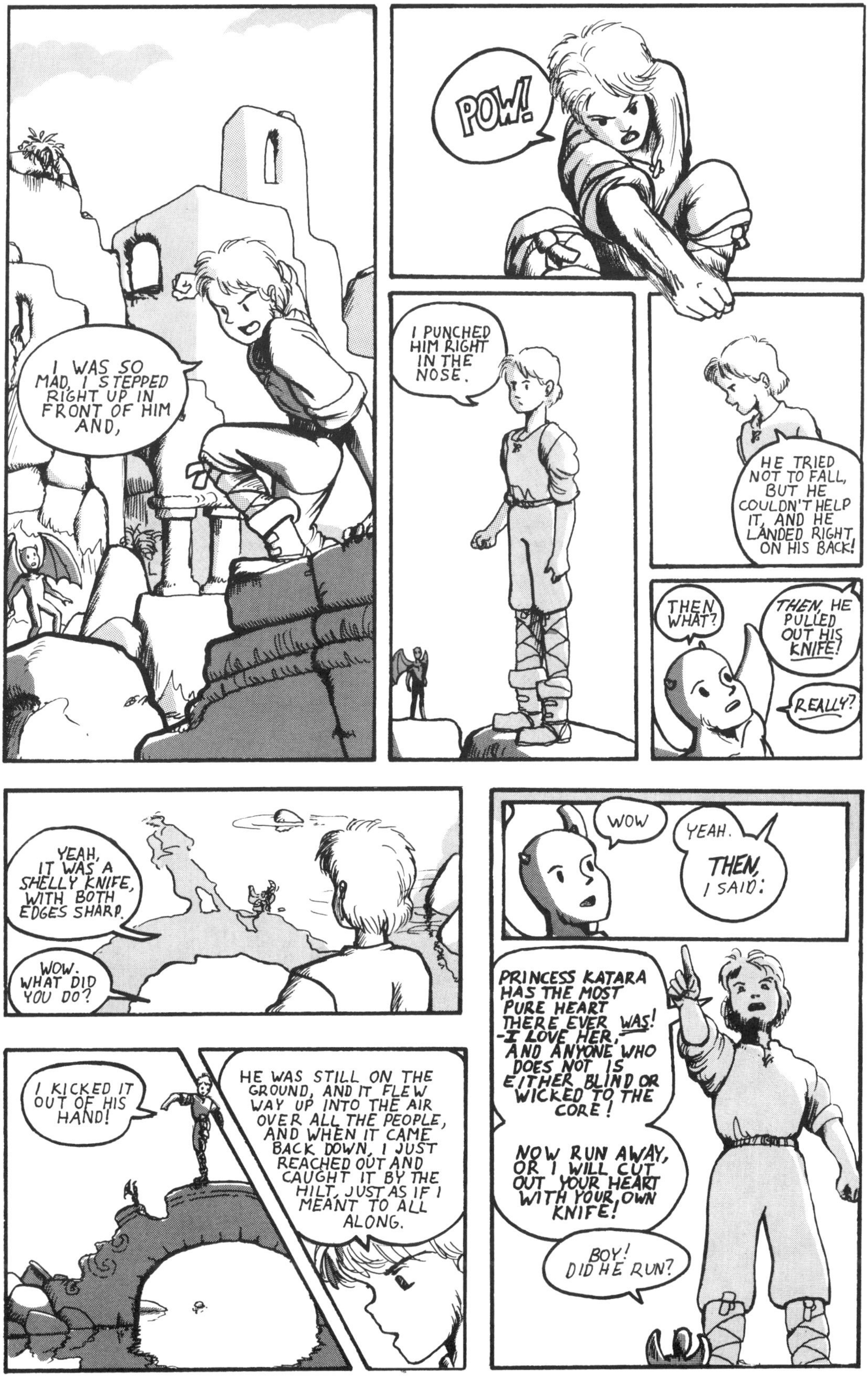
I WAS SO MAD, I STEPPED RIGHT UP IN FRONT OF HIM AND,
POW!
I PUNCHED HIM RIGHT IN THE NOSE.
HE TRIED NOT TO FALL, BUT HE COULDN'T HELP IT, AND HE LANDED RIGHT ON HIS BACK!
THEN WHAT?
THEN, HE PULLED OUT HIS KNIFE!
REALLY?
YEAH, IT WAS A SHELLY KNIFE, WITH BOTH EDGES SHARP.
WOW. WHAT DID YOU DO?
I KICKED IT OUT OF HIS HAND!
HE WAS STILL ON THE GROUND, AND IT FLEW WAY UP INTO THE AIR OVER ALL THE PEOPLE, AND WHEN IT CAME BACK DOWN, I JUST REACHED OUT AND CAUGHT IT BY THE HILT, JUST AS IF I MEANT TO ALL ALONG.
WOW
YEAH. THEN, I SAID:
PRINCESS KATARA HAS THE MOST PURE HEART THERE EVER WAS! -I LOVE HER, AND ANYONE WHO DOES NOT IS EITHER BLIND OR WICKED TO THE CORE!
NOW RUN AWAY, OR I WILL CUT OUT YOUR HEART WITH YOUR OWN KNIFE!
BOY! DID HE RUN?

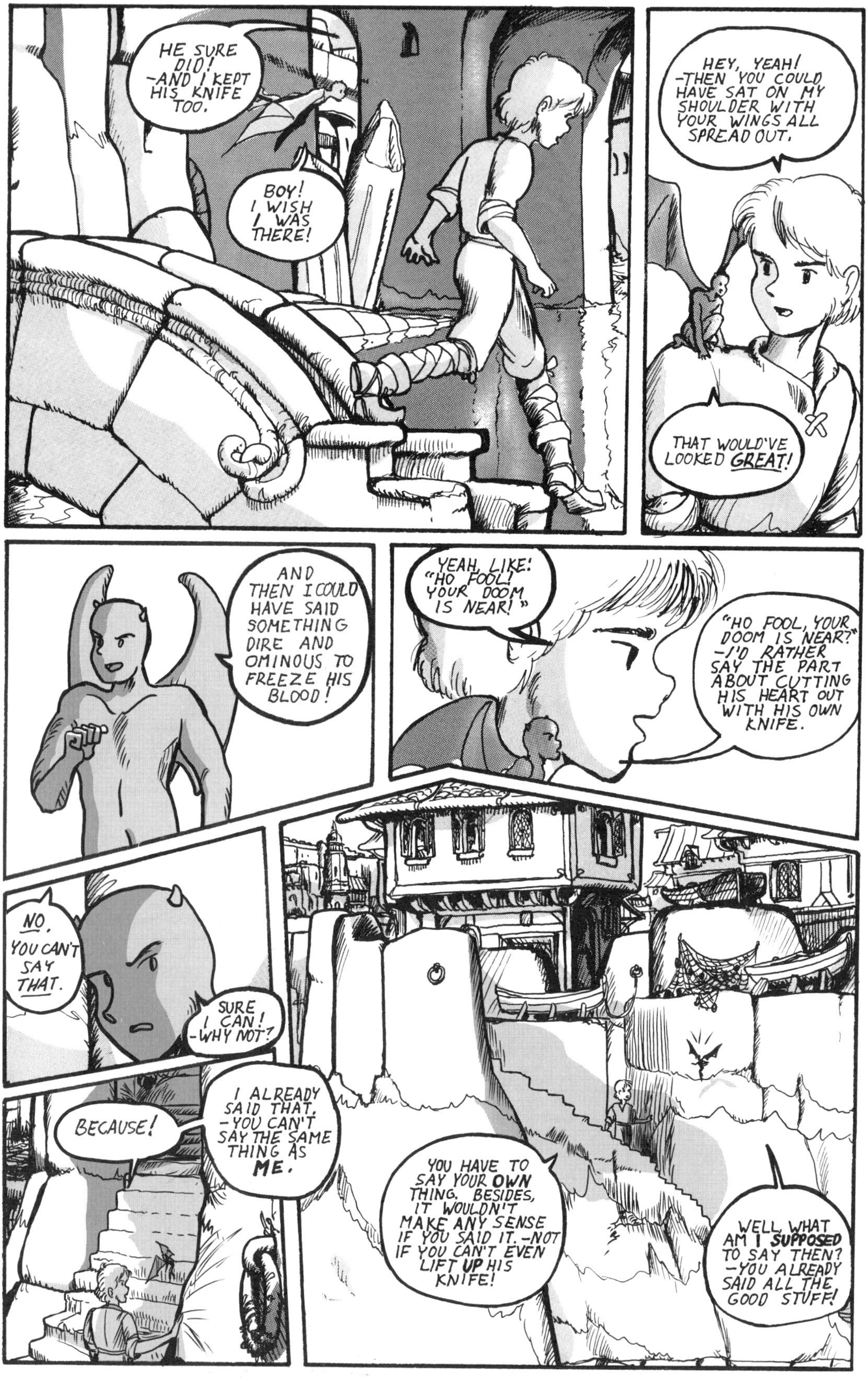
HE SURE DID! -AND I KEPT HIS KNIFE TOO.
BOY! I WISH I WAS THERE!
HEY, YEAH! -THEN YOU COULD HAVE SAT ON MY SHOULDER WITH YOUR WINGS ALL SPREAD OUT.
THAT WOULD'VE LOOKED GREAT!
AND THEN I COULD HAVE SAID SOMETHING DIRE AND OMINOUS TO FREEZE HIS BLOOD!
YEAH, LIKE: "HO FOOL! YOUR DOOM IS NEAR!"
"HO FOOL, YOUR DOOM IS NEAR?" -I'D RATHER SAY THE PART ABOUT CUTTING HIS HEART OUT WITH HIS OWN KNIFE.
NO. YOU CAN'T SAY THAT.
SURE I CAN! -WHY NOT?
BECAUSE!
I ALREADY SAID THAT. -YOU CAN'T SAY THE SAME THING AS ME.
YOU HAVE TO SAY YOUR OWN THING. BESIDES, IT WOULDN'T MAKE ANY SENSE IF YOU SAID IT. -NOT IF YOU CAN'T EVEN LIFT UP HIS KNIFE!
WELL, WHAT AM I SUPPOSED TO SAY THEN? -YOU ALREADY SAID ALL THE GOOD STUFF!

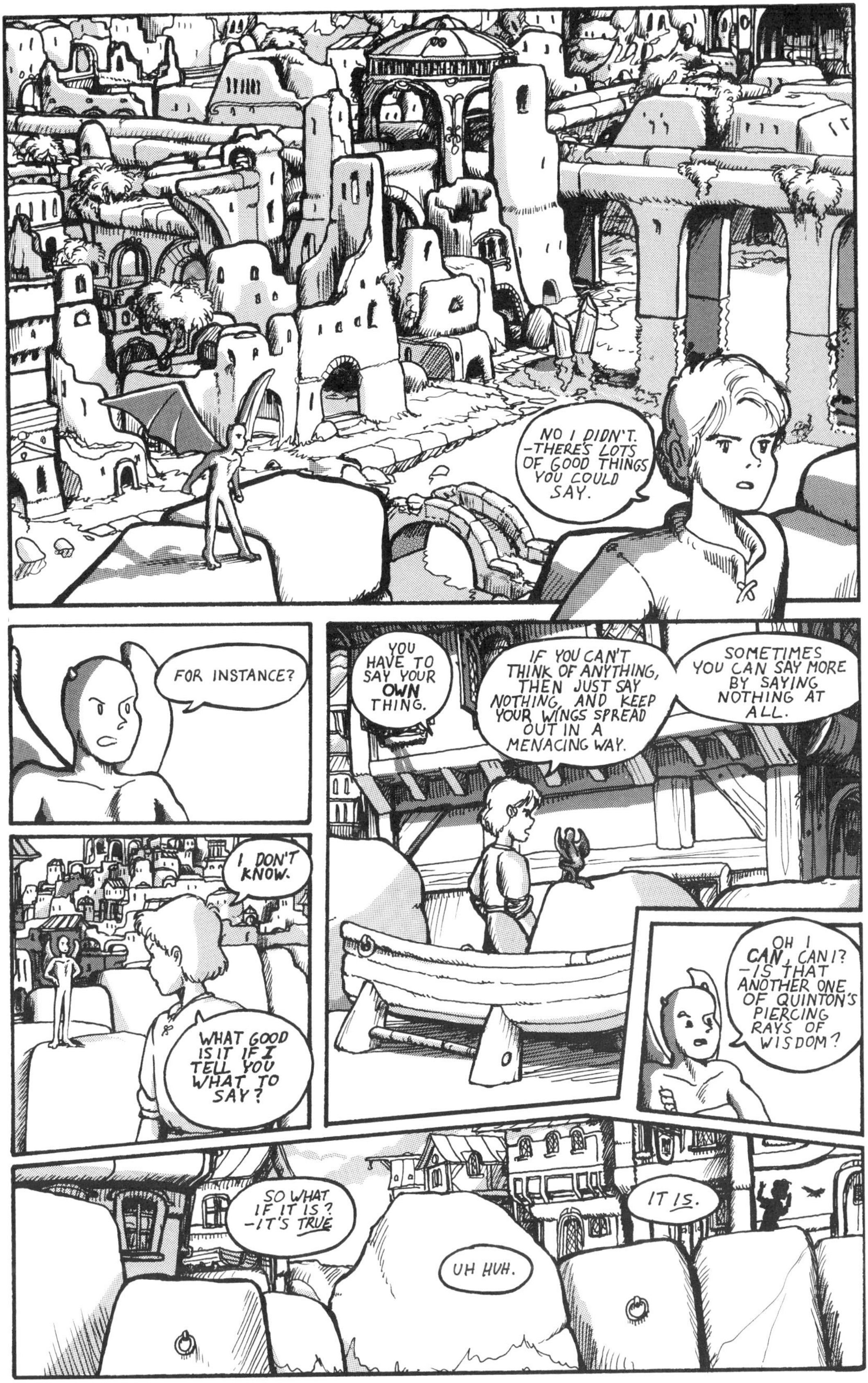
NO I DIDN'T. -THERE'S LOTS OF GOOD THINGS YOU COULD SAY.
FOR INSTANCE?
I DON'T KNOW.
WHAT GOOD IS IT IF I TELL YOU WHAT TO SAY?
YOU HAVE TO SAY YOUR OWN THING.
IF YOU CAN'T THINK OF ANYTHING, THEN JUST SAY NOTHING, AND KEEP YOUR WINGS SPREAD OUT IN A MENACING WAY.
SOMETIMES YOU CAN SAY MORE BY SAYING NOTHING AT ALL.
OH I CAN, CAN I? -IS THAT ANOTHER ONE OF QUINTON'S PIERCING RAYS OF WISDOM?
SO WHAT IF IT IS? -IT'S TRUE
UH HUH.
IT IS.

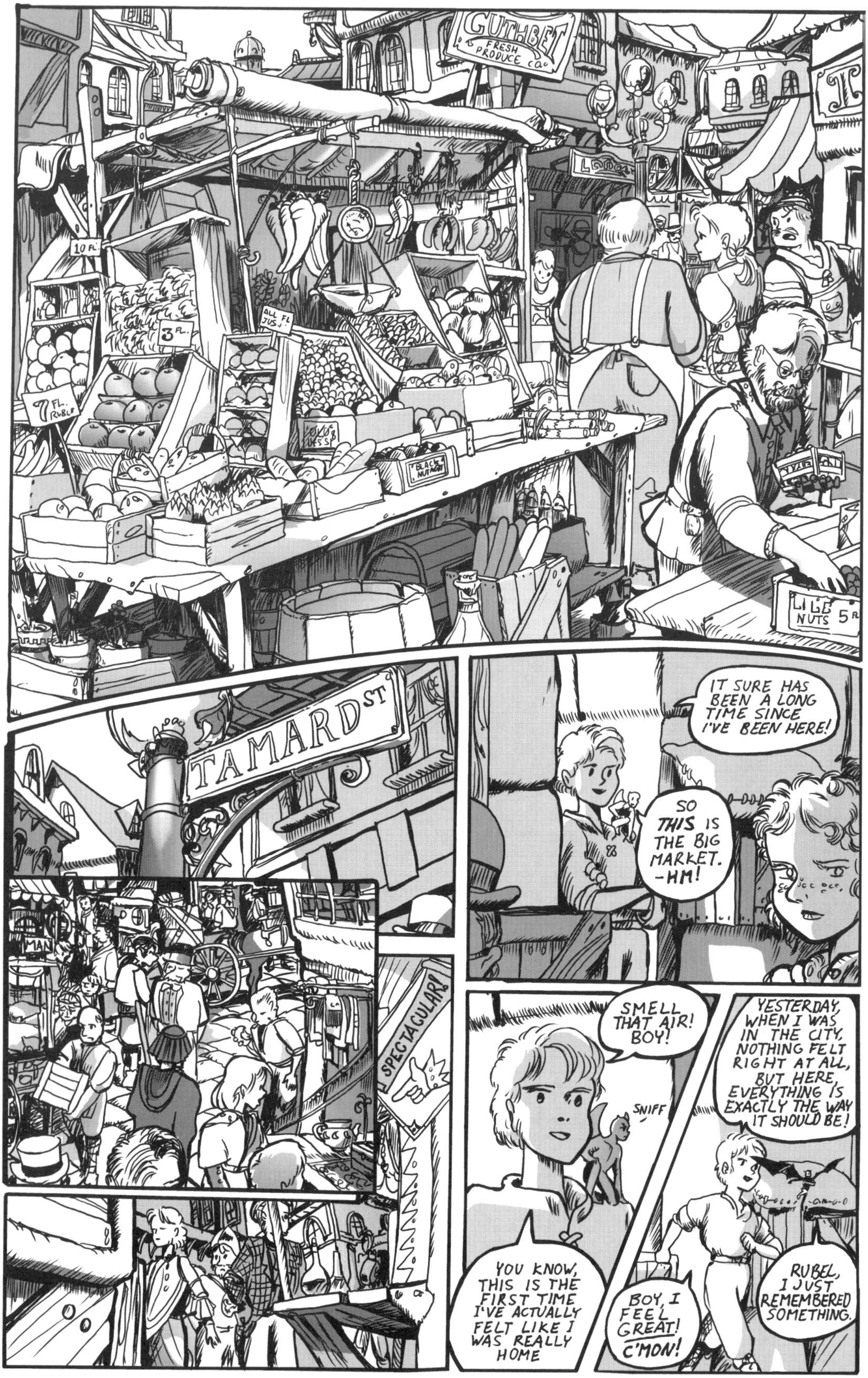
GUTHBET FRESH PRODUCE CO.
10 FL.
3 FL.
7 FL. RUBLE
BLACK NUTMEG
LILB NUTS 5 FL.
TAMARD ST
IT SURE HAS BEEN A LONG TIME SINCE I'VE BEEN HERE!
SO THIS IS THE BIG MARKET. -HM!
SPECTACULAR!
SMELL THAT AIR! BOY!
SNIFF
YESTERDAY, WHEN I WAS IN THE CITY, NOTHING FELT RIGHT AT ALL, BUT HERE, EVERYTHING IS EXACTLY THE WAY IT SHOULD BE!
YOU KNOW, THIS IS THE FIRST TIME I'VE ACTUALLY FELT LIKE I WAS REALLY HOME
BOY, I FEEL GREAT! C'MON!
RUBEL, I JUST REMEMBERED SOMETHING.

IT WAS SOMETHING ABOUT QUINTON.

WHAT ABOUT HIM?

I DON'T REMEMBER EXACTLY. —IT WAS A LONG TIME AGO.

YOU WERE ONLY THREE.

THREE..?

IT WAS SOMETHING HE SAID...

NO, NO..! IT WAS SOMETHING FROM LAST NIGHT!

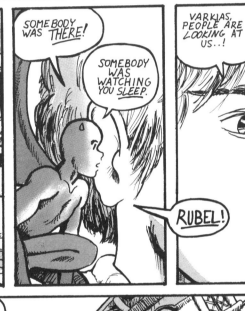

SOMEBODY WAS THERE!

SOMEBODY WAS WATCHING YOU SLEEP.

VARKIAS, PEOPLE ARE LOOKING AT US..!

RUBEL!

WE SHOULD LEAVE HERE!

WE SHOULD LEAVE HERE RIGHT AWAY!

WE HAVE TO LEAVE, BEFORE...

MA! LOOK'IT! —ON THAT KID'S SHOULDER! —A LITTLE MAN WITH BAT'S WINGS!

Chapter 3

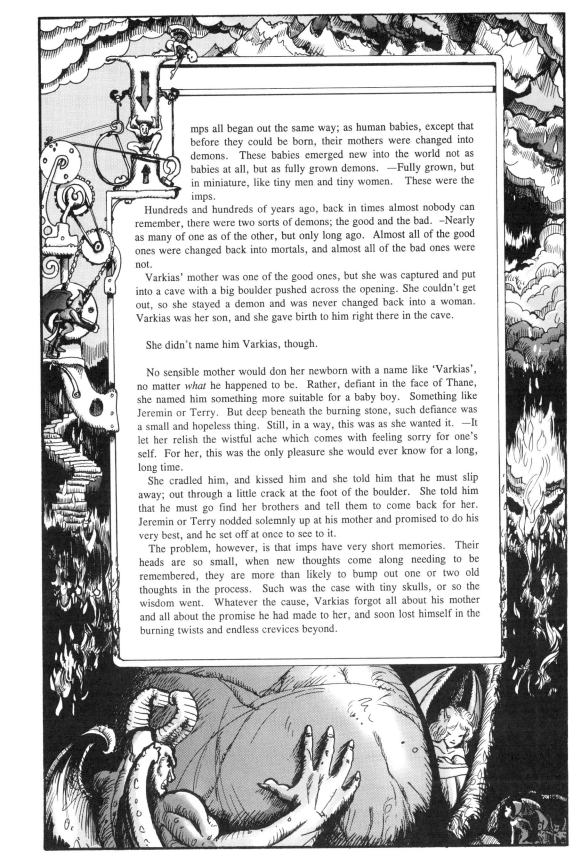

mps all began out the same way; as human babies, except that before they could be born, their mothers were changed into demons. These babies emerged new into the world not as babies at all, but as fully grown demons. —Fully grown, but in miniature, like tiny men and tiny women. These were the imps.

Hundreds and hundreds of years ago, back in times almost nobody can remember, there were two sorts of demons; the good and the bad. —Nearly as many of one as of the other, but only long ago. Almost all of the good ones were changed back into mortals, and almost all of the bad ones were not.

Varkias' mother was one of the good ones, but she was captured and put into a cave with a big boulder pushed across the opening. She couldn't get out, so she stayed a demon and was never changed back into a woman. Varkias was her son, and she gave birth to him right there in the cave.

She didn't name him Varkias, though.

No sensible mother would don her newborn with a name like 'Varkias', no matter *what* he happened to be. Rather, defiant in the face of Thane, she named him something more suitable for a baby boy. Something like Jeremin or Terry. But deep beneath the burning stone, such defiance was a small and hopeless thing. Still, in a way, this was as she wanted it. —It let her relish the wistful ache which comes with feeling sorry for one's self. For her, this was the only pleasure she would ever know for a long, long time.

She cradled him, and kissed him and she told him that he must slip away; out through a little crack at the foot of the boulder. She told him that he must go find her brothers and tell them to come back for her. Jeremin or Terry nodded solemnly up at his mother and promised to do his very best, and he set off at once to see to it.

The problem, however, is that imps have very short memories. Their heads are so small, when new thoughts come along needing to be remembered, they are more than likely to bump out one or two old thoughts in the process. Such was the case with tiny skulls, or so the wisdom went. Whatever the cause, Varkias forgot all about his mother and all about the promise he had made to her, and soon lost himself in the burning twists and endless crevices beyond.

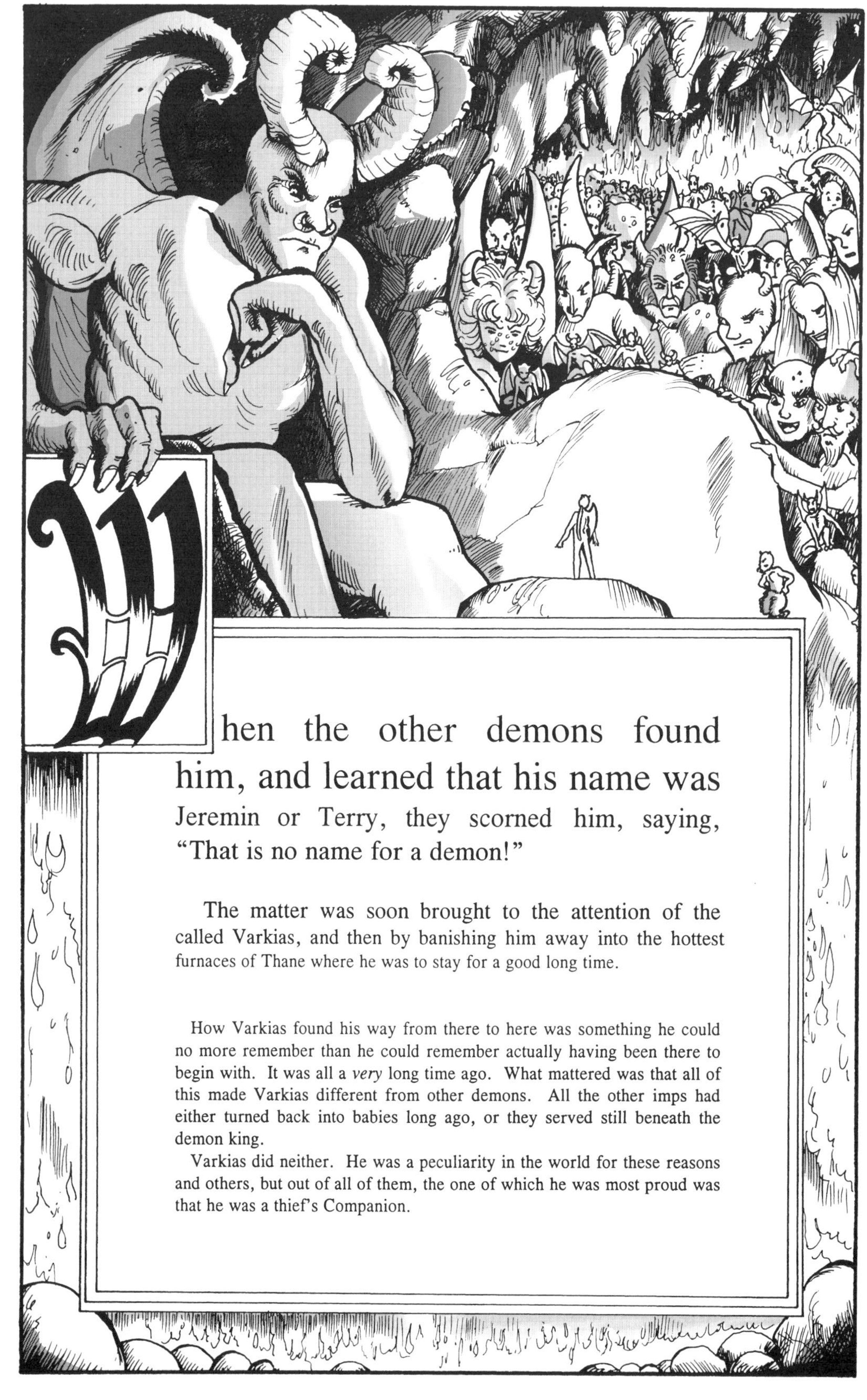

When the other demons found him, and learned that his name was Jeremin or Terry, they scorned him, saying, "That is no name for a demon!"

The matter was soon brought to the attention of the called Varkias, and then by banishing him away into the hottest furnaces of Thane where he was to stay for a good long time.

How Varkias found his way from there to here was something he could no more remember than he could remember actually having been there to begin with. It was all a *very* long time ago. What mattered was that all of this made Varkias different from other demons. All the other imps had either turned back into babies long ago, or they served still beneath the demon king.

Varkias did neither. He was a peculiarity in the world for these reasons and others, but out of all of them, the one of which he was most proud was that he was a thief's Companion.

Only Rubel was Rubel. He was not just any thief. (There were hardly any thieves out there as it was. *Real* thieves, that is). Rubel was a *real* thief. And a *princess's* thief no less. Rubel was the sort who'd fought and won against monsters. Monsters, like Chead and the Shadow Lady. Rubel was the sort of thief who punched greasy Geropian bullies flat on their backs with single smashes to their noses. —And stole their knives afterwards for good measure. Varkias was *his* imp.

The problem was that people knew all about *demons.*

Not necessarily all the correct things. Not even things they entirely believed in. Still, being what they are, preconceptions are always the first things people have in their heads when it comes down to meeting up with new people and new things.

And so, people knew all about *demons.*

Even tiny ones like him. *Especially* tiny ones like him. Imps meant trouble.

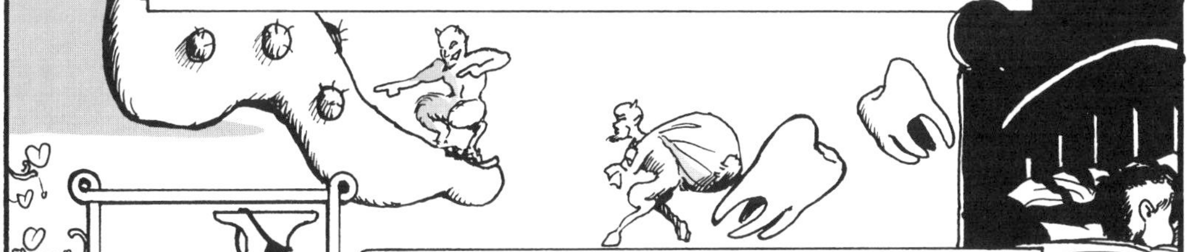

It was said that an imp could make you sick by spitting up your nose, or give you a wart just by poking you. They could blind you by kicking you in the eye, even with your eyelid shut. It was said that if you left your window open at night, an imp might come in and steal your teeth right from your gums while you slept. Everyone who had ever heard a nursery rhyme knew about imps! Imps were nearly as bad as fairies! (Except that fairies could also be nice if they wanted to, whereas imps were bad through and through).

The fact of the matter, however, was that most people had never actually *seen* an imp. Never a *real* one. It's difficult to believe in magic things, (no matter how much you might like to), when the only kind of magic you've ever known is the sort that a friend once heard about happening to somebody. —Or the laborious, mechanical kind of magic performed with cards and balls and metal rings; that sort looks nice but doesn't really fool anybody.

Thus, the fascination of seeing an actual, live imp; one with bat's wings and tiny horns and everything, easily out-matched everybody's fear of warts and stolen teeth. Particularly in such a sunny, friendly setting as Tamard street.

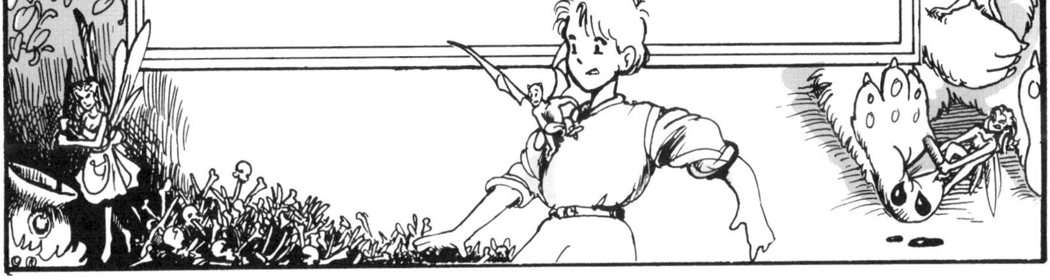

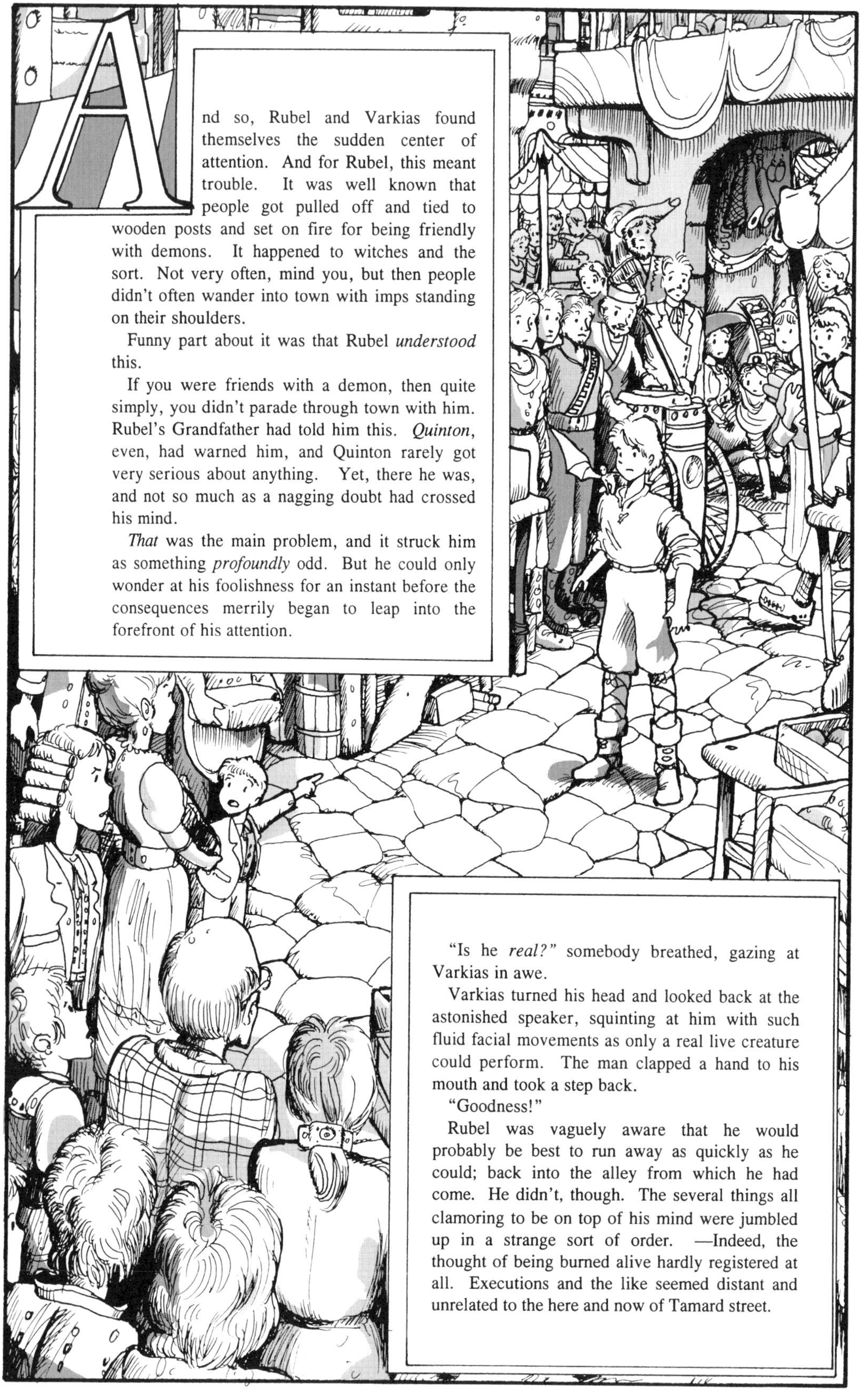

And so, Rubel and Varkias found themselves the sudden center of attention. And for Rubel, this meant trouble. It was well known that people got pulled off and tied to wooden posts and set on fire for being friendly with demons. It happened to witches and the sort. Not very often, mind you, but then people didn't often wander into town with imps standing on their shoulders.

Funny part about it was that Rubel *understood* this.

If you were friends with a demon, then quite simply, you didn't parade through town with him. Rubel's Grandfather had told him this. *Quinton*, even, had warned him, and Quinton rarely got very serious about anything. Yet, there he was, and not so much as a nagging doubt had crossed his mind.

That was the main problem, and it struck him as something *profoundly* odd. But he could only wonder at his foolishness for an instant before the consequences merrily began to leap into the forefront of his attention.

"Is he *real?"* somebody breathed, gazing at Varkias in awe.

Varkias turned his head and looked back at the astonished speaker, squinting at him with such fluid facial movements as only a real live creature could perform. The man clapped a hand to his mouth and took a step back.

"Goodness!"

Rubel was vaguely aware that he would probably be best to run away as quickly as he could; back into the alley from which he had come. He didn't, though. The several things all clamoring to be on top of his mind were jumbled up in a strange sort of order. —Indeed, the thought of being burned alive hardly registered at all. Executions and the like seemed distant and unrelated to the here and now of Tamard street.

ow at the very top of all his jumbled thoughts, was the grumble in his stomach. For some reason, his hunger was the thing making most sense. He'd come here with honest money to spend; nearly a whole fistful of silver and brass, with even a coin or two of gold in the lot. He'd come to buy himself some well deserved breakfast, and he had done nothing bad to anybody. Running away would only leave him panting and guilty and most of all, still hungry.

So instead, Rubel told them all quite firmly, "Yes. He's real."

The crowd made a sound of wonder. They had been waiting on his answer.

"Am I *real*?" Varkias snorted beneath his breath.

"Goodness," said the man again.

"Where did you find him?" asked the boy who had first cried everybody's attention upon the imp and thief.

"In the forest," Rubel told him.

The boy's eyes to opened wider.

"In the Sleeping Wood," he put in for good measure.

"The *Sleeping wood?*" the boy chimed. "Wow!"

"He's not evil," Rubel added.

"He's *good?*"

Varkias snorted again, this time with contempt. The audience reacted with uncertainty.

"Can he *talk?*" the boy asked. "How come you have him? Can he *fly?*"

Everybody looked to Rubel.

ubel felt an impatient movement on his shoulder.

"What do you mean, can I *talk?* Of course I can *talk,*" Varkias answered the boy loudly enough for all to hear. He sounded not quite irritable, but close to it. (Varkias hadn't yet decided on what his mood ought to be for such an occasion as this. Probably irritable. Irritable generally served).

The audience made more sounds of wonder when they heard his voice.

"Wow!" the boy wowed. "How come you have him? Are there more in the forest? How did you *get* him?"

Rubel frowned and felt a flurry of powerful anger burst somewhere inside him. —Easily mastered and only very brief, though he could only guess from where it had come.

"*Get* him?" he asked. "You don't go and *get* friends. I've known him ever since I was born."

"Ever since you were *born*?" the boy repeated, his eyes now flashing like a pair of green flames. "You were born in the *forest*. . ? Are you a *thief?*"

Quick as lightning, that. Even Rubel should have been taken aback, except he wasn't. The inside of his head had gone a little fuzzy again. Not so that he felt confused. Just a little light. Everybody leaned in, quiet enough to give that block of sunny Tamard an unreal air. Rubel returned their looks solidly. His stomach grumbled.

"Yes," he said. "I am a thief."

A buzz swept through the market, half in whispers.

"But if you call the guardsmen and the jailers," he told them loudly, "I'll be gone as fast as wind, and they won't see even a hair on my head!"

From the expression people gave, anybody could tell that not one of them would have dreamed of calling guardsmen or jailers. What, with the air smelling so fresh and new amidst the bright market about them, and the shining boy and his magic imp before them.

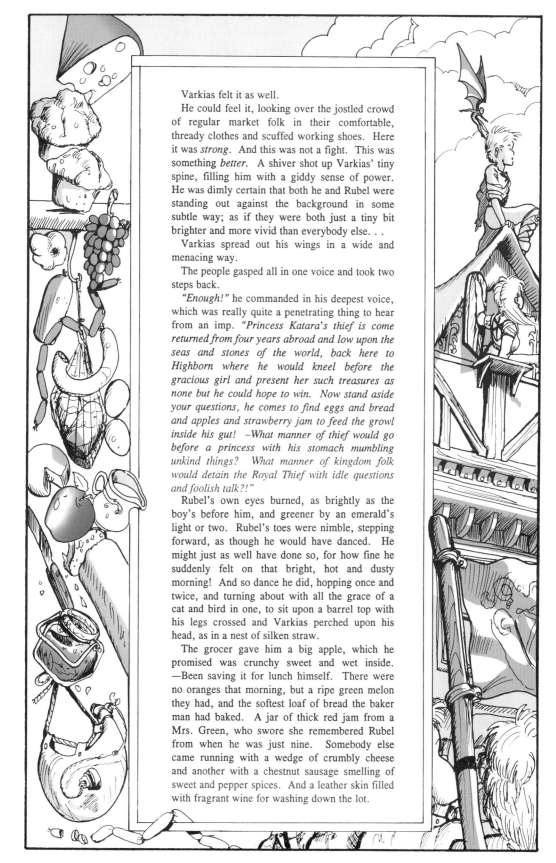

Varkias felt it as well.

He could feel it, looking over the jostled crowd of regular market folk in their comfortable, thready clothes and scuffed working shoes. Here it was *strong*. And this was not a fight. This was something *better*. A shiver shot up Varkias' tiny spine, filling him with a giddy sense of power. He was dimly certain that both he and Rubel were standing out against the background in some subtle way; as if they were both just a tiny bit brighter and more vivid than everybody else. . .

Varkias spread out his wings in a wide and menacing way.

The people gasped all in one voice and took two steps back.

"Enough!" he commanded in his deepest voice, which was really quite a penetrating thing to hear from an imp. *"Princess Katara's thief is come returned from four years abroad and low upon the seas and stones of the world, back here to Highborn where he would kneel before the gracious girl and present her such treasures as none but he could hope to win. Now stand aside your questions, he comes to find eggs and bread and apples and strawberry jam to feed the growl inside his gut! –What manner of thief would go before a princess with his stomach mumbling unkind things? What manner of kingdom folk would detain the Royal Thief with idle questions and foolish talk?!"*

Rubel's own eyes burned, as brightly as the boy's before him, and greener by an emerald's light or two. Rubel's toes were nimble, stepping forward, as though he would have danced. He might just as well have done so, for how fine he suddenly felt on that bright, hot and dusty morning! And so dance he did, hopping once and twice, and turning about with all the grace of a cat and bird in one, to sit upon a barrel top with his legs crossed and Varkias perched upon his head, as in a nest of silken straw.

The grocer gave him a big apple, which he promised was crunchy sweet and wet inside. —Been saving it for lunch himself. There were no oranges that morning, but a ripe green melon they had, and the softest loaf of bread the baker man had baked. A jar of thick red jam from a Mrs. Green, who swore she remembered Rubel from when he was just nine. Somebody else came running with a wedge of crumbly cheese and another with a chestnut sausage smelling of sweet and pepper spices. And a leather skin filled with fragrant wine for washing down the lot.

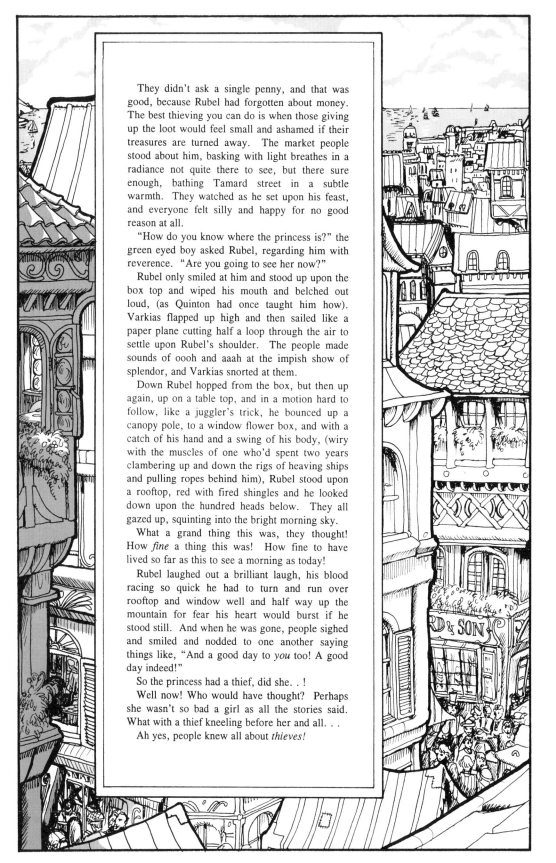

They didn't ask a single penny, and that was good, because Rubel had forgotten about money. The best thieving you can do is when those giving up the loot would feel small and ashamed if their treasures are turned away. The market people stood about him, basking with light breathes in a radiance not quite there to see, but there sure enough, bathing Tamard street in a subtle warmth. They watched as he set upon his feast, and everyone felt silly and happy for no good reason at all.

"How do you know where the princess is?" the green eyed boy asked Rubel, regarding him with reverence. "Are you going to see her now?"

Rubel only smiled at him and stood up upon the box top and wiped his mouth and belched out loud, (as Quinton had once taught him how). Varkias flapped up high and then sailed like a paper plane cutting half a loop through the air to settle upon Rubel's shoulder. The people made sounds of oooh and aaah at the impish show of splendor, and Varkias snorted at them.

Down Rubel hopped from the box, but then up again, up on a table top, and in a motion hard to follow, like a juggler's trick, he bounced up a canopy pole, to a window flower box, and with a catch of his hand and a swing of his body, (wiry with the muscles of one who'd spent two years clambering up and down the rigs of heaving ships and pulling ropes behind him), Rubel stood upon a rooftop, red with fired shingles and he looked down upon the hundred heads below. They all gazed up, squinting into the bright morning sky.

What a grand thing this was, they thought! How *fine* a thing this was! How fine to have lived so far as this to see a morning as today!

Rubel laughed out a brilliant laugh, his blood racing so quick he had to turn and run over rooftop and window well and half way up the mountain for fear his heart would burst if he stood still. And when he was gone, people sighed and smiled and nodded to one another saying things like, "And a good day to *you* too! A good day indeed!"

So the princess had a thief, did she. . !

Well now! Who would have thought? Perhaps she wasn't so bad a girl as all the stories said. What with a thief kneeling before her and all. . .

Ah yes, people knew all about *thieves!*

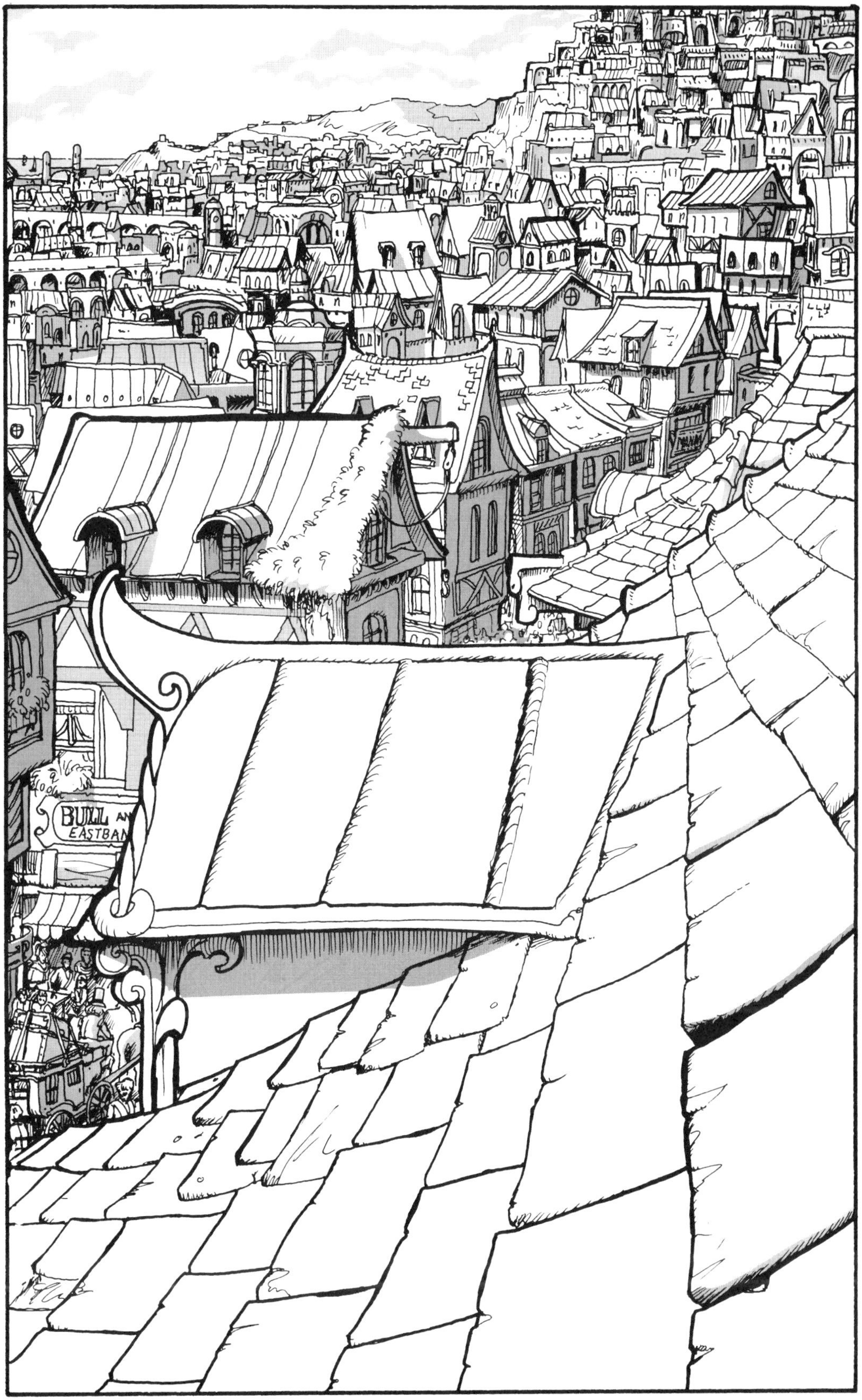
BULL AN
EASTBAN

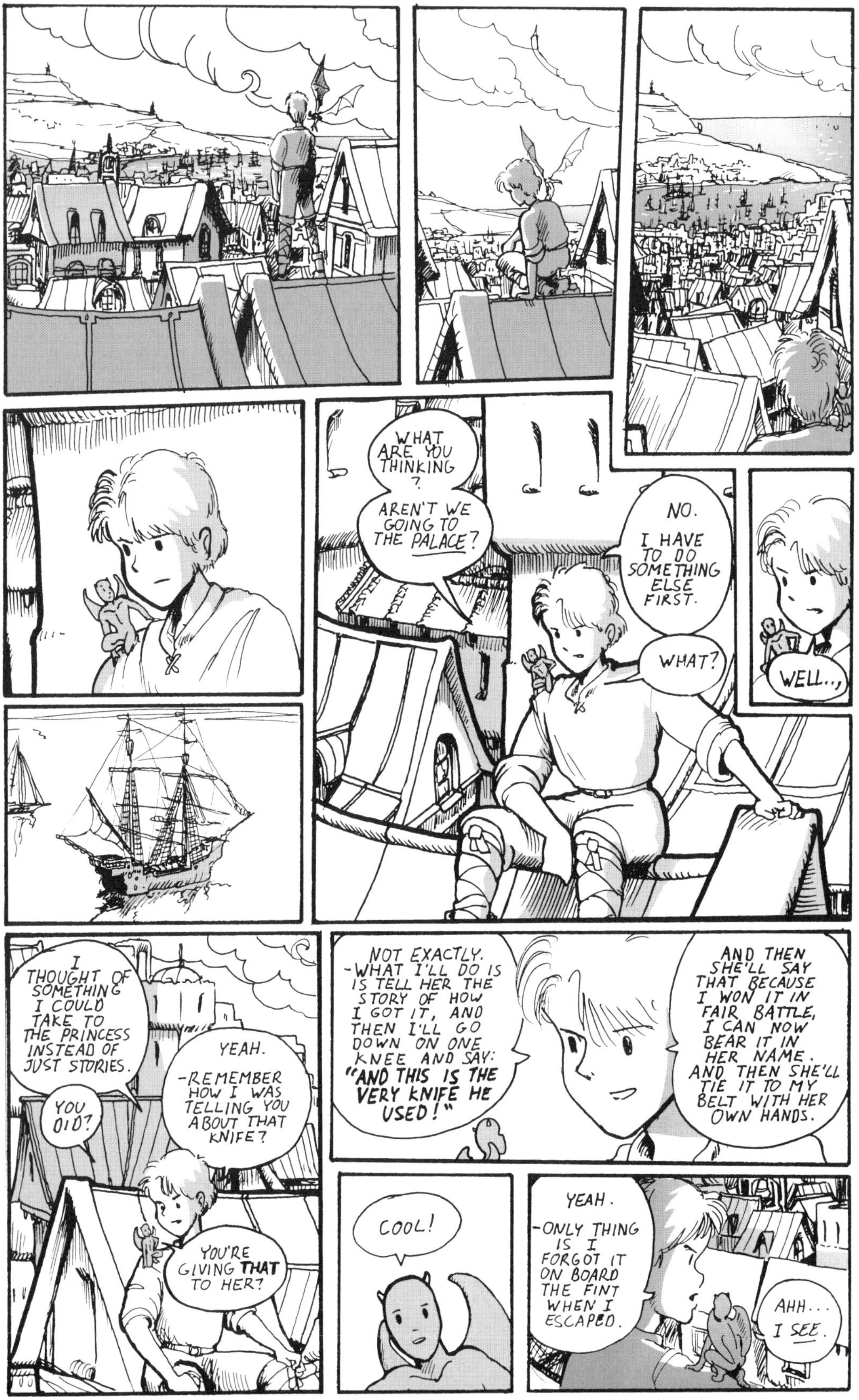

WHAT ARE YOU THINKING ?
AREN'T WE GOING TO THE PALACE?
NO.
I HAVE TO DO SOMETHING ELSE FIRST.
WHAT?
WELL..,
I THOUGHT OF SOMETHING I COULD TAKE TO THE PRINCESS INSTEAD OF JUST STORIES.
YOU DID?
YEAH.
-REMEMBER HOW I WAS TELLING YOU ABOUT THAT KNIFE?
YOU'RE GIVING **THAT** TO HER?
NOT EXACTLY. -WHAT I'LL DO IS IS TELL HER THE STORY OF HOW I GOT IT, AND THEN I'LL GO DOWN ON ONE KNEE AND SAY: **"AND THIS IS THE VERY KNIFE HE USED!"**
AND THEN SHE'LL SAY THAT BECAUSE I WON IT IN FAIR BATTLE, I CAN NOW BEAR IT IN HER NAME. AND THEN SHE'LL TIE IT TO MY BELT WITH HER OWN HANDS.
COOL!
YEAH.
-ONLY THING IS I FORGOT IT ON BOARD THE FINT WHEN I ESCAPED.
AHH... I SEE.

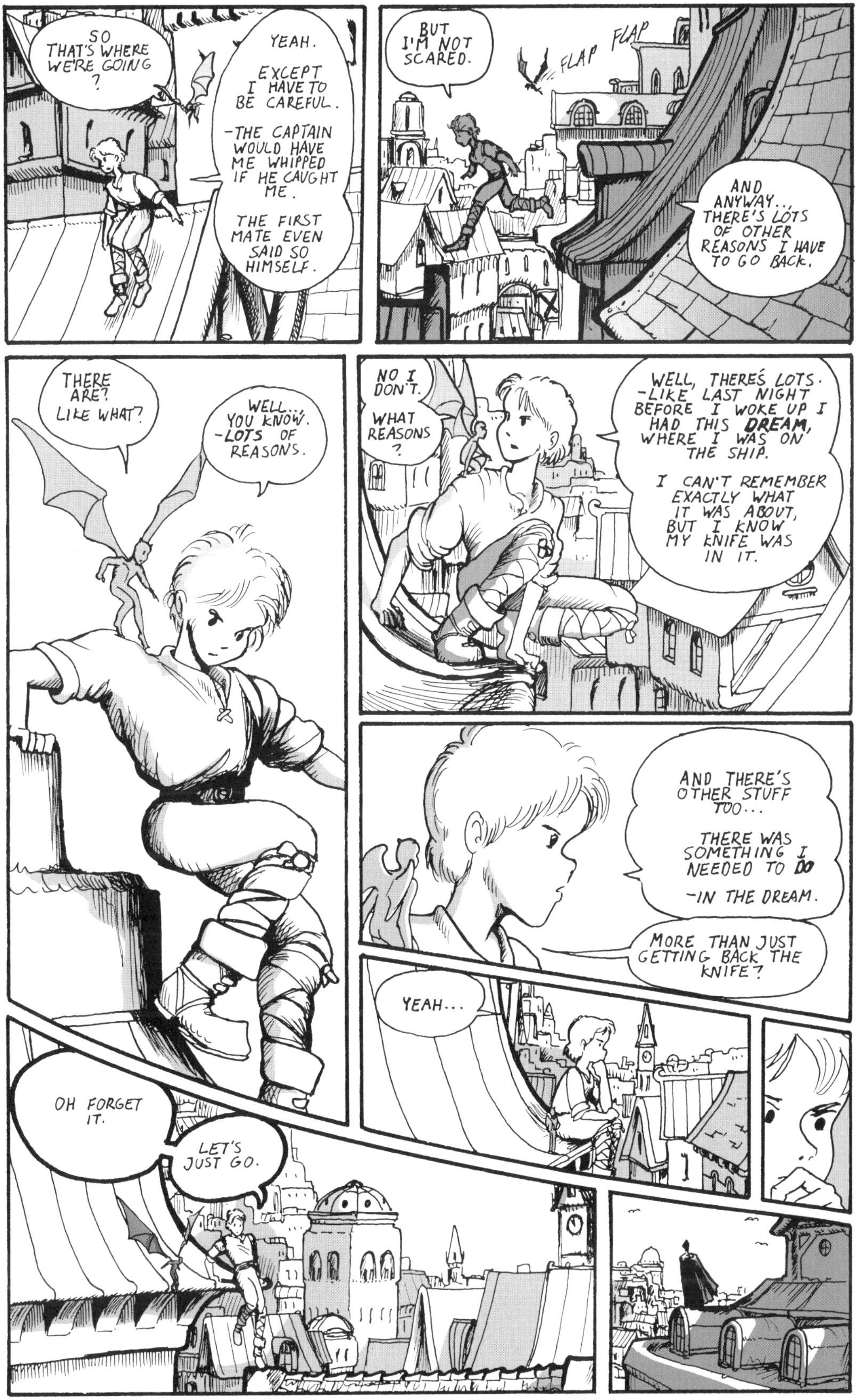
SO THAT'S WHERE WE'RE GOING ?
YEAH.
EXCEPT I HAVE TO BE CAREFUL.
-THE CAPTAIN WOULD HAVE ME WHIPPED IF HE CAUGHT ME.
THE FIRST MATE EVEN SAID SO HIMSELF.
BUT I'M NOT SCARED.
FLAP FLAP
AND ANYWAY... THERE'S LOTS OF OTHER REASONS I HAVE TO GO BACK.
THERE ARE? LIKE WHAT?
WELL... YOU KNOW. -**LOTS** OF REASONS.
NO I DON'T.
WHAT REASONS ?
WELL, THERE'S LOTS. -LIKE LAST NIGHT BEFORE I WOKE UP I HAD THIS **DREAM**, WHERE I WAS ON THE SHIP.
I CAN'T REMEMBER EXACTLY WHAT IT WAS ABOUT, BUT I KNOW MY KNIFE WAS IN IT.
AND THERE'S OTHER STUFF TOO...
THERE WAS SOMETHING I NEEDED TO **DO**
-IN THE DREAM.
MORE THAN JUST GETTING BACK THE KNIFE?
YEAH...
OH FORGET IT.
LET'S JUST GO.

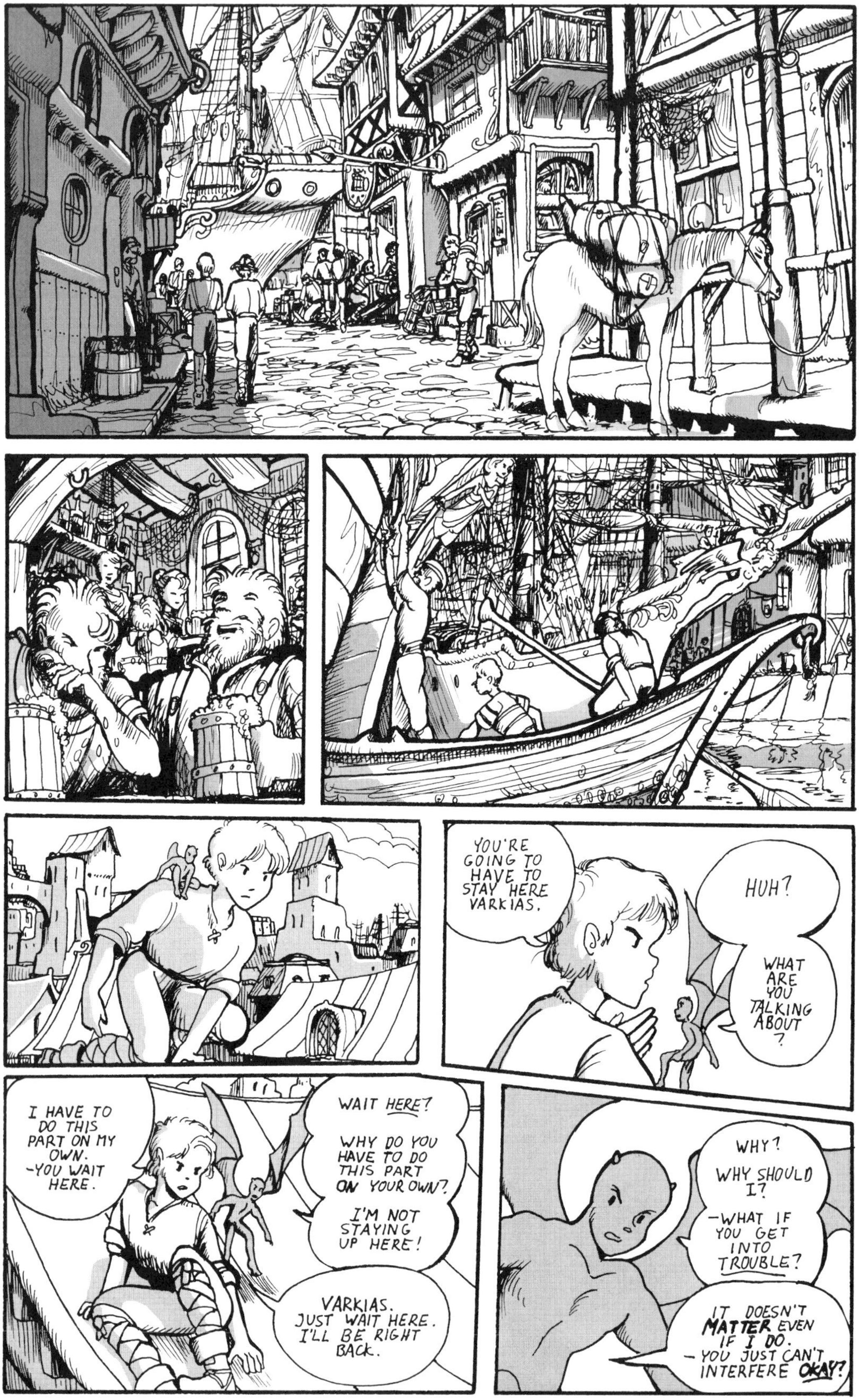
YOU'RE GOING TO HAVE TO STAY HERE VARKIAS.
HUH?
WHAT ARE YOU TALKING ABOUT?
I HAVE TO DO THIS PART ON MY OWN. -YOU WAIT HERE.
WAIT HERE?
WHY DO YOU HAVE TO DO THIS PART ON YOUR OWN?
I'M NOT STAYING UP HERE!
VARKIAS. JUST WAIT HERE. I'LL BE RIGHT BACK.
WHY?
WHY SHOULD I?
-WHAT IF YOU GET INTO TROUBLE?
IT DOESN'T MATTER EVEN IF I DO. -YOU JUST CAN'T INTERFERE OKAY?

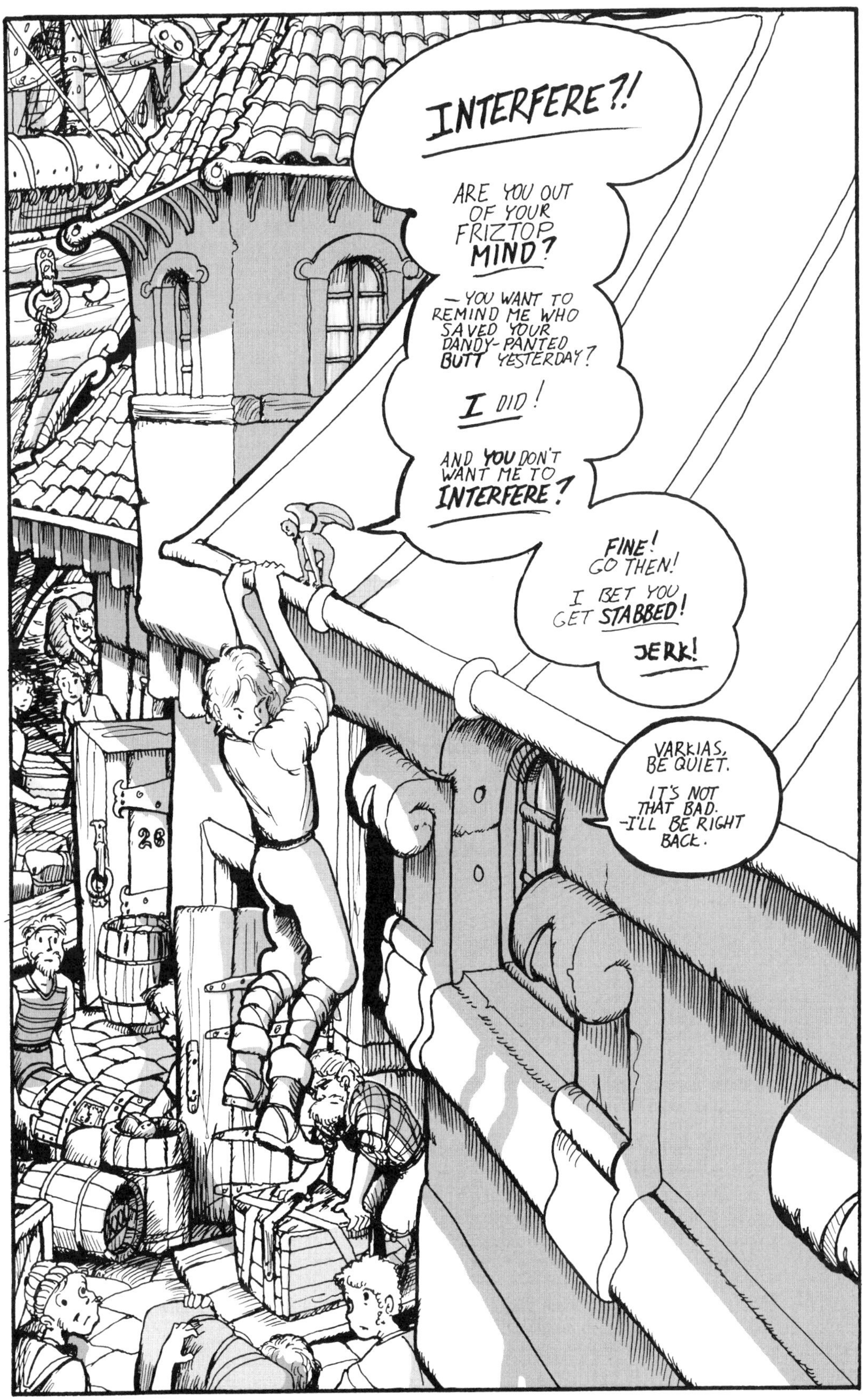

INTERFERE?!
ARE YOU OUT OF YOUR FRIZTOP MIND?
—YOU WANT TO REMIND ME WHO SAVED YOUR DANDY-PANTED BUTT YESTERDAY?
I DID!
AND YOU DON'T WANT ME TO INTERFERE?
FINE! GO THEN!
I BET YOU GET STABBED!
JERK!
VARKIAS, BE QUIET.
IT'S NOT THAT BAD. —I'LL BE RIGHT BACK.
26

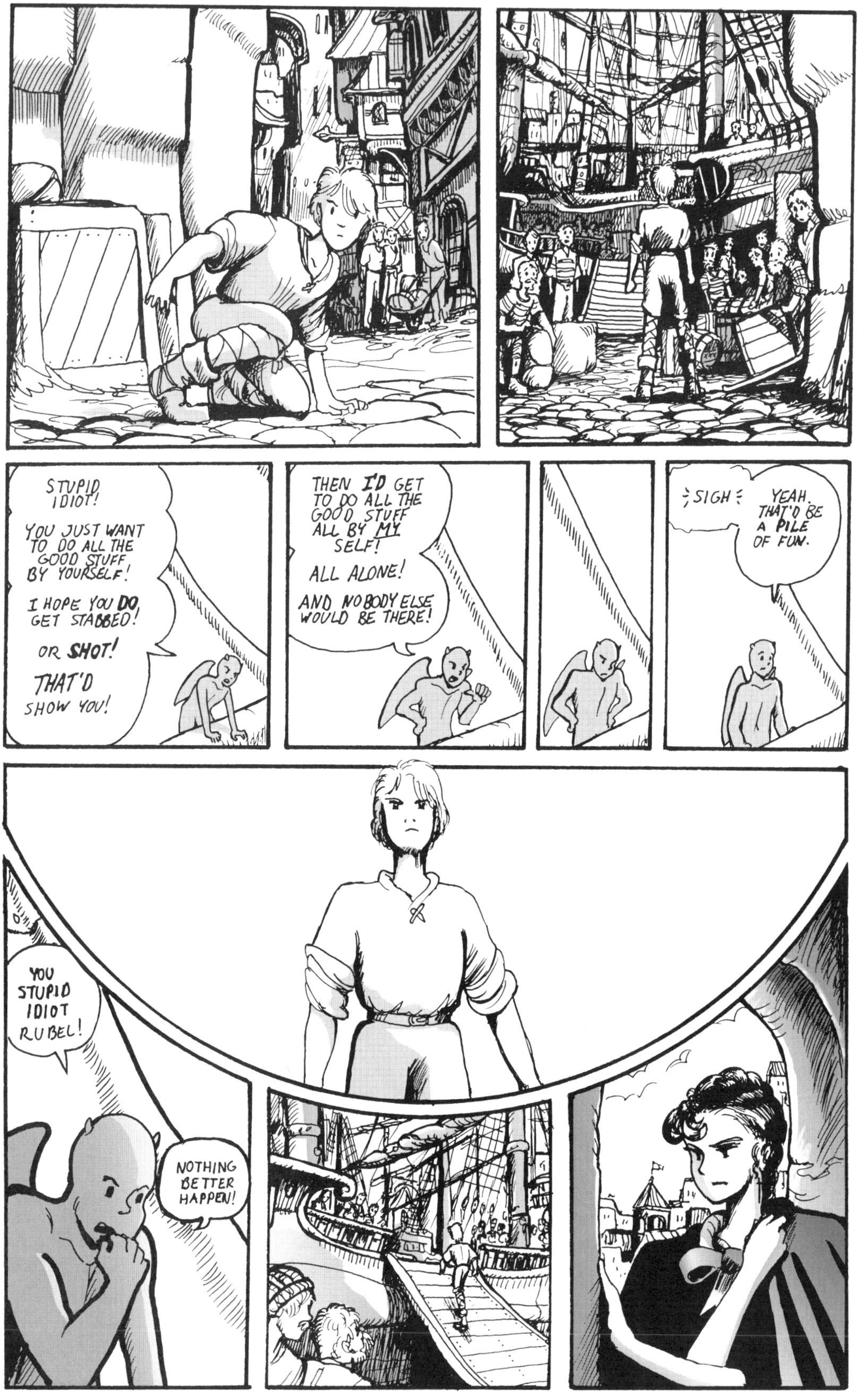
STUPID IDIOT!
YOU JUST WANT TO DO ALL THE GOOD STUFF BY YOURSELF!
I HOPE YOU DO GET STABBED!
OR SHOT!
THAT'D SHOW YOU!
THEN I'D GET TO DO ALL THE GOOD STUFF ALL BY MY SELF!
ALL ALONE!
AND NOBODY ELSE WOULD BE THERE!
SIGH
YEAH. THAT'D BE A PILE OF FUN.
YOU STUPID IDIOT RUBEL!
NOTHING BETTER HAPPEN!

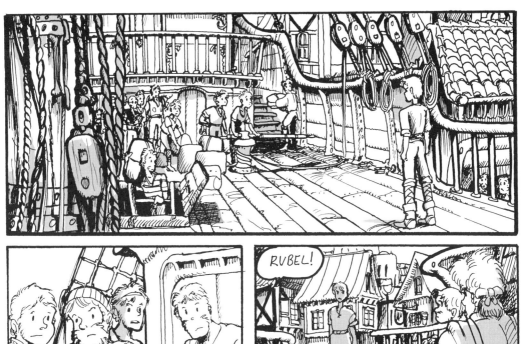

RUBEL!

YOU SHOULDN'T BE BACK HERE. —THE CAPTAIN WOULD BE FURIOUS!

WILLIAM! —I'VE COME BACK TO GET MY THINGS.

WHERE ARE THEY?

NONE OF US TOUCHED ANYTHING! —IT'S ALL IN THE SHIP'S OFFICE.

THE CAPTAIN LOCKED IT ALL UP AND KEPT IT. —HE THOUGHT YOU MIGHT COME BACK AND LOOK FOR IT.

RUBEL, HE'S ONLY GONE FOR A LITTLE WHILE. HE COULD COME BACK ANY TIME!

RUBEL!

WHAT ARE YOU DOING?

BUT YOU CAN'T GET IN. —HE LOCKED THE DOOR.

DON'T BE FOOLISH!

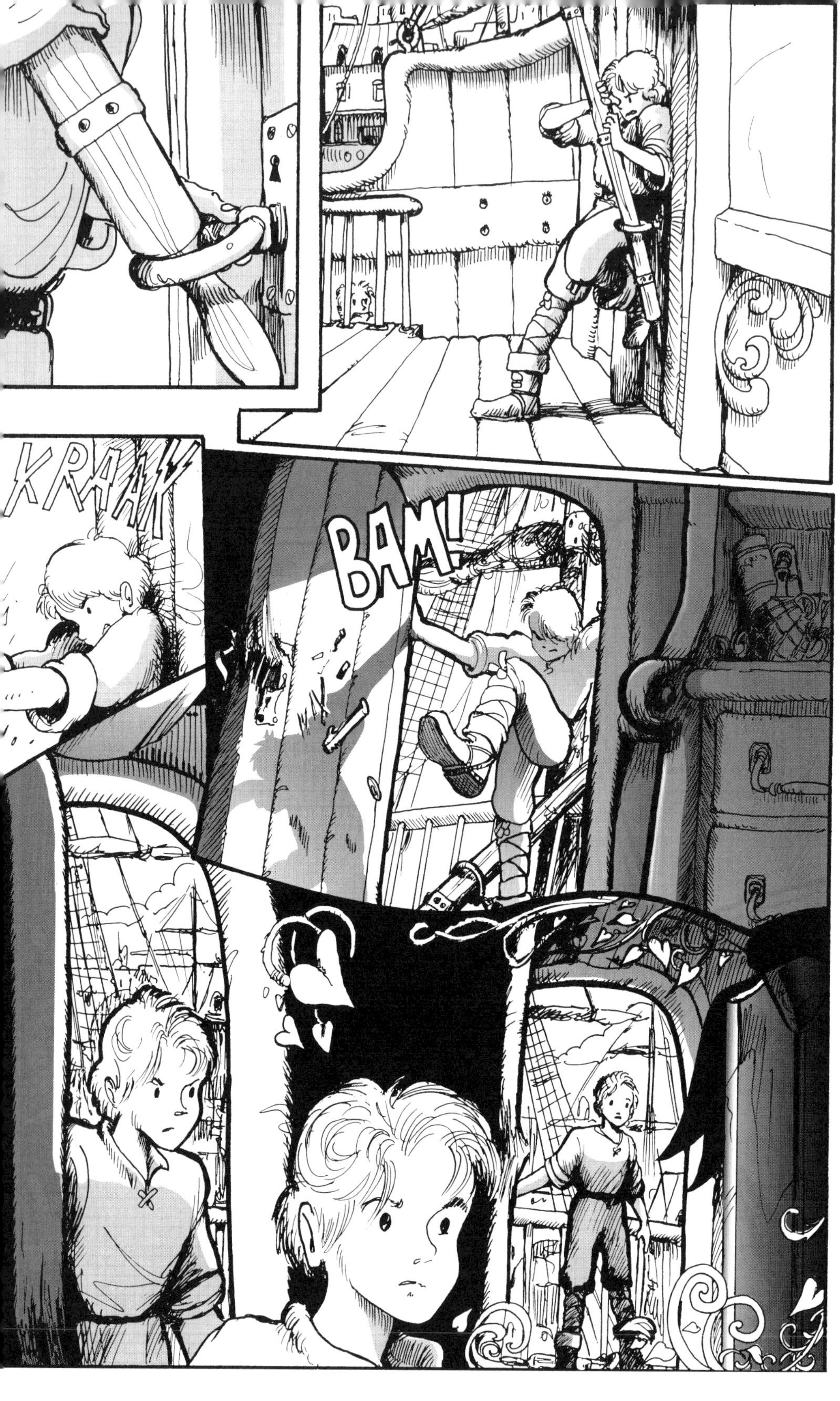
KRAAK
BAM!

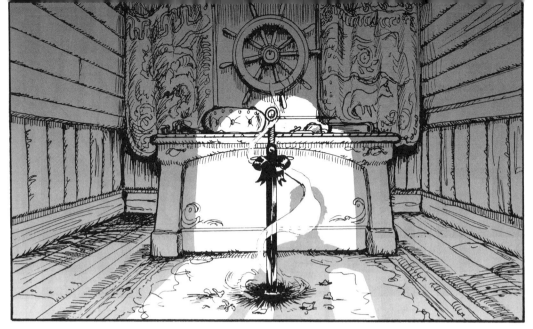

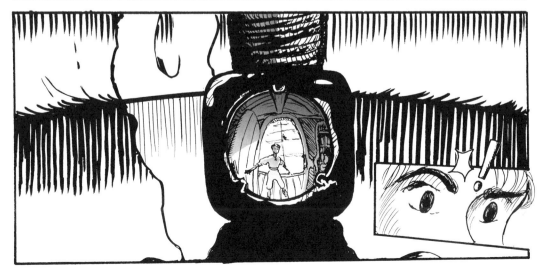

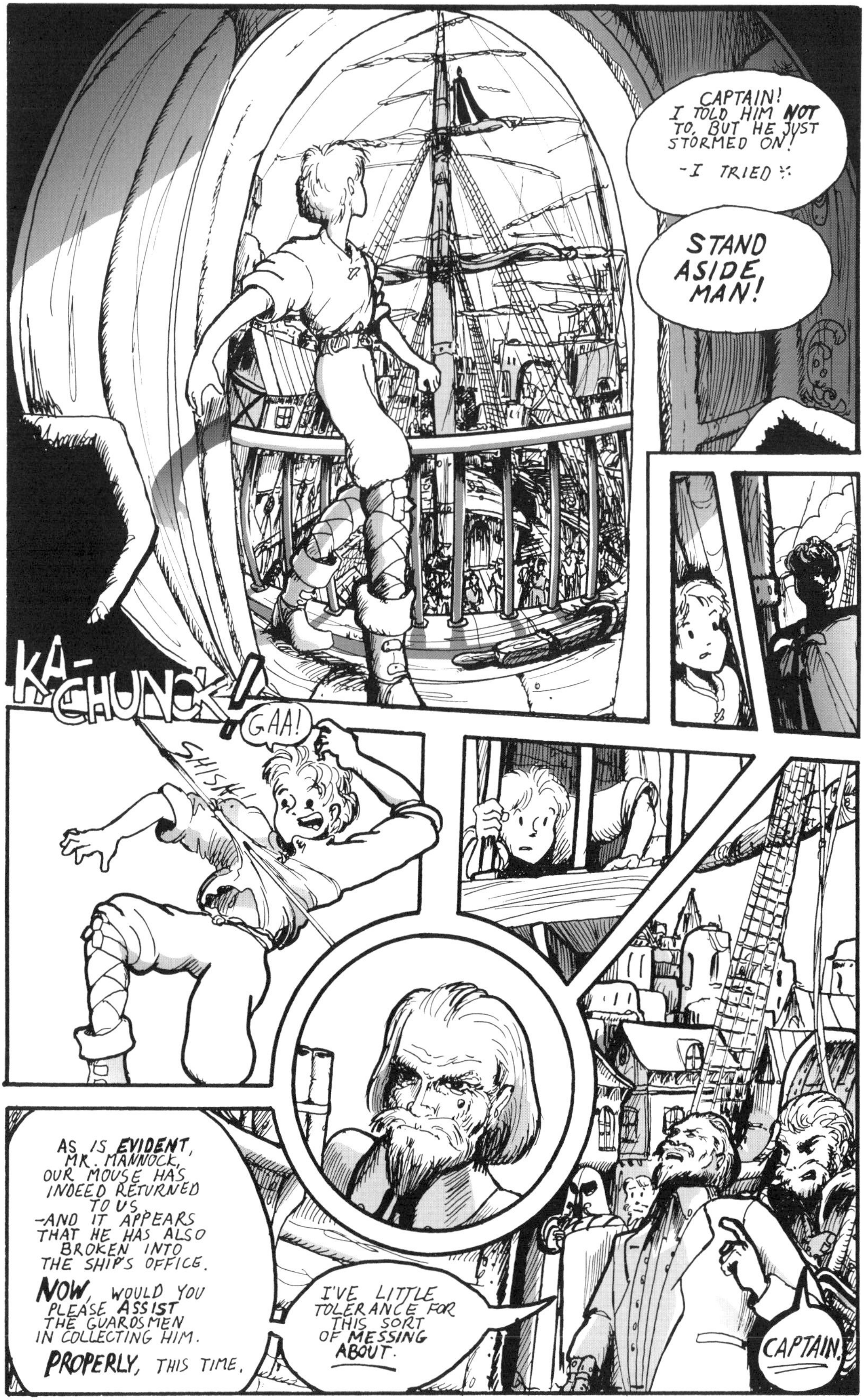
CAPTAIN! I TOLD HIM NOT TO, BUT HE JUST STORMED ON! -I TRIED
STAND ASIDE, MAN!
KA-CHUNCK!
SHISH!
GAA!
AS IS EVIDENT, MR. MANNOCK, OUR MOUSE HAS INDEED RETURNED TO US -AND IT APPEARS THAT HE HAS ALSO BROKEN INTO THE SHIP'S OFFICE.
NOW, WOULD YOU PLEASE ASSIST THE GUARDSMEN IN COLLECTING HIM.
PROPERLY, THIS TIME.
I'VE LITTLE TOLERANCE FOR THIS SORT OF MESSING ABOUT.
CAPTAIN.

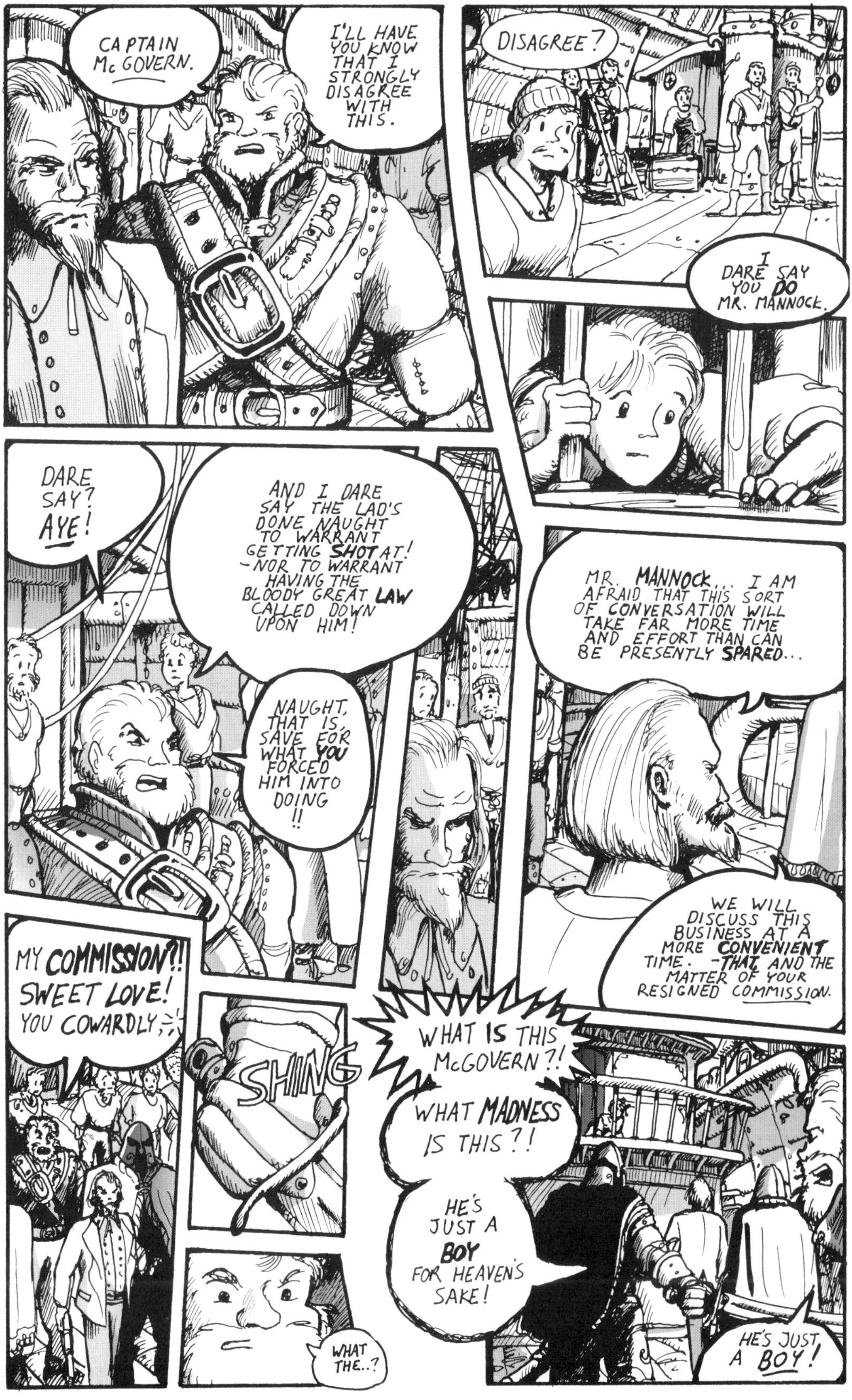
CAPTAIN McGOVERN.
I'LL HAVE YOU KNOW THAT I STRONGLY DISAGREE WITH THIS.
DISAGREE?
I DARE SAY YOU DO MR. MANNOCK.
DARE SAY? AYE!
AND I DARE SAY THE LAD'S DONE NAUGHT TO WARRANT GETTING SHOT AT! -NOR TO WARRANT HAVING THE BLOODY GREAT LAW CALLED DOWN UPON HIM!
NAUGHT, THAT IS, SAVE FOR WHAT YOU FORCED HIM INTO DOING!!
MR. MANNOCK... I AM AFRAID THAT THIS SORT OF CONVERSATION WILL TAKE FAR MORE TIME AND EFFORT THAN CAN BE PRESENTLY SPARED...
WE WILL DISCUSS THIS BUSINESS AT A MORE CONVENIENT TIME. -THAT, AND THE MATTER OF YOUR RESIGNED COMMISSION.
MY COMMISSION?!! SWEET LOVE! YOU COWARDLY,-!
SHING
WHAT THE..?
WHAT IS THIS McGOVERN?!
WHAT MADNESS IS THIS?!
HE'S JUST A BOY FOR HEAVEN'S SAKE!
HE'S JUST A BOY!

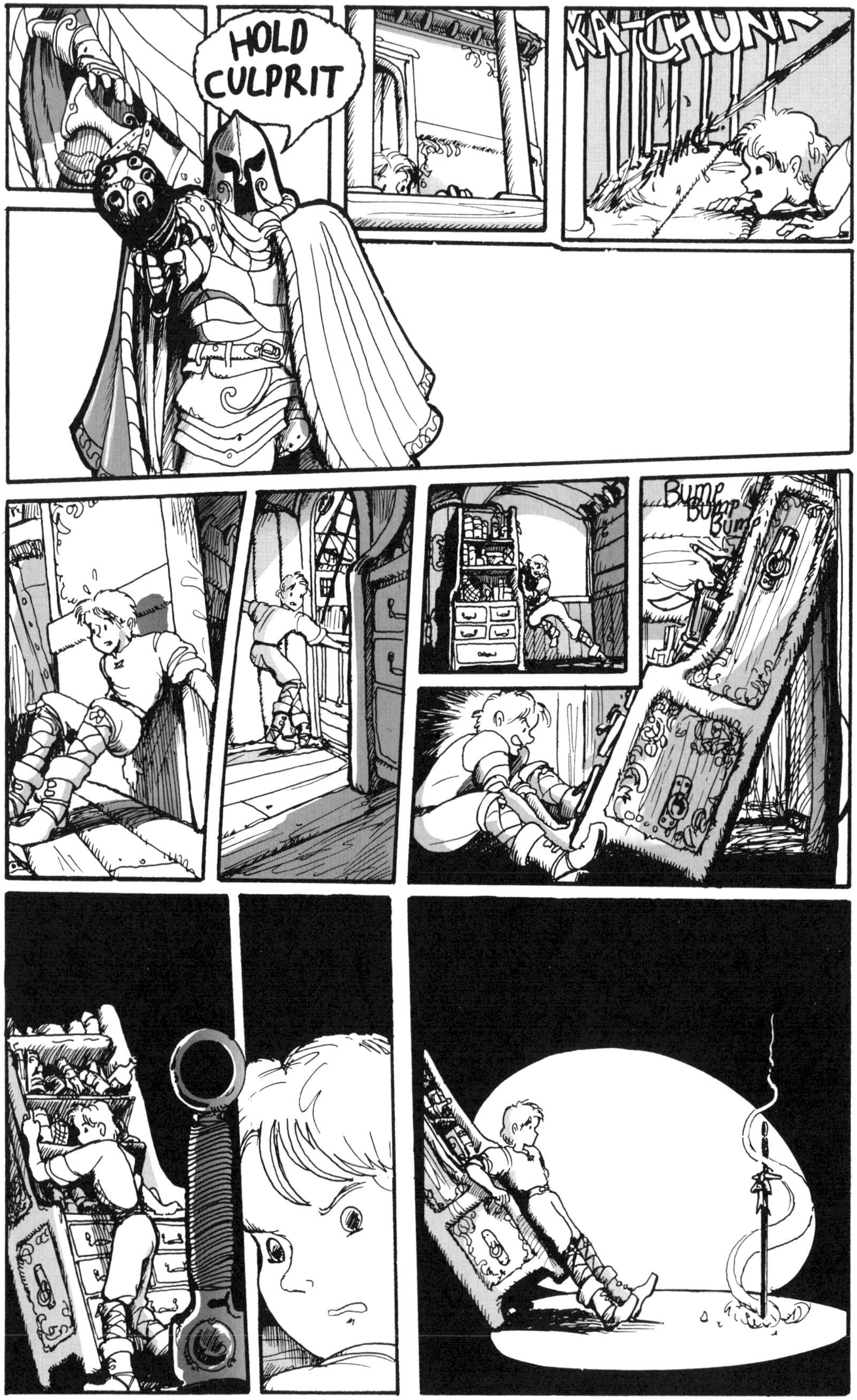
HOLD CULPRIT
KA-CHUNK
Bump
Bump
Bump

Chapter 4

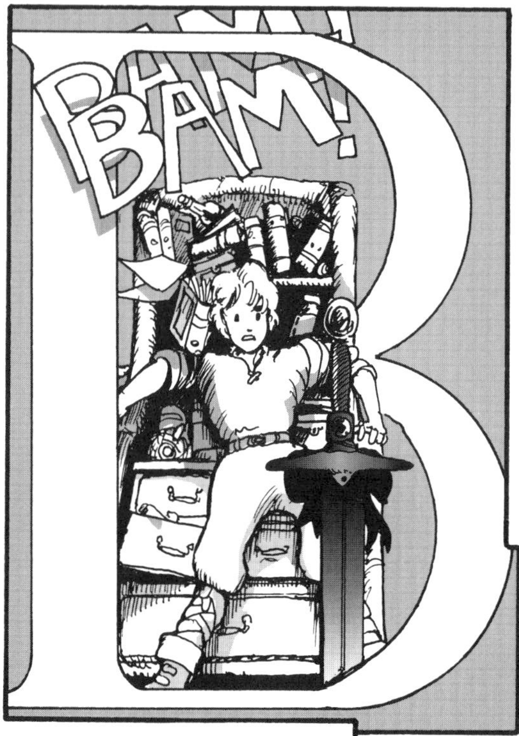
BAM!

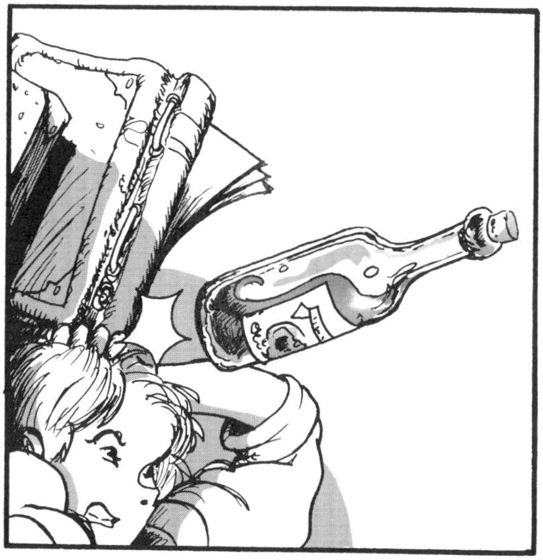

AM! BAM! went the door. Assorted objects rattled and fell around Rubel's ears as he struggled to hold fast his impromptu fortification. With heels jammed into the floor boards and his back pressed into knobbles of wood, book and bolt, he braced the shuddering barricade.

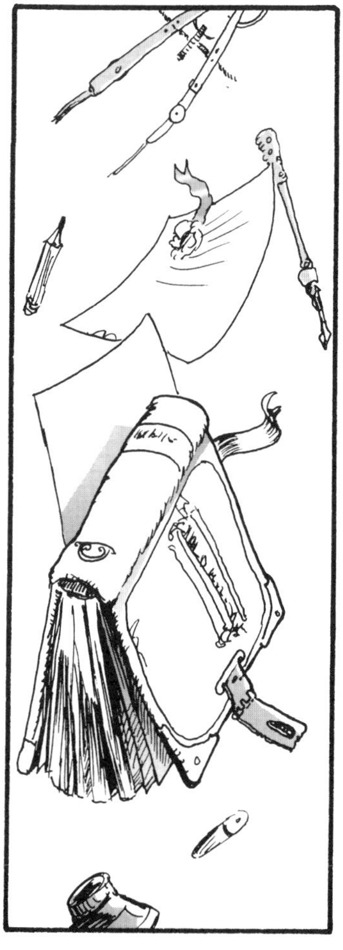

BAM! BAM! BAM!

And the black sword stood silent before him. It gazed at him darkly through a veil of magic that smelled of old and wet autumn leaves, and the black ribbon bow tied about its hilt moved gently in some invisible breeze. Rubel knew who the sword belonged to, and he had a fairly good idea as to why it was there. He was also certain beyond any shadow of a doubt that touching it would be an *astonishingly* bad idea.

BAM! BAM! *SPLINTER!*

Rubel bit his lip and pushed an anxious hand through his hair. What *was* he going to do?

The sword seemed aware of his dilemma, and it throbbed with an unwholesome sort of glee. "Yes, little boy, take hold of me!" it seemed to laugh. "Slide your fingers around my hilt and I shall be your *Sword!* —And you shall be my Boy! If you do not, they'll have your head! I know it! And *you* do as well, I think, but only *I* know why!"

It could cut through metal, Rubel thought with a start. Through *armor*. It would cut their armor as though slicing sheets of wet clay. She would not have placed it there if it could not. Rubel felt the truth of this sink right down to the pit of his stomach. So, he thought, she *is* trustworthy. . , after her own frightful manner.

And who were *they?* He'd never seen before such guardsmen as those now beating outside the door. —Encased in blackened metal from brow to toe; old metal too. *Old.* The sense of age clung about them as it did with family silverware; like the *good* forks people save for occasions.

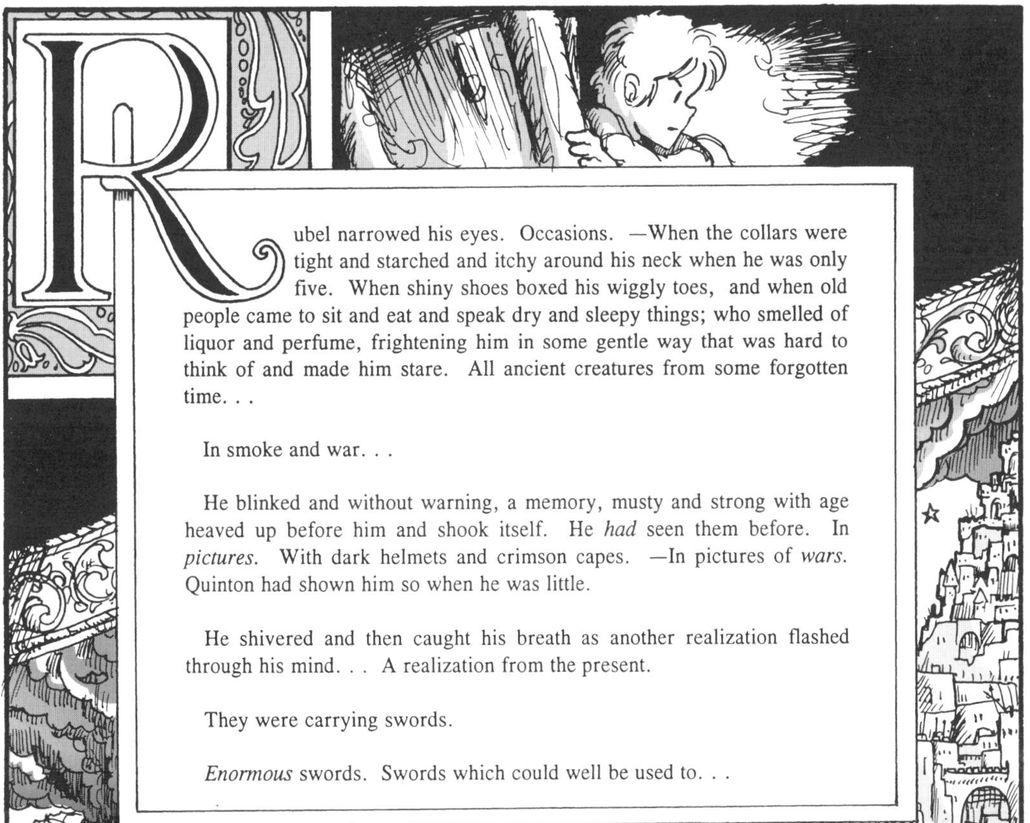

Rubel narrowed his eyes. Occasions. —When the collars were tight and starched and itchy around his neck when he was only five. When shiny shoes boxed his wiggly toes, and when old people came to sit and eat and speak dry and sleepy things; who smelled of liquor and perfume, frightening him in some gentle way that was hard to think of and made him stare. All ancient creatures from some forgotten time. . .

In smoke and war. . .

He blinked and without warning, a memory, musty and strong with age heaved up before him and shook itself. He *had* seen them before. In *pictures.* With dark helmets and crimson capes. —In pictures of *wars.* Quinton had shown him so when he was little.

He shivered and then caught his breath as another realization flashed through his mind. . . A realization from the present.

They were carrying swords.

Enormous swords. Swords which could well be used to. . .

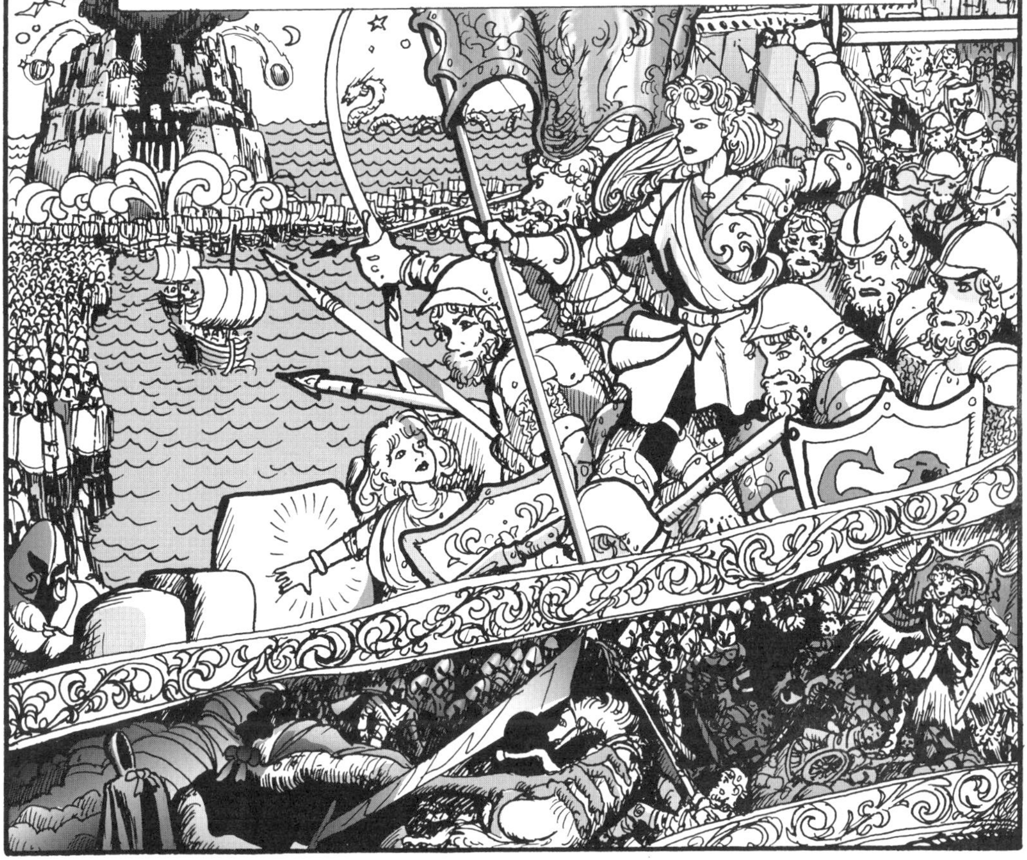

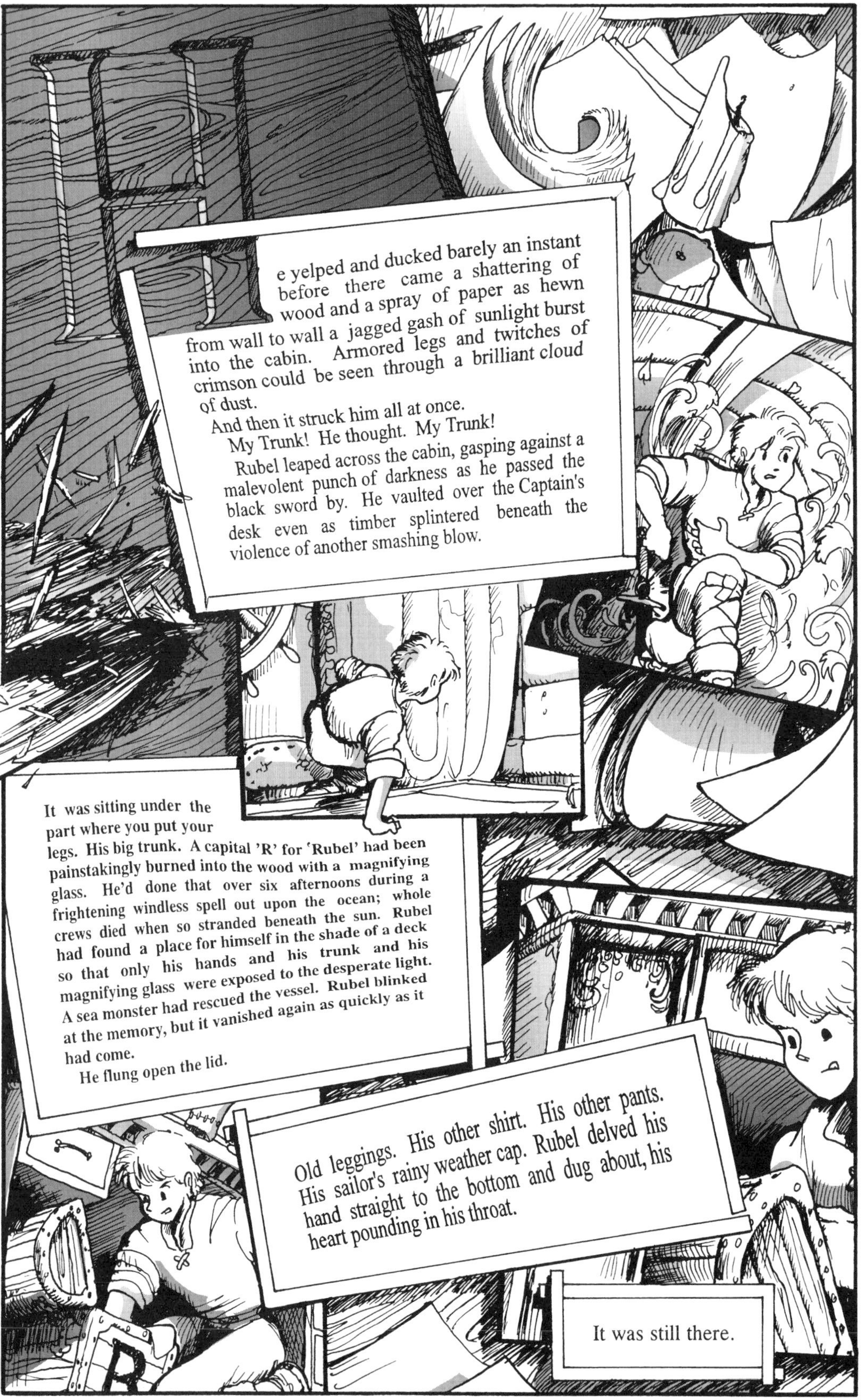
He yelped and ducked barely an instant before there came a shattering of wood and a spray of paper as hewn from wall to wall a jagged gash of sunlight burst into the cabin. Armored legs and twitches of crimson could be seen through a brilliant cloud of dust.
And then it struck him all at once.
My Trunk! He thought. My Trunk!
Rubel leaped across the cabin, gasping against a malevolent punch of darkness as he passed the black sword by. He vaulted over the Captain's desk even as timber splintered beneath the violence of another smashing blow.
It was sitting under the part where you put your legs. His big trunk. A capital 'R' for 'Rubel' had been painstakingly burned into the wood with a magnifying glass. He'd done that over six afternoons during a frightening windless spell out upon the ocean; whole crews died when so stranded beneath the sun. Rubel had found a place for himself in the shade of a deck so that only his hands and his trunk and his magnifying glass were exposed to the desperate light. A sea monster had rescued the vessel. Rubel blinked at the memory, but it vanished again as quickly as it had come.
He flung open the lid.
Old leggings. His other shirt. His other pants. His sailor's rainy weather cap. Rubel delved his hand straight to the bottom and dug about, his heart pounding in his throat.
It was still there.

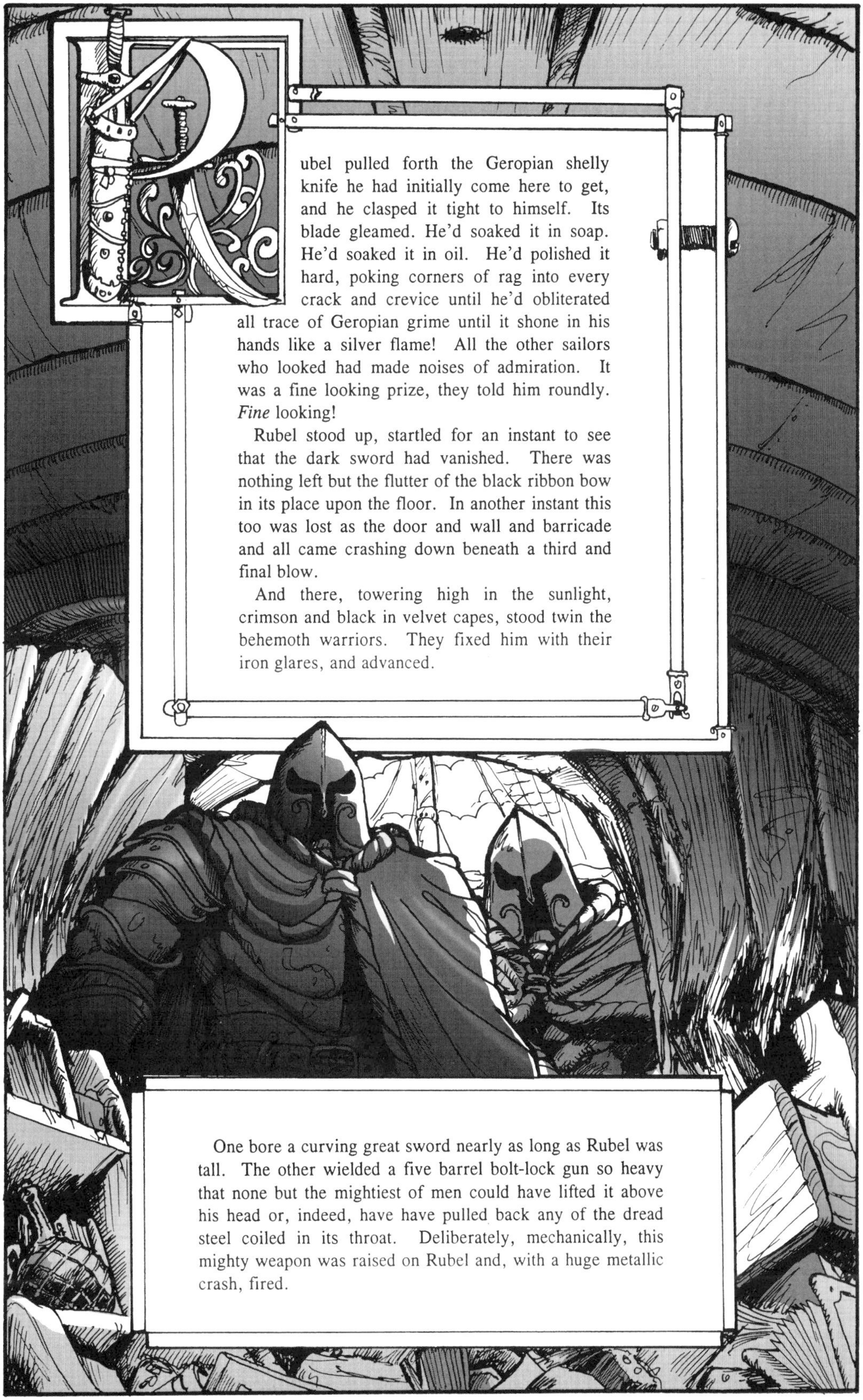

Rubel pulled forth the Geropian shelly knife he had initially come here to get, and he clasped it tight to himself. Its blade gleamed. He'd soaked it in soap. He'd soaked it in oil. He'd polished it hard, poking corners of rag into every crack and crevice until he'd obliterated all trace of Geropian grime until it shone in his hands like a silver flame! All the other sailors who looked had made noises of admiration. It was a fine looking prize, they told him roundly. *Fine* looking!

Rubel stood up, startled for an instant to see that the dark sword had vanished. There was nothing left but the flutter of the black ribbon bow in its place upon the floor. In another instant this too was lost as the door and wall and barricade and all came crashing down beneath a third and final blow.

And there, towering high in the sunlight, crimson and black in velvet capes, stood twin the behemoth warriors. They fixed him with their iron glares, and advanced.

One bore a curving great sword nearly as long as Rubel was tall. The other wielded a five barrel bolt-lock gun so heavy that none but the mightiest of men could have lifted it above his head or, indeed, have have pulled back any of the dread steel coiled in its throat. Deliberately, mechanically, this mighty weapon was raised on Rubel and, with a huge metallic crash, fired.

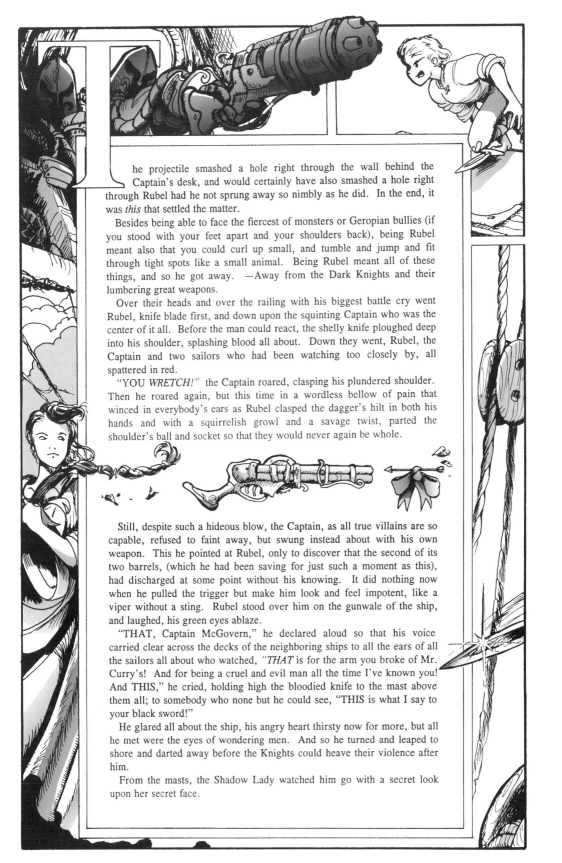

he projectile smashed a hole right through the wall behind the Captain's desk, and would certainly have also smashed a hole right through Rubel had he not sprung away so nimbly as he did. In the end, it was *this* that settled the matter.

Besides being able to face the fiercest of monsters or Geropian bullies (if you stood with your feet apart and your shoulders back), being Rubel meant also that you could curl up small, and tumble and jump and fit through tight spots like a small animal. Being Rubel meant all of these things, and so he got away. —Away from the Dark Knights and their lumbering great weapons.

Over their heads and over the railing with his biggest battle cry went Rubel, knife blade first, and down upon the squinting Captain who was the center of it all. Before the man could react, the shelly knife ploughed deep into his shoulder, splashing blood all about. Down they went, Rubel, the Captain and two sailors who had been watching too closely by, all spattered in red.

"YOU *WRETCH!*" the Captain roared, clasping his plundered shoulder. Then he roared again, but this time in a wordless bellow of pain that winced in everybody's ears as Rubel clasped the dagger's hilt in both his hands and with a squirrelish growl and a savage twist, parted the shoulder's ball and socket so that they would never again be whole.

Still, despite such a hideous blow, the Captain, as all true villains are so capable, refused to faint away, but swung instead about with his own weapon. This he pointed at Rubel, only to discover that the second of its two barrels, (which he had been saving for just such a moment as this), had discharged at some point without his knowing. It did nothing now when he pulled the trigger but make him look and feel impotent, like a viper without a sting. Rubel stood over him on the gunwale of the ship, and laughed, his green eyes ablaze.

"THAT, Captain McGovern," he declared aloud so that his voice carried clear across the decks of the neighboring ships to all the ears of all the sailors all about who watched, *"THAT* is for the arm you broke of Mr. Curry's! And for being a cruel and evil man all the time I've known you! And THIS," he cried, holding high the bloodied knife to the mast above them all; to somebody who none but he could see, "THIS is what I say to your black sword!"

He glared all about the ship, his angry heart thirsty now for more, but all he met were the eyes of wondering men. And so he turned and leaped to shore and darted away before the Knights could heave their violence after him.

From the masts, the Shadow Lady watched him go with a secret look upon her secret face.

AYE LAD.
POINT MADE.
POINT MADE.
WILL SOMEBODY PLEASE SHOOT THAT WRETCH?!

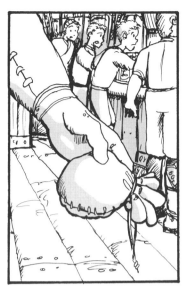

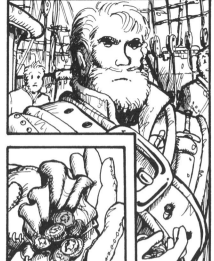

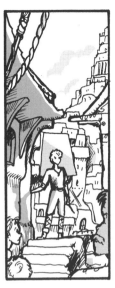

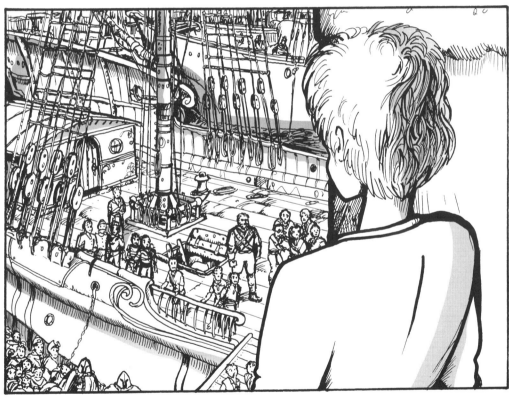

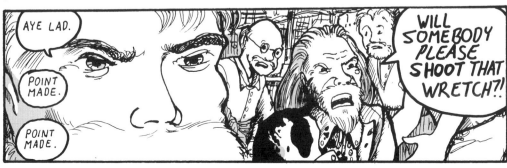

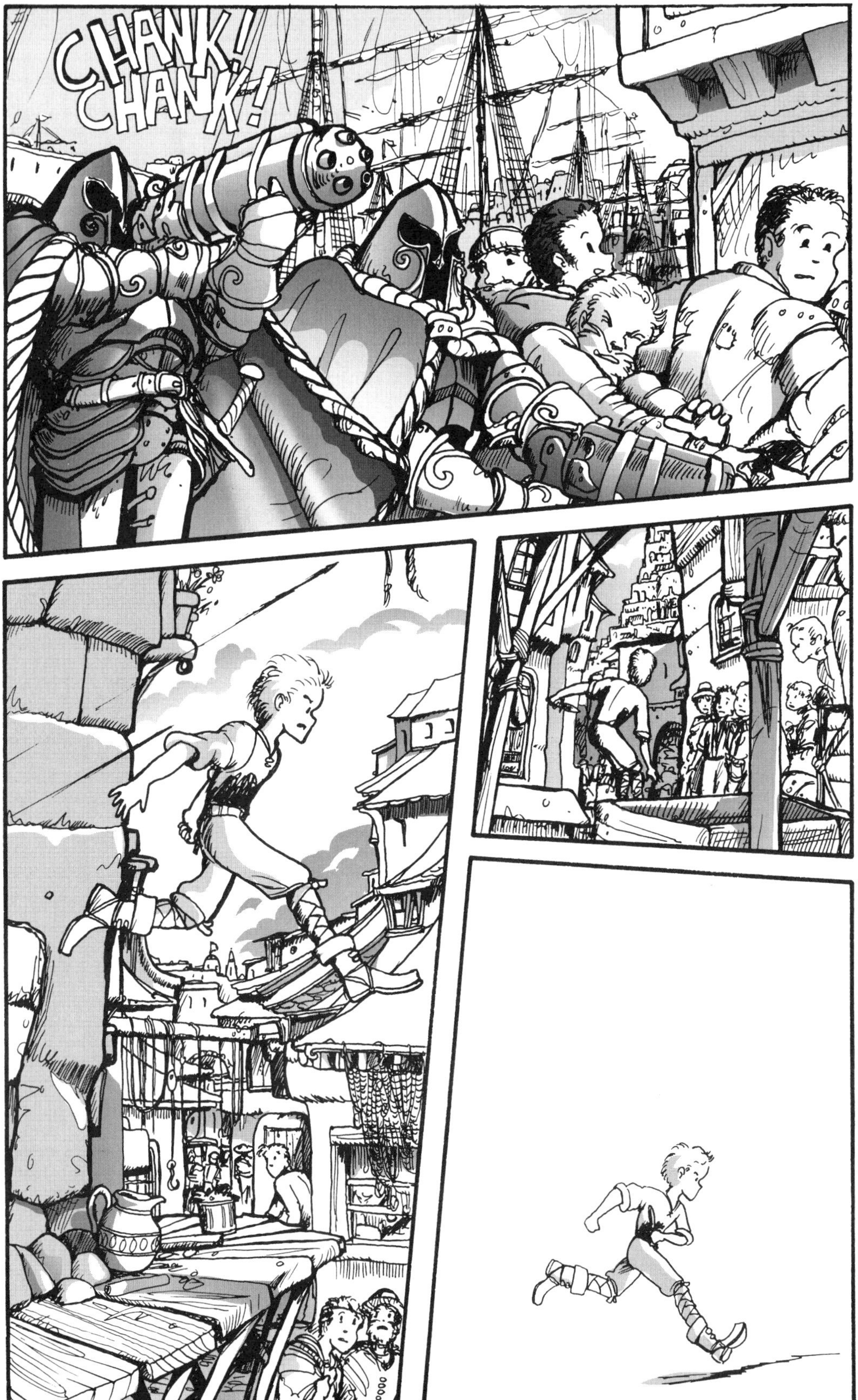
CHANK! CHANK!

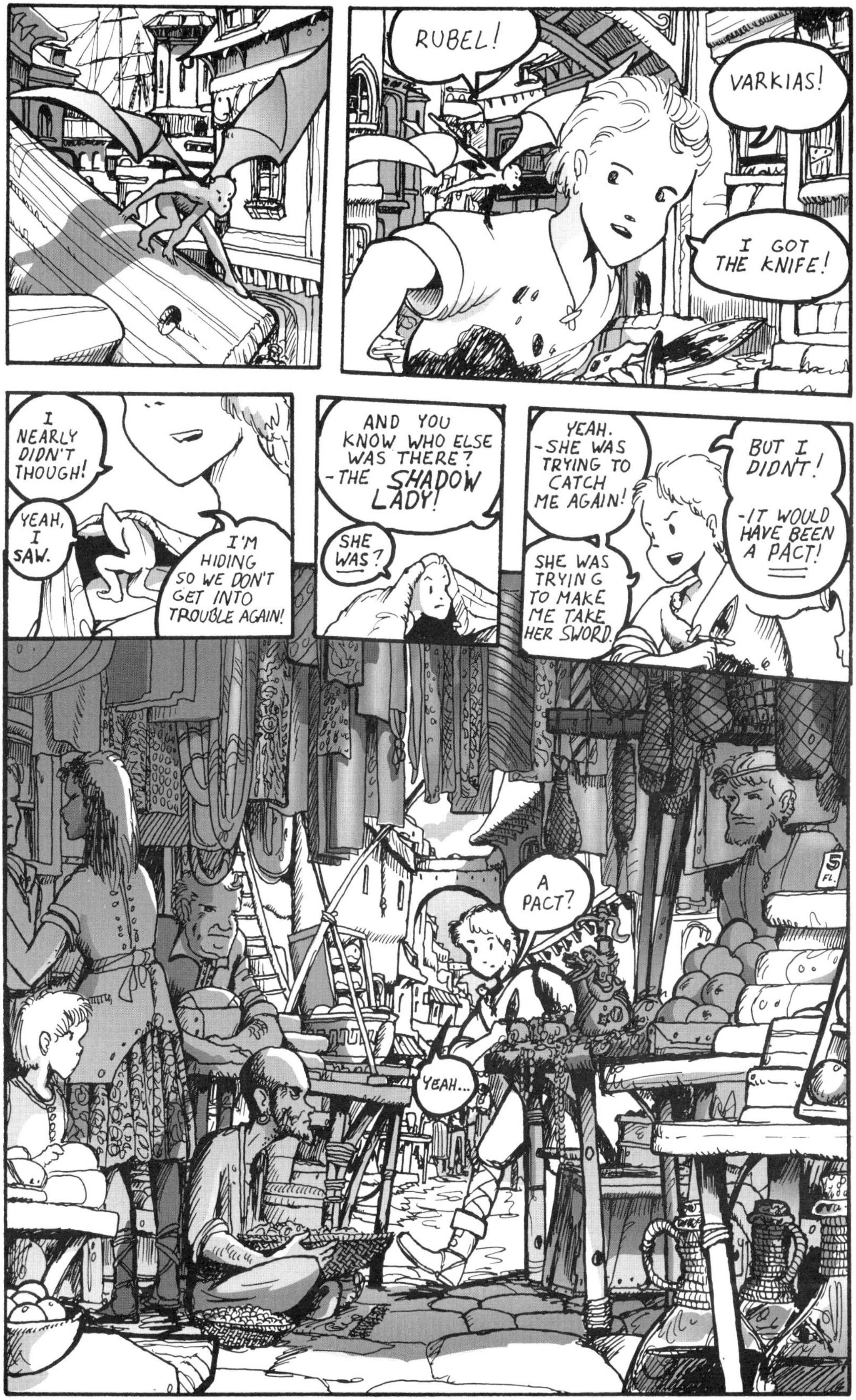
RUBEL!
VARKIAS!
I GOT THE KNIFE!
I NEARLY DIDN'T THOUGH!
YEAH, I SAW.
I'M HIDING SO WE DON'T GET INTO TROUBLE AGAIN!
AND YOU KNOW WHO ELSE WAS THERE? -THE SHADOW LADY!
SHE WAS?
YEAH. -SHE WAS TRYING TO CATCH ME AGAIN!
SHE WAS TRYING TO MAKE ME TAKE HER SWORD.
BUT I DIDN'T!
-IT WOULD HAVE BEEN A PACT!
A PACT?
YEAH...
5 FL.

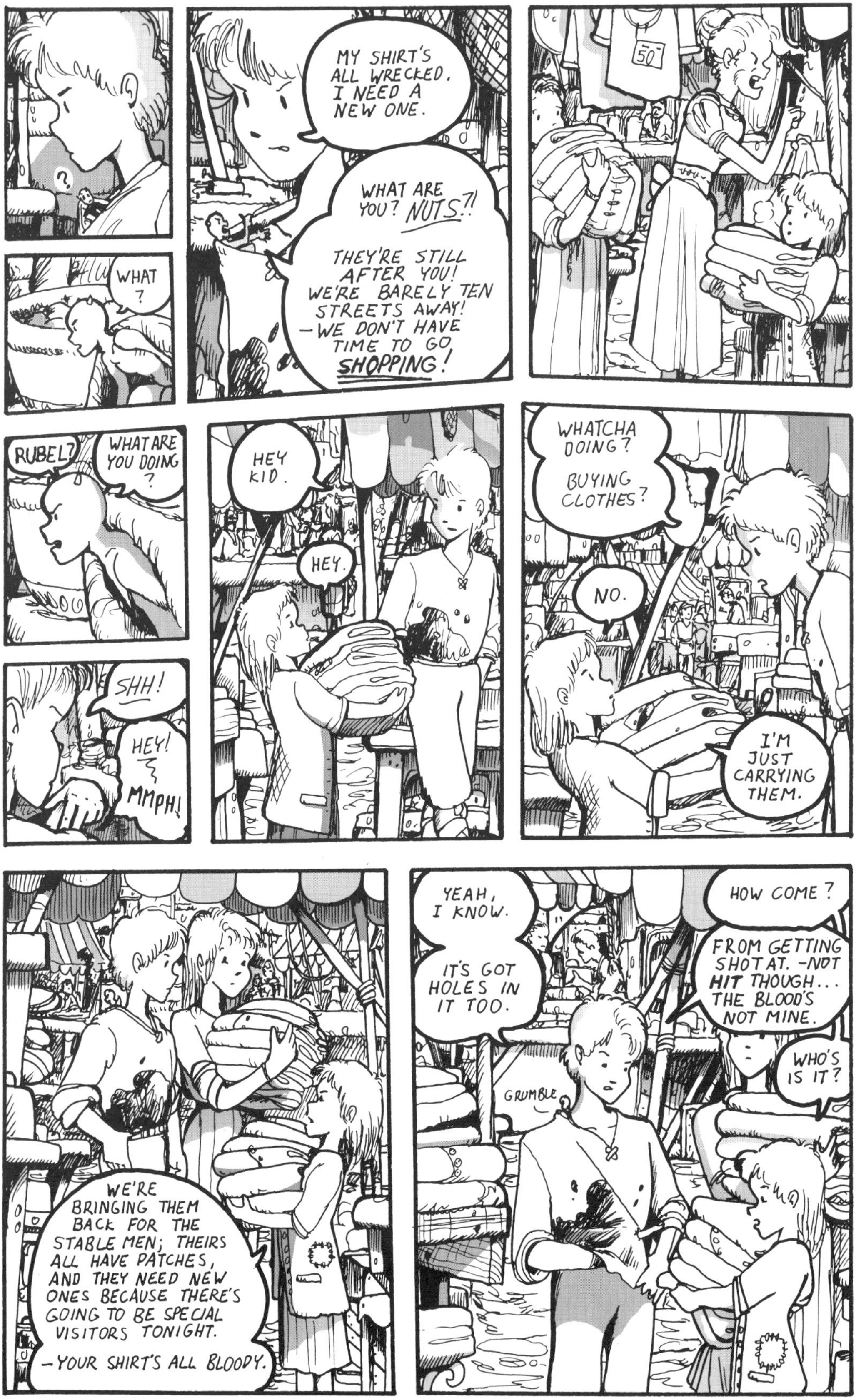
?
MY SHIRT'S ALL WRECKED. I NEED A NEW ONE.
WHAT?
WHAT ARE YOU? NUTS?!
THEY'RE STILL AFTER YOU! WE'RE BARELY TEN STREETS AWAY! —WE DON'T HAVE TIME TO GO SHOPPING!
50
RUBEL?
WHAT ARE YOU DOING?
SHH!
HEY!
MMPH!
HEY KID.
HEY.
WHATCHA DOING? BUYING CLOTHES?
NO.
I'M JUST CARRYING THEM.
WE'RE BRINGING THEM BACK FOR THE STABLE MEN; THEIRS ALL HAVE PATCHES, AND THEY NEED NEW ONES BECAUSE THERE'S GOING TO BE SPECIAL VISITORS TONIGHT.
—YOUR SHIRT'S ALL BLOODY.
YEAH, I KNOW.
IT'S GOT HOLES IN IT TOO.
HOW COME?
FROM GETTING SHOT AT. —NOT HIT THOUGH... THE BLOOD'S NOT MINE.
GRUMBLE
WHO'S IS IT?

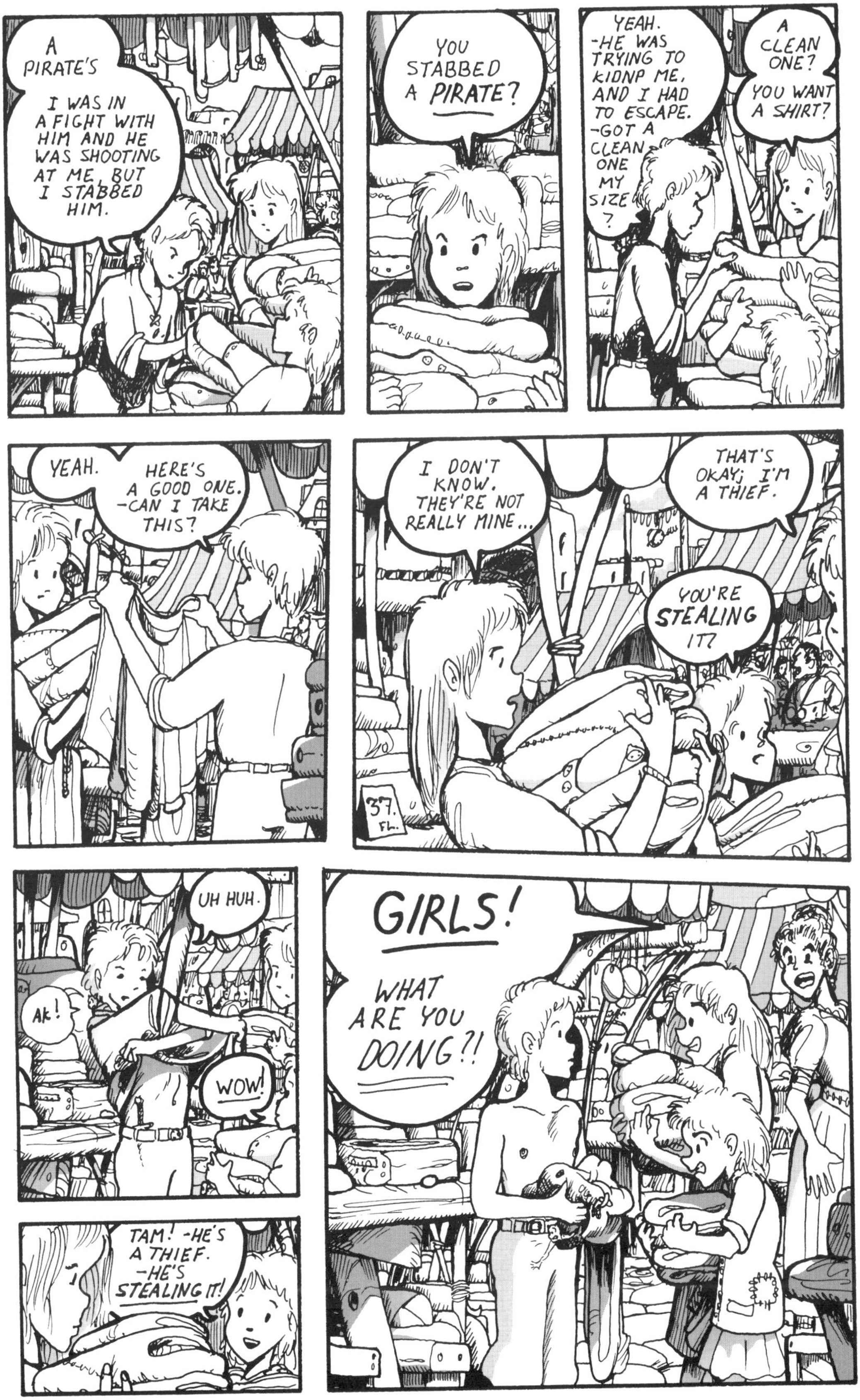

A PIRATE'S
I WAS IN A FIGHT WITH HIM AND HE WAS SHOOTING AT ME, BUT I STABBED HIM.
YOU STABBED A PIRATE?
YEAH. -HE WAS TRYING TO KIDNP ME, AND I HAD TO ESCAPE. -GOT A CLEAN ONE MY SIZE?
A CLEAN ONE?
YOU WANT A SHIRT?
YEAH.
HERE'S A GOOD ONE. -CAN I TAKE THIS?
I DON'T KNOW. THEY'RE NOT REALLY MINE...
THAT'S OKAY; I'M A THIEF.
YOU'RE STEALING IT?
37. FL.
UH HUH.
AK!
WOW!
TAM! -HE'S A THIEF. -HE'S STEALING IT!
GIRLS!
WHAT ARE YOU DOING?!

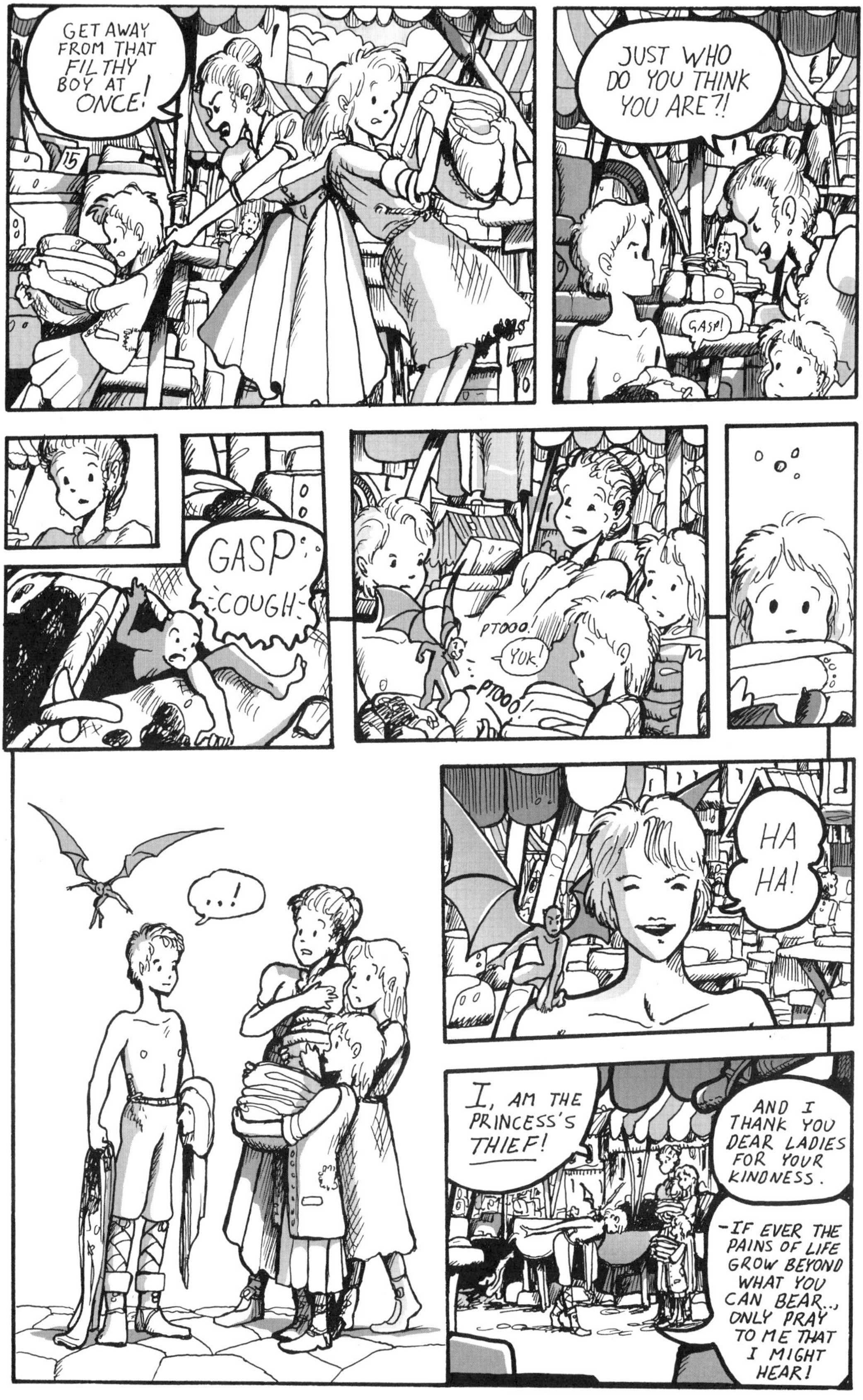
GET AWAY FROM THAT FILTHY BOY AT ONCE!
JUST WHO DO YOU THINK YOU ARE?!
GASP!
GASP COUGH
PTOOO!
YUK!
PTOOO!
...!
HA HA!
I, AM THE PRINCESS'S THIEF!
AND I THANK YOU DEAR LADIES FOR YOUR KINDNESS.
-IF EVER THE PAINS OF LIFE GROW BEYOND WHAT YOU CAN BEAR.., ONLY PRAY TO ME THAT I MIGHT HEAR!

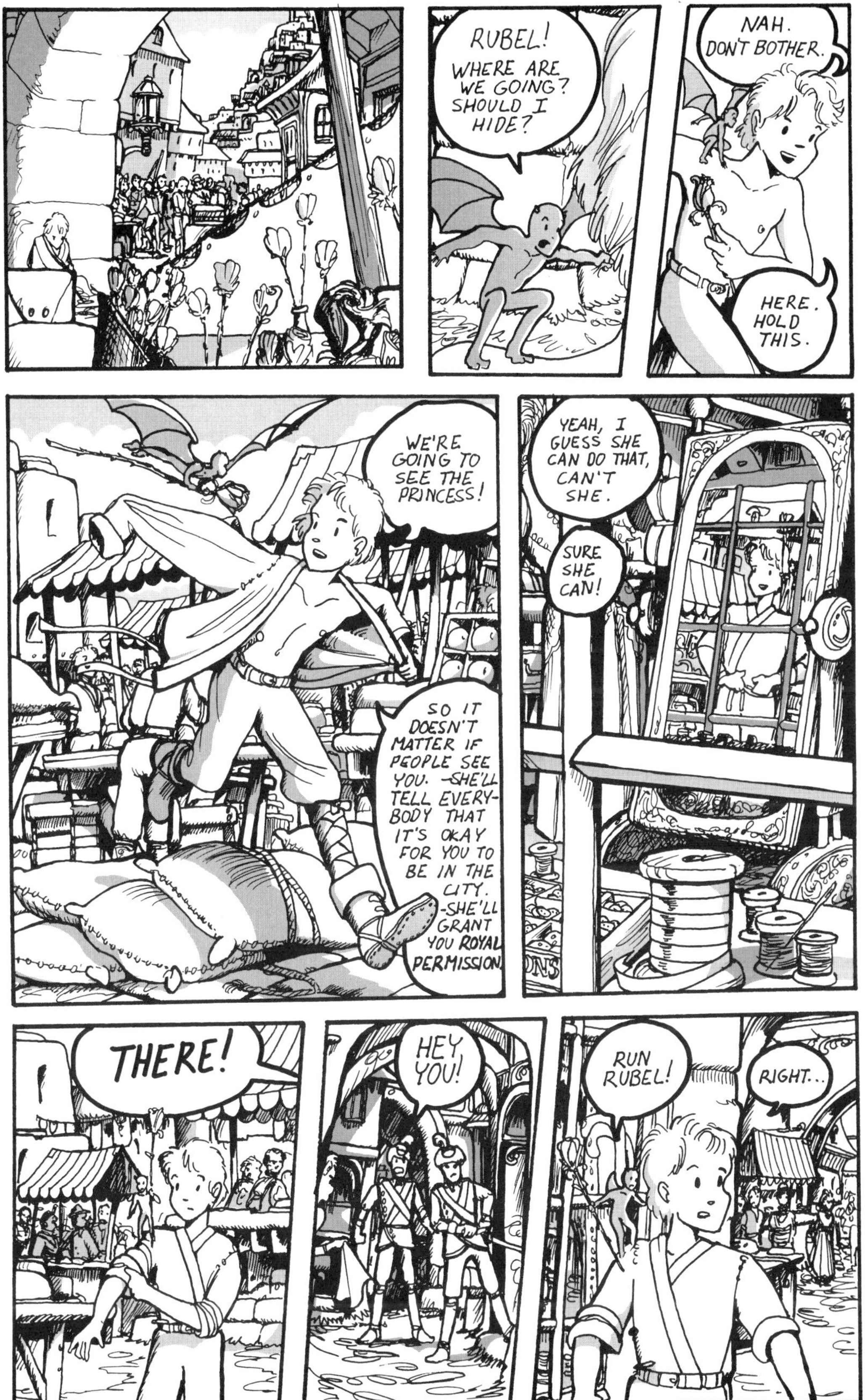
RUBEL! WHERE ARE WE GOING? SHOULD I HIDE?
NAH. DON'T BOTHER.
HERE. HOLD THIS.
WE'RE GOING TO SEE THE PRINCESS!
SO IT DOESN'T MATTER IF PEOPLE SEE YOU. –SHE'LL TELL EVERYBODY THAT IT'S OKAY FOR YOU TO BE IN THE CITY. –SHE'LL GRANT YOU ROYAL PERMISSION!
YEAH, I GUESS SHE CAN DO THAT, CAN'T SHE.
SURE SHE CAN!
THERE!
HEY YOU!
RUN RUBEL!
RIGHT...

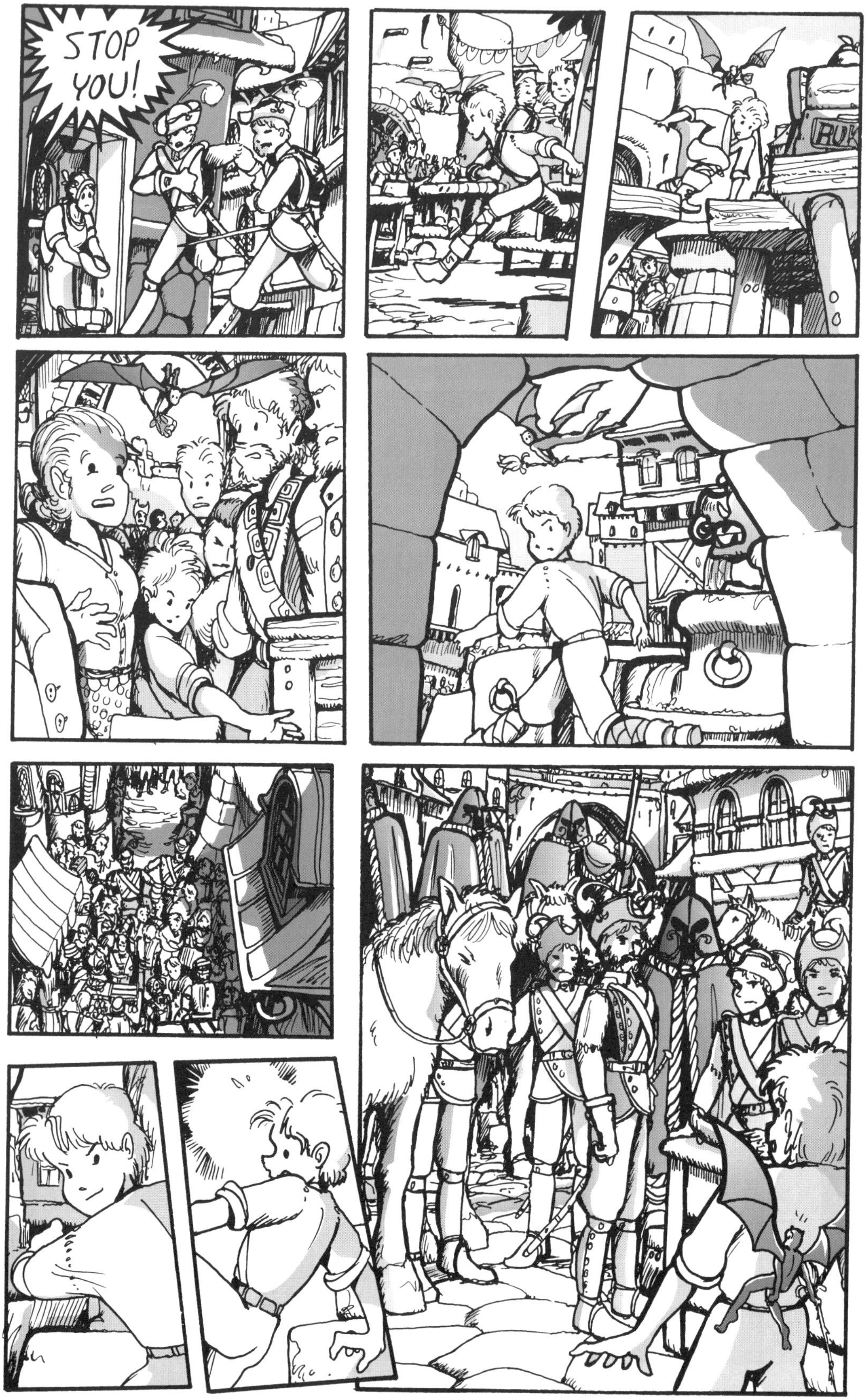
STOP YOU!
RUK

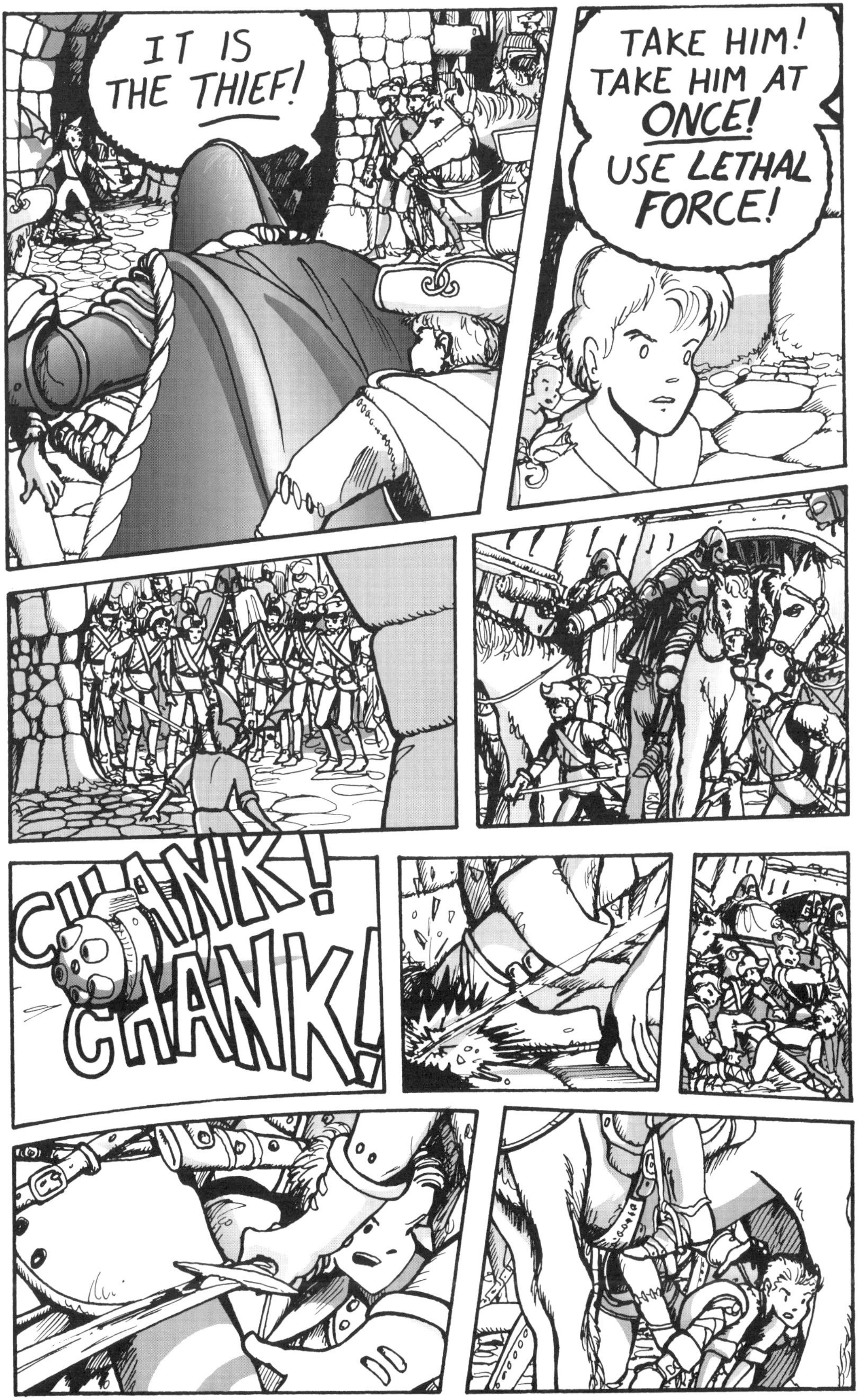
IT IS THE THIEF!
TAKE HIM! TAKE HIM AT ONCE! USE LETHAL FORCE!
CHANK! CHANK!

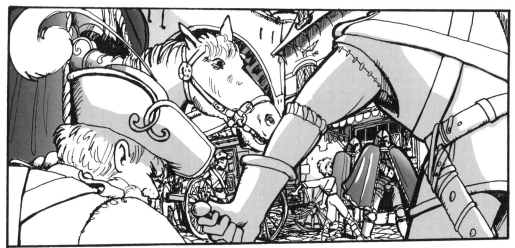

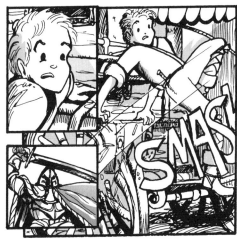

SMASH

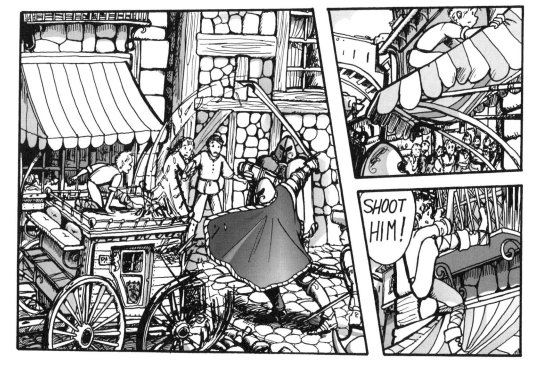

SHOOT HIM!

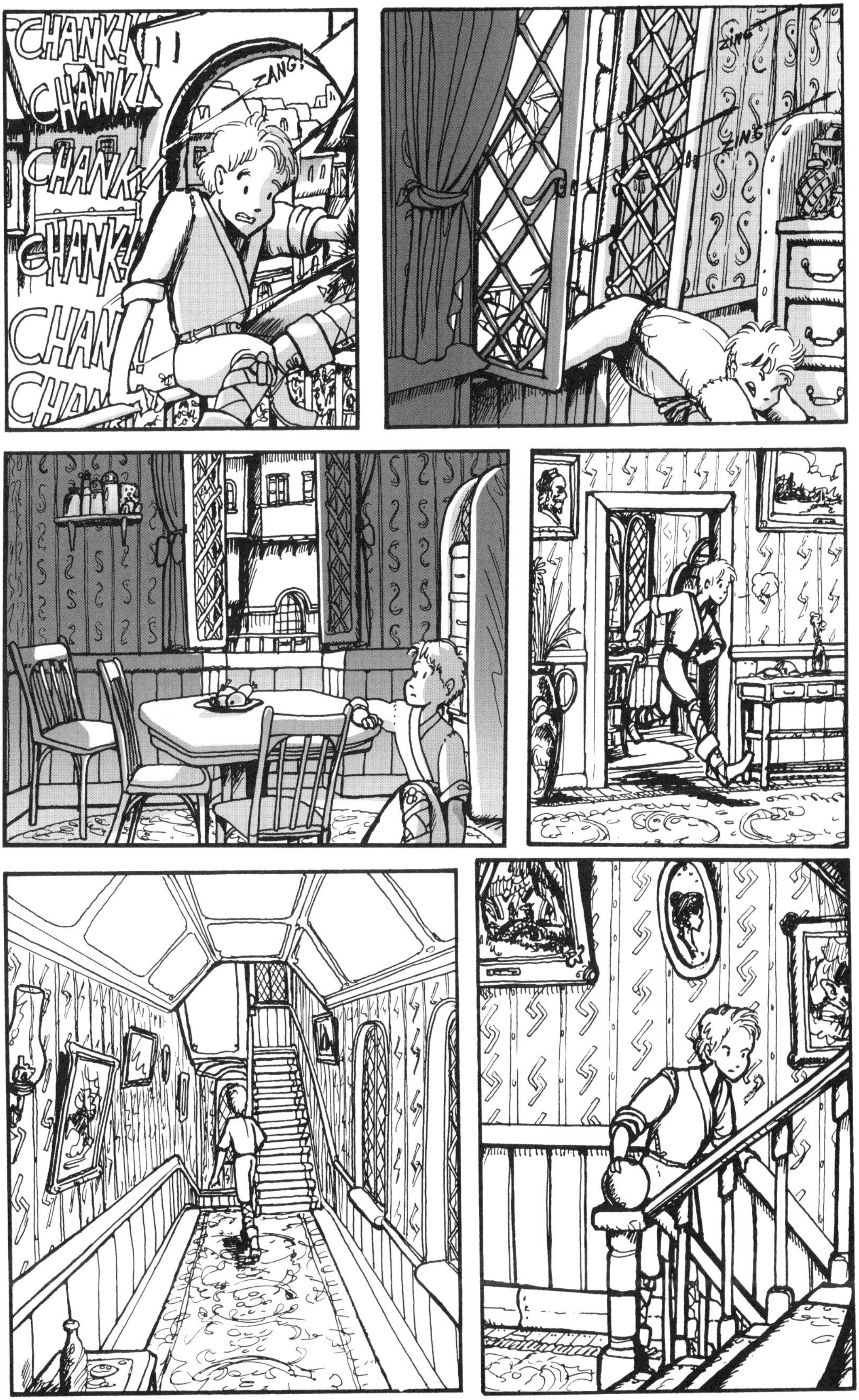
CHANK!
CHANK!
CHANK!
CHANK!
CHANK!
ZANG!
ZING
ZING

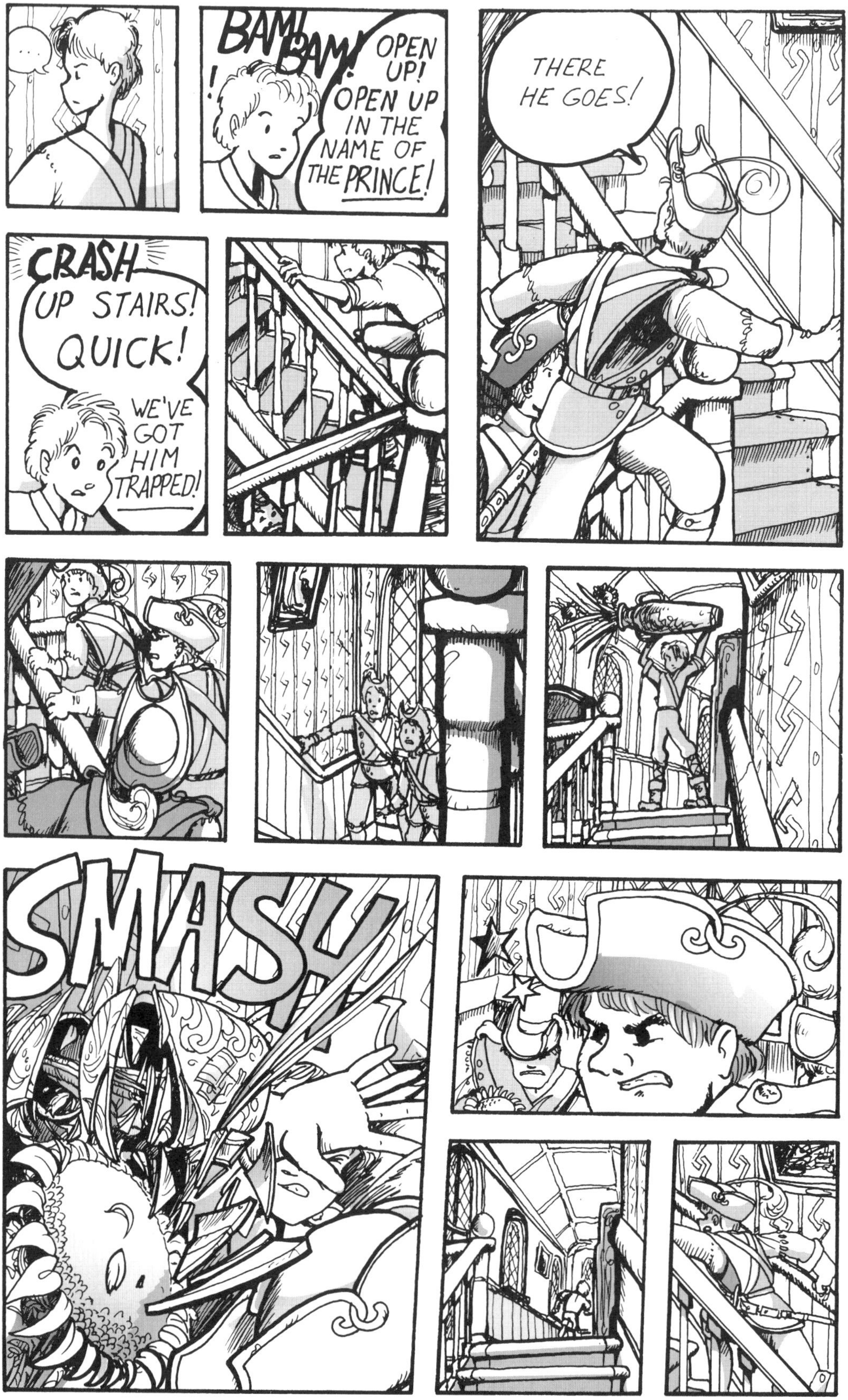
. . .
BAM! BAM!
!
OPEN UP! OPEN UP IN THE NAME OF THE PRINCE!
THERE HE GOES!
CRASH
UP STAIRS! QUICK!
WE'VE GOT HIM TRAPPED!
SMASH

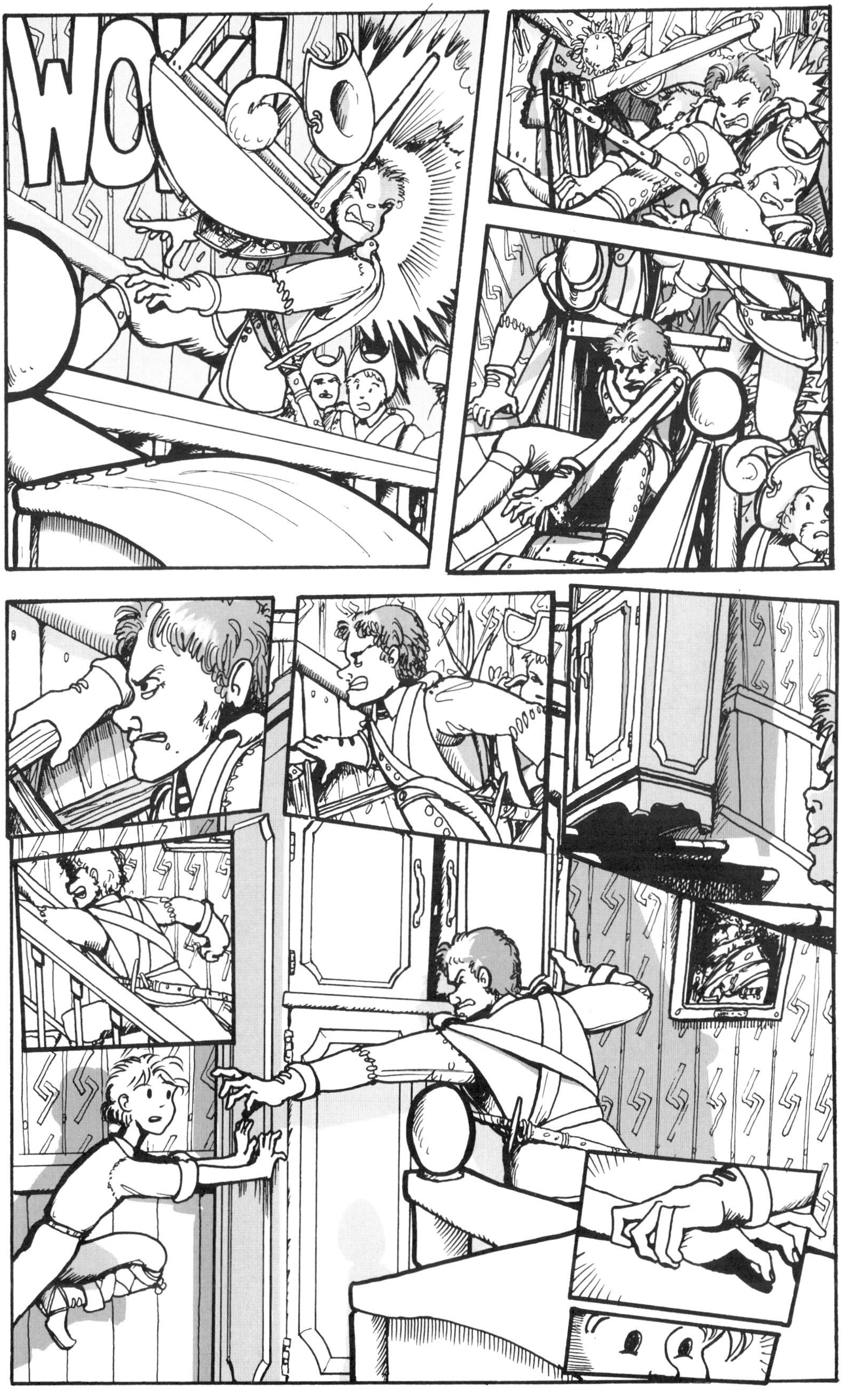

Chapter 5

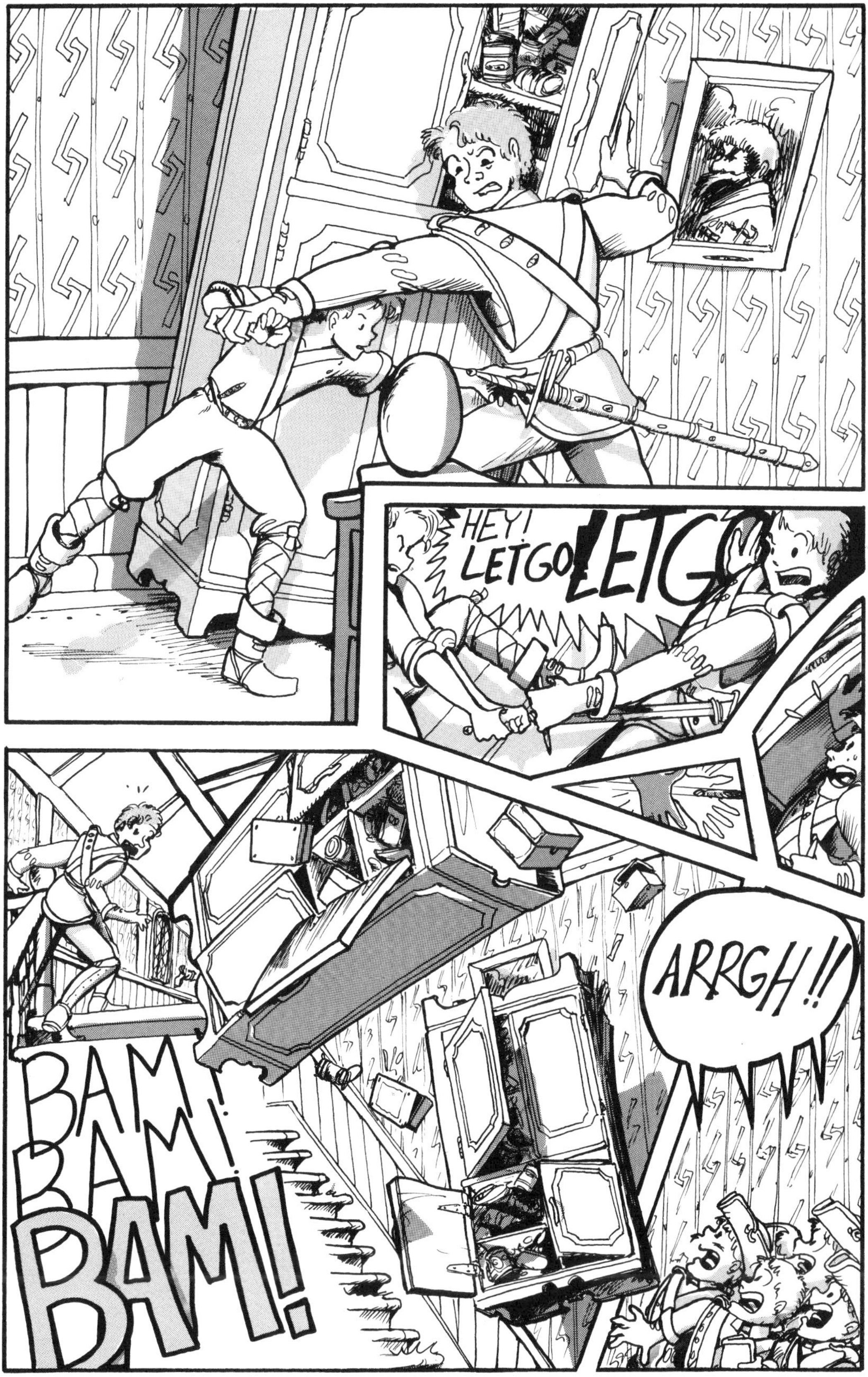
HEY!
LETGO
LETGO
ARRGH!!
BAM!
BAM!
BAM!

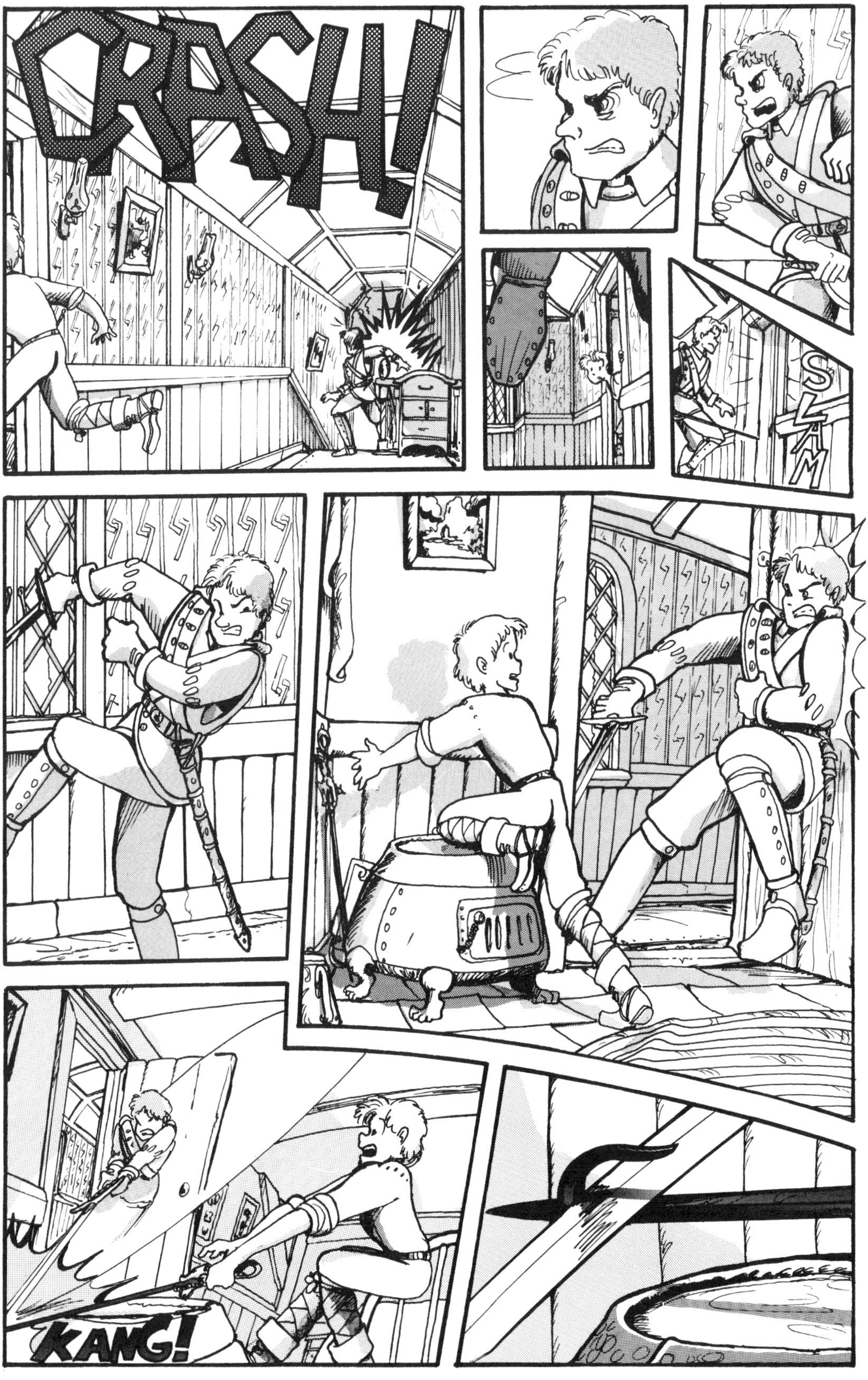
CRASH!
SLAM
KANG!

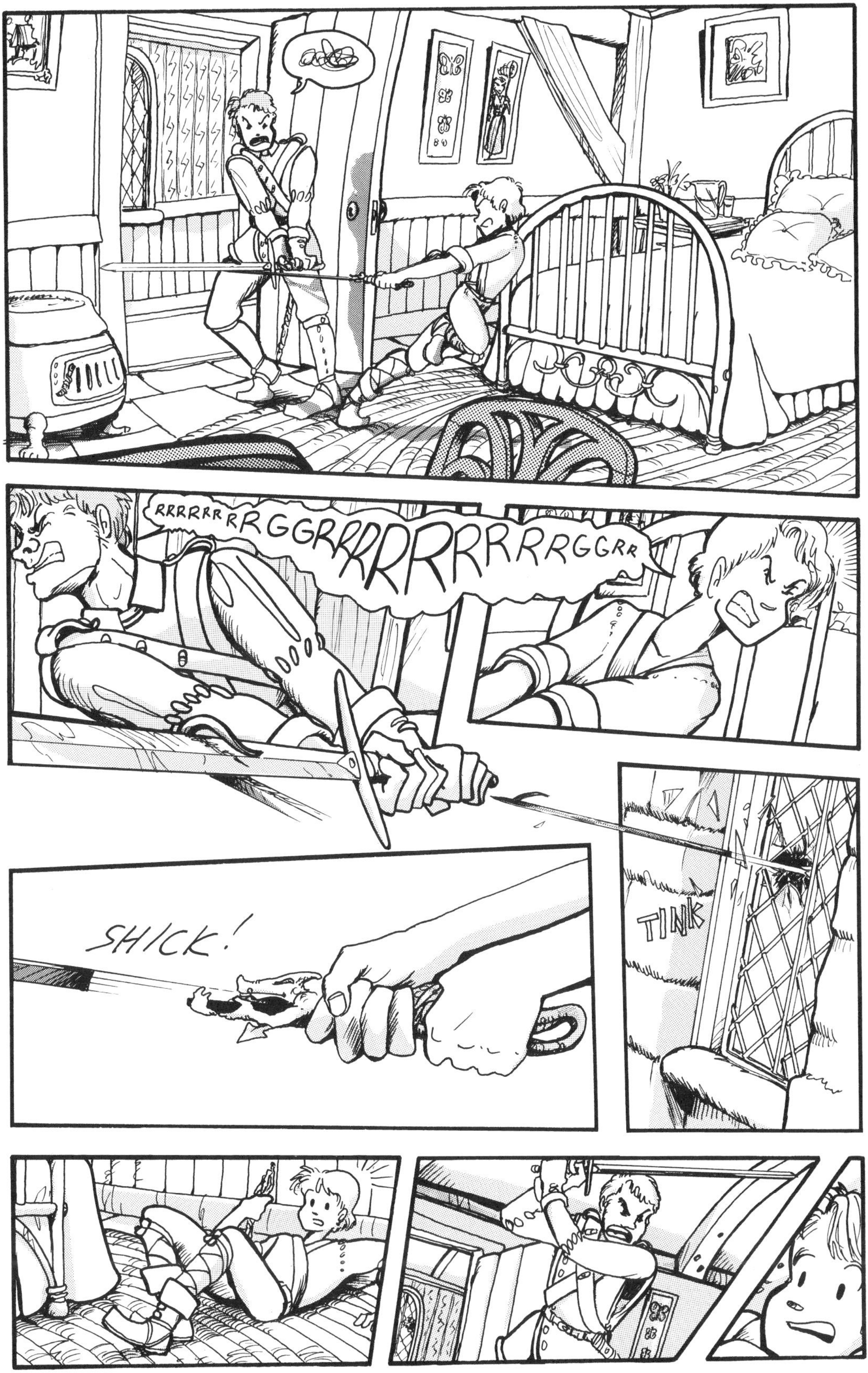
RRRRRRRRGGRRRRRRRRRRRGGRR
TINK
SHICK!

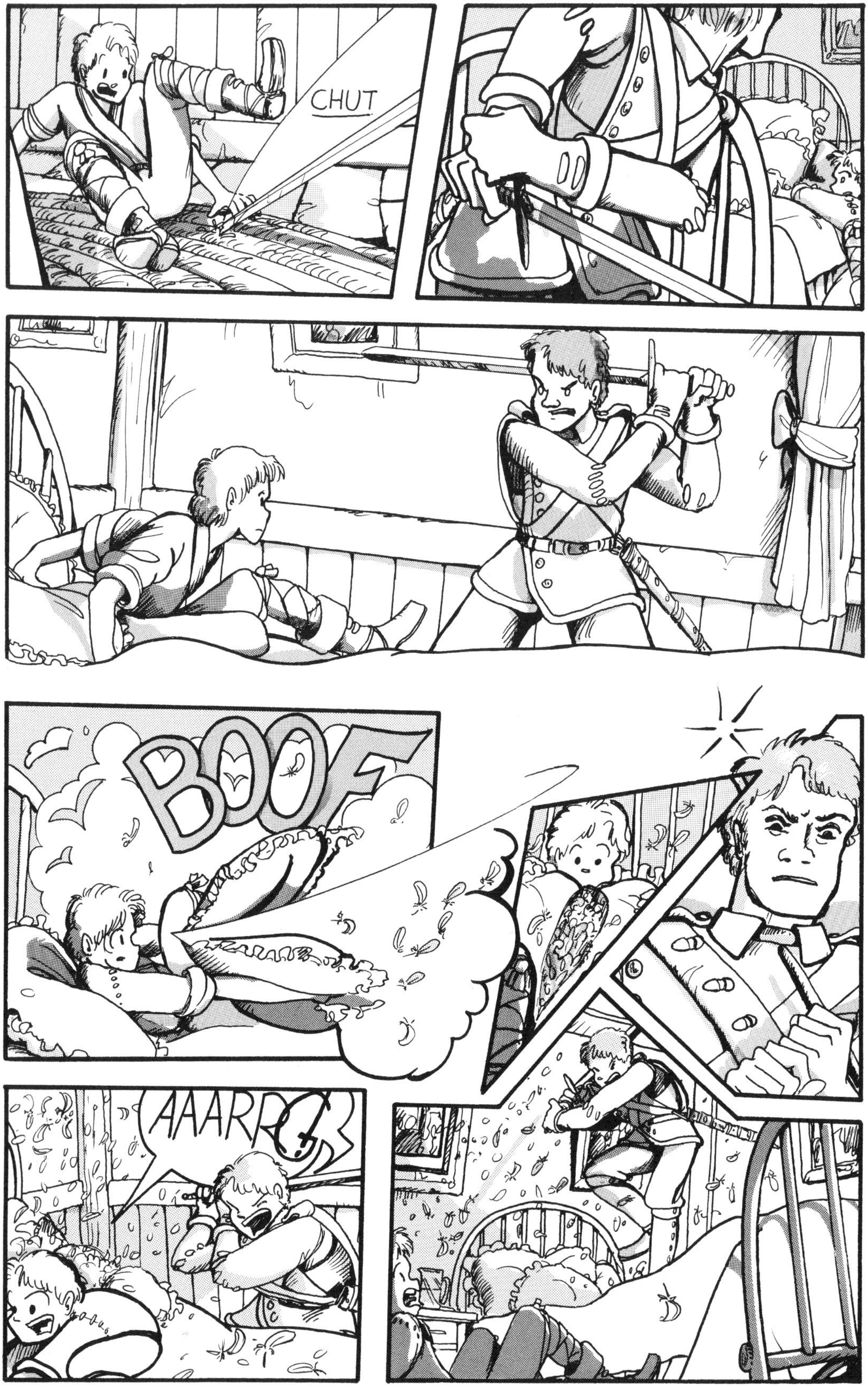
CHUT
BOOF
AAARRG

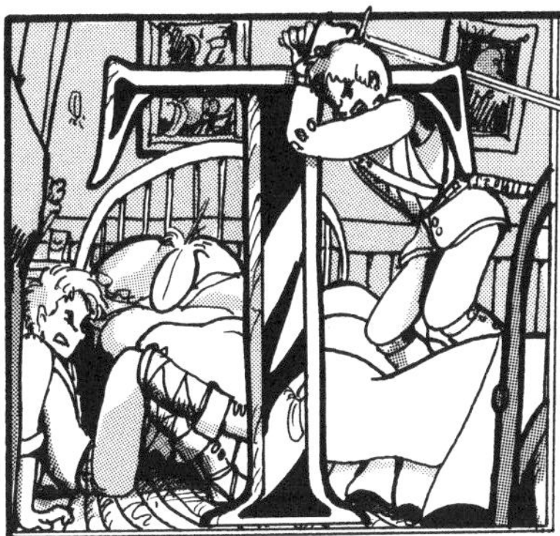

Throwing his weight against the wall, Rubel pushed mightily with both feet on the bed frame. The bed slid back and the guardsman fell forward, dropping his sword in order to catch himself from smashing headlong into the floor, which he did anyway.

Rubel darted for the door.

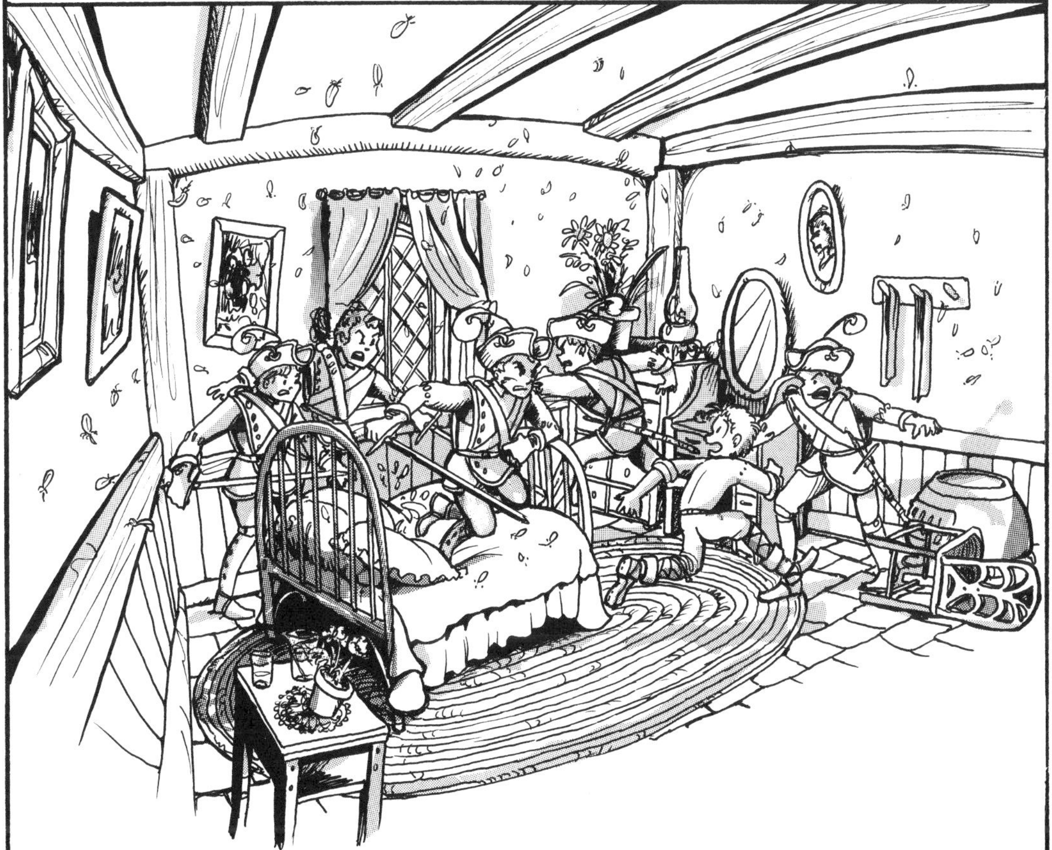

Just as he reached it, in tumbled all the other guardsmen, all looking sore and mean. Rubel yelped and reversed his direction. With swords drawn and faces red, the guardsmen leaped after him.

Around and around the tiny room they all went, knocking things over and treading on the bed with their dusty boots, and stirring up the air so that it was difficult to breathe without inhaling feathers. Yet, try as they might, Rubel always managed to stay half a finger's breadth away from capture, and this frustrated the guardsmen so that they sweated and puffed and ran harder still.

Each time around the room, Rubel tried to slip out the door, but each time he always found a flashing sword or a guardsman blocking the way, and so around he went again. And with each revolution, Rubel felt his luck growing more and more impatient to leave, and so at last he made a desperate choice and lunged for the window.

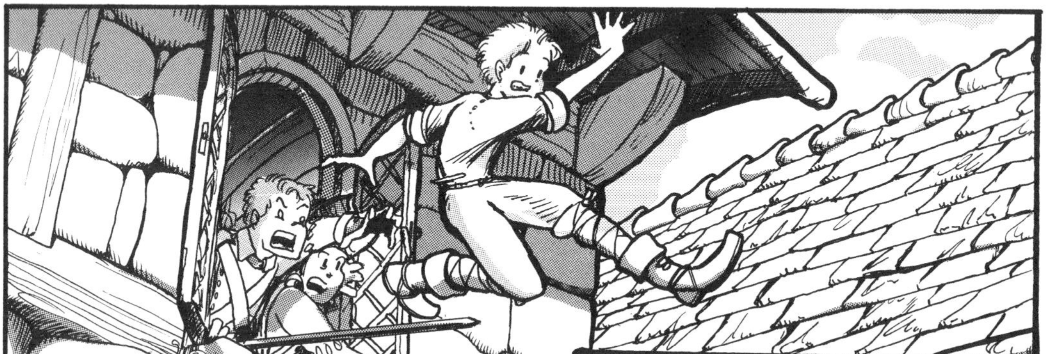

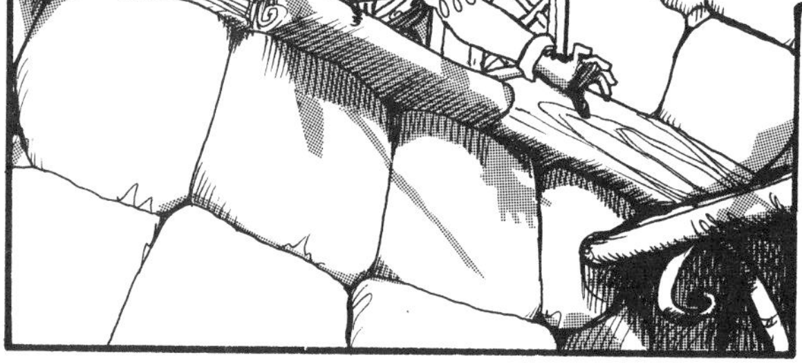

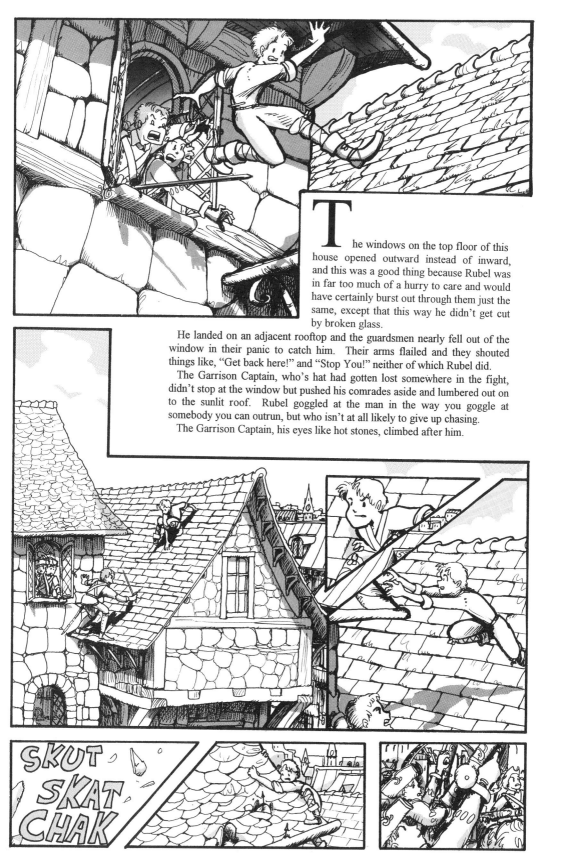

The windows on the top floor of this house opened outward instead of inward, and this was a good thing because Rubel was in far too much of a hurry to care and would have certainly burst out through them just the same, except that this way he didn't get cut by broken glass.

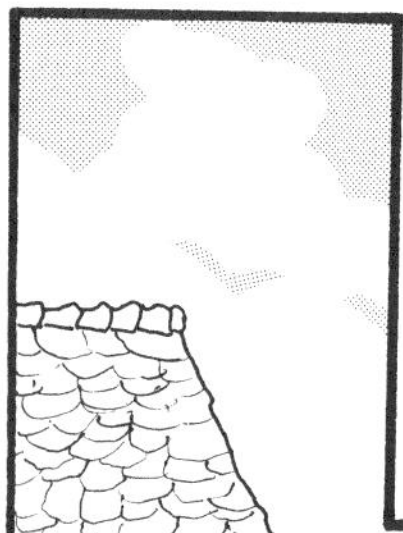

He landed on an adjacent rooftop and the guardsmen nearly fell out of the window in their panic to catch him. Their arms flailed and they shouted things like, "Get back here!" and "Stop You!" neither of which Rubel did.

The Garrison Captain, who's hat had gotten lost somewhere in the fight, didn't stop at the window but pushed his comrades aside and lumbered out on to the sunlit roof. Rubel goggled at the man in the way you goggle at somebody you can outrun, but who isn't at all likely to give up chasing.

The Garrison Captain, his eyes like hot stones, climbed after him.

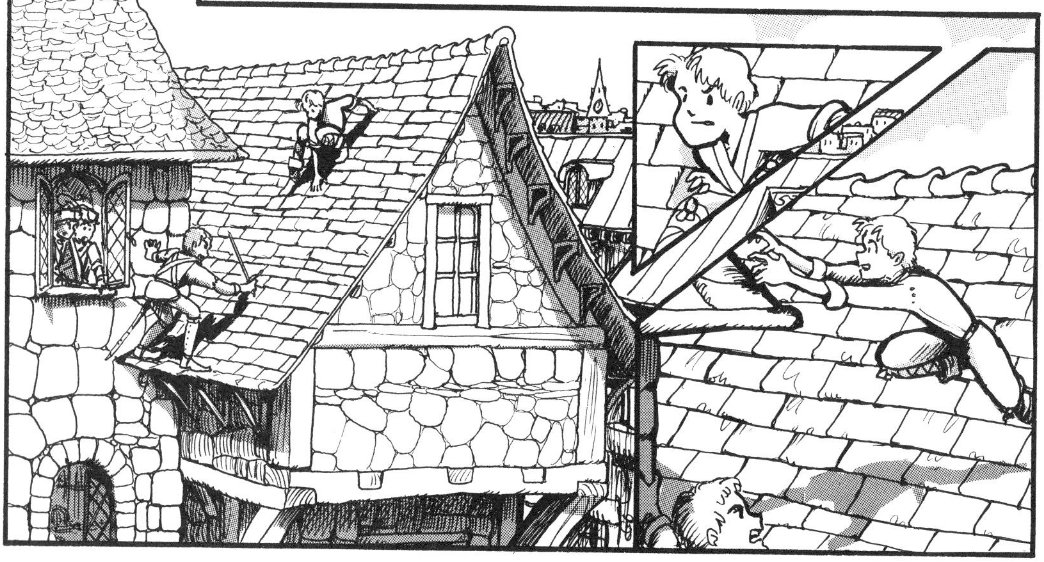

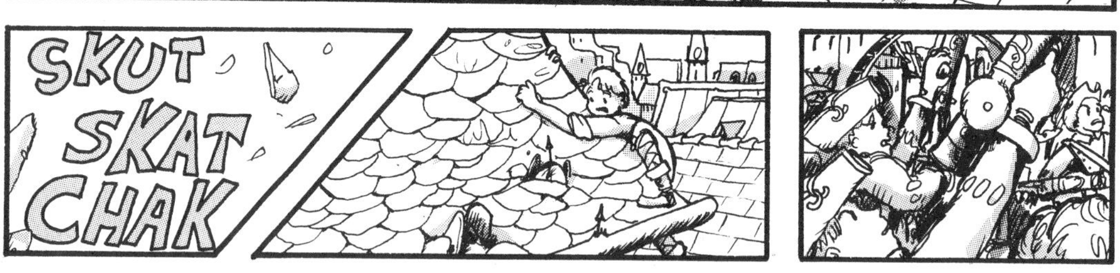
SKUT
SKAT
CHAK

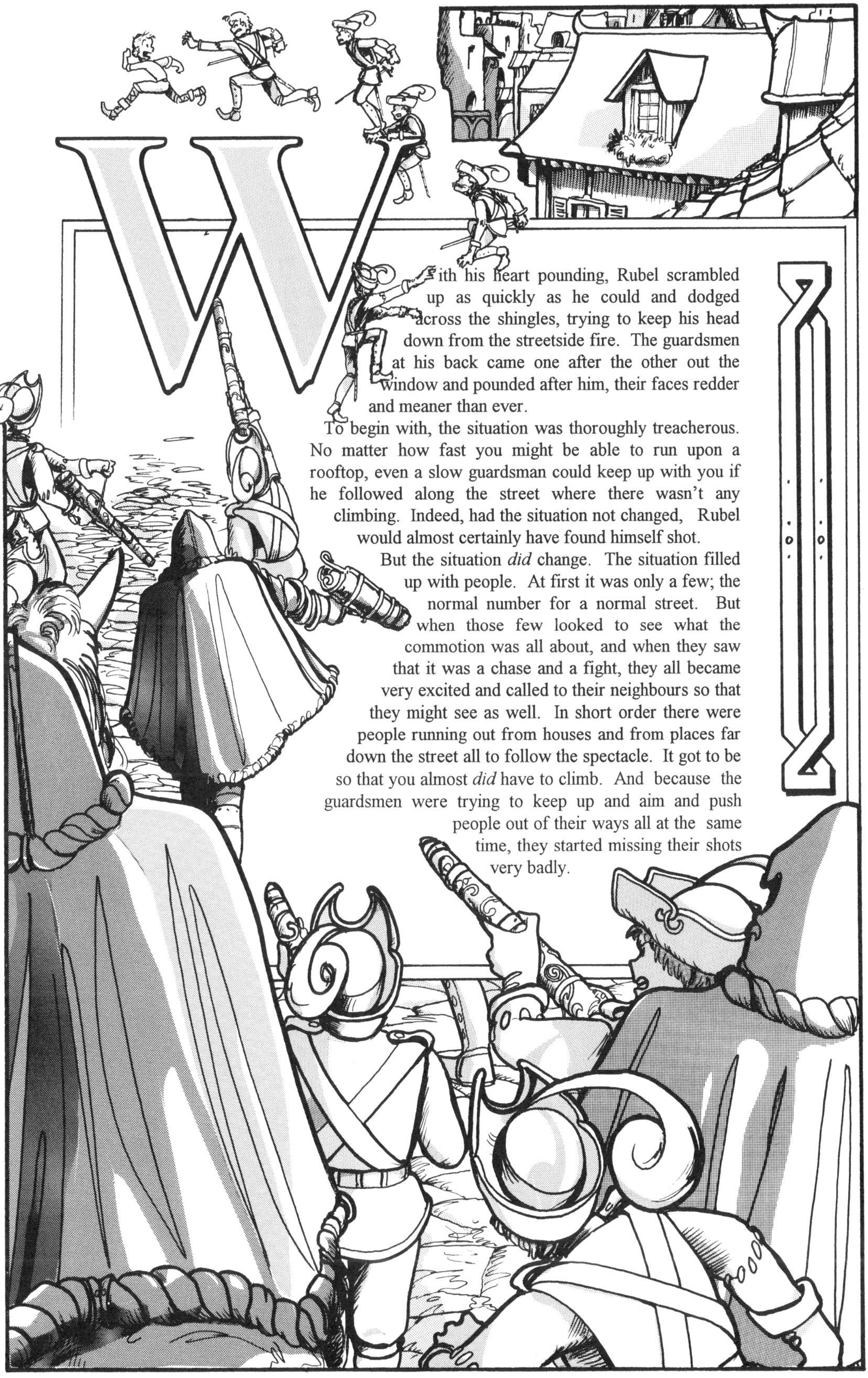

With his heart pounding, Rubel scrambled up as quickly as he could and dodged across the shingles, trying to keep his head down from the streetside fire. The guardsmen at his back came one after the other out the window and pounded after him, their faces redder and meaner than ever.

To begin with, the situation was thoroughly treacherous. No matter how fast you might be able to run upon a rooftop, even a slow guardsman could keep up with you if he followed along the street where there wasn't any climbing. Indeed, had the situation not changed, Rubel would almost certainly have found himself shot.

But the situation *did* change. The situation filled up with people. At first it was only a few; the normal number for a normal street. But when those few looked to see what the commotion was all about, and when they saw that it was a chase and a fight, they all became very excited and called to their neighbours so that they might see as well. In short order there were people running out from houses and from places far down the street all to follow the spectacle. It got to be so that you almost *did* have to climb. And because the guardsmen were trying to keep up and aim and push people out of their ways all at the same time, they started missing their shots very badly.

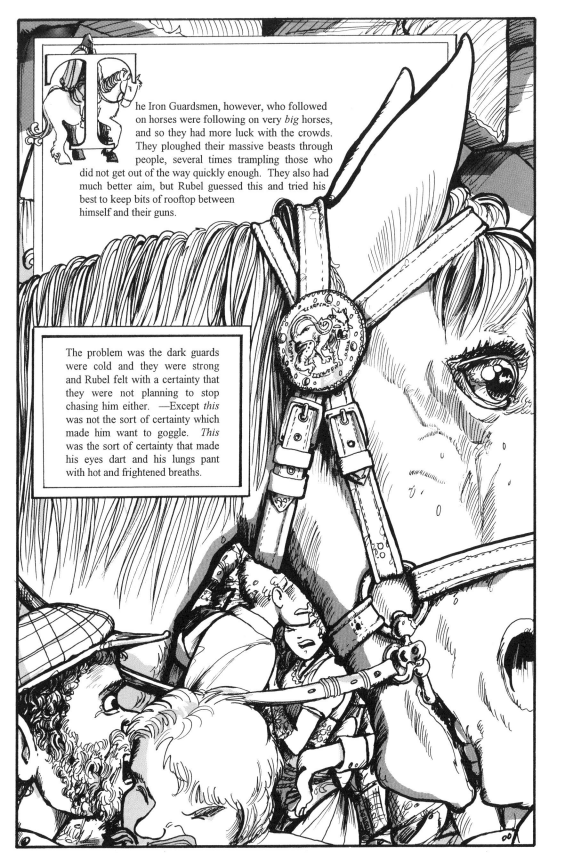

The Iron Guardsmen, however, who followed on horses were following on very *big* horses, and so they had more luck with the crowds. They ploughed their massive beasts through people, several times trampling those who did not get out of the way quickly enough. They also had much better aim, but Rubel guessed this and tried his best to keep bits of rooftop between himself and their guns.

The problem was the dark guards were cold and they were strong and Rubel felt with a certainty that they were not planning to stop chasing him either. —Except *this* was not the sort of certainty which made him want to goggle. *This* was the sort of certainty that made his eyes dart and his lungs pant with hot and frightened breaths.

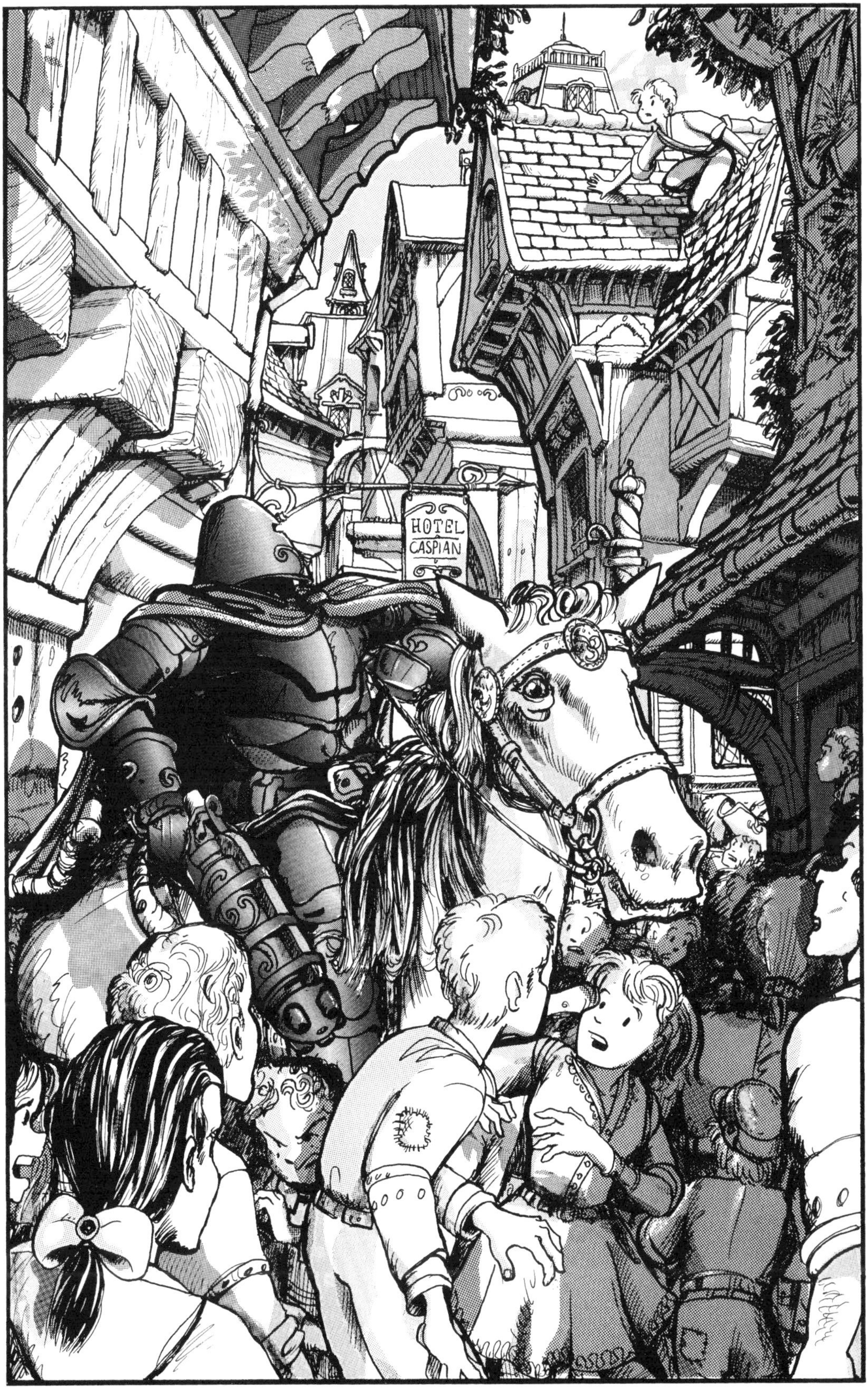
HOTEL
CASPIAN

Even massive horses, however, had their limits. There were simply far too many people filling up streets which were much too narrow to digest such confusion. So trample and stamp as they might, the white beasts of the Iron Guard were soon so thoroughly muddled that they could make no headway, and were left behind like war ships foundering in mud. Further, with the five red faced guardsmen unused to rooftops and unable to run as quickly as Rubel in any case, it began to look all of a sudden as though the boy might just get away. When this realization dawned upon him, Rubel's fright, which had become very tightly wound indeed, loosed all at once, turning into something ticklish and laughing and entirely unexpected.

"HA HA!" he turned and sang, feeling bright and saucy all at once. "YOU CAN'T CATCH ME! YOU CAN'T CATCH ME! I AM THE PRINCESSES' THIEF, I AM!"

And then he ran out of rooftops.

"Nice going," Varkias said, lighting on Rubel's shoulder, still clutching the rose meant for Katara. "I think you should have turned a different way a couple of houses back."

The five guardsmen came puffing up wearing expressions which were quite black.

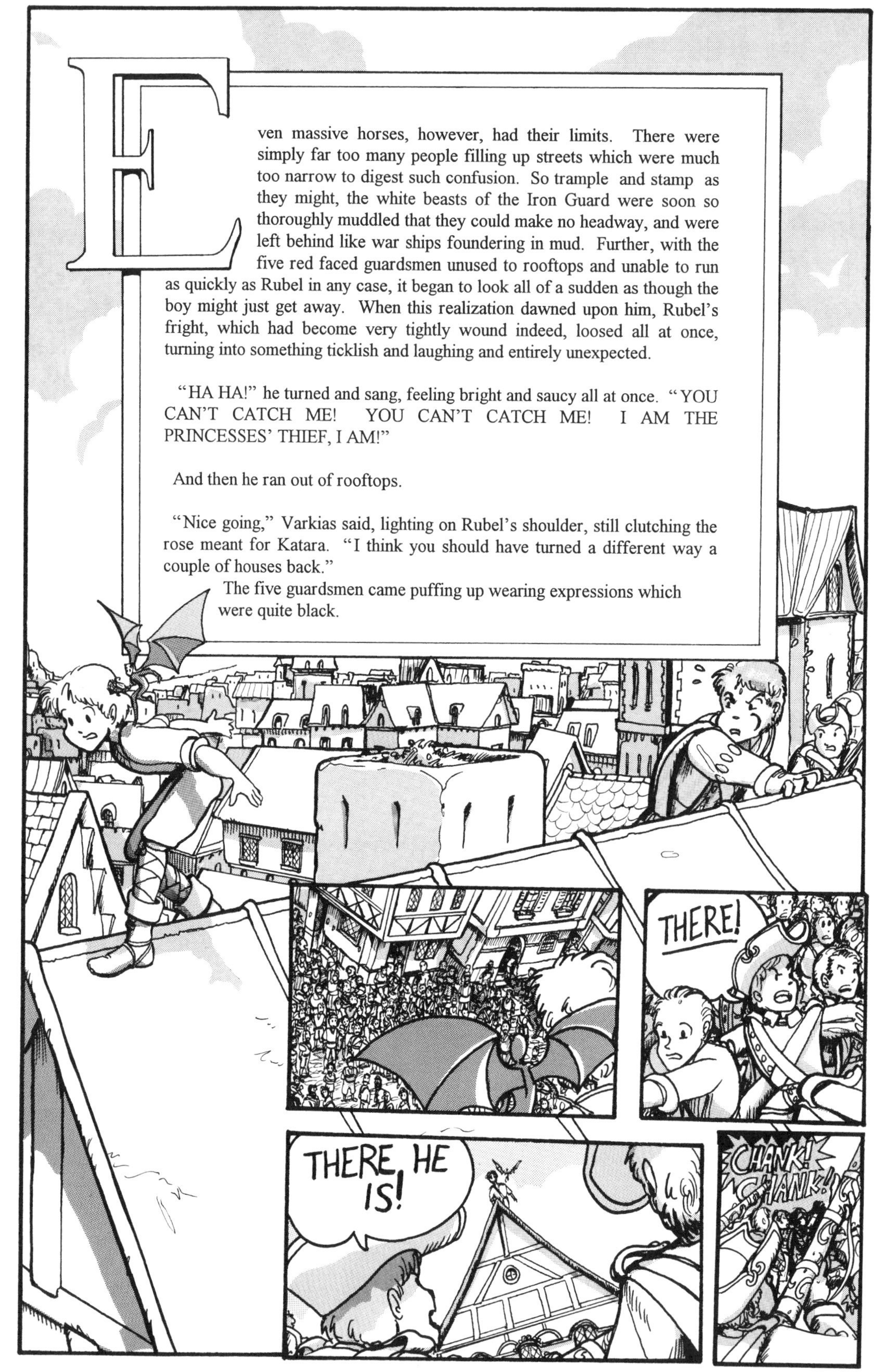
THERE!
THERE, HE IS!
CHANK! CHANK!

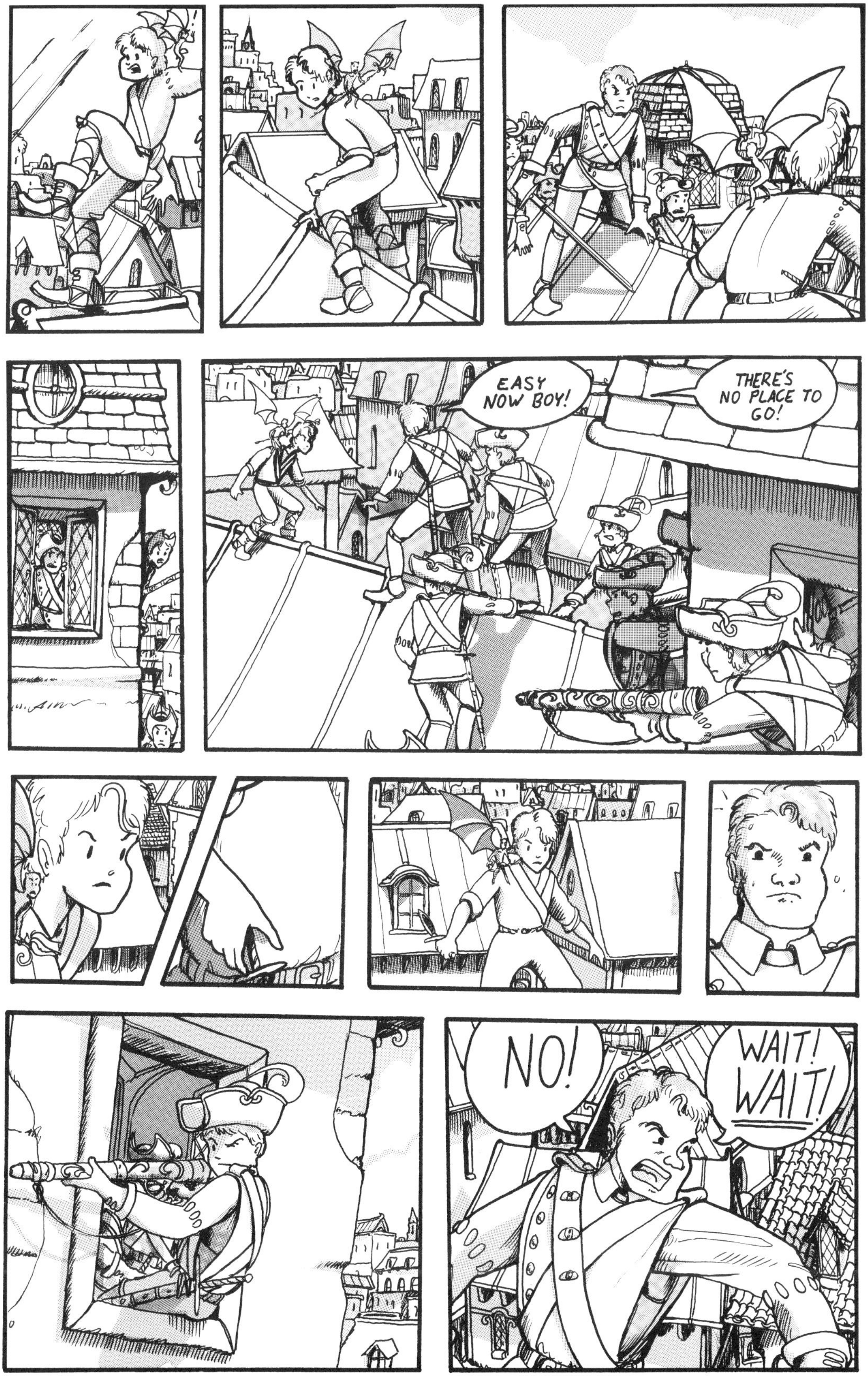
EASY NOW BOY!
THERE'S NO PLACE TO GO!
NO!
WAIT! WAIT!

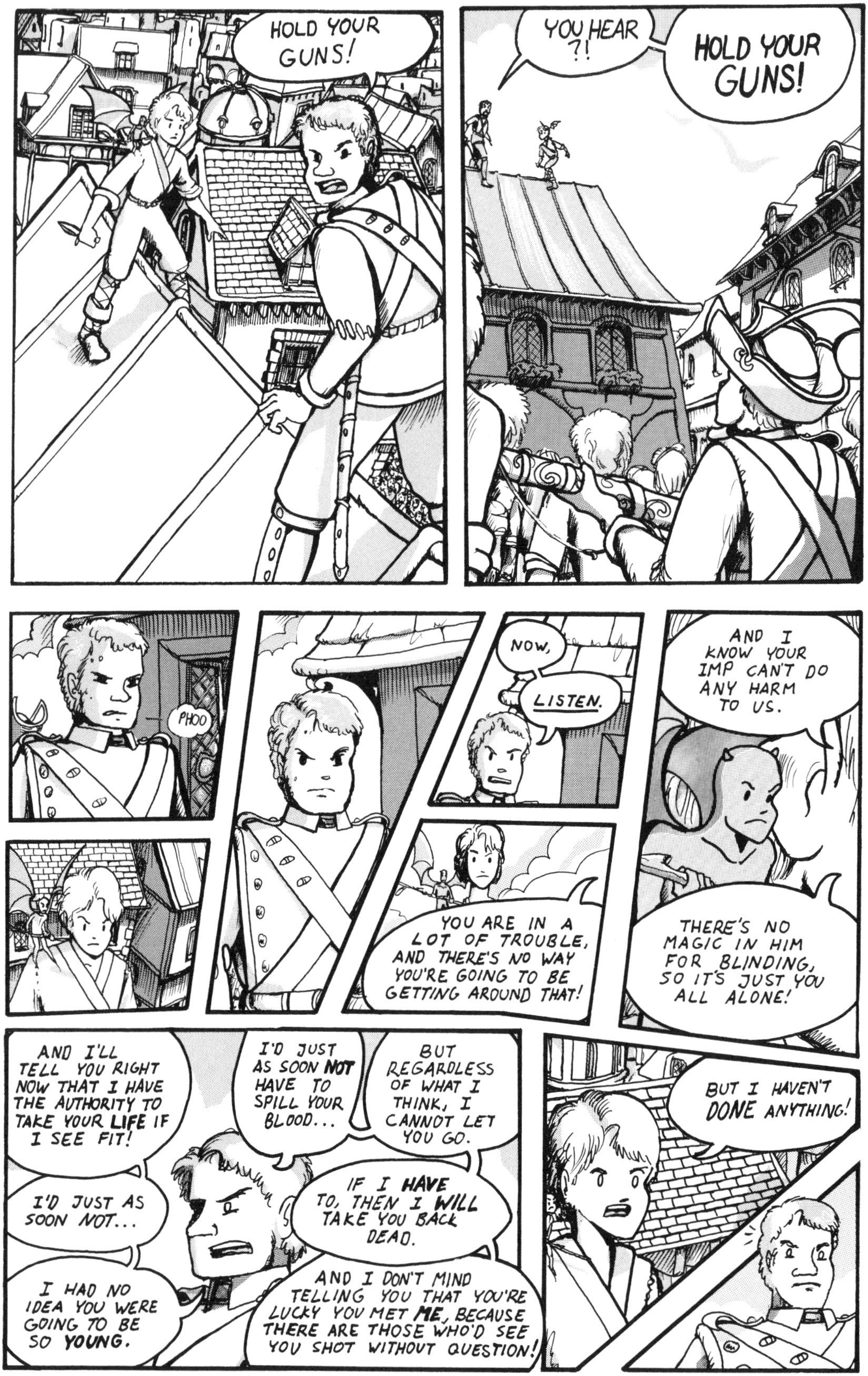
HOLD YOUR GUNS!
YOU HEAR ?!
HOLD YOUR GUNS!
PHOO
NOW,
LISTEN.
AND I KNOW YOUR IMP CAN'T DO ANY HARM TO US.
YOU ARE IN A LOT OF TROUBLE, AND THERE'S NO WAY YOU'RE GOING TO BE GETTING AROUND THAT!
THERE'S NO MAGIC IN HIM FOR BLINDING, SO IT'S JUST YOU ALL ALONE!
AND I'LL TELL YOU RIGHT NOW THAT I HAVE THE AUTHORITY TO TAKE YOUR LIFE IF I SEE FIT!
I'D JUST AS SOON NOT...
I HAD NO IDEA YOU WERE GOING TO BE SO YOUNG.
I'D JUST AS SOON NOT HAVE TO SPILL YOUR BLOOD...
BUT REGARDLESS OF WHAT I THINK, I CANNOT LET YOU GO.
IF I HAVE TO, THEN I WILL TAKE YOU BACK DEAD.
AND I DON'T MIND TELLING YOU THAT YOU'RE LUCKY YOU MET ME, BECAUSE THERE ARE THOSE WHO'D SEE YOU SHOT WITHOUT QUESTION!
BUT I HAVEN'T DONE ANYTHING!

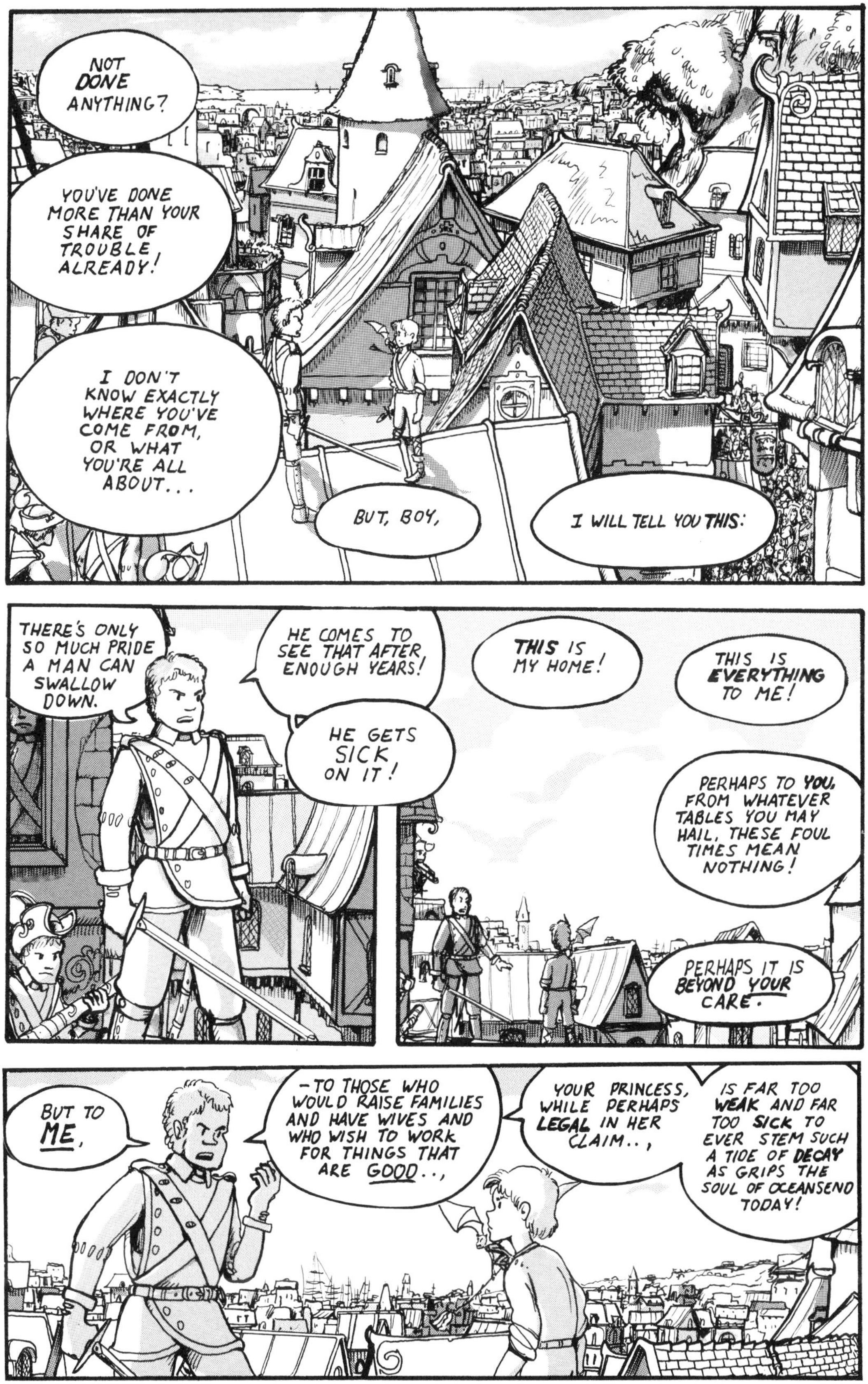
NOT DONE ANYTHING?
YOU'VE DONE MORE THAN YOUR SHARE OF TROUBLE, ALREADY!
I DON'T KNOW EXACTLY WHERE YOU'VE COME FROM, OR WHAT YOU'RE ALL ABOUT...
BUT, BOY,
I WILL TELL YOU THIS:
THERE'S ONLY SO MUCH PRIDE A MAN CAN SWALLOW DOWN.
HE COMES TO SEE THAT AFTER ENOUGH YEARS!
HE GETS SICK, ON IT!
THIS IS MY HOME!
THIS IS EVERYTHING TO ME!
PERHAPS TO YOU, FROM WHATEVER TABLES YOU MAY HAIL, THESE FOUL TIMES MEAN NOTHING!
PERHAPS IT IS BEYOND YOUR CARE.
BUT TO ME,
–TO THOSE WHO WOULD RAISE FAMILIES AND HAVE WIVES AND WHO WISH TO WORK FOR THINGS THAT ARE GOOD..,
YOUR PRINCESS, WHILE PERHAPS LEGAL IN HER CLAIM..,
IS FAR TOO WEAK AND FAR TOO SICK TO EVER STEM SUCH A TIDE OF DECAY AS GRIPS THE SOUL OF OCEANSEND TODAY!

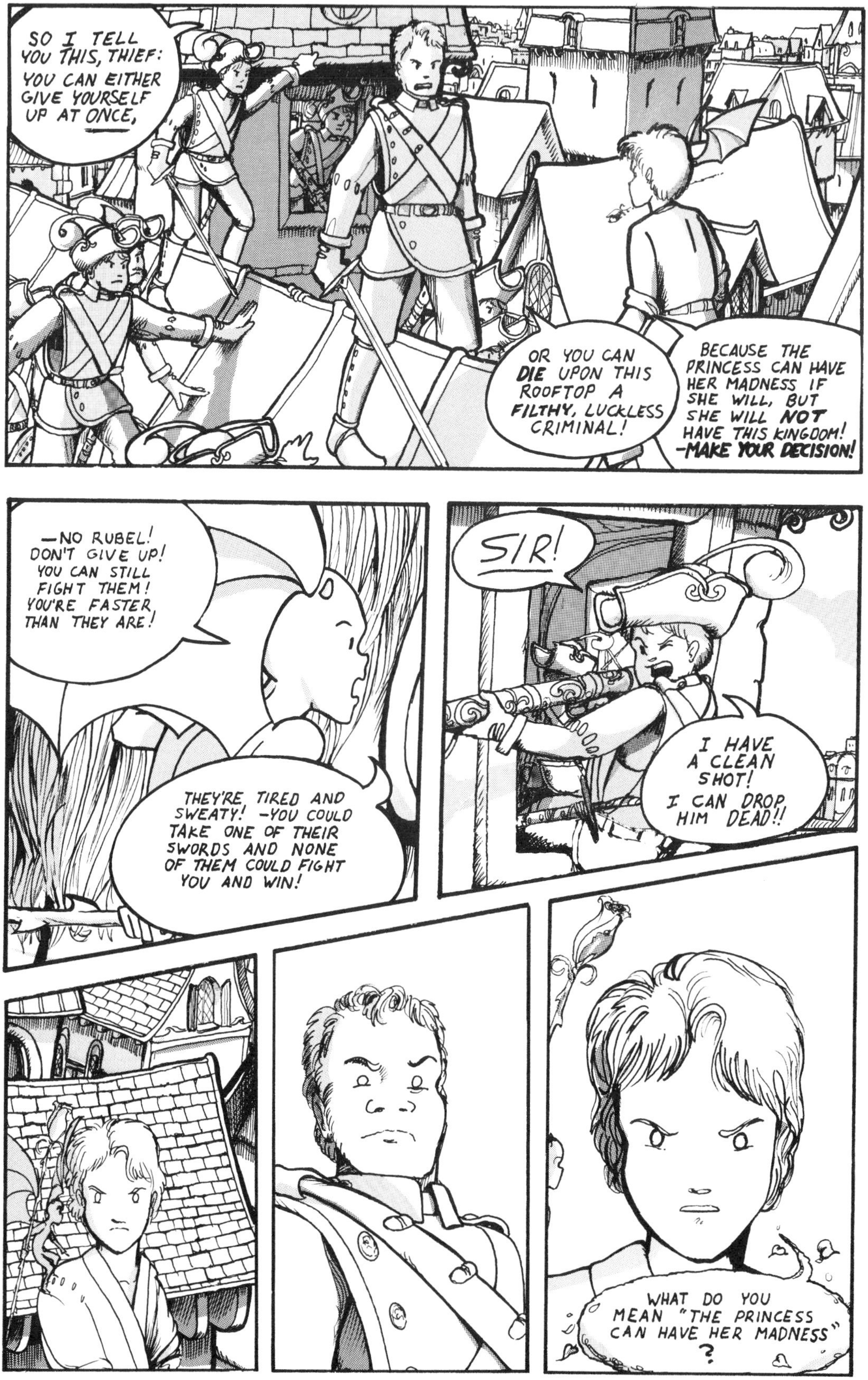
SO I TELL YOU THIS, THIEF: YOU CAN EITHER GIVE YOURSELF UP AT ONCE,
OR YOU CAN DIE UPON THIS ROOFTOP A FILTHY, LUCKLESS CRIMINAL!
BECAUSE THE PRINCESS CAN HAVE HER MADNESS IF SHE WILL, BUT SHE WILL NOT HAVE THIS KINGDOM! —MAKE YOUR DECISION!
—NO RUBEL! DON'T GIVE UP! YOU CAN STILL FIGHT THEM! YOU'RE FASTER THAN THEY ARE!
THEY'RE TIRED AND SWEATY! —YOU COULD TAKE ONE OF THEIR SWORDS AND NONE OF THEM COULD FIGHT YOU AND WIN!
SIR!
I HAVE A CLEAN SHOT! I CAN DROP HIM DEAD!!
WHAT DO YOU MEAN "THE PRINCESS CAN HAVE HER MADNESS"?

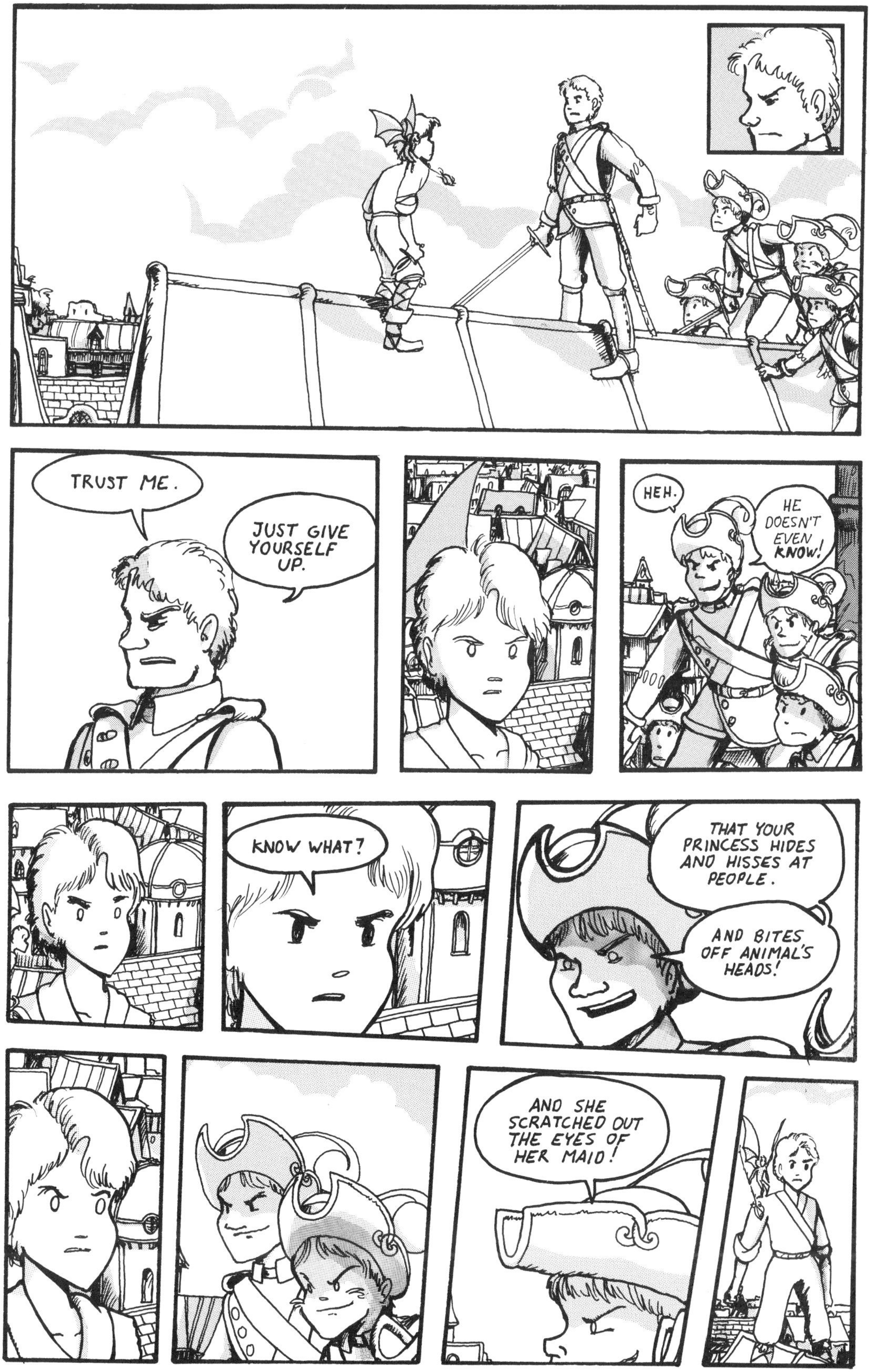
TRUST ME.
JUST GIVE YOURSELF UP.
HEH.
HE DOESN'T EVEN KNOW!
KNOW WHAT?
THAT YOUR PRINCESS HIDES AND HISSES AT PEOPLE.
AND BITES OFF ANIMAL'S HEADS!
AND SHE SCRATCHED OUT THE EYES OF HER MAID!

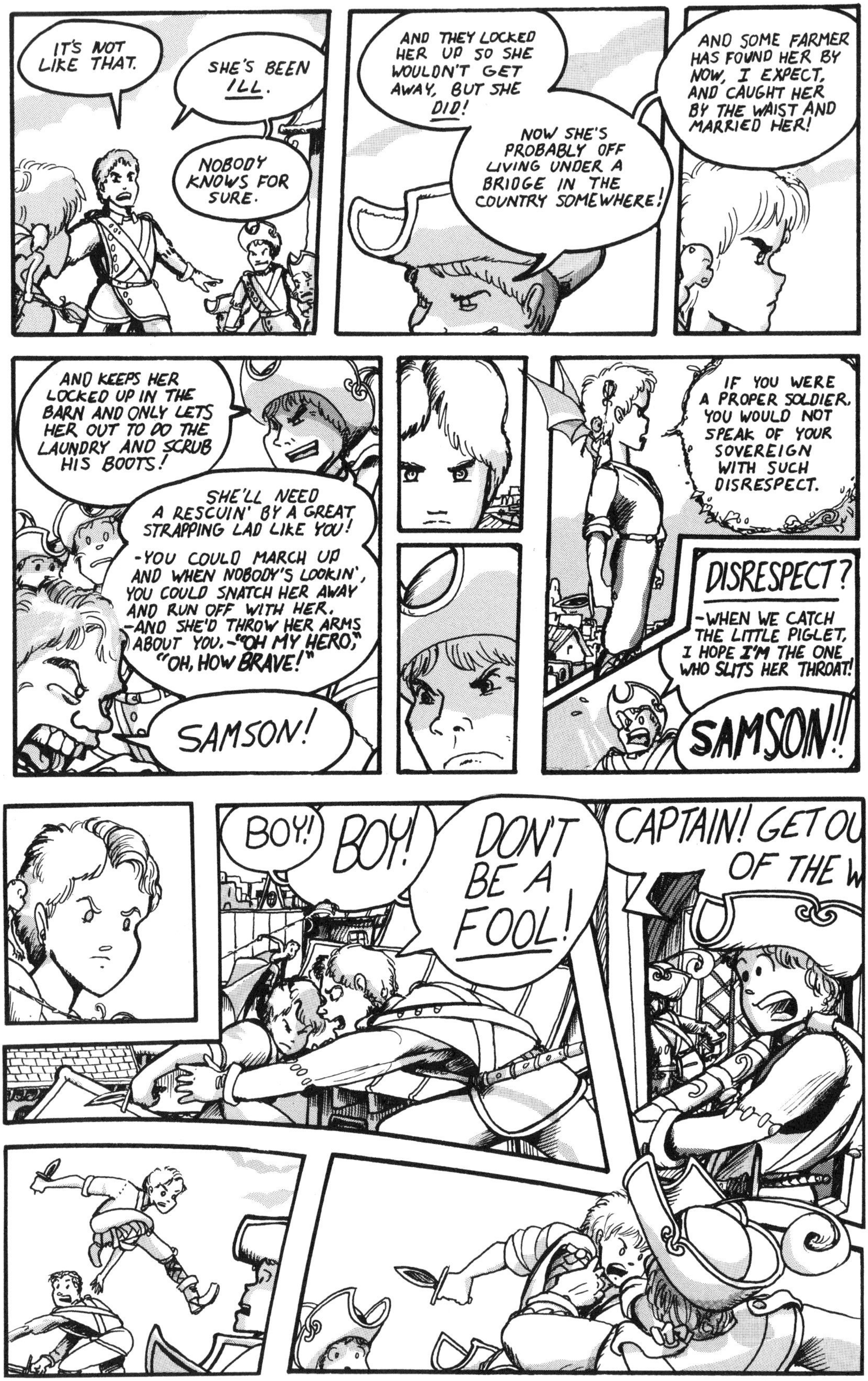
IT'S NOT LIKE THAT.
SHE'S BEEN ILL.
NOBODY KNOWS FOR SURE.
AND THEY LOCKED HER UP SO SHE WOULDN'T GET AWAY, BUT SHE DID!
NOW SHE'S PROBABLY OFF LIVING UNDER A BRIDGE IN THE COUNTRY SOMEWHERE!
AND SOME FARMER HAS FOUND HER BY NOW, I EXPECT, AND CAUGHT HER BY THE WAIST AND MARRIED HER!
AND KEEPS HER LOCKED UP IN THE BARN AND ONLY LETS HER OUT TO DO THE LAUNDRY AND SCRUB HIS BOOTS!
SHE'LL NEED A RESCUIN' BY A GREAT STRAPPING LAD LIKE YOU! -YOU COULD MARCH UP AND WHEN NOBODY'S LOOKIN', YOU COULD SNATCH HER AWAY AND RUN OFF WITH HER. -AND SHE'D THROW HER ARMS ABOUT YOU. -"OH MY HERO," "OH, HOW BRAVE!"
SAMSON!
IF YOU WERE A PROPER SOLDIER, YOU WOULD NOT SPEAK OF YOUR SOVEREIGN WITH SUCH DISRESPECT.
DISRESPECT? -WHEN WE CATCH THE LITTLE PIGLET, I HOPE I'M THE ONE WHO SLITS HER THROAT!
SAMSON!!
BOY!
BOY!
DON'T BE A FOOL!
CAPTAIN! GET OU OF THE W

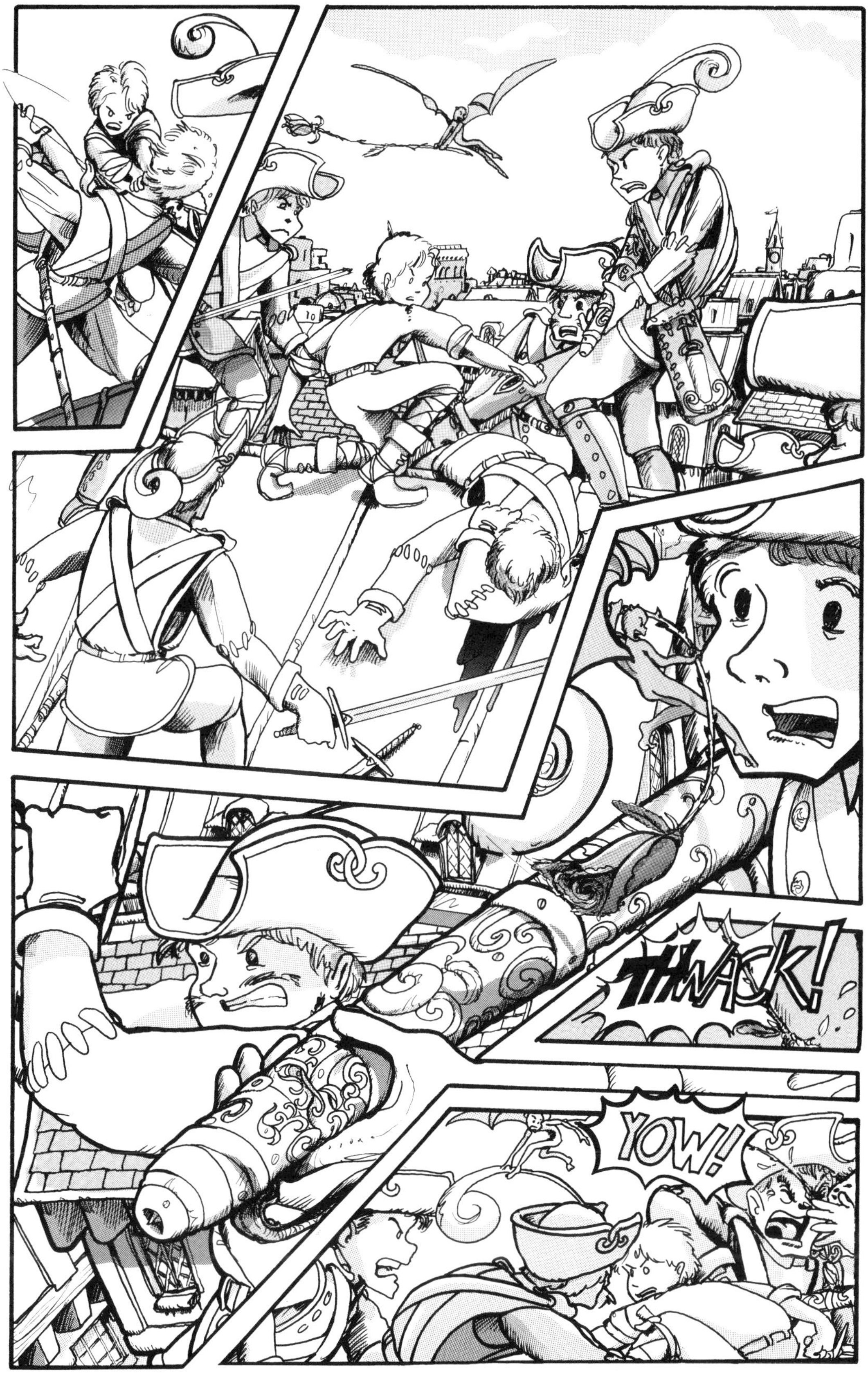
THWACK!
YOW!

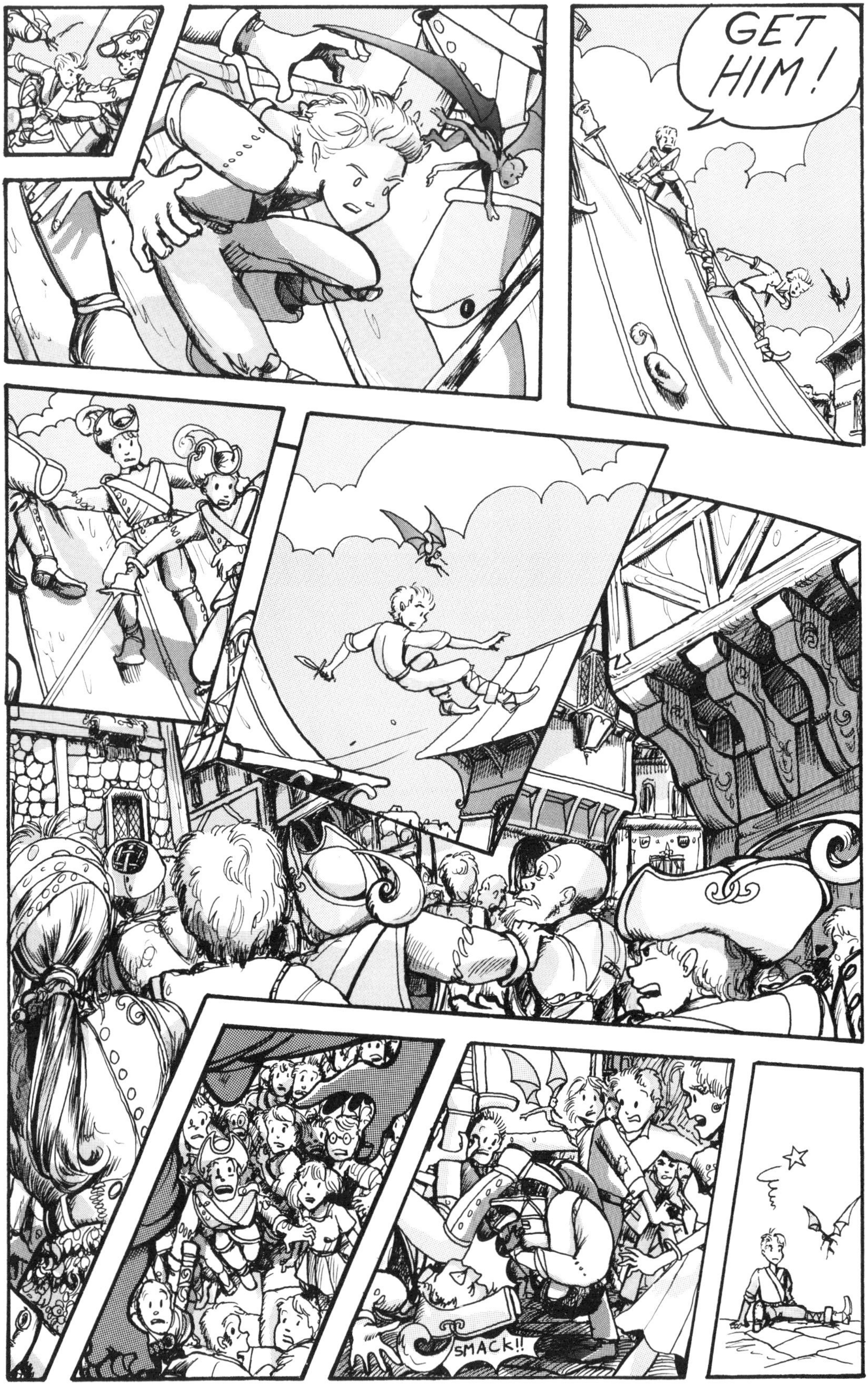
GET HIM!
SMACK!!

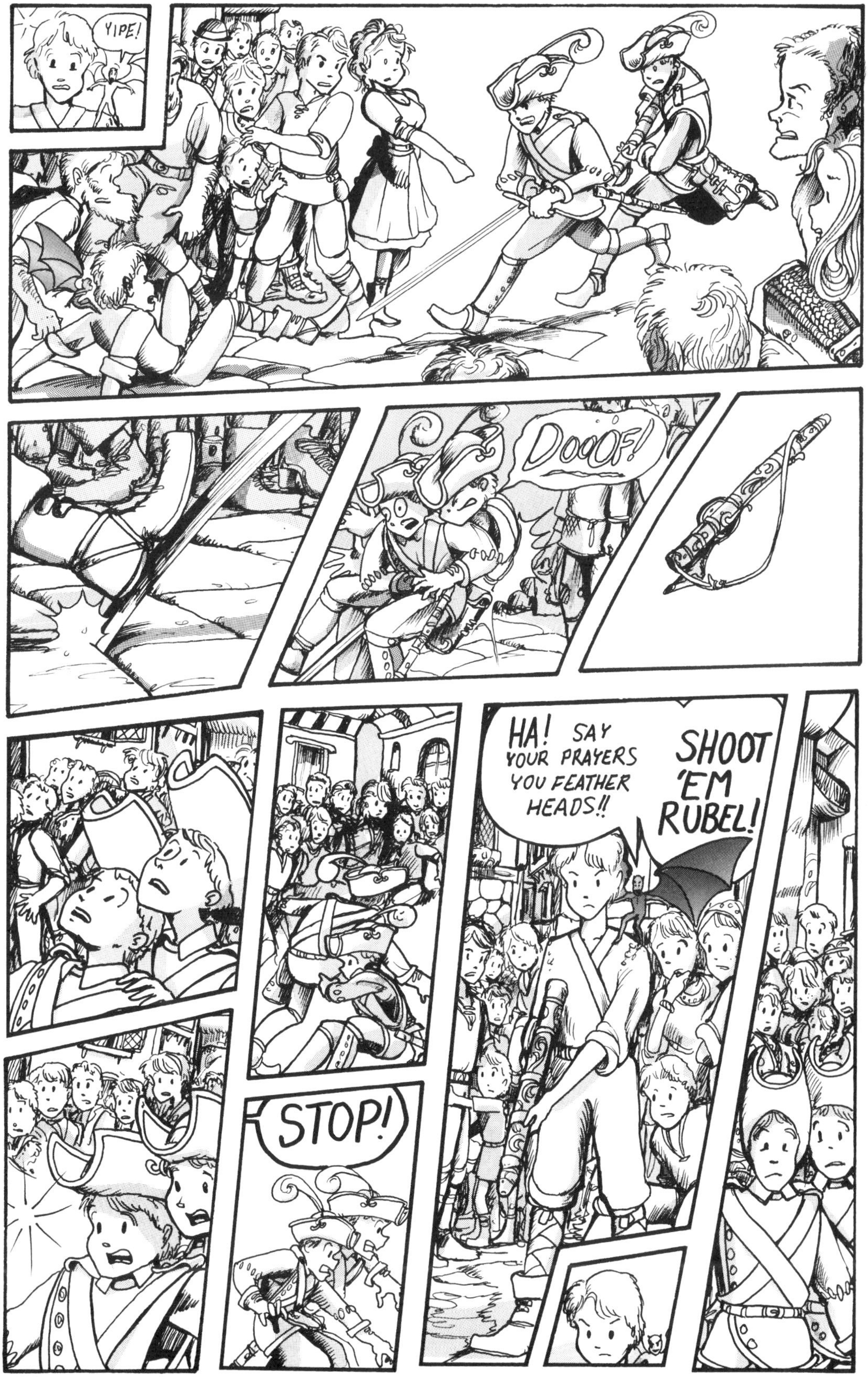
YIPE!
DOOOF!
HA! SAY YOUR PRAYERS YOU FEATHER HEADS!!
SHOOT 'EM RUBEL!
STOP!

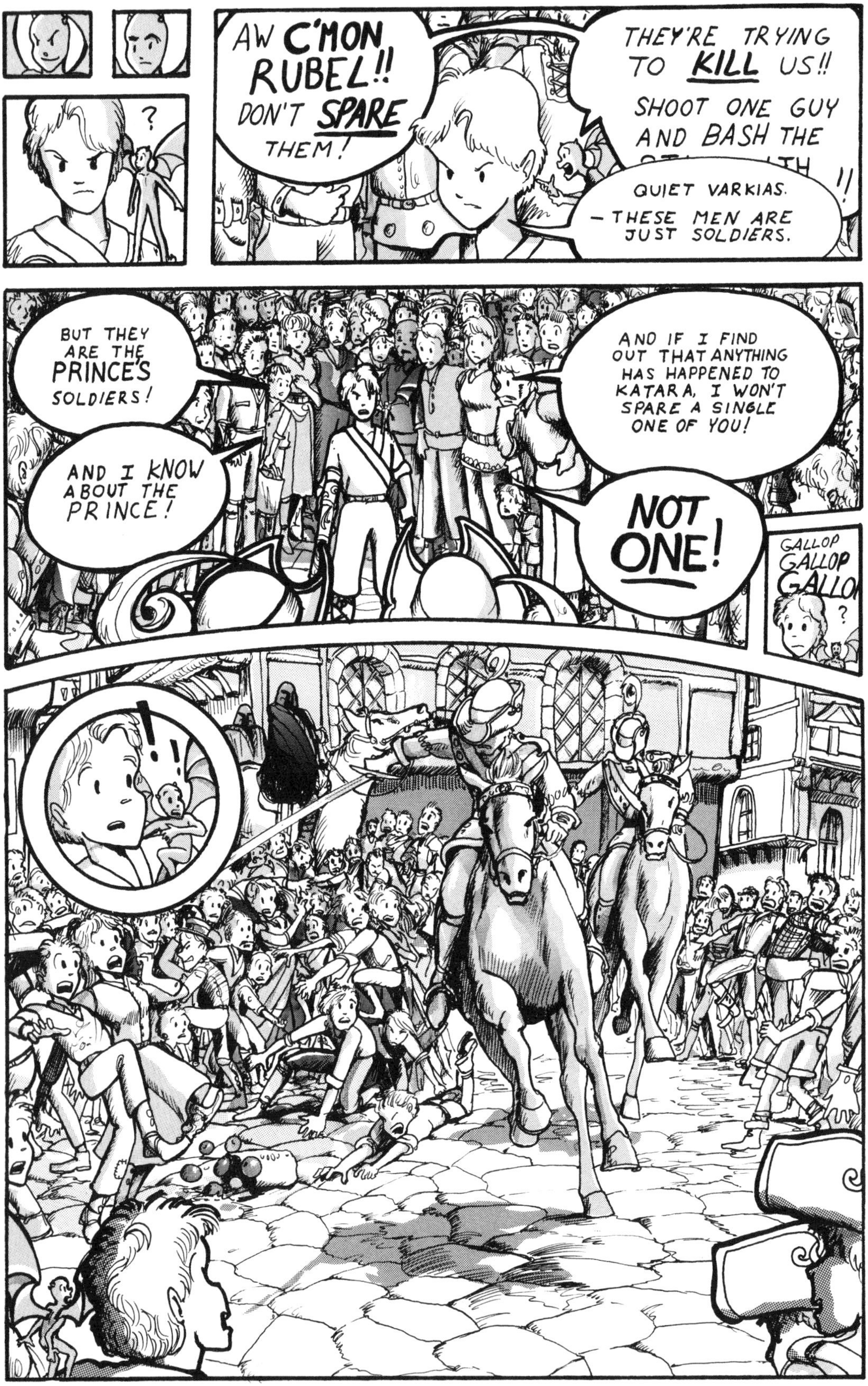
AW C'MON RUBEL!! DON'T SPARE THEM!
THEY'RE TRYING TO KILL US!! SHOOT ONE GUY AND BASH THE
!!
QUIET VARKIAS. — THESE MEN ARE JUST SOLDIERS.
BUT THEY ARE THE PRINCE'S SOLDIERS!
AND I KNOW ABOUT THE PRINCE!
AND IF I FIND OUT THAT ANYTHING HAS HAPPENED TO KATARA, I WON'T SPARE A SINGLE ONE OF YOU!
NOT ONE!
GALLOP
GALLOP

Chapter 6

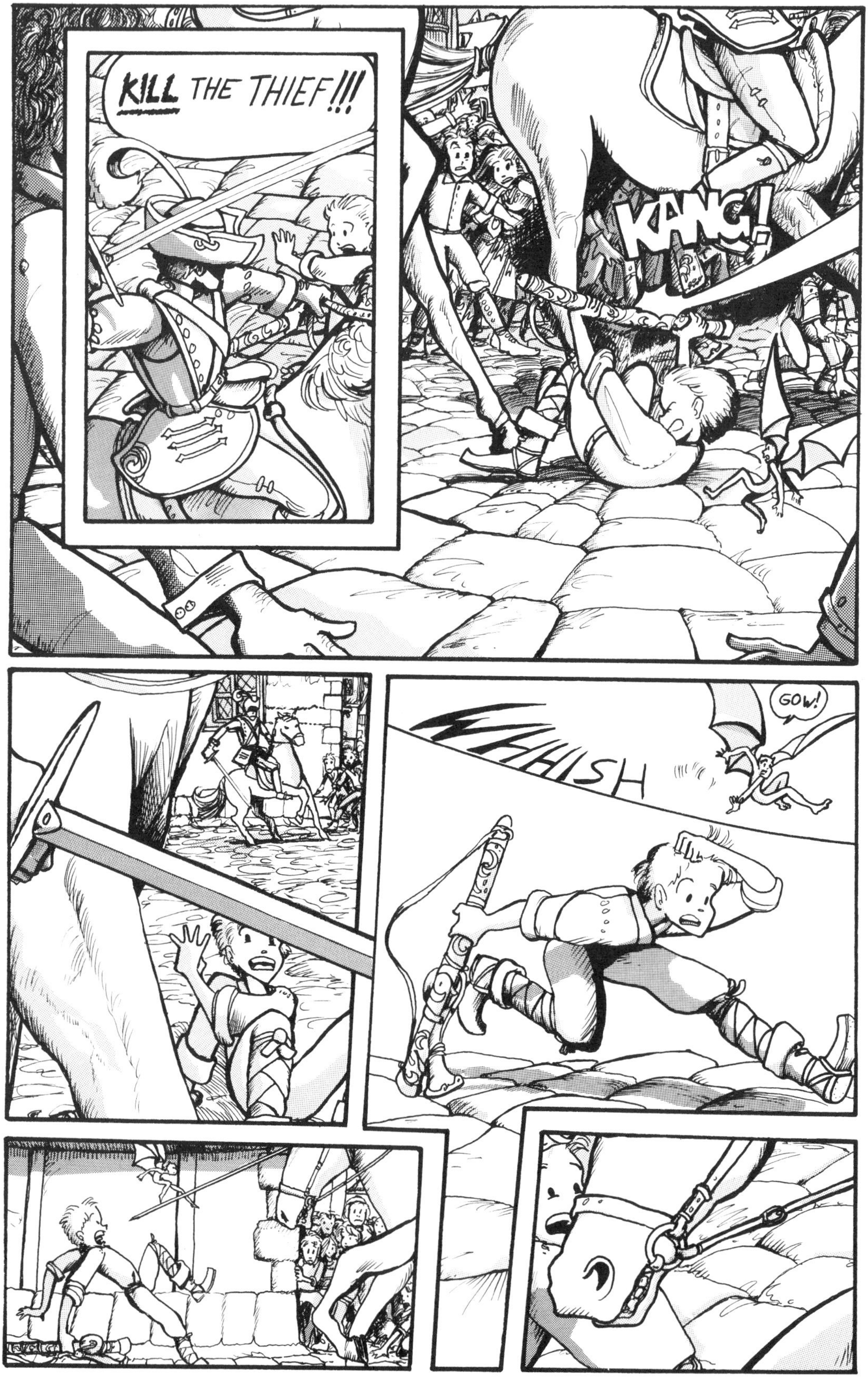
KILL THE THIEF!!!
KANG!
WHHISH
GOW!

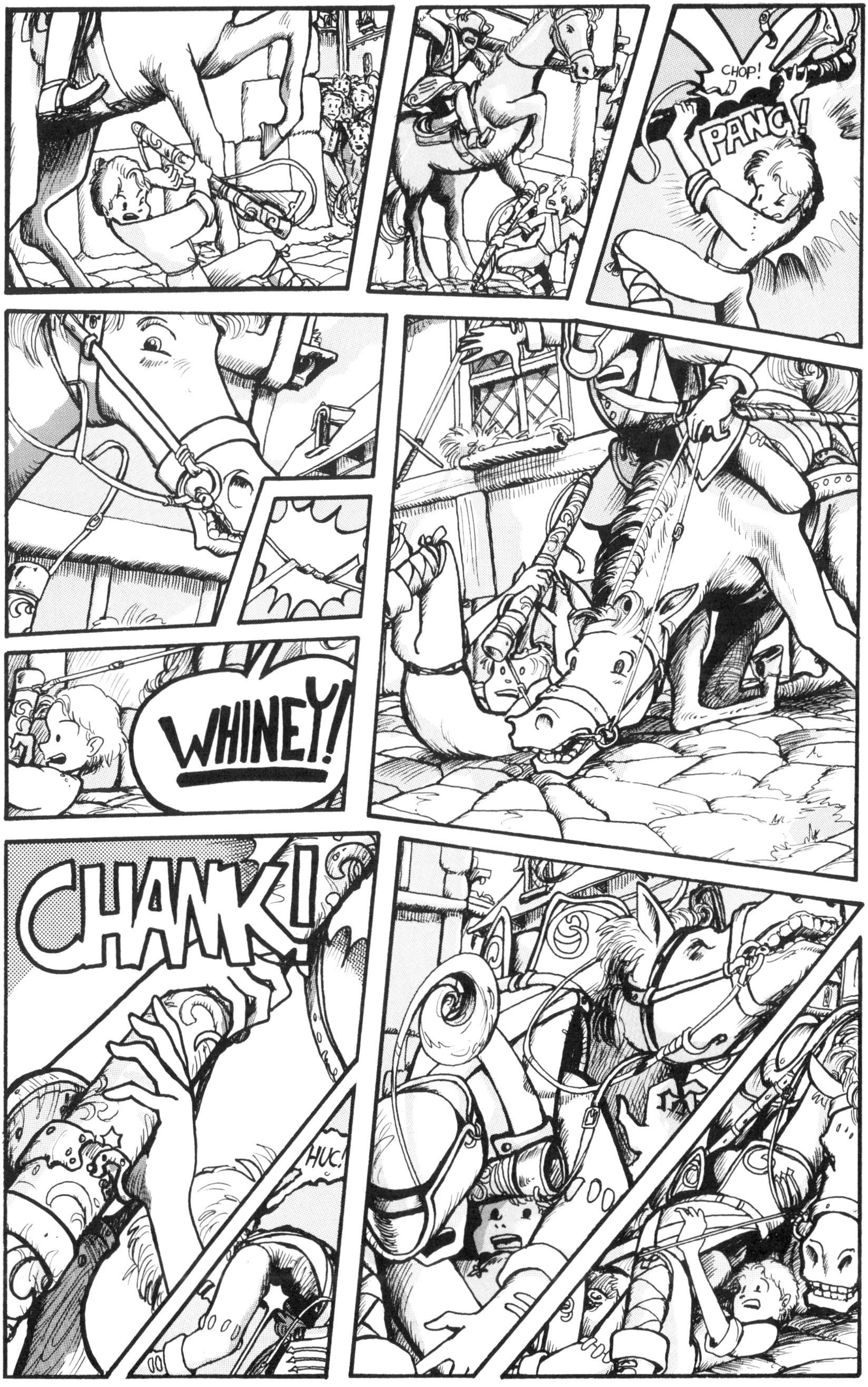
CHOP!
PANG!
WHINEY!
CHANK!
HUC!

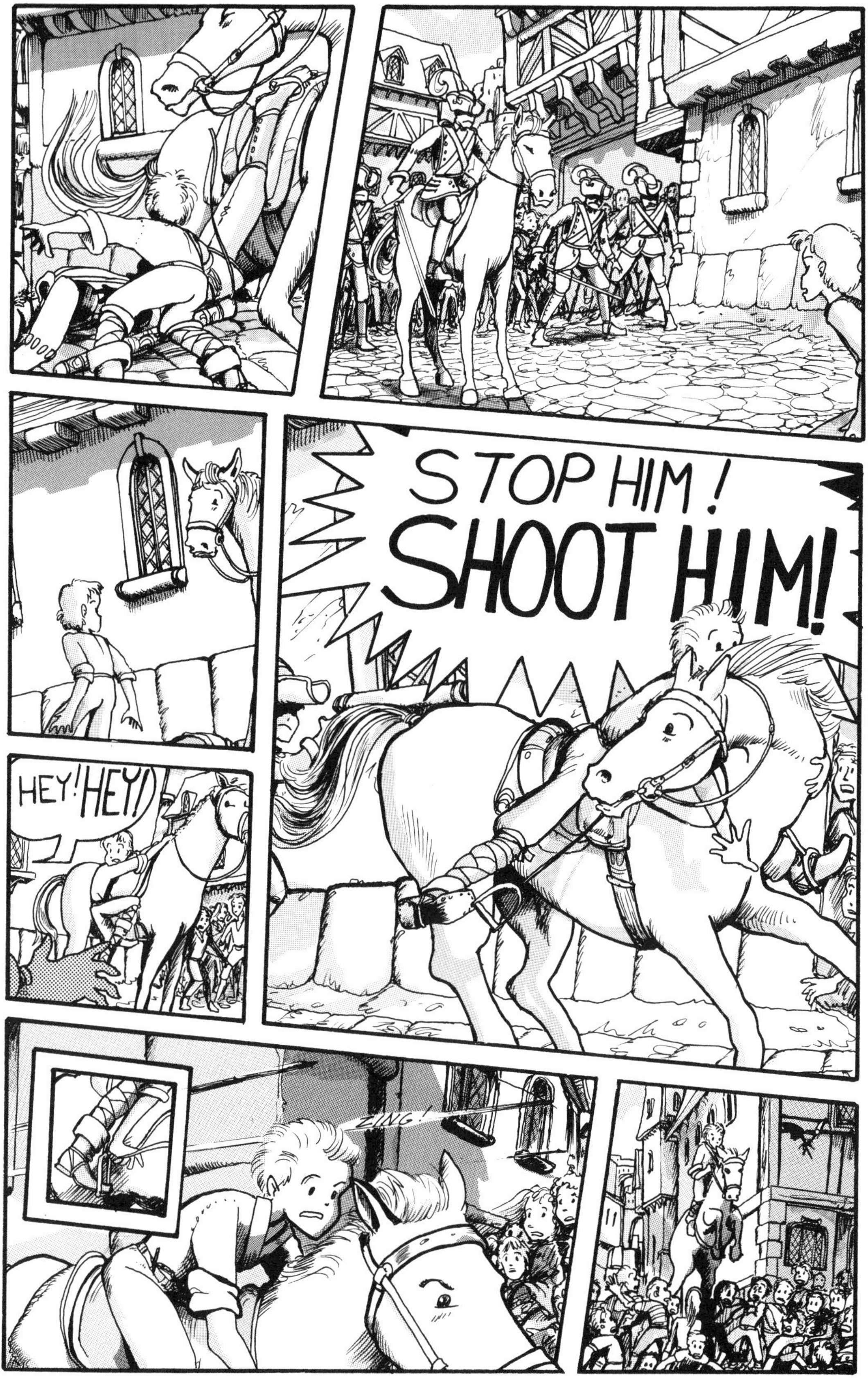
STOP HIM!
SHOOT HIM!
HEY! HEY!
ZING!

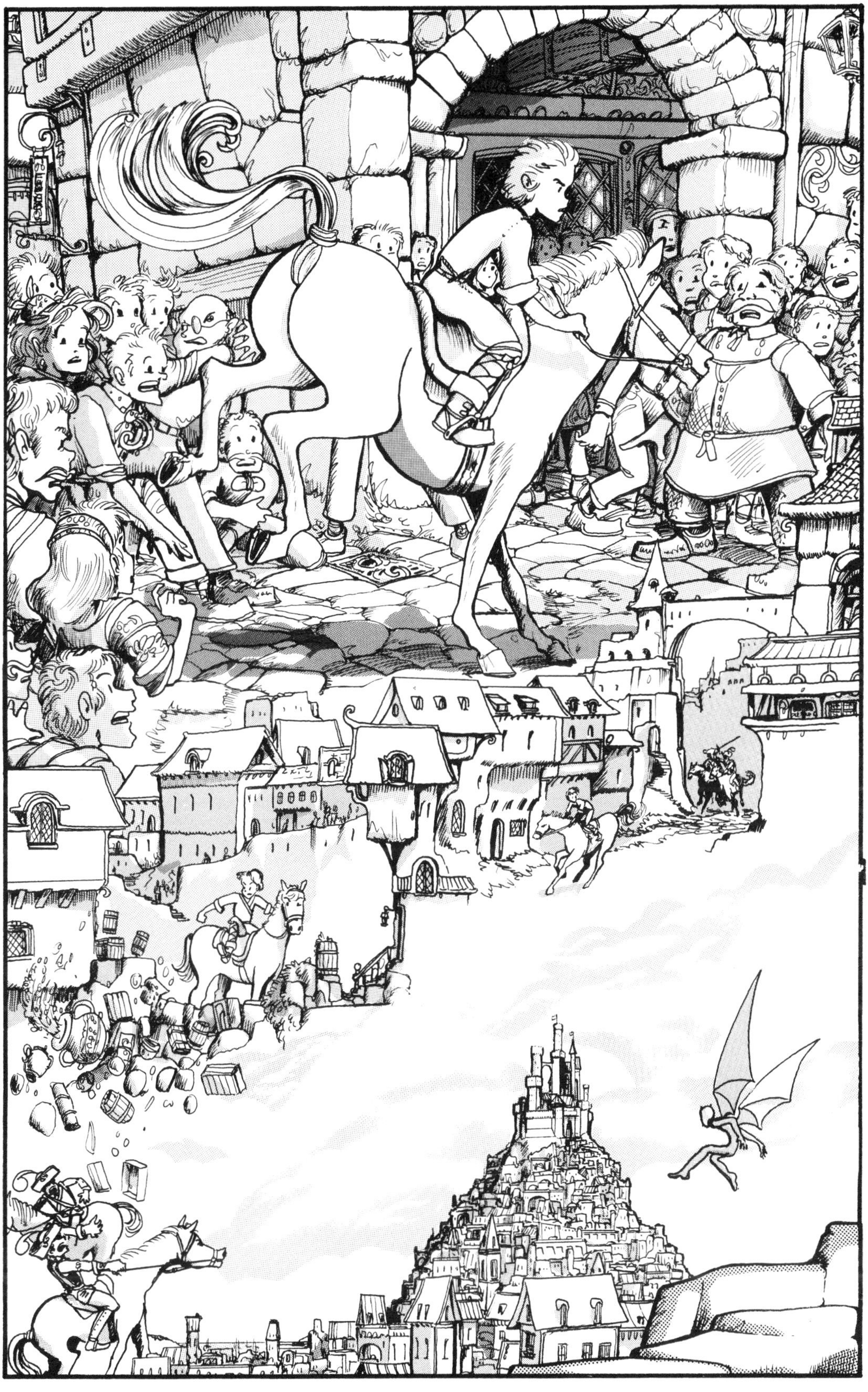

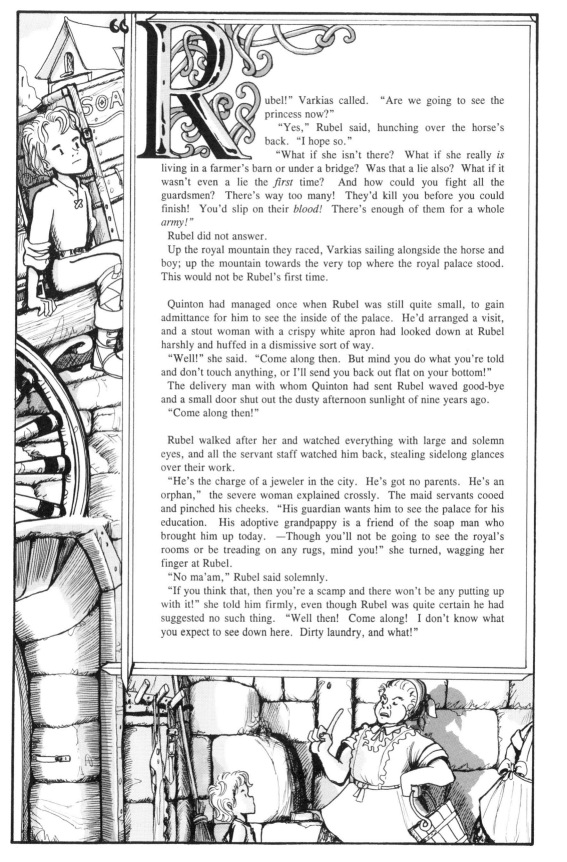

"R ubel!" Varkias called. "Are we going to see the princess now?"

"Yes," Rubel said, hunching over the horse's back. "I hope so."

"What if she isn't there? What if she really *is* living in a farmer's barn or under a bridge? Was that a lie also? What if it wasn't even a lie the *first* time? And how could you fight all the guardsmen? There's way too many! They'd kill you before you could finish! You'd slip on their *blood!* There's enough of them for a whole *army!*"

Rubel did not answer.

Up the royal mountain they raced, Varkias sailing alongside the horse and boy; up the mountain towards the very top where the royal palace stood. This would not be Rubel's first time.

Quinton had managed once when Rubel was still quite small, to gain admittance for him to see the inside of the palace. He'd arranged a visit, and a stout woman with a crispy white apron had looked down at Rubel harshly and huffed in a dismissive sort of way.

"Well!" she said. "Come along then. But mind you do what you're told and don't touch anything, or I'll send you back out flat on your bottom!"

The delivery man with whom Quinton had sent Rubel waved good-bye and a small door shut out the dusty afternoon sunlight of nine years ago.

"Come along then!"

Rubel walked after her and watched everything with large and solemn eyes, and all the servant staff watched him back, stealing sidelong glances over their work.

"He's the charge of a jeweler in the city. He's got no parents. He's an orphan," the severe woman explained crossly. The maid servants cooed and pinched his cheeks. "His guardian wants him to see the palace for his education. His adoptive grandpappy is a friend of the soap man who brought him up today. —Though you'll not be going to see the royal's rooms or be treading on any rugs, mind you!" she turned, wagging her finger at Rubel.

"No ma'am," Rubel said solemnly.

"If you think that, then you're a scamp and there won't be any putting up with it!" she told him firmly, even though Rubel was quite certain he had suggested no such thing. "Well then! Come along! I don't know what you expect to see down here. Dirty laundry, and what!"

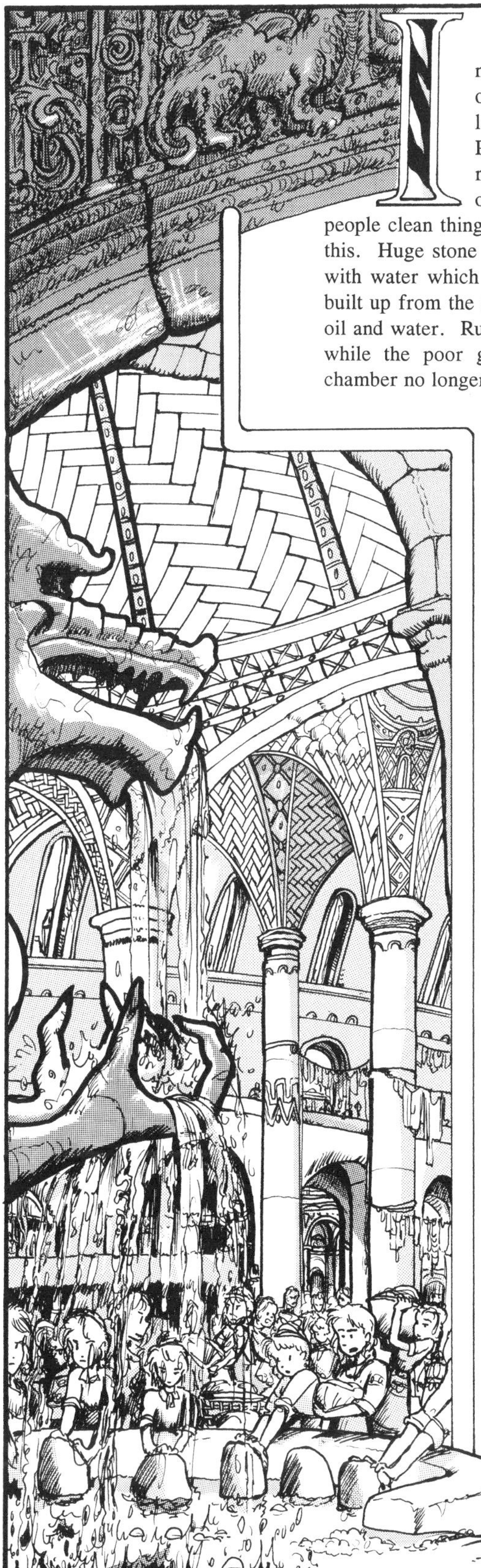

Indeed, they were in a room which seemed very full of laundry; it was the place where all the dirty laundry from the whole castle came to be washed. Piles and piles of it, and girls with their sleeves rolled up scrubbing and beating cloth and blowing out the sides of their mouths. Rubel had seen people clean things before, but never at such a height of industry as this. Huge stone pools carved right there into the floor were filled with water which came from the mouth of a twisting stone dragon built up from the floor; a stone dragon with stone scales shiny from oil and water. Rubel stood quietly to one side, watching the dragon while the poor girls cleaned expensive cloth, until the laundry chamber no longer interested him.

"Could I see the kitchen?" he asked the severe woman, who turned on him with her worst look, trying to frighten him. He returned her glare with the clear eyes of one who does not understand when he is supposed to be frightened, and the servant maidens glanced from one another and laughed into their work, delighted to see their mistress challenged as such.

There were three kitchens, one of which was only used for making bread, and the other two for making everything else. The kitchen master was a big man with enormous arms which looked like legs of ham, and he roared and bellowed and made his underlings scurry about their tasks.

"This is Rubel," the severe woman informed the man. "He's here for his education. He's got no parents and his guardian is a jeweler in the city. He asked if he could see the kitchen."

"Oh Ho!" the man Ho'd, in exactly the way you might expect a cook with ham arms to do.

Rubel looked up at him earnestly.

"I know a bread maker on my friend's street," he told the man. "He chases me sometimes with a rolling pin, but I think his bread isn't that good anyway. I told him he should put sunflower seeds in it, but he said he only makes *good* bread, but I *like* bread with sunflower seeds. What kind of bread does the king like?"

The kitchen master looked at him with astonishment, and laughed again his booming laugh.

"I'll come back for him in a bit," the severe woman advised, exchanging a look with the man.

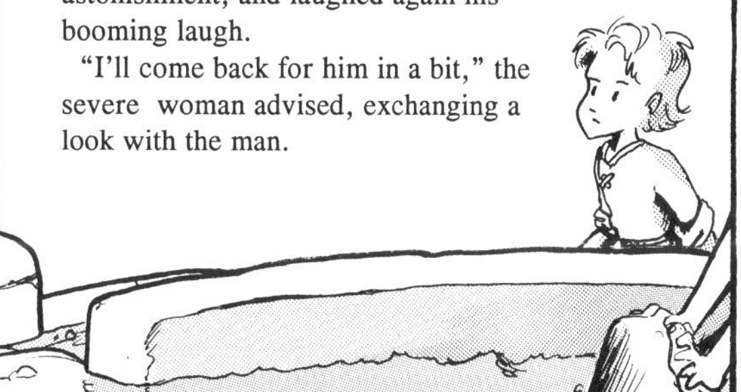

he kitchen master took an interest in Rubel, and showed him all the various parts of the three kitchens. He showed Rubel the giant bread ovens and he showed him how to chop up a pig into all the right bits, which he did, slapping and turning the meat with his fat palms with such speed and skill Rubel had to gaze in wonder. Then he let Rubel open and close the kitchen windows high up in the vaulted ceiling by using the grand metal hand cranks with their ancient waxy wooden handles. All the kitchen workers paused in their tasks to watch, each remembering when opening and closing the windows was a thrill for them as well and not just another job to do. The kitchen master said that Rubel must come back during the winter to watch the snowflakes fly in and puff into steam upon the oven stones, and sit with his back against a sack of flour with his toes stretched out before the flames with a plate of roast beef drippings in his lap and a pile of hard bread crusts to dip. Rubel said he would like that very much.

He also said that he would like to see the royal stables. The kitchen master escorted him out across a wide yard and into a place where they kept horses and carts and wagons.

The stables were large and interesting, but Rubel had been in places like that before.

"The king's own mount, eh?" the kitchen master and the stable master mused together.

Rubel looked up at them with his gaze honest and unwavering while they mused. The two men talked and then a third man was consulted; a man with a fine collar and expensive buttons and an officer's sword hanging at his belt. This third man stood and listened without saying a word, and he examined Rubel up and down.

"Nothing so special about being an orphan you know," he told Rubel after a long silence.

"It is if you were born in the forest," Rubel told him back. "I'm a thief."

The kitchen master and the stable master both blinked and broke into wide smiles and more, "Oh Ho's!" The officer's eyebrows went up a notch, but he did not smile.

"Oh you are, are you?" he asked quite seriously. "And you think the king would want a thief going over his horses, do you? Knowing how to get in and out? That's quite the education, I'll warrant young man!"

"I wouldn't steal anything from the king," Rubel told him, with equal seriousness. "Not unless he deserved it, and I like the king."

The kitchen master and the stable master watched the officer for his reaction. The officer stroked his chin in thought.

"Fine then," he said, "follow me, but mind you don't misbehave."

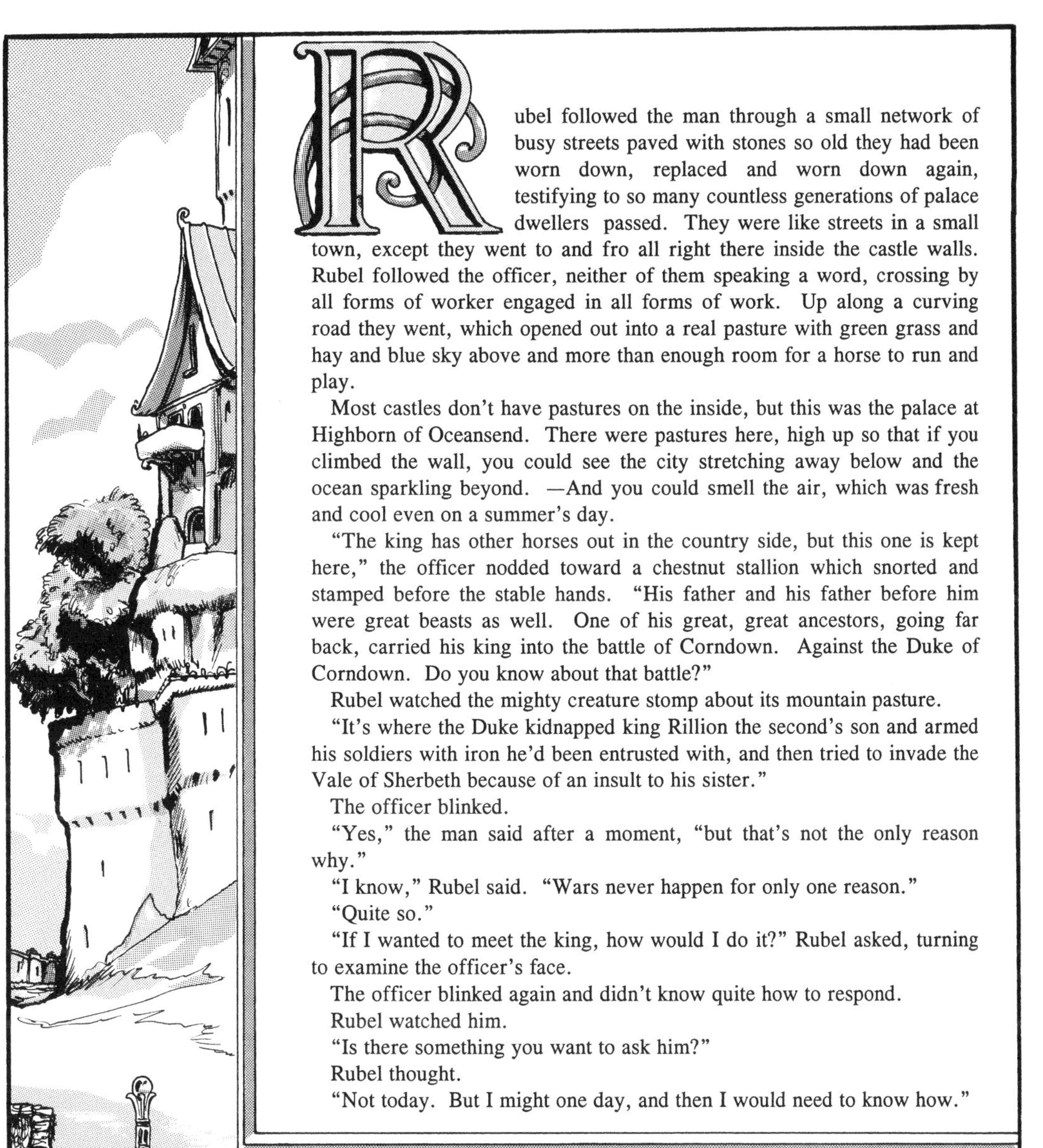

Rubel followed the man through a small network of busy streets paved with stones so old they had been worn down, replaced and worn down again, testifying to so many countless generations of palace dwellers passed. They were like streets in a small town, except they went to and fro all right there inside the castle walls. Rubel followed the officer, neither of them speaking a word, crossing by all forms of worker engaged in all forms of work. Up along a curving road they went, which opened out into a real pasture with green grass and hay and blue sky above and more than enough room for a horse to run and play.

Most castles don't have pastures on the inside, but this was the palace at Highborn of Oceansend. There were pastures here, high up so that if you climbed the wall, you could see the city stretching away below and the ocean sparkling beyond. —And you could smell the air, which was fresh and cool even on a summer's day.

"The king has other horses out in the country side, but this one is kept here," the officer nodded toward a chestnut stallion which snorted and stamped before the stable hands. "His father and his father before him were great beasts as well. One of his great, great ancestors, going far back, carried his king into the battle of Corndown. Against the Duke of Corndown. Do you know about that battle?"

Rubel watched the mighty creature stomp about its mountain pasture.

"It's where the Duke kidnapped king Rillion the second's son and armed his soldiers with iron he'd been entrusted with, and then tried to invade the Vale of Sherbeth because of an insult to his sister."

The officer blinked.

"Yes," the man said after a moment, "but that's not the only reason why."

"I know," Rubel said. "Wars never happen for only one reason."

"Quite so."

"If I wanted to meet the king, how would I do it?" Rubel asked, turning to examine the officer's face.

The officer blinked again and didn't know quite how to respond.

Rubel watched him.

"Is there something you want to ask him?"

Rubel thought.

"Not today. But I might one day, and then I would need to know how."

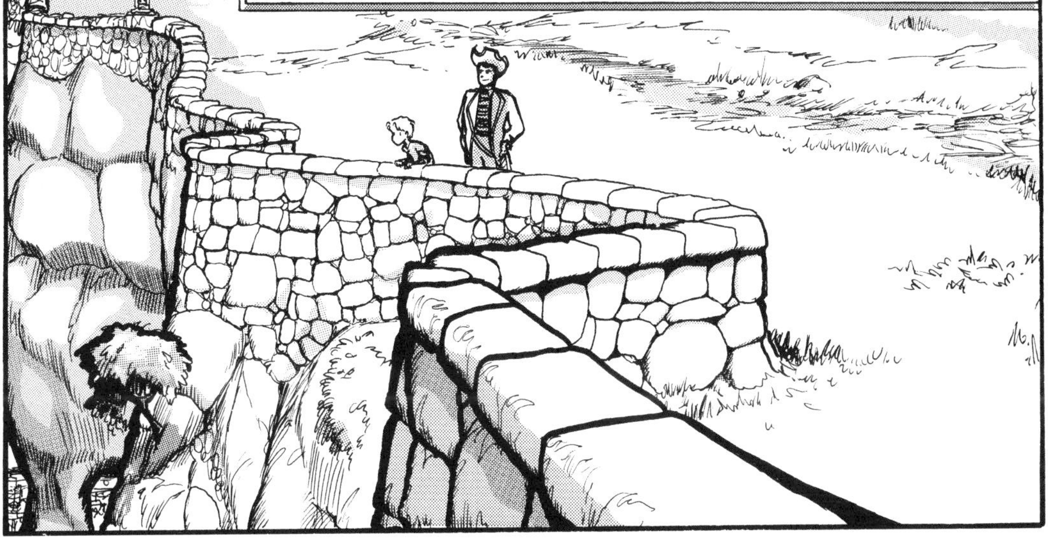

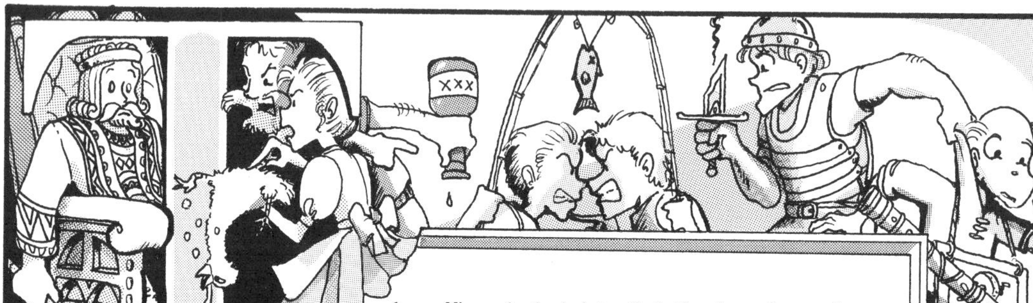
XXX

The officer looked into Rubel's face for a long moment before he decided, for lack of any better idea, to answer the boy as completely as he could. He gathered his thoughts to do so.

"Well. . ," he began, "the first thing to understand is that the king is a man, and because this is so, he moves about his business as any man might be expected."

Rubel absorbed this.

"So if somebody wanted to find *you,* how would they do it?" the officer asked, turning the explanation into a question as adults who consider themselves good with children often do.

Rubel thought.

"They would look for me where they knew I sometimes was?"

"And if they didn't know you or your habits?"

Rubel thought some more.

"They would ask somebody who *did* know me. –So I would ask somebody where the king was? But would they tell me? What if I was an assassin?"

"Well," the officer said, warming to the subject, "if a strange person came about asking where they might find one of your friends, would you tell them right away? Or would you want to find out more about them?"

"I'd want to find out more about them," Rubel said. "So they'd ask me who I was first?"

"Follow me," the officer said with a wry smile and set off at a brisk walk.

Rubel got down from the wall and followed the officer back through the bustling castle village.

As they went, the officer explained, "the truth of the matter is that not just *anybody* can have an audience with the king. If that were the case, then there would be a line up waiting to see him with every matter you could possibly imagine. —Some people think that there is a throne room with a big chair in the middle of it, and that all the king ever does is sit on it all day and solve problems for everybody who comes calling."

Rubel didn't say anything. This was very close to what he had always believed. Especially about the big chair.

"If you want to see the king, the officer told him, "you first have to talk to somebody who *knows* the king. And then *that* person will go to the king and tell him that you wish to have an audience with his majesty. Then the king will decide whether or not he wants to see *you.* He'll want to know in advance what business you mean to discuss with him so that he can think about it and have an answer ready for you. —Or if he doesn't like the sound of the question you want to bring to him, he may well decide that he doesn't want to see you at all."

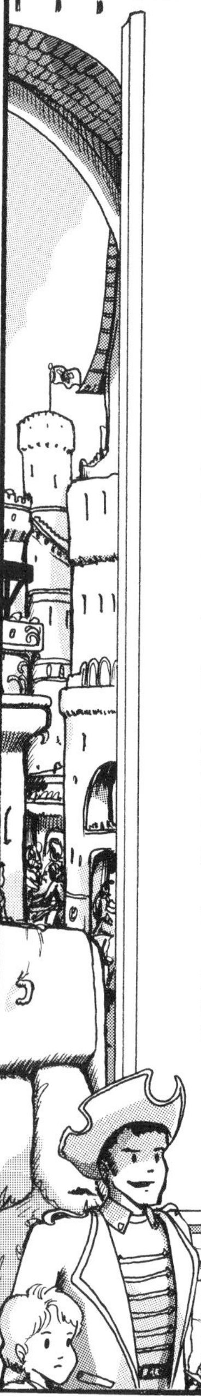

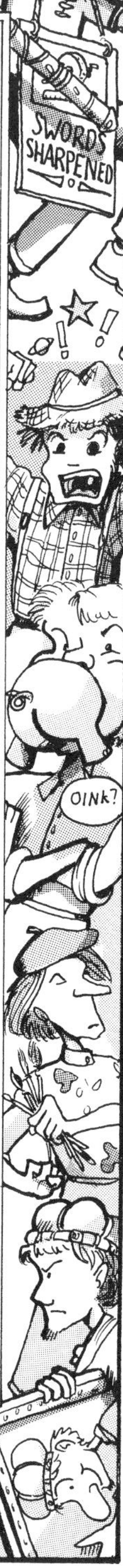
SWORDS SHARPENED
OINK?

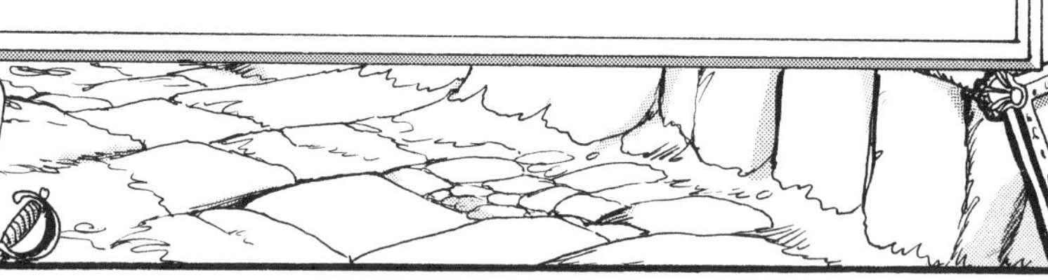

ubel frowned.

"So he doesn't have to talk to you at *all* if he doesn't want to? Even if you have *very* good reason to see him?"

The officer nodded with his wry smile and added, "And sometimes, even if he *would* want to see you, his advisors might not pass your question on to him. Sometimes, if the king doesn't chose his court well, he may find himself surrounded by people who try to do his thinking for him. –Or try not to let him think at all. Sometimes the king is surrounded by people who abuse their power and try to serve their own ends."

Rubel looked up at the officer, squinting.

"So that means," he hazarded, "that even if it was an *emergency* and even if you *had* to talk to him. . . I mean, even if it was *really* important and the king would want to hear you, they might not let you tell him because they might *want* something bad to happen?" His expression was quite suddenly ablaze as the implications of this thought raced several times around the inside of his head.

"Worse than that," the officer added in a hushed voice, "They might even throw you in the dungeon just to keep you from telling! And the king would never even know!"

Rubel chewed his lip and his young and perfect forehead knitted up as he considered. He was taking it all very gravely.

"That's very bad," he declared after a space.

The officer laughed.

"Well yes, except you know, you do have an advantage, if you really are a *thief*. You see here?"

The officer turned about and pointed. They had walked all the way to the massive main gate through which everything leaving or entering the palace had to pass. "If you absolutely needed to get into the palace, all you would have to remember is that during the day, these gates are always open. —Unless, of course, there was a war or something like that going on. For the most part, though, the king relies on his guardsmen watching the entrance. And any thief worth his salt could get in past a few measly guardsmen, don't you think?"

Rubel examined the gate for a long moment. It seemed to him that it was more of a tunnel than it was a gate. —Short perhaps, but a tunnel nonetheless. He ran back and forth through it a couple of times, his head craning all about in order to examine it fully.

This short tunnel had a huge drawbridge at its mouth which was made from enormous oaken beams, each carved from nearly a whole tree, and each strapped and bolted with broad strips of black metal. It crossed a chasm to a stone bridge on the far side, which in turn, led down the spiral of the mountain roadway. There also appeared, when he looked up, to be two other gates, one at each end of the tunnel. Both were the sort you could drop at once to stop people, or kill them if they didn't move in time.

Dotted all along the roof of the tunnel, and up and down the two towers placed to either side of the tunnel's mouth, were dark slit windows for guardsmen to shoot or drop things through. Any intruder caught in the tunnel could be quickly killed, and any intruder who hung about in front would find himself just as quickly filled up with arrows and bolt lock bolts if he didn't run away. The whole affair seemed to Rubel a very sound arrangement for a palace to have at its entrance.

"So?" the officer inquired, looking amused. "Easy enough?"

"No," Rubel said at length. "Not easy, I don't think. But probably if it was open, and if you were fast enough and if nobody was expecting you, you could get through."

"Just my point exactly," the officer laughed. "Just my point exactly! Thieves have an advantage over armies! A band of rogues would find themselves shot down quick enough, but a *thief* might just have a chance! Now come and I'll show you something else."

The officer set off with Rubel at his heel. The man was feeling an odd sense of elation at the way the tour was developing. He was having fun. His wry grin was playing more and more often across his face, and it became less and less wry as it did. The guardsmen who had been listening to the conversation exchanged smiles, and one called out after Rubel.

"Aye, there lad! Trying to figure a break in, are you?"

"Only if I have to!" Rubel called back to him over his shoulder, with such earnestness that the guards couldn't help but laugh.

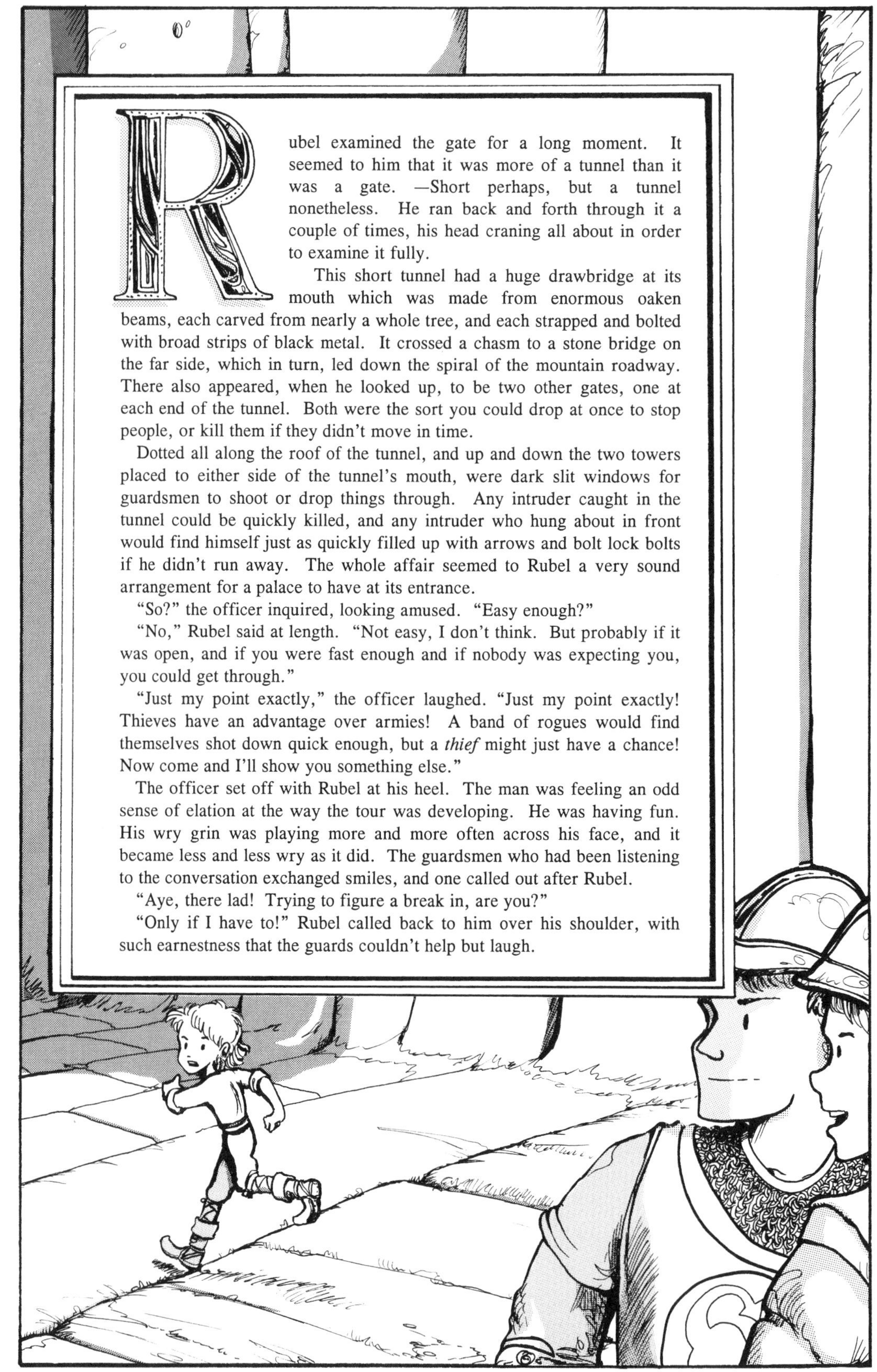

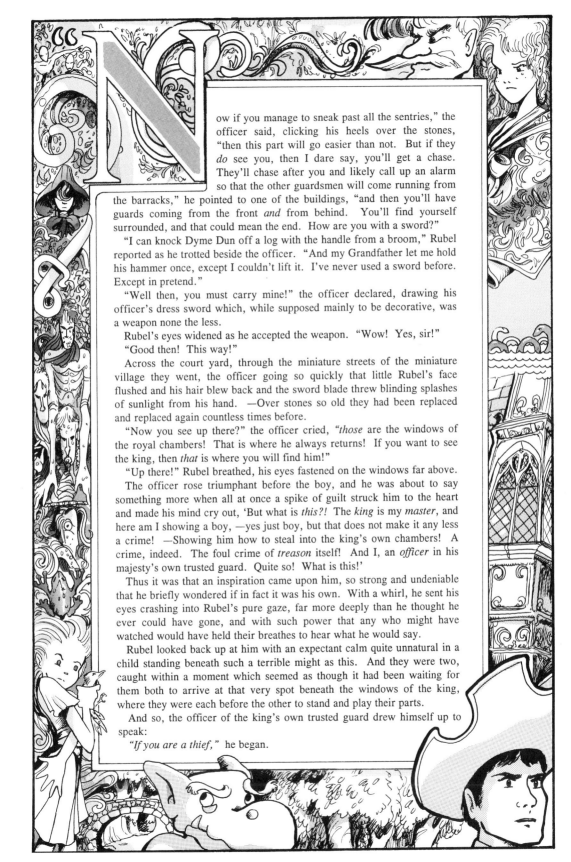

"Now if you manage to sneak past all the sentries," the officer said, clicking his heels over the stones, "then this part will go easier than not. But if they *do* see you, then I dare say, you'll get a chase. They'll chase after you and likely call up an alarm so that the other guardsmen will come running from the barracks," he pointed to one of the buildings, "and then you'll have guards coming from the front *and* from behind. You'll find yourself surrounded, and that could mean the end. How are you with a sword?"

"I can knock Dyme Dun off a log with the handle from a broom," Rubel reported as he trotted beside the officer. "And my Grandfather let me hold his hammer once, except I couldn't lift it. I've never used a sword before. Except in pretend."

"Well then, you must carry mine!" the officer declared, drawing his officer's dress sword which, while supposed mainly to be decorative, was a weapon none the less.

Rubel's eyes widened as he accepted the weapon. "Wow! Yes, sir!"

"Good then! This way!"

Across the court yard, through the miniature streets of the miniature village they went, the officer going so quickly that little Rubel's face flushed and his hair blew back and the sword blade threw blinding splashes of sunlight from his hand. —Over stones so old they had been replaced and replaced again countless times before.

"Now you see up there?" the officer cried, "*those* are the windows of the royal chambers! That is where he always returns! If you want to see the king, then *that* is where you will find him!"

"Up there!" Rubel breathed, his eyes fastened on the windows far above.

The officer rose triumphant before the boy, and he was about to say something more when all at once a spike of guilt struck him to the heart and made his mind cry out, 'But what is *this?!* The *king* is my *master*, and here am I showing a boy, —yes just boy, but that does not make it any less a crime! —Showing him how to steal into the king's own chambers! A crime, indeed. The foul crime of *treason* itself! And I, an *officer* in his majesty's own trusted guard. Quite so! What is this!'

Thus it was that an inspiration came upon him, so strong and undeniable that he briefly wondered if in fact it was his own. With a whirl, he sent his eyes crashing into Rubel's pure gaze, far more deeply than he thought he ever could have gone, and with such power that any who might have watched would have held their breathes to hear what he would say.

Rubel looked back up at him with an expectant calm quite unnatural in a child standing beneath such a terrible might as this. And they were two, caught within a moment which seemed as though it had been waiting for them both to arrive at that very spot beneath the windows of the king, where they were each before the other to stand and play their parts.

And so, the officer of the king's own trusted guard drew himself up to speak:

"If you are a thief," he began.

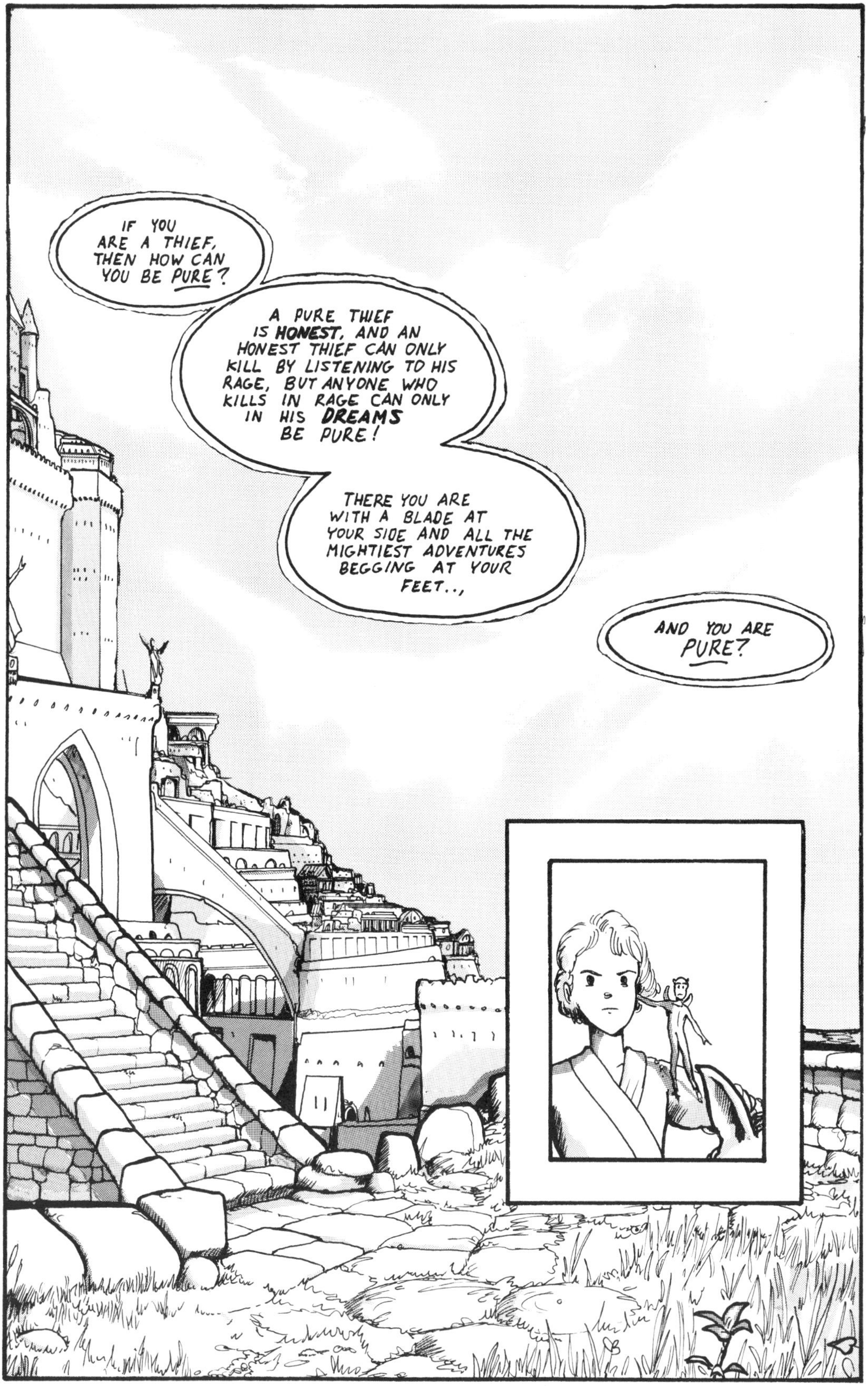
IF YOU ARE A THIEF, THEN HOW CAN YOU BE PURE?
A PURE THIEF IS HONEST, AND AN HONEST THIEF CAN ONLY KILL BY LISTENING TO HIS RAGE, BUT ANYONE WHO KILLS IN RAGE CAN ONLY IN HIS DREAMS BE PURE!
THERE YOU ARE WITH A BLADE AT YOUR SIDE AND ALL THE MIGHTIEST ADVENTURES BEGGING AT YOUR FEET..,
AND YOU ARE PURE?

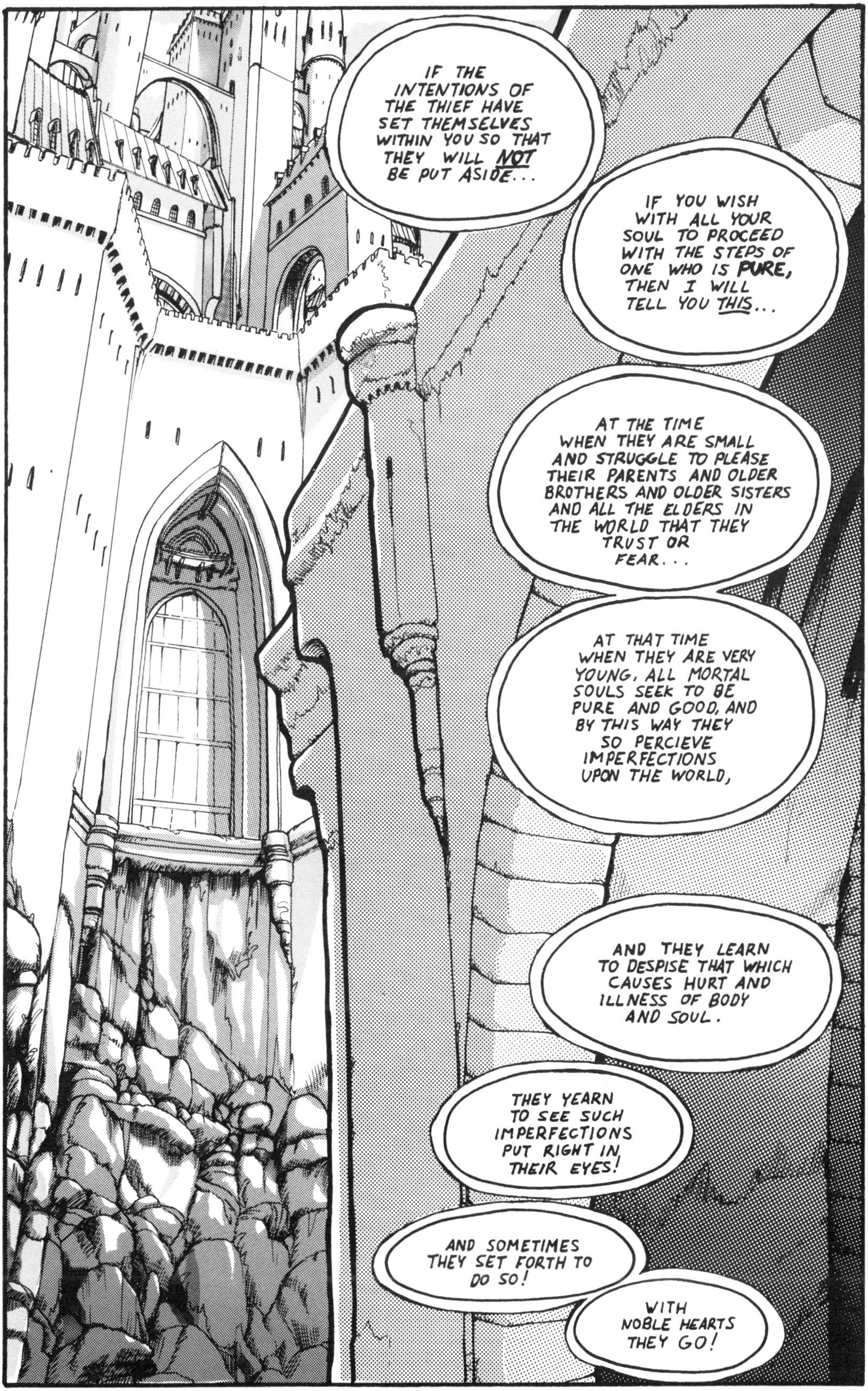
IF THE INTENTIONS OF THE THIEF HAVE SET THEMSELVES WITHIN YOU SO THAT THEY WILL NOT BE PUT ASIDE...
IF YOU WISH WITH ALL YOUR SOUL TO PROCEED WITH THE STEPS OF ONE WHO IS PURE, THEN I WILL TELL YOU THIS...
AT THE TIME WHEN THEY ARE SMALL AND STRUGGLE TO PLEASE THEIR PARENTS AND OLDER BROTHERS AND OLDER SISTERS AND ALL THE ELDERS IN THE WORLD THAT THEY TRUST OR FEAR...
AT THAT TIME WHEN THEY ARE VERY YOUNG, ALL MORTAL SOULS SEEK TO BE PURE AND GOOD, AND BY THIS WAY THEY SO PERCIEVE IMPERFECTIONS UPON THE WORLD,
AND THEY LEARN TO DESPISE THAT WHICH CAUSES HURT AND ILLNESS OF BODY AND SOUL.
THEY YEARN TO SEE SUCH IMPERFECTIONS PUT RIGHT IN THEIR EYES!
AND SOMETIMES THEY SET FORTH TO DO SO!
WITH NOBLE HEARTS THEY GO!

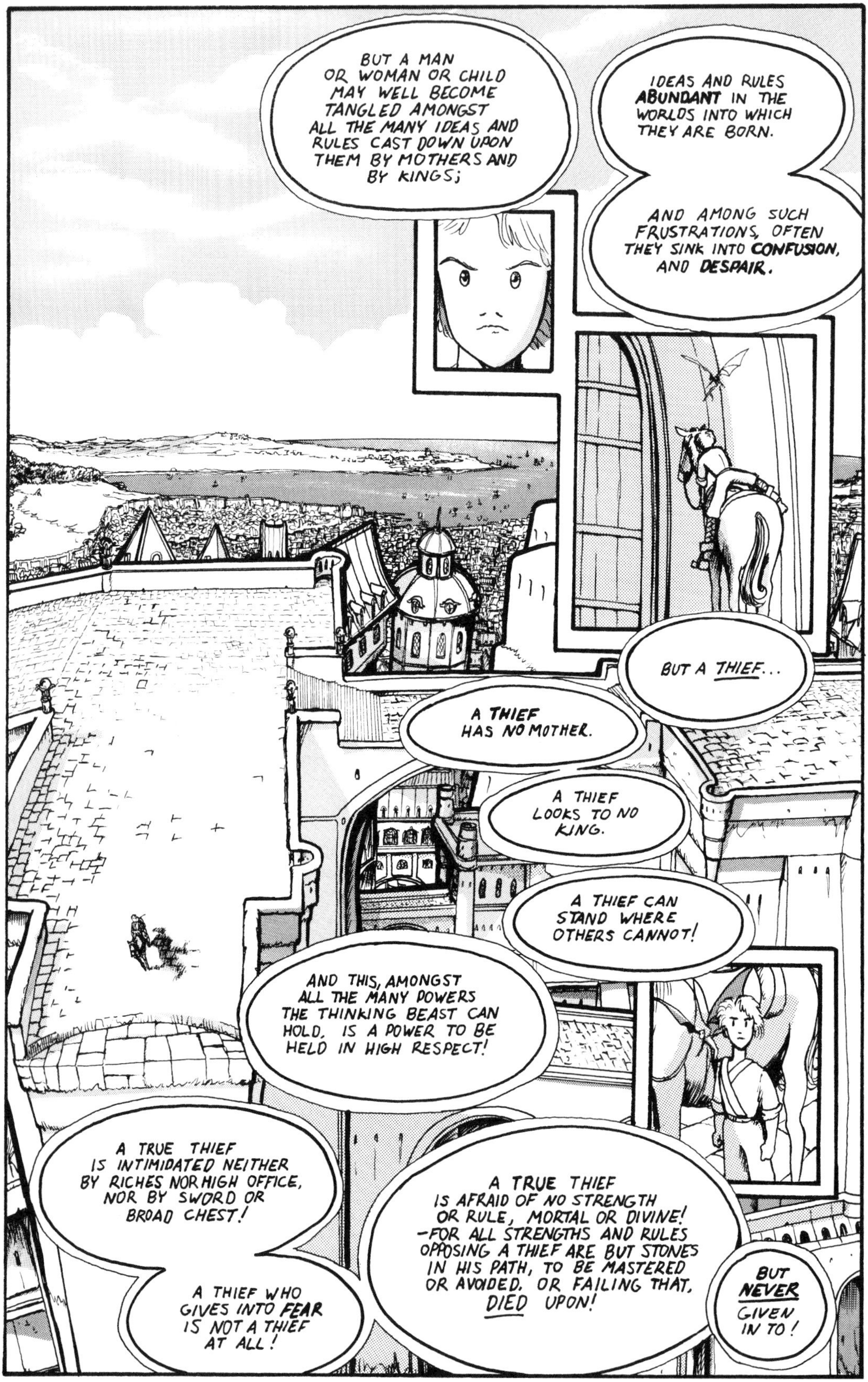
BUT A MAN OR WOMAN OR CHILD MAY WELL BECOME TANGLED AMONGST ALL THE MANY IDEAS AND RULES CAST DOWN UPON THEM BY MOTHERS AND BY KINGS;
IDEAS AND RULES ABUNDANT IN THE WORLDS INTO WHICH THEY ARE BORN.
AND AMONG SUCH FRUSTRATIONS, OFTEN THEY SINK INTO CONFUSION, AND DESPAIR.
BUT A THIEF...
A THIEF HAS NO MOTHER.
A THIEF LOOKS TO NO KING.
A THIEF CAN STAND WHERE OTHERS CANNOT!
AND THIS, AMONGST ALL THE MANY POWERS THE THINKING BEAST CAN HOLD, IS A POWER TO BE HELD IN HIGH RESPECT!
A TRUE THIEF IS INTIMIDATED NEITHER BY RICHES NOR HIGH OFFICE, NOR BY SWORD OR BROAD CHEST!
A THIEF WHO GIVES INTO FEAR IS NOT A THIEF AT ALL!
A TRUE THIEF IS AFRAID OF NO STRENGTH OR RULE, MORTAL OR DIVINE! -FOR ALL STRENGTHS AND RULES OPPOSING A THIEF ARE BUT STONES IN HIS PATH, TO BE MASTERED OR AVOIDED. OR FAILING THAT, DIED UPON!
BUT NEVER GIVEN IN TO!

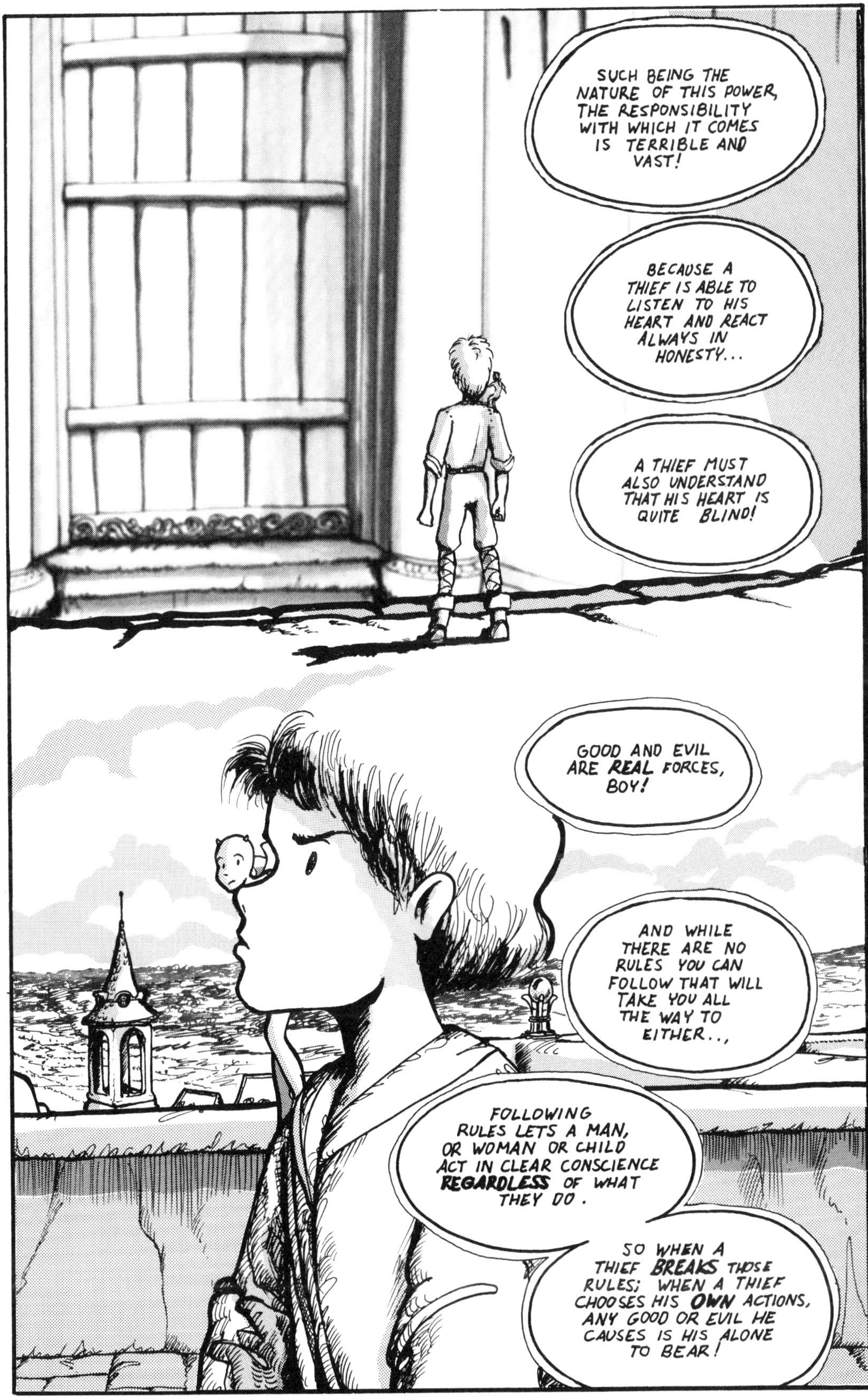
SUCH BEING THE NATURE OF THIS POWER, THE RESPONSIBILITY WITH WHICH IT COMES IS TERRIBLE AND VAST!
BECAUSE A THIEF IS ABLE TO LISTEN TO HIS HEART AND REACT ALWAYS IN HONESTY...
A THIEF MUST ALSO UNDERSTAND THAT HIS HEART IS QUITE BLIND!
GOOD AND EVIL ARE **REAL** FORCES, BOY!
AND WHILE THERE ARE NO RULES YOU CAN FOLLOW THAT WILL TAKE YOU ALL THE WAY TO EITHER..,
FOLLOWING RULES LETS A MAN, OR WOMAN OR CHILD ACT IN CLEAR CONSCIENCE **REGARDLESS** OF WHAT THEY DO.
SO WHEN A THIEF **BREAKS** THOSE RULES; WHEN A THIEF CHOOSES HIS **OWN** ACTIONS, ANY GOOD OR EVIL HE CAUSES IS HIS ALONE TO BEAR!

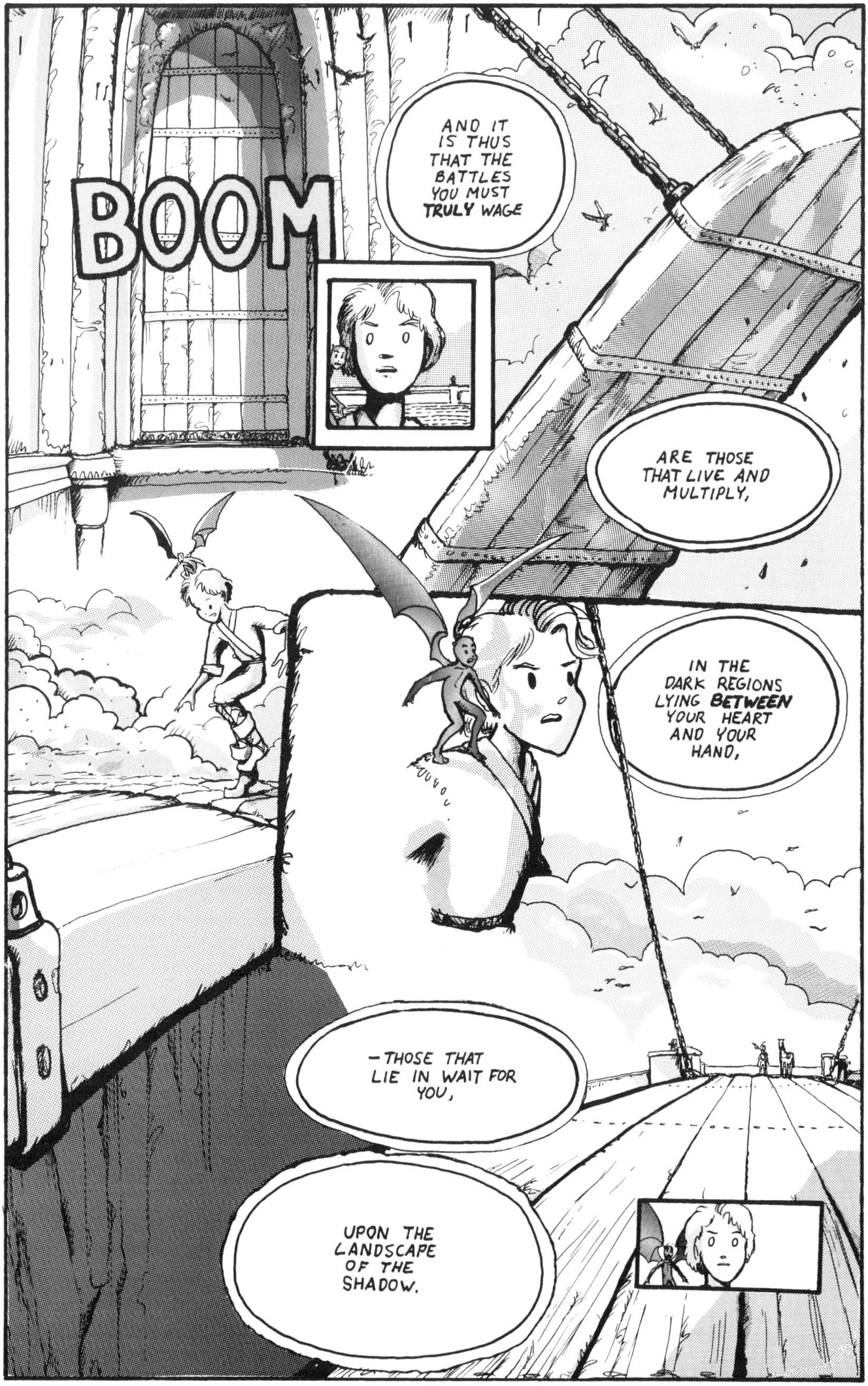
BOOM
AND IT IS THUS THAT THE BATTLES YOU MUST TRULY WAGE
ARE THOSE THAT LIVE AND MULTIPLY,
IN THE DARK REGIONS LYING BETWEEN YOUR HEART AND YOUR HAND,
-THOSE THAT LIE IN WAIT FOR YOU,
UPON THE LANDSCAPE OF THE SHADOW.

Interlude...

Thieves & Kings

Presents...

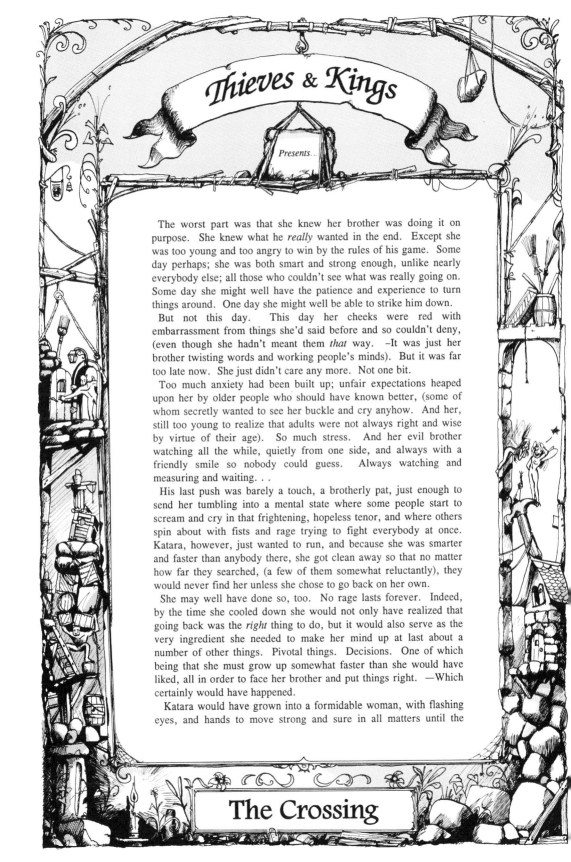

The worst part was that she knew her brother was doing it on purpose. She knew what he *really* wanted in the end. Except she was too young and too angry to win by the rules of his game. Some day perhaps; she was both smart and strong enough, unlike nearly everybody else; all those who couldn't see what was really going on. Some day she might well have the patience and experience to turn things around. One day she might well be able to strike him down.

But not this day. This day her cheeks were red with embarrassment from things she'd said before and so couldn't deny, (even though she hadn't meant them *that* way. –It was just her brother twisting words and working people's minds). But it was far too late now. She just didn't care any more. Not one bit.

Too much anxiety had been built up; unfair expectations heaped upon her by older people who should have known better, (some of whom secretly wanted to see her buckle and cry anyhow. And her, still too young to realize that adults were not always right and wise by virtue of their age). So much stress. And her evil brother watching all the while, quietly from one side, and always with a friendly smile so nobody could guess. Always watching and measuring and waiting. . .

His last push was barely a touch, a brotherly pat, just enough to send her tumbling into a mental state where some people start to scream and cry in that frightening, hopeless tenor, and where others spin about with fists and rage trying to fight everybody at once. Katara, however, just wanted to run, and because she was smarter and faster than anybody there, she got clean away so that no matter how far they searched, (a few of them somewhat reluctantly), they would never find her unless she chose to go back on her own.

She may well have done so, too. No rage lasts forever. Indeed, by the time she cooled down she would not only have realized that going back was the *right* thing to do, but it would also serve as the very ingredient she needed to make her mind up at last about a number of other things. Pivotal things. Decisions. One of which being that she must grow up somewhat faster than she would have liked, all in order to face her brother and put things right. —Which certainly would have happened.

Katara would have grown into a formidable woman, with flashing eyes, and hands to move strong and sure in all matters until the

The Crossing

world would come to both fear her and love her above all else. Except in the Sleeping Wood, angry, tearful states like hers were nearly always the keys for unlocking *other* things. . . The Sleeping Wood, at the mouth of which her brother had insisted the picnic be held. . .

The Wood felt her darting beneath its boughs; a tiny bundle of fury and sadness and loneliness which made its roots ache as she passed. Though while it had little patience for such things, it did have a place to keep them, deep within its magic gut where uncompromising creatures could be digested and quietly forgotten. And so, with grumbling nudges and shifting roots, Katara's blind race was diverted along hidden pathways and secret trails until she was far away from where she had begun, and far more lost than she could begin to understand. . .

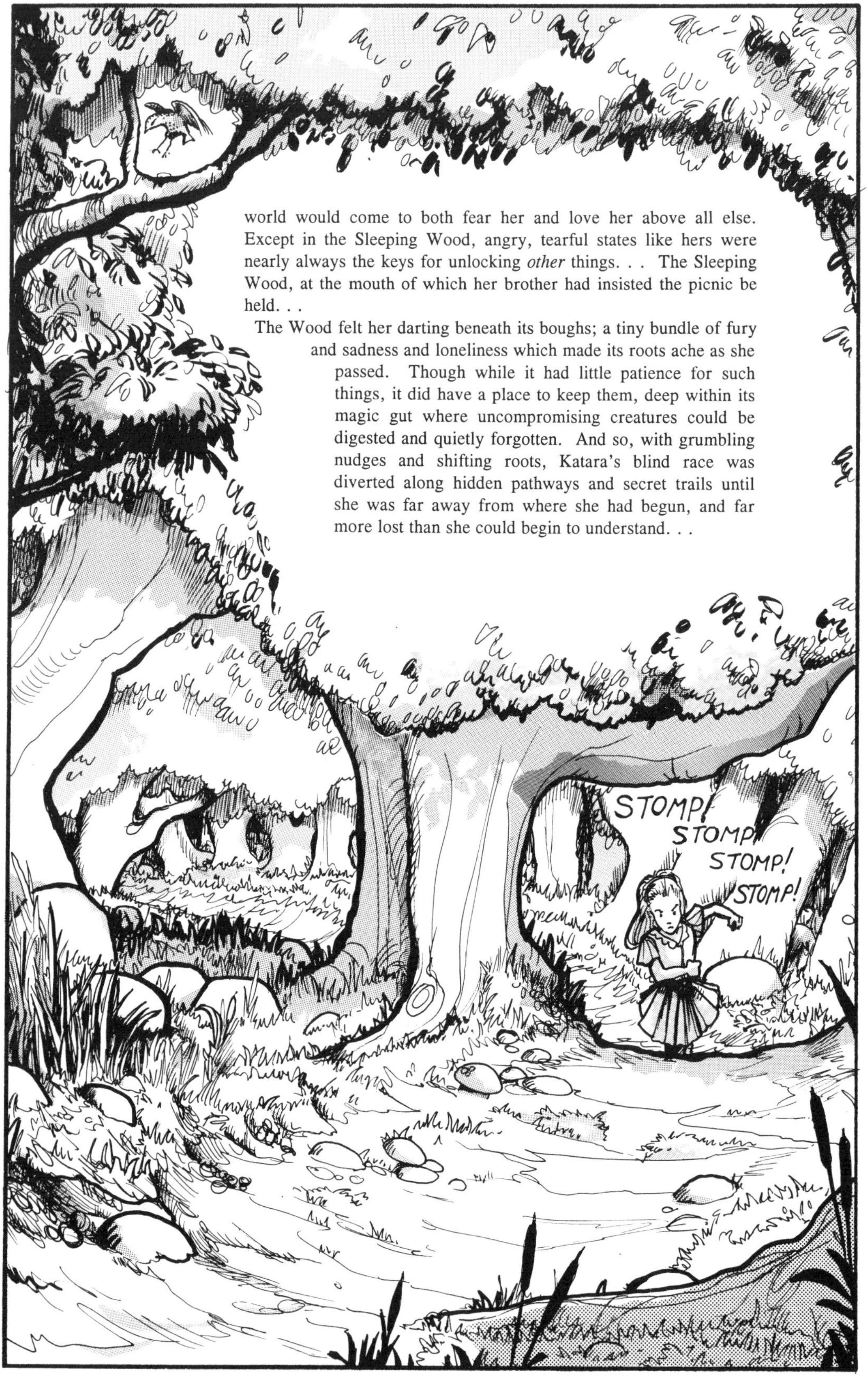

STOMP!
STOMP!
STOMP!
STOMP!

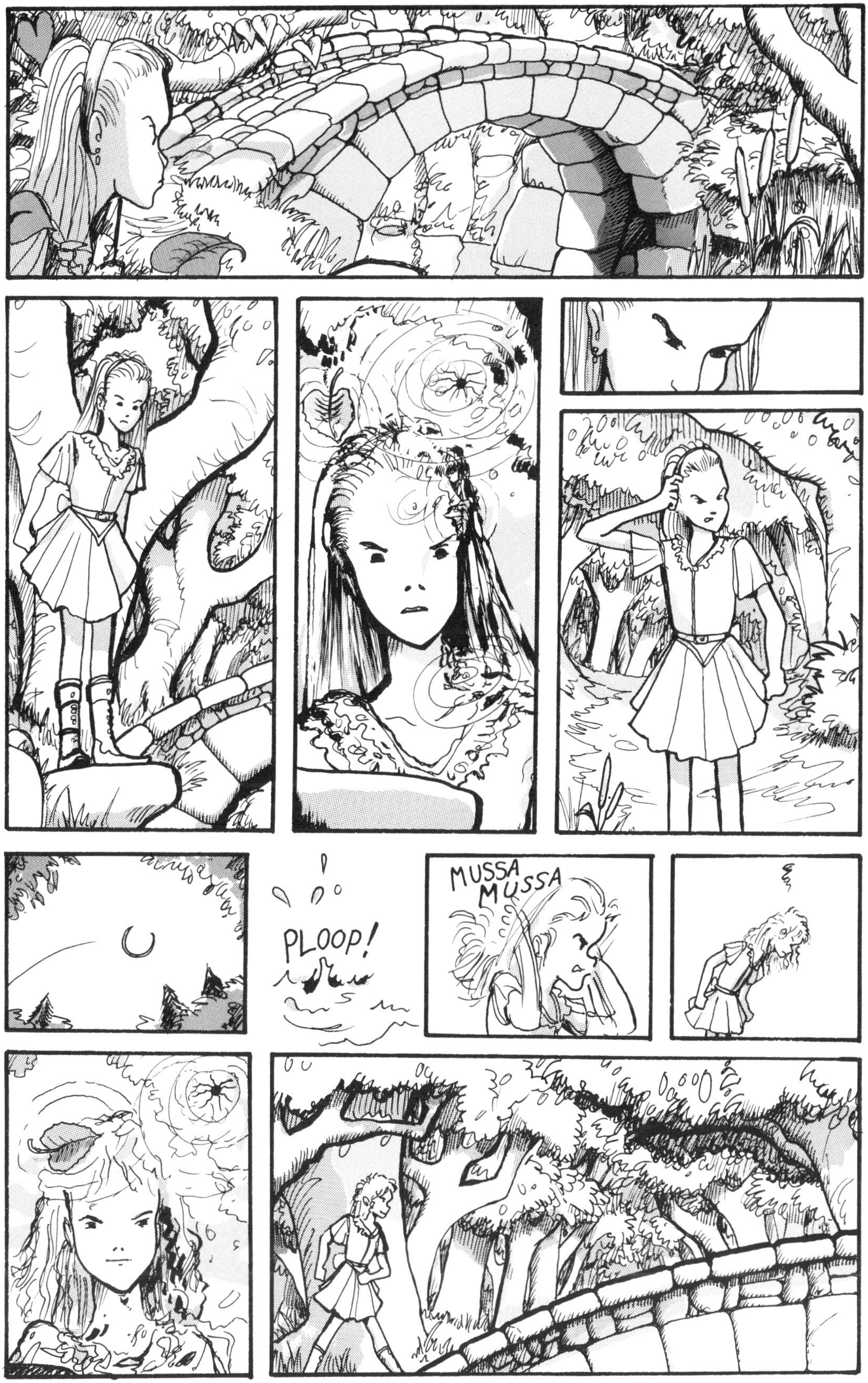
PLOOP!
MUSSA MUSSA

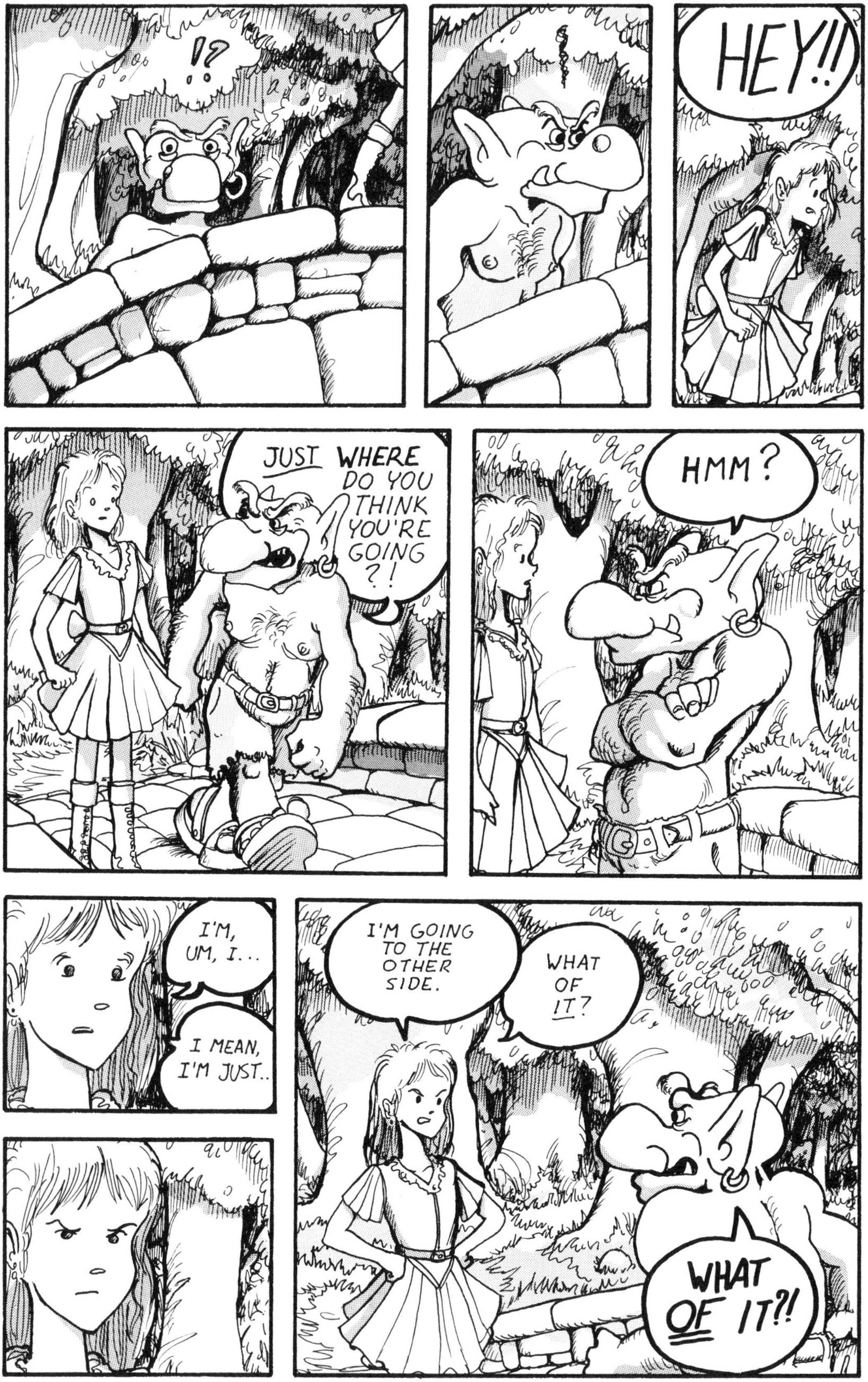

!?
HEY!!
JUST WHERE DO YOU THINK YOU'RE GOING ?!
HMM?
I'M, UM, I...
I MEAN, I'M JUST..
I'M GOING TO THE OTHER SIDE.
WHAT OF IT?
WHAT OF IT?!

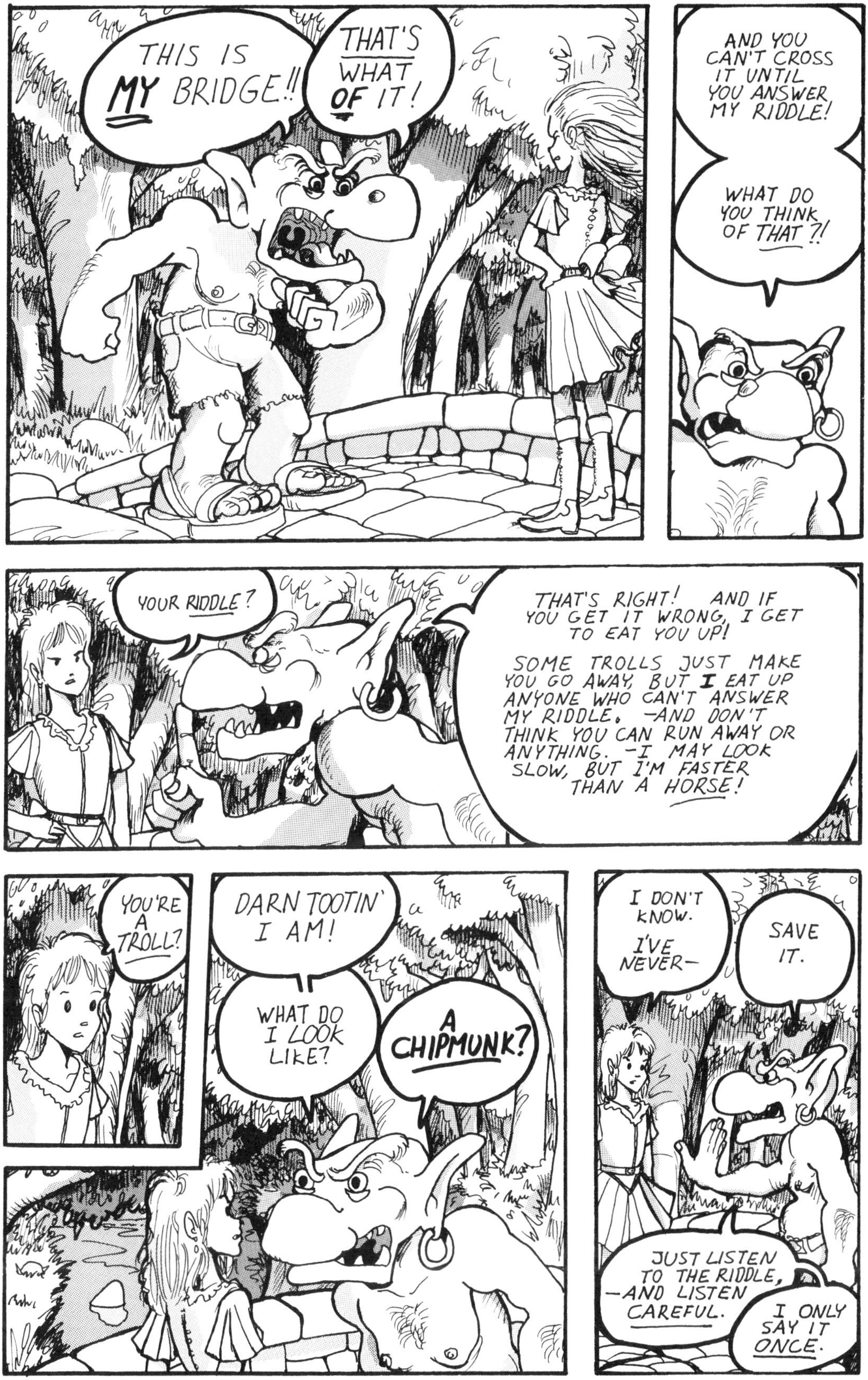
THIS IS MY BRIDGE!!
THAT'S WHAT OF IT!
AND YOU CAN'T CROSS IT UNTIL YOU ANSWER MY RIDDLE!
WHAT DO YOU THINK OF THAT?!
YOUR RIDDLE?
THAT'S RIGHT! AND IF YOU GET IT WRONG, I GET TO EAT YOU UP!
SOME TROLLS JUST MAKE YOU GO AWAY, BUT I EAT UP ANYONE WHO CAN'T ANSWER MY RIDDLE. —AND DON'T THINK YOU CAN RUN AWAY OR ANYTHING. —I MAY LOOK SLOW, BUT I'M FASTER THAN A HORSE!
YOU'RE A TROLL?
DARN TOOTIN' I AM!
WHAT DO I LOOK LIKE?
A CHIPMUNK?
I DON'T KNOW.
I'VE NEVER—
SAVE IT.
JUST LISTEN TO THE RIDDLE, —AND LISTEN CAREFUL.
I ONLY SAY IT ONCE.

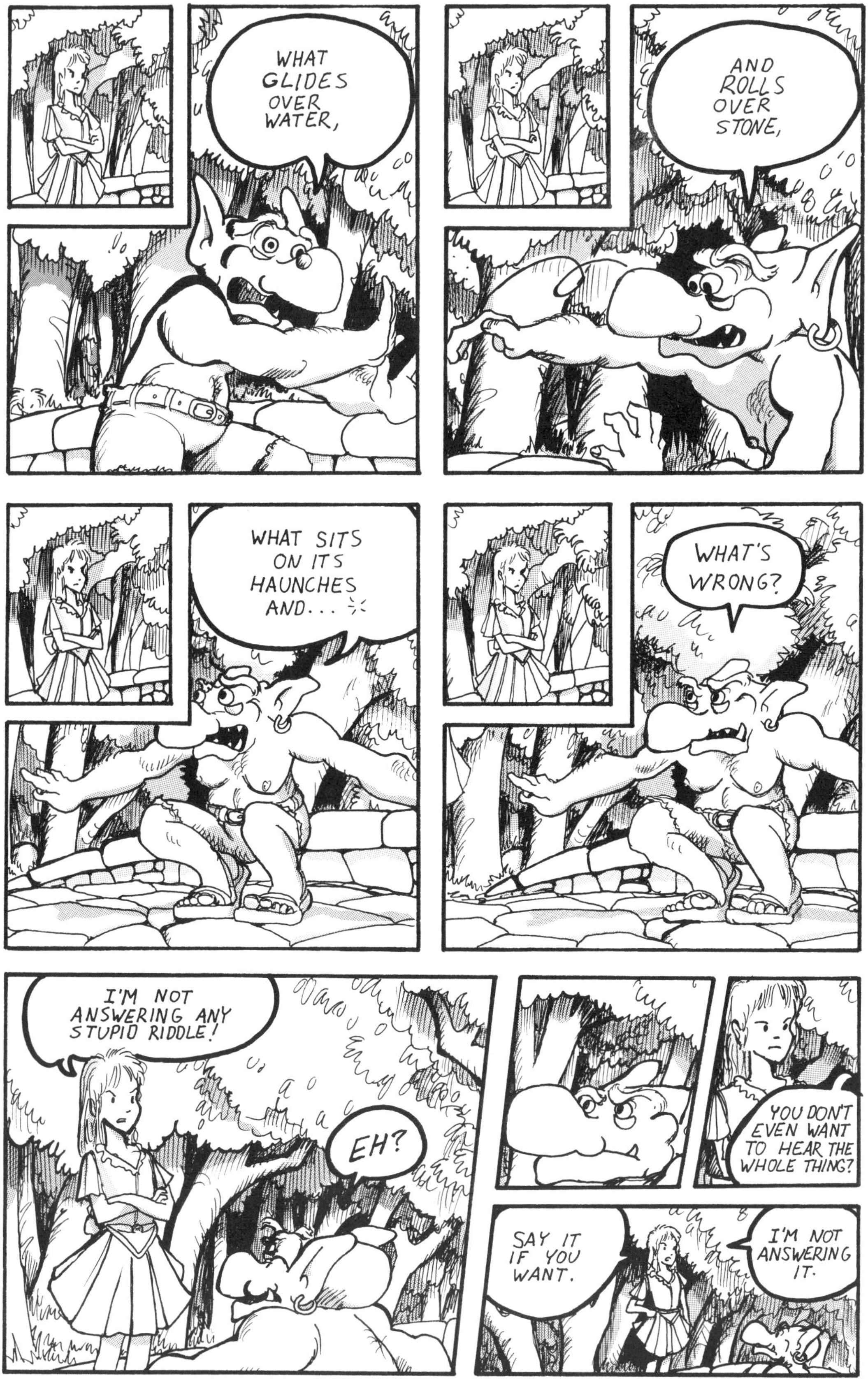

WHAT GLIDES OVER WATER,
AND ROLLS OVER STONE,
WHAT SITS ON ITS HAUNCHES AND...
WHAT'S WRONG?
I'M NOT ANSWERING ANY STUPID RIDDLE!
EH?
YOU DON'T EVEN WANT TO HEAR THE WHOLE THING?
SAY IT IF YOU WANT.
I'M NOT ANSWERING IT.

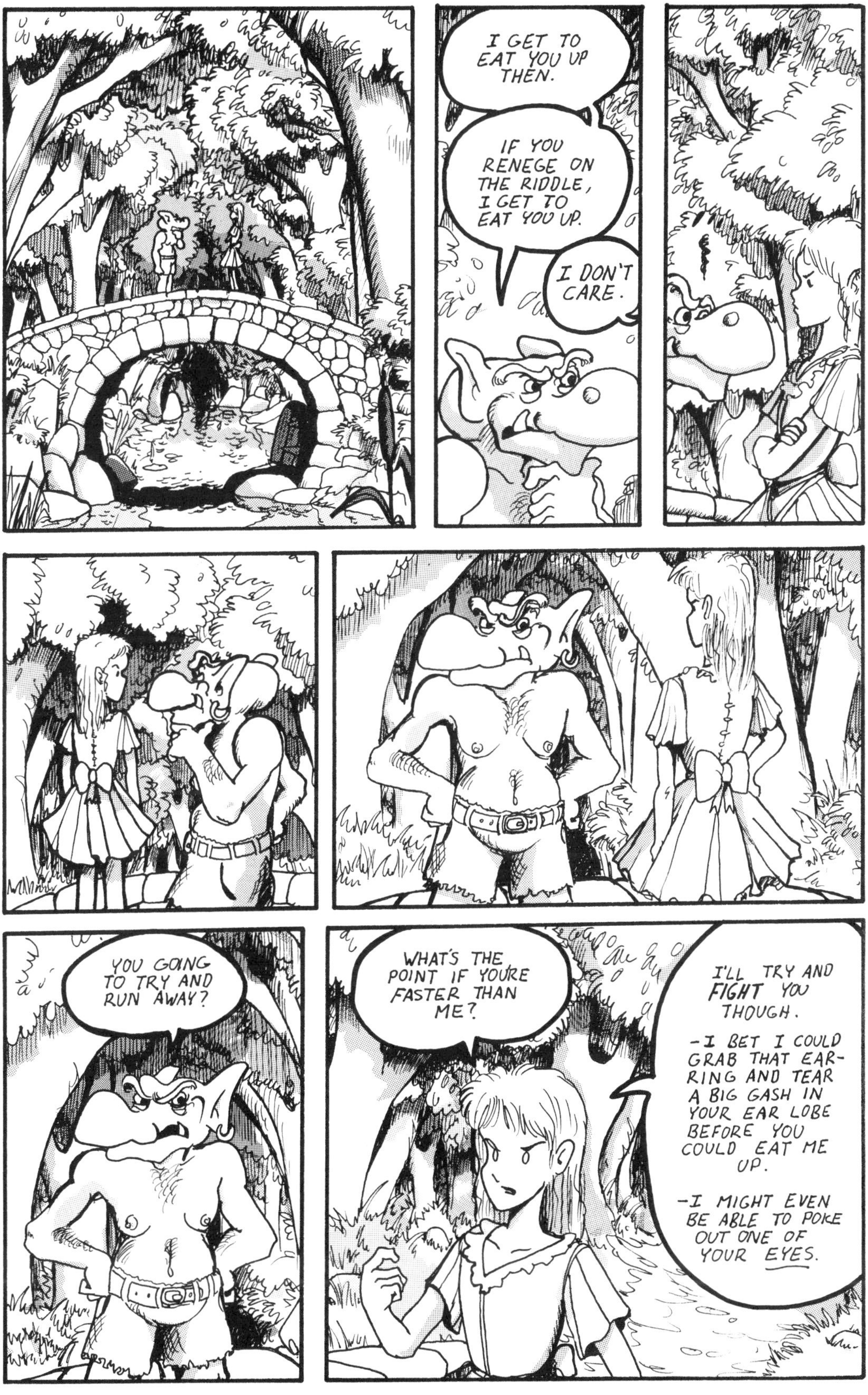
I GET TO EAT YOU UP THEN.
IF YOU RENEGE ON THE RIDDLE, I GET TO EAT YOU UP.
I DON'T CARE.
YOU GOING TO TRY AND RUN AWAY?
WHAT'S THE POINT IF YOU'RE FASTER THAN ME?
I'LL TRY AND FIGHT YOU THOUGH.
-I BET I COULD GRAB THAT EAR-RING AND TEAR A BIG GASH IN YOUR EAR LOBE BEFORE YOU COULD EAT ME UP.
-I MIGHT EVEN BE ABLE TO POKE OUT ONE OF YOUR EYES.

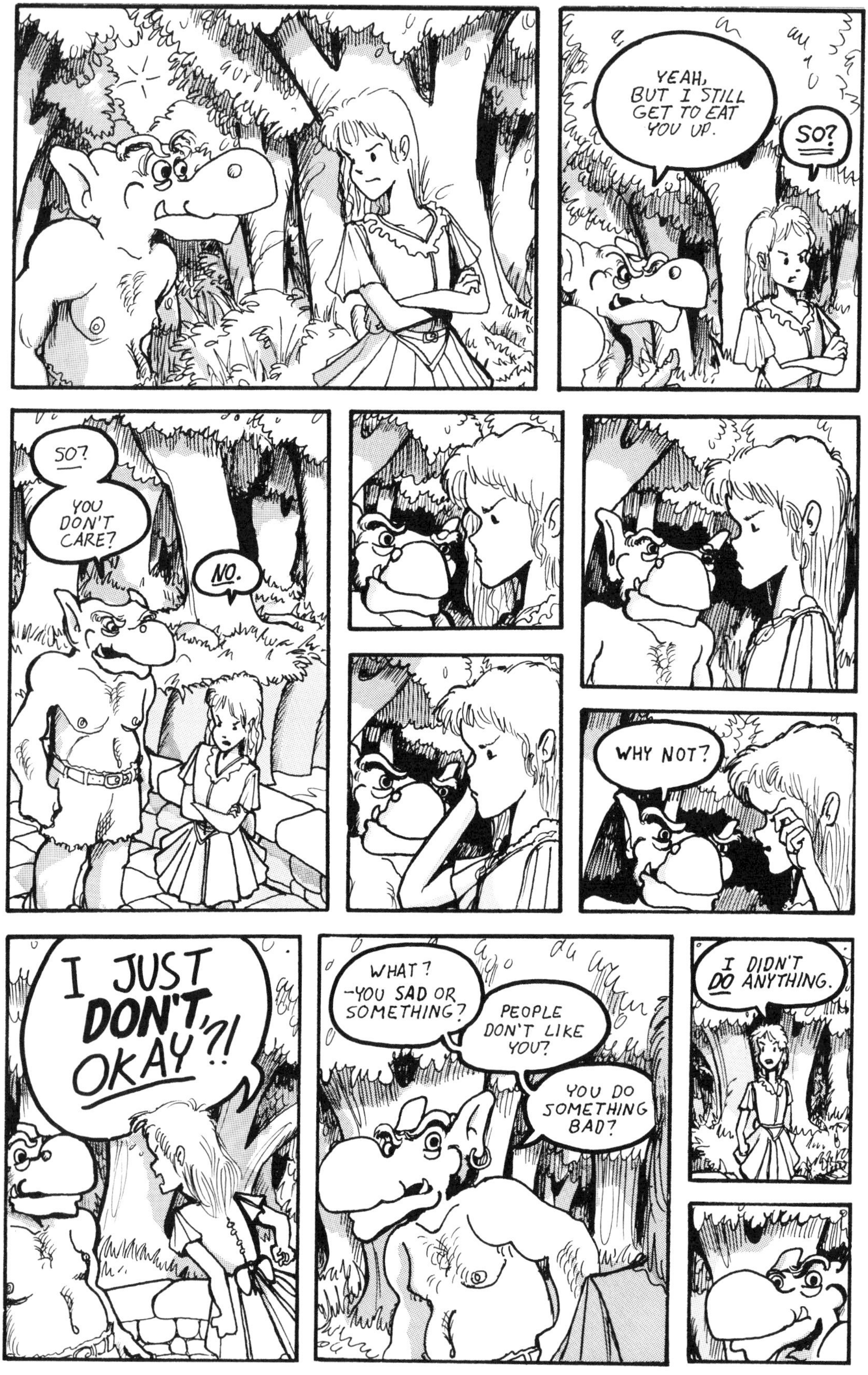
YEAH, BUT I STILL GET TO EAT YOU UP.
SO?
SO?
YOU DON'T CARE?
NO.
WHY NOT?
I JUST DON'T, OKAY?!
WHAT? -YOU SAD OR SOMETHING?
PEOPLE DON'T LIKE YOU?
YOU DO SOMETHING BAD?
I DIDN'T DO ANYTHING.

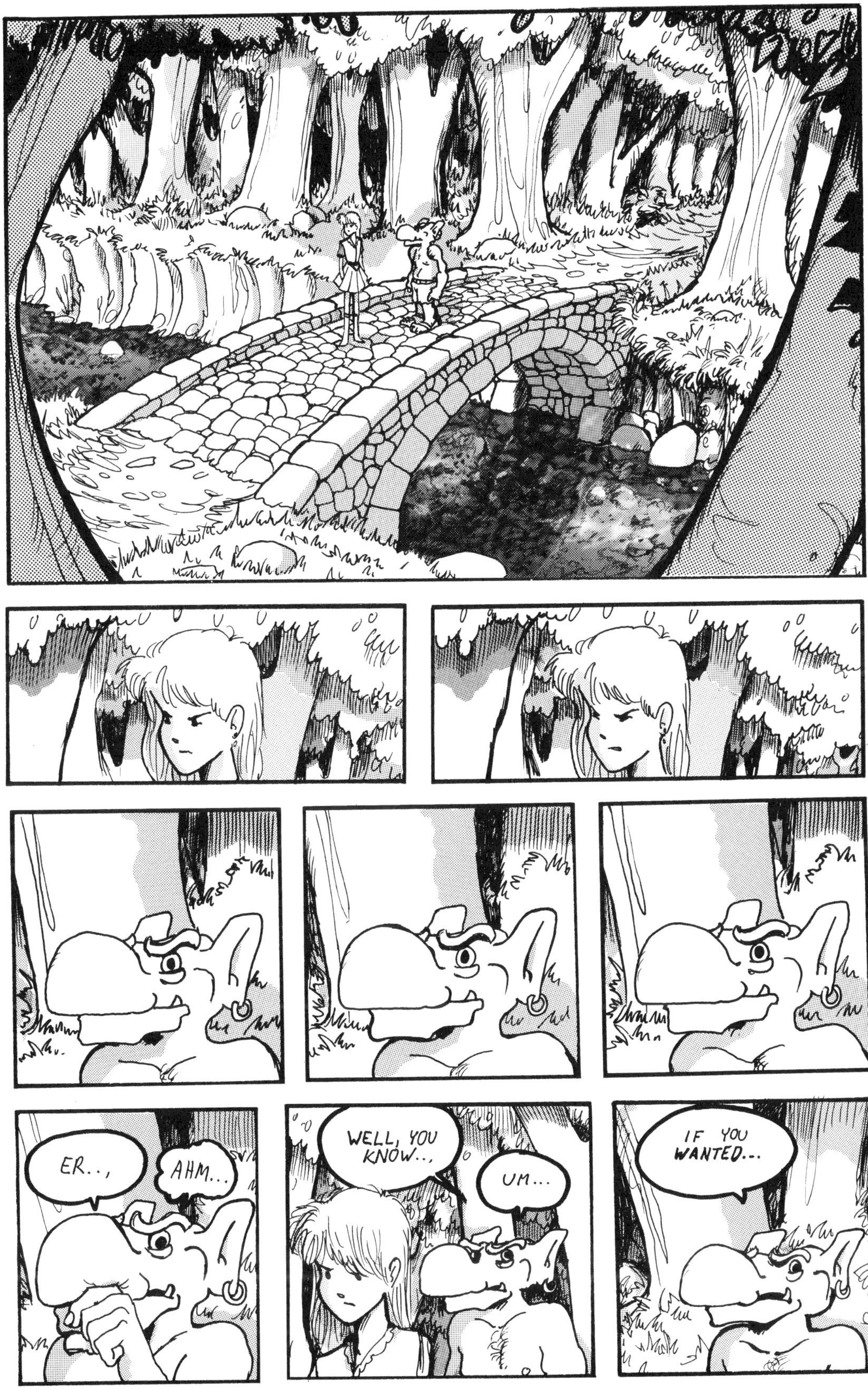
ER..,
AHM...
WELL, YOU KNOW..,
UM...
IF YOU WANTED...

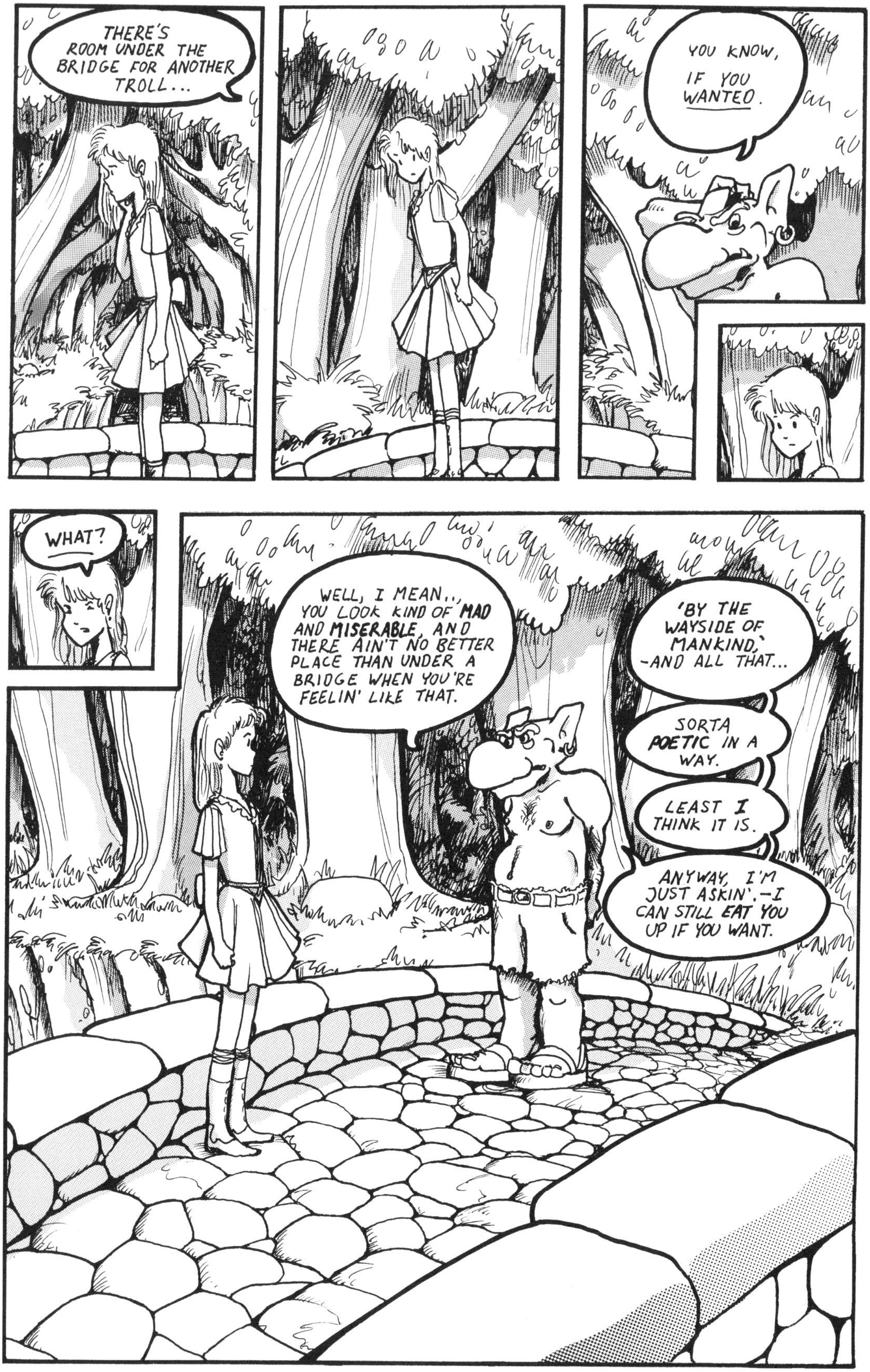

THERE'S ROOM UNDER THE BRIDGE FOR ANOTHER TROLL...
YOU KNOW, IF YOU WANTED.
WHAT?
WELL, I MEAN... YOU LOOK KIND OF MAD AND MISERABLE, AND THERE AIN'T NO BETTER PLACE THAN UNDER A BRIDGE WHEN YOU'RE FEELIN' LIKE THAT.
'BY THE WAYSIDE OF MANKIND,' -AND ALL THAT...
SORTA POETIC IN A WAY.
LEAST I THINK IT IS.
ANYWAY, I'M JUST ASKIN'. -I CAN STILL EAT YOU UP IF YOU WANT.

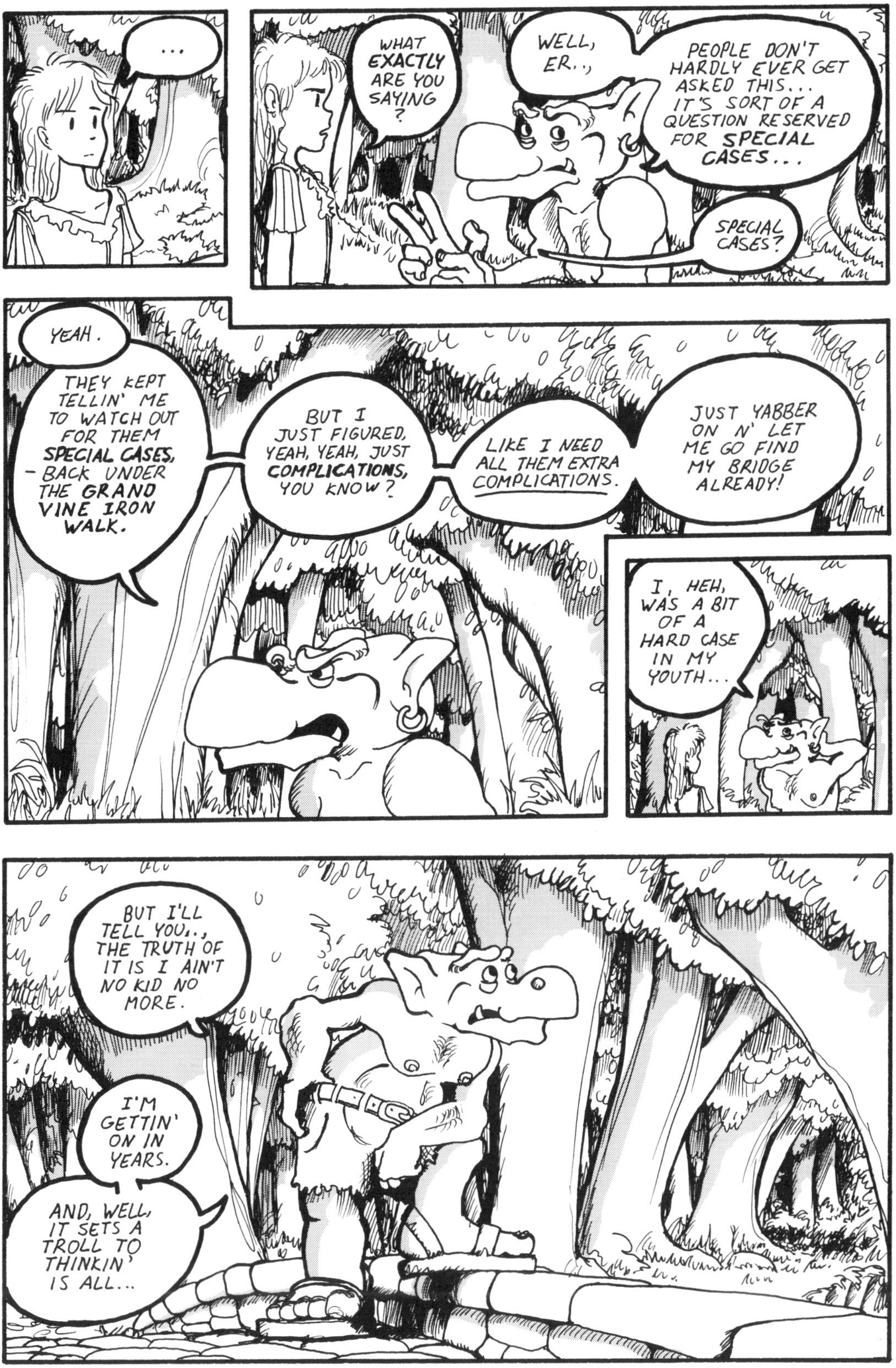
...
WHAT EXACTLY ARE YOU SAYING?
WELL, ER..,
PEOPLE DON'T HARDLY EVER GET ASKED THIS... IT'S SORT OF A QUESTION RESERVED FOR SPECIAL CASES...
SPECIAL CASES?
YEAH.
THEY KEPT TELLIN' ME TO WATCH OUT FOR THEM SPECIAL CASES, - BACK UNDER THE GRAND VINE IRON WALK.
BUT I JUST FIGURED, YEAH, YEAH, JUST COMPLICATIONS, YOU KNOW?
LIKE I NEED ALL THEM EXTRA COMPLICATIONS.
JUST YABBER ON N' LET ME GO FIND MY BRIDGE ALREADY!
I, HEH, WAS A BIT OF A HARD CASE IN MY YOUTH...
BUT I'LL TELL YOU.., THE TRUTH OF IT IS I AIN'T NO KID NO MORE.
I'M GETTIN' ON IN YEARS.
AND, WELL, IT SETS A TROLL TO THINKIN' IS ALL...

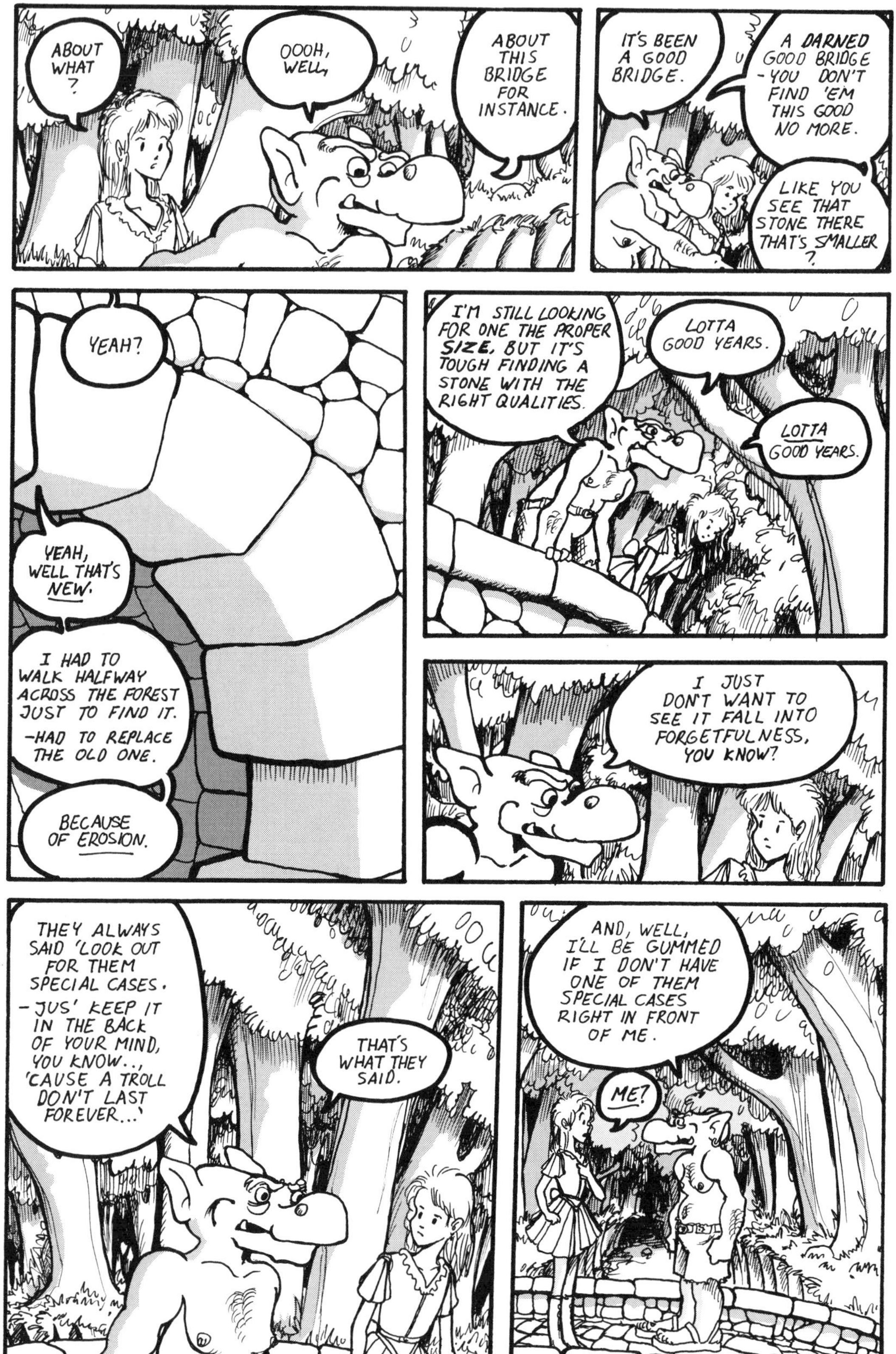
ABOUT WHAT ?
OOOH, WELL,
ABOUT THIS BRIDGE FOR INSTANCE.
IT'S BEEN A GOOD BRIDGE.
A DARNED GOOD BRIDGE -YOU DON'T FIND 'EM THIS GOOD NO MORE.
LIKE YOU SEE THAT STONE THERE THAT'S SMALLER ?
YEAH?
YEAH, WELL THAT'S NEW.
I HAD TO WALK HALFWAY ACROSS THE FOREST JUST TO FIND IT. -HAD TO REPLACE THE OLD ONE.
BECAUSE OF EROSION.
I'M STILL LOOKING FOR ONE THE PROPER SIZE, BUT IT'S TOUGH FINDING A STONE WITH THE RIGHT QUALITIES.
LOTTA GOOD YEARS.
LOTTA GOOD YEARS.
I JUST DON'T WANT TO SEE IT FALL INTO FORGETFULNESS, YOU KNOW?
THEY ALWAYS SAID 'LOOK OUT FOR THEM SPECIAL CASES. -JUS' KEEP IT IN THE BACK OF YOUR MIND, YOU KNOW.., 'CAUSE A TROLL DON'T LAST FOREVER...'
THAT'S WHAT THEY SAID.
AND, WELL, I'LL BE GUMMED IF I DON'T HAVE ONE OF THEM SPECIAL CASES RIGHT IN FRONT OF ME.
ME?

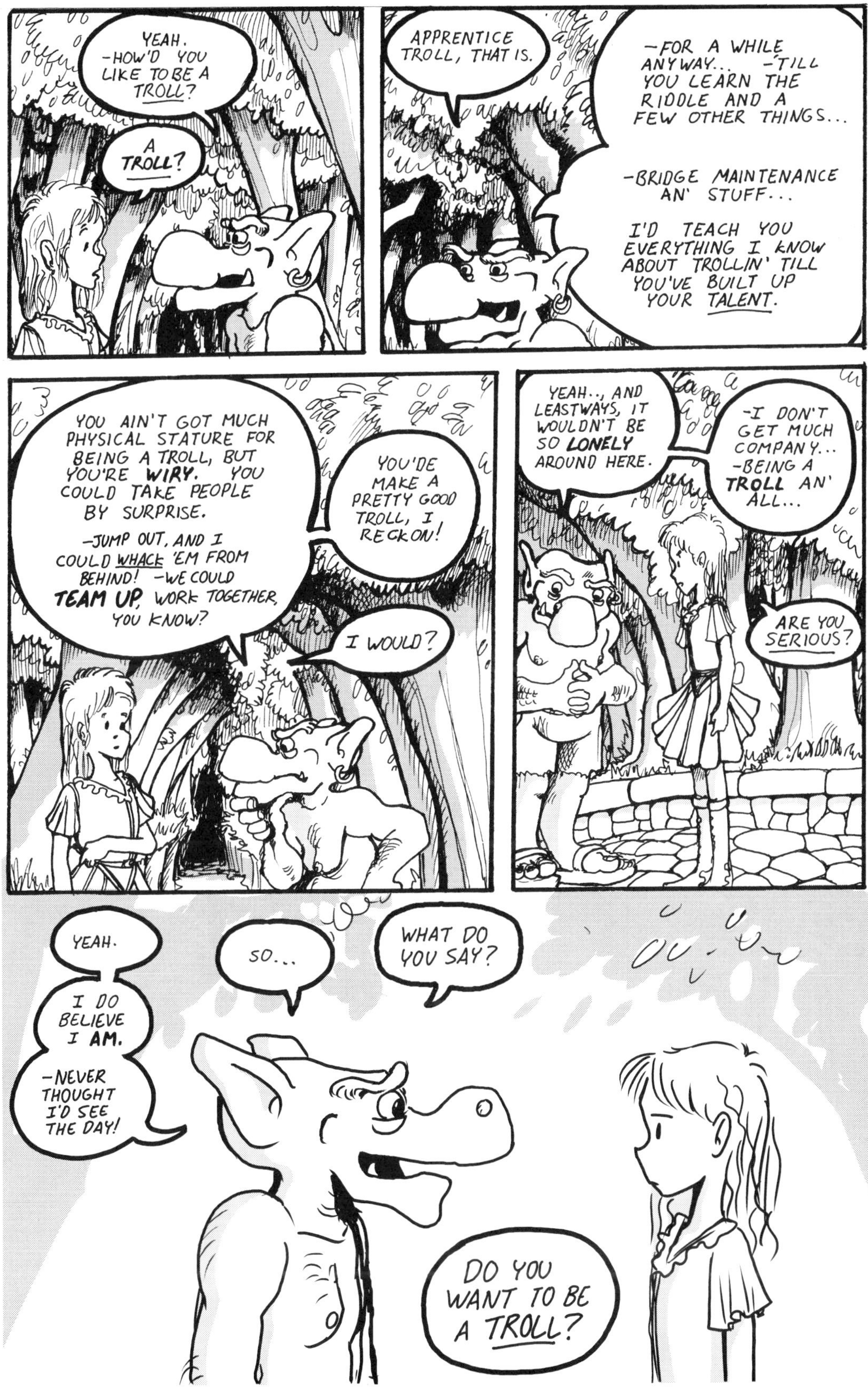

YEAH. -HOW'D YOU LIKE TO BE A TROLL?
A TROLL?
APPRENTICE TROLL, THAT IS.
-FOR A WHILE ANYWAY... -TILL YOU LEARN THE RIDDLE AND A FEW OTHER THINGS...
-BRIDGE MAINTENANCE AN' STUFF...
I'D TEACH YOU EVERYTHING I KNOW ABOUT TROLLIN' TILL YOU'VE BUILT UP YOUR TALENT.
YOU AIN'T GOT MUCH PHYSICAL STATURE FOR BEING A TROLL, BUT YOU'RE WIRY. YOU COULD TAKE PEOPLE BY SURPRISE.
-JUMP OUT, AND I COULD WHACK 'EM FROM BEHIND! -WE COULD TEAM UP, WORK TOGETHER, YOU KNOW?
YOU'DE MAKE A PRETTY GOOD TROLL, I RECKON!
I WOULD?
YEAH.., AND LEASTWAYS, IT WOULDN'T BE SO LONELY AROUND HERE.
-I DON'T GET MUCH COMPANY... -BEING A TROLL AN' ALL...
ARE YOU SERIOUS?
YEAH.
I DO BELIEVE I AM.
-NEVER THOUGHT I'D SEE THE DAY!
SO...
WHAT DO YOU SAY?
DO YOU WANT TO BE A TROLL?

Interlude part 2

The Madman of Millbrook

The Millbrook Strips. . .

The following comic strips feature the very first, very *oldest* incarnations of the *Thieves & Kings* world you're ever apt to come across. Back when the larger story was still just a sprawling collection of notes and maps and loose sketches, these strips came into being. They were the *first* tentative steps into the world I'd been building from behind the safety of a desk. Faced with all that history, those mountains, kingdoms and oceans.., well it was all a bit daunting for a first time explorer. Did I want to launch immediately into a huge comic book campaign? No way. Send in a scouting party first! Or a spy. *Quinton* performs both functions rather well; a tiny drop of high charisma capable of catalyzing the whole of reality. Yeah. Send *that* guy in first.

The classic four-frame newspaper gag strip had always been something I'd wanted to try my hand at ever since I was a boy. I figured, "How hard can it be? It's only four frames, right?" Heh. Turns out, 'Funny' is one of the most difficult things to achieve; Ask any writer. Drama? Action? Romance? All in a day's work. But making your audience *laugh?* Now *that's* tough. On top of that, these strips are *also* some of my first explorations into the world of pen and ink cartooning, and boy, they look it! My hand has become a great deal more steady since those early days.

So why include these old strips here?

Well, partly because, despite their being so young and rough around the edges, they still make me laugh, and *that's* something! But also... These strips comprise certain *foundation stones* upon which a number of other important events will soon be laid. Because, as it turns out, Quinton *was* a good scout and spy. A catalyst which *did* have a huge impact on reality.

And so. . , the *Millbrook Strips* take place during a period in the T&K world history, about 1000 years before the events surrounding Rubel and Varkias begin...

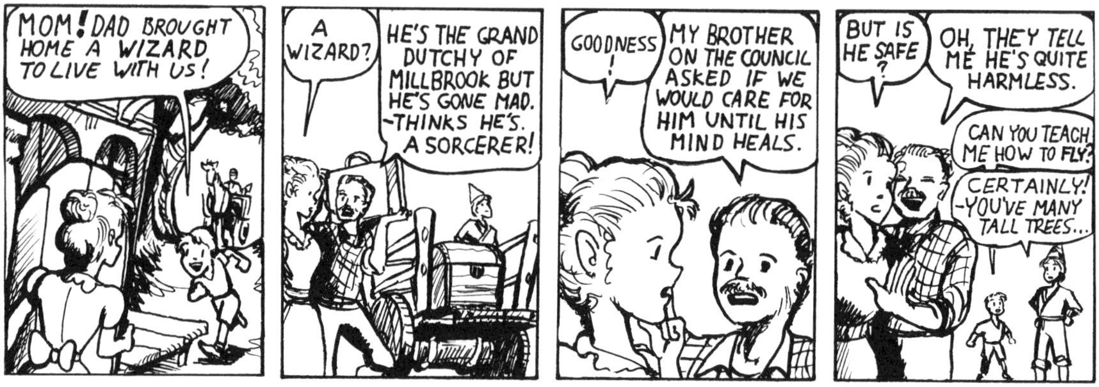
MOM! DAD BROUGHT HOME A WIZARD TO LIVE WITH US!
A WIZARD?
HE'S THE GRAND DUTCHY OF MILLBROOK BUT HE'S GONE MAD. -THINKS HE'S. A SORCERER!
GOODNESS!
MY BROTHER ON THE COUNCIL ASKED IF WE WOULD CARE FOR HIM UNTIL HIS MIND HEALS.
BUT IS HE SAFE?
OH, THEY TELL ME HE'S QUITE HARMLESS.
CAN YOU TEACH ME HOW TO FLY?
CERTAINLY! -YOU'VE MANY TALL TREES...

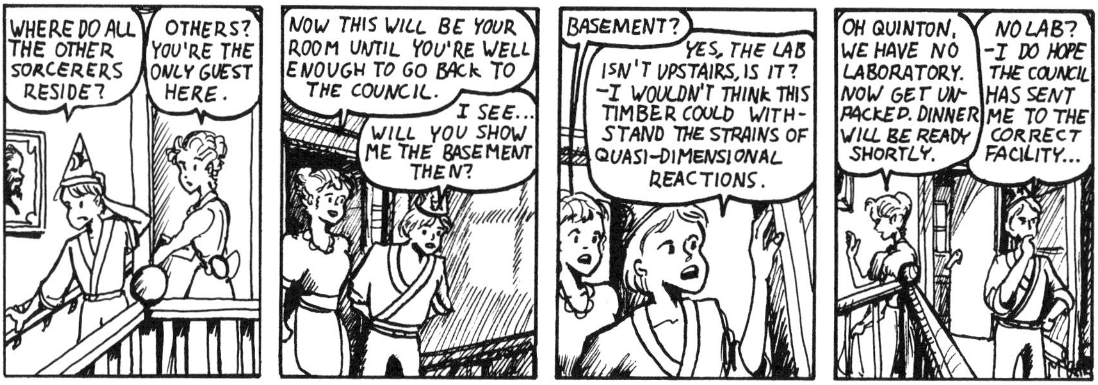
WHERE DO ALL THE OTHER SORCERERS RESIDE?
OTHERS? YOU'RE THE ONLY GUEST HERE.
NOW THIS WILL BE YOUR ROOM UNTIL YOU'RE WELL ENOUGH TO GO BACK TO THE COUNCIL.
I SEE... WILL YOU SHOW ME THE BASEMENT THEN?
BASEMENT?
YES, THE LAB ISN'T UPSTAIRS, IS IT? -I WOULDN'T THINK THIS TIMBER COULD WITHSTAND THE STRAINS OF QUASI-DIMENSIONAL REACTIONS.
OH QUINTON, WE HAVE NO LABORATORY. NOW GET UNPACKED. DINNER WILL BE READY SHORTLY.
NO LAB? -I DO HOPE THE COUNCIL HAS SENT ME TO THE CORRECT FACILITY...

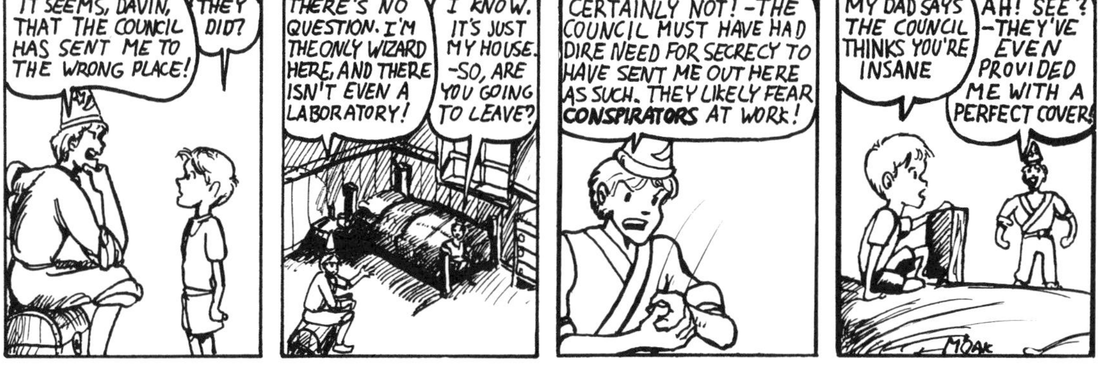
IT SEEMS, DAVIN, THAT THE COUNCIL HAS SENT ME TO THE WRONG PLACE!
THEY DID?
THERE'S NO QUESTION. I'M THE ONLY WIZARD HERE, AND THERE ISN'T EVEN A LABORATORY!
I KNOW. IT'S JUST MY HOUSE. -SO, ARE YOU GOING TO LEAVE?
CERTAINLY NOT! -THE COUNCIL MUST HAVE HAD DIRE NEED FOR SECRECY TO HAVE SENT ME OUT HERE AS SUCH. THEY LIKELY FEAR CONSPIRATORS AT WORK!
MY DAD SAYS THE COUNCIL THINKS YOU'RE INSANE
AH! SEE? -THEY'VE EVEN PROVIDED ME WITH A PERFECT COVER!
MOAK

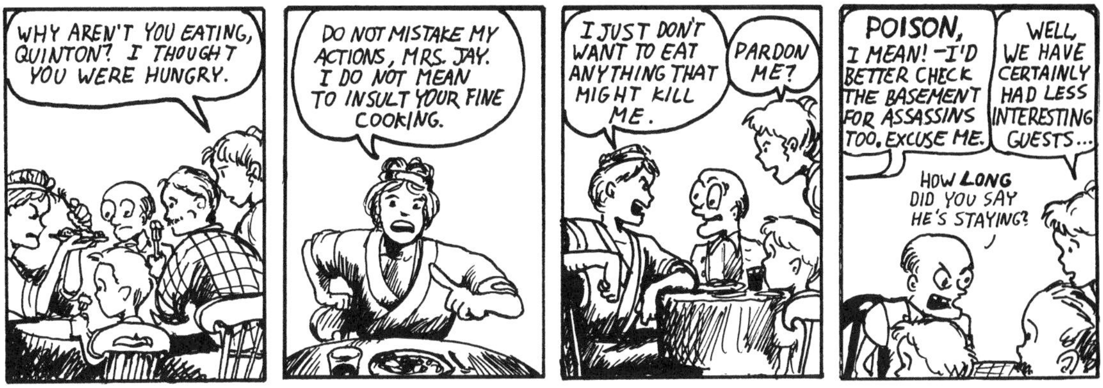
WHY AREN'T YOU EATING, QUINTON? I THOUGHT YOU WERE HUNGRY.
DO NOT MISTAKE MY ACTIONS, MRS. JAY. I DO NOT MEAN TO INSULT YOUR FINE COOKING.
I JUST DON'T WANT TO EAT ANYTHING THAT MIGHT KILL ME.
PARDON ME?
POISON, I MEAN! —I'D BETTER CHECK THE BASEMENT FOR ASSASSINS TOO. EXCUSE ME.
WELL, WE HAVE CERTAINLY HAD LESS INTERESTING GUESTS...
HOW **LONG** DID YOU SAY HE'S STAYING?

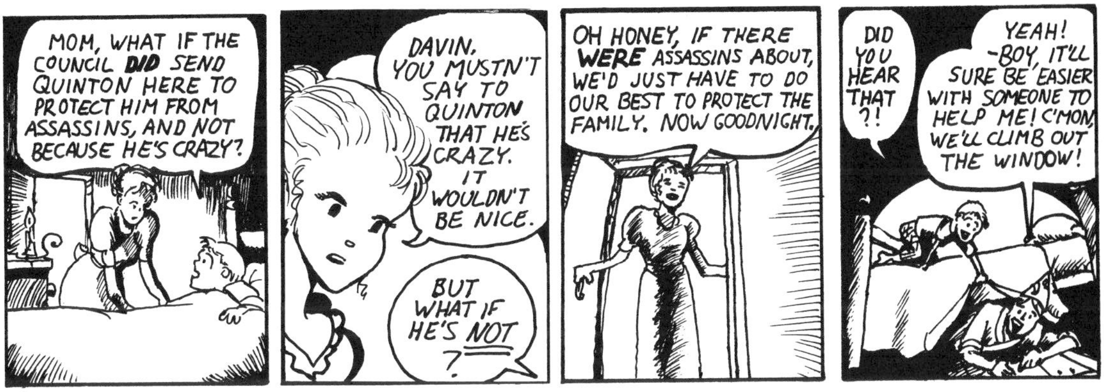
MOM, WHAT IF THE COUNCIL **DID** SEND QUINTON HERE TO PROTECT HIM FROM ASSASSINS, AND NOT BECAUSE HE'S CRAZY?
DAVIN, YOU MUSTN'T SAY TO QUINTON THAT HE'S CRAZY. IT WOULDN'T BE NICE.
BUT WHAT IF HE'S NOT?
OH HONEY, IF THERE **WERE** ASSASSINS ABOUT, WE'D JUST HAVE TO DO OUR BEST TO PROTECT THE FAMILY. NOW GOODNIGHT.
DID YOU HEAR THAT?!
YEAH! —BOY, IT'LL SURE BE EASIER WITH SOMEONE TO HELP ME! C'MON, WE'LL CLIMB OUT THE WINDOW!

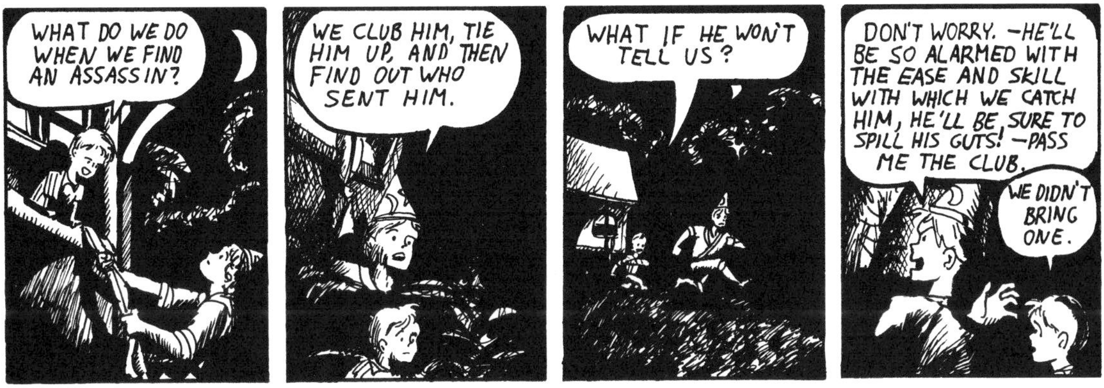
WHAT DO WE DO WHEN WE FIND AN ASSASSIN?
WE CLUB HIM, TIE HIM UP, AND THEN FIND OUT WHO SENT HIM.
WHAT IF HE WON'T TELL US?
DON'T WORRY. —HE'LL BE SO ALARMED WITH THE EASE AND SKILL WITH WHICH WE CATCH HIM, HE'LL BE SURE TO SPILL HIS GUTS! —PASS ME THE CLUB.
WE DIDN'T BRING ONE.

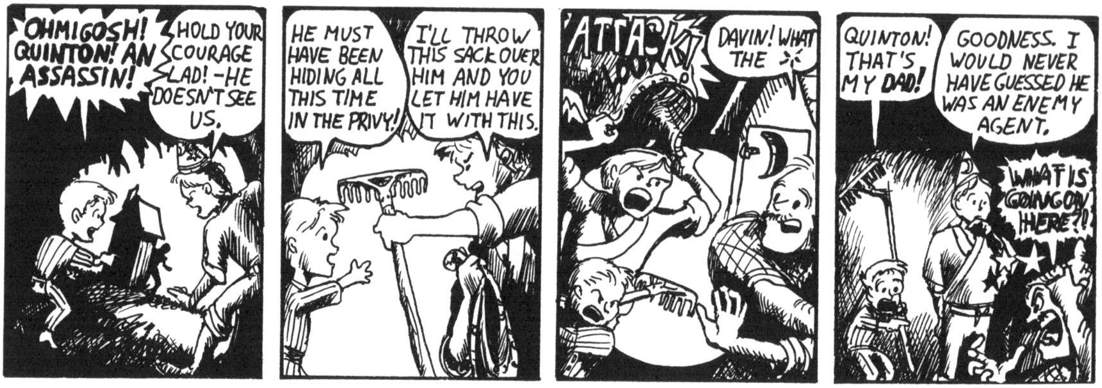
OHMIGOSH! QUINTON! AN ASSASSIN!
HOLD YOUR COURAGE LAD! -HE DOESN'T SEE US.
HE MUST HAVE BEEN HIDING ALL THIS TIME IN THE PRIVY!
I'LL THROW THIS SACK OVER HIM AND YOU LET HIM HAVE IT WITH THIS.
ATTACK!
DAVIN! WHAT THE
QUINTON! THAT'S MY DAD!
GOODNESS. I WOULD NEVER HAVE GUESSED HE WAS AN ENEMY AGENT.
WHAT IS GOING ON HERE?!

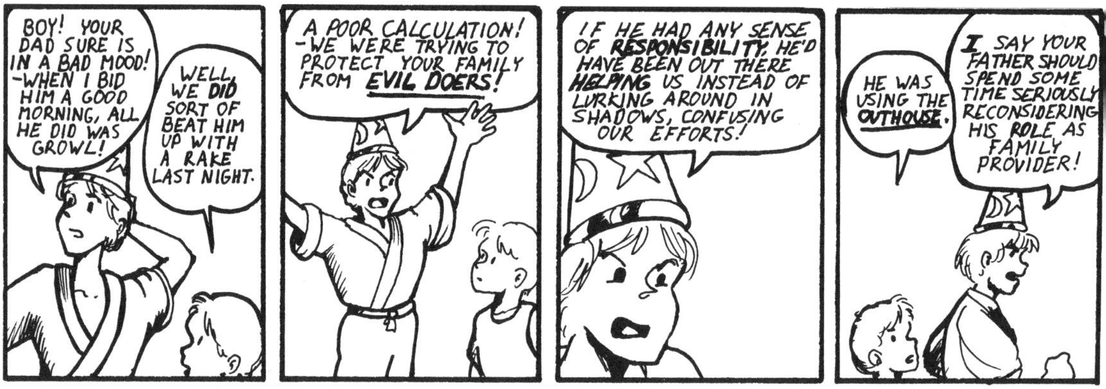
BOY! YOUR DAD SURE IS IN A BAD MOOD! -WHEN I BID HIM A GOOD MORNING, ALL HE DID WAS GROWL!
WELL, WE DID SORT OF BEAT HIM UP WITH A RAKE LAST NIGHT.
A POOR CALCULATION! -WE WERE TRYING TO PROTECT YOUR FAMILY FROM EVIL DOERS!
IF HE HAD ANY SENSE OF RESPONSIBILITY, HE'D HAVE BEEN OUT THERE HELPING US INSTEAD OF LURKING AROUND IN SHADOWS, CONFUSING OUR EFFORTS!
HE WAS USING THE OUTHOUSE.
I SAY YOUR FATHER SHOULD SPEND SOME TIME SERIOUSLY RECONSIDERING HIS ROLE AS FAMILY PROVIDER!

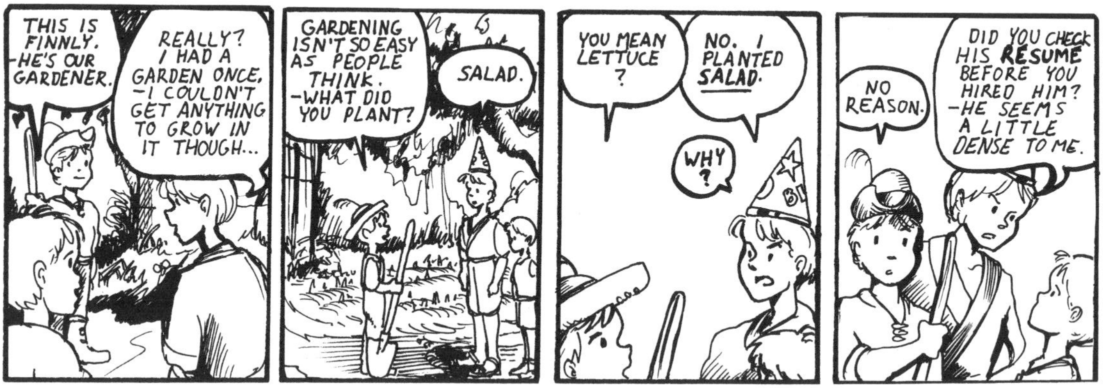
THIS IS FINNLY. -HE'S OUR GARDENER.
REALLY? I HAD A GARDEN ONCE, -I COULDN'T GET ANYTHING TO GROW IN IT THOUGH...
GARDENING ISN'T SO EASY AS PEOPLE THINK. -WHAT DID YOU PLANT?
SALAD.
YOU MEAN LETTUCE?
NO. I PLANTED SALAD.
WHY?
NO REASON.
DID YOU CHECK HIS RESUME BEFORE YOU HIRED HIM? -HE SEEMS A LITTLE DENSE TO ME.

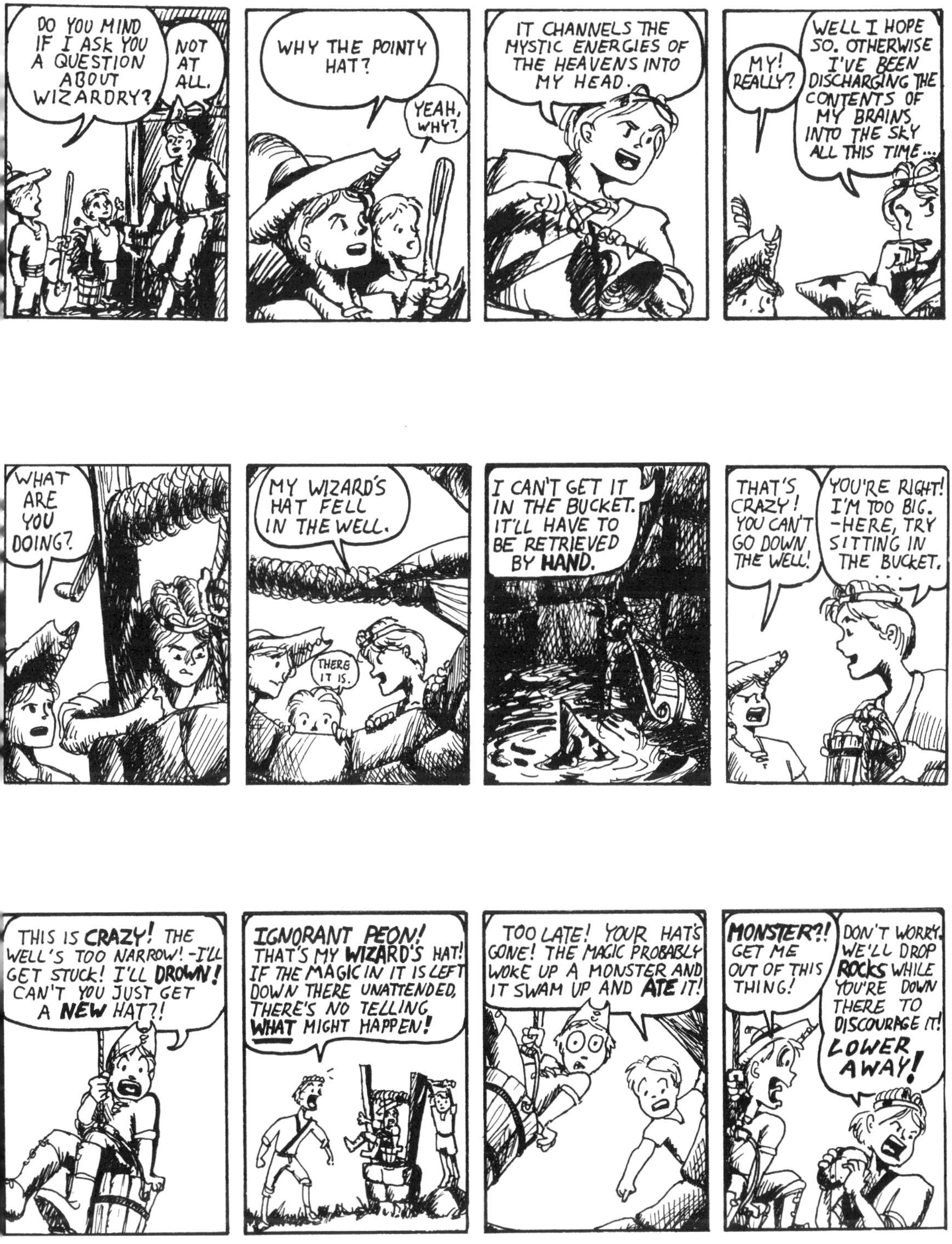
DO YOU MIND IF I ASK YOU A QUESTION ABOUT WIZARDRY?
NOT AT ALL.
WHY THE POINTY HAT?
YEAH, WHY?
IT CHANNELS THE MYSTIC ENERGIES OF THE HEAVENS INTO MY HEAD.
MY! REALLY?
WELL I HOPE SO. OTHERWISE I'VE BEEN DISCHARGING THE CONTENTS OF MY BRAINS INTO THE SKY ALL THIS TIME...
WHAT ARE YOU DOING?
MY WIZARD'S HAT FELL IN THE WELL.
THERE IT IS.
I CAN'T GET IT IN THE BUCKET. IT'LL HAVE TO BE RETRIEVED BY **HAND**.
THAT'S CRAZY! YOU CAN'T GO DOWN THE WELL!
YOU'RE RIGHT! I'M TOO BIG. -HERE, TRY SITTING IN THE BUCKET. . . .
THIS IS **CRAZY**! THE WELL'S TOO NARROW! -I'LL GET STUCK! I'LL **DROWN**! CAN'T YOU JUST GET A **NEW** HAT?!
IGNORANT PEON! THAT'S MY **WIZARD'S** HAT! IF THE **MAGIC** IN IT IS LEFT DOWN THERE UNATTENDED, THERE'S NO TELLING **WHAT** MIGHT HAPPEN!
TOO LATE! YOUR HAT'S GONE! THE MAGIC PROBABLY WOKE UP A MONSTER AND IT SWAM UP AND **ATE** IT!
MONSTER?! GET ME OUT OF THIS THING!
DON'T WORRY. WE'LL DROP **ROCKS** WHILE YOU'RE DOWN THERE TO DISCOURAGE IT! **LOWER AWAY!**

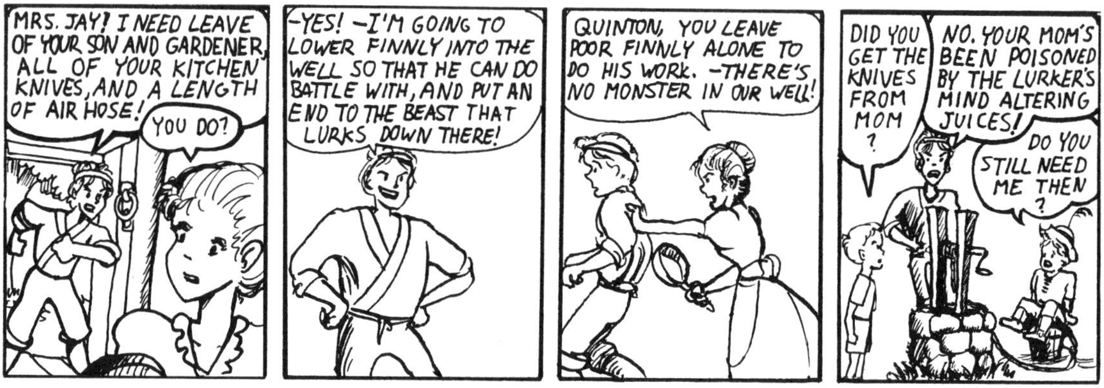
MRS. JAY! I NEED LEAVE OF YOUR SON AND GARDENER, ALL OF YOUR KITCHEN KNIVES, AND A LENGTH OF AIR HOSE!
YOU DO?
-YES! -I'M GOING TO LOWER FINNLY INTO THE WELL SO THAT HE CAN DO BATTLE WITH, AND PUT AN END TO THE BEAST THAT LURKS DOWN THERE!
QUINTON, YOU LEAVE POOR FINNLY ALONE TO DO HIS WORK. -THERE'S NO MONSTER IN OUR WELL!
DID YOU GET THE KNIVES FROM MOM?
NO. YOUR MOM'S BEEN POISONED BY THE LURKER'S MIND ALTERING JUICES!
DO YOU STILL NEED ME THEN?

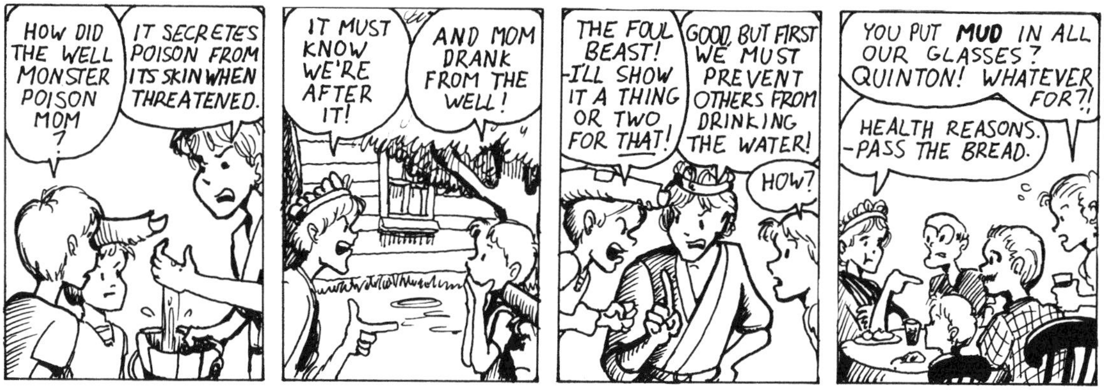
HOW DID THE WELL MONSTER POISON MOM?
IT SECRETES POISON FROM ITS SKIN WHEN THREATENED.
IT MUST KNOW WE'RE AFTER IT!
AND MOM DRANK FROM THE WELL!
THE FOUL BEAST! -I'LL SHOW IT A THING OR TWO FOR THAT!
GOOD, BUT FIRST WE MUST PREVENT OTHERS FROM DRINKING THE WATER!
HOW?
YOU PUT MUD IN ALL OUR GLASSES? QUINTON! WHATEVER FOR?!
HEALTH REASONS. -PASS THE BREAD.

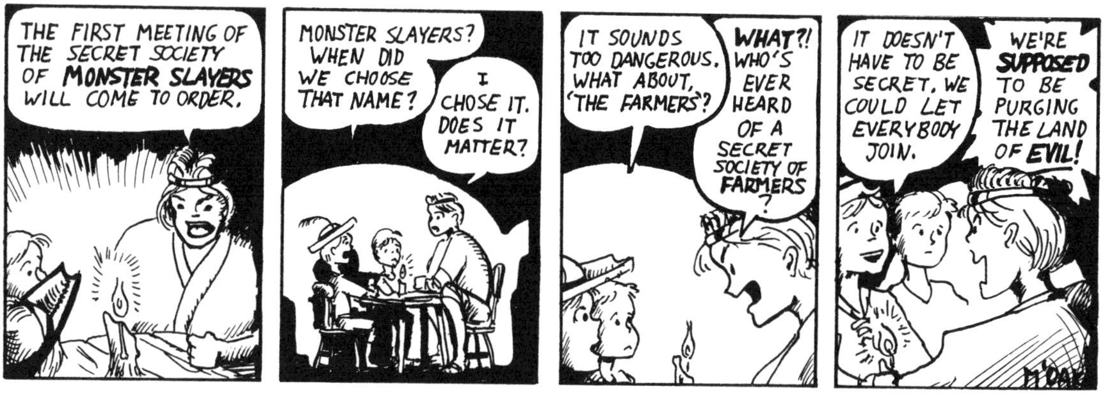
THE FIRST MEETING OF THE SECRET SOCIETY OF MONSTER SLAYERS WILL COME TO ORDER.
MONSTER SLAYERS? WHEN DID WE CHOOSE THAT NAME?
I CHOSE IT. DOES IT MATTER?
IT SOUNDS TOO DANGEROUS. WHAT ABOUT, 'THE FARMERS'?
WHAT?! WHO'S EVER HEARD OF A SECRET SOCIETY OF FARMERS?
IT DOESN'T HAVE TO BE SECRET. WE COULD LET EVERYBODY JOIN.
WE'RE SUPPOSED TO BE PURGING THE LAND OF EVIL!
M'DAL

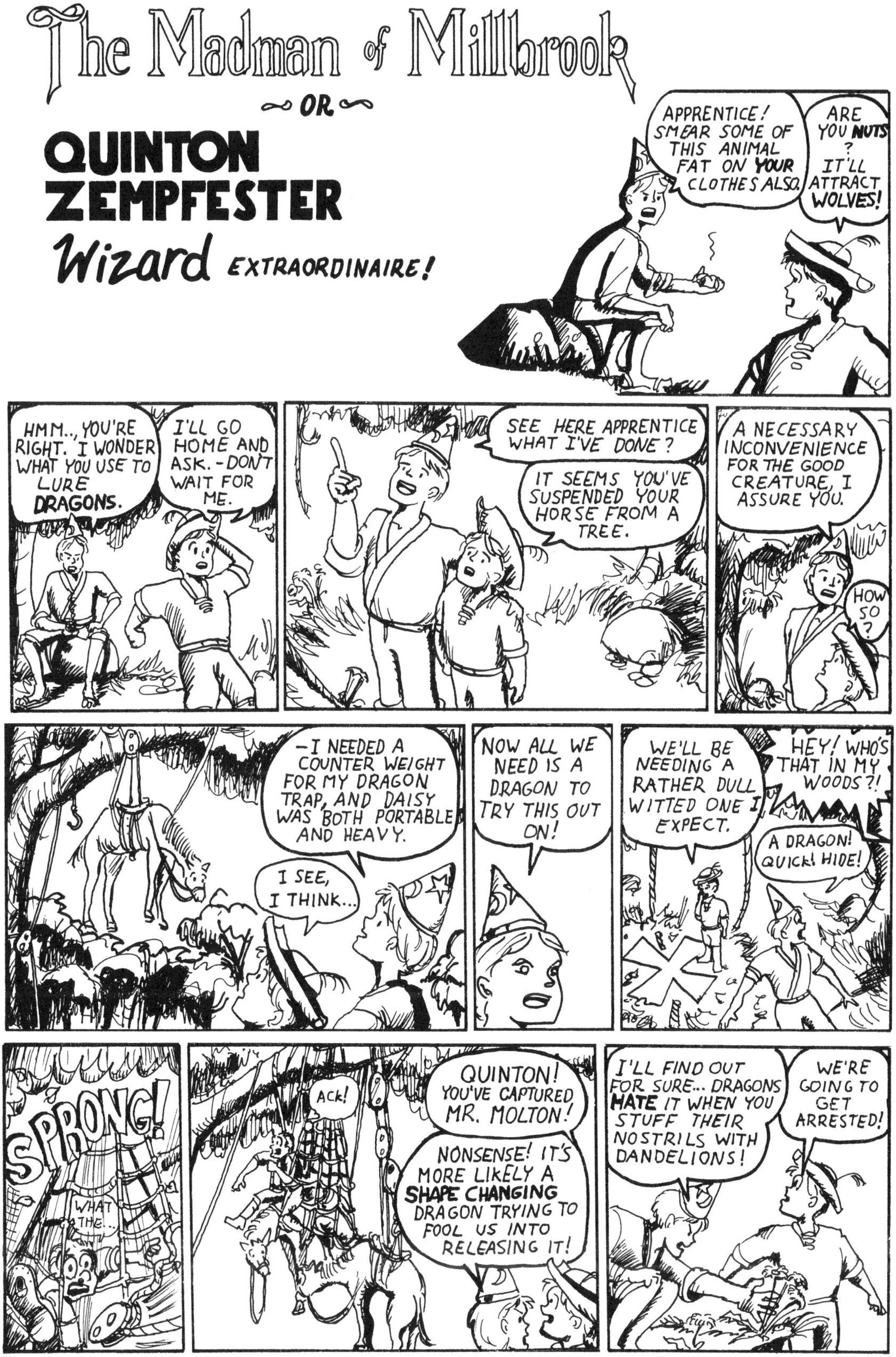
The Madman of Millbrook
OR
QUINTON ZEMPFESTER
Wizard EXTRAORDINAIRE!
APPRENTICE! SMEAR SOME OF THIS ANIMAL FAT ON YOUR CLOTHES ALSO.
ARE YOU NUTS? IT'LL ATTRACT WOLVES!
HMM.., YOU'RE RIGHT. I WONDER WHAT YOU USE TO LURE DRAGONS.
I'LL GO HOME AND ASK. -DON'T WAIT FOR ME.
SEE HERE APPRENTICE WHAT I'VE DONE?
IT SEEMS YOU'VE SUSPENDED YOUR HORSE FROM A TREE.
A NECESSARY INCONVENIENCE FOR THE GOOD CREATURE, I ASSURE YOU.
HOW SO?
-I NEEDED A COUNTER WEIGHT FOR MY DRAGON TRAP, AND DAISY WAS BOTH PORTABLE AND HEAVY.
I SEE, I THINK...
NOW ALL WE NEED IS A DRAGON TO TRY THIS OUT ON!
WE'LL BE NEEDING A RATHER DULL WITTED ONE I EXPECT.
HEY! WHO'S THAT IN MY WOODS?!
A DRAGON! QUICK! HIDE!
SPRONG!
WHAT THE...
ACK!
QUINTON! YOU'VE CAPTURED MR. MOLTON!
NONSENSE! IT'S MORE LIKELY A SHAPE CHANGING DRAGON TRYING TO FOOL US INTO RELEASING IT!
I'LL FIND OUT FOR SURE... DRAGONS HATE IT WHEN YOU STUFF THEIR NOSTRILS WITH DANDELIONS!
WE'RE GOING TO GET ARRESTED!

Chapter 7

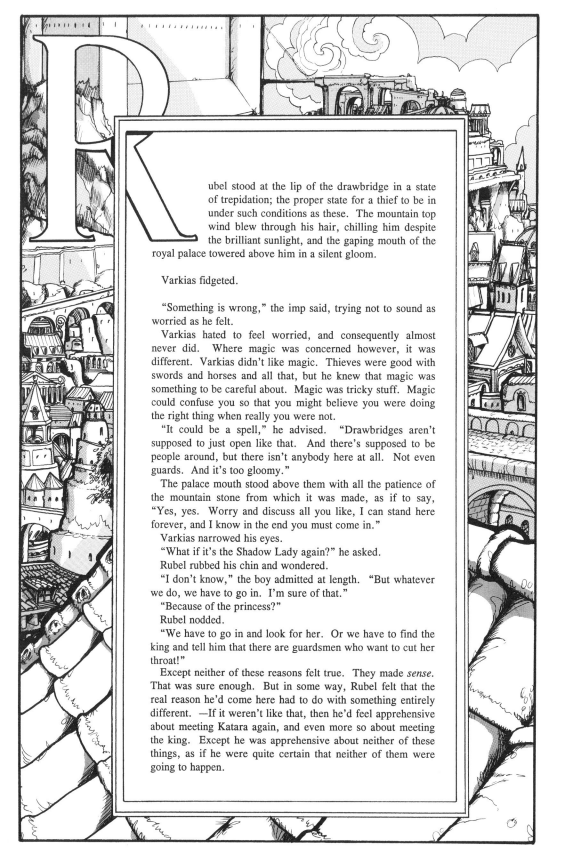

Rubel stood at the lip of the drawbridge in a state of trepidation; the proper state for a thief to be in under such conditions as these. The mountain top wind blew through his hair, chilling him despite the brilliant sunlight, and the gaping mouth of the royal palace towered above him in a silent gloom.

Varkias fidgeted.

"Something is wrong," the imp said, trying not to sound as worried as he felt.

Varkias hated to feel worried, and consequently almost never did. Where magic was concerned however, it was different. Varkias didn't like magic. Thieves were good with swords and horses and all that, but he knew that magic was something to be careful about. Magic was tricky stuff. Magic could confuse you so that you might believe you were doing the right thing when really you were not.

"It could be a spell," he advised. "Drawbridges aren't supposed to just open like that. And there's supposed to be people around, but there isn't anybody here at all. Not even guards. And it's too gloomy."

The palace mouth stood above them with all the patience of the mountain stone from which it was made, as if to say, "Yes, yes. Worry and discuss all you like, I can stand here forever, and I know in the end you must come in."

Varkias narrowed his eyes.

"What if it's the Shadow Lady again?" he asked.

Rubel rubbed his chin and wondered.

"I don't know," the boy admitted at length. "But whatever we do, we have to go in. I'm sure of that."

"Because of the princess?"

Rubel nodded.

"We have to go in and look for her. Or we have to find the king and tell him that there are guardsmen who want to cut her throat!"

Except neither of these reasons felt true. They made *sense*. That was sure enough. But in some way, Rubel felt that the real reason he'd come here had to do with something entirely different. —If it weren't like that, then he'd feel apprehensive about meeting Katara again, and even more so about meeting the king. Except he was apprehensive about neither of these things, as if he were quite certain that neither of them were going to happen.

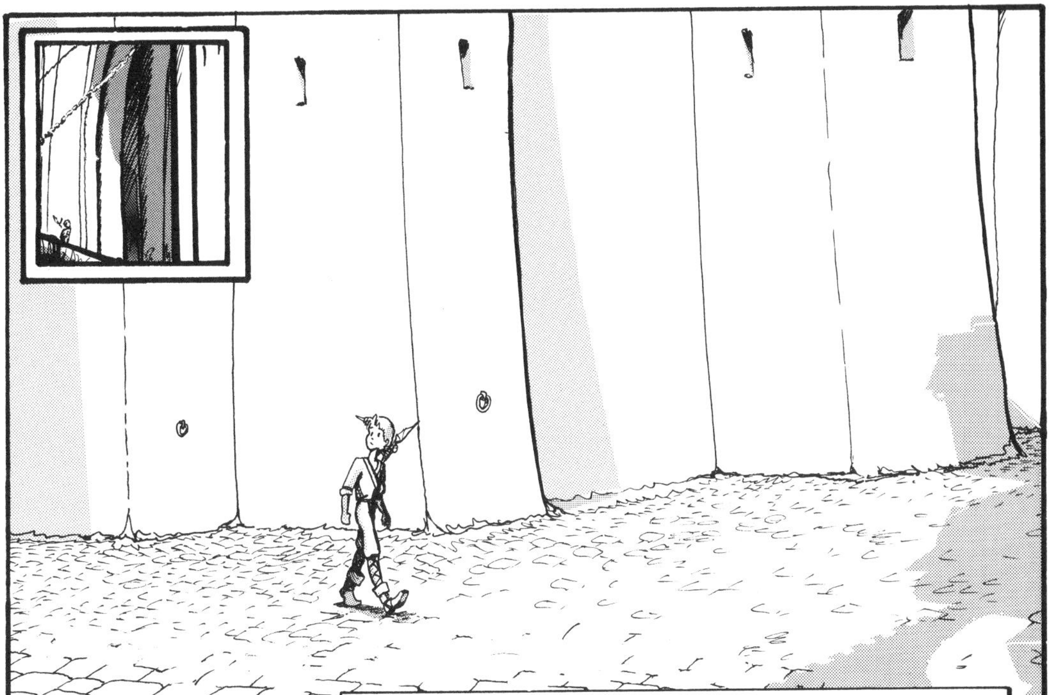

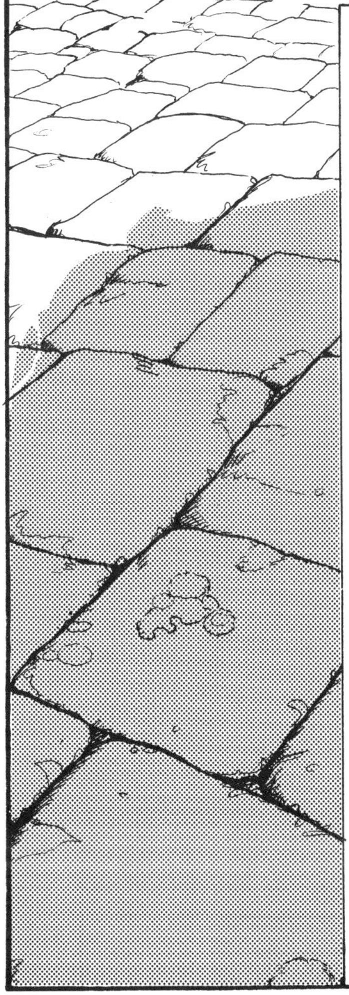

Indeed, the whole act of coming to the palace and of fighting before with the city guardsmen; all of that had seemed somehow abrupt and misplaced. Not entirely right. It was a quiet, unsettling sort of feeling, and it had grown less quiet and more unsettling until it was now sitting in his mind like a very plain object, impatient to be noticed, but cast at a frustrating attitude which made it impossible to recognize. This feeling urged him forward, seeming to know all about where he was supposed to go, if only he would follow. . .

Rubel shook himself like a wet dog and made impatient huffing noises.

"Huff!" he went in a firm and final way which he hoped would bolster his courage and make the odd feeling go away. It worked, but only a little.

"Huff!" Varkias concurred.

And so, there not seeming to be much choice, Rubel clenched his teeth and adjusted his knife. He paused, touched once the warm surface of the fob watch still tucked beneath his belt, and then taking a deep breath, he stepped out upon the centuries old timber. Keeping to the very middle of the drawbridge, he and Varkias crossed into the ominous silence of the royal palace.

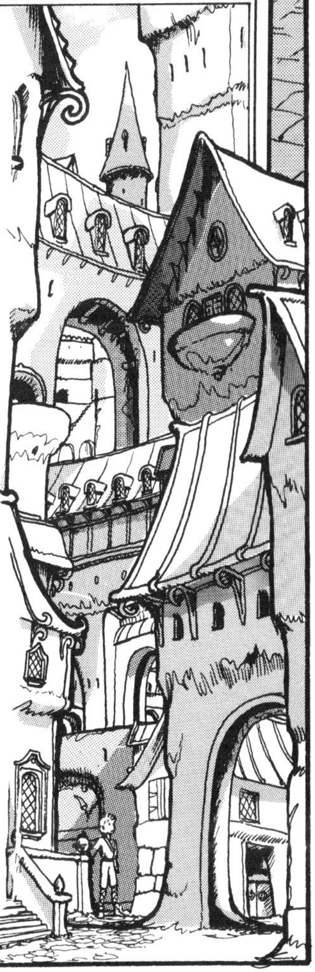

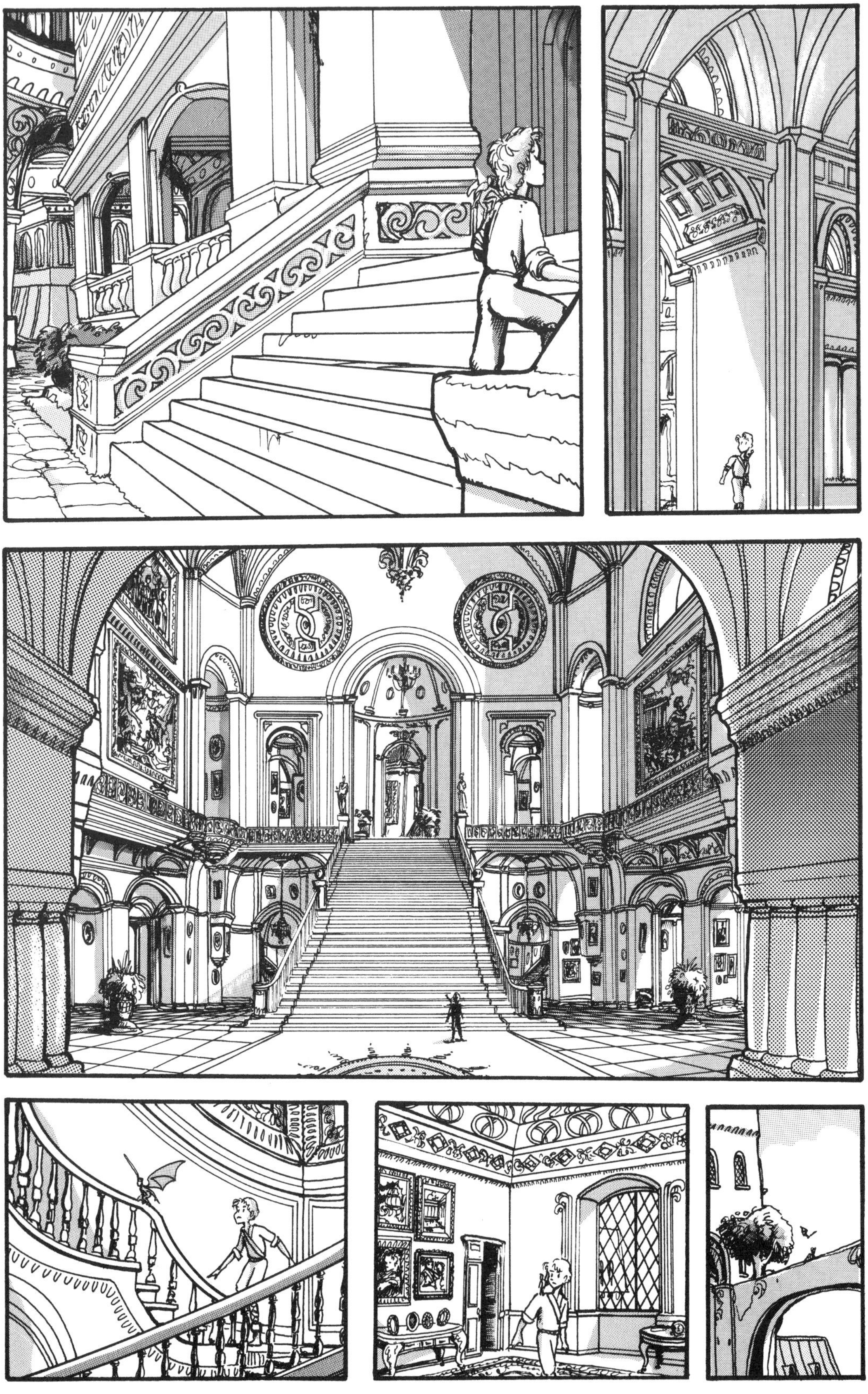

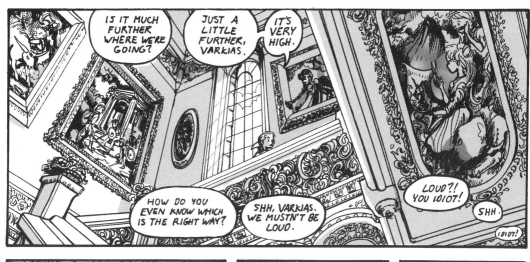

IS IT MUCH FURTHER WHERE WE'RE GOING?

JUST A LITTLE FURTHER, VARKIAS.

IT'S VERY HIGH.

LOUD?! YOU IDIOT!

SHH.

IDIOT!

HOW DO YOU EVEN KNOW WHICH IS THE RIGHT WAY?

SHH, VARKIAS. WE MUSTN'T BE LOUD.

SO?

IS THIS IT?

IS THAT WHERE THE PRINCESS IS?

NO.

I DON'T THINK SHE'S IN THE PALACE AT ALL.

YOU HAVE TO STAY CLOSE TO ME, VARKIAS.

WE'RE STRONGER WHEN WE'RE TOGETHER.

I WILL.

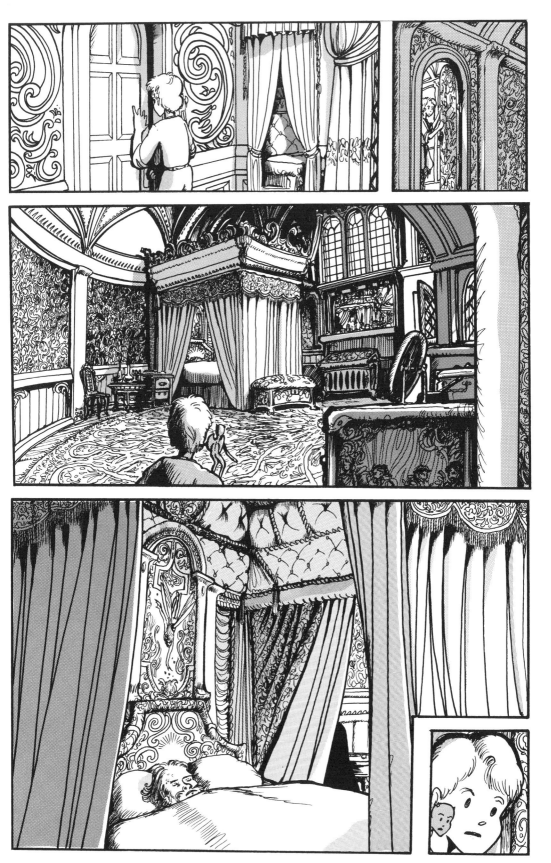

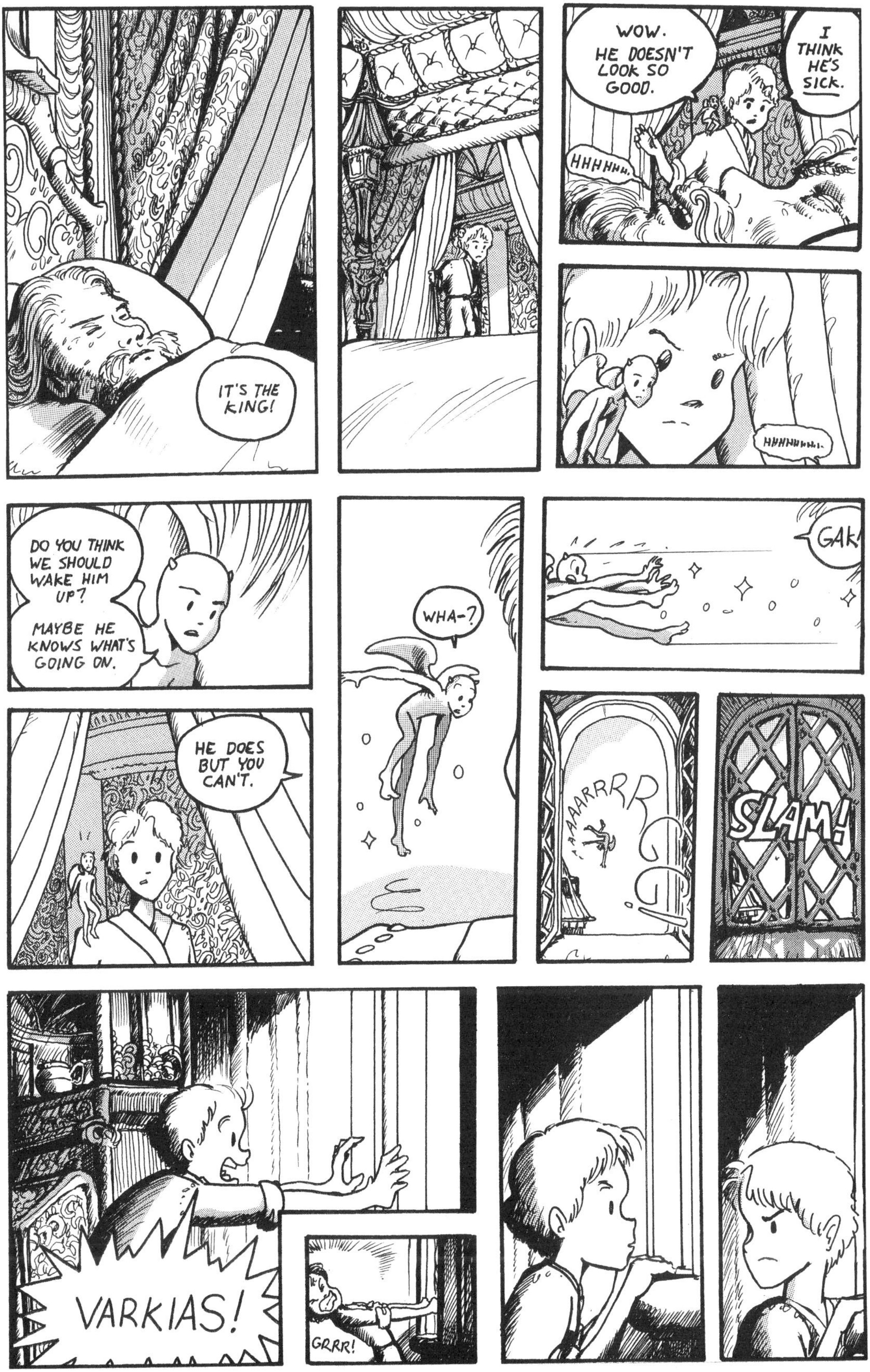

IT'S THE KING!
WOW. HE DOESN'T LOOK SO GOOD.
I THINK HE'S SICK.
HHHHHH...
HHHHHHH...
DO YOU THINK WE SHOULD WAKE HIM UP?
MAYBE HE KNOWS WHAT'S GOING ON.
HE DOES BUT YOU CAN'T.
WHA-?
GAK!
AAAARRRR
SLAM!
VARKIAS!
GRRR!

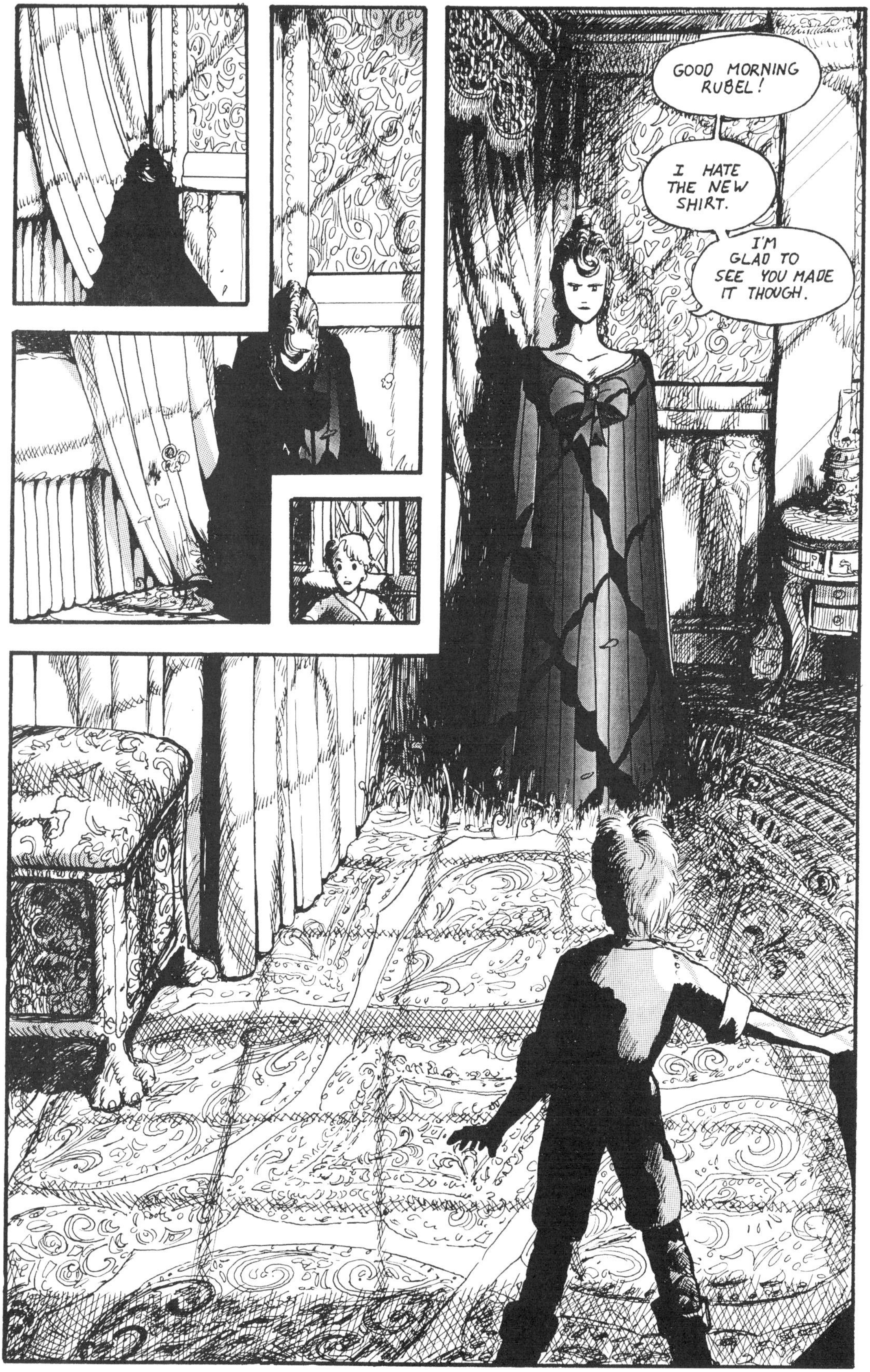
GOOD MORNING RUBEL!
I HATE THE NEW SHIRT.
I'M GLAD TO SEE YOU MADE IT THOUGH.

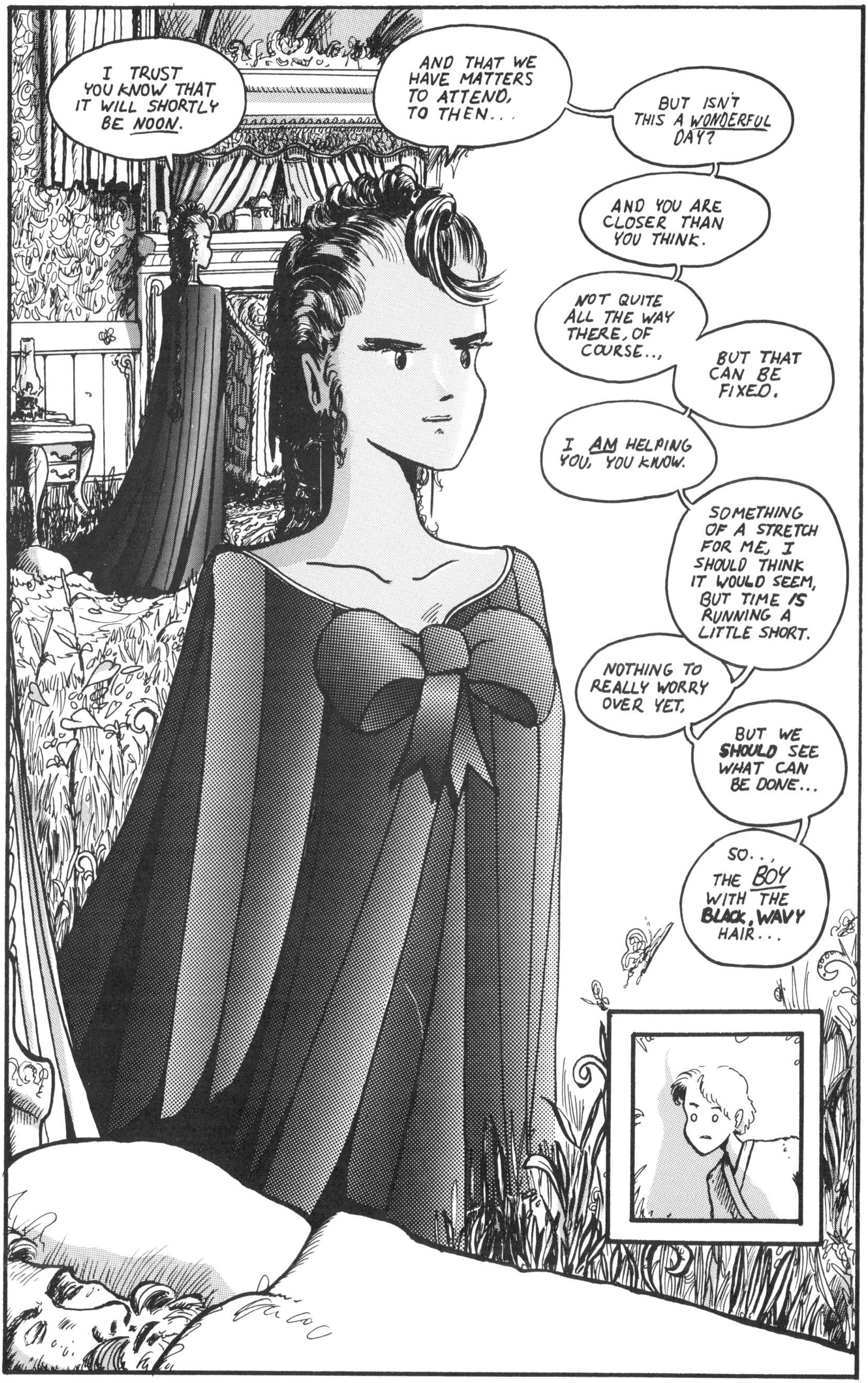
I TRUST YOU KNOW THAT IT WILL SHORTLY BE NOON.
AND THAT WE HAVE MATTERS TO ATTEND, TO THEN...
BUT ISN'T THIS A WONDERFUL DAY?
AND YOU ARE CLOSER THAN YOU THINK.
NOT QUITE ALL THE WAY THERE, OF COURSE..,
BUT THAT CAN BE FIXED.
I AM HELPING YOU, YOU KNOW.
SOMETHING OF A STRETCH FOR ME, I SHOULD THINK IT WOULD SEEM, BUT TIME IS RUNNING A LITTLE SHORT.
NOTHING TO REALLY WORRY OVER YET,
BUT WE SHOULD SEE WHAT CAN BE DONE...
SO.., THE BOY WITH THE BLACK, WAVY HAIR...

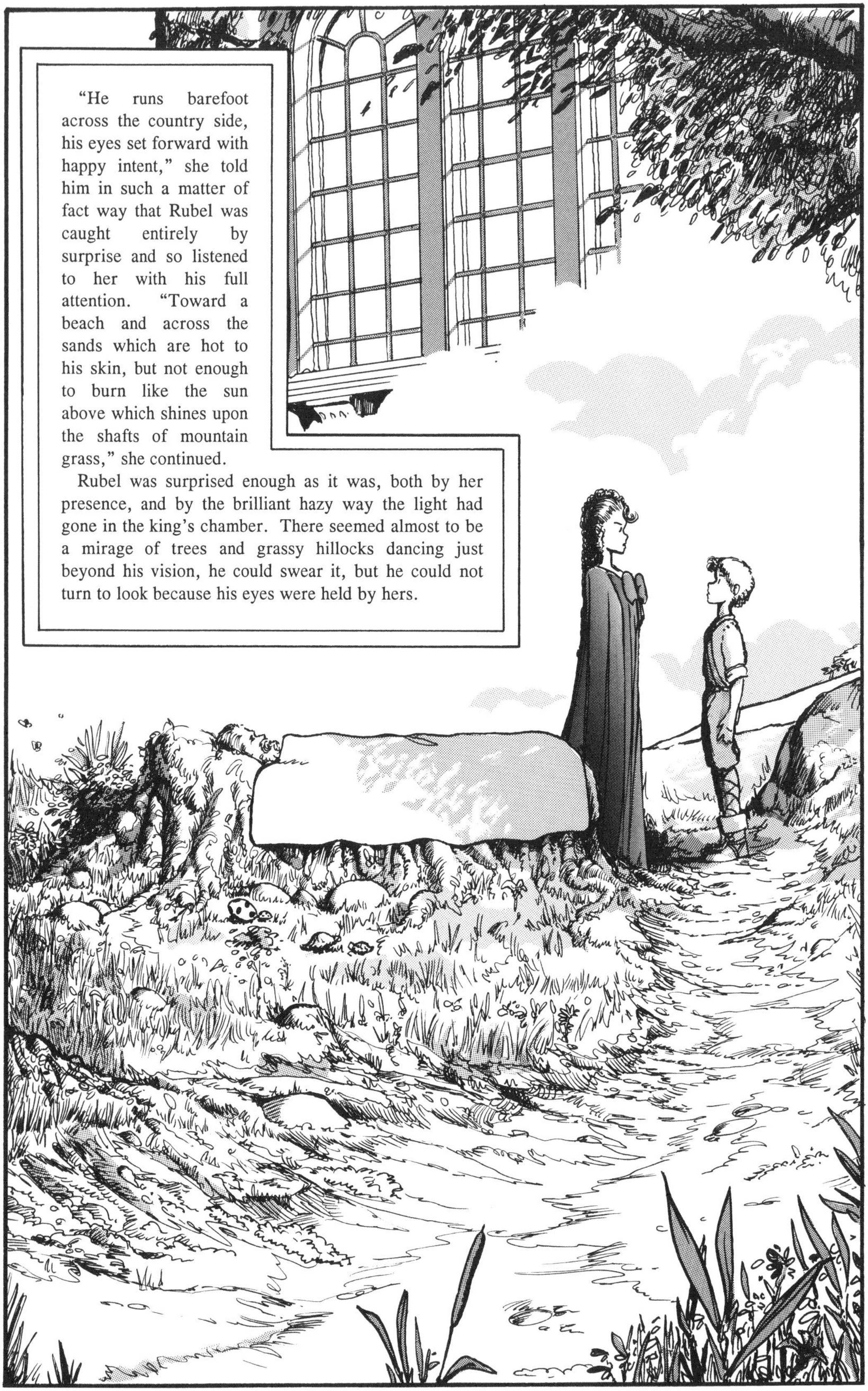

"He runs barefoot across the country side, his eyes set forward with happy intent," she told him in such a matter of fact way that Rubel was caught entirely by surprise and so listened to her with his full attention. "Toward a beach and across the sands which are hot to his skin, but not enough to burn like the sun above which shines upon the shafts of mountain grass," she continued.

Rubel was surprised enough as it was, both by her presence, and by the brilliant hazy way the light had gone in the king's chamber. There seemed almost to be a mirage of trees and grassy hillocks dancing just beyond his vision, he could swear it, but he could not turn to look because his eyes were held by hers.

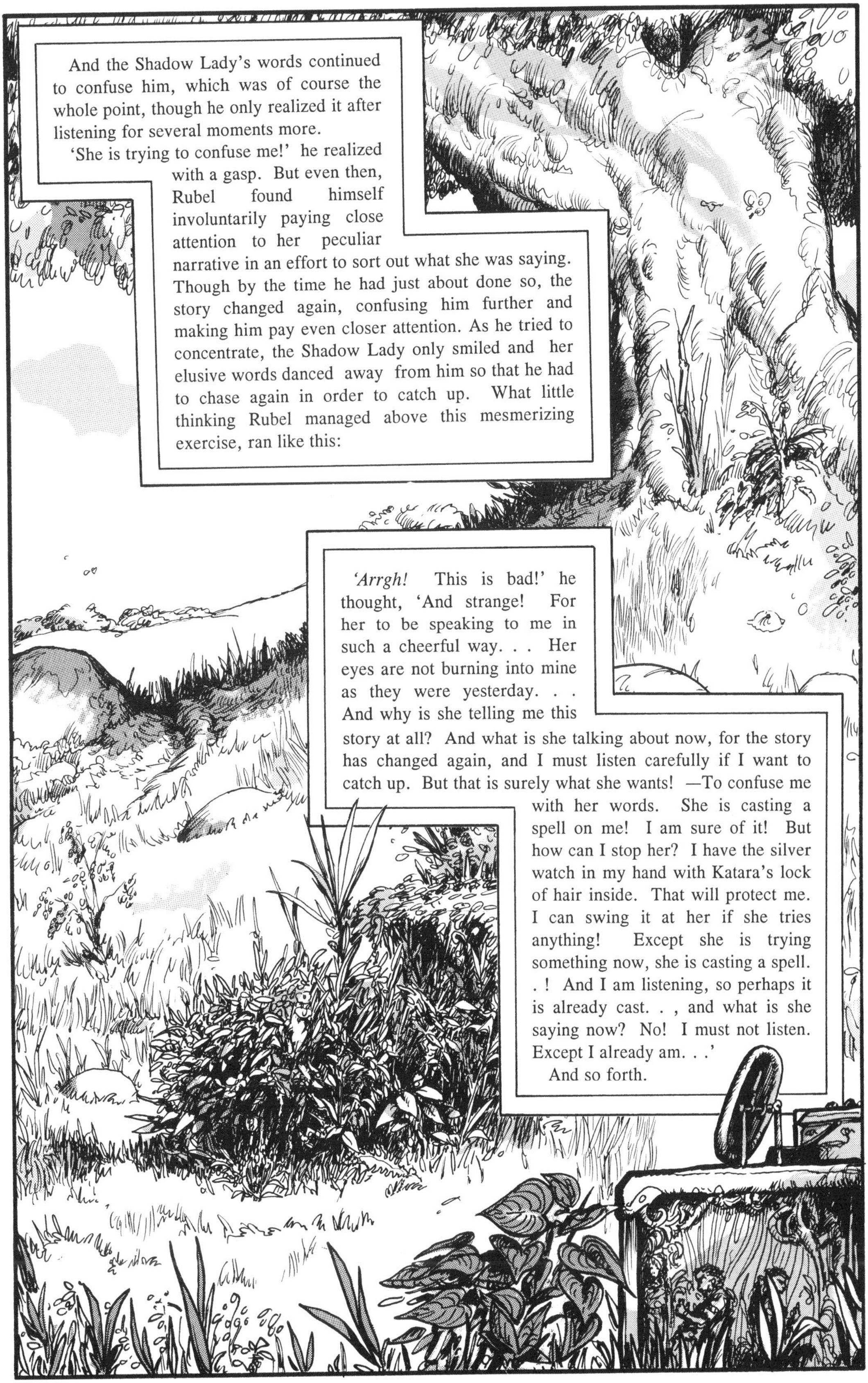
And the Shadow Lady's words continued to confuse him, which was of course the whole point, though he only realized it after listening for several moments more.
'She is trying to confuse me!' he realized with a gasp. But even then, Rubel found himself involuntarily paying close attention to her peculiar narrative in an effort to sort out what she was saying. Though by the time he had just about done so, the story changed again, confusing him further and making him pay even closer attention. As he tried to concentrate, the Shadow Lady only smiled and her elusive words danced away from him so that he had to chase again in order to catch up. What little thinking Rubel managed above this mesmerizing exercise, ran like this:
'Arrgh! This is bad!' he thought, 'And strange! For her to be speaking to me in such a cheerful way. . . Her eyes are not burning into mine as they were yesterday. . . And why is she telling me this story at all? And what is she talking about now, for the story has changed again, and I must listen carefully if I want to catch up. But that is surely what she wants! —To confuse me with her words. She is casting a spell on me! I am sure of it! But how can I stop her? I have the silver watch in my hand with Katara's lock of hair inside. That will protect me. I can swing it at her if she tries anything! Except she is trying something now, she is casting a spell. . ! And I am listening, so perhaps it is already cast. . , and what is she saying now? No! I must not listen. Except I already am. . .'
And so forth.

In the end, the struggle to make sense of it all caused Rubel's thinking to become so taxed and confused that the effort of trying to think at all began to seem altogether too much bother. Thus, without another thought, Rubel glided entirely beneath the Shadow Lady's influence, letting the story take him where it would.

It was then that it started to say things to him directly.

"Take this Rubel, and put it on," she said, holding out something to him. "Take the other one off first."
He did.
The thing she handed to him was his old shirt. The one he'd gotten rid of because it had been stained with captain McGovern's blood. Except, he was told, it wasn't really captain McGovern's blood at all. It was *his* blood; from where he had been struck at point blank by the captain's personal gun. —A fact he marveled at for having so easily overlooked. . .

And so, with a gasp of pain, Rubel was shocked back into full awareness. The hazy light flashed out as he collapsed to the floor.

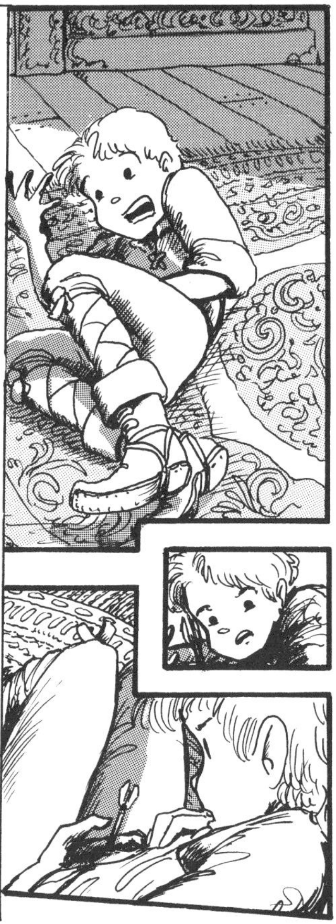

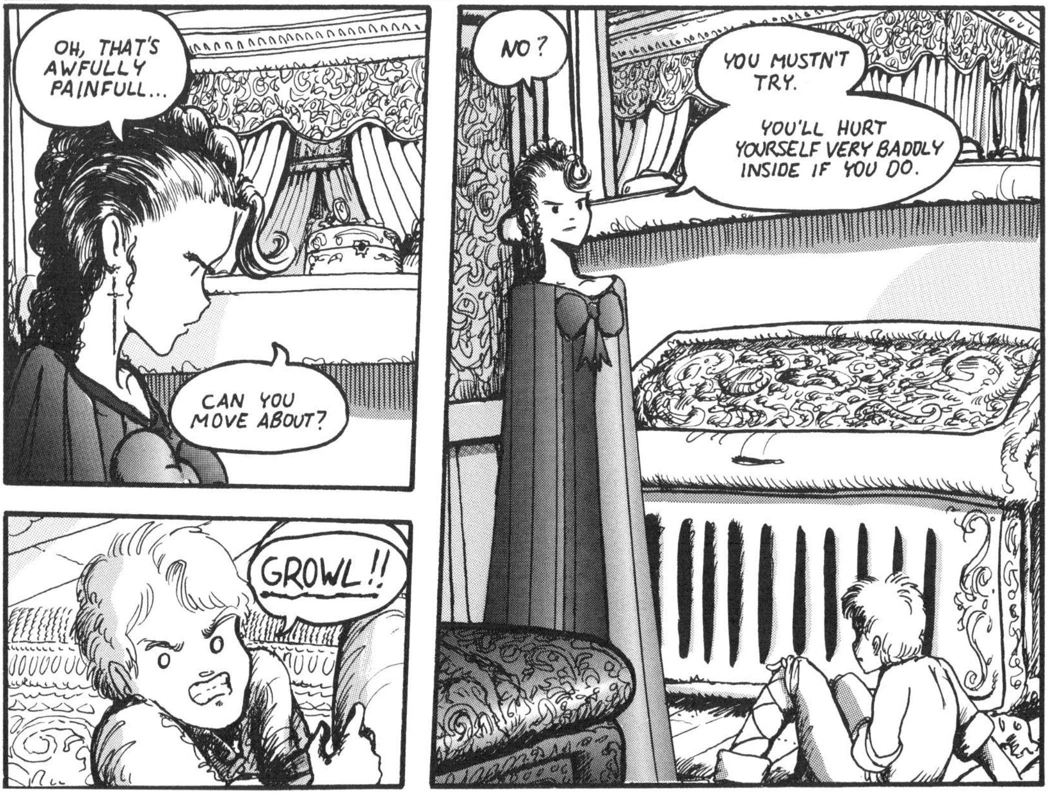
OH, THAT'S AWFULLY PAINFULL...
CAN YOU MOVE ABOUT?
GROWL!!
NO?
YOU MUSTN'T TRY.
YOU'LL HURT YOURSELF VERY BADDLY INSIDE IF YOU DO.

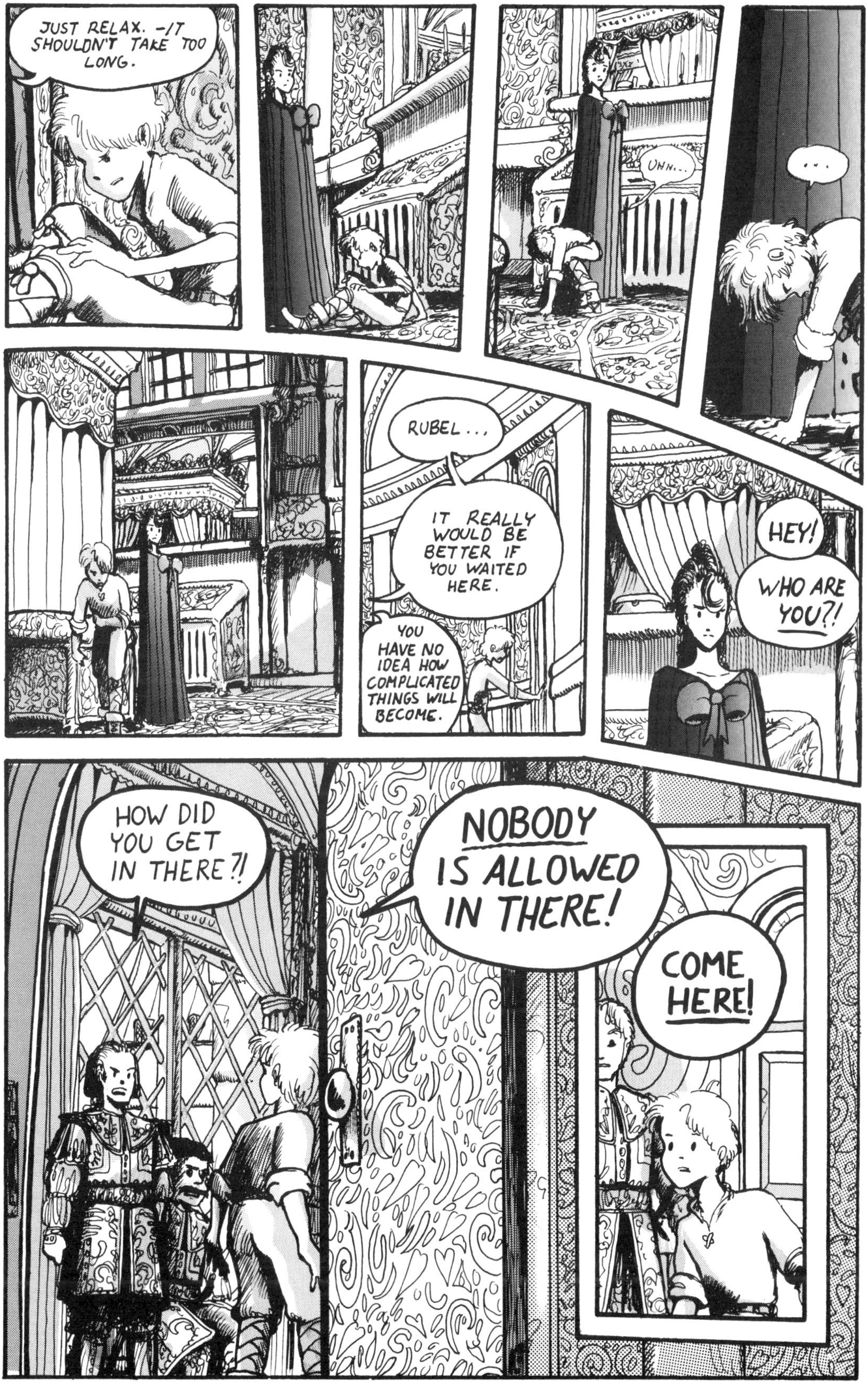
JUST RELAX. -IT SHOULDN'T TAKE TOO LONG.
UHN...
...
RUBEL...
IT REALLY WOULD BE BETTER IF YOU WAITED HERE.
YOU HAVE NO IDEA HOW COMPLICATED THINGS WILL BECOME.
HEY!
WHO ARE YOU?!
HOW DID YOU GET IN THERE?!
NOBODY IS ALLOWED IN THERE!
COME HERE!

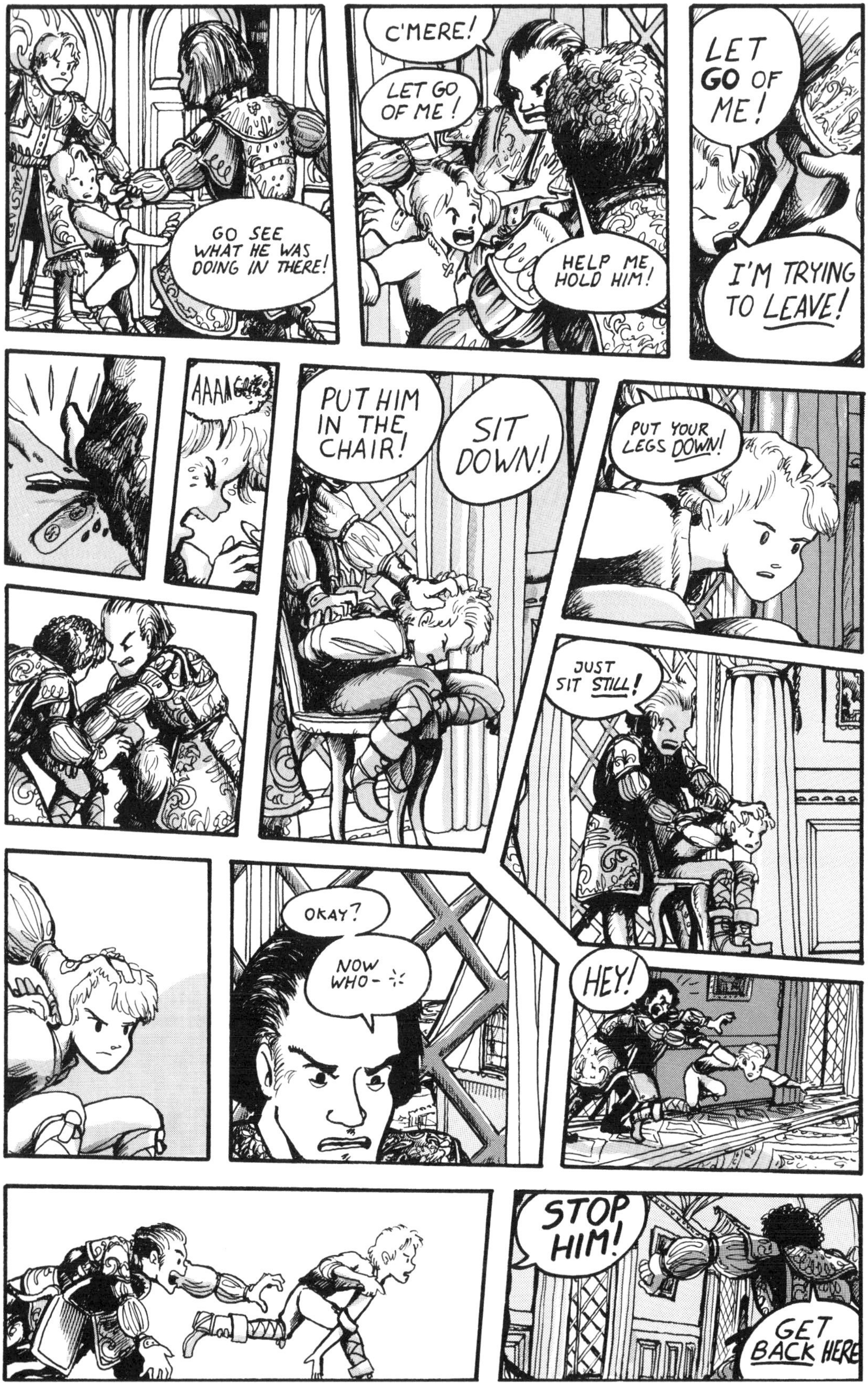
C'MERE!
LET GO OF ME!
GO SEE WHAT HE WAS DOING IN THERE!
HELP ME HOLD HIM!
LET GO OF ME!
I'M TRYING TO LEAVE!
AAAA
PUT HIM IN THE CHAIR!
SIT DOWN!
PUT YOUR LEGS DOWN!
JUST SIT STILL!
OKAY?
NOW WHO-
HEY!
STOP HIM!
GET BACK HERE

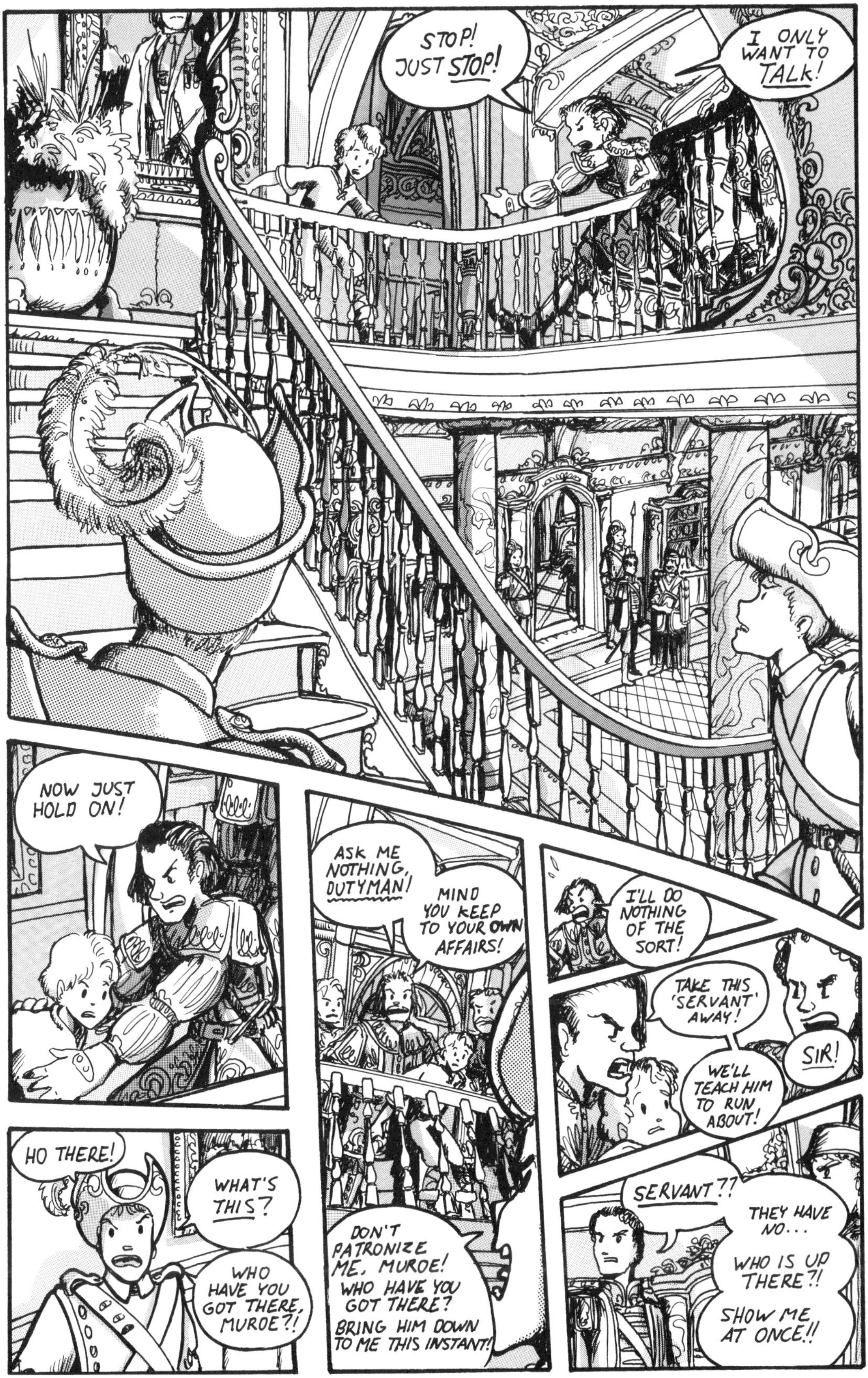
STOP! JUST STOP!
I ONLY WANT TO TALK!
NOW JUST HOLD ON!
ASK ME NOTHING, DUTYMAN!
MIND YOU KEEP TO YOUR OWN AFFAIRS!
I'LL DO NOTHING OF THE SORT!
TAKE THIS 'SERVANT' AWAY!
SIR!
WE'LL TEACH HIM TO RUN ABOUT!
HO THERE!
WHAT'S THIS?
WHO HAVE YOU GOT THERE, MUROE?!
DON'T PATRONIZE ME, MUROE!
WHO HAVE YOU GOT THERE?
BRING HIM DOWN TO ME THIS INSTANT!
SERVANT?!
THEY HAVE NO...
WHO IS UP THERE?!
SHOW ME AT ONCE!!

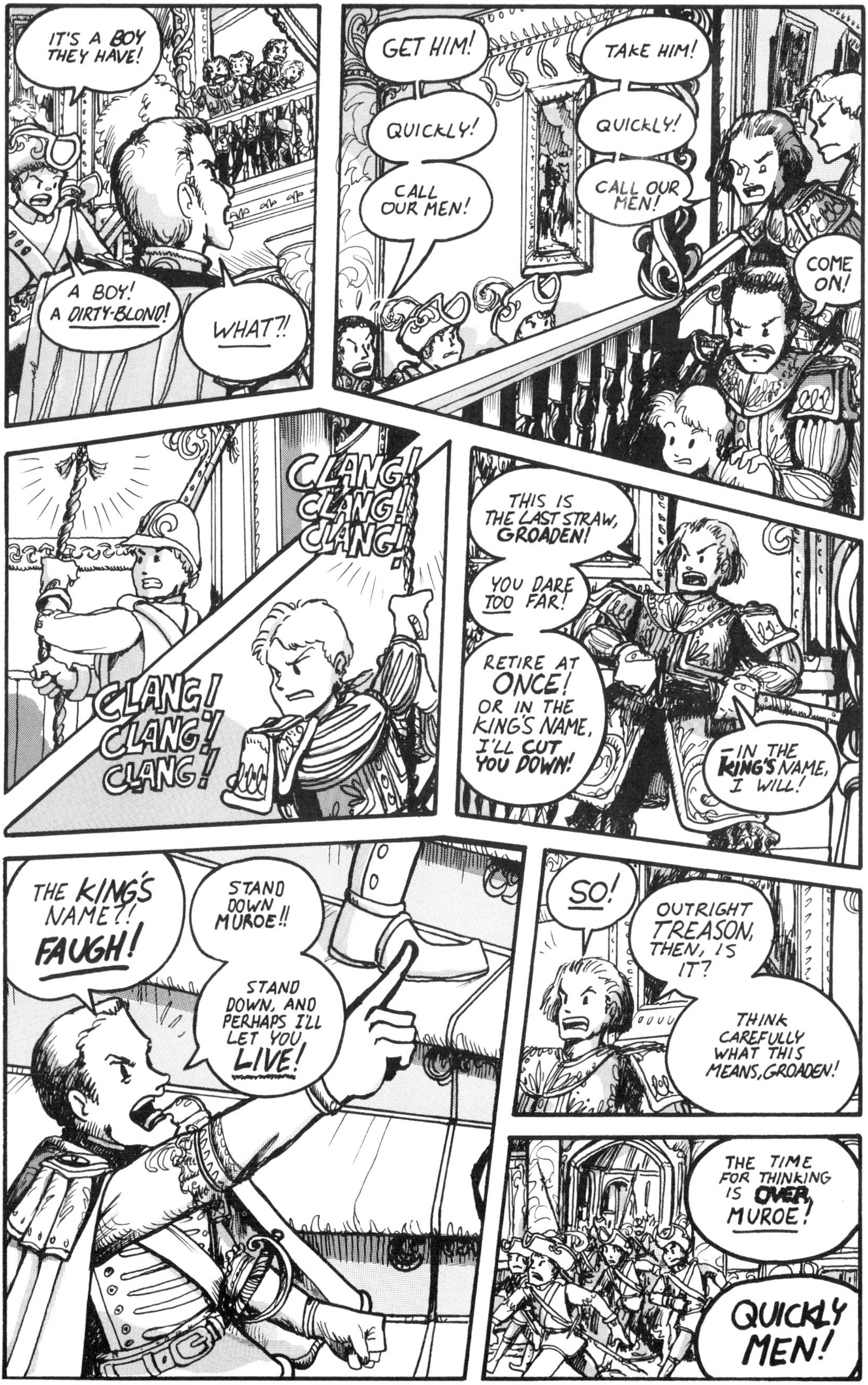

IT'S A BOY THEY HAVE!
A BOY! A DIRTY-BLOND!
WHAT?!
GET HIM!
QUICKLY!
CALL OUR MEN!
TAKE HIM!
QUICKLY!
CALL OUR MEN!
COME ON!
CLANG! CLANG! CLANG!
CLANG! CLANG! CLANG!
THIS IS THE LAST STRAW, GROADEN!
YOU DARE TOO FAR!
RETIRE AT ONCE! OR IN THE KING'S NAME, I'LL CUT YOU DOWN!
—IN THE KING'S NAME, I WILL!
THE KING'S NAME?! FAUGH!
STAND DOWN MUROE!!
STAND DOWN, AND PERHAPS I'LL LET YOU LIVE!
SO!
OUTRIGHT TREASON, THEN, IS IT?
THINK CAREFULLY WHAT THIS MEANS, GROADEN!
THE TIME FOR THINKING IS OVER, MUROE!
QUICKLY MEN!

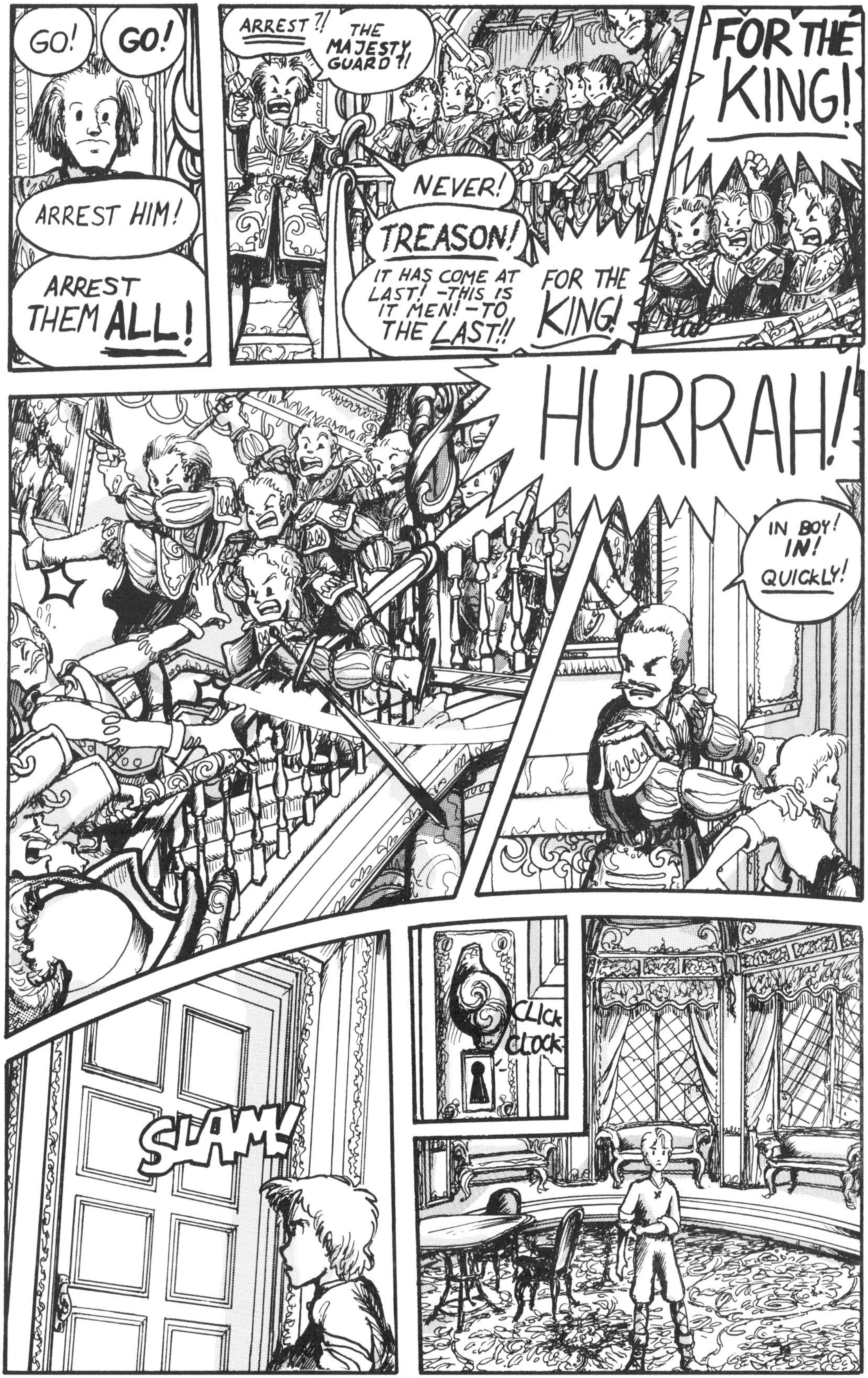

GO!
GO!
ARREST HIM!
ARREST THEM ALL!
ARREST?!
THE MAJESTY GUARD?!
NEVER!
TREASON!
IT HAS COME AT LAST! -THIS IS IT MEN! -TO THE LAST!!
FOR THE KING!
FOR THE KING!
HURRAH!
IN BOY! IN! QUICKLY!
SLAM!
CLICK
CLOCK

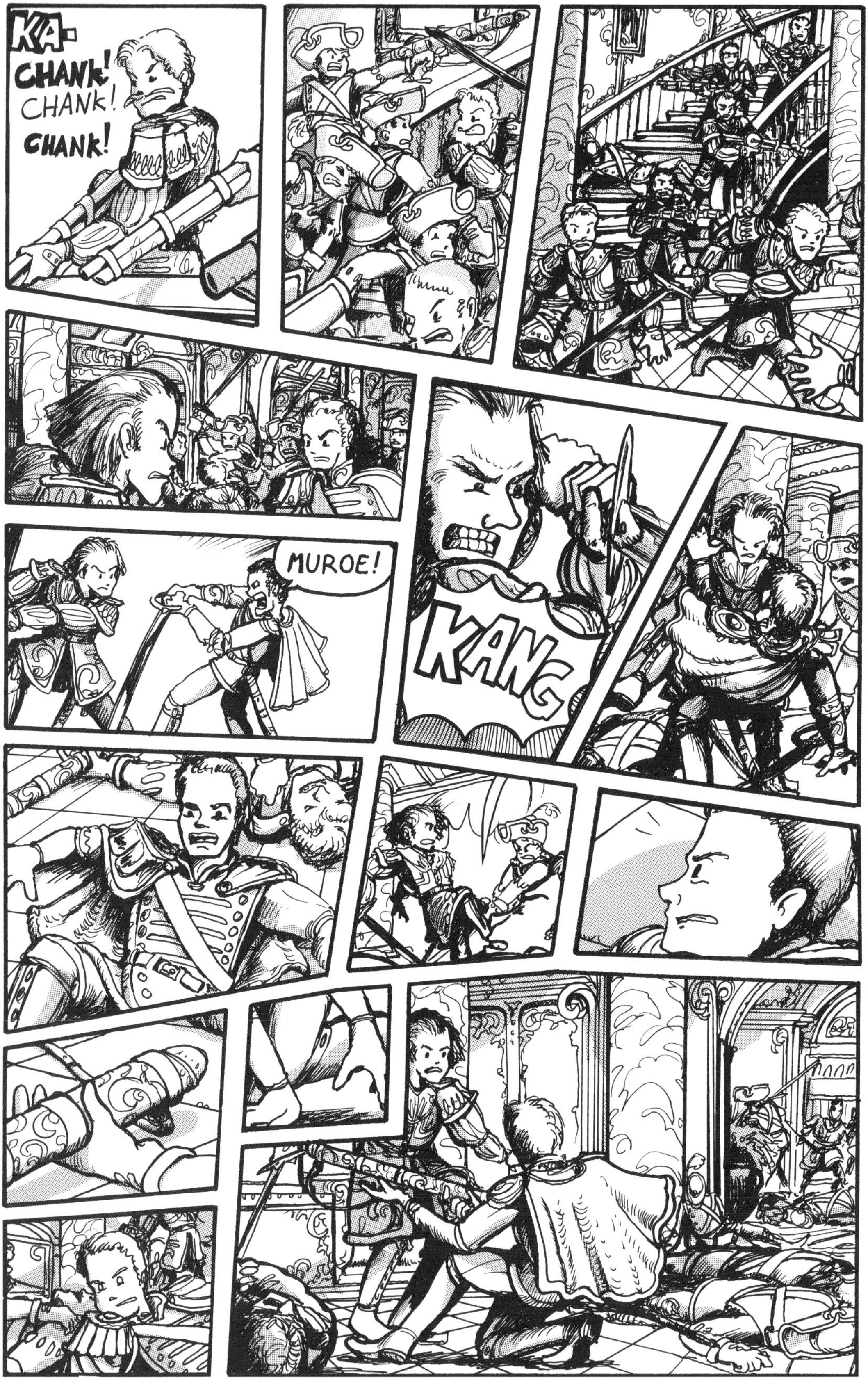
KA-
CHANK!
CHANK!
CHANK!
MUROE!
KANG

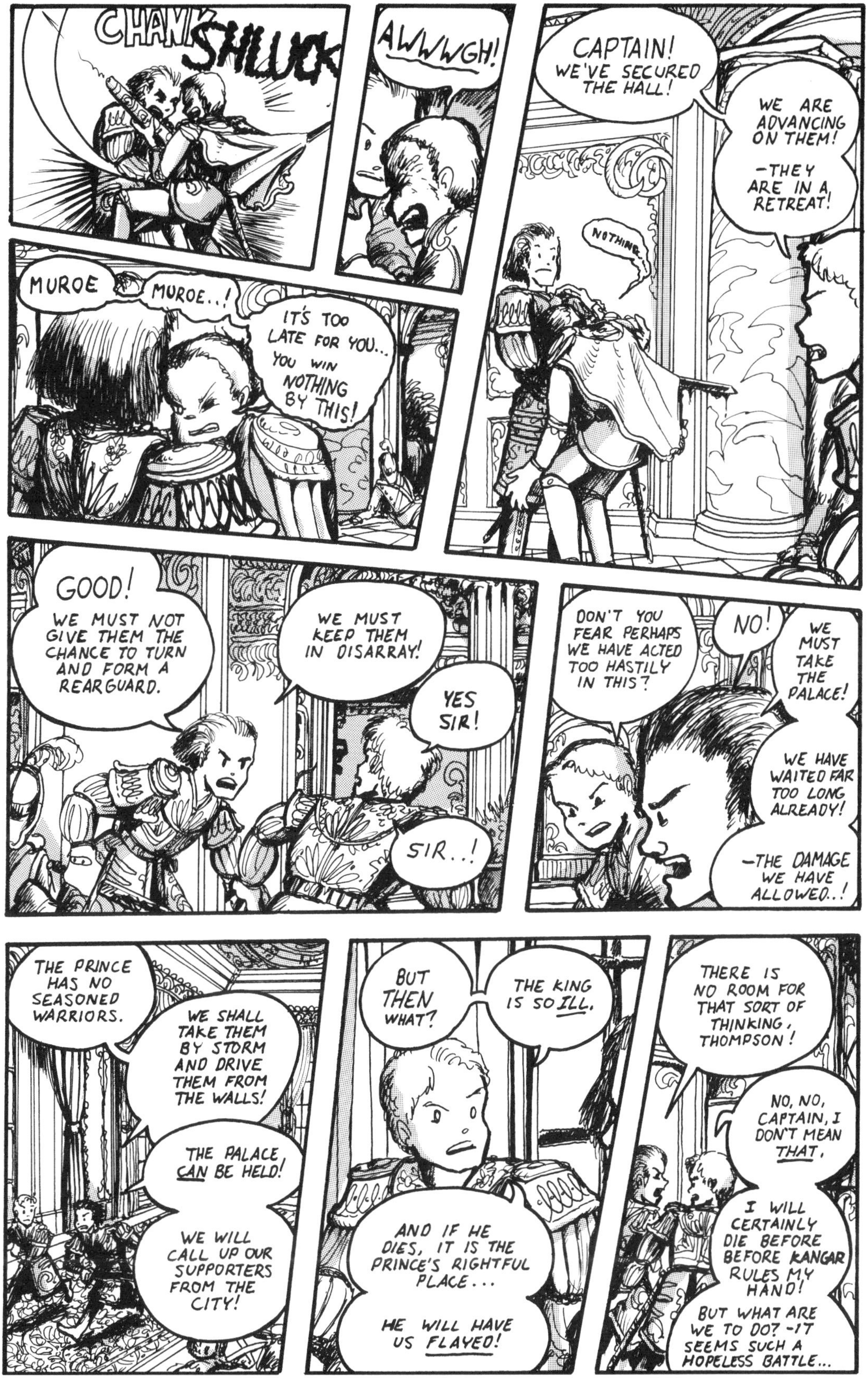

CHANK
SHLUCK
AWWWGH!
CAPTAIN! WE'VE SECURED THE HALL!
WE ARE ADVANCING ON THEM!
-THEY ARE IN A RETREAT!
MUROE
MUROE..!
IT'S TOO LATE FOR YOU... YOU WIN NOTHING BY THIS!
NOTHING.
GOOD!
WE MUST NOT GIVE THEM THE CHANCE TO TURN AND FORM A REARGUARD.
WE MUST KEEP THEM IN DISARRAY!
YES SIR!
SIR..!
DON'T YOU FEAR PERHAPS WE HAVE ACTED TOO HASTILY IN THIS?
NO!
WE MUST TAKE THE PALACE!
WE HAVE WAITED FAR TOO LONG ALREADY!
-THE DAMAGE WE HAVE ALLOWED..!
THE PRINCE HAS NO SEASONED WARRIORS.
WE SHALL TAKE THEM BY STORM AND DRIVE THEM FROM THE WALLS!
THE PALACE CAN BE HELD!
WE WILL CALL UP OUR SUPPORTERS FROM THE CITY!
BUT THEN WHAT?
THE KING IS SO ILL.
AND IF HE DIES, IT IS THE PRINCE'S RIGHTFUL PLACE...
HE WILL HAVE US FLAYED!
THERE IS NO ROOM FOR THAT SORT OF THINKING, THOMPSON!
NO, NO, CAPTAIN, I DON'T MEAN THAT.
I WILL CERTAINLY DIE BEFORE BEFORE KANGAR RULES MY HAND!
BUT WHAT ARE WE TO DO? -IT SEEMS SUCH A HOPELESS BATTLE...

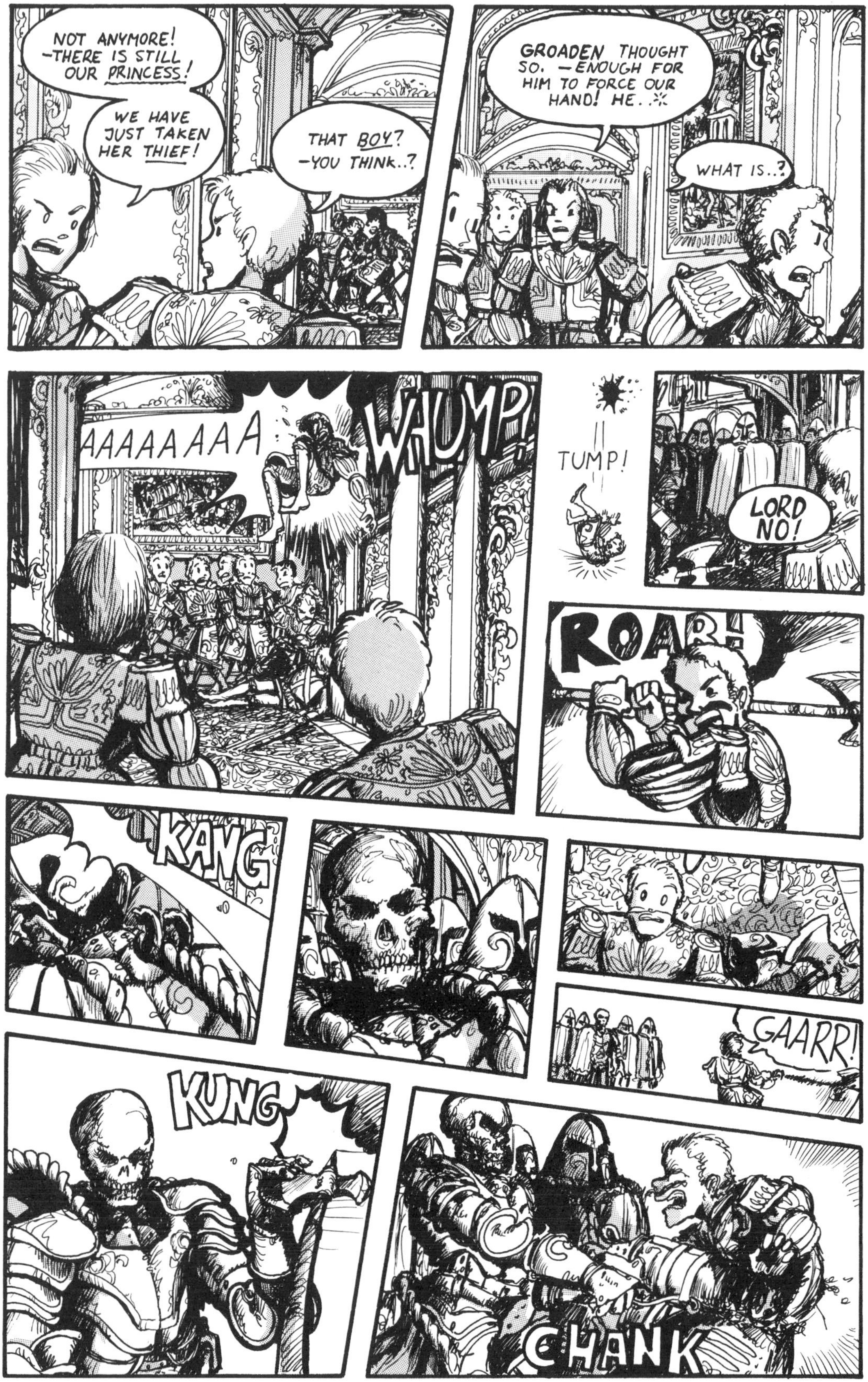
NOT ANYMORE! -THERE IS STILL OUR PRINCESS!
WE HAVE JUST TAKEN HER THIEF!
THAT BOY? -YOU THINK..?
GROADEN THOUGHT SO. -ENOUGH FOR HIM TO FORCE OUR HAND! HE..
WHAT IS..?
AAAAAAAA
WHUMP!
TUMP!
LORD NO!
ROAR!
KANG
GAARR!
KUNG
CHANK

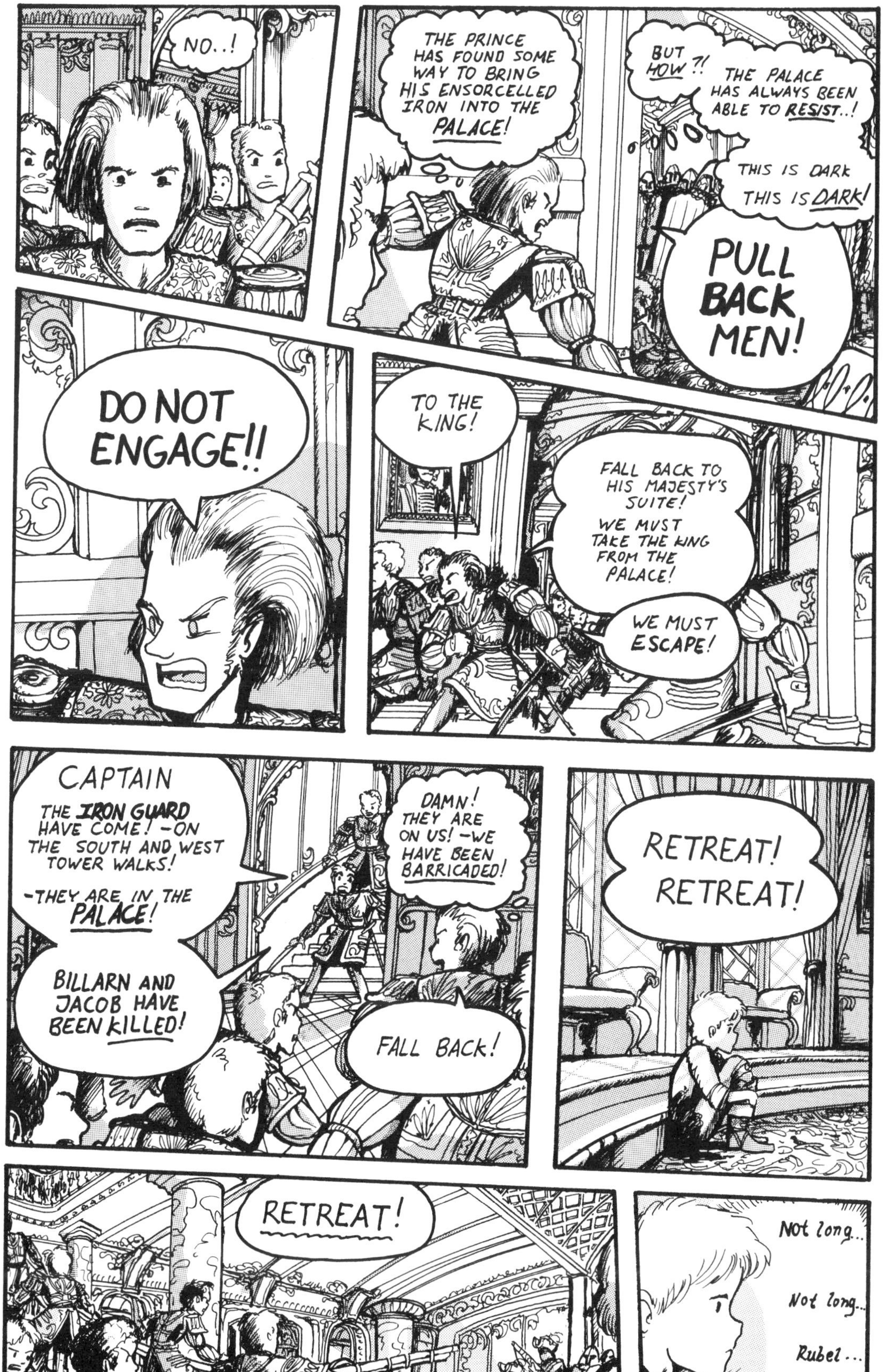
NO..!
THE PRINCE HAS FOUND SOME WAY TO BRING HIS ENSORCELLED IRON INTO THE PALACE!
BUT HOW?!
THE PALACE HAS ALWAYS BEEN ABLE TO RESIST..!
THIS IS DARK
THIS IS DARK!
PULL BACK MEN!
DO NOT ENGAGE!!
TO THE KING!
FALL BACK TO HIS MAJESTY'S SUITE!
WE MUST TAKE THE KING FROM THE PALACE!
WE MUST ESCAPE!
CAPTAIN
THE IRON GUARD HAVE COME! –ON THE SOUTH AND WEST TOWER WALKS!
–THEY ARE IN THE PALACE!
BILLARN AND JACOB HAVE BEEN KILLED!
DAMN! THEY ARE ON US! –WE HAVE BEEN BARRICADED!
FALL BACK!
RETREAT! RETREAT!
RETREAT!
Not long...
Not long...
Rubel...

Chapter 8

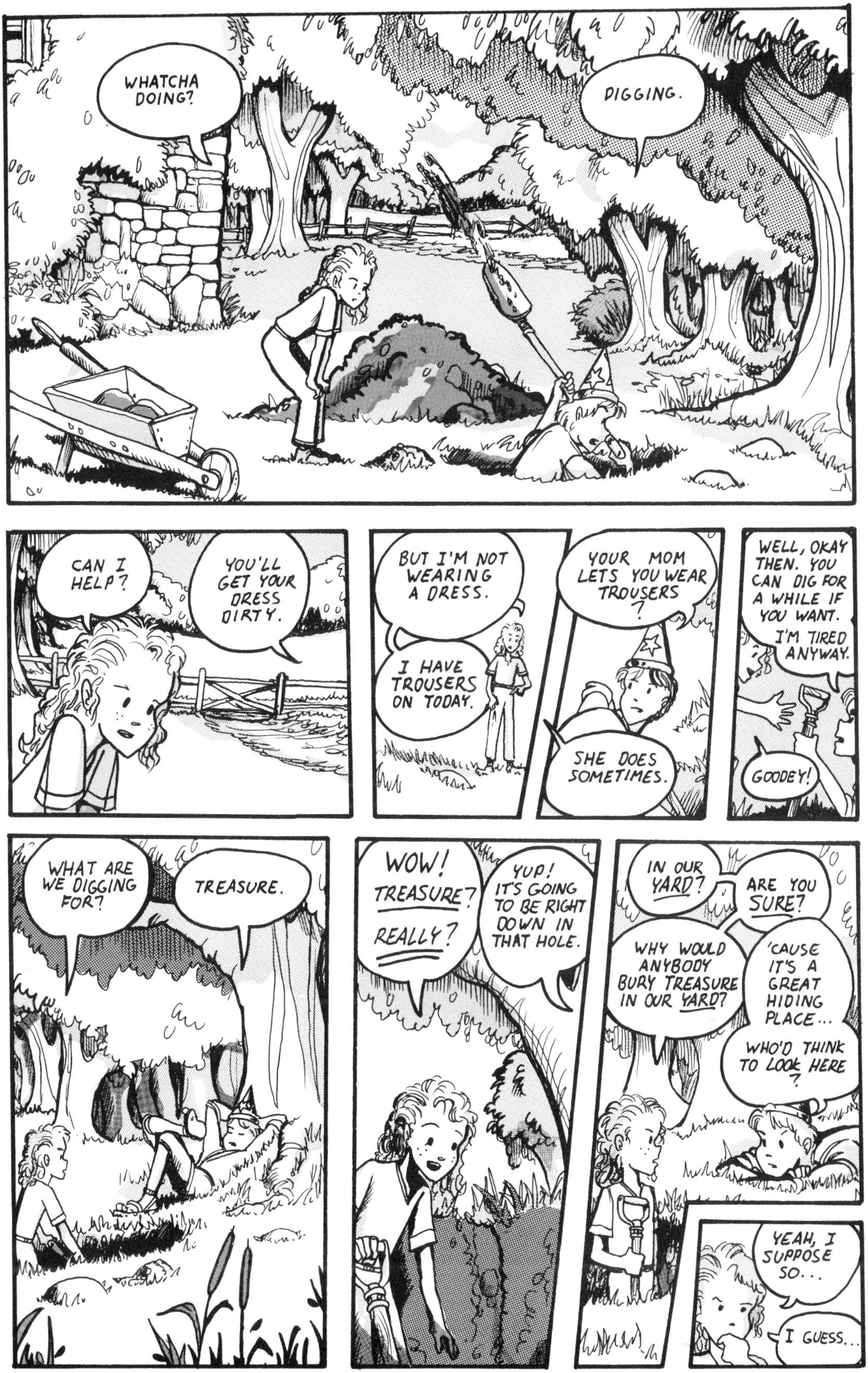
WHATCHA DOING?
DIGGING.
CAN I HELP?
YOU'LL GET YOUR DRESS DIRTY.
BUT I'M NOT WEARING A DRESS.
I HAVE TROUSERS ON TODAY.
YOUR MOM LETS YOU WEAR TROUSERS?
SHE DOES SOMETIMES.
WELL, OKAY THEN. YOU CAN DIG FOR A WHILE IF YOU WANT.
I'M TIRED ANYWAY.
GOODEY!
WHAT ARE WE DIGGING FOR?
TREASURE.
WOW! TREASURE? REALLY?
YUP! IT'S GOING TO BE RIGHT DOWN IN THAT HOLE.
IN OUR YARD?
ARE YOU SURE?
WHY WOULD ANYBODY BURY TREASURE IN OUR YARD?
'CAUSE IT'S A GREAT HIDING PLACE...
WHO'D THINK TO LOOK HERE?
YEAH, I SUPPOSE SO...
I GUESS...

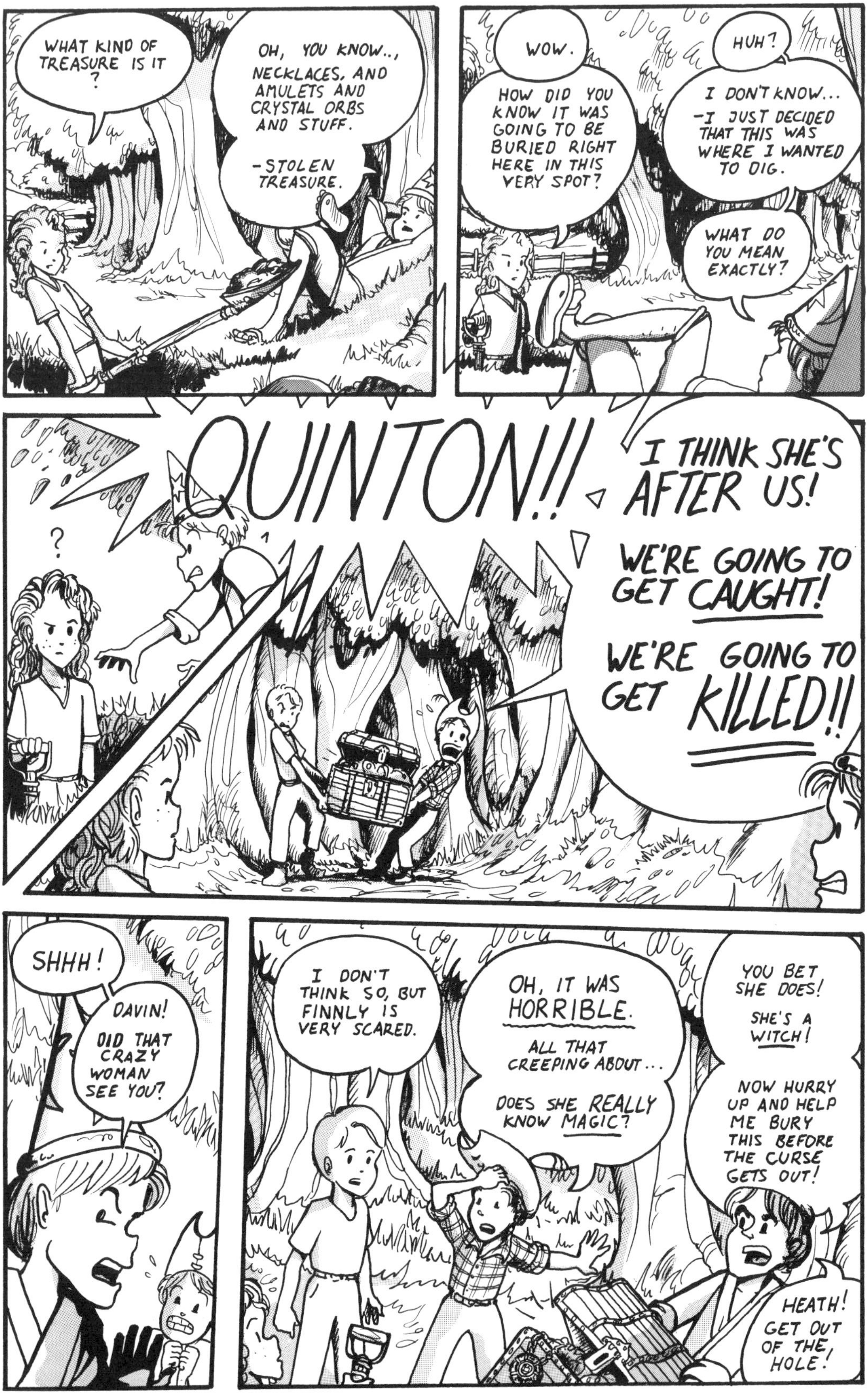
WHAT KIND OF TREASURE IS IT ?
OH, YOU KNOW.., NECKLACES, AND AMULETS AND CRYSTAL ORBS AND STUFF.
-STOLEN TREASURE.
WOW.
HOW DID YOU KNOW IT WAS GOING TO BE BURIED RIGHT HERE IN THIS VERY SPOT?
HUH?
I DON'T KNOW...
-I JUST DECIDED THAT THIS WAS WHERE I WANTED TO DIG.
WHAT DO YOU MEAN EXACTLY?
QUINTON!!
I THINK SHE'S AFTER US!
WE'RE GOING TO GET CAUGHT!
WE'RE GOING TO GET KILLED!!
?
SHHH!
DAVIN! DID THAT CRAZY WOMAN SEE YOU?
I DON'T THINK SO, BUT FINNLY IS VERY SCARED.
OH, IT WAS HORRIBLE.
ALL THAT CREEPING ABOUT...
DOES SHE REALLY KNOW MAGIC?
YOU BET SHE DOES!
SHE'S A WITCH!
NOW HURRY UP AND HELP ME BURY THIS BEFORE THE CURSE GETS OUT!
HEATH! GET OUT OF THE HOLE!

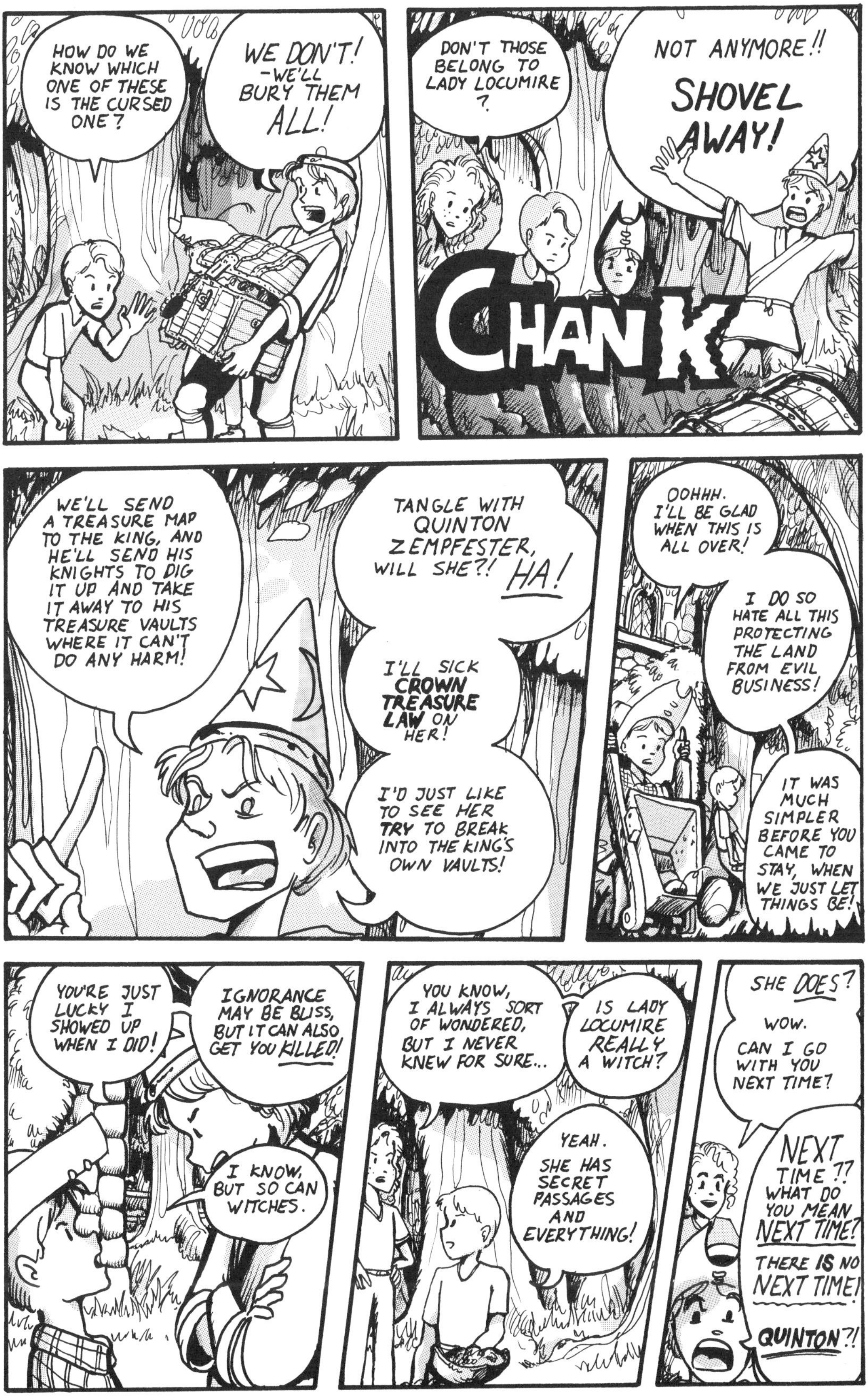

HOW DO WE KNOW WHICH ONE OF THESE IS THE CURSED ONE?
WE DON'T! -WE'LL BURY THEM ALL!
DON'T THOSE BELONG TO LADY LOCUMIRE ?.
NOT ANYMORE!! SHOVEL AWAY!
CHANK
WE'LL SEND A TREASURE MAP TO THE KING, AND HE'LL SEND HIS KNIGHTS TO DIG IT UP AND TAKE IT AWAY TO HIS TREASURE VAULTS WHERE IT CAN'T DO ANY HARM!
TANGLE WITH QUINTON ZEMPFESTER, WILL SHE?! HA!
I'LL SICK CROWN TREASURE LAW ON HER!
I'D JUST LIKE TO SEE HER TRY TO BREAK INTO THE KING'S OWN VAULTS!
OOHHH. I'LL BE GLAD WHEN THIS IS ALL OVER!
I DO SO HATE ALL THIS PROTECTING THE LAND FROM EVIL BUSINESS!
IT WAS MUCH SIMPLER BEFORE YOU CAME TO STAY, WHEN WE JUST LET THINGS BE!
YOU'RE JUST LUCKY I SHOWED UP WHEN I DID!
IGNORANCE MAY BE BLISS, BUT IT CAN ALSO GET YOU KILLED!
I KNOW, BUT SO CAN WITCHES.
YOU KNOW, I ALWAYS SORT OF WONDERED, BUT I NEVER KNEW FOR SURE...
IS LADY LOCUMIRE REALLY A WITCH?
YEAH. SHE HAS SECRET PASSAGES AND EVERYTHING!
SHE DOES?
WOW. CAN I GO WITH YOU NEXT TIME?
NEXT TIME?? WHAT DO YOU MEAN NEXT TIME? THERE IS NO NEXT TIME!
QUINTON?!

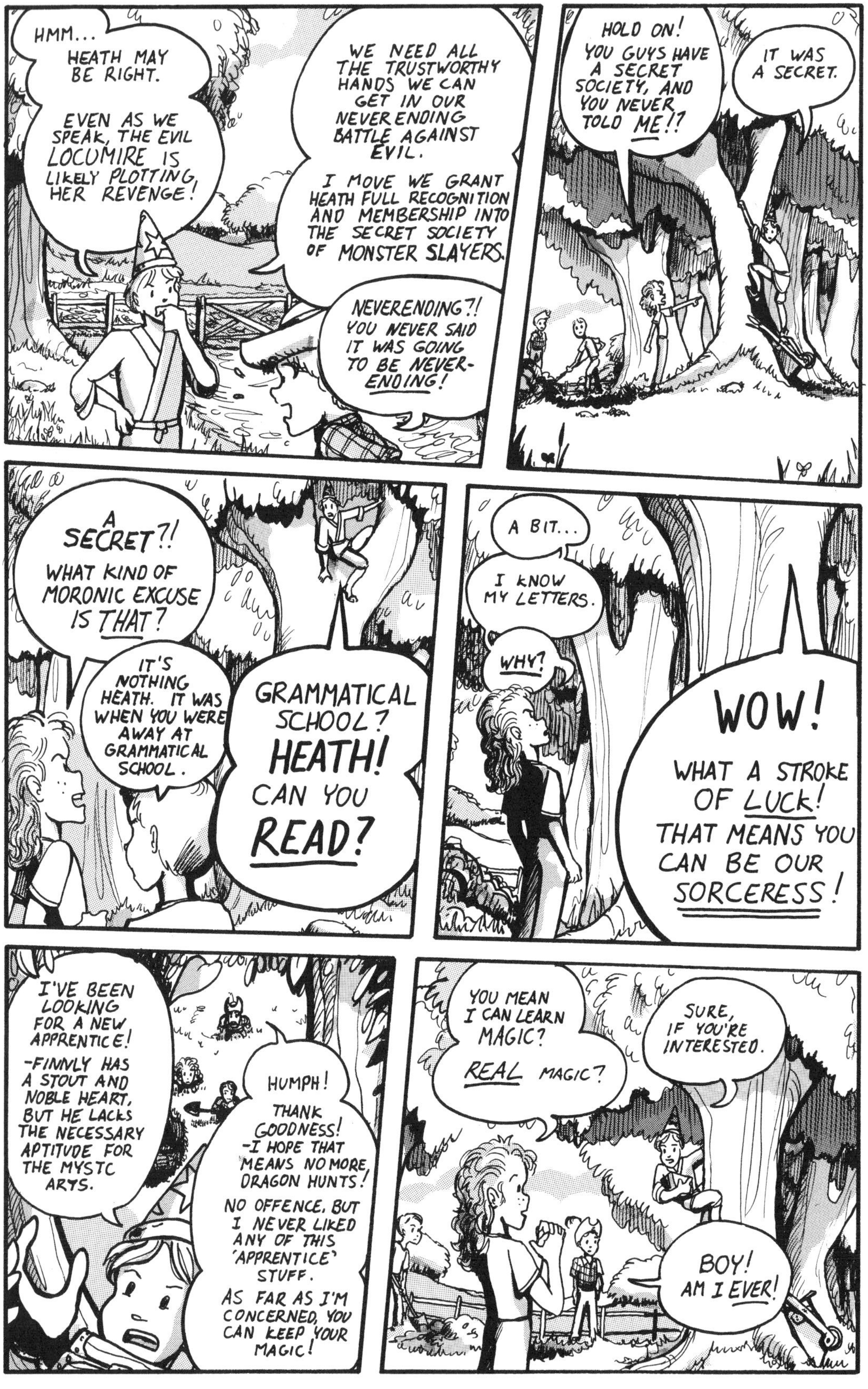
HMM... HEATH MAY BE RIGHT.
EVEN AS WE SPEAK, THE EVIL LOCUMIRE IS LIKELY PLOTTING HER REVENGE!
WE NEED ALL THE TRUSTWORTHY HANDS WE CAN GET IN OUR NEVERENDING BATTLE AGAINST EVIL.
I MOVE WE GRANT HEATH FULL RECOGNITION AND MEMBERSHIP INTO THE SECRET SOCIETY OF MONSTER SLAYERS.
NEVERENDING?! YOU NEVER SAID IT WAS GOING TO BE NEVER-ENDING!
HOLD ON! YOU GUYS HAVE A SECRET SOCIETY, AND YOU NEVER TOLD ME!?
IT WAS A SECRET.
A SECRET?! WHAT KIND OF MORONIC EXCUSE IS THAT?
IT'S NOTHING HEATH. IT WAS WHEN YOU WERE AWAY AT GRAMMATICAL SCHOOL.
GRAMMATICAL SCHOOL? HEATH! CAN YOU READ?
A BIT...
I KNOW MY LETTERS.
WHY?
WOW! WHAT A STROKE OF LUCK! THAT MEANS YOU CAN BE OUR SORCERESS!
I'VE BEEN LOOKING FOR A NEW APPRENTICE! -FINNLY HAS A STOUT AND NOBLE HEART, BUT HE LACKS THE NECESSARY APTITUDE FOR THE MYSTC ARTS.
HUMPH! THANK GOODNESS! -I HOPE THAT MEANS NO MORE DRAGON HUNTS!
NO OFFENCE, BUT I NEVER LIKED ANY OF THIS 'APPRENTICE' STUFF.
AS FAR AS I'M CONCERNED, YOU CAN KEEP YOUR MAGIC!
YOU MEAN I CAN LEARN MAGIC? REAL MAGIC?
SURE, IF YOU'RE INTERESTED.
BOY! AM I EVER!

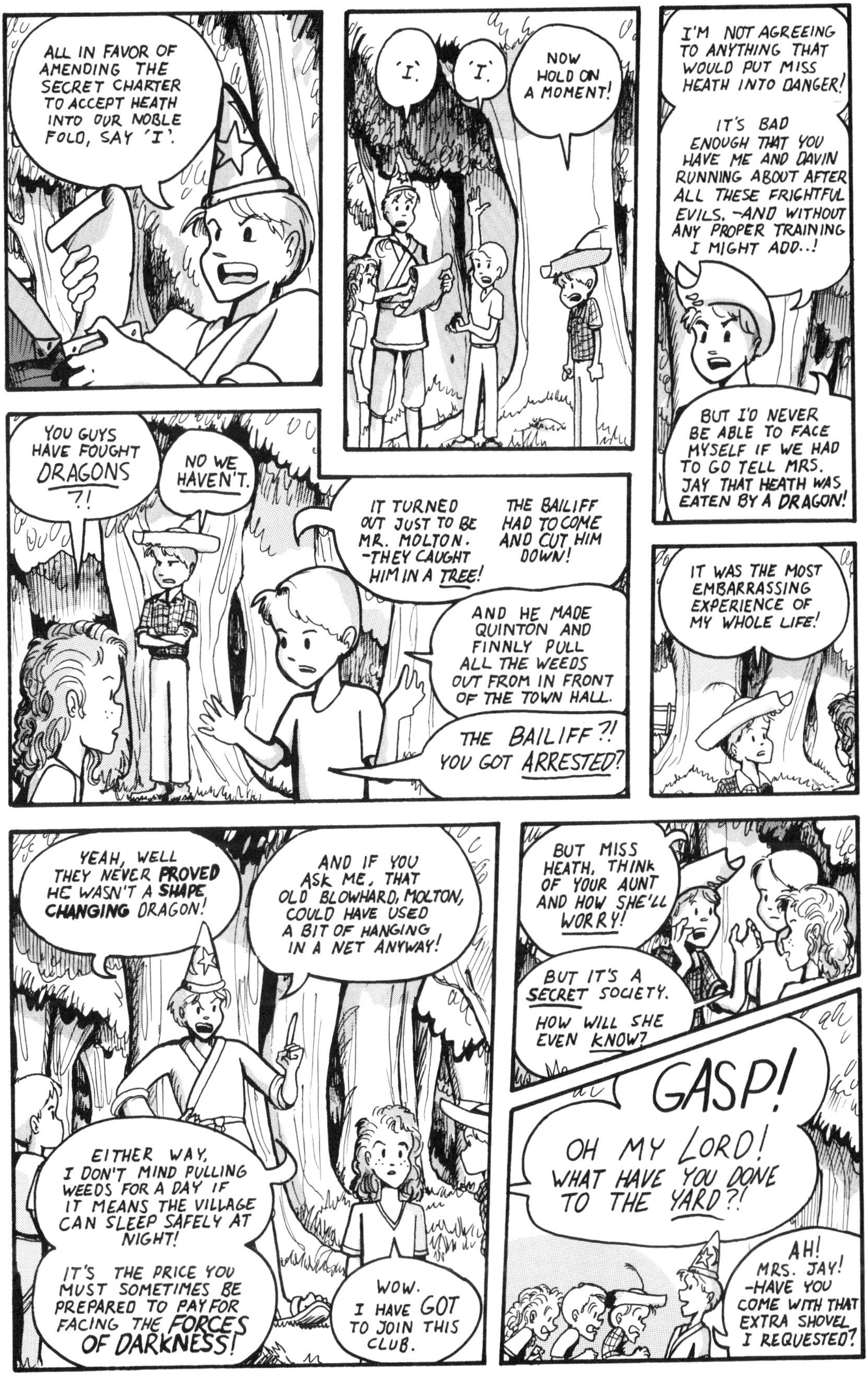
ALL IN FAVOR OF AMENDING THE SECRET CHARTER TO ACCEPT HEATH INTO OUR NOBLE FOLD, SAY 'I'.
'I'.
'I'.
NOW HOLD ON A MOMENT!
I'M NOT AGREEING TO ANYTHING THAT WOULD PUT MISS HEATH INTO DANGER!
IT'S BAD ENOUGH THAT YOU HAVE ME AND DAVIN RUNNING ABOUT AFTER ALL THESE FRIGHTFUL EVILS. -AND WITHOUT ANY PROPER TRAINING I MIGHT ADD..!
BUT I'D NEVER BE ABLE TO FACE MYSELF IF WE HAD TO GO TELL MRS. JAY THAT HEATH WAS EATEN BY A DRAGON!
YOU GUYS HAVE FOUGHT DRAGONS ?!
NO WE HAVEN'T.
IT TURNED OUT JUST TO BE MR. MOLTON. -THEY CAUGHT HIM IN A TREE!
THE BAILIFF HAD TO COME AND CUT HIM DOWN!
AND HE MADE QUINTON AND FINNLY PULL ALL THE WEEDS OUT FROM IN FRONT OF THE TOWN HALL.
THE BAILIFF ?! YOU GOT ARRESTED?
IT WAS THE MOST EMBARRASSING EXPERIENCE OF MY WHOLE LIFE!
YEAH, WELL THEY NEVER PROVED HE WASN'T A SHAPE CHANGING DRAGON!
AND IF YOU ASK ME, THAT OLD BLOWHARD, MOLTON, COULD HAVE USED A BIT OF HANGING IN A NET ANYWAY!
EITHER WAY, I DON'T MIND PULLING WEEDS FOR A DAY IF IT MEANS THE VILLAGE CAN SLEEP SAFELY AT NIGHT!
IT'S THE PRICE YOU MUST SOMETIMES BE PREPARED TO PAY FOR FACING THE FORCES OF DARKNESS!
WOW. I HAVE GOT TO JOIN THIS CLUB.
BUT MISS HEATH, THINK OF YOUR AUNT AND HOW SHE'LL WORRY!
BUT IT'S A SECRET SOCIETY.
HOW WILL SHE EVEN KNOW?
GASP!
OH MY LORD! WHAT HAVE YOU DONE TO THE YARD?!
AH! MRS. JAY! -HAVE YOU COME WITH THAT EXTRA SHOVEL I REQUESTED?

Chapter 9

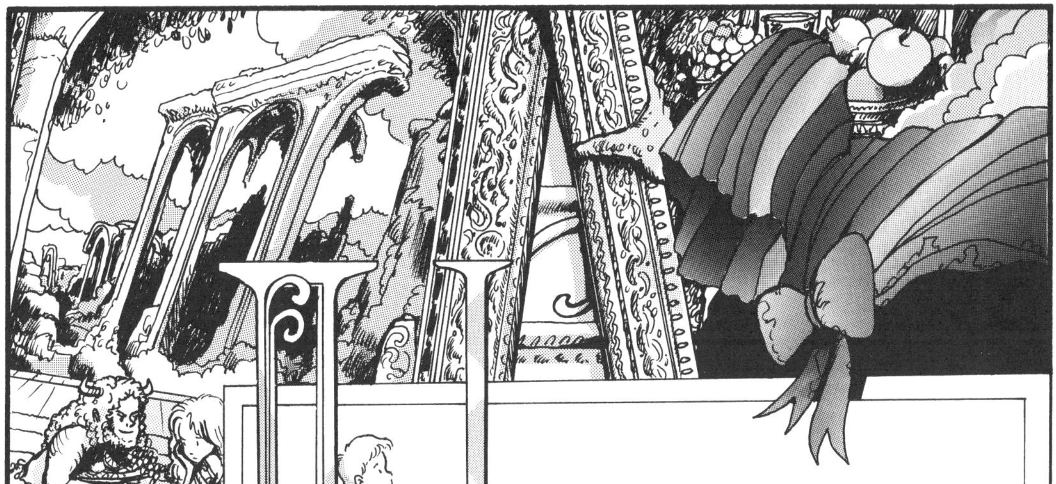

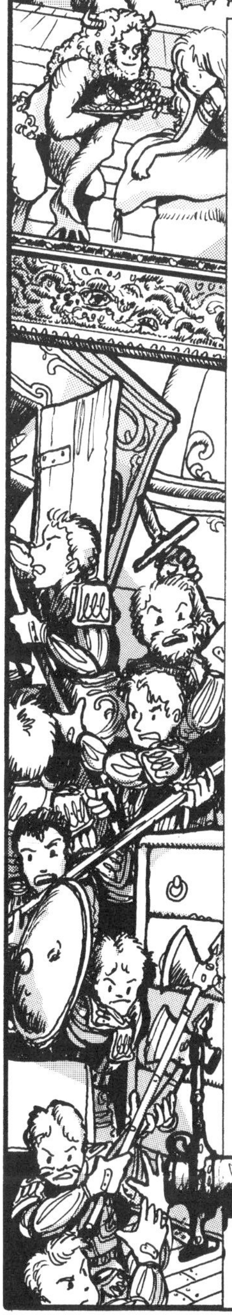

Upon the wall there was a picture.

In the picture, there was a shadow.

It watched from within and Rubel, unable to do anything else, watched it back. It moved and watched and moved again, doing so with the same silky, heavy motion common in the sort of cats that live in jungles.

The name of this beast was Jurid, but Rubel did not know that. He knew only to watch it and rock gently on his heels while the world grew fuzzy in his vision and the blood clotted around the stub of metal in his side.

Through the haze of his perception, he could hear the majesty guard outside the door barking to one another in tight voices; men of acute patriotic devotion and ability who, as the enemy pressed them, quickly lost the roguish attitude they had born when their strength and casual efficiency had easily outmatched that of prince Kangar's blue backs.

Before such juggernaut force as the iron clad giants, the men under lieutenant captain Earl Muroe's command fell back. They fell back until, for some reason not altogether clear to Rubel but which seemed of the utmost importance to the soldiers, the retreat was called to a halt. With a tense command, Muroe's men raced off and produced heavy swords and war axes and iron shafted spears from hidden caches, (all weapons made for two hands).

Three very large and very old bolt lock cannons were brought out from dusty window closets; guns which had been designed at one time to be used against such things as dragons and other airborne targets, (the likes of which nobody had seen for many countless ages, and which explained the great degree to which the canons had been allowed to decay). —Only one of them was serviceable at all, while the other two seized hopelessly, rusted at every moving part.

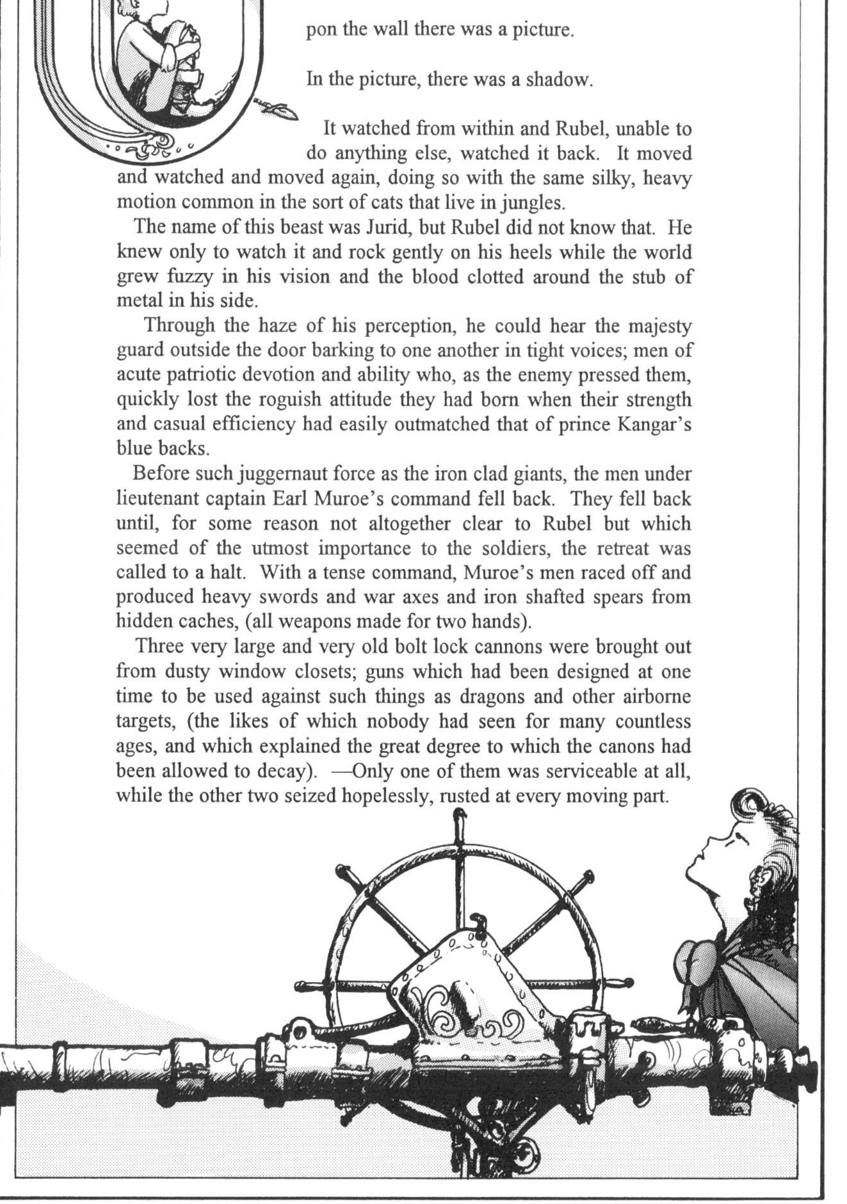

This single cannon was dragged with hasty effort into position at the head of a stairwell, leaving long and ugly scrapes upon the polished wooden floor. Armed with one of the antique iron missile shafts also rescued from the dust, the cannon was brought into action. Its mere presence had a powerful bolstering effect upon the king's soldiers. Their hearts all sprang as one, each man made giddy by both a racing heart and the sudden possibility that the battle might be turning in their favor.

According to old wisdom passed down and held in the stores of knowledge kept by such groups as the majesty guard, the enchanted iron warriors could, in theory, be destroyed. It required that the great helm of an undead soldier be smashed or wrenched away and that the skeleton head once exposed be severed at the neck with an aptly swung blade.

Of course, this could only be achieved at great personal risk to the attacking party, but the majesty guard existed for precisely such purposes, and they set themselves upon the task with a murderous energy.

Two iron guards were successfully annihilated in this manner, (one of which had already lost its helmet), and a third was toppled in a thunderous crash as the bolt lock cannon hurled its missile, smashing it through the breast plate of the giant. The king's men let out a grand hurrah as each behemoth fell, and for several breathless moments it seemed to all that the battle might indeed be won.

But this was not to be.

The cannon, in discharging, had damaged itself beyond further use, and the warrior it had struck did not stay down. Though with a shattered cavity in its chest, the iron beast brought itself back up again. Glaring in cold fury upon the king's men, the behemoth resumed its advance, crushing a wounded man to death with one terrible tromp of its mighty foot. Another raised its own great weapon and loosed all six chambers into a knot of soldiers still struggling with the broken canon.

And so it went, the loss of life escalating at such an alarming rate that the majesty guard would certainly have been exterminated had not Muroe raised his voice. He had been watching the killing with a terrible anxiety. —The sort you feel when horrible things are happening, but which you cannot stop until a foolish, and incidental task is completed. (In this case, it was the rescuing of some documents and the destruction of some others; papers and maps which had almost been forgotten in the fray, and which could under no circumstances be left to the enemy). And so, with this foolish task secured, he gave at last the command to resume their retreat and abandon the palace. —A move he knew which carried with it vast ramifications.

f least importance, the decision meant giving up their foothold within the castle. —Even though such a position would prove extremely difficult to regain once lost, the palace could never be entirely closed off to the majesty guard. If they felt like fighting hard enough then, even with the drawbridge up and all the windows shuttered tight, the palace could still be taken back. It was possible because of hidden passage ways and secret doors.

Within the castle architecture there existed such secret and mystical elements as were known to only a very few. Of course, owing to both the enormous age of the palace and to the genius with which it had been constructed, a great many of those secrets had been forgotten long, long ago. The majesty guard was, however, a brotherhood spanning nearly three centuries. —And while three hundred years might not seem like much when measured against the age of the palace, (which was very much older, indeed), it was certainly long enough for a company of clever men to acquire at least a few secrets. And it was one of those very secrets through which Muroe intended to evacuate both the king and his men.

So the real significance, Muroe knew, did not lie in actually leaving the palace to the enemy. It did not lie in the strategic placement of troops or guns. The real significance was of a less tangible variety, though one which struck a deep chord in his heart.

There is a type of special person who, while their gift may seem at first to be of wonderful advantage, actually finds it more difficult to excel in positions of high responsibility than another person might. Muroe was one of these.

Muroe had exceptional 'sight'. Subtle or gross, he was able to see quite clearly the currents and moods of a society acting upon its people. Currents and moods which were often virtually invisible to others. And it caused him to worry. Out of natural habit, he always tried to sort out how best to position himself in the unceasing flow of time and events so that he might help things work out in ways that were right and good.

He was always so *serious,* people would accuse. And he had become even more so of late. Despite his best efforts, events were right then barreling down a route he had long ago foreseen. In Muroe's eyes, quitting the palace was final proof of more than just a battle gone sour.

Four years ago when prince Kangar was just 13 years old, the boy asked his father if he might be granted a division of soldiers for his very own. —A group of soldiers who would be like his father's majesty guard, except that Kangar would call them the 'prince guard' and they would only be for him. The king was not happy about this idea at all.

The king had grown of late to find the job of being a father an increasingly difficult one. True, it had never been easy for him to love and trust his young son, but in recent years things had gotten worse.

Small children have many ways to show when they are angry, but usually a fit of rage is quickly over and then easily put aside, both by the child and parent alike. The times, however, were coming to an end when the king's children could only run and deal with their anger in the small ways allowed to children. Kangar was on the verge of turning into a young man with all the powers young men have, and as this time approached, things became decidedly strained between father and son.

On occasion, the king would attempt to prove to his son, (as well as to himself), that he really did trust and love the boy, just as much as he perceived good fathers ought. So he granted Kangar his wish and gave him some soldiers, quietly hoping that doing so would provide Kangar with a place into which all those unhappy energies with which the boy was so filled might be channeled and transformed into something healthy and good. The king had no extraordinary wisdom, but he did know that sometimes happiness and contentment could be found when a person toils upon something loved.

And so, dressed in finely cut uniforms of brand new design and rich blue material, sixty men were selected and granted titles and stations in their own small division, and they were given over to the prince to be commanded as the boy saw fit. Kangar was delighted. He paraded his beaming new soldiers up and down the streets of the city, much to the satisfaction of the people, who loved him. And though the king felt ill at ease, the man smiled and waved to his son.

It was during this uneasy time that a great blow was dealt to the king for which he was entirely unprepared. His daughter, princess Katara, ran away into the Sleeping Wood where no one and no effort could find her.

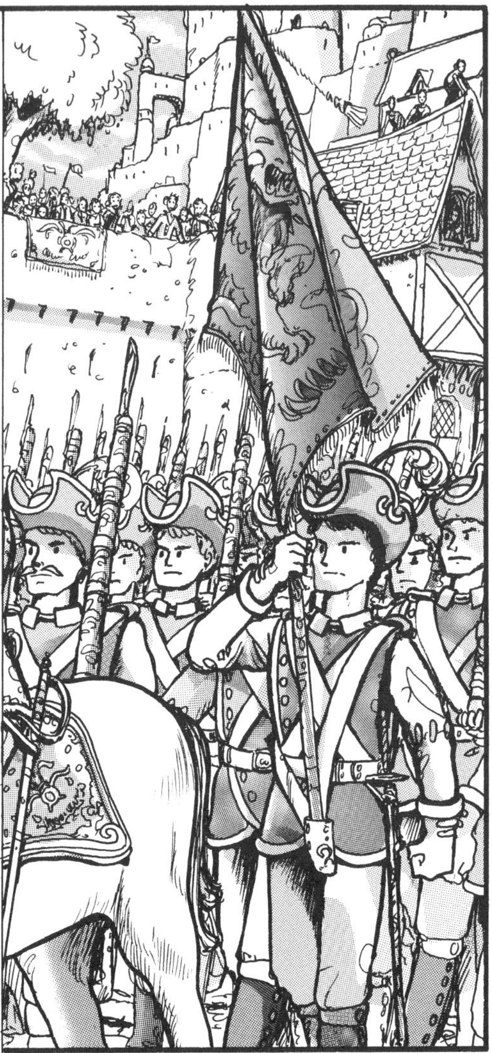

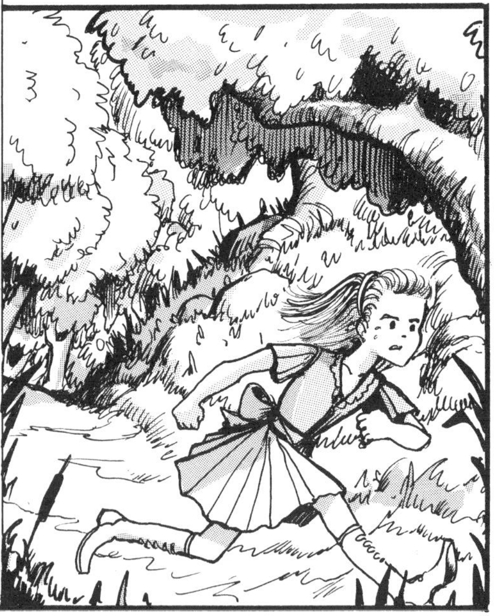

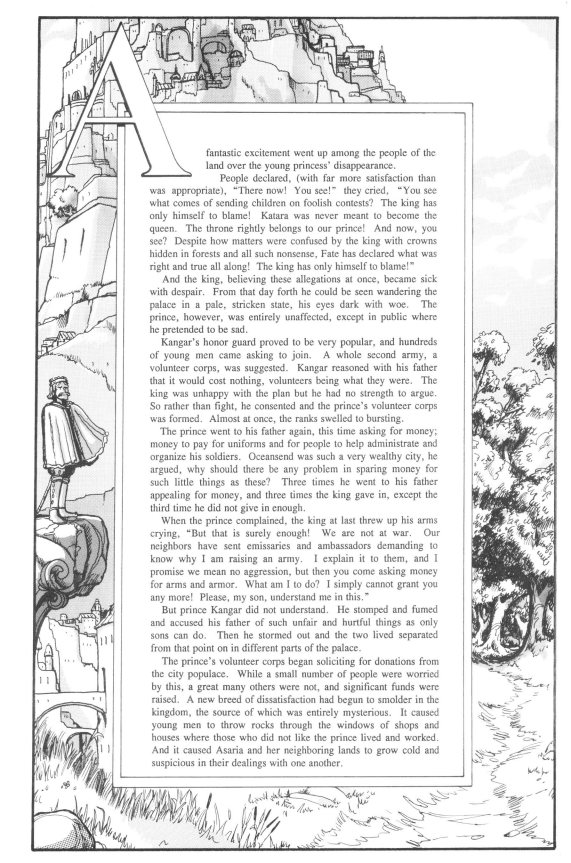

A fantastic excitement went up among the people of the land over the young princess' disappearance.

People declared, (with far more satisfaction than was appropriate), "There now! You see!" they cried, "You see what comes of sending children on foolish contests? The king has only himself to blame! Katara was never meant to become the queen. The throne rightly belongs to our prince! And now, you see? Despite how matters were confused by the king with crowns hidden in forests and all such nonsense, Fate has declared what was right and true all along! The king has only himself to blame!"

And the king, believing these allegations at once, became sick with despair. From that day forth he could be seen wandering the palace in a pale, stricken state, his eyes dark with woe. The prince, however, was entirely unaffected, except in public where he pretended to be sad.

Kangar's honor guard proved to be very popular, and hundreds of young men came asking to join. A whole second army, a volunteer corps, was suggested. Kangar reasoned with his father that it would cost nothing, volunteers being what they were. The king was unhappy with the plan but he had no strength to argue. So rather than fight, he consented and the prince's volunteer corps was formed. Almost at once, the ranks swelled to bursting.

The prince went to his father again, this time asking for money; money to pay for uniforms and for people to help administrate and organize his soldiers. Oceansend was such a very wealthy city, he argued, why should there be any problem in sparing money for such little things as these? Three times he went to his father appealing for money, and three times the king gave in, except the third time he did not give in enough.

When the prince complained, the king at last threw up his arms crying, "But that is surely enough! We are not at war. Our neighbors have sent emissaries and ambassadors demanding to know why I am raising an army. I explain it to them, and I promise we mean no aggression, but then you come asking money for arms and armor. What am I to do? I simply cannot grant you any more! Please, my son, understand me in this."

But prince Kangar did not understand. He stomped and fumed and accused his father of such unfair and hurtful things as only sons can do. Then he stormed out and the two lived separated from that point on in different parts of the palace.

The prince's volunteer corps began soliciting for donations from the city populace. While a small number of people were worried by this, a great many others were not, and significant funds were raised. A new breed of dissatisfaction had begun to smolder in the kingdom, the source of which was entirely mysterious. It caused young men to throw rocks through the windows of shops and houses where those who did not like the prince lived and worked. And it caused Asaria and her neighboring lands to grow cold and suspicious in their dealings with one another.

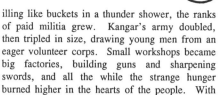

Filling like buckets in a thunder shower, the ranks of paid militia grew. Kangar's army doubled, then tripled in size, drawing young men from an eager volunteer corps. Small workshops became big factories, building guns and sharpening swords, and all the while the strange hunger burned higher in the hearts of the people. With very little effort the prince had in but three and a half years, come to occupy a position of high authority and rapidly increasing power.

The king woke up each morning with more and more worries, and a paler and paler face until, on the very same morning of the prince's 17th birthday, the king did not wake up at all. Laboring beneath the pall of his strange illness, the simple man with his simple heart lay in a tortured, murmuring state, doomed to waste away while doctors administered liquids directly into his body through a set of ugly metal tubes. That same day, the iron guard, donned in brilliant red capes, made their first appearance, marching in the prince's birthday parade.

The mysterious armored giants were admired and feared by all for their strength and silent devotion to the rising prince, who would surely soon be king. The people cheered and prince Kangar shone before them in military dress, young and handsome with his sword and breast plate flashing in the sun.

And so, in flanks which held the tops of stairwells and hallways leading to the king's suite, the majesty guard fell back. Each flank doing its best to protect the one before it.

While the official documents and ceremonies were perhaps weeks or even many months away from being signed and performed, Muroe knew that this morning marked the true end of his master's rein. The man he was sworn to protect had been brought to the very brink of death, and Muroe had been unable to stop it.

But there were *other* forces at work. Forces which ran deeper than did the knowledge of the majesty guard. There were *thieves*. Thieves of an old cast and mind. And if the most secret whispers were true, then the princess herself had such a thief beneath her rule; there was the strange boy, of whom Muroe knew precious little, and until that morning had even doubted the existence of, (and if the truth were known, doubted even now). But whatever the case, the prince was frightened of that boy. And that was something in a day when the prince feared neither his father nor the might of other nations.

Indeed, there was still the princess.

GET UP. WE MUST LEAVE AT ONCE!

YOU WILL BE KILLED IF YOU STAY HERE!

CAN YOU WALK?

QUICKLY!

THERE ISN'T ANY TIME!

GO! GO RUBEL! THIS IS SERIOUS!

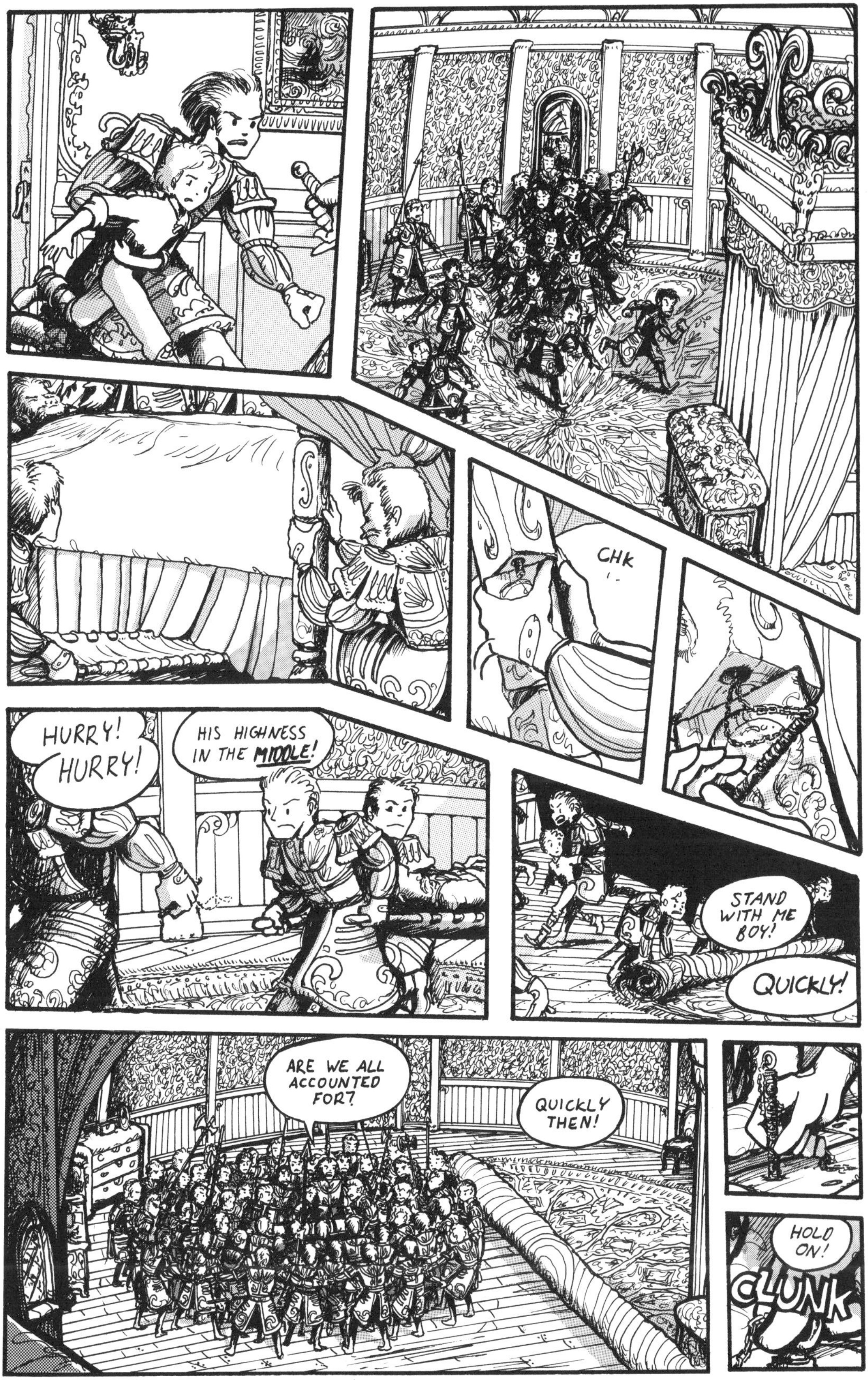
CHK
HURRY! HURRY!
HIS HIGHNESS IN THE MIDDLE!
STAND WITH ME BOY!
QUICKLY!
ARE WE ALL ACCOUNTED FOR?
QUICKLY THEN!
HOLD ON!
CLUNK

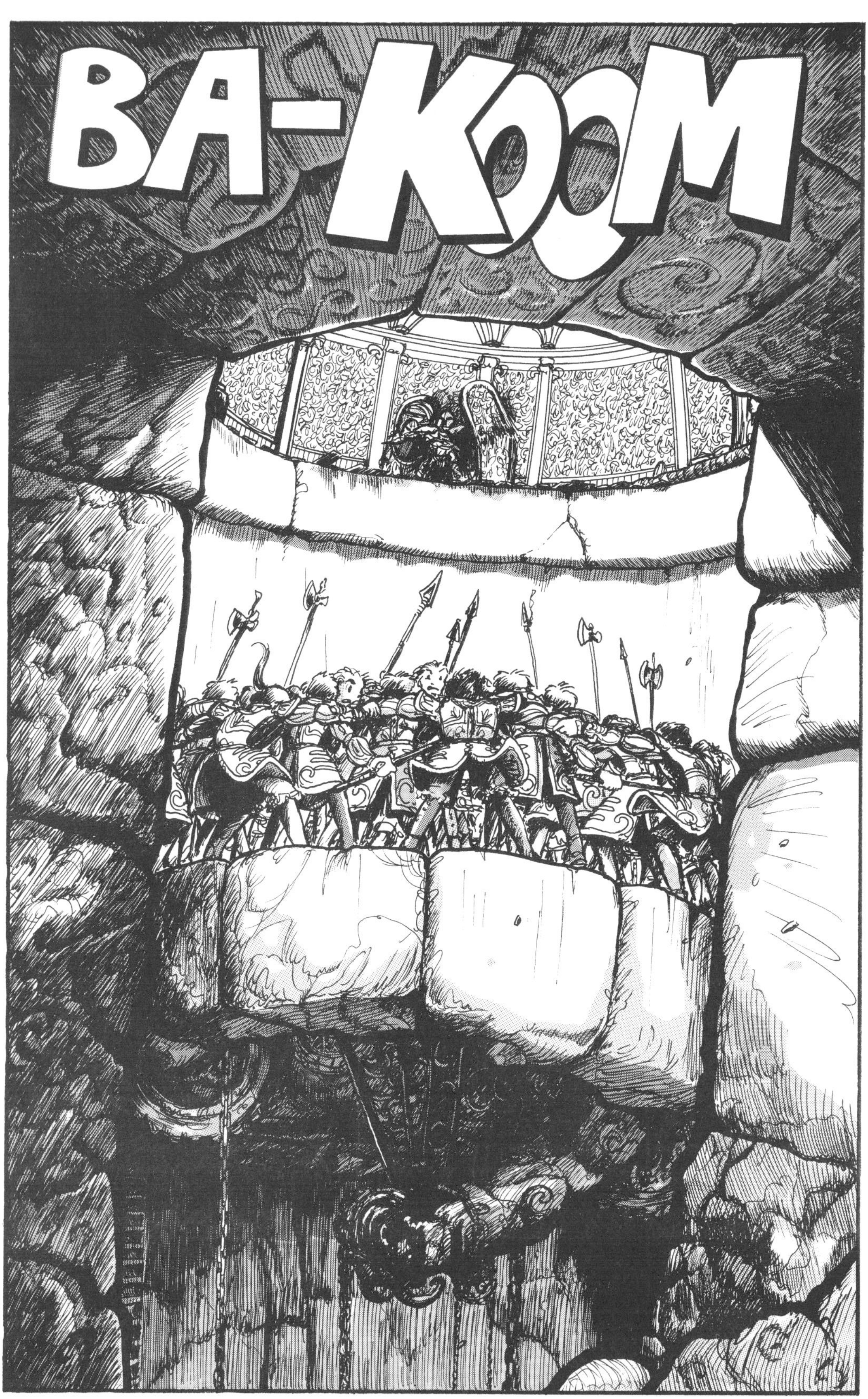
BA-KOOM

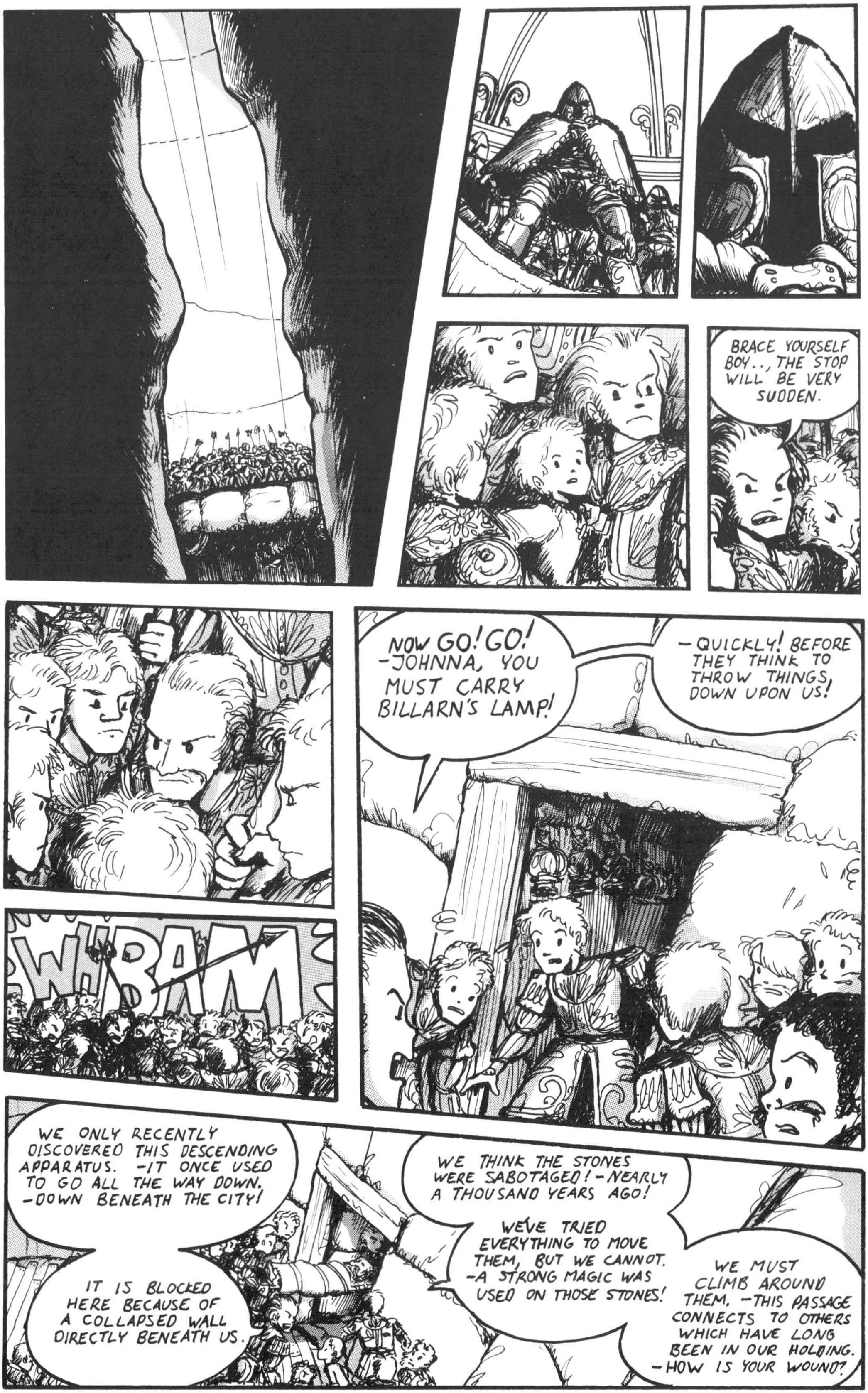
BRACE YOURSELF BOY.., THE STOP WILL BE VERY SUDDEN.
NOW GO! GO! -JOHNNA, YOU MUST CARRY BILLARN'S LAMP!
-QUICKLY! BEFORE THEY THINK TO THROW THINGS DOWN UPON US!
WHBAM
WE ONLY RECENTLY DISCOVERED THIS DESCENDING APPARATUS. -IT ONCE USED TO GO ALL THE WAY DOWN. -DOWN BENEATH THE CITY!
IT IS BLOCKED HERE BECAUSE OF A COLLAPSED WALL DIRECTLY BENEATH US.
WE THINK THE STONES WERE SABOTAGED! -NEARLY A THOUSAND YEARS AGO!
WE'VE TRIED EVERYTHING TO MOVE THEM, BUT WE CANNOT. -A STRONG MAGIC WAS USED ON THOSE STONES!
WE MUST CLIMB AROUND THEM. -THIS PASSAGE CONNECTS TO OTHERS WHICH HAVE LONG BEEN IN OUR HOLDING. -HOW IS YOUR WOUND?

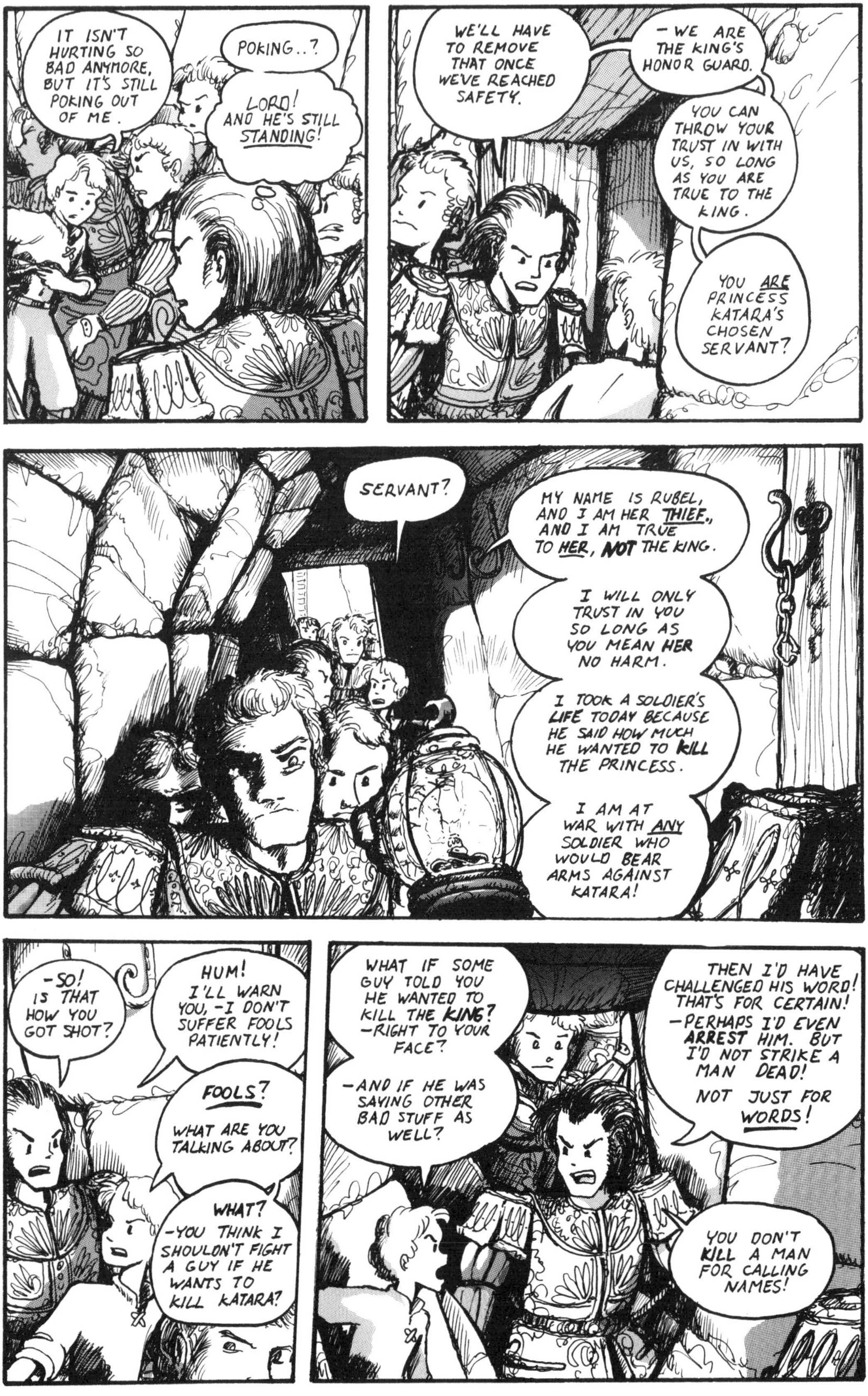
IT ISN'T HURTING SO BAD ANYMORE, BUT IT'S STILL POKING OUT OF ME.
POKING..?
LORD! AND HE'S STILL STANDING!
WE'LL HAVE TO REMOVE THAT ONCE WE'VE REACHED SAFETY.
-WE ARE THE KING'S HONOR GUARD.
YOU CAN THROW YOUR TRUST IN WITH US, SO LONG AS YOU ARE TRUE TO THE KING.
YOU ARE PRINCESS KATARA'S CHOSEN SERVANT?
SERVANT?
MY NAME IS RUBEL, AND I AM HER THIEF., AND I AM TRUE TO HER, NOT THE KING.
I WILL ONLY TRUST IN YOU SO LONG AS YOU MEAN HER NO HARM.
I TOOK A SOLDIER'S LIFE TODAY BECAUSE HE SAID HOW MUCH HE WANTED TO KILL THE PRINCESS.
I AM AT WAR WITH ANY SOLDIER WHO WOULD BEAR ARMS AGAINST KATARA!
-SO! IS THAT HOW YOU GOT SHOT?
HUM! I'LL WARN YOU, -I DON'T SUFFER FOOLS PATIENTLY!
FOOLS?
WHAT ARE YOU TALKING ABOUT?
WHAT? -YOU THINK I SHOULDN'T FIGHT A GUY IF HE WANTS TO KILL KATARA?
WHAT IF SOME GUY TOLD YOU HE WANTED TO KILL THE KING? -RIGHT TO YOUR FACE?
-AND IF HE WAS SAYING OTHER BAD STUFF AS WELL?
THEN I'D HAVE CHALLENGED HIS WORD! THAT'S FOR CERTAIN! -PERHAPS I'D EVEN ARREST HIM. BUT I'D NOT STRIKE A MAN DEAD!
NOT JUST FOR WORDS!
YOU DON'T KILL A MAN FOR CALLING NAMES!

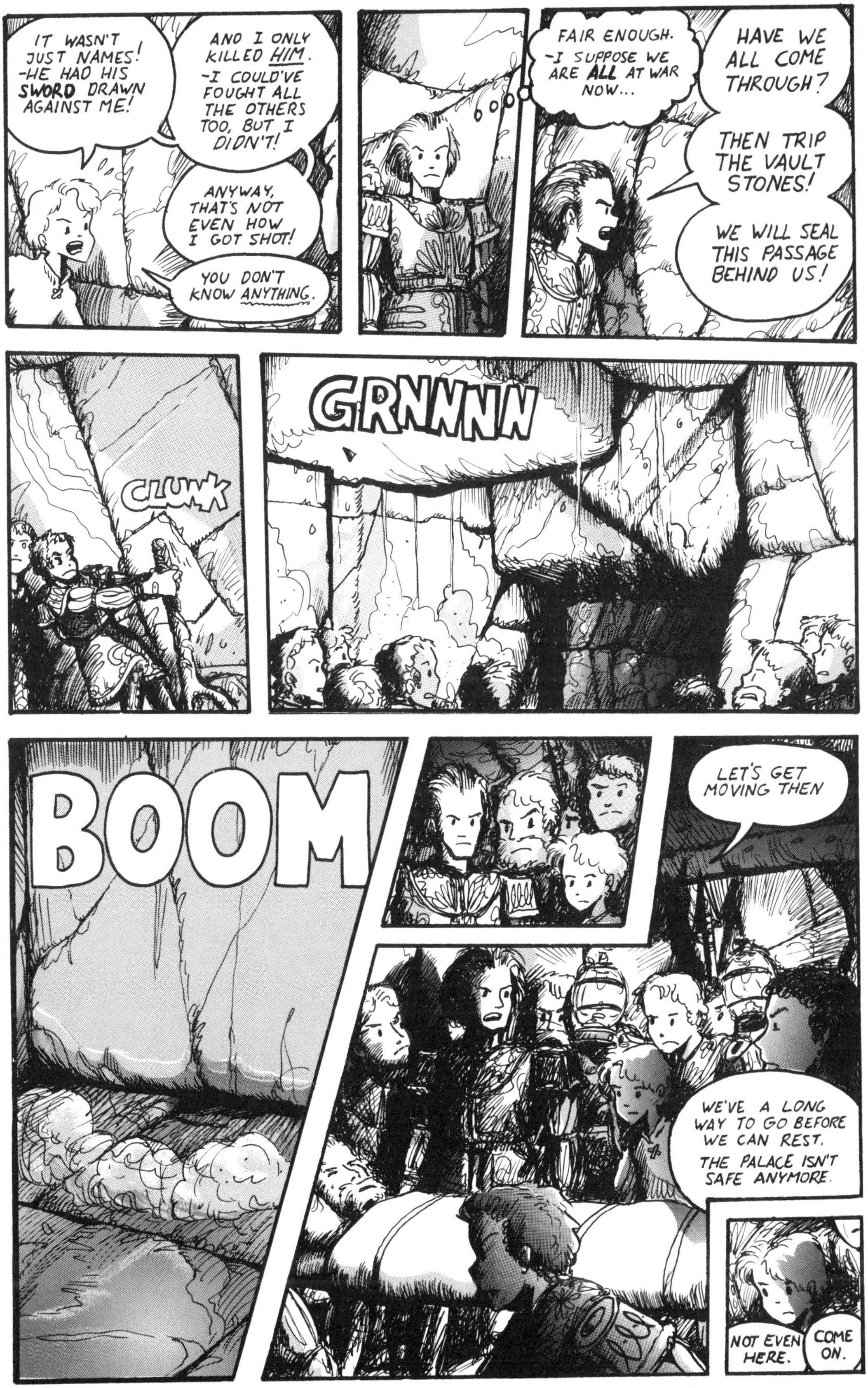
IT WASN'T JUST NAMES! -HE HAD HIS SWORD DRAWN AGAINST ME!
AND I ONLY KILLED HIM. -I COULD'VE FOUGHT ALL THE OTHERS TOO, BUT I DIDN'T!
ANYWAY, THAT'S NOT EVEN HOW I GOT SHOT!
YOU DON'T KNOW ANYTHING.
FAIR ENOUGH. -I SUPPOSE WE ARE ALL AT WAR NOW...
HAVE WE ALL COME THROUGH?
THEN TRIP THE VAULT STONES!
WE WILL SEAL THIS PASSAGE BEHIND US!
CLUNK
GRNNNN
BOOM
LET'S GET MOVING THEN
WE'VE A LONG WAY TO GO BEFORE WE CAN REST.
THE PALACE ISN'T SAFE ANYMORE.
NOT EVEN HERE.
COME ON.

Chapter 10

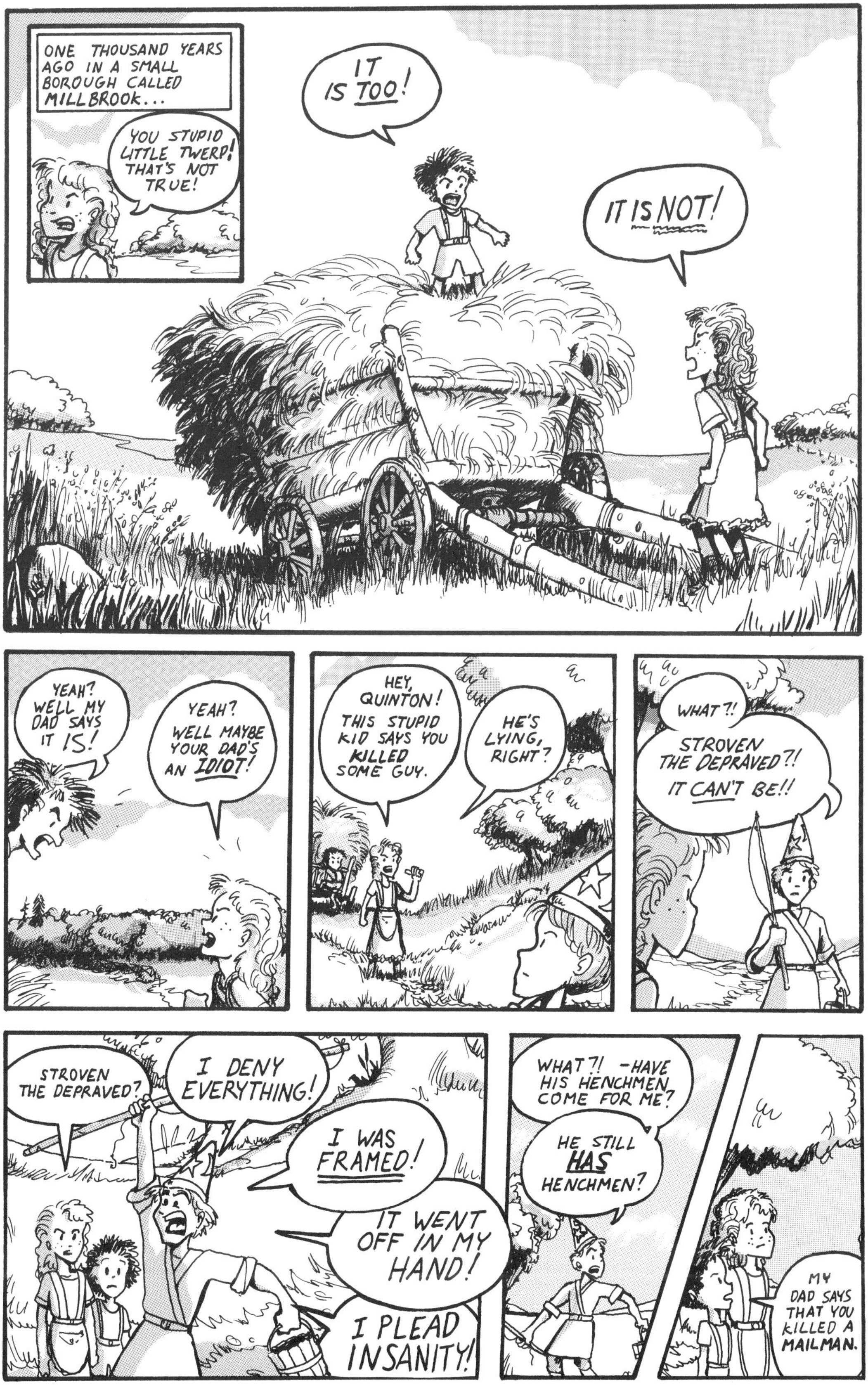
ONE THOUSAND YEARS AGO IN A SMALL BOROUGH CALLED MILLBROOK...
YOU STUPID LITTLE TWERP! THAT'S NOT TRUE!
IT IS TOO!
IT IS NOT!
YEAH? WELL MY DAD SAYS IT IS!
YEAH? WELL MAYBE YOUR DAD'S AN IDIOT!
HEY, QUINTON! THIS STUPID KID SAYS YOU KILLED SOME GUY.
HE'S LYING, RIGHT?
WHAT?!
STROVEN THE DEPRAVED?! IT CAN'T BE!!
STROVEN THE DEPRAVED?
I DENY EVERYTHING!
I WAS FRAMED!
IT WENT OFF IN MY HAND!
I PLEAD INSANITY!
WHAT?! -HAVE HIS HENCHMEN COME FOR ME?
HE STILL HAS HENCHMEN?
MY DAD SAYS THAT YOU KILLED A MAILMAN.

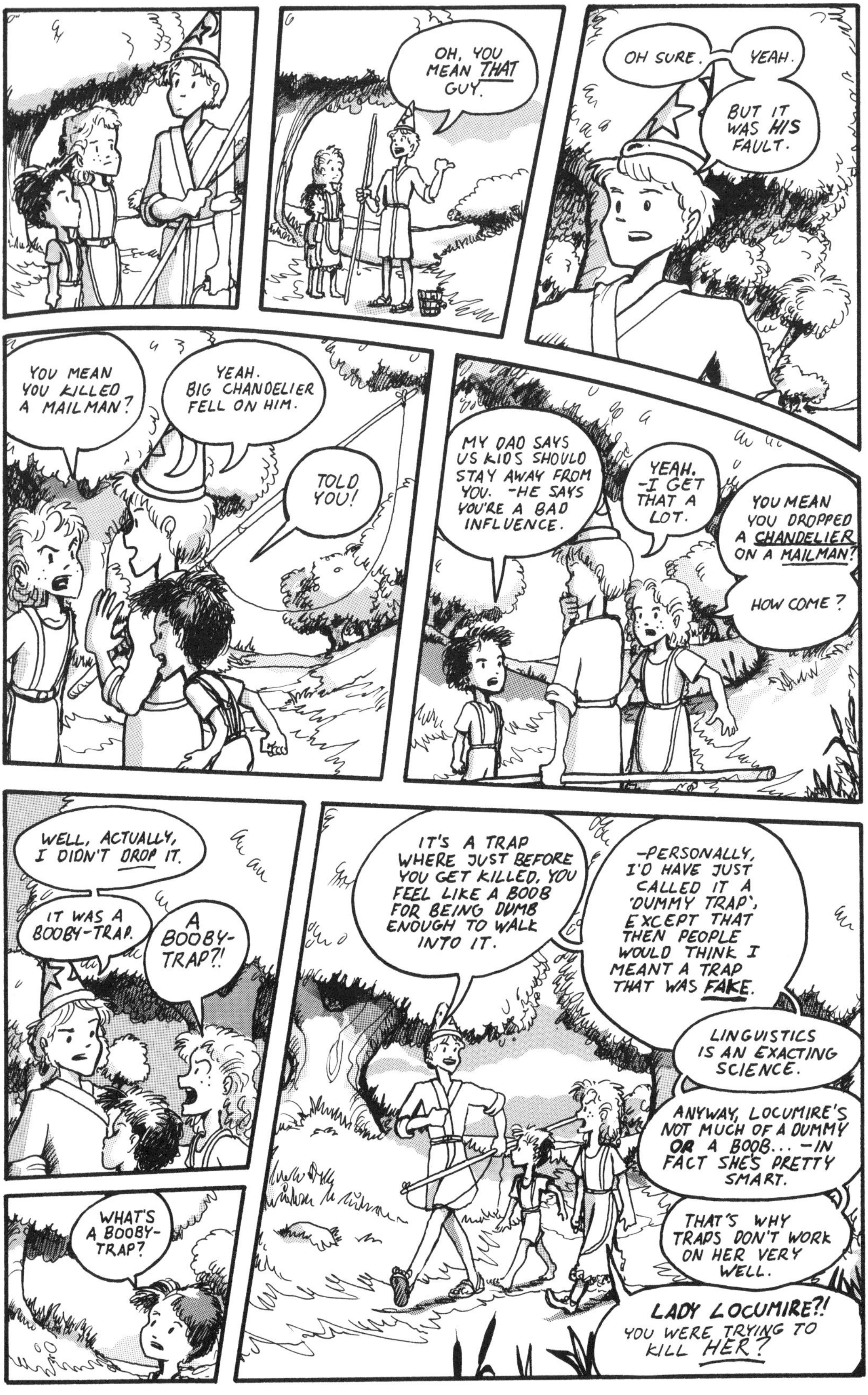
OH, YOU MEAN THAT GUY.
OH SURE.
YEAH.
BUT IT WAS HIS FAULT.
YOU MEAN YOU KILLED A MAILMAN?
YEAH. BIG CHANDELIER FELL ON HIM.
TOLD YOU!
MY DAD SAYS US KIDS SHOULD STAY AWAY FROM YOU. -HE SAYS YOU'RE A BAD INFLUENCE.
YEAH. -I GET THAT A LOT.
YOU MEAN YOU DROPPED A CHANDELIER ON A MAILMAN?
HOW COME?
WELL, ACTUALLY, I DIDN'T DROP IT.
IT WAS A BOOBY-TRAP.
A BOOBY-TRAP?!
WHAT'S A BOOBY-TRAP?
IT'S A TRAP WHERE JUST BEFORE YOU GET KILLED, YOU FEEL LIKE A BOOB FOR BEING DUMB ENOUGH TO WALK INTO IT.
-PERSONALLY, I'D HAVE JUST CALLED IT A 'DUMMY TRAP', EXCEPT THAT THEN PEOPLE WOULD THINK I MEANT A TRAP THAT WAS FAKE.
LINGUISTICS IS AN EXACTING SCIENCE.
ANYWAY, LOCUMIRE'S NOT MUCH OF A DUMMY OR A BOOB... -IN FACT SHE'S PRETTY SMART.
THAT'S WHY TRAPS DON'T WORK ON HER VERY WELL.
LADY LOCUMIRE?! YOU WERE TRYING TO KILL HER?

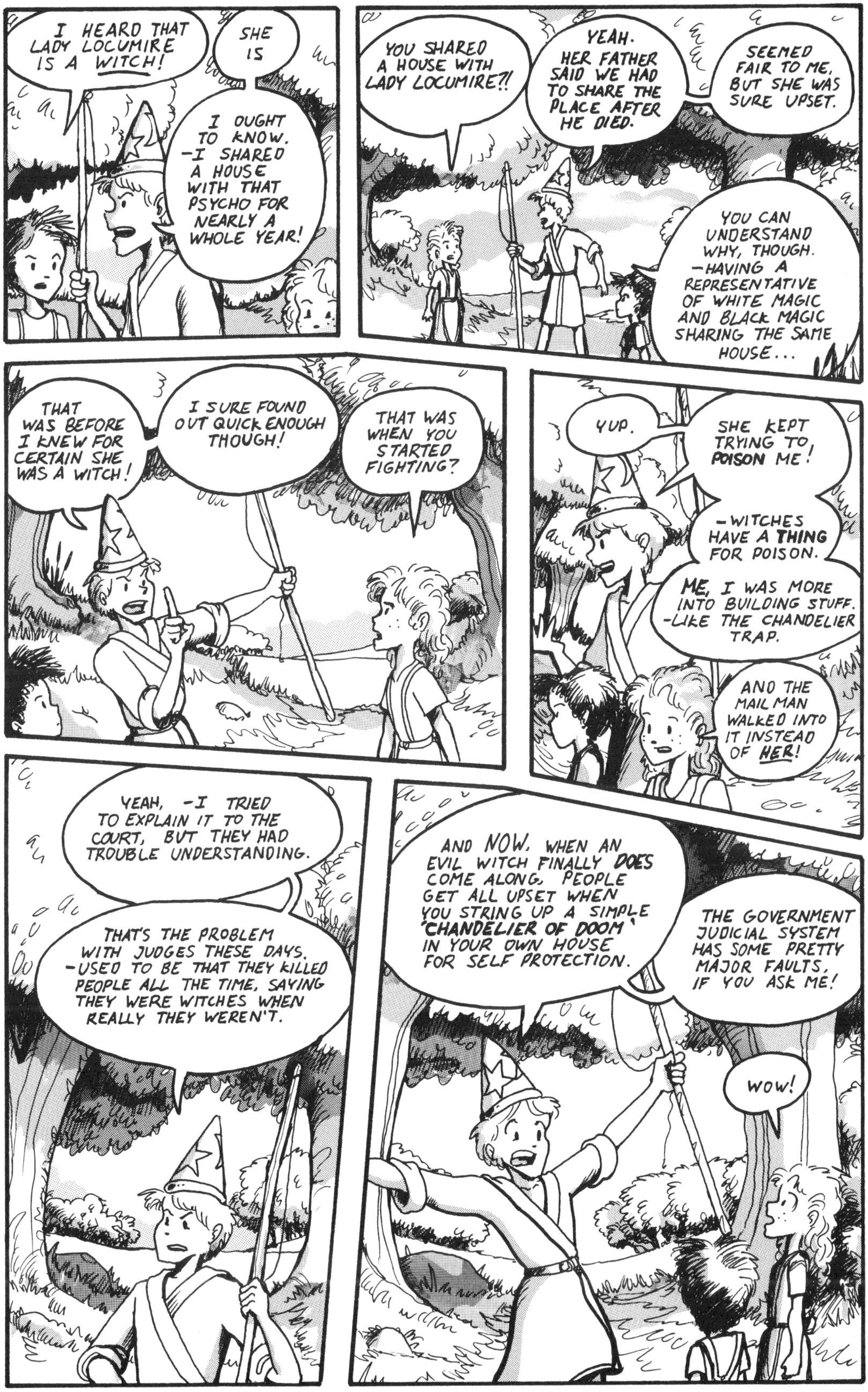

I HEARD THAT LADY LOCUMIRE IS A WITCH!
SHE IS
I OUGHT TO KNOW. -I SHARED A HOUSE WITH THAT PSYCHO FOR NEARLY A WHOLE YEAR!
YOU SHARED A HOUSE WITH LADY LOCUMIRE?!
YEAH. HER FATHER SAID WE HAD TO SHARE THE PLACE AFTER HE DIED.
SEEMED FAIR TO ME, BUT SHE WAS SURE UPSET.
YOU CAN UNDERSTAND WHY, THOUGH. -HAVING A REPRESENTATIVE OF WHITE MAGIC AND BLACK MAGIC SHARING THE SAME HOUSE...
THAT WAS BEFORE I KNEW FOR CERTAIN SHE WAS A WITCH!
I SURE FOUND OUT QUICK ENOUGH THOUGH!
THAT WAS WHEN YOU STARTED FIGHTING?
YUP.
SHE KEPT TRYING TO, POISON ME!
-WITCHES HAVE A THING FOR POISON.
ME, I WAS MORE INTO BUILDING STUFF. -LIKE THE CHANDELIER TRAP.
AND THE MAIL MAN WALKED INTO IT INSTEAD OF HER!
YEAH, -I TRIED TO EXPLAIN IT TO THE COURT, BUT THEY HAD TROUBLE UNDERSTANDING.
THAT'S THE PROBLEM WITH JUDGES THESE DAYS. -USED TO BE THAT THEY KILLED PEOPLE ALL THE TIME, SAYING THEY WERE WITCHES WHEN REALLY THEY WEREN'T.
AND NOW, WHEN AN EVIL WITCH FINALLY DOES COME ALONG, PEOPLE GET ALL UPSET WHEN YOU STRING UP A SIMPLE 'CHANDELIER OF DOOM' IN YOUR OWN HOUSE FOR SELF PROTECTION.
THE GOVERNMENT JUDICIAL SYSTEM HAS SOME PRETTY MAJOR FAULTS, IF YOU ASK ME!
WOW!

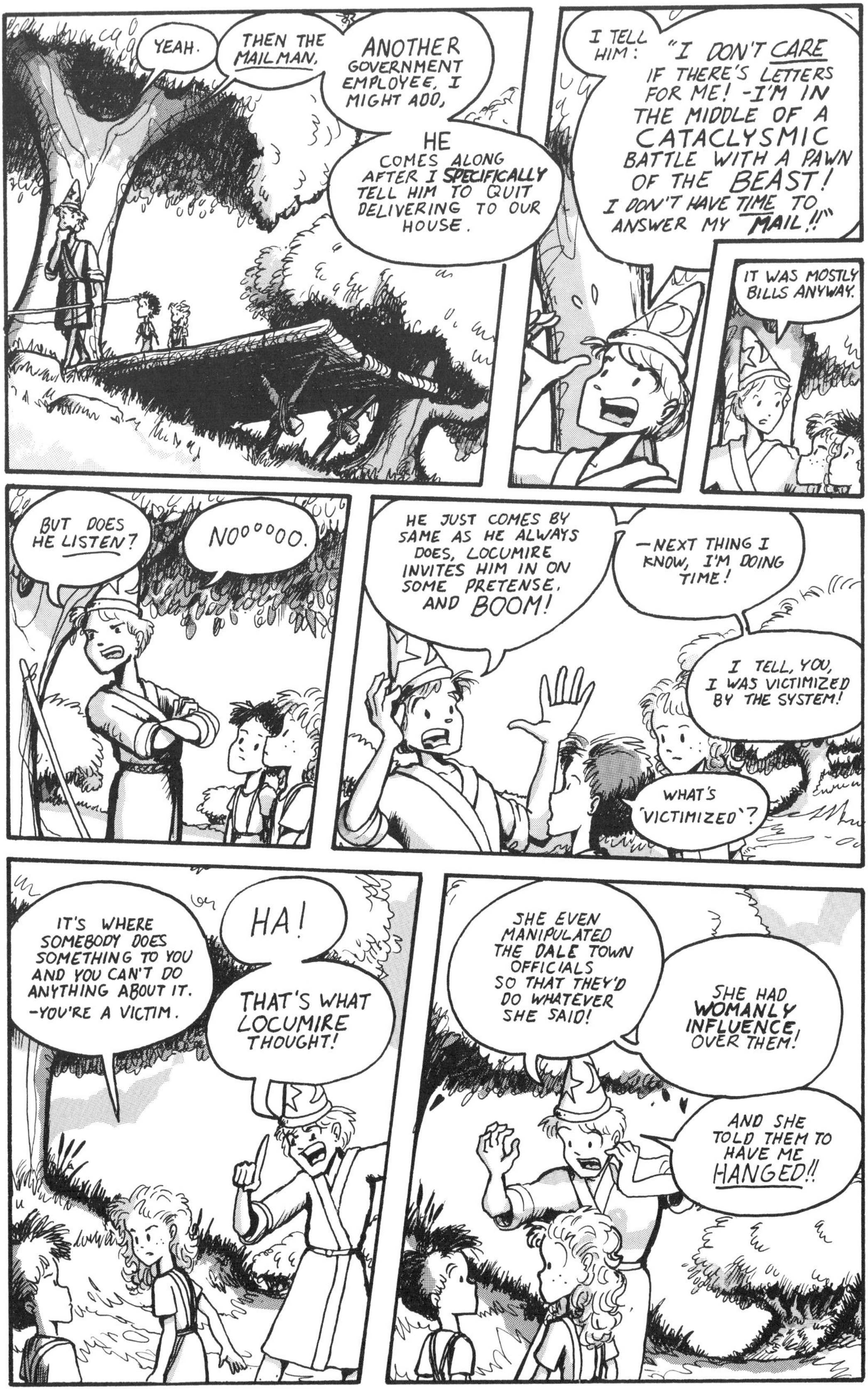
YEAH.
THEN THE MAILMAN,
ANOTHER GOVERNMENT EMPLOYEE, I MIGHT ADD,
HE COMES ALONG AFTER I SPECIFICALLY TELL HIM TO QUIT DELIVERING TO OUR HOUSE.
I TELL HIM: "I DON'T CARE IF THERE'S LETTERS FOR ME! -I'M IN THE MIDDLE OF A CATACLYSMIC BATTLE WITH A PAWN OF THE BEAST! I DON'T HAVE TIME TO ANSWER MY MAIL!!"
IT WAS MOSTLY BILLS ANYWAY.
BUT DOES HE LISTEN?
NOºººOO.
HE JUST COMES BY SAME AS HE ALWAYS DOES, LOCUMIRE INVITES HIM IN ON SOME PRETENSE, AND BOOM!
-NEXT THING I KNOW, I'M DOING TIME!
I TELL, YOU, I WAS VICTIMIZED BY THE SYSTEM!
WHAT'S 'VICTIMIZED'?
IT'S WHERE SOMEBODY DOES SOMETHING TO YOU AND YOU CAN'T DO ANYTHING ABOUT IT. -YOU'RE A VICTIM.
HA!
THAT'S WHAT LOCUMIRE THOUGHT!
SHE EVEN MANIPULATED THE DALE TOWN OFFICIALS SO THAT THEY'D DO WHATEVER SHE SAID!
SHE HAD WOMANLY INFLUENCE, OVER THEM!
AND SHE TOLD THEM TO HAVE ME HANGED!!

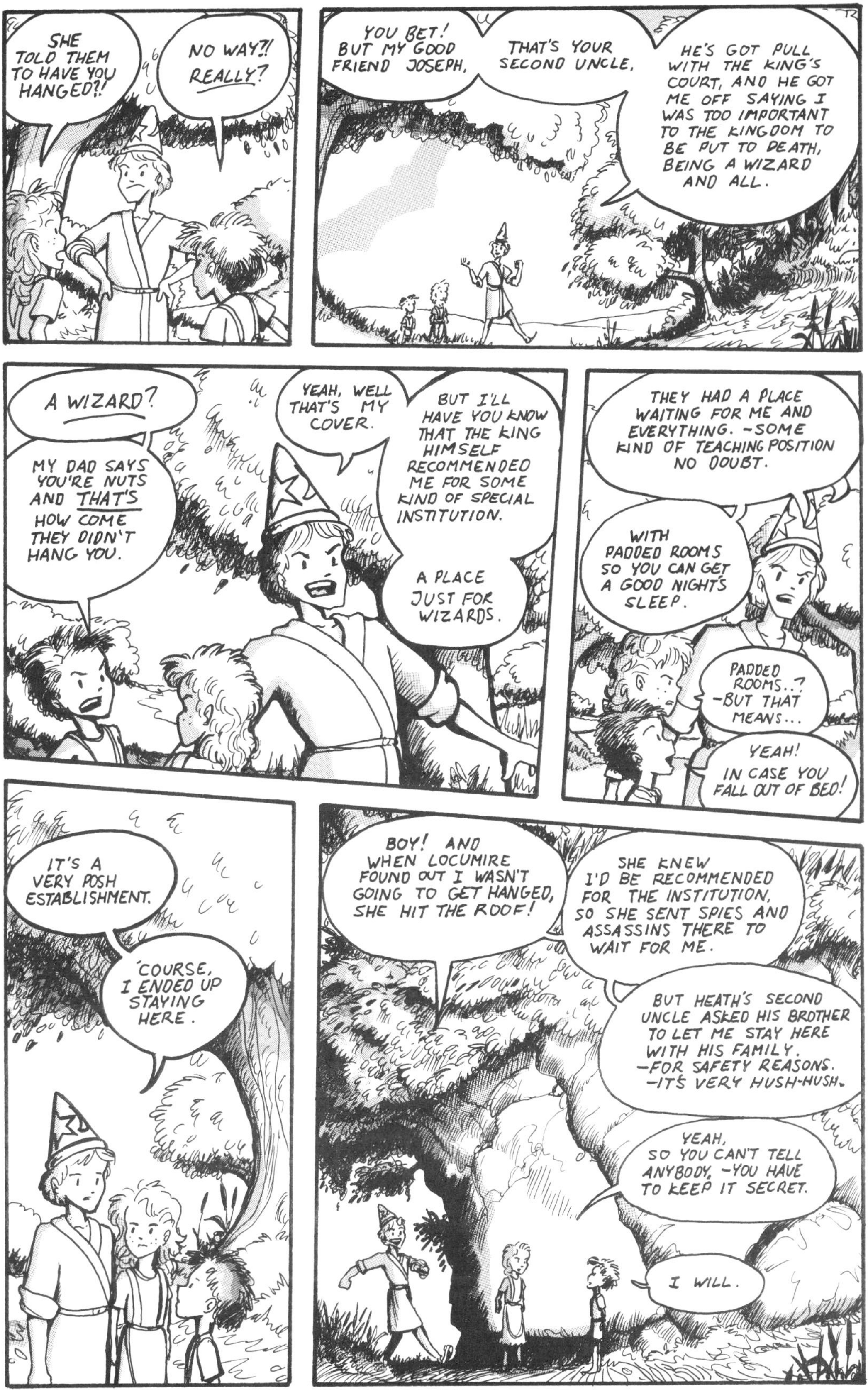
SHE TOLD THEM TO HAVE YOU HANGED?!
NO WAY?! REALLY?
YOU BET! BUT MY GOOD FRIEND JOSEPH,
THAT'S YOUR SECOND UNCLE,
HE'S GOT PULL WITH THE KING'S COURT, AND HE GOT ME OFF SAYING I WAS TOO IMPORTANT TO THE KINGDOM TO BE PUT TO DEATH, BEING A WIZARD AND ALL.
A WIZARD?
MY DAD SAYS YOU'RE NUTS AND THAT'S HOW COME THEY DIDN'T HANG YOU.
YEAH, WELL THAT'S MY COVER.
BUT I'LL HAVE YOU KNOW THAT THE KING HIMSELF RECOMMENDED ME FOR SOME KIND OF SPECIAL INSTITUTION.
A PLACE JUST FOR WIZARDS.
THEY HAD A PLACE WAITING FOR ME AND EVERYTHING. -SOME KIND OF TEACHING POSITION NO DOUBT.
WITH PADDED ROOMS SO YOU CAN GET A GOOD NIGHT'S SLEEP.
PADDED ROOMS..? -BUT THAT MEANS...
YEAH! IN CASE YOU FALL OUT OF BED!
IT'S A VERY POSH ESTABLISHMENT.
'COURSE, I ENDED UP STAYING HERE.
BOY! AND WHEN LOCUMIRE FOUND OUT I WASN'T GOING TO GET HANGED, SHE HIT THE ROOF!
SHE KNEW I'D BE RECOMMENDED FOR THE INSTITUTION, SO SHE SENT SPIES AND ASSASSINS THERE TO WAIT FOR ME.
BUT HEATH'S SECOND UNCLE ASKED HIS BROTHER TO LET ME STAY HERE WITH HIS FAMILY. -FOR SAFETY REASONS. -IT'S VERY HUSH-HUSH.
YEAH, SO YOU CAN'T TELL ANYBODY, -YOU HAVE TO KEEP IT SECRET.
I WILL.

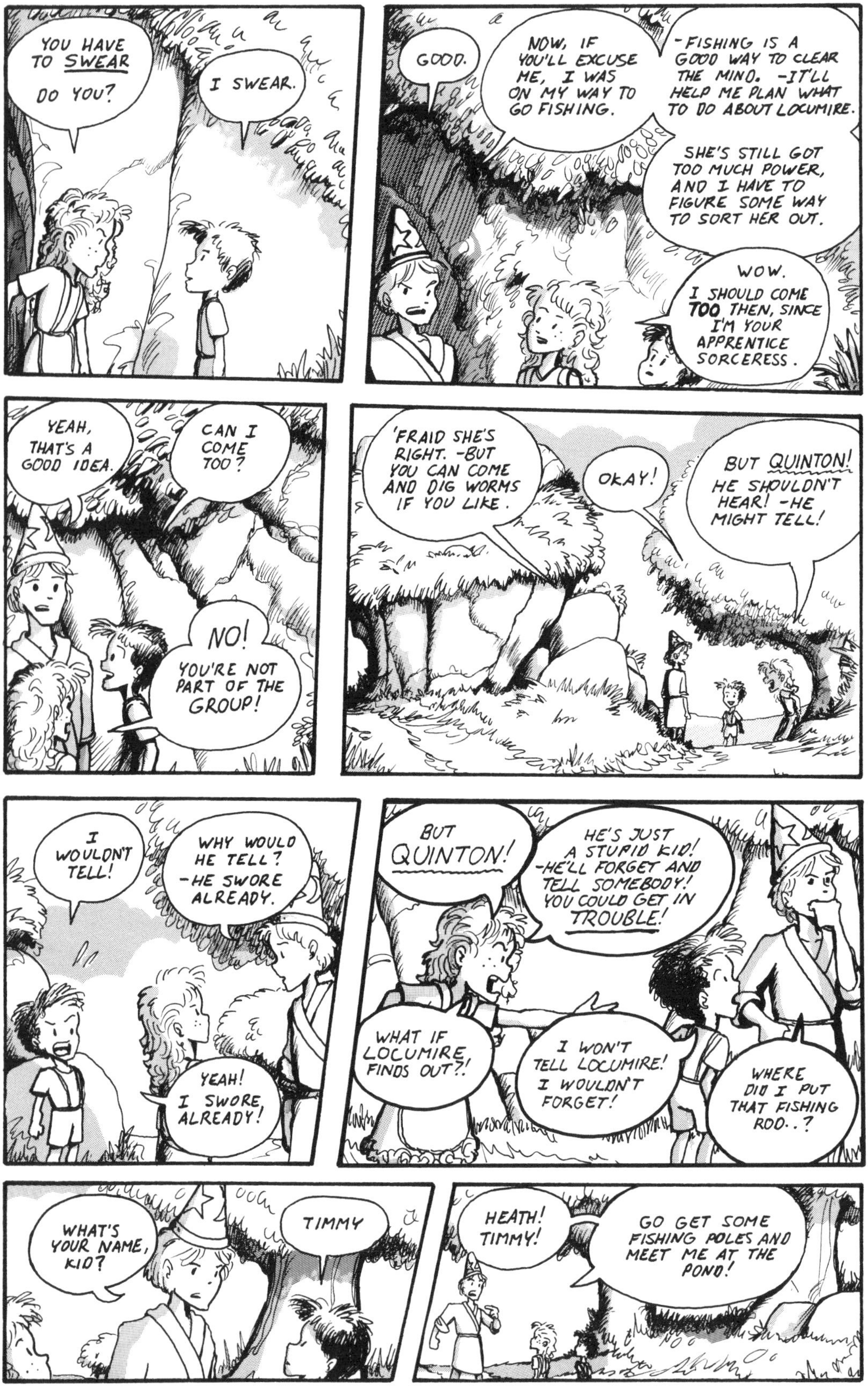
YOU HAVE TO SWEAR DO YOU?
I SWEAR.
GOOD.
NOW, IF YOU'LL EXCUSE ME, I WAS ON MY WAY TO GO FISHING.
-FISHING IS A GOOD WAY TO CLEAR THE MIND. -IT'LL HELP ME PLAN WHAT TO DO ABOUT LOCUMIRE.
SHE'S STILL GOT TOO MUCH POWER, AND I HAVE TO FIGURE SOME WAY TO SORT HER OUT.
WOW. I SHOULD COME TOO THEN, SINCE I'M YOUR APPRENTICE SORCERESS.
YEAH, THAT'S A GOOD IDEA.
CAN I COME TOO?
NO! YOU'RE NOT PART OF THE GROUP!
'FRAID SHE'S RIGHT. -BUT YOU CAN COME AND DIG WORMS IF YOU LIKE.
OKAY!
BUT QUINTON! HE SHOULDN'T HEAR! -HE MIGHT TELL!
I WOULDN'T TELL!
WHY WOULD HE TELL? -HE SWORE ALREADY.
YEAH! I SWORE ALREADY!
BUT QUINTON!
HE'S JUST A STUPID KID! -HE'LL FORGET AND TELL SOMEBODY! YOU COULD GET IN TROUBLE!
WHAT IF LOCUMIRE FINDS OUT?!
I WON'T TELL LOCUMIRE! I WOULDN'T FORGET!
WHERE DID I PUT THAT FISHING ROD..?
WHAT'S YOUR NAME, KID?
TIMMY
HEATH! TIMMY!
GO GET SOME FISHING POLES AND MEET ME AT THE POND!

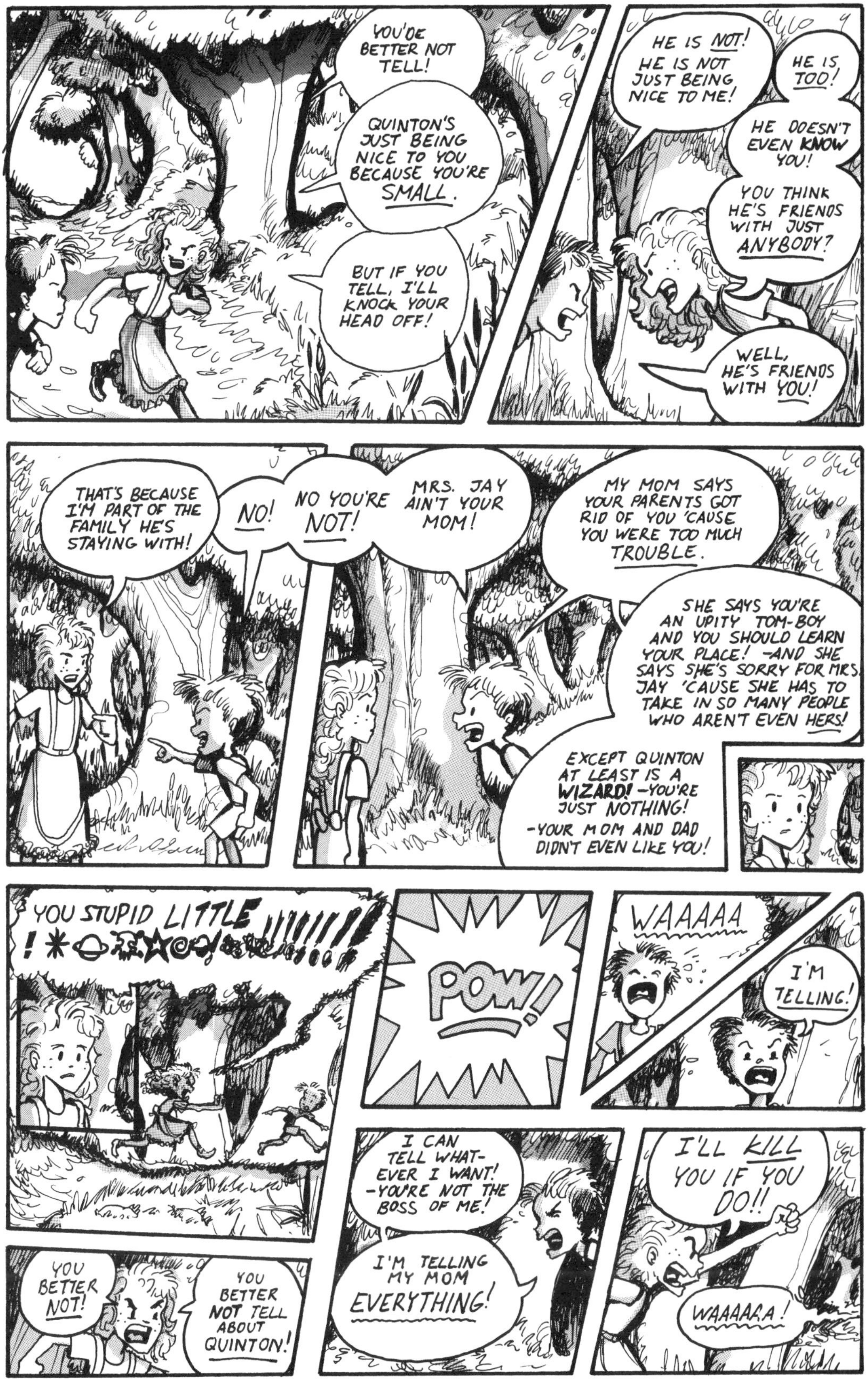
YOU'DE BETTER NOT TELL!
QUINTON'S JUST BEING NICE TO YOU BECAUSE YOU'RE SMALL.
BUT IF YOU TELL, I'LL KNOCK YOUR HEAD OFF!
HE IS NOT! HE IS NOT JUST BEING NICE TO ME!
HE IS TOO!
HE DOESN'T EVEN KNOW YOU!
YOU THINK HE'S FRIENDS WITH JUST ANYBODY?
WELL, HE'S FRIENDS WITH YOU!
THAT'S BECAUSE I'M PART OF THE FAMILY HE'S STAYING WITH!
NO!
NO YOU'RE NOT!
MRS. JAY AIN'T YOUR MOM!
MY MOM SAYS YOUR PARENTS GOT RID OF YOU 'CAUSE YOU WERE TOO MUCH TROUBLE.
SHE SAYS YOU'RE AN UPITY TOM-BOY AND YOU SHOULD LEARN YOUR PLACE! -AND SHE SAYS SHE'S SORRY FOR MRS. JAY 'CAUSE SHE HAS TO TAKE IN SO MANY PEOPLE WHO AREN'T EVEN HERS!
EXCEPT QUINTON AT LEAST IS A WIZARD! -YOU'RE JUST NOTHING! -YOUR MOM AND DAD DIDN'T EVEN LIKE YOU!
YOU STUPID LITTLE
POW!
WAAAAA
I'M TELLING!
YOU BETTER NOT!
YOU BETTER NOT TELL ABOUT QUINTON!
I CAN TELL WHAT-EVER I WANT! -YOU'RE NOT THE BOSS OF ME!
I'M TELLING MY MOM EVERYTHING!
I'LL KILL YOU IF YOU DO!!
WAAAAAA!

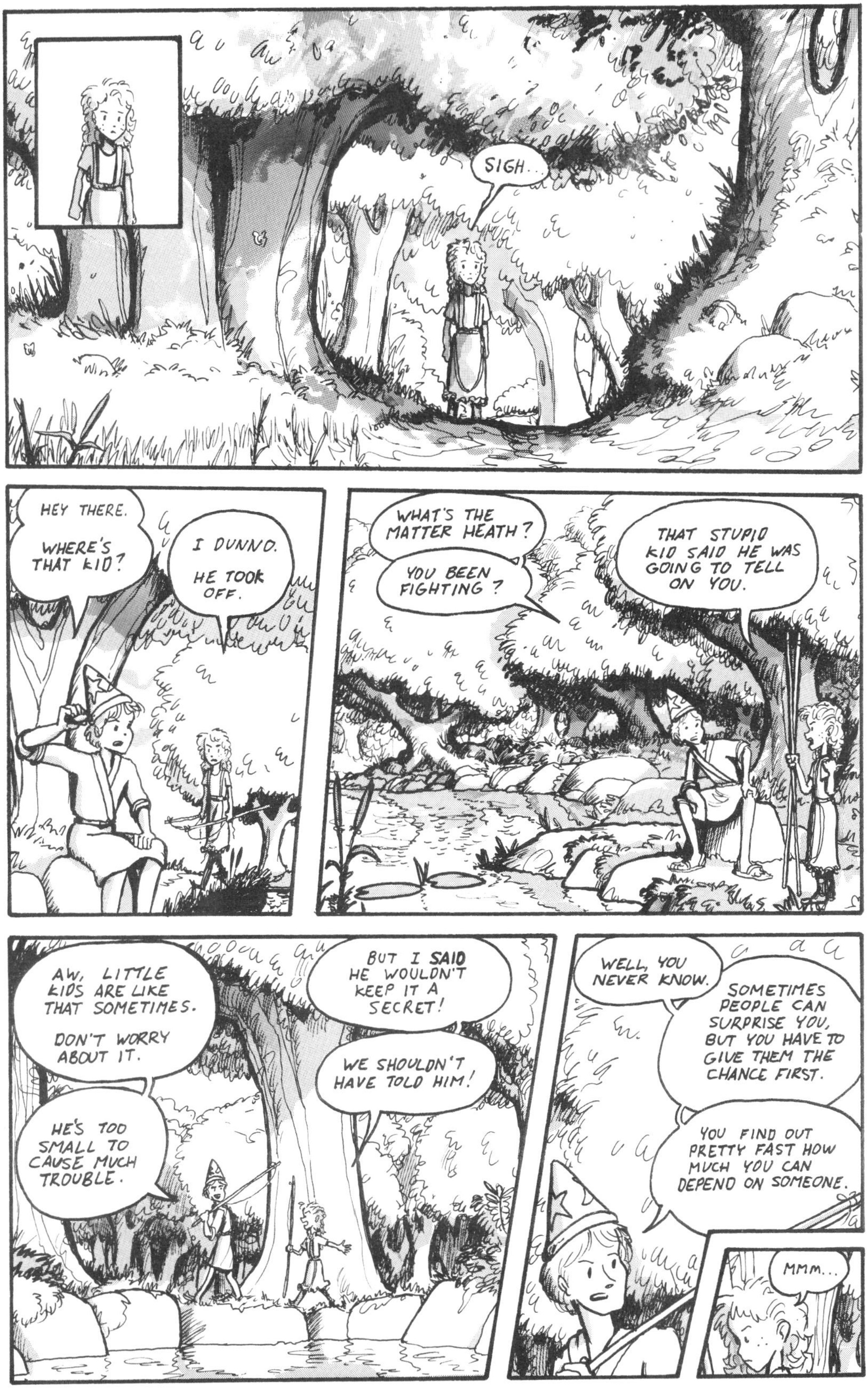

SIGH...
HEY THERE.
WHERE'S THAT KID?
I DUNNO.
HE TOOK OFF.
WHAT'S THE MATTER HEATH?
YOU BEEN FIGHTING?
THAT STUPID KID SAID HE WAS GOING TO TELL ON YOU.
AW, LITTLE KIDS ARE LIKE THAT SOMETIMES.
DON'T WORRY ABOUT IT.
BUT I SAID HE WOULDN'T KEEP IT A SECRET!
WE SHOULDN'T HAVE TOLD HIM!
HE'S TOO SMALL TO CAUSE MUCH TROUBLE.
WELL, YOU NEVER KNOW.
SOMETIMES PEOPLE CAN SURPRISE YOU, BUT YOU HAVE TO GIVE THEM THE CHANCE FIRST.
YOU FIND OUT PRETTY FAST HOW MUCH YOU CAN DEPEND ON SOMEONE.
MMM...

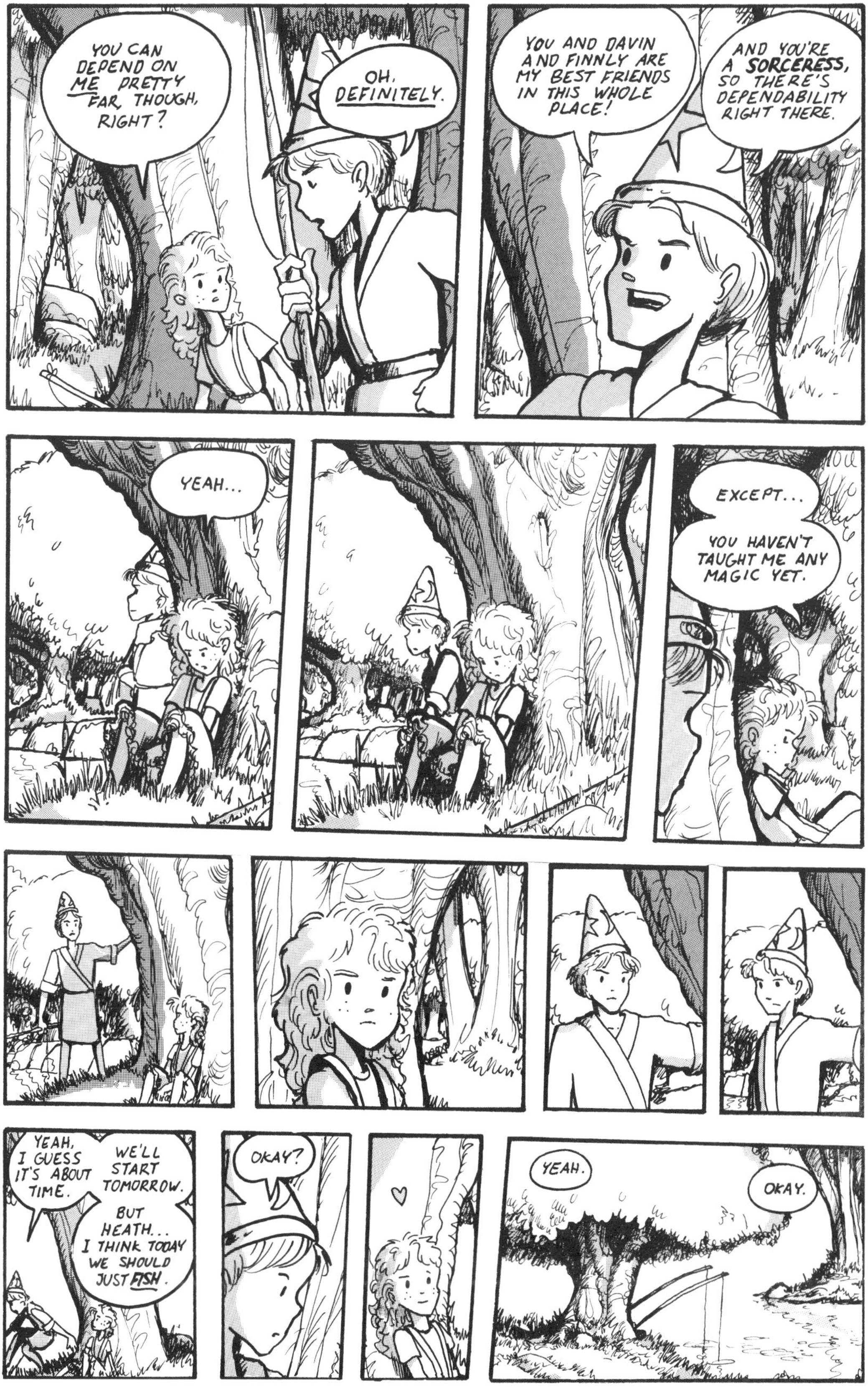
YOU CAN DEPEND ON ME PRETTY FAR, THOUGH, RIGHT?
OH, DEFINITELY.
YOU AND DAVIN AND FINNLY ARE MY BEST FRIENDS IN THIS WHOLE PLACE!
AND YOU'RE A SORCERESS, SO THERE'S DEPENDABILITY RIGHT THERE.
YEAH...
EXCEPT...
YOU HAVEN'T TAUGHT ME ANY MAGIC YET.
YEAH, I GUESS IT'S ABOUT TIME.
WE'LL START TOMORROW.
BUT HEATH... I THINK TODAY WE SHOULD JUST FISH.
OKAY?
YEAH.
OKAY.

Chapter 11

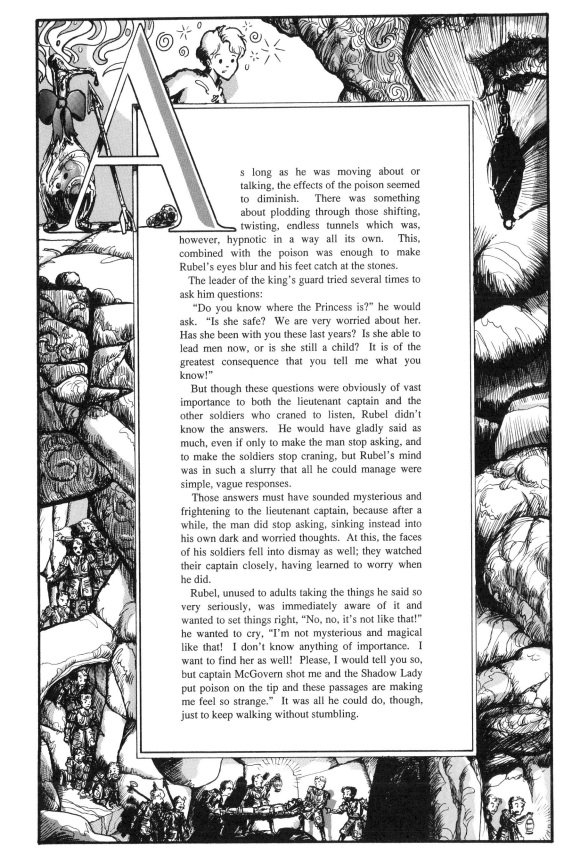

As long as he was moving about or talking, the effects of the poison seemed to diminish. There was something about plodding through those shifting, twisting, endless tunnels which was, however, hypnotic in a way all its own. This, combined with the poison was enough to make Rubel's eyes blur and his feet catch at the stones.

The leader of the king's guard tried several times to ask him questions:

"Do you know where the Princess is?" he would ask. "Is she safe? We are very worried about her. Has she been with you these last years? Is she able to lead men now, or is she still a child? It is of the greatest consequence that you tell me what you know!"

But though these questions were obviously of vast importance to both the lieutenant captain and the other soldiers who craned to listen, Rubel didn't know the answers. He would have gladly said as much, even if only to make the man stop asking, and to make the soldiers stop craning, but Rubel's mind was in such a slurry that all he could manage were simple, vague responses.

Those answers must have sounded mysterious and frightening to the lieutenant captain, because after a while, the man did stop asking, sinking instead into his own dark and worried thoughts. At this, the faces of his soldiers fell into dismay as well; they watched their captain closely, having learned to worry when he did.

Rubel, unused to adults taking the things he said so very seriously, was immediately aware of it and wanted to set things right, "No, no, it's not like that!" he wanted to cry, "I'm not mysterious and magical like that! I don't know anything of importance. I want to find her as well! Please, I would tell you so, but captain McGovern shot me and the Shadow Lady put poison on the tip and these passages are making me feel so strange." It was all he could do, though, just to keep walking without stumbling.

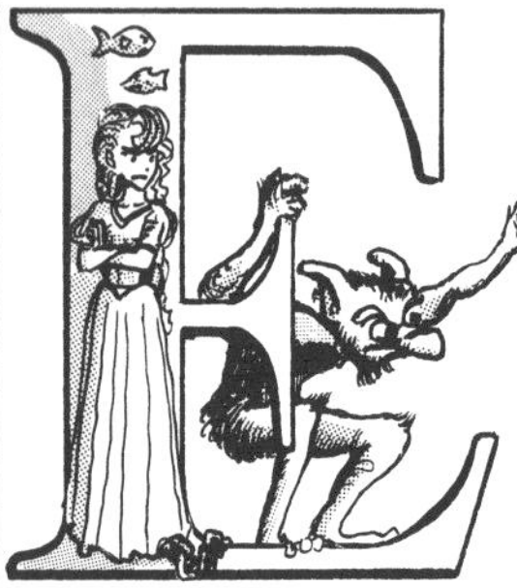

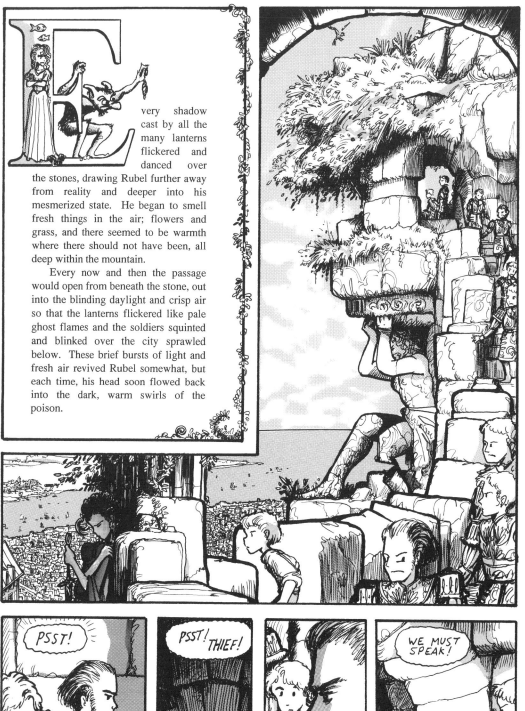

Every shadow cast by all the many lanterns flickered and danced over the stones, drawing Rubel further away from reality and deeper into his mesmerized state. He began to smell fresh things in the air; flowers and grass, and there seemed to be warmth where there should not have been, all deep within the mountain.

Every now and then the passage would open from beneath the stone, out into the blinding daylight and crisp air so that the lanterns flickered like pale ghost flames and the soldiers squinted and blinked over the city sprawled below. These brief bursts of light and fresh air revived Rubel somewhat, but each time, his head soon flowed back into the dark, warm swirls of the poison.

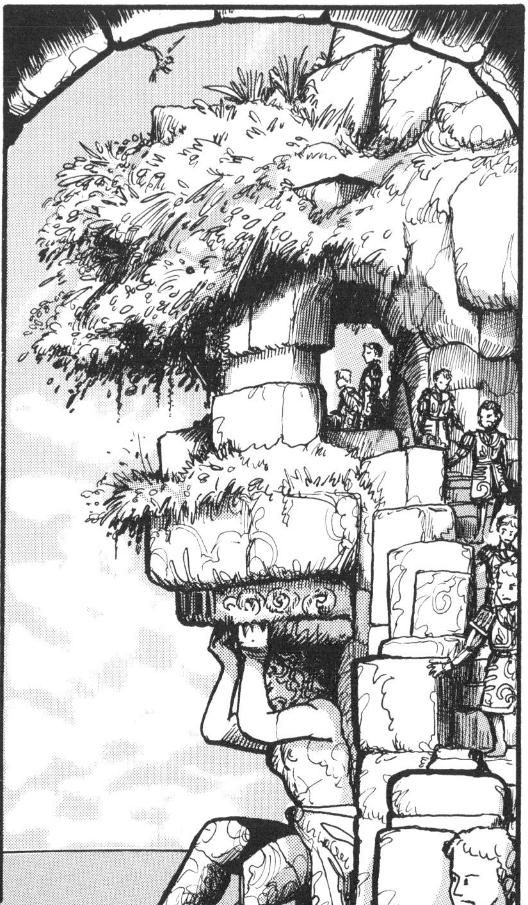

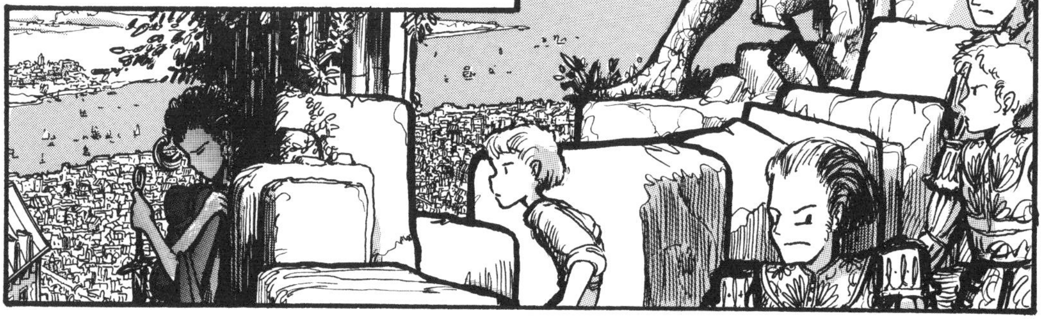

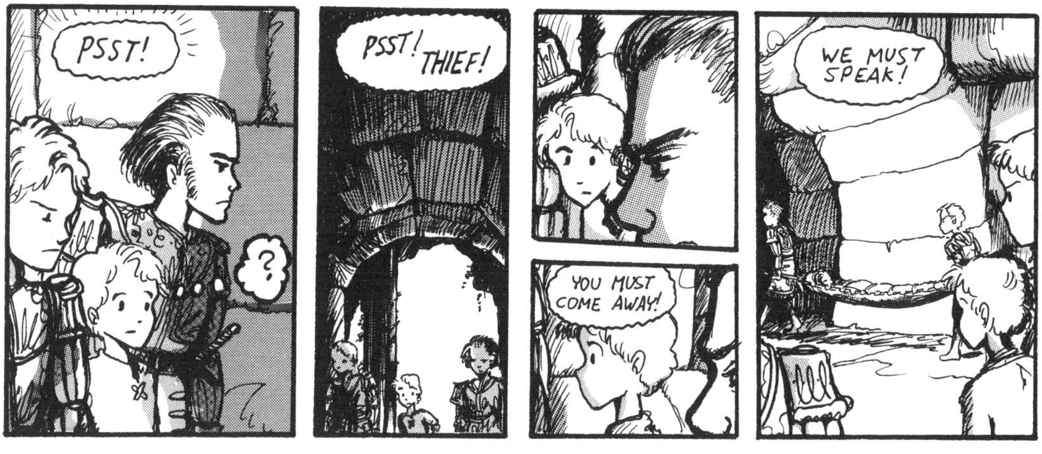
PSST!
?
PSST! THIEF!
YOU MUST COME AWAY!
WE MUST SPEAK!

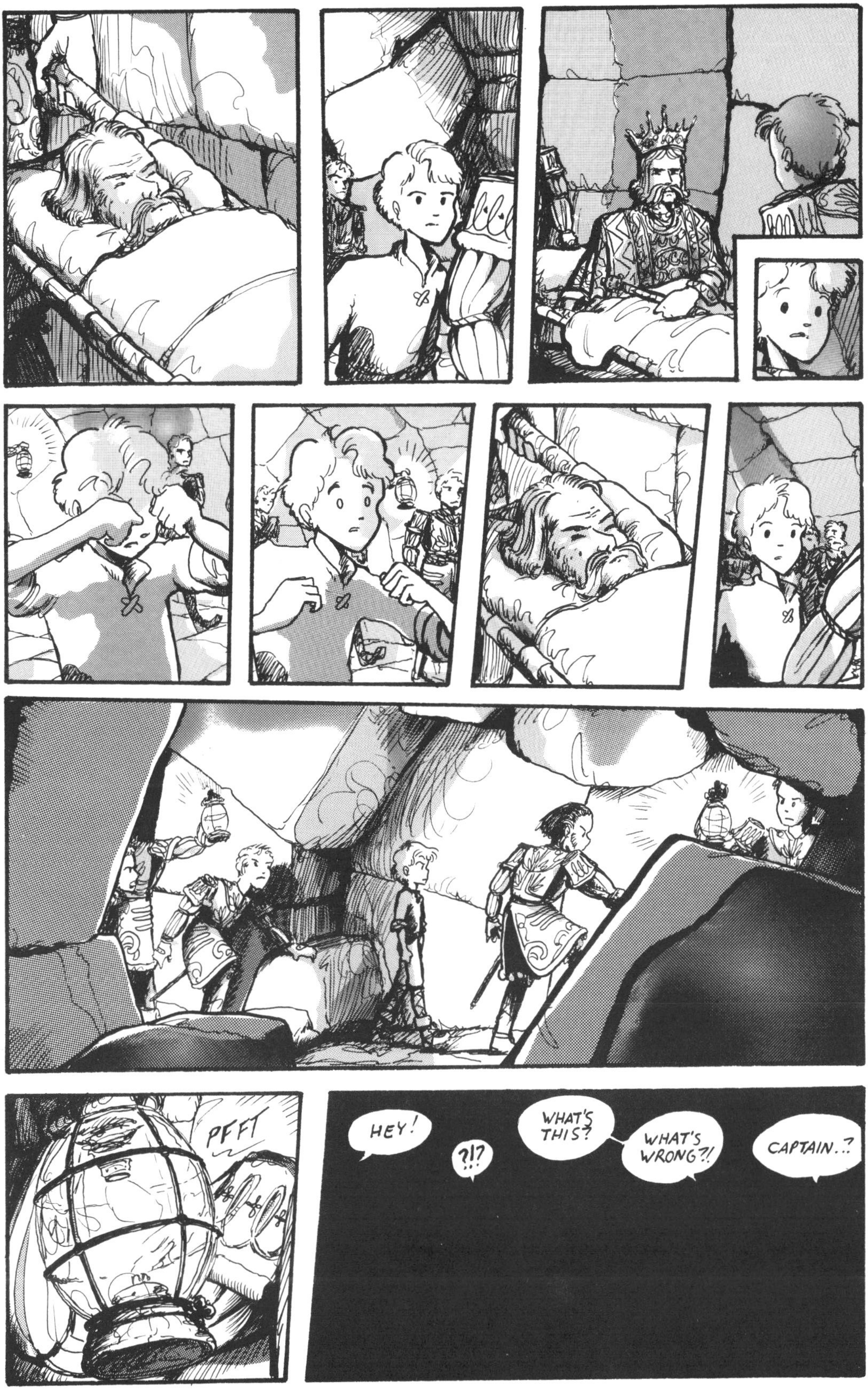
PFFT
HEY!
?!?
WHAT'S THIS?
WHAT'S WRONG?!
CAPTAIN..?

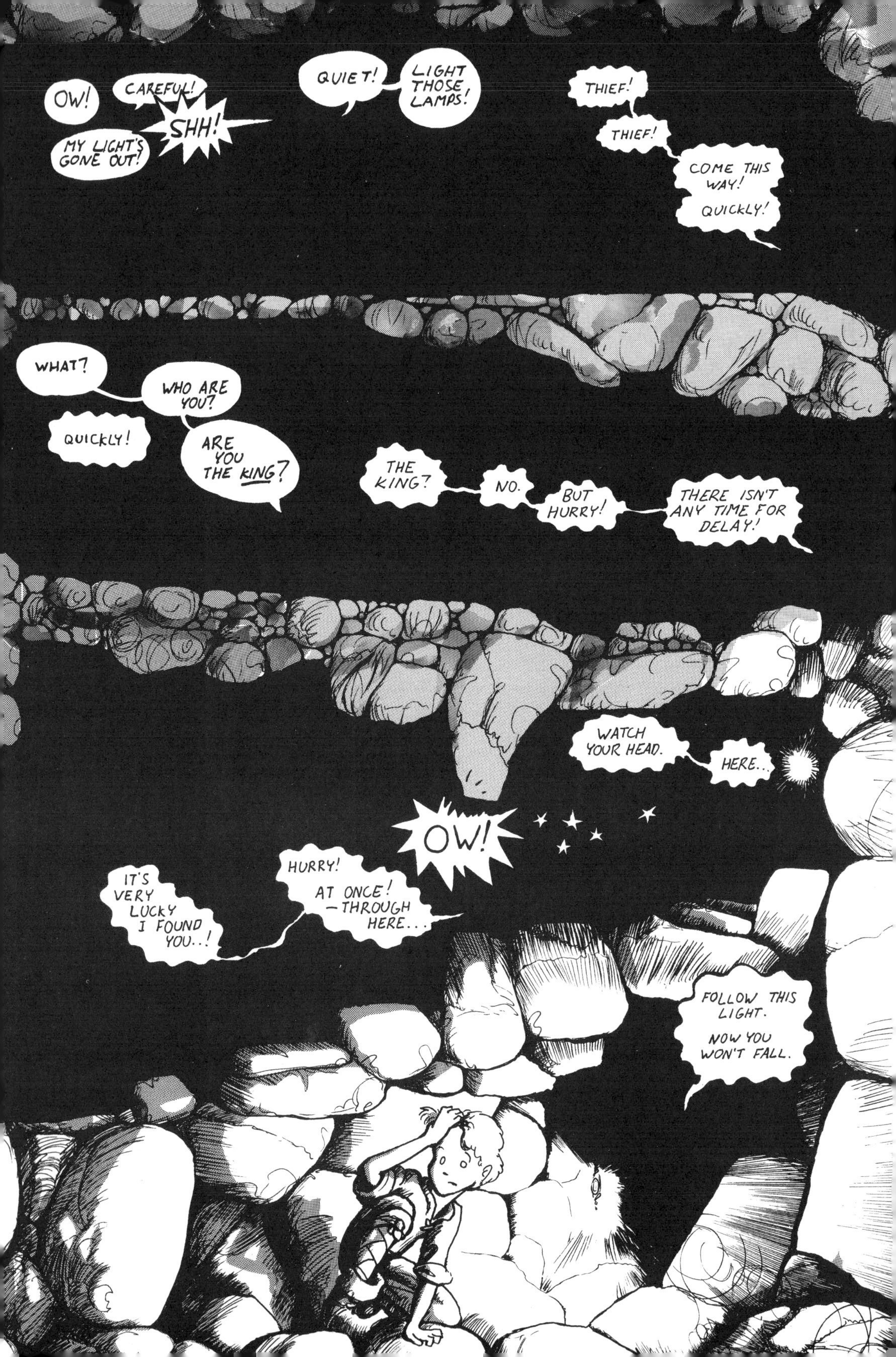
OW!
CAREFUL!
SHH!
MY LIGHT'S GONE OUT!
QUIET!
LIGHT THOSE LAMPS!
THIEF!
THIEF!
COME THIS WAY!
QUICKLY!
WHAT?
WHO ARE YOU?
QUICKLY!
ARE YOU THE KING?
THE KING?
NO.
BUT HURRY!
THERE ISN'T ANY TIME FOR DELAY!
WATCH YOUR HEAD.
HERE...
OW!
HURRY!
AT ONCE! —THROUGH HERE...
IT'S VERY LUCKY I FOUND YOU..!
FOLLOW THIS LIGHT.
NOW YOU WON'T FALL.

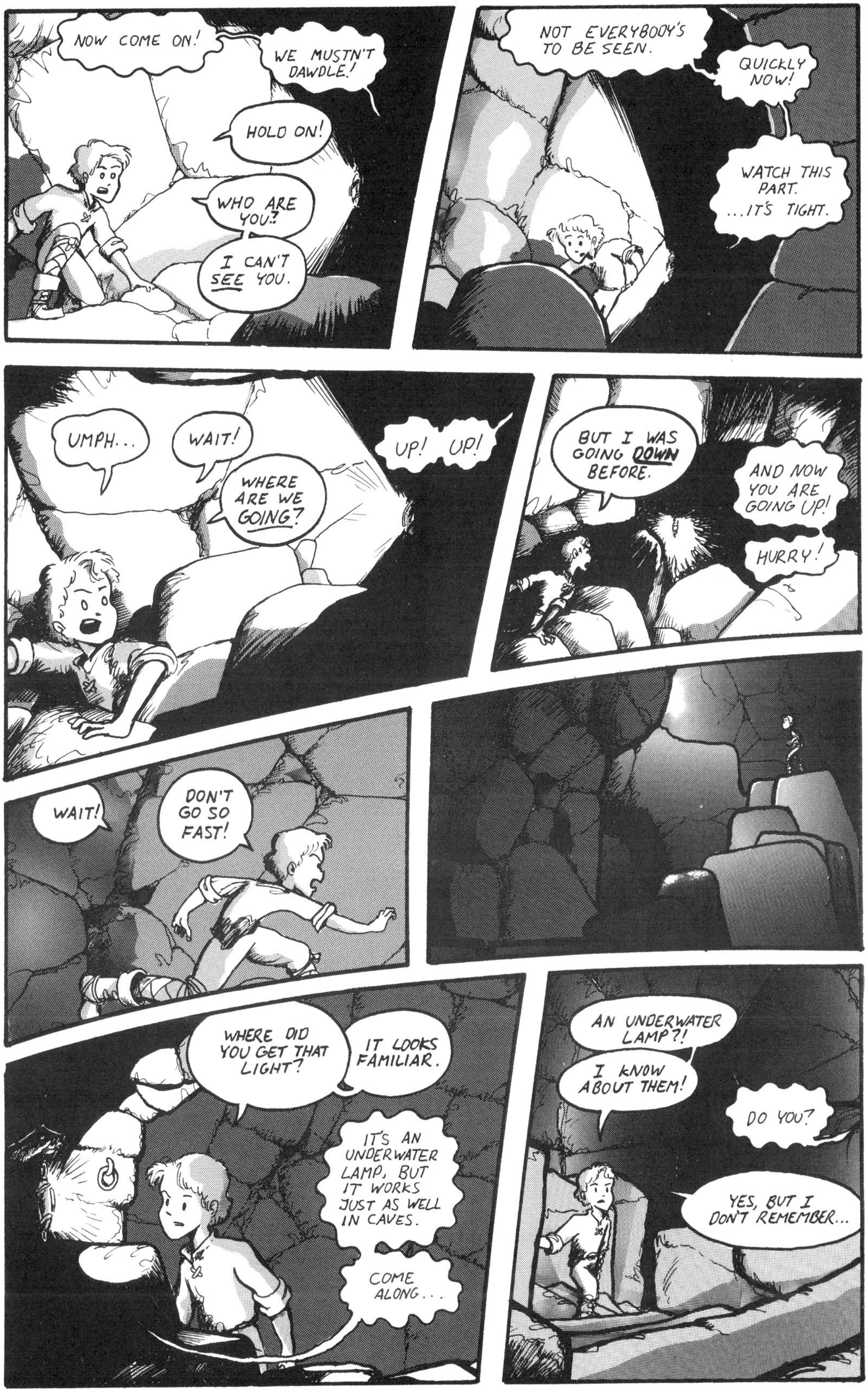
NOW COME ON!
WE MUSTN'T DAWDLE!
HOLD ON!
WHO ARE YOU?
I CAN'T SEE YOU.
NOT EVERYBODY'S TO BE SEEN.
QUICKLY NOW!
WATCH THIS PART. ...IT'S TIGHT.
UMPH...
WAIT!
WHERE ARE WE GOING?
UP! UP!
BUT I WAS GOING DOWN BEFORE.
AND NOW YOU ARE GOING UP!
HURRY!
WAIT!
DON'T GO SO FAST!
WHERE DID YOU GET THAT LIGHT?
IT LOOKS FAMILIAR.
IT'S AN UNDERWATER LAMP, BUT IT WORKS JUST AS WELL IN CAVES.
COME ALONG...
AN UNDERWATER LAMP?!
I KNOW ABOUT THEM!
DO YOU?
YES, BUT I DON'T REMEMBER...

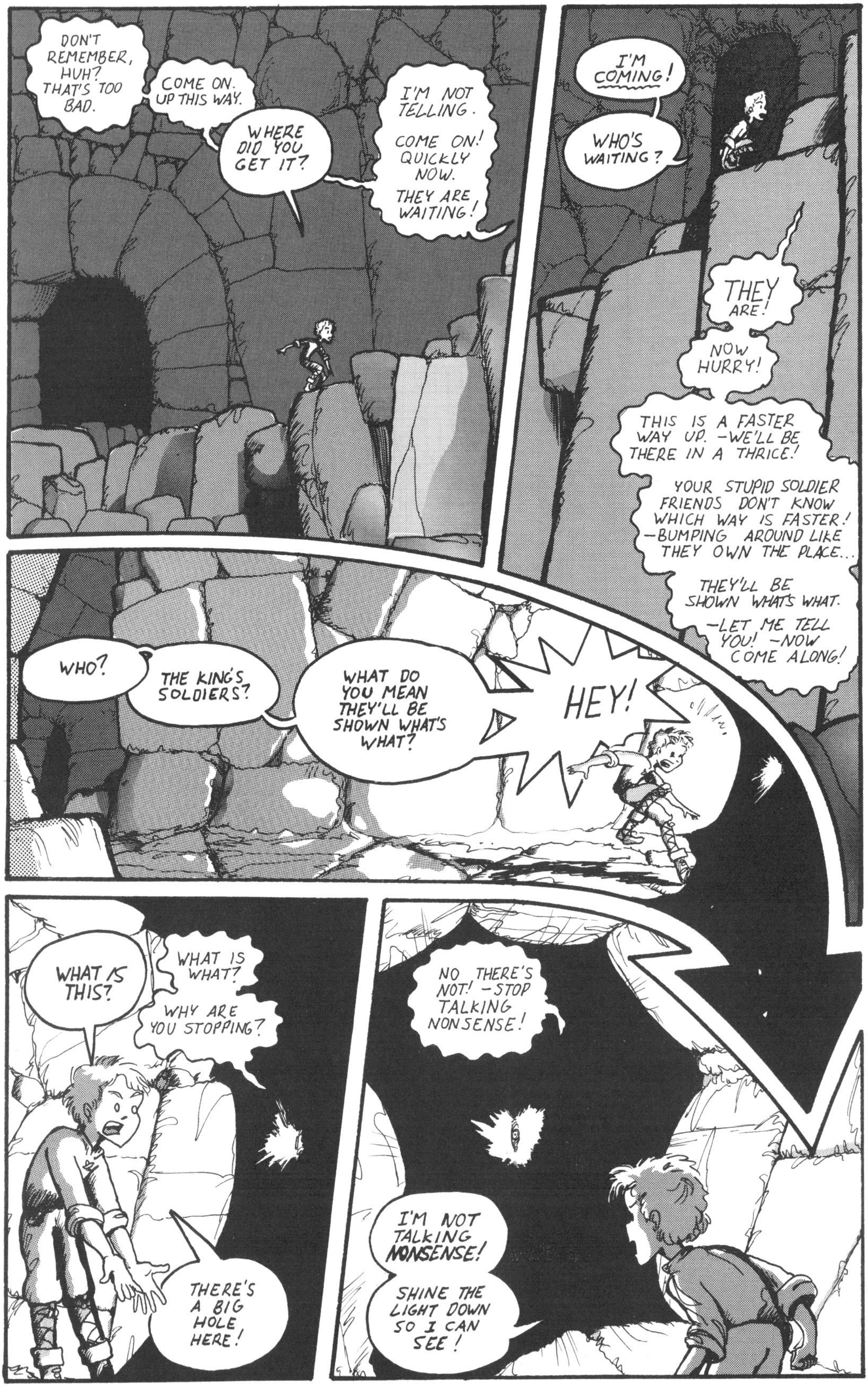
DON'T REMEMBER, HUH? THAT'S TOO BAD.
COME ON. UP THIS WAY.
WHERE DID YOU GET IT?
I'M NOT TELLING.
COME ON! QUICKLY NOW.
THEY ARE WAITING!
I'M COMING!
WHO'S WAITING?
THEY ARE!
NOW HURRY!
THIS IS A FASTER WAY UP. —WE'LL BE THERE IN A THRICE!
YOUR STUPID SOLDIER FRIENDS DON'T KNOW WHICH WAY IS FASTER! —BUMPING AROUND LIKE THEY OWN THE PLACE...
THEY'LL BE SHOWN WHAT'S WHAT.
—LET ME TELL YOU! —NOW COME ALONG!
WHO?
THE KING'S SOLDIERS?
WHAT DO YOU MEAN THEY'LL BE SHOWN WHAT'S WHAT?
HEY!
WHAT IS THIS?
WHAT IS WHAT?
WHY ARE YOU STOPPING?
THERE'S A BIG HOLE HERE!
NO THERE'S NOT! —STOP TALKING NONSENSE!
I'M NOT TALKING NONSENSE!
SHINE THE LIGHT DOWN SO I CAN SEE!

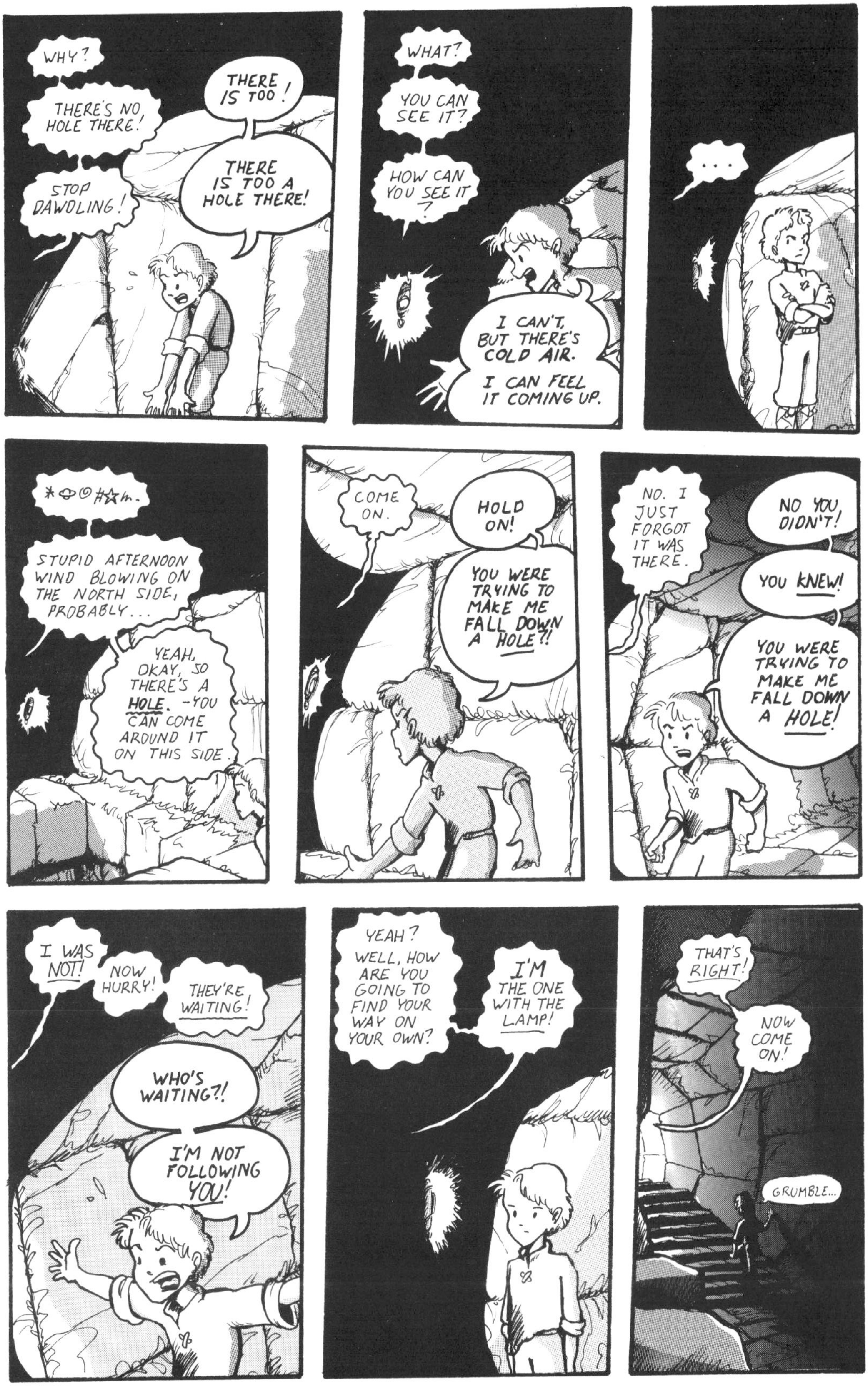
WHY?
THERE'S NO HOLE THERE!
STOP DAWDLING!
THERE IS TOO!
THERE IS TOO A HOLE THERE!
WHAT?
YOU CAN SEE IT?
HOW CAN YOU SEE IT?
I CAN'T, BUT THERE'S COLD AIR.
I CAN FEEL IT COMING UP.
. . .
*♁©#☆m.
STUPID AFTERNOON WIND BLOWING ON THE NORTH SIDE, PROBABLY...
YEAH, OKAY, SO THERE'S A HOLE. -YOU CAN COME AROUND IT ON THIS SIDE.
COME ON.
HOLD ON!
YOU WERE TRYING TO MAKE ME FALL DOWN A HOLE?!
NO. I JUST FORGOT IT WAS THERE.
NO YOU DIDN'T!
YOU KNEW!
YOU WERE TRYING TO MAKE ME FALL DOWN A HOLE!
I WAS NOT!
NOW HURRY!
THEY'RE WAITING!
WHO'S WAITING?!
I'M NOT FOLLOWING YOU!
YEAH?
WELL, HOW ARE YOU GOING TO FIND YOUR WAY ON YOUR OWN?
I'M THE ONE WITH THE LAMP!
THAT'S RIGHT!
NOW COME ON!
GRUMBLE...

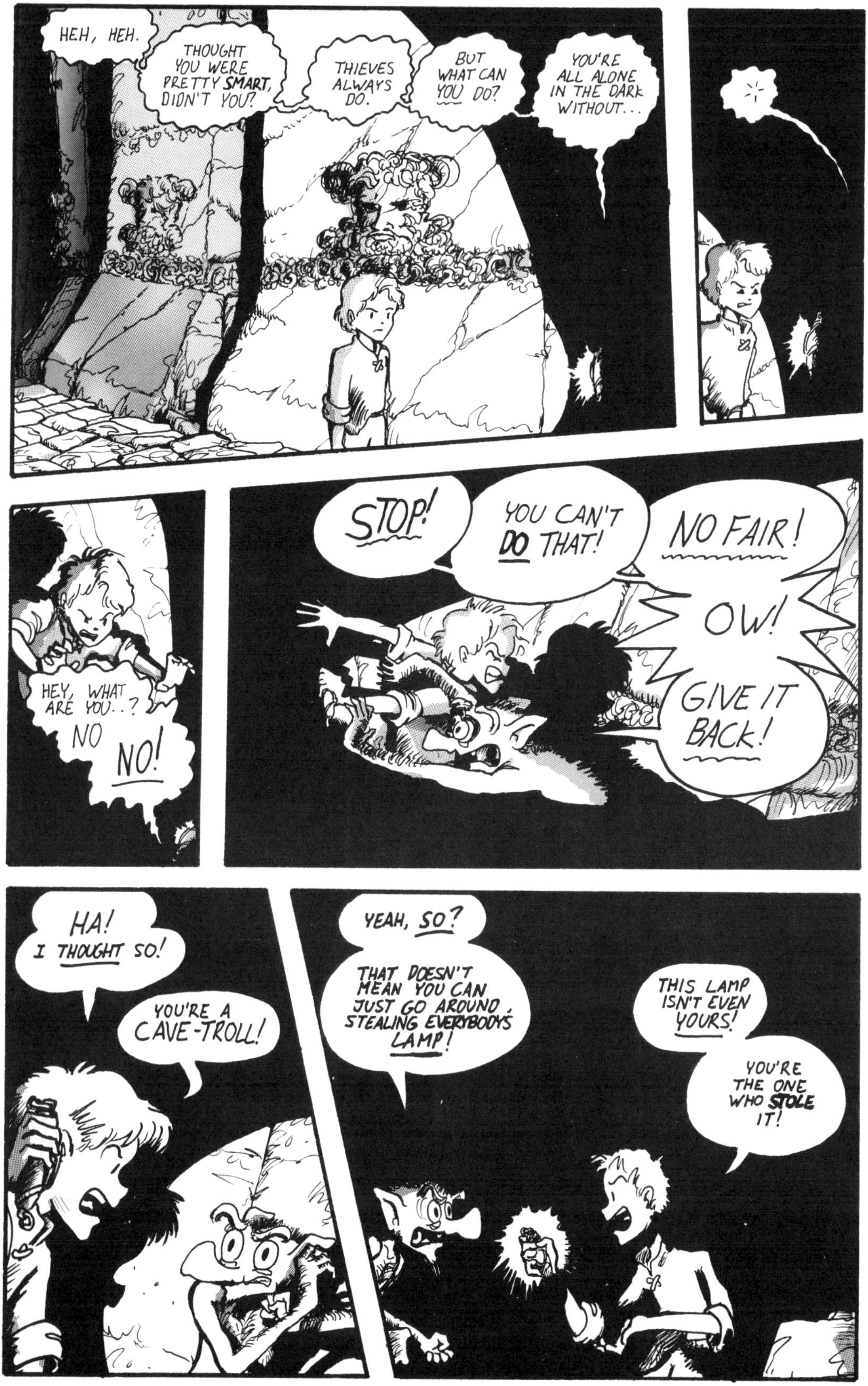
HEH, HEH.
THOUGHT YOU WERE PRETTY SMART, DIDN'T YOU?
THIEVES ALWAYS DO.
BUT WHAT CAN YOU DO?
YOU'RE ALL ALONE IN THE DARK WITHOUT...
HEY, WHAT ARE YOU..? NO NO!
STOP!
YOU CAN'T DO THAT!
NO FAIR!
OW!
GIVE IT BACK!
HA! I THOUGHT SO!
YOU'RE A CAVE-TROLL!
YEAH, SO?
THAT DOESN'T MEAN YOU CAN JUST GO AROUND, STEALING EVERYBODY'S LAMP!
THIS LAMP ISN'T EVEN YOURS!
YOU'RE THE ONE WHO STOLE IT!

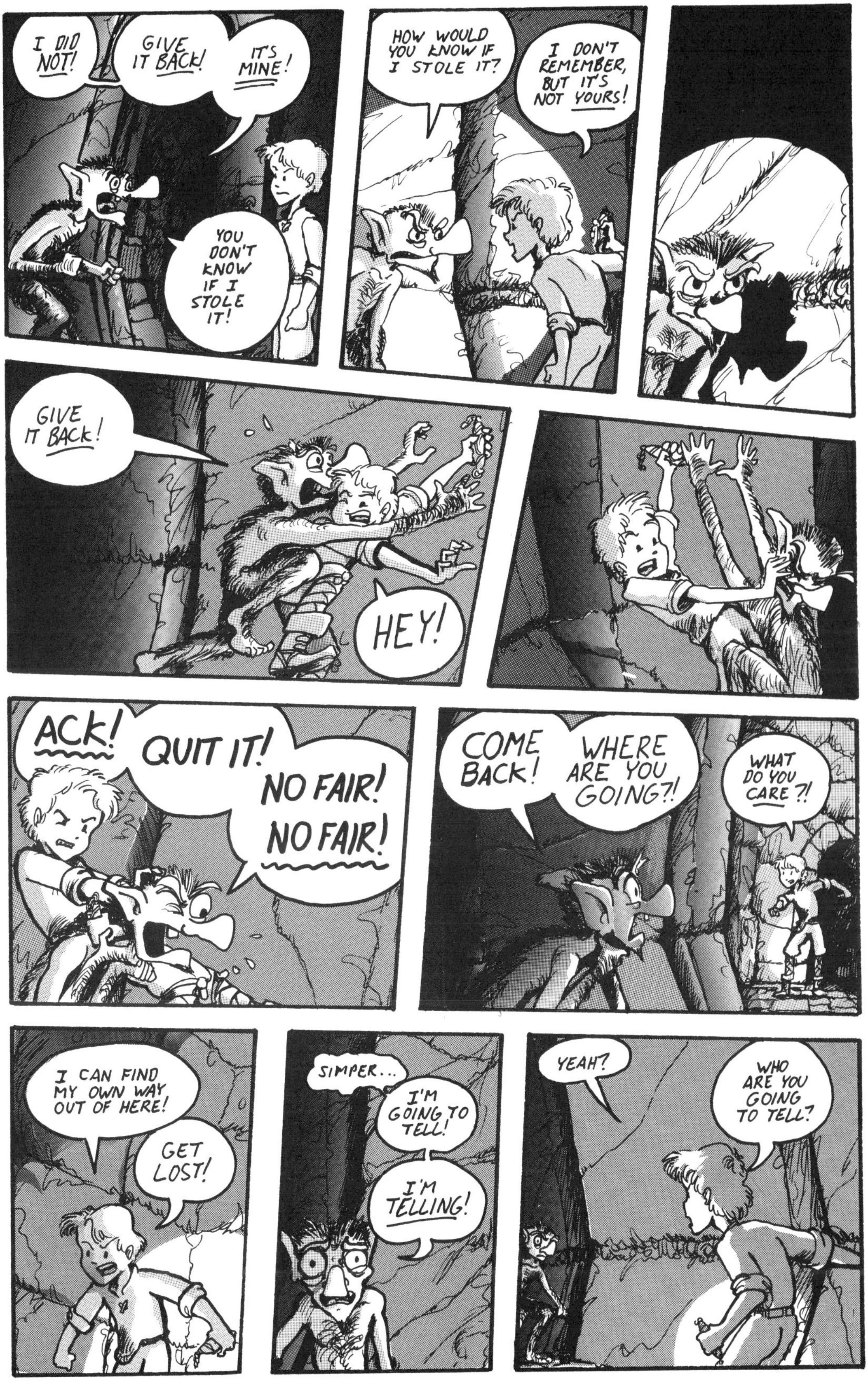
I DID NOT!
GIVE IT BACK!
IT'S MINE!
YOU DON'T KNOW IF I STOLE IT!
HOW WOULD YOU KNOW IF I STOLE IT?
I DON'T REMEMBER, BUT IT'S NOT YOURS!
GIVE IT BACK!
HEY!
ACK!
QUIT IT!
NO FAIR! NO FAIR!
COME BACK!
WHERE ARE YOU GOING?!
WHAT DO YOU CARE?!
I CAN FIND MY OWN WAY OUT OF HERE!
GET LOST!
SIMPER...
I'M GOING TO TELL!
I'M TELLING!
YEAH?
WHO ARE YOU GOING TO TELL?

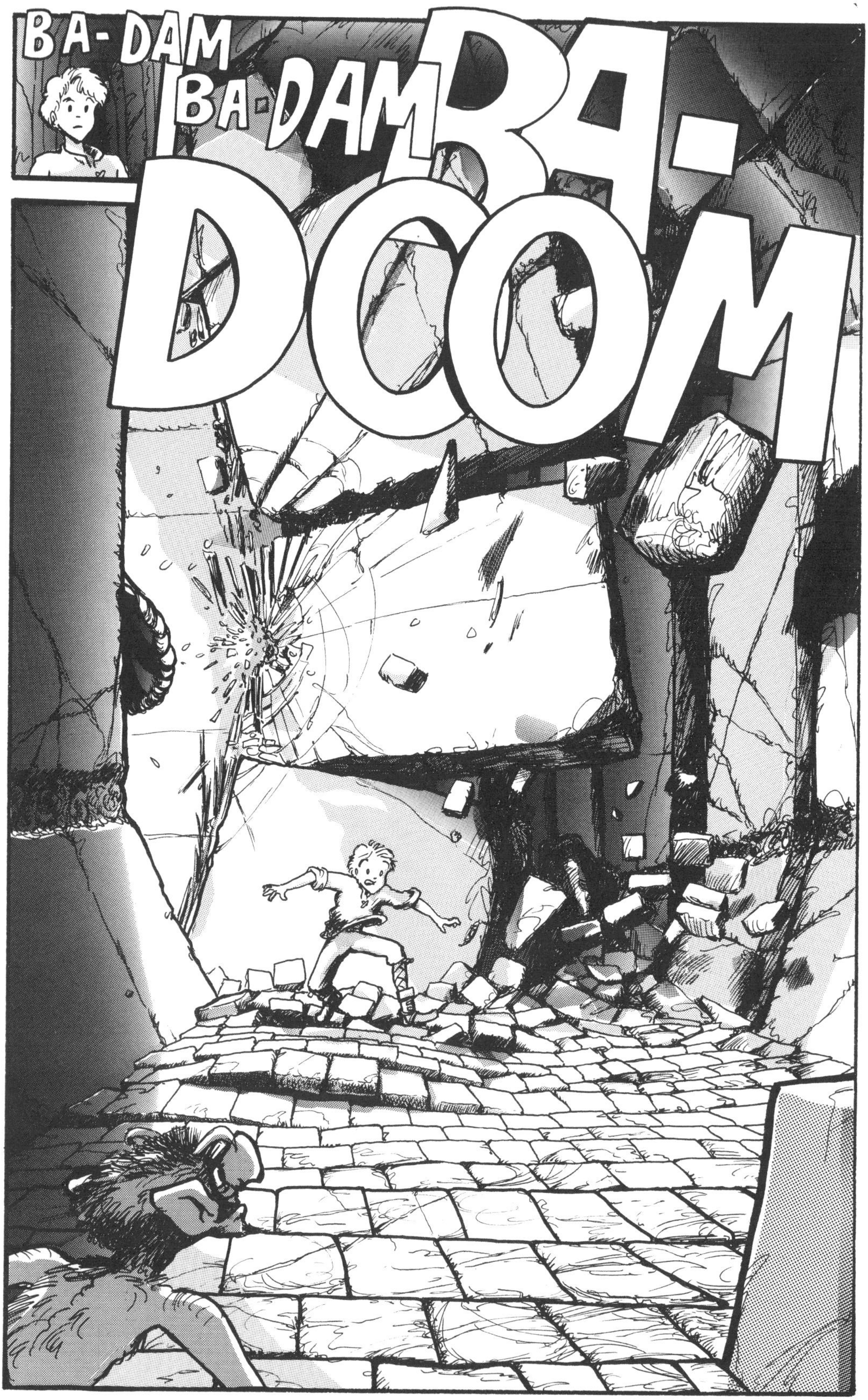
BA-DAM
BA-DAM
BA-DOOM

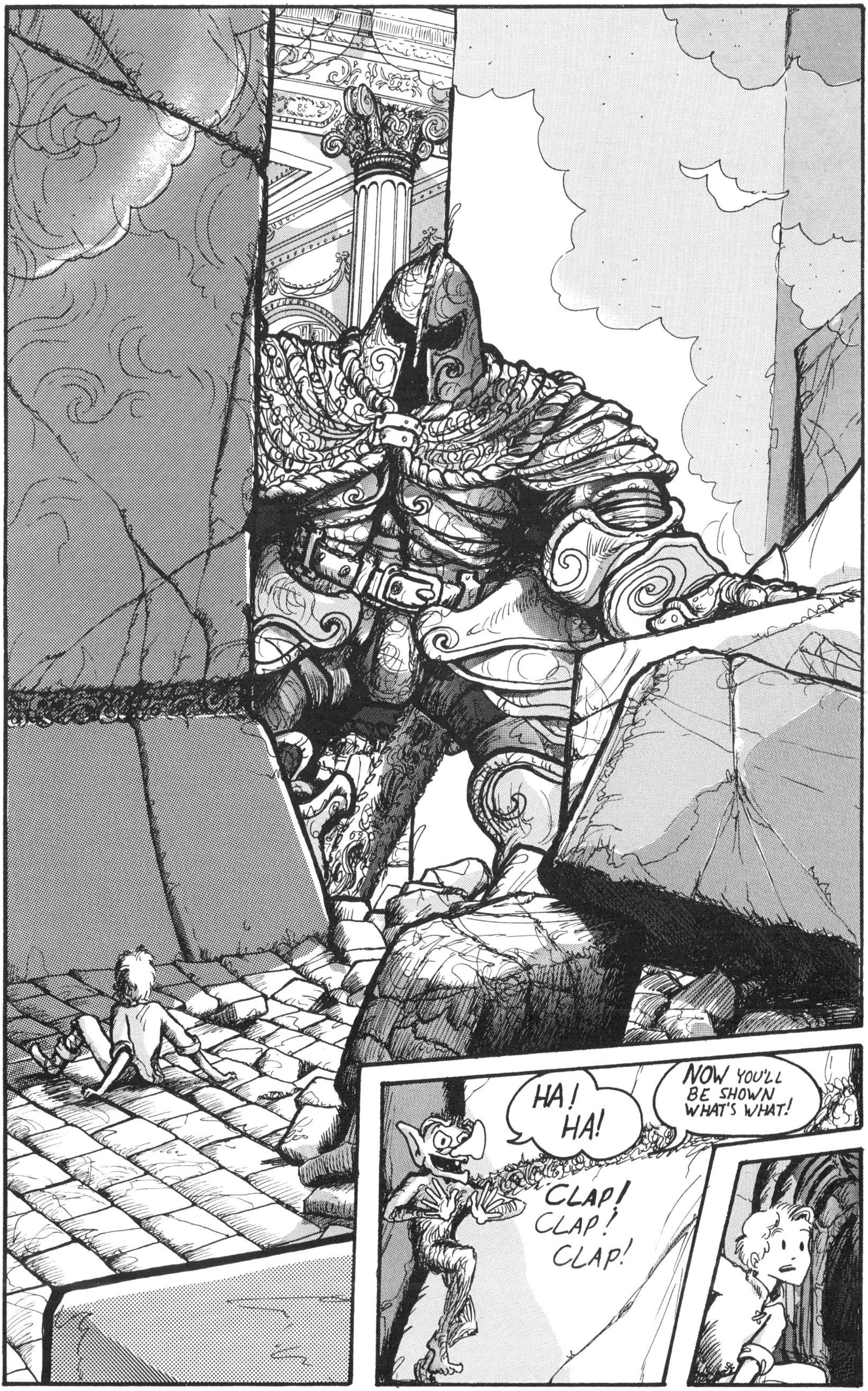
HA! HA!
NOW YOU'LL BE SHOWN WHAT'S WHAT!
CLAP! CLAP! CLAP!

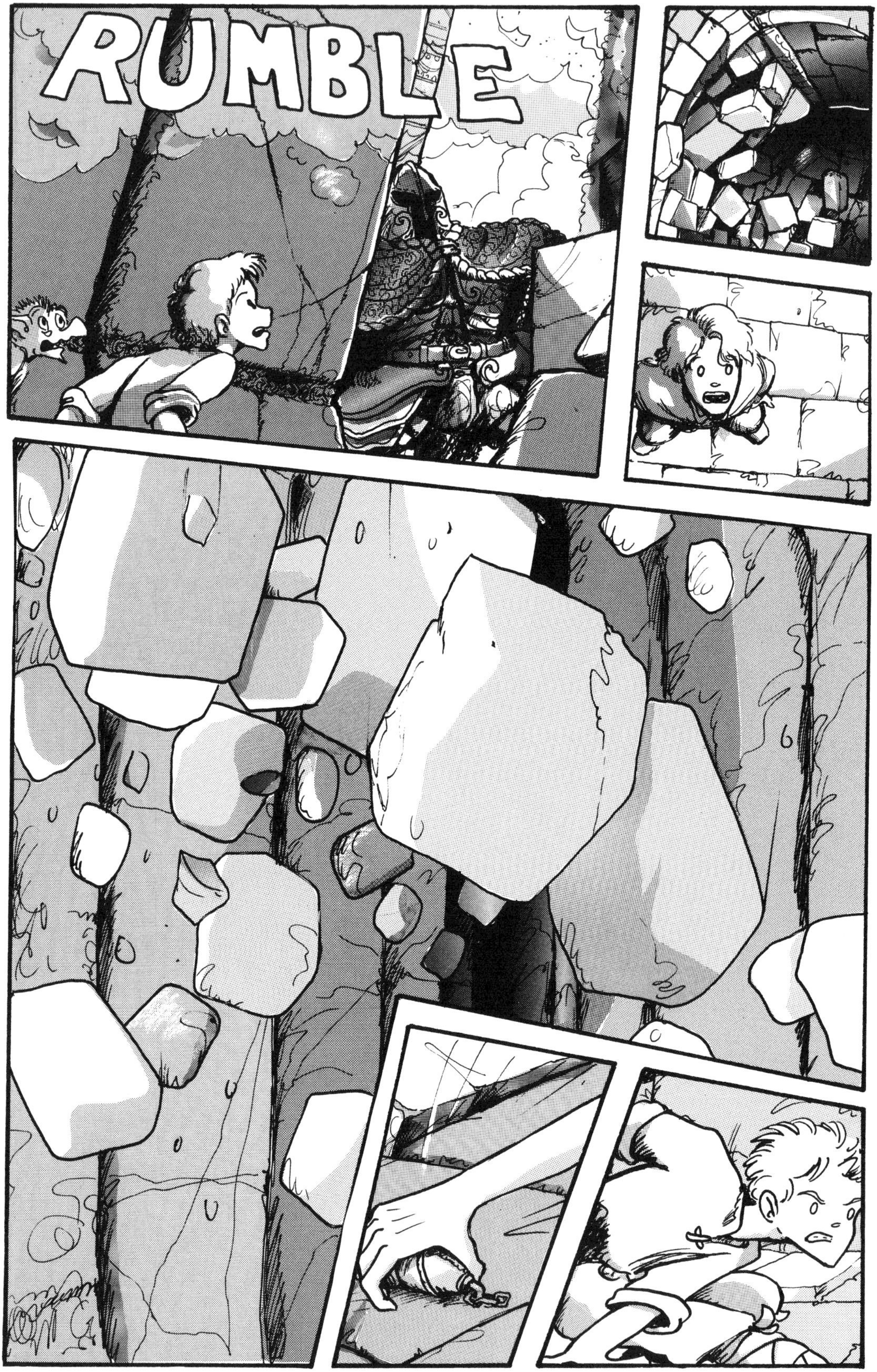
RUMBLE

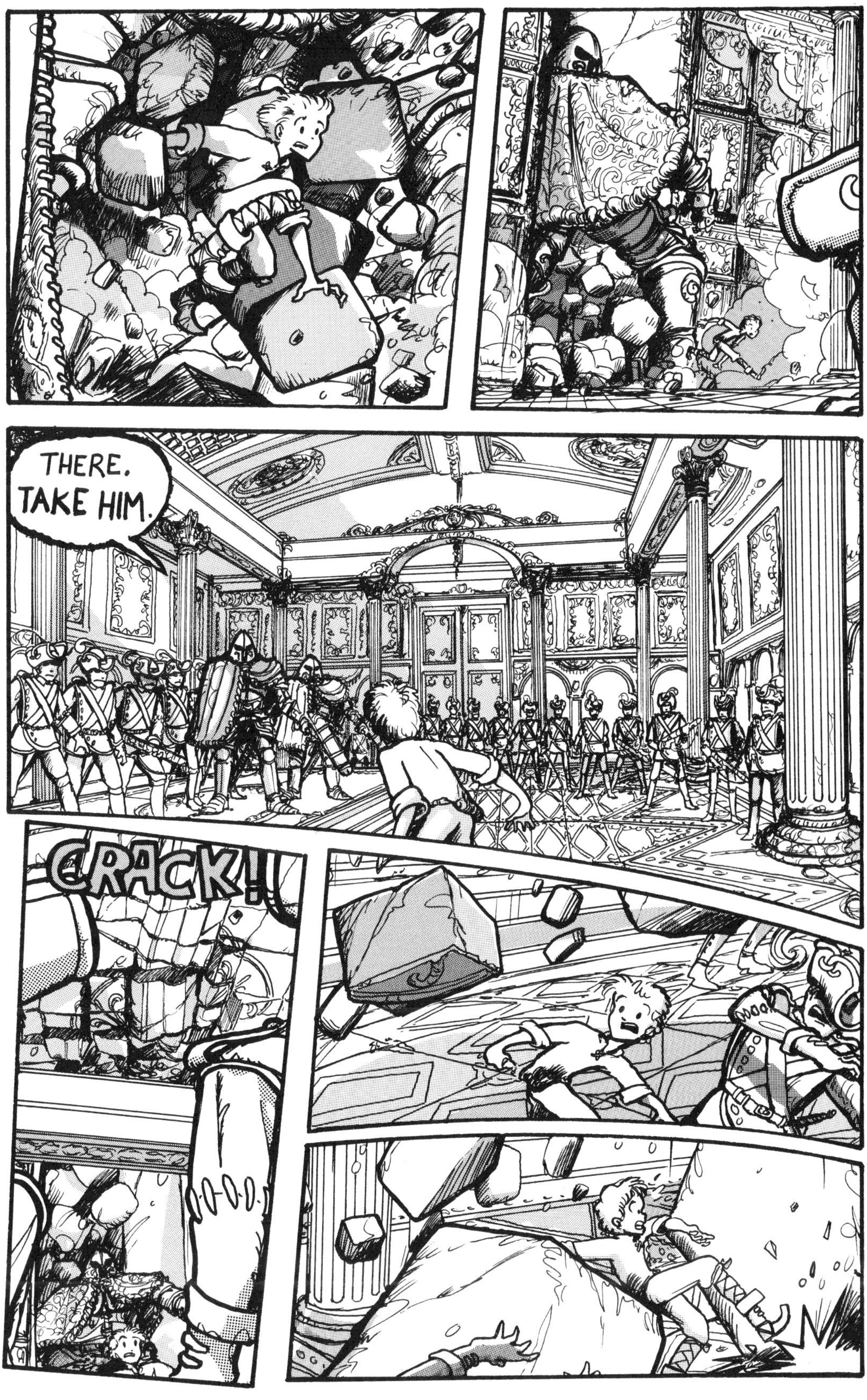
THERE. TAKE HIM.
CRACK!

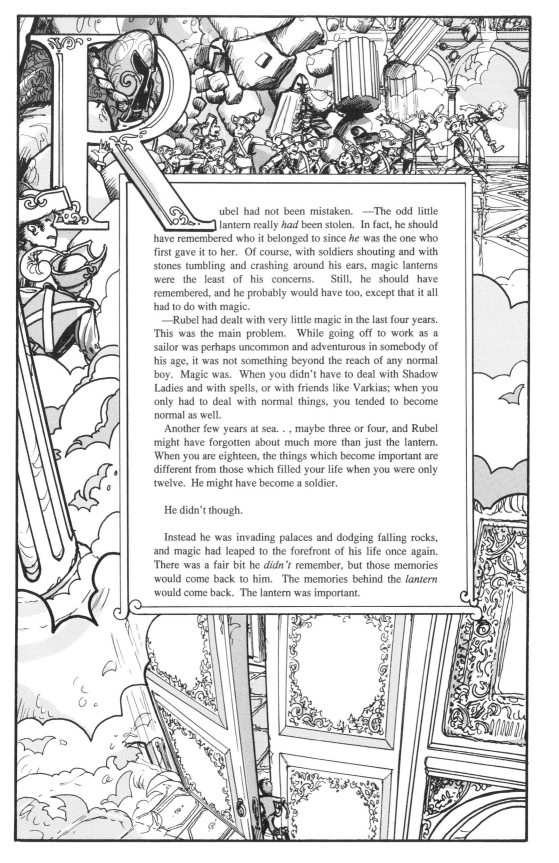

ubel had not been mistaken. —The odd little lantern really *had* been stolen. In fact, he should have remembered who it belonged to since *he* was the one who first gave it to her. Of course, with soldiers shouting and with stones tumbling and crashing around his ears, magic lanterns were the least of his concerns. Still, he should have remembered, and he probably would have too, except that it all had to do with magic.

—Rubel had dealt with very little magic in the last four years. This was the main problem. While going off to work as a sailor was perhaps uncommon and adventurous in somebody of his age, it was not something beyond the reach of any normal boy. Magic was. When you didn't have to deal with Shadow Ladies and with spells, or with friends like Varkias; when you only had to deal with normal things, you tended to become normal as well.

Another few years at sea. . , maybe three or four, and Rubel might have forgotten about much more than just the lantern. When you are eighteen, the things which become important are different from those which filled your life when you were only twelve. He might have become a soldier.

He didn't though.

Instead he was invading palaces and dodging falling rocks, and magic had leaped to the forefront of his life once again. There was a fair bit he *didn't* remember, but those memories would come back to him. The memories behind the *lantern* would come back. The lantern was important.

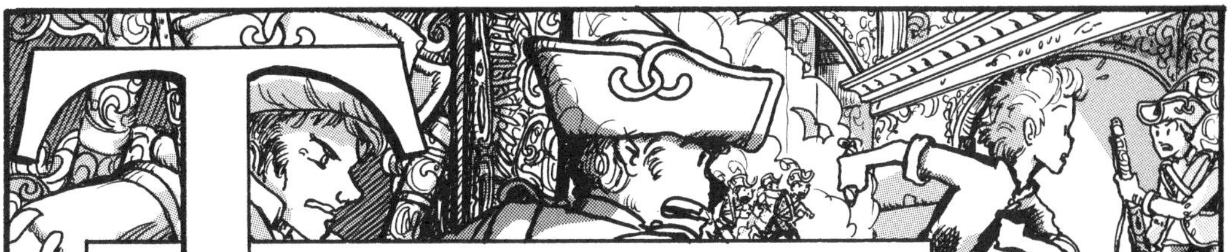

The story of the lantern began a long time ago, long before Rubel was born, but it started in that same city, and it started with a man who was a little bit like Rubel in some ways. —The man's name was Ben, and he was enchanted.

Ben was very handsome and very strong and amazingly, *instantly* talented in whatever he touched or did. He could take a flute or harp and play it as though he were a long experienced musician, which he was not. He could pick up a chisel and carve stone like a master, even if he had never carved a thing in his life. Without trying, he was the very best at everything, and this was enough to make people both despise and worship him.

Being worshipped, however, wasn't the same as having friends, and it hurt Ben to be despised, so he cursed his talents and all the things which made him special. Except cursing did not make them go away.

Now, when people are confronted by the likes of Ben, one of the ways to avoid feeling unimportant is to offer *advice.* —Not because he especially *needed* any, but because people wanted him to *listen* and acknowledge that even though he was wonderful, they must also be special in some way. —Certainly they *must* be if one so wonderful as Ben listened and squinted and nodded his head while they spoke. —And he did. Ben took to doing this even with ideas that weren't actually worth very much, (as is the case with many ideas).

"Yes, well that's not *bad*," people would say, gaining confidence, "but here, let me tell you what you *should* do."

Then, because Ben was so very gifted, he always managed to make the advice work brilliantly, and always after that, people puffed with pride. "Ah, but look how clever I am," they would think, "and look how simple Ben is! Being handsome and talented is fine, but what use is it without somebody like *me* to tell him how things are? Oh, what a likable fellow Ben is!"

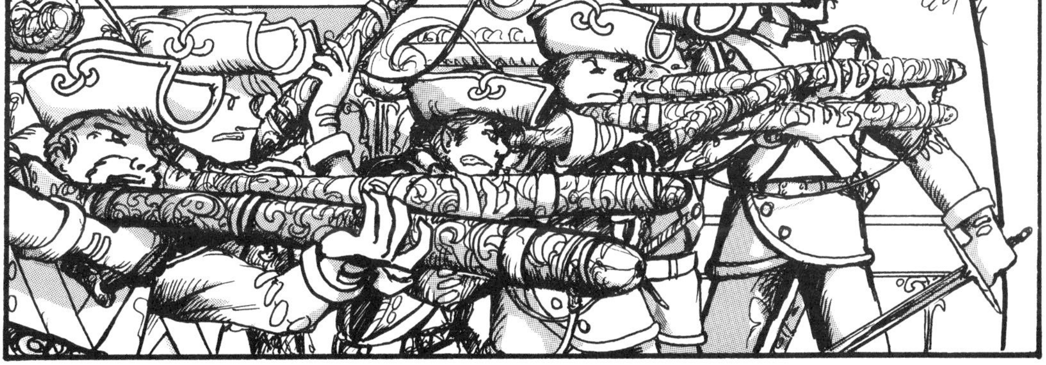

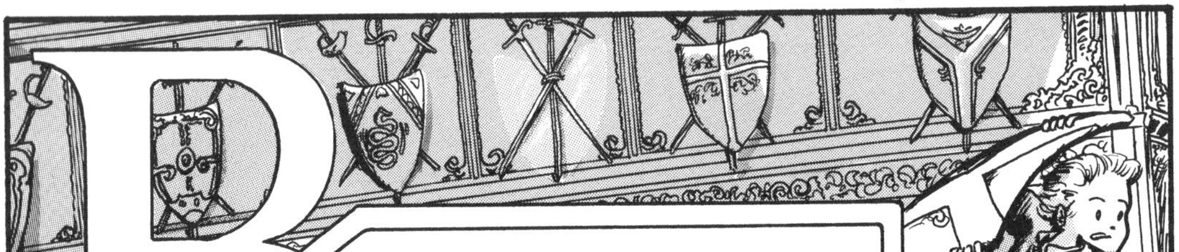

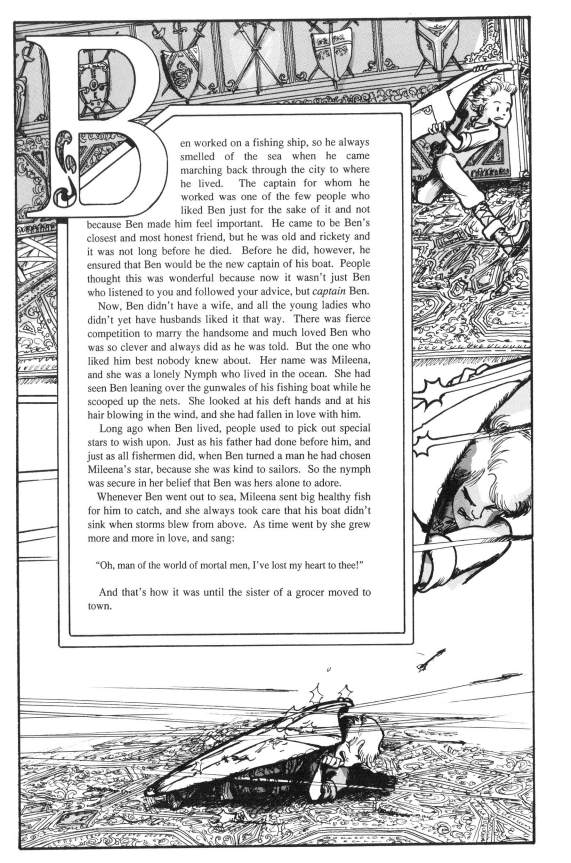

Ben worked on a fishing ship, so he always smelled of the sea when he came marching back through the city to where he lived. The captain for whom he worked was one of the few people who liked Ben just for the sake of it and not because Ben made him feel important. He came to be Ben's closest and most honest friend, but he was old and rickety and it was not long before he died. Before he did, however, he ensured that Ben would be the new captain of his boat. People thought this was wonderful because now it wasn't just Ben who listened to you and followed your advice, but *captain* Ben.

Now, Ben didn't have a wife, and all the young ladies who didn't yet have husbands liked it that way. There was fierce competition to marry the handsome and much loved Ben who was so clever and always did as he was told. But the one who liked him best nobody knew about. Her name was Mileena, and she was a lonely Nymph who lived in the ocean. She had seen Ben leaning over the gunwales of his fishing boat while he scooped up the nets. She looked at his deft hands and at his hair blowing in the wind, and she had fallen in love with him.

Long ago when Ben lived, people used to pick out special stars to wish upon. Just as his father had done before him, and just as all fishermen did, when Ben turned a man he had chosen Mileena's star, because she was kind to sailors. So the nymph was secure in her belief that Ben was hers alone to adore.

Whenever Ben went out to sea, Mileena sent big healthy fish for him to catch, and she always took care that his boat didn't sink when storms blew from above. As time went by she grew more and more in love, and sang:

"Oh, man of the world of mortal men, I've lost my heart to thee!"

And that's how it was until the sister of a grocer moved to town.

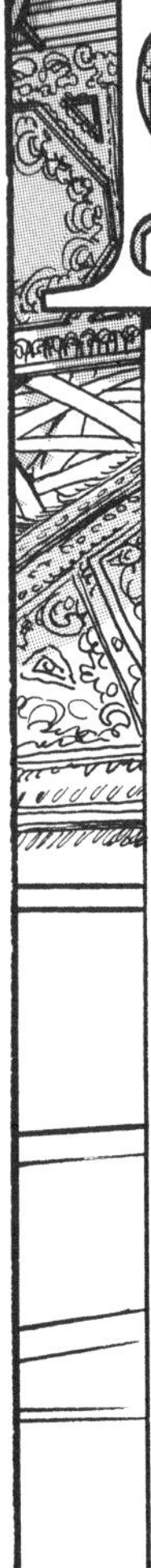

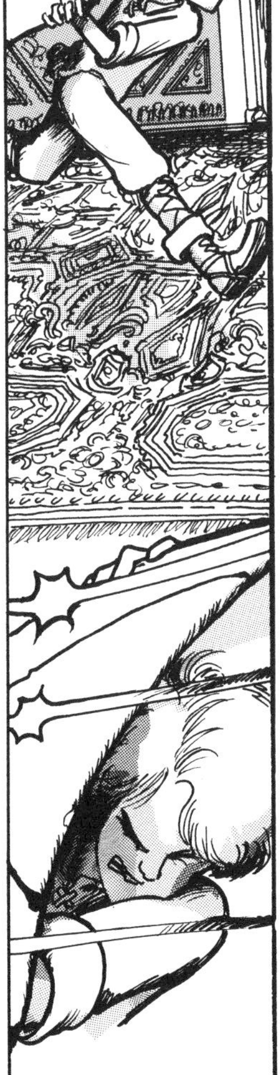

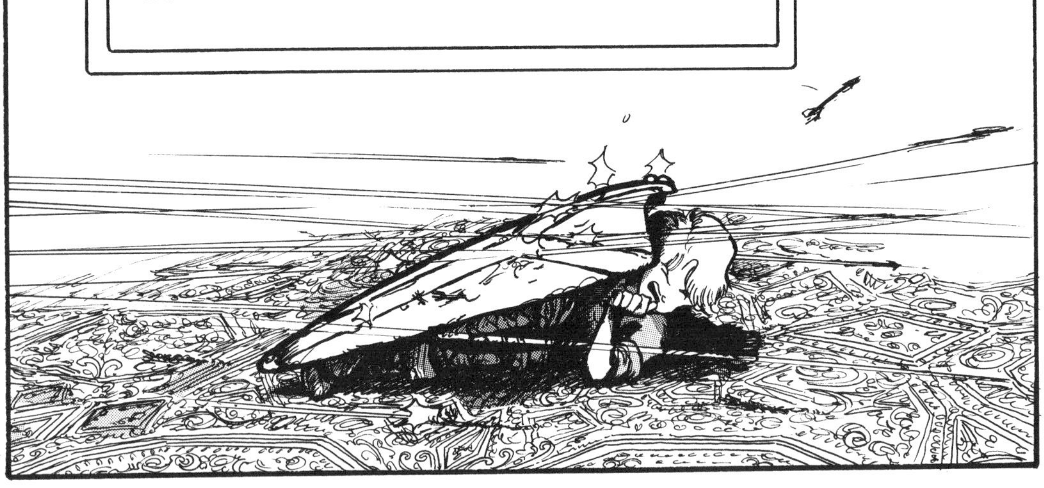

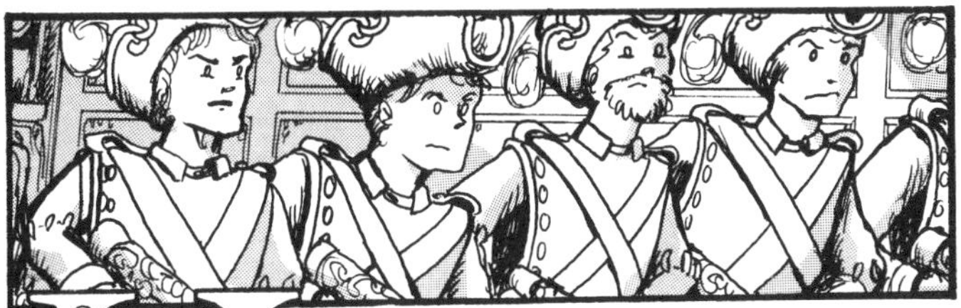

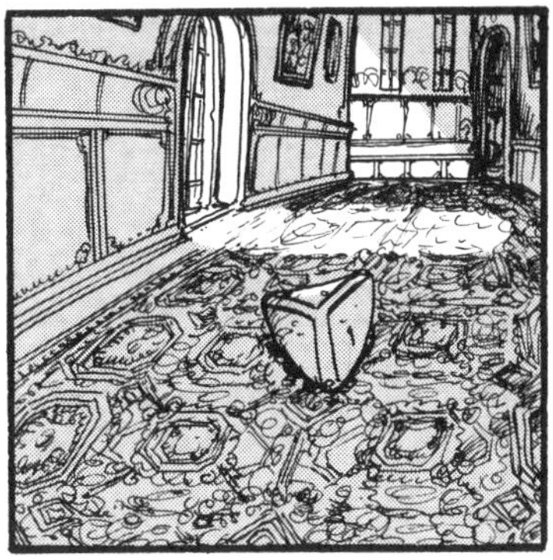

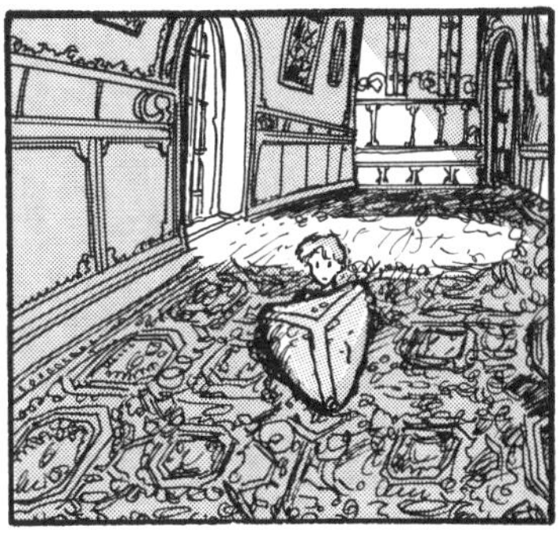

Her name was Julin, and she was beautiful and clever and it wasn't long before she decided that she would marry Ben. None of the other girls stood a chance beside her and the wedding was soon announced.

When the nymph Mileena heard about the wedding, she cried and raged and sank ships, drowning men who never knew why. But though she hated and loathed, Mileena could not bring herself to despise Ben. She kept her wrath from him. It was Julin for whom she held her anger.

If ever Julin set foot upon a boat, the nymph swore, she would wash that ship out to sea and there torture the woman with storms and bleaching sunlight until her life was shriveled up and gone. She swore it and dreamed it and writhed in her hatred, but Julin didn't know so didn't care, and since she never went aboard ships, (boats were such awful, *dirty* things, she'd say), Mileena was unable to do a thing. The nymph could only go mad to think of Julin standing smug and self satisfied at Ben's side.

Time passed and Julin decided that she would be a mother. Soon after she became pregnant. The rounder she got, the more smug and self satisfied she became and Ben ran to and fro to please her. When Mileena learned of the coming child, it made her insane with jealousy.

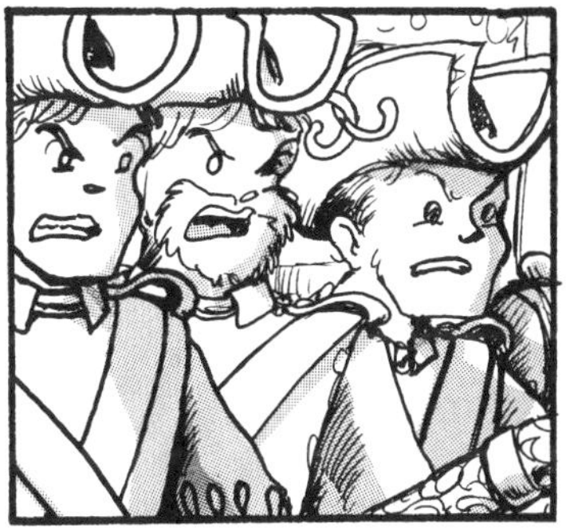

The baby was born, and her mother decided to name her Sara, but the child's eyes sparkled like her father's, and as she grew, it became clear that she shared Ben's enchantment.

Sara was quick and bright and strong, and the people lost their hearts to her at once. She had the magic of her father, and the will of her mother, and in this she was a sight! Ben loved her, but Julin fought bitterly with the girl. —Julin was used to people doing as they were told, but Sara only did what suited her. She disobeyed and always with results that made people cry, "How clever! How wonderful! How splendid Sara is!"

Julin spent much of her motherhood livid with frustration, and it only got worse when Sara decided that she wanted to become a sailor like her father.

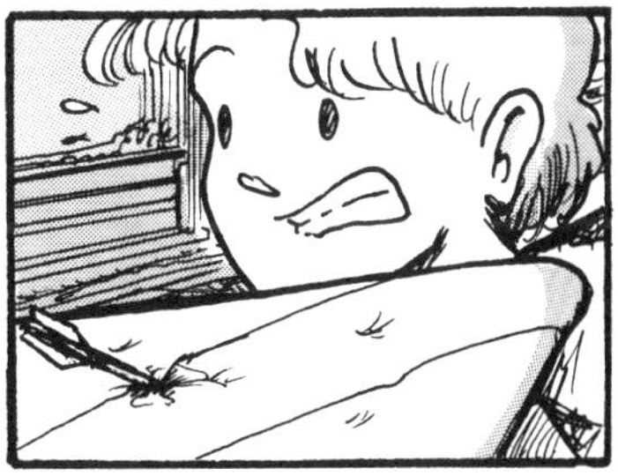

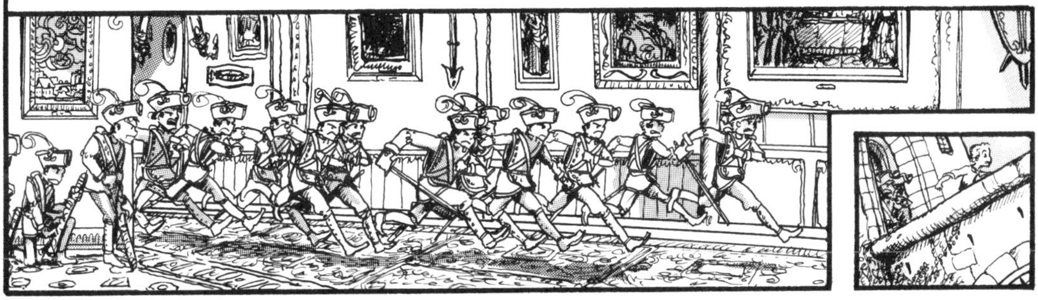

Mileena frowned on this; Sara was the daughter of the woman she hated most, so she tried her best to make things difficult for the girl. She made the waves choppy and she sent the coldest water up from the ocean floor and several times knocked Sara into the sea. She considered even drowning her out of spite, but decided against it, for fear of breaking Ben's heart, for she knew he loved the girl. —But even through all of this, Sara shone. She braved the coldest waters and swam like a fish, and indeed, learned to sail better even than her father. Even Mileena found herself grudgingly impressed, but refused to lose her heart to the girl. "Perhaps if she were *my* daughter. But she isn't and I do not like her one bit!"

Julin was upset as well, but for different reasons. She looked between herself and Ben, and then at Sara who didn't want to be like her, and she said, "No daughter of mine. . !"

Mileena laughed at this, and began to favor Sara just because it made the girl's mother hurt inside. She used her will to make sure that Sara was successful in all she did upon the water. —This, when added to Sara's enchantment made the girl seem all the more divine. People marveled at her and adored her, and Sara adored them back.

When the time came for Sara to choose a star, she picked out Mileena's, doing so in all the honesty of youth. She meant her best and hoped that Mileena would love her. The nymph only snorted.

Now when all this came about, Julin complained bitterly, which was nothing new. What *was* new, however, was that on the very night of her daughter's ceremony, she looked upon her own star and made many bitter wishes. Girls were supposed to choose their mother's stars, *not* their father's.

"Something must be done!" she said.

The nymph whose star she wished upon was named Auril, and she agreed, but not for the reasons Julin thought were important, and at first, not even for reasons Auril understood herself.

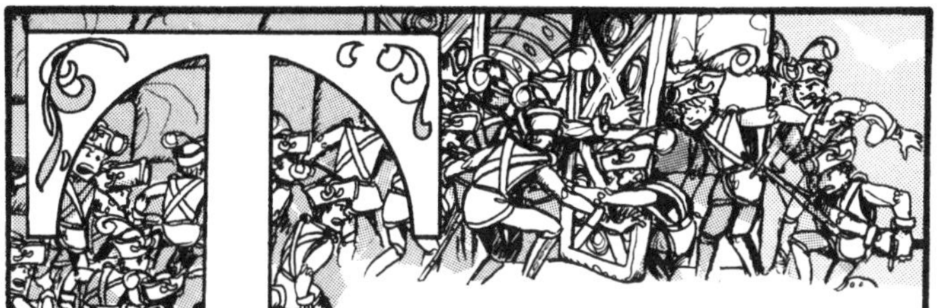

The nymph Auril worried and wondered but she could not see clearly what made things feel wrong. "Ben and Sara, Ben and Sara," she said to herself. "Why does that ring false?" She decided that she would watch, and it was not long before she spied Ben and his daughter returning home one day from the ocean. She saw Ben's deft hands, and she saw his hair blowing in the wind, and she saw how gaily Sara sprang to shore, and how the boat was filled with the beautiful fish Mileena had sent them. She saw all of these things and understood, exclaiming. "Ah, but what is *this? This* cannot be! But these are two with *Faerie* blood in them, here among the world of mortal kind! This cannot be! This cannot be!" And with that, she sent the nets flying into the air so that they spun about Ben's head and snapped his neck.

Ben's spirit flew up into the air and Auril caught it, telling him, "Dear Ben, you are not supposed to be here. You must come away to where you belong. And your daughter must come too."

Auril would have taken Sara then as well, but Mileena came to stop her, crying, "No, Auril! What are you doing? These two are *mine.* I forbid you!"

But Auril turned upon her, saying, "Mileena, you should know better. These are not for you. They may have chosen so, but they must come away. I must take them back to the borders of Nove, where their kind live."

But the water nymph shook her head, seeing only that Julin had sent Auril to hurt her.

"No!" She cried. "You cannot! You *must* not! They are mine!"

She could do nothing, though; Ben was already gone, and Sara stood upon dry land. All she could do was look up through the waves in rage.

"Foolish girl!" she cried at Sara. "Foolish girl! You swore yourself to me! Come to me at once! Come into the *water!"*

But Sara was stricken with fear, and she did not move.

"Oh, Mileena!" Auril sighed.

Mileena only hissed and vanished beneath the brine.

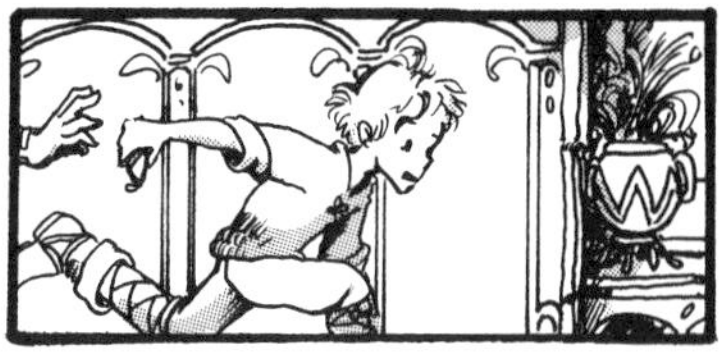

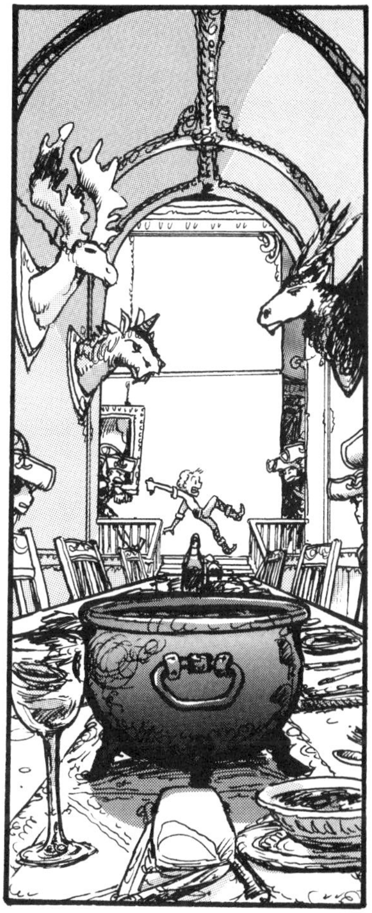

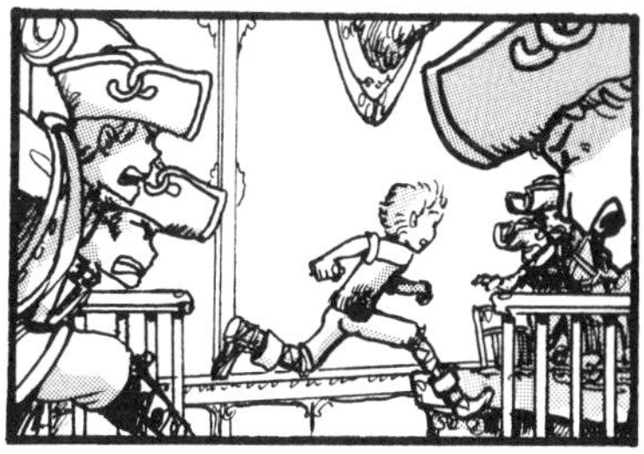

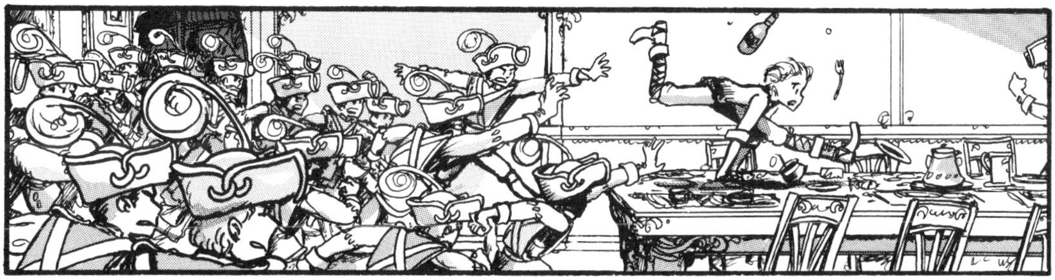

Auril was sorry she had struck Ben dead so abruptly as she had done, and turned to poor Sara, who understood little of what had happened.

"Sara Blue, Sara Blue," she said, her words rising in halos, "I must take you away. I will reach down for you at dusk. You will stand upon your balcony and wait for me. You must bid your mother and your friends good-bye, but then I must take you away."

And with that she flew off into the sky.

Stricken by this news, the fishermen all wept as they made their way back to Sara's home. They came up the hill, a sorry parade for all to see, and everybody felt their heart strings ache. The gossips were quiet and sober as they passed the news to all the ears that cared to hear.

Sara made her good-byes as best she could, and all the people who loved her dressed her up and brought flowers for her hair, saying that Sara must look her best, though really they just didn't know what else they ought to do. Julin scowled into the white of her daughter's dress as she tied the ribbons, hiding her tears from the girl. Sara hugged her anyway, and Julin cried openly, saying that she was so very sorry, though she could not have said exactly what she was sorry for. At dusk, young Sara stood bravely upon her balcony, shifting her bare feet while she watched the sky. It was then that Mileena struck.

Up through the sewers and cracks the water came; a thousand icy wet fingers clutching at the stone. Even as Auril swept down to take Sara, the sea crashed in upon the city with all its pounding might. None is stronger than the sea, and thus Mileena caught Sara away from Auril as she might have snatched a doll.

All the people of Highborn at Oceansend cried out as half their city crumbled and vanished beneath the black water. Mileena held Sara there, and she did not let her go until all the air ran out of the girl's lungs and she died.

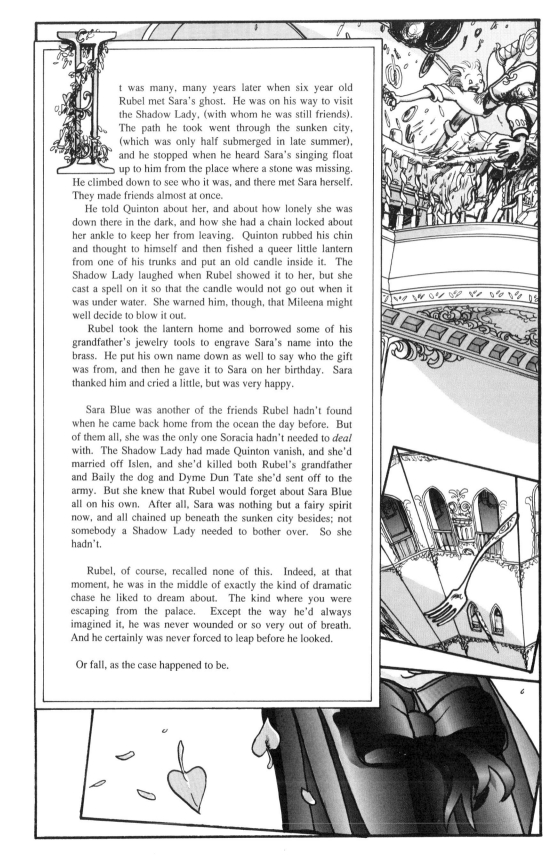

It was many, many years later when six year old Rubel met Sara's ghost. He was on his way to visit the Shadow Lady, (with whom he was still friends). The path he took went through the sunken city, (which was only half submerged in late summer), and he stopped when he heard Sara's singing float up to him from the place where a stone was missing. He climbed down to see who it was, and there met Sara herself. They made friends almost at once.

He told Quinton about her, and about how lonely she was down there in the dark, and how she had a chain locked about her ankle to keep her from leaving. Quinton rubbed his chin and thought to himself and then fished a queer little lantern from one of his trunks and put an old candle inside it. The Shadow Lady laughed when Rubel showed it to her, but she cast a spell on it so that the candle would not go out when it was under water. She warned him, though, that Mileena might well decide to blow it out.

Rubel took the lantern home and borrowed some of his grandfather's jewelry tools to engrave Sara's name into the brass. He put his own name down as well to say who the gift was from, and then he gave it to Sara on her birthday. Sara thanked him and cried a little, but was very happy.

Sara Blue was another of the friends Rubel hadn't found when he came back home from the ocean the day before. But of them all, she was the only one Soracia hadn't needed to *deal* with. The Shadow Lady had made Quinton vanish, and she'd married off Islen, and she'd killed both Rubel's grandfather and Baily the dog and Dyme Dun Tate she'd sent off to the army. But she knew that Rubel would forget about Sara Blue all on his own. After all, Sara was nothing but a fairy spirit now, and all chained up beneath the sunken city besides; not somebody a Shadow Lady needed to bother over. So she hadn't.

Rubel, of course, recalled none of this. Indeed, at that moment, he was in the middle of exactly the kind of dramatic chase he liked to dream about. The kind where you were escaping from the palace. Except the way he'd always imagined it, he was never wounded or so very out of breath. And he certainly was never forced to leap before he looked.

Or fall, as the case happened to be.

Chapter 12

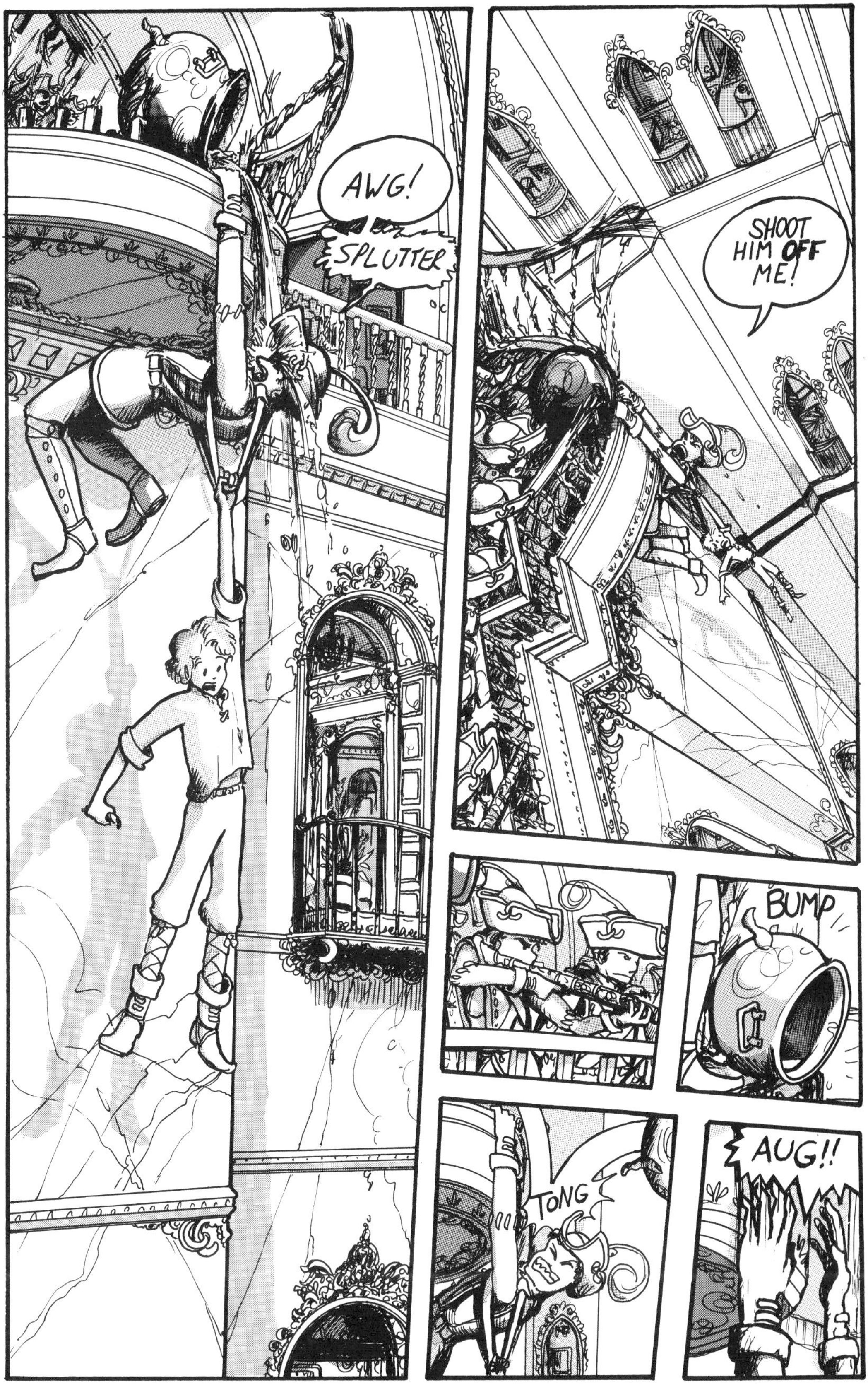
AWG!
SPLUTTER
SHOOT HIM OFF ME!
BUMP
TONG
AUG!!

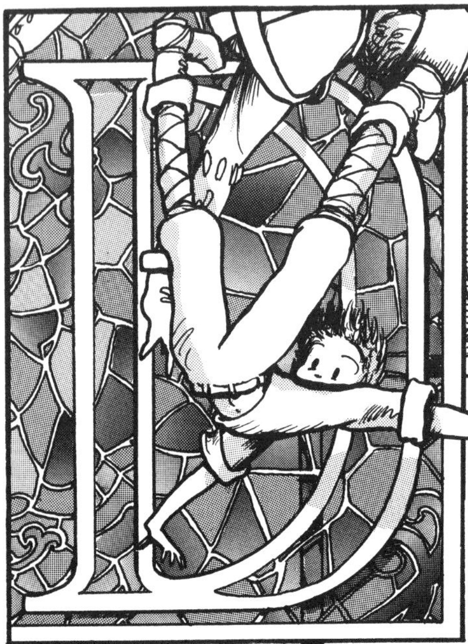
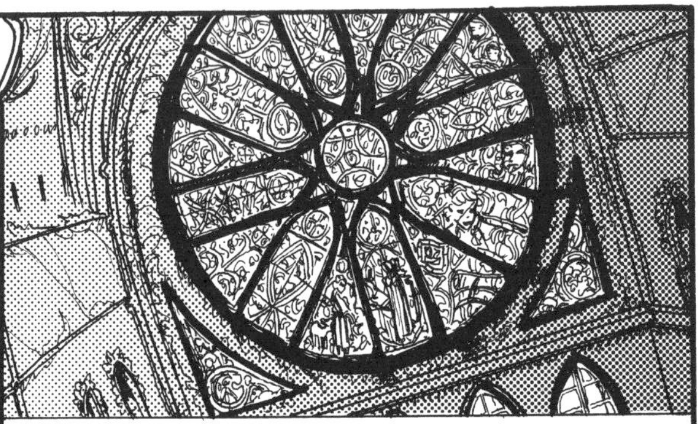

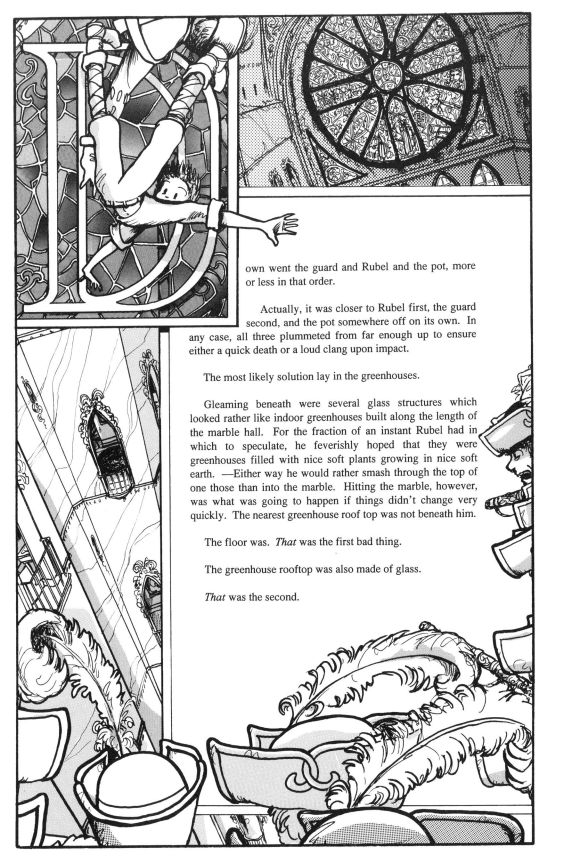

Down went the guard and Rubel and the pot, more or less in that order.

Actually, it was closer to Rubel first, the guard second, and the pot somewhere off on its own. In any case, all three plummeted from far enough up to ensure either a quick death or a loud clang upon impact.

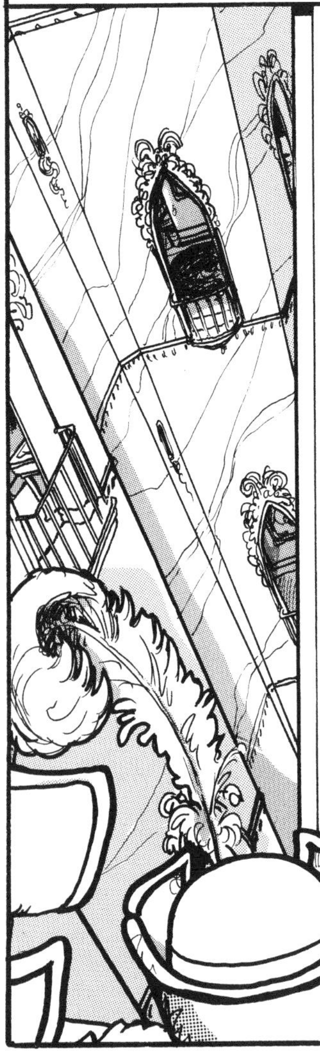

The most likely solution lay in the greenhouses.

Gleaming beneath were several glass structures which looked rather like indoor greenhouses built along the length of the marble hall. For the fraction of an instant Rubel had in which to speculate, he feverishly hoped that they were greenhouses filled with nice soft plants growing in nice soft earth. —Either way he would rather smash through the top of one those than into the marble. Hitting the marble, however, was what was going to happen if things didn't change very quickly. The nearest greenhouse roof top was not beneath him.

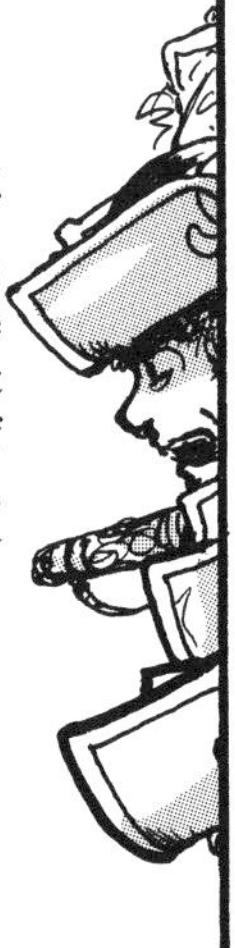

The floor was. *That* was the first bad thing.

The greenhouse rooftop was also made of glass.

That was the second.

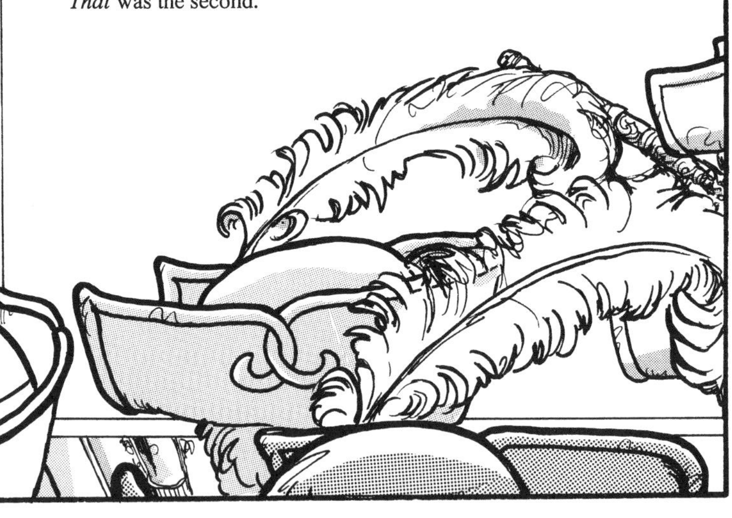

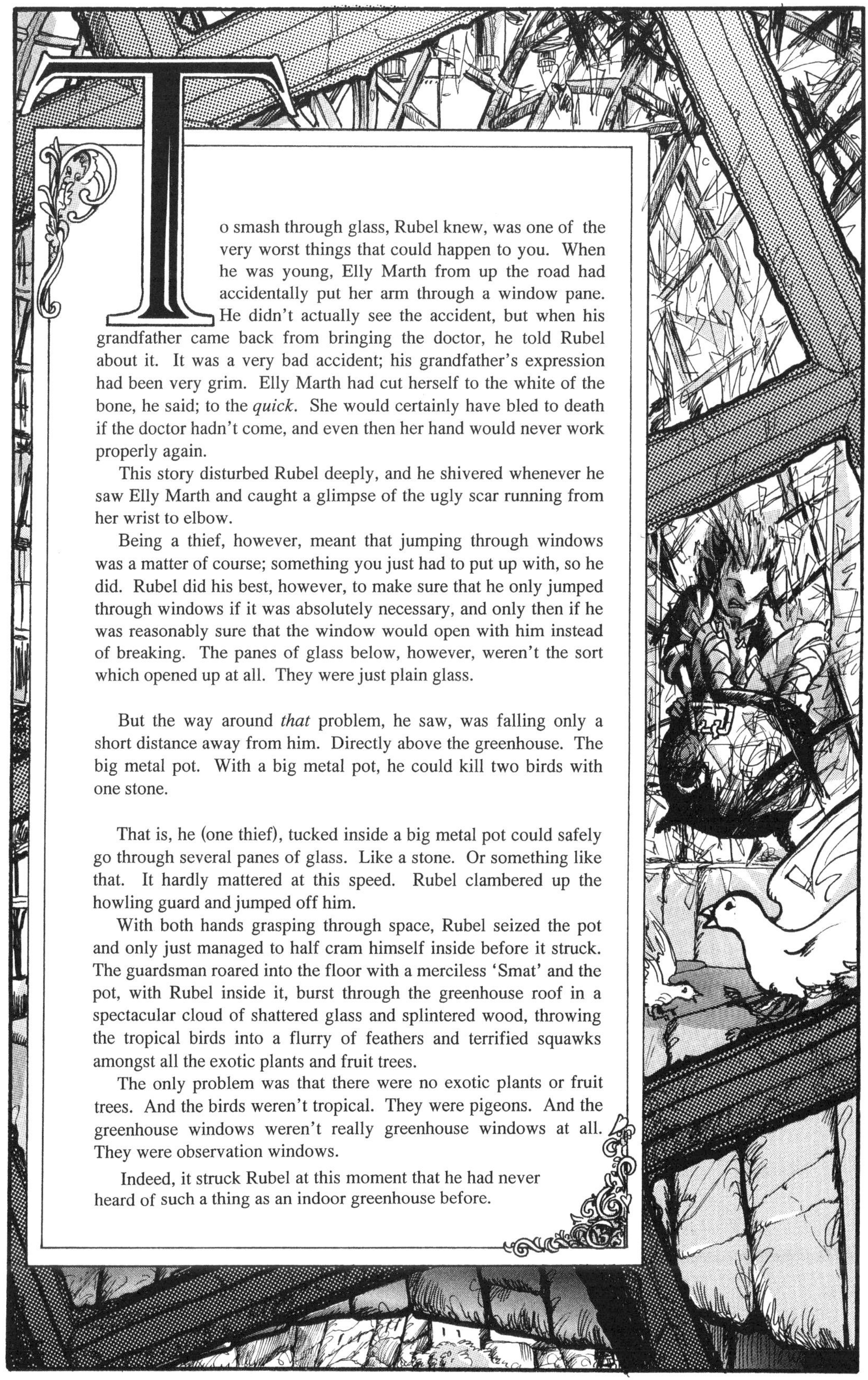

To smash through glass, Rubel knew, was one of the very worst things that could happen to you. When he was young, Elly Marth from up the road had accidentally put her arm through a window pane. He didn't actually see the accident, but when his grandfather came back from bringing the doctor, he told Rubel about it. It was a very bad accident; his grandfather's expression had been very grim. Elly Marth had cut herself to the white of the bone, he said; to the *quick*. She would certainly have bled to death if the doctor hadn't come, and even then her hand would never work properly again.

This story disturbed Rubel deeply, and he shivered whenever he saw Elly Marth and caught a glimpse of the ugly scar running from her wrist to elbow.

Being a thief, however, meant that jumping through windows was a matter of course; something you just had to put up with, so he did. Rubel did his best, however, to make sure that he only jumped through windows if it was absolutely necessary, and only then if he was reasonably sure that the window would open with him instead of breaking. The panes of glass below, however, weren't the sort which opened up at all. They were just plain glass.

But the way around *that* problem, he saw, was falling only a short distance away from him. Directly above the greenhouse. The big metal pot. With a big metal pot, he could kill two birds with one stone.

That is, he (one thief), tucked inside a big metal pot could safely go through several panes of glass. Like a stone. Or something like that. It hardly mattered at this speed. Rubel clambered up the howling guard and jumped off him.

With both hands grasping through space, Rubel seized the pot and only just managed to half cram himself inside before it struck. The guardsman roared into the floor with a merciless 'Smat' and the pot, with Rubel inside it, burst through the greenhouse roof in a spectacular cloud of shattered glass and splintered wood, throwing the tropical birds into a flurry of feathers and terrified squawks amongst all the exotic plants and fruit trees.

The only problem was that there were no exotic plants or fruit trees. And the birds weren't tropical. They were pigeons. And the greenhouse windows weren't really greenhouse windows at all. They were observation windows.

Indeed, it struck Rubel at this moment that he had never heard of such a thing as an indoor greenhouse before.

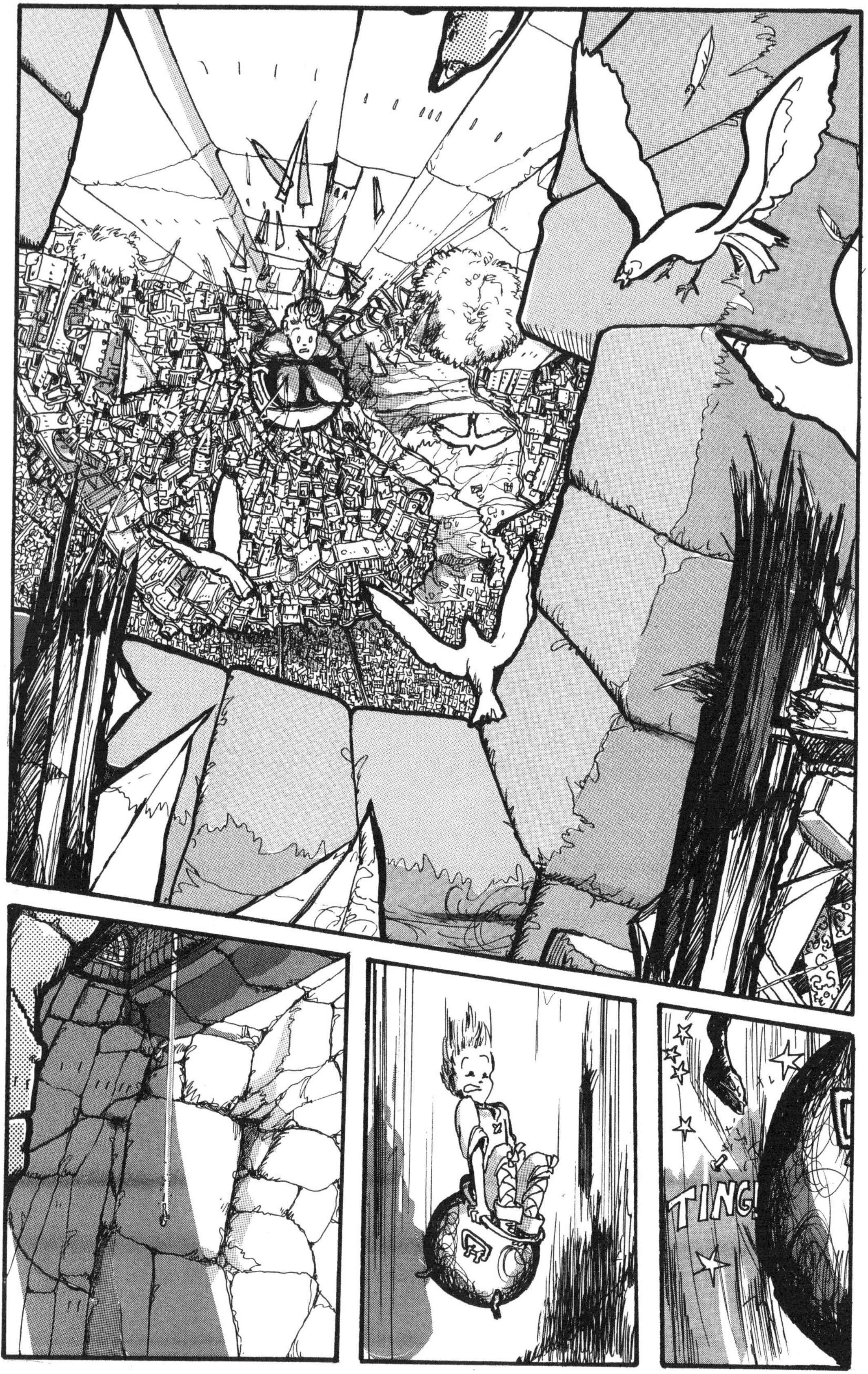
TING!

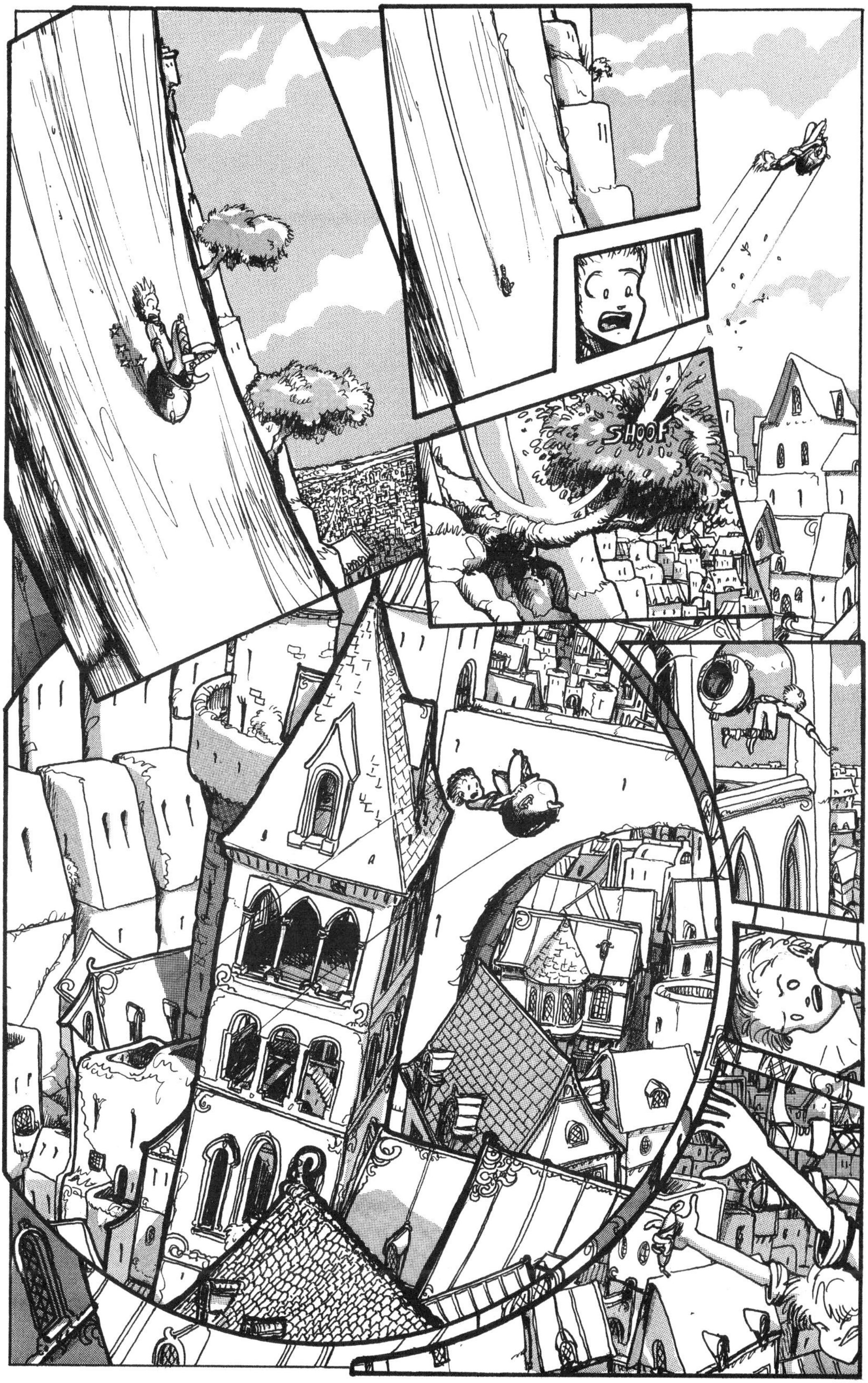
SHOOF

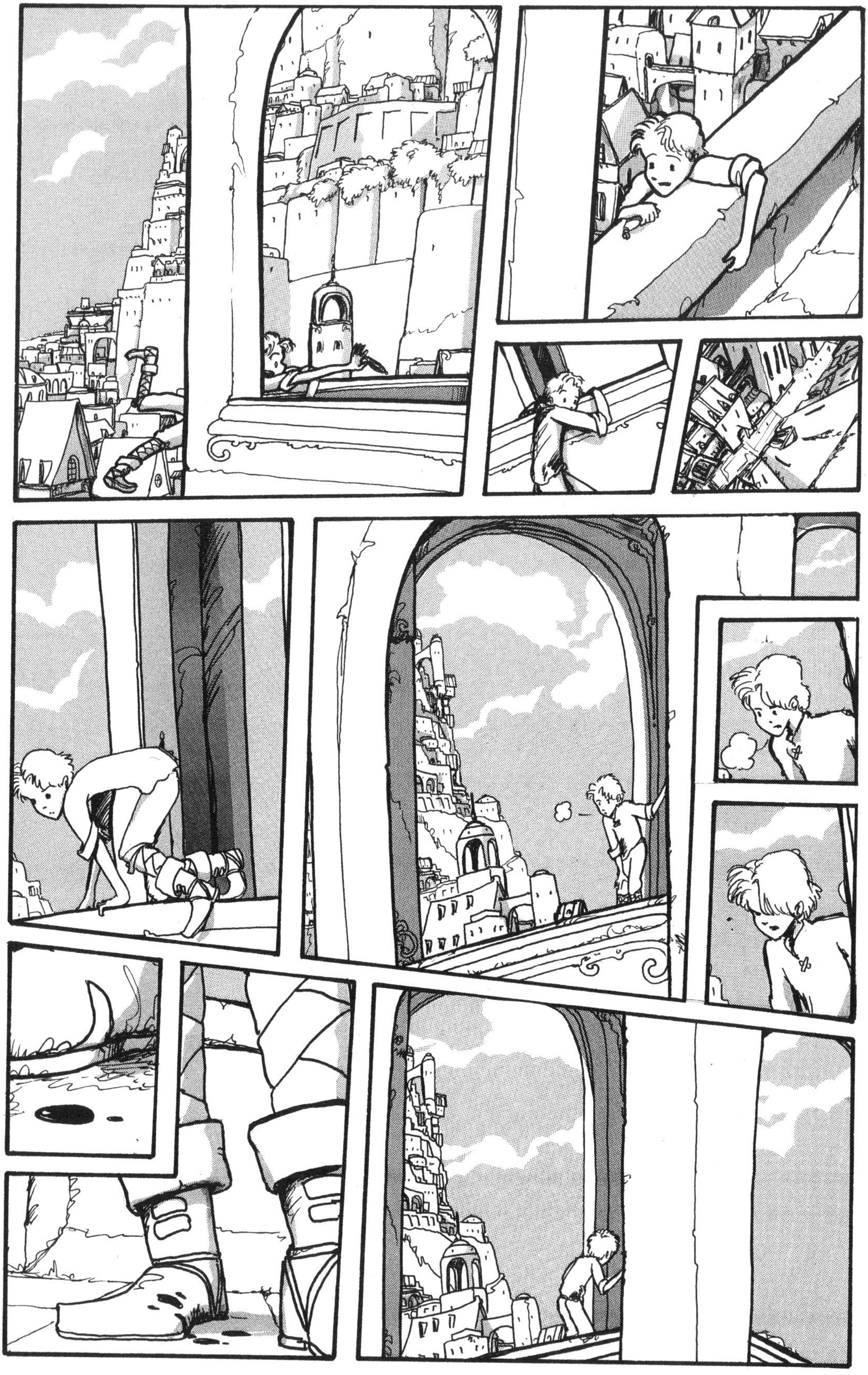

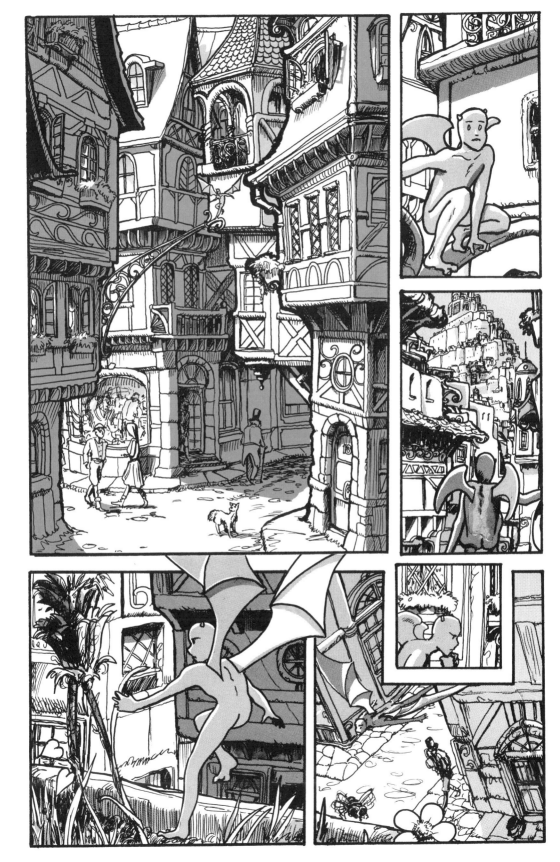

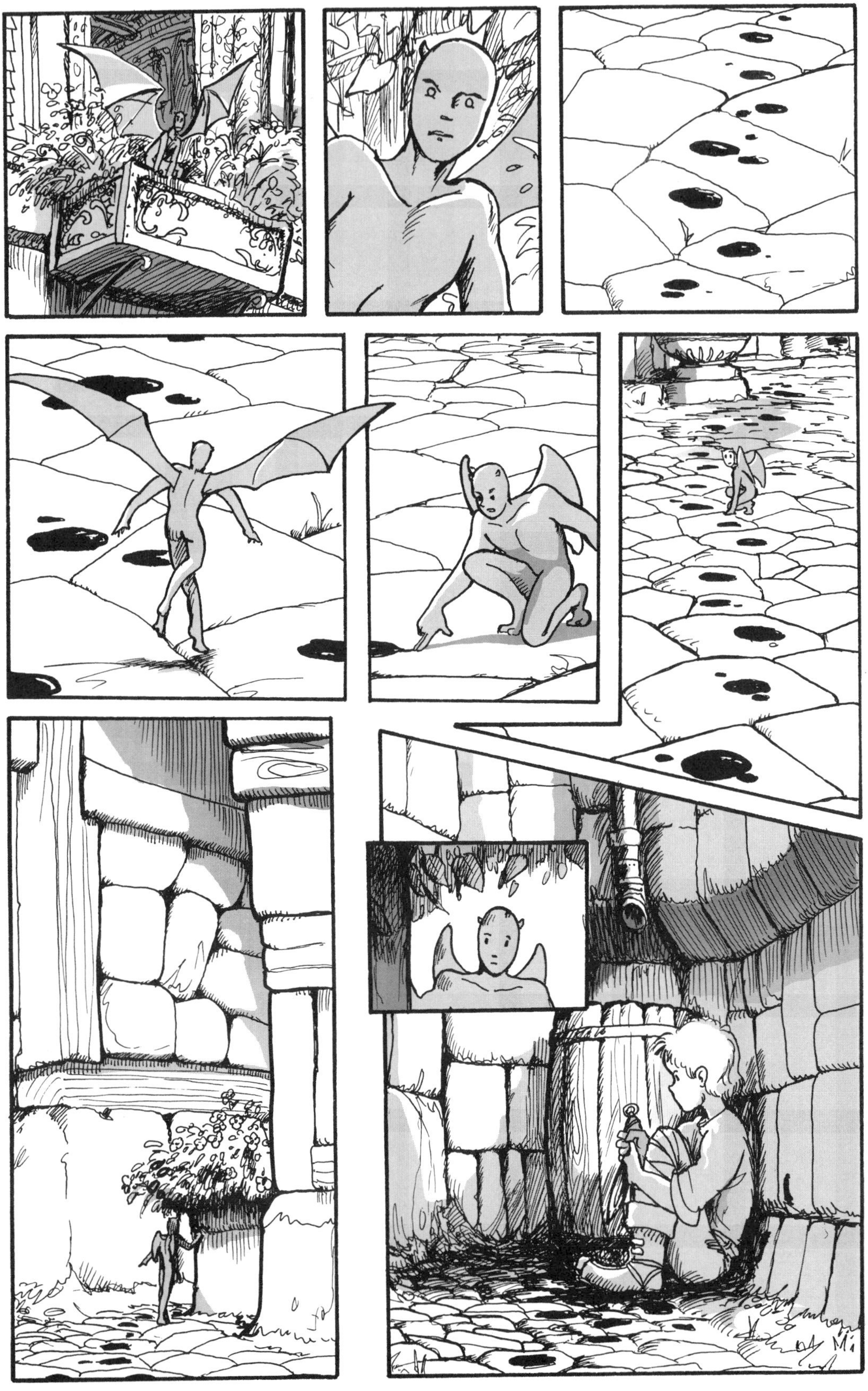

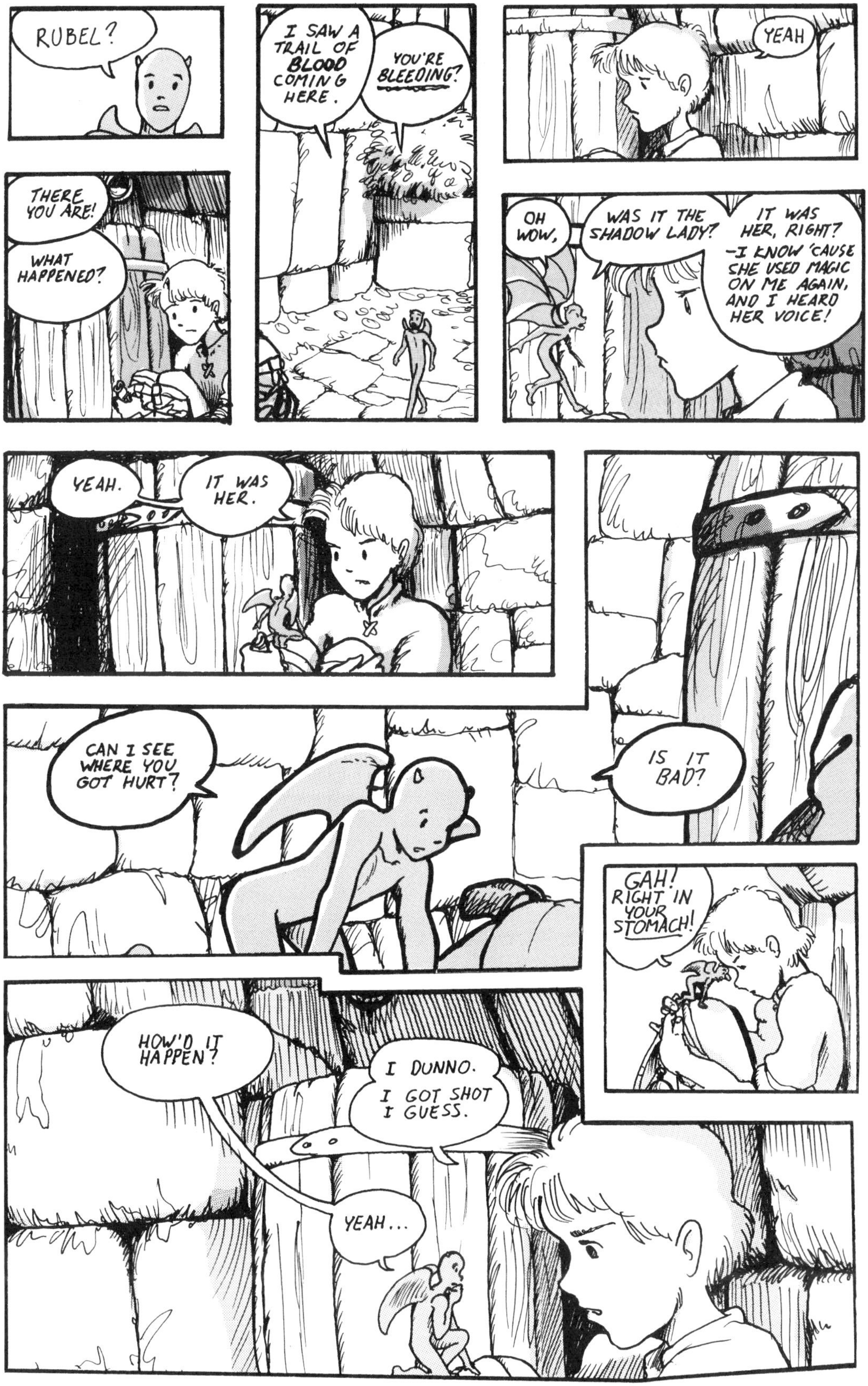

RUBEL?
I SAW A TRAIL OF BLOOD COMING HERE.
YOU'RE BLEEDING?
YEAH
THERE YOU ARE!
WHAT HAPPENED?
OH WOW,
WAS IT THE SHADOW LADY?
IT WAS HER, RIGHT? -I KNOW 'CAUSE SHE USED MAGIC ON ME AGAIN, AND I HEARD HER VOICE!
YEAH.
IT WAS HER.
CAN I SEE WHERE YOU GOT HURT?
IS IT BAD?
GAH! RIGHT IN YOUR STOMACH!
HOW'D IT HAPPEN?
I DUNNO.
I GOT SHOT I GUESS.
YEAH...

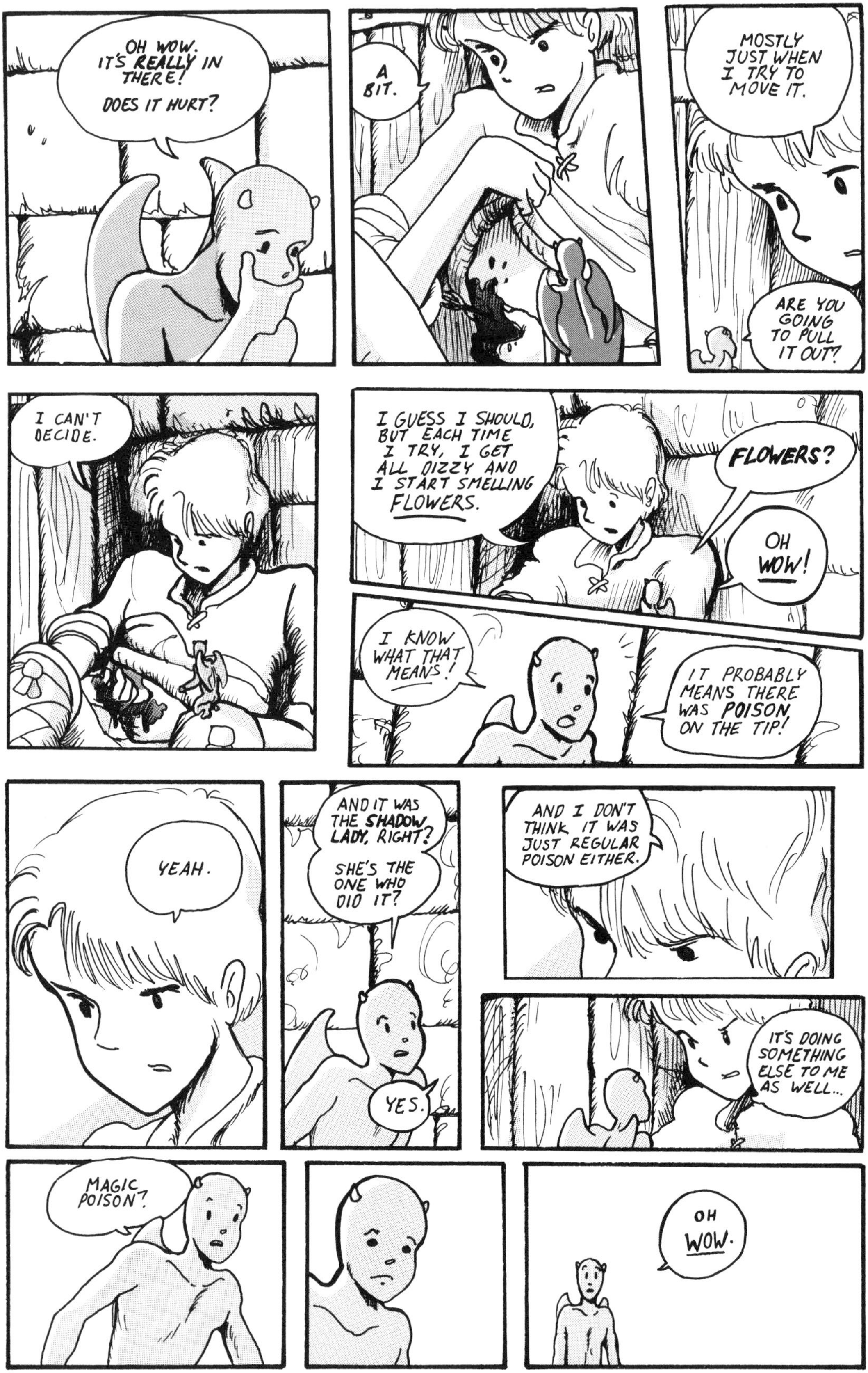
OH WOW. IT'S REALLY IN THERE!
DOES IT HURT?
A BIT.
MOSTLY JUST WHEN I TRY TO MOVE IT.
ARE YOU GOING TO PULL IT OUT?
I CAN'T DECIDE.
I GUESS I SHOULD, BUT EACH TIME I TRY, I GET ALL DIZZY AND I START SMELLING FLOWERS.
FLOWERS?
OH WOW!
I KNOW WHAT THAT MEANS!
IT PROBABLY MEANS THERE WAS POISON ON THE TIP!
YEAH.
AND IT WAS THE SHADOW LADY, RIGHT?
SHE'S THE ONE WHO DID IT?
YES.
AND I DON'T THINK IT WAS JUST REGULAR POISON EITHER.
IT'S DOING SOMETHING ELSE TO ME AS WELL...
MAGIC POISON?
OH WOW.

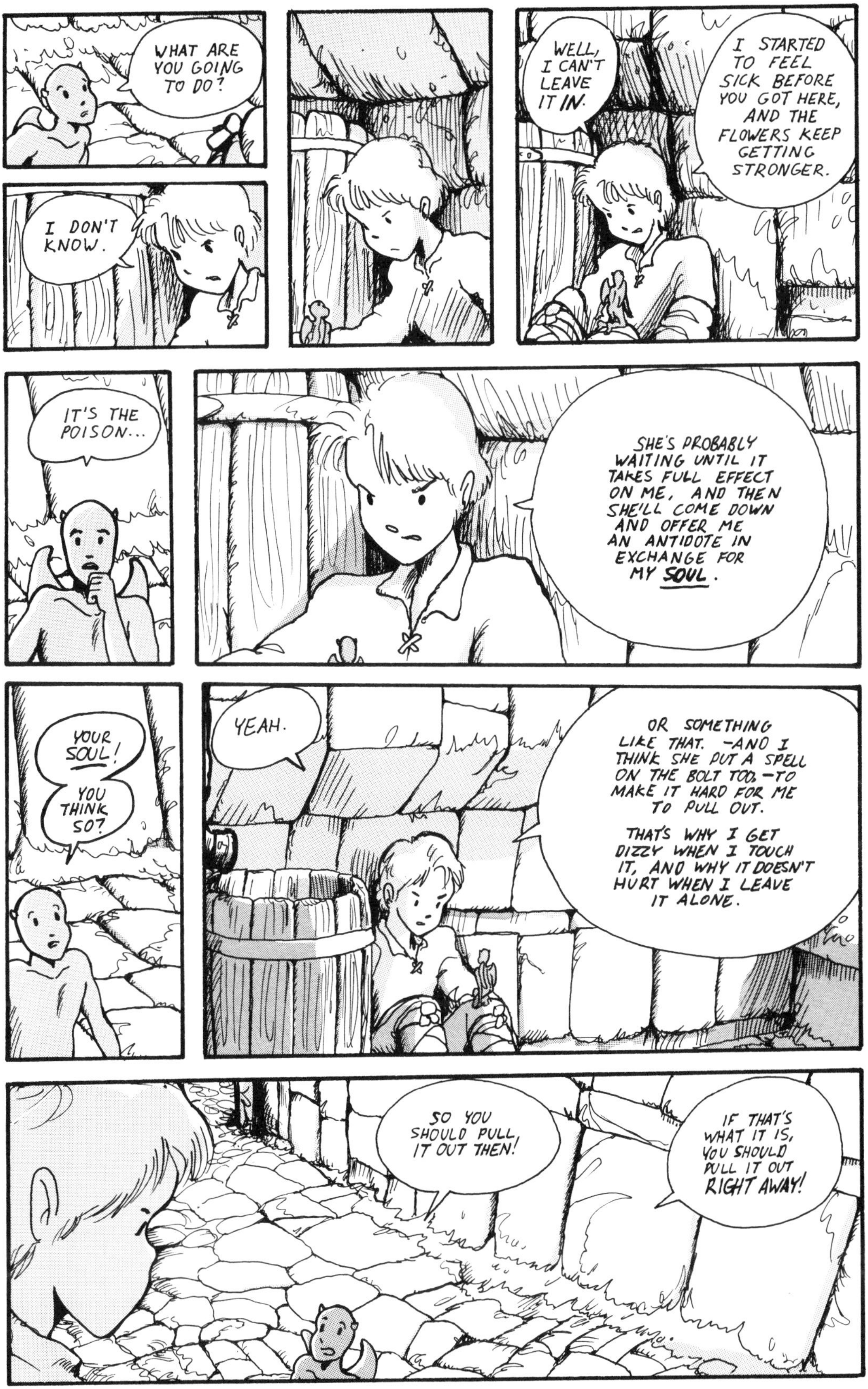

WHAT ARE YOU GOING TO DO?
I DON'T KNOW.
WELL, I CAN'T LEAVE IT IN.
I STARTED TO FEEL SICK BEFORE YOU GOT HERE, AND THE FLOWERS KEEP GETTING STRONGER.
IT'S THE POISON...
SHE'S PROBABLY WAITING UNTIL IT TAKES FULL EFFECT ON ME, AND THEN SHE'LL COME DOWN AND OFFER ME AN ANTIDOTE IN EXCHANGE FOR MY SOUL.
YOUR SOUL!
YOU THINK SO?
YEAH.
OR SOMETHING LIKE THAT. —AND I THINK SHE PUT A SPELL ON THE BOLT TOO,—TO MAKE IT HARD FOR ME TO PULL OUT.
THAT'S WHY I GET DIZZY WHEN I TOUCH IT, AND WHY IT DOESN'T HURT WHEN I LEAVE IT ALONE.
SO YOU SHOULD PULL IT OUT THEN!
IF THAT'S WHAT IT IS, YOU SHOULD PULL IT OUT RIGHT AWAY!

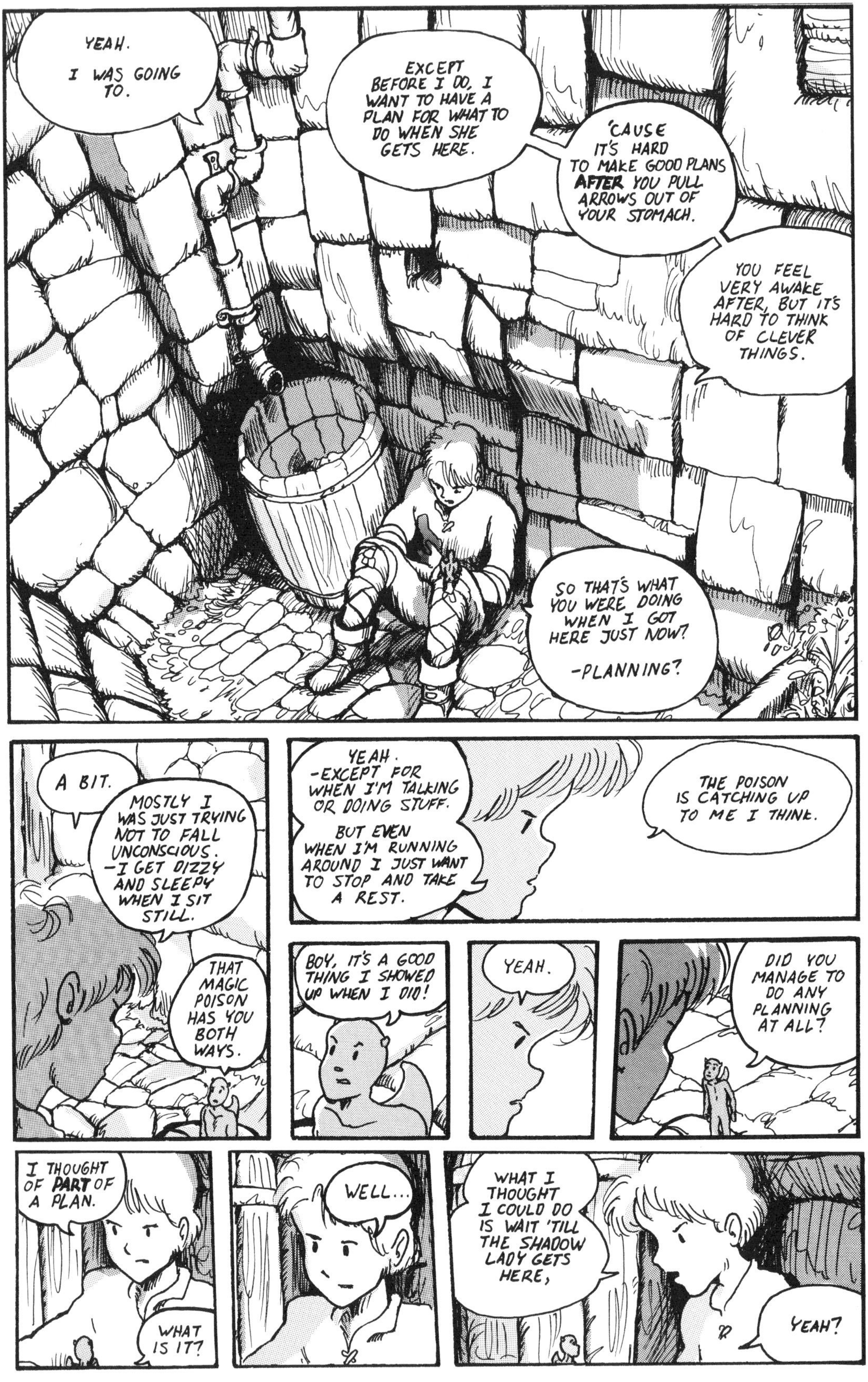
YEAH.
I WAS GOING TO.
EXCEPT BEFORE I DO, I WANT TO HAVE A PLAN FOR WHAT TO DO WHEN SHE GETS HERE.
'CAUSE IT'S HARD TO MAKE GOOD PLANS **AFTER** YOU PULL ARROWS OUT OF YOUR STOMACH.
YOU FEEL VERY AWAKE AFTER, BUT IT'S HARD TO THINK OF CLEVER THINGS.
SO THAT'S WHAT YOU WERE DOING WHEN I GOT HERE JUST NOW?
-PLANNING?
A BIT.
MOSTLY I WAS JUST TRYING NOT TO FALL UNCONSCIOUS. -I GET DIZZY AND SLEEPY WHEN I SIT STILL.
THAT MAGIC POISON HAS YOU BOTH WAYS.
YEAH. -EXCEPT FOR WHEN I'M TALKING OR DOING STUFF.
BUT EVEN WHEN I'M RUNNING AROUND I JUST WANT TO STOP AND TAKE A REST.
THE POISON IS CATCHING UP TO ME I THINK.
BOY, IT'S A GOOD THING I SHOWED UP WHEN I DID!
YEAH.
DID YOU MANAGE TO DO ANY PLANNING AT ALL?
I THOUGHT OF **PART** OF A PLAN.
WHAT IS IT?
WELL...
WHAT I THOUGHT I COULD DO IS WAIT 'TILL THE SHADOW LADY GETS HERE,
YEAH?

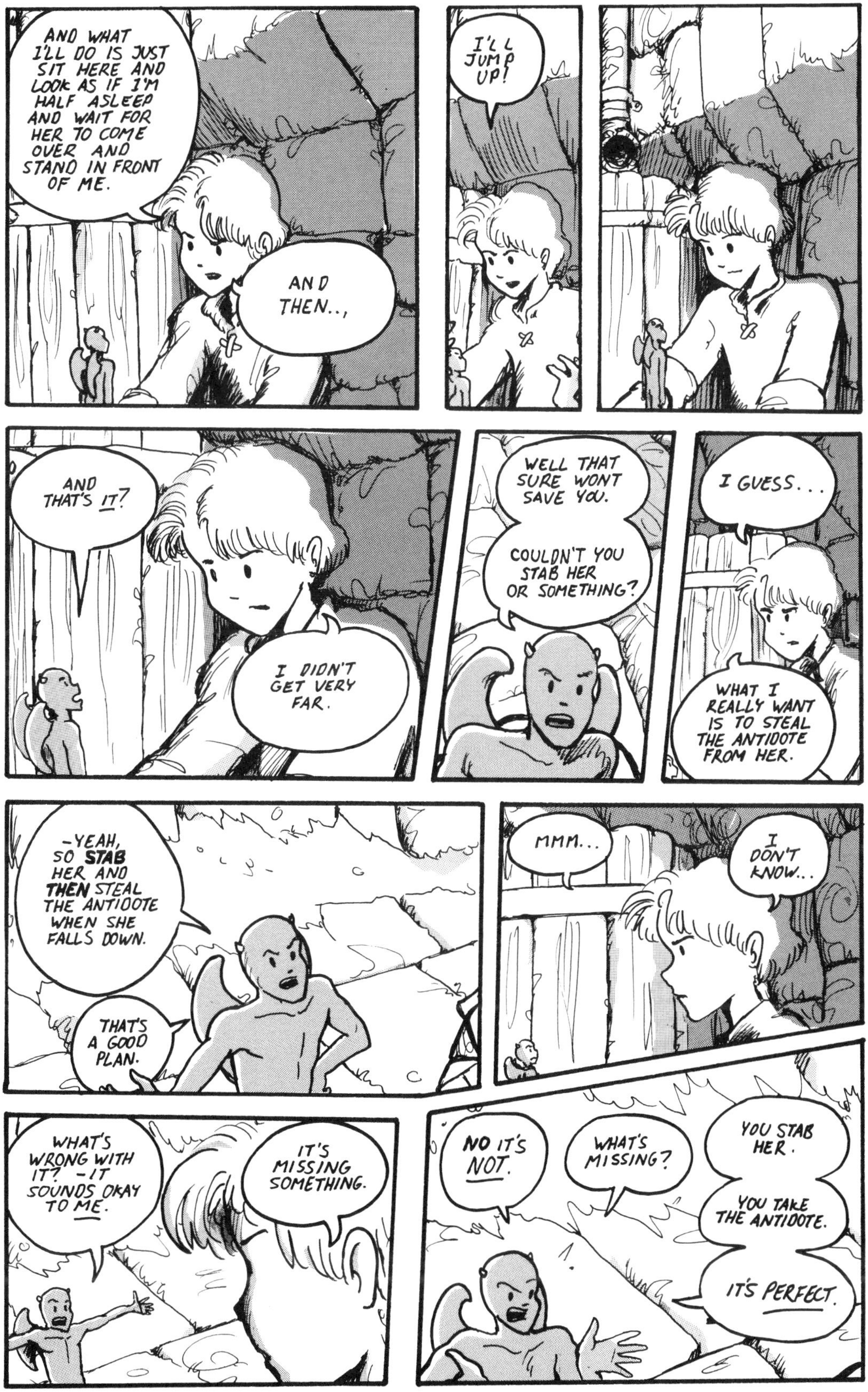
AND WHAT I'LL DO IS JUST SIT HERE AND LOOK AS IF I'M HALF ASLEEP AND WAIT FOR HER TO COME OVER AND STAND IN FRONT OF ME.
AND THEN..,
I'LL JUMP UP!
AND THAT'S IT?
I DIDN'T GET VERY FAR.
WELL THAT SURE WONT SAVE YOU.
COULDN'T YOU STAB HER OR SOMETHING?
I GUESS...
WHAT I REALLY WANT IS TO STEAL THE ANTIDOTE FROM HER.
-YEAH, SO STAB HER AND THEN STEAL THE ANTIDOTE WHEN SHE FALLS DOWN.
THAT'S A GOOD PLAN.
MMM...
I DON'T KNOW...
WHAT'S WRONG WITH IT? -IT SOUNDS OKAY TO ME.
IT'S MISSING SOMETHING.
NO IT'S NOT.
WHAT'S MISSING?
YOU STAB HER.
YOU TAKE THE ANTIDOTE.
IT'S PERFECT.

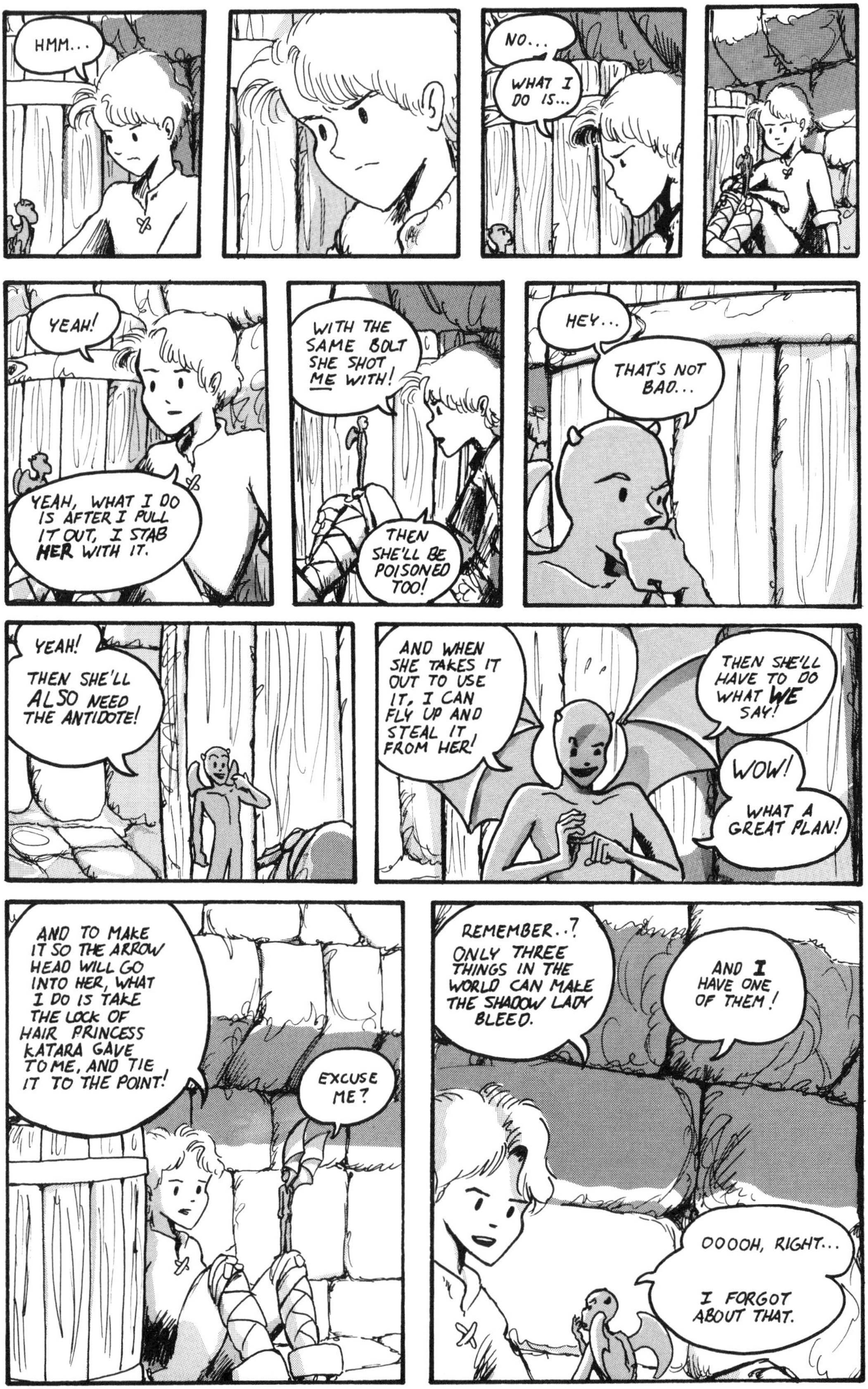
HMM...
NO...
WHAT I DO IS...
YEAH!
YEAH, WHAT I DO IS AFTER I PULL IT OUT, I STAB HER WITH IT.
WITH THE SAME BOLT SHE SHOT ME WITH!
THEN SHE'LL BE POISONED TOO!
HEY...
THAT'S NOT BAD...
YEAH!
THEN SHE'LL ALSO NEED THE ANTIDOTE!
AND WHEN SHE TAKES IT OUT TO USE IT, I CAN FLY UP AND STEAL IT FROM HER!
THEN SHE'LL HAVE TO DO WHAT WE SAY!
WOW!
WHAT A GREAT PLAN!
AND TO MAKE IT SO THE ARROW HEAD WILL GO INTO HER, WHAT I DO IS TAKE THE LOCK OF HAIR PRINCESS KATARA GAVE TO ME, AND TIE IT TO THE POINT!
EXCUSE ME?
REMEMBER..?
ONLY THREE THINGS IN THE WORLD CAN MAKE THE SHADOW LADY BLEED.
AND I HAVE ONE OF THEM!
OOOOH, RIGHT...
I FORGOT ABOUT THAT.

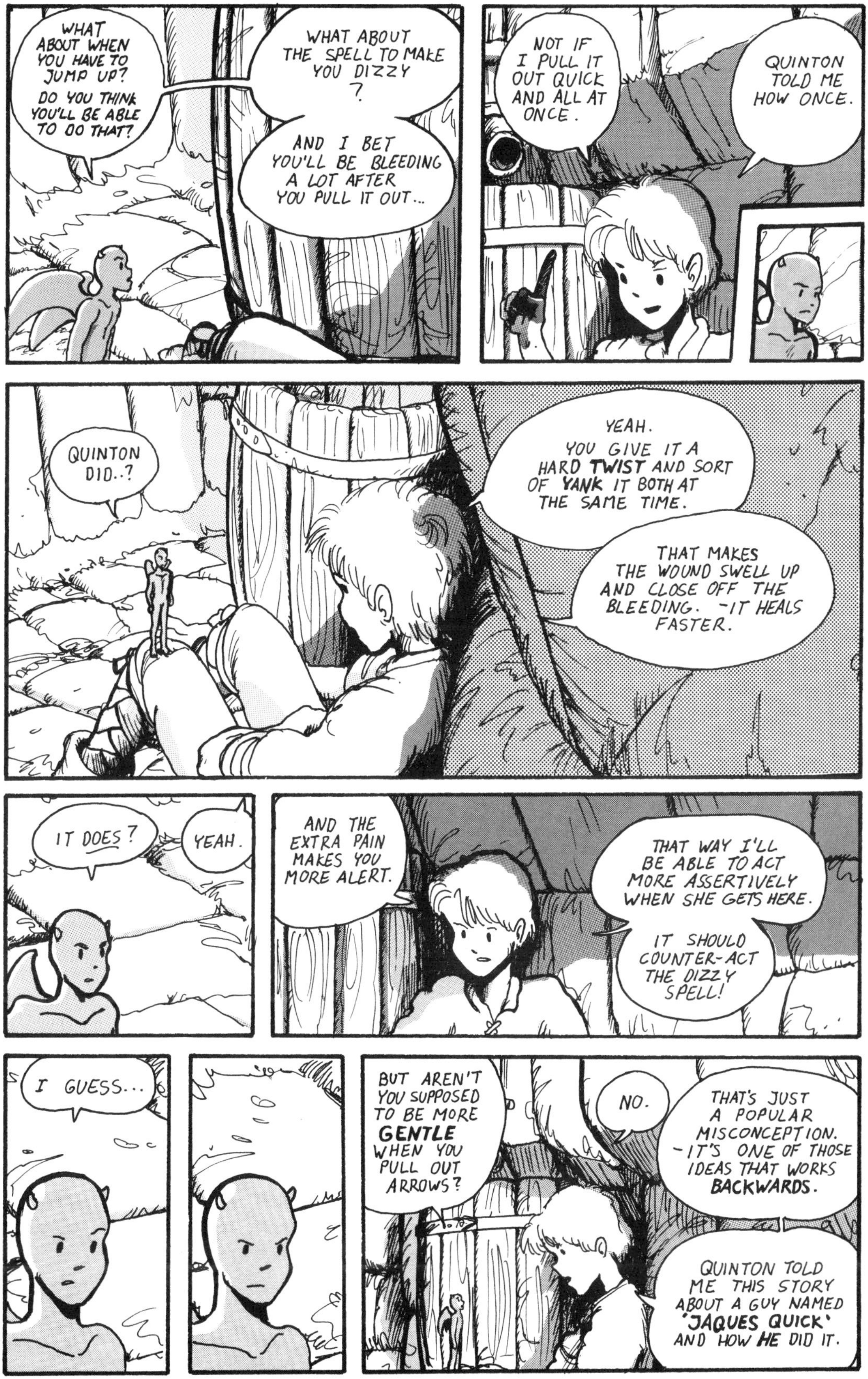
WHAT ABOUT WHEN YOU HAVE TO JUMP UP? DO YOU THINK YOU'LL BE ABLE TO DO THAT?
WHAT ABOUT THE SPELL TO MAKE YOU DIZZY ?
AND I BET YOU'LL BE BLEEDING A LOT AFTER YOU PULL IT OUT...
NOT IF I PULL IT OUT QUICK AND ALL AT ONCE.
QUINTON TOLD ME HOW ONCE.
QUINTON DID..?
YEAH. YOU GIVE IT A HARD TWIST AND SORT OF YANK IT BOTH AT THE SAME TIME.
THAT MAKES THE WOUND SWELL UP AND CLOSE OFF THE BLEEDING. -IT HEALS FASTER.
IT DOES?
YEAH.
AND THE EXTRA PAIN MAKES YOU MORE ALERT.
THAT WAY I'LL BE ABLE TO ACT MORE ASSERTIVELY WHEN SHE GETS HERE.
IT SHOULD COUNTER-ACT THE DIZZY SPELL!
I GUESS...
BUT AREN'T YOU SUPPOSED TO BE MORE GENTLE WHEN YOU PULL OUT ARROWS?
NO.
THAT'S JUST A POPULAR MISCONCEPTION. -IT'S ONE OF THOSE IDEAS THAT WORKS BACKWARDS.
QUINTON TOLD ME THIS STORY ABOUT A GUY NAMED 'JAQUES QUICK' AND HOW HE DID IT.

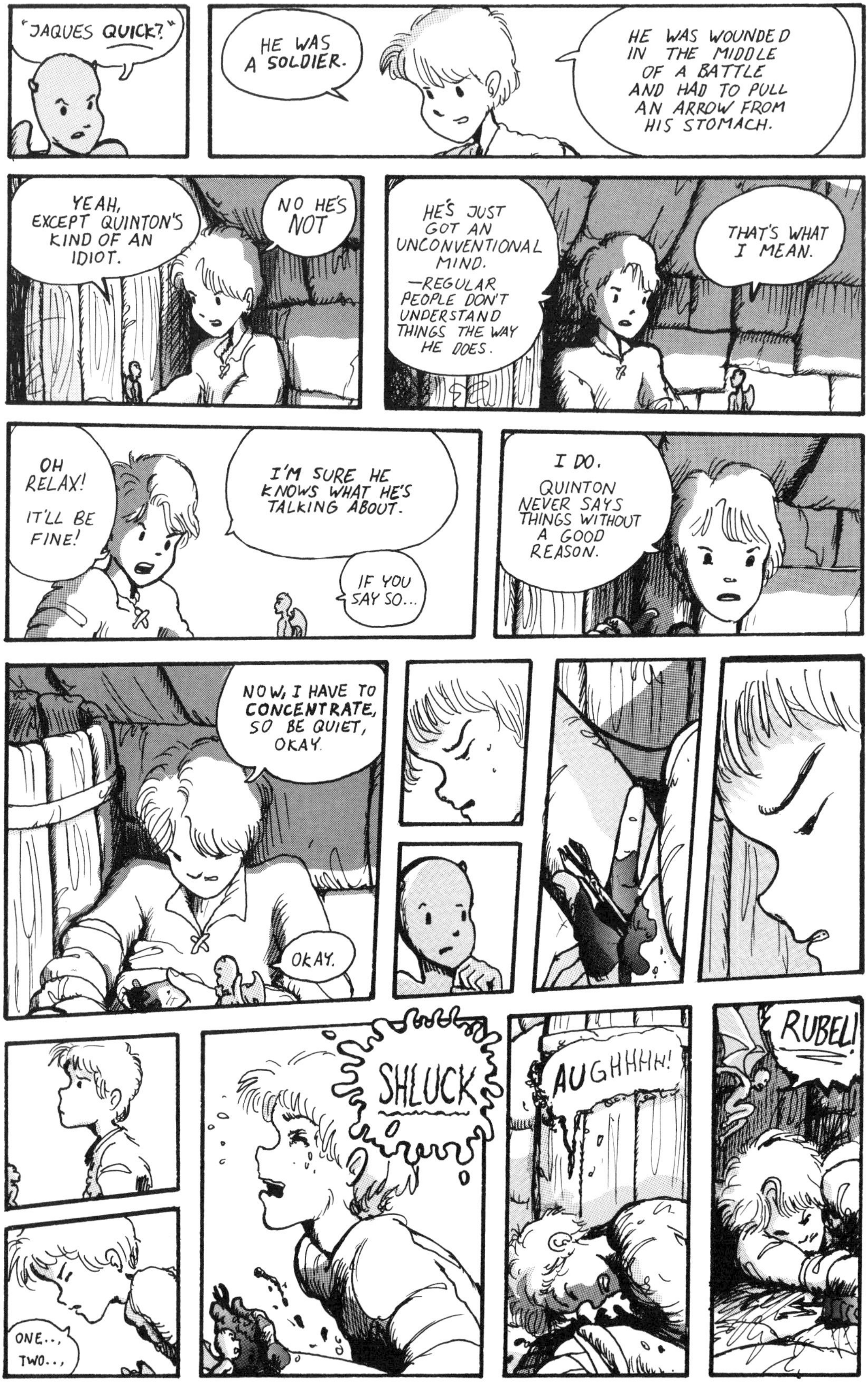
"JAQUES QUICK?"
HE WAS A SOLDIER.
HE WAS WOUNDED IN THE MIDDLE OF A BATTLE AND HAD TO PULL AN ARROW FROM HIS STOMACH.
YEAH, EXCEPT QUINTON'S KIND OF AN IDIOT.
NO HE'S NOT
HE'S JUST GOT AN UNCONVENTIONAL MIND.
—REGULAR PEOPLE DON'T UNDERSTAND THINGS THE WAY HE DOES.
THAT'S WHAT I MEAN.
OH RELAX!
IT'LL BE FINE!
I'M SURE HE KNOWS WHAT HE'S TALKING ABOUT.
IF YOU SAY SO...
I DO.
QUINTON NEVER SAYS THINGS WITHOUT A GOOD REASON.
NOW, I HAVE TO CONCENTRATE, SO BE QUIET, OKAY.
OKAY.
ONE.., TWO..,
SHLUCK
AUGHHHH!
RUBEL!

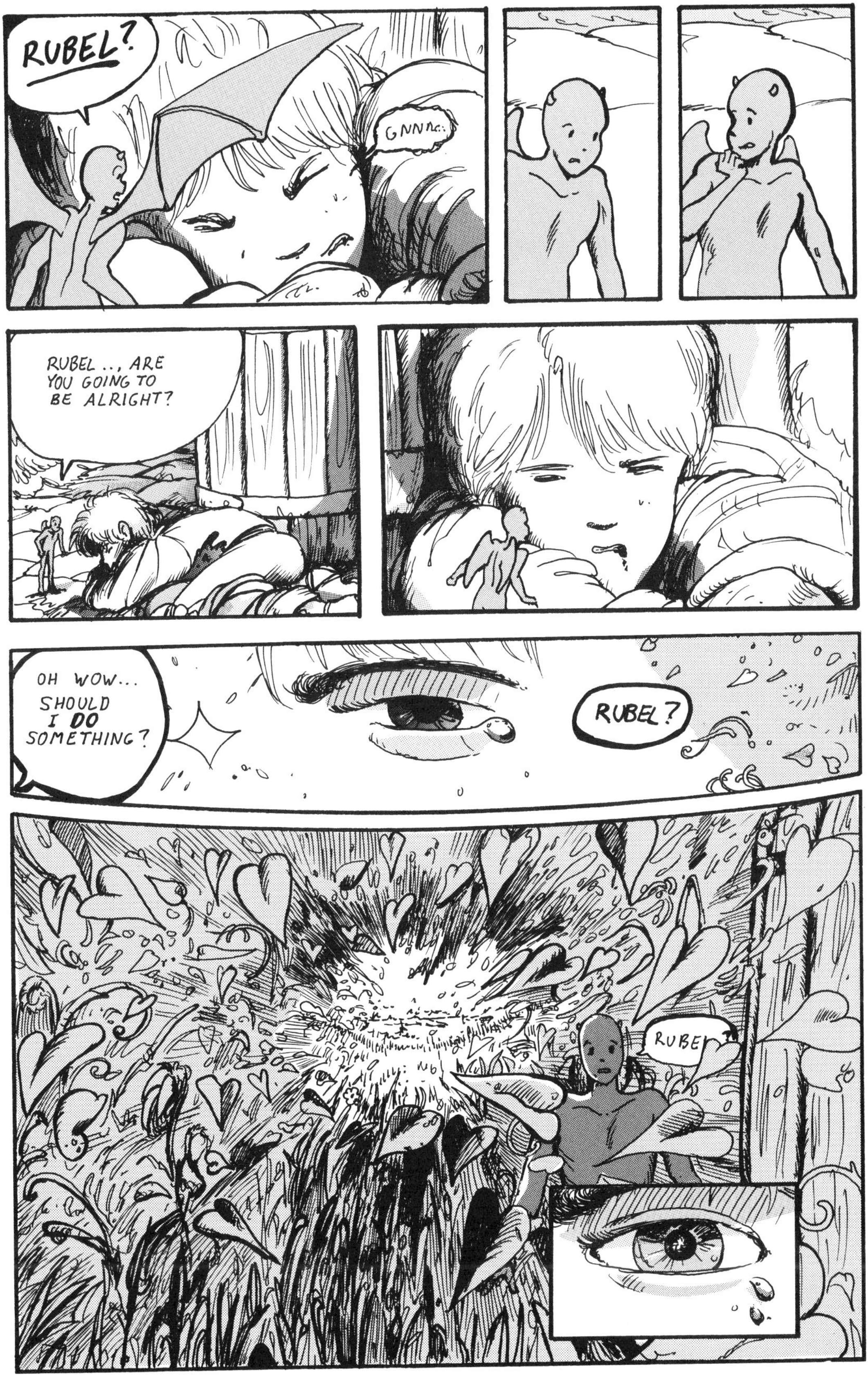
RUBEL?
GNNN...
RUBEL..., ARE YOU GOING TO BE ALRIGHT?
OH WOW... SHOULD I DO SOMETHING?
RUBEL?
RUBE

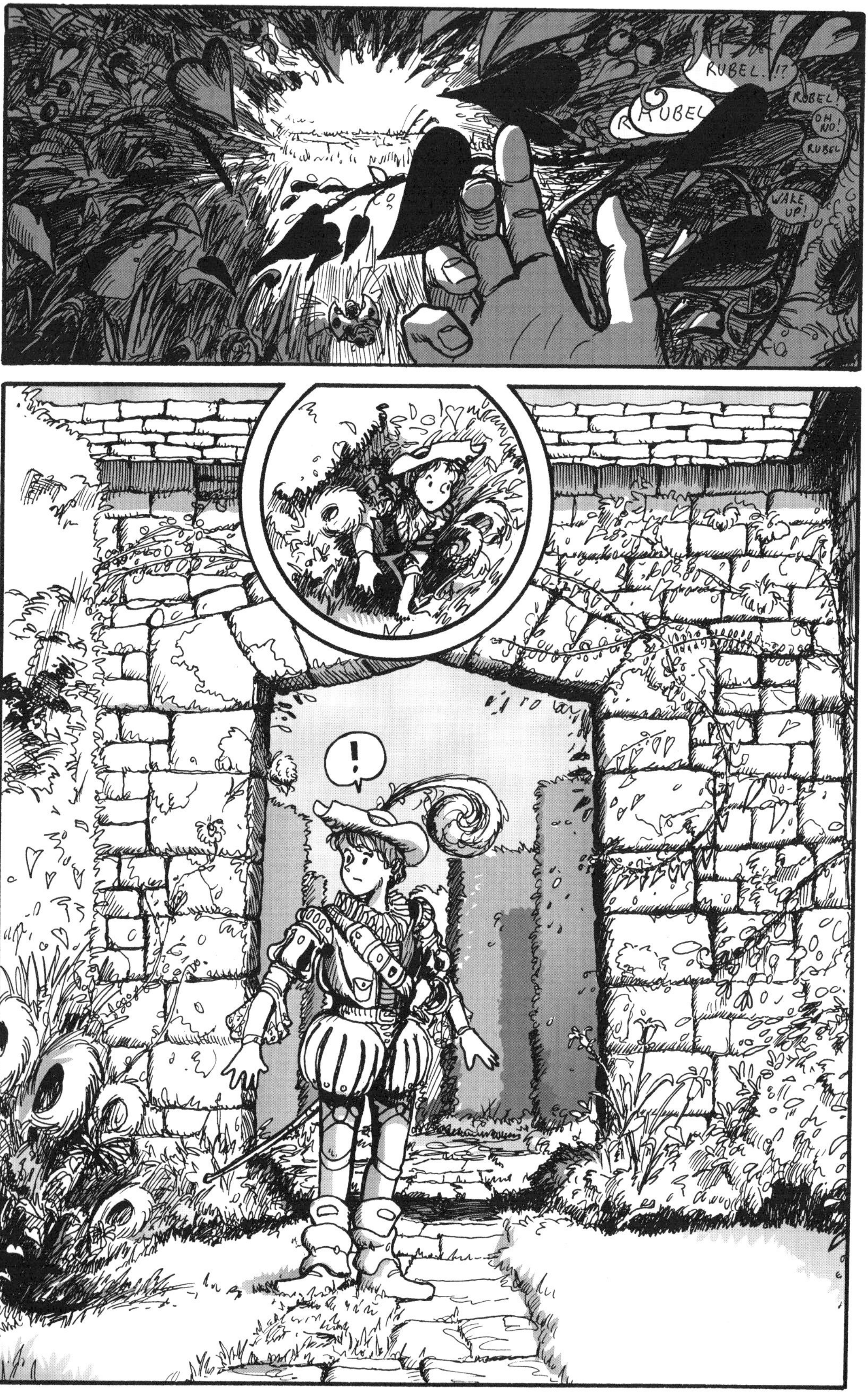
RUBEL..!?
R RUBEL
RUBEL!
OH NO!
RUBEL
WAKE UP!
!

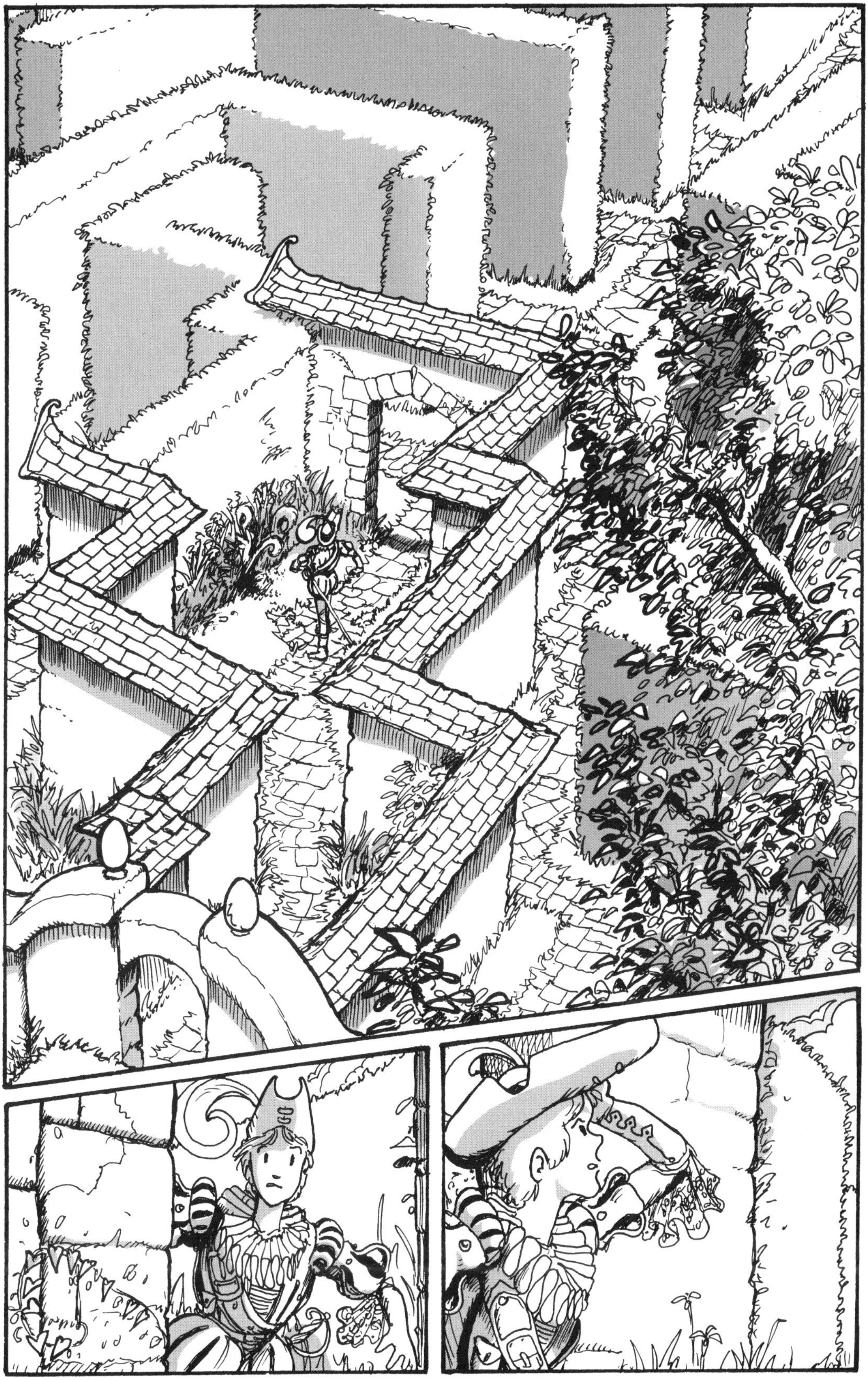

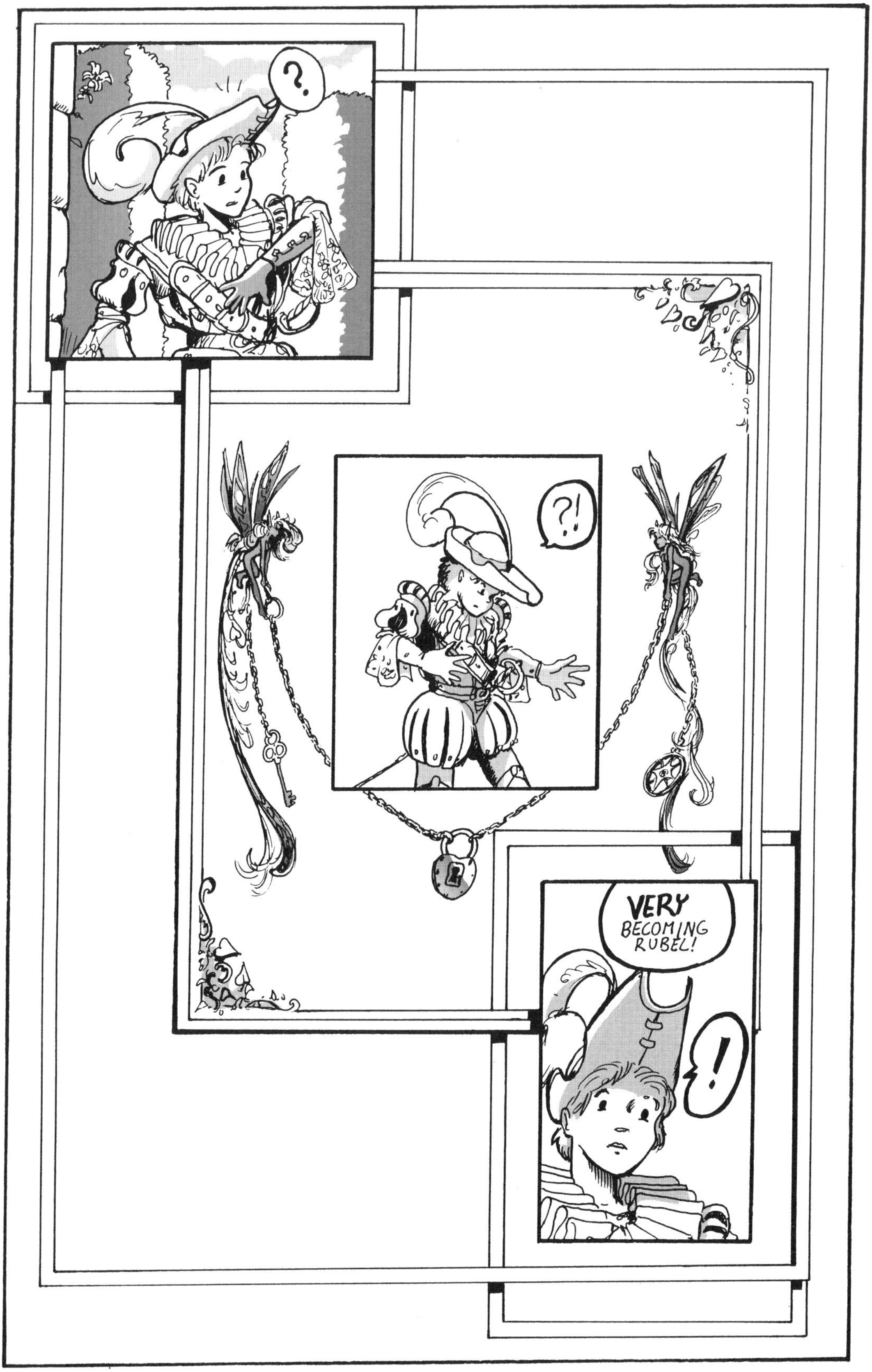
?
?!
VERY BECOMING RUBEL!
!

Chapter 13

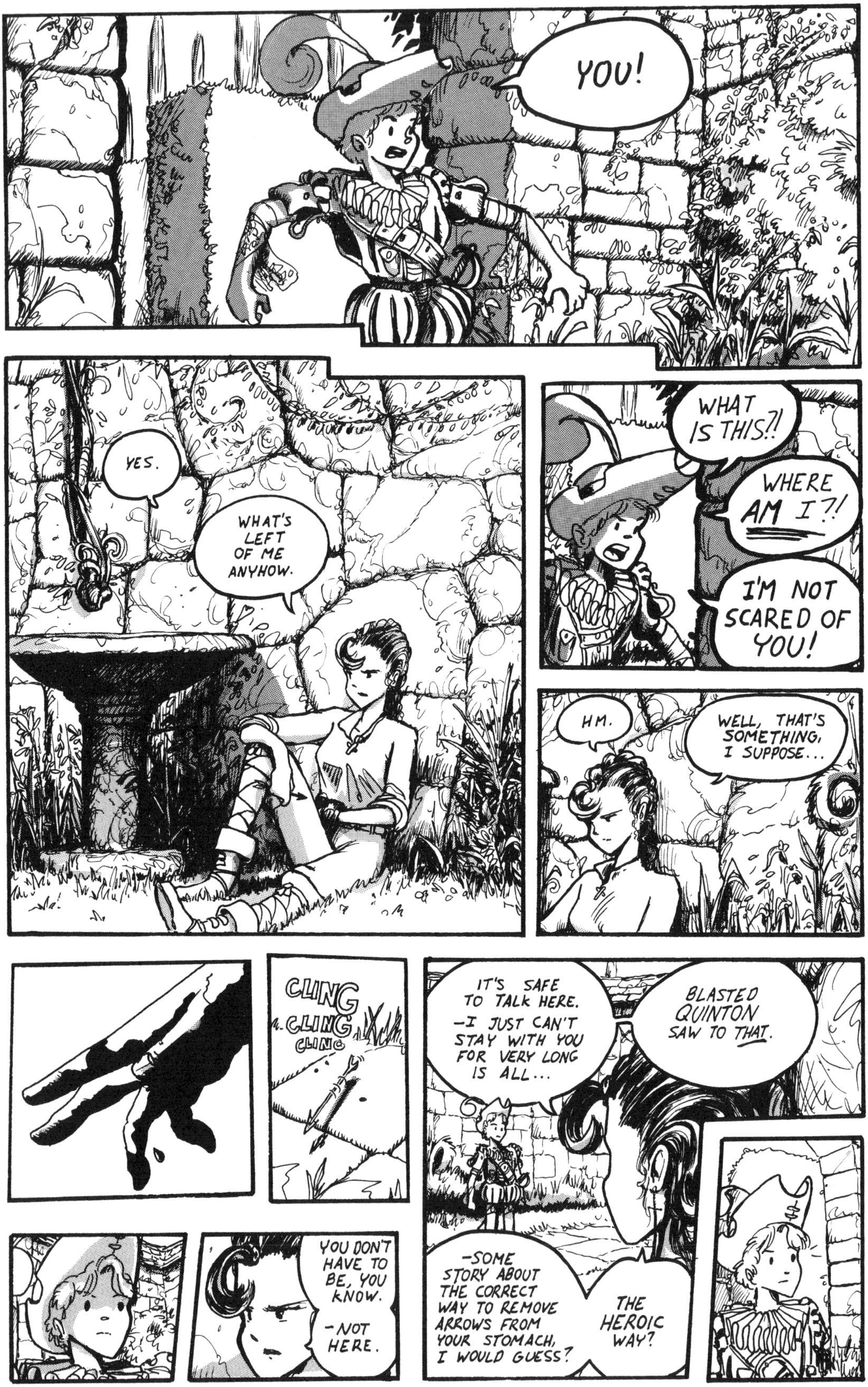
YOU!
YES.
WHAT'S LEFT OF ME ANYHOW.
WHAT IS THIS?!
WHERE AM I?!
I'M NOT SCARED OF YOU!
HM.
WELL, THAT'S SOMETHING, I SUPPOSE...
CLING
CLING
CLING
IT'S SAFE TO TALK HERE.
–I JUST CAN'T STAY WITH YOU FOR VERY LONG IS ALL...
BLASTED QUINTON SAW TO THAT.
–SOME STORY ABOUT THE CORRECT WAY TO REMOVE ARROWS FROM YOUR STOMACH, I WOULD GUESS?
THE HEROIC WAY?
YOU DON'T HAVE TO BE, YOU KNOW.
–NOT HERE.

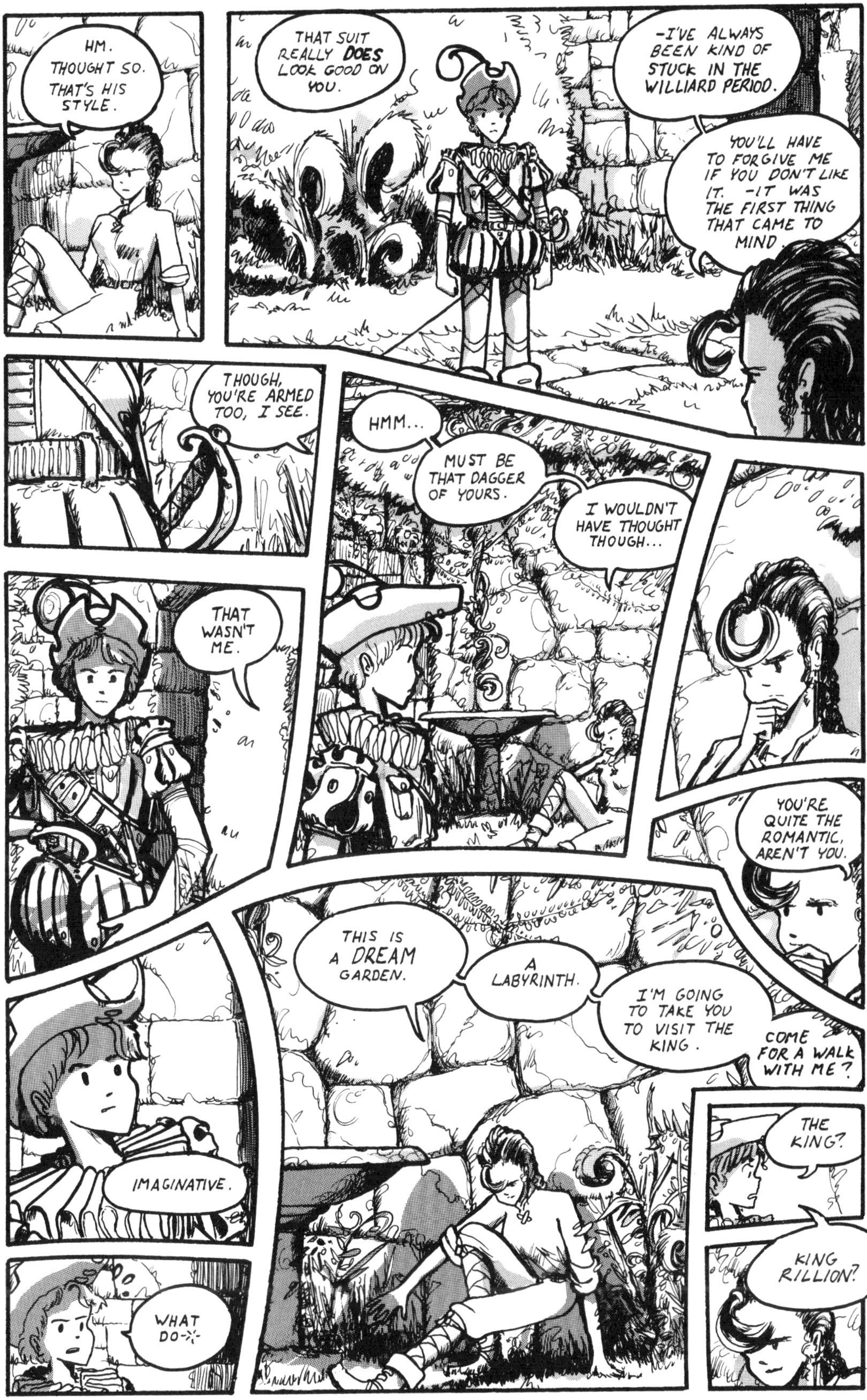
HM. THOUGHT SO. THAT'S HIS STYLE.
THAT SUIT REALLY DOES LOOK GOOD ON YOU.
-I'VE ALWAYS BEEN KIND OF STUCK IN THE WILLIARD PERIOD.
YOU'LL HAVE TO FORGIVE ME IF YOU DON'T LIKE IT. -IT WAS THE FIRST THING THAT CAME TO MIND.
THOUGH, YOU'RE ARMED TOO, I SEE.
HMM...
MUST BE THAT DAGGER OF YOURS.
I WOULDN'T HAVE THOUGHT THOUGH...
THAT WASN'T ME.
YOU'RE QUITE THE ROMANTIC, AREN'T YOU.
IMAGINATIVE.
THIS IS A DREAM GARDEN.
A LABYRINTH.
I'M GOING TO TAKE YOU TO VISIT THE KING.
COME FOR A WALK WITH ME?
THE KING?
KING RILLION?
WHAT DO-

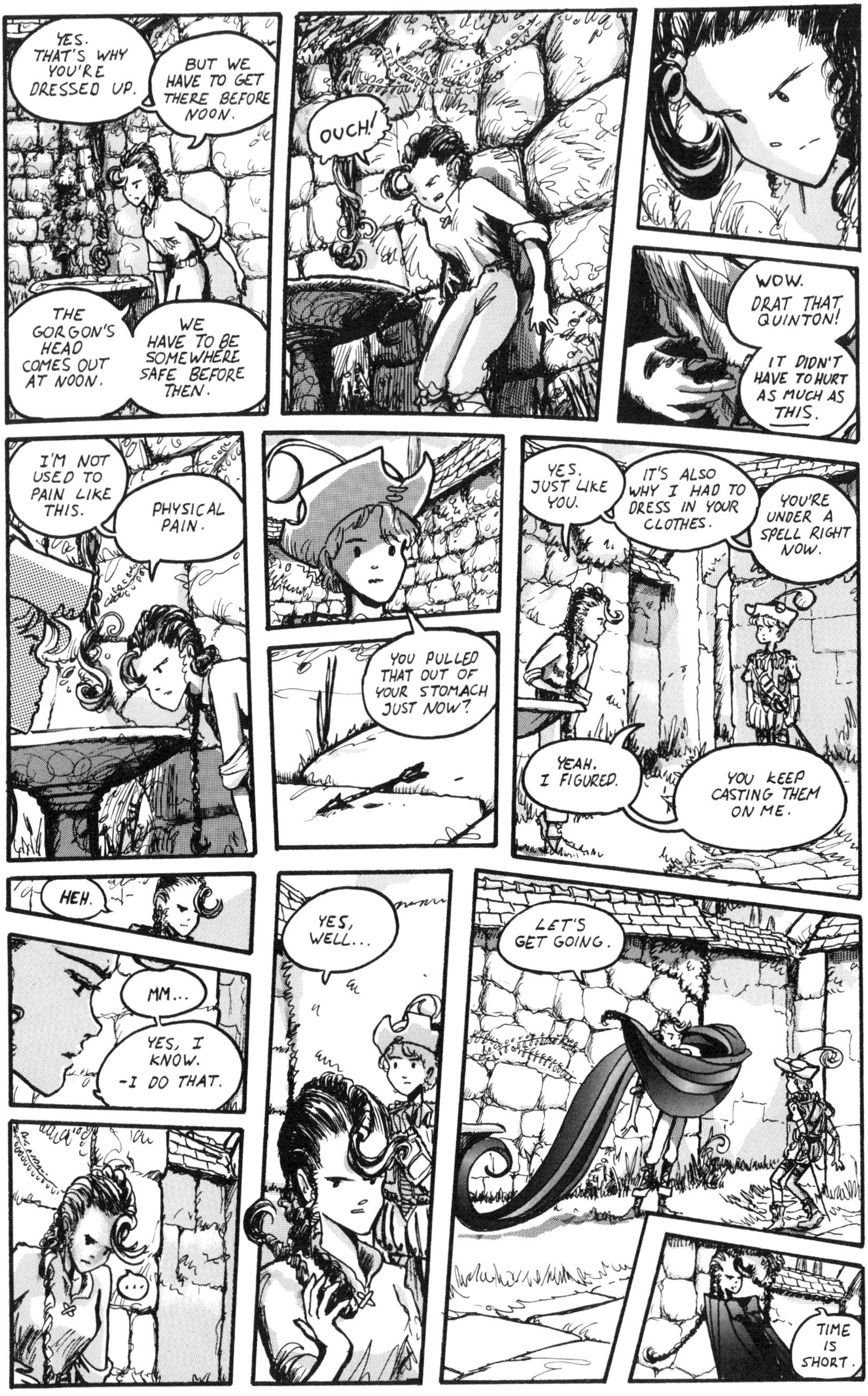
YES. THAT'S WHY YOU'RE DRESSED UP.
BUT WE HAVE TO GET THERE BEFORE NOON.
THE GORGON'S HEAD COMES OUT AT NOON.
WE HAVE TO BE SOMEWHERE SAFE BEFORE THEN.
OUCH!
WOW. DRAT THAT QUINTON!
IT DIDN'T HAVE TO HURT AS MUCH AS THIS.
I'M NOT USED TO PAIN LIKE THIS.
PHYSICAL PAIN.
YOU PULLED THAT OUT OF YOUR STOMACH JUST NOW?
YES. JUST LIKE YOU.
IT'S ALSO WHY I HAD TO DRESS IN YOUR CLOTHES.
YOU'RE UNDER A SPELL RIGHT NOW.
YEAH. I FIGURED.
YOU KEEP CASTING THEM ON ME.
HEH.
MM...
YES, I KNOW. -I DO THAT.
YES, WELL...
LET'S GET GOING.
TIME IS SHORT.

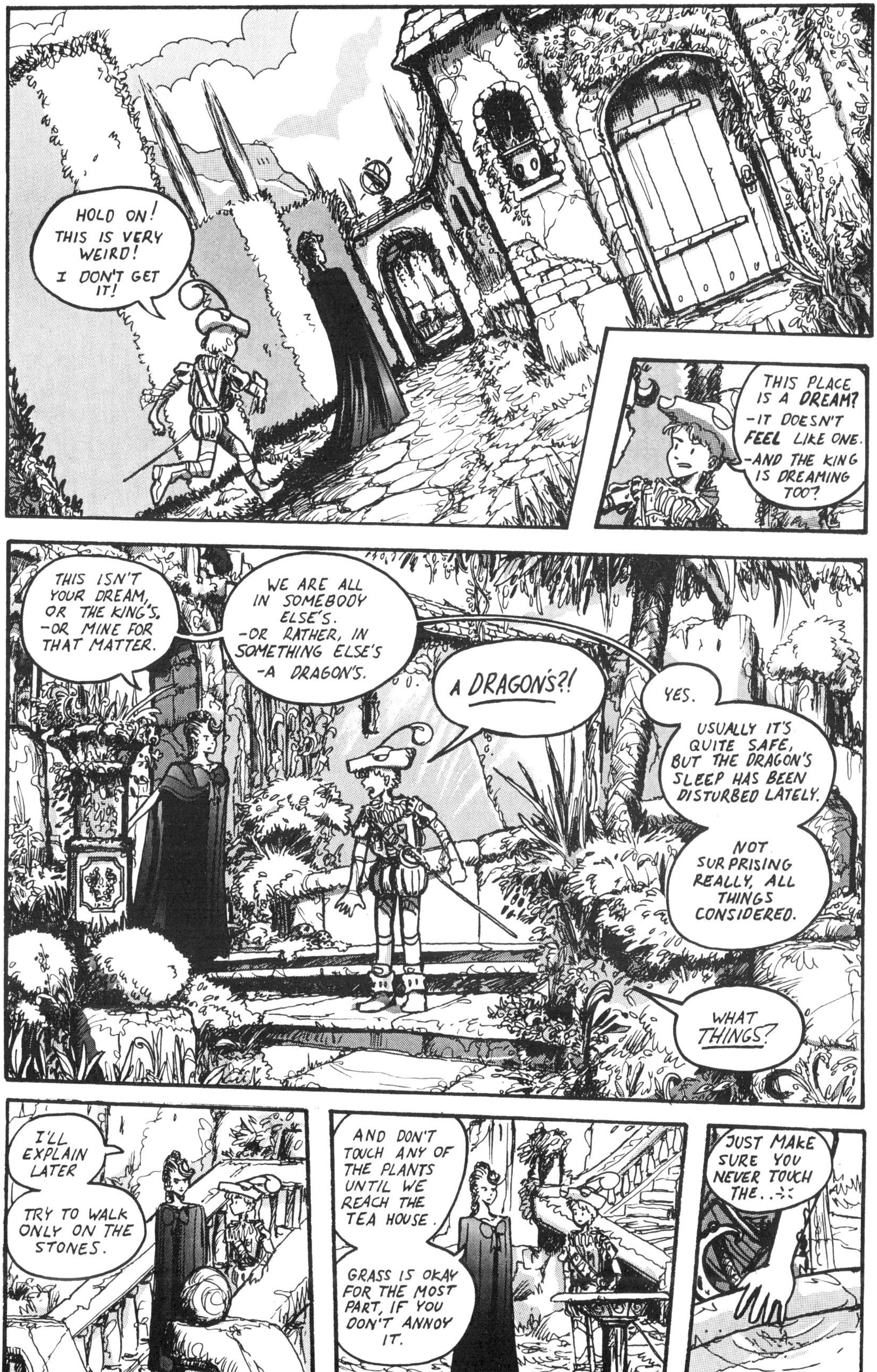
HOLD ON! THIS IS VERY WEIRD! I DON'T GET IT!
THIS PLACE IS A DREAM? -IT DOESN'T FEEL LIKE ONE. -AND THE KING IS DREAMING TOO?
THIS ISN'T YOUR DREAM, OR THE KING'S. -OR MINE FOR THAT MATTER.
WE ARE ALL IN SOMEBODY ELSE'S. -OR RATHER, IN SOMETHING ELSE'S -A DRAGON'S.
A DRAGON'S?!
YES.
USUALLY IT'S QUITE SAFE, BUT THE DRAGON'S SLEEP HAS BEEN DISTURBED LATELY.
NOT SURPRISING REALLY, ALL THINGS CONSIDERED.
WHAT THINGS?
I'LL EXPLAIN LATER
TRY TO WALK ONLY ON THE STONES.
AND DON'T TOUCH ANY OF THE PLANTS UNTIL WE REACH THE TEA HOUSE.
GRASS IS OKAY FOR THE MOST PART, IF YOU DON'T ANNOY IT.
JUST MAKE SURE YOU NEVER TOUCH THE..:-:

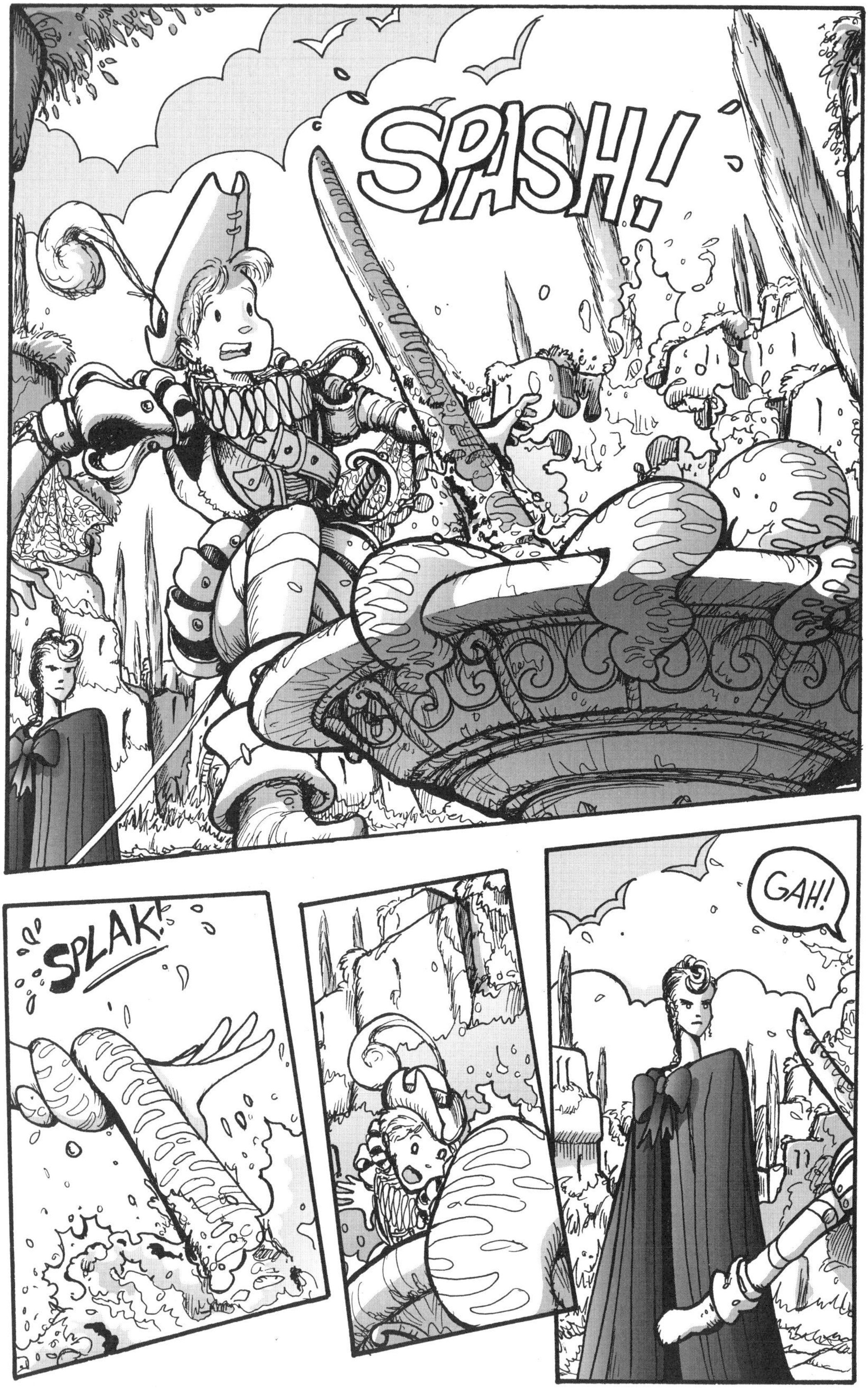
SPLASH!
SPLAK!
GAH!

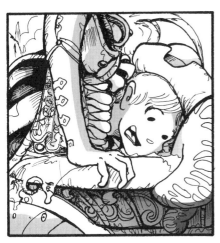

CAREFUL.

I EXPECT IT HAS TEETH.

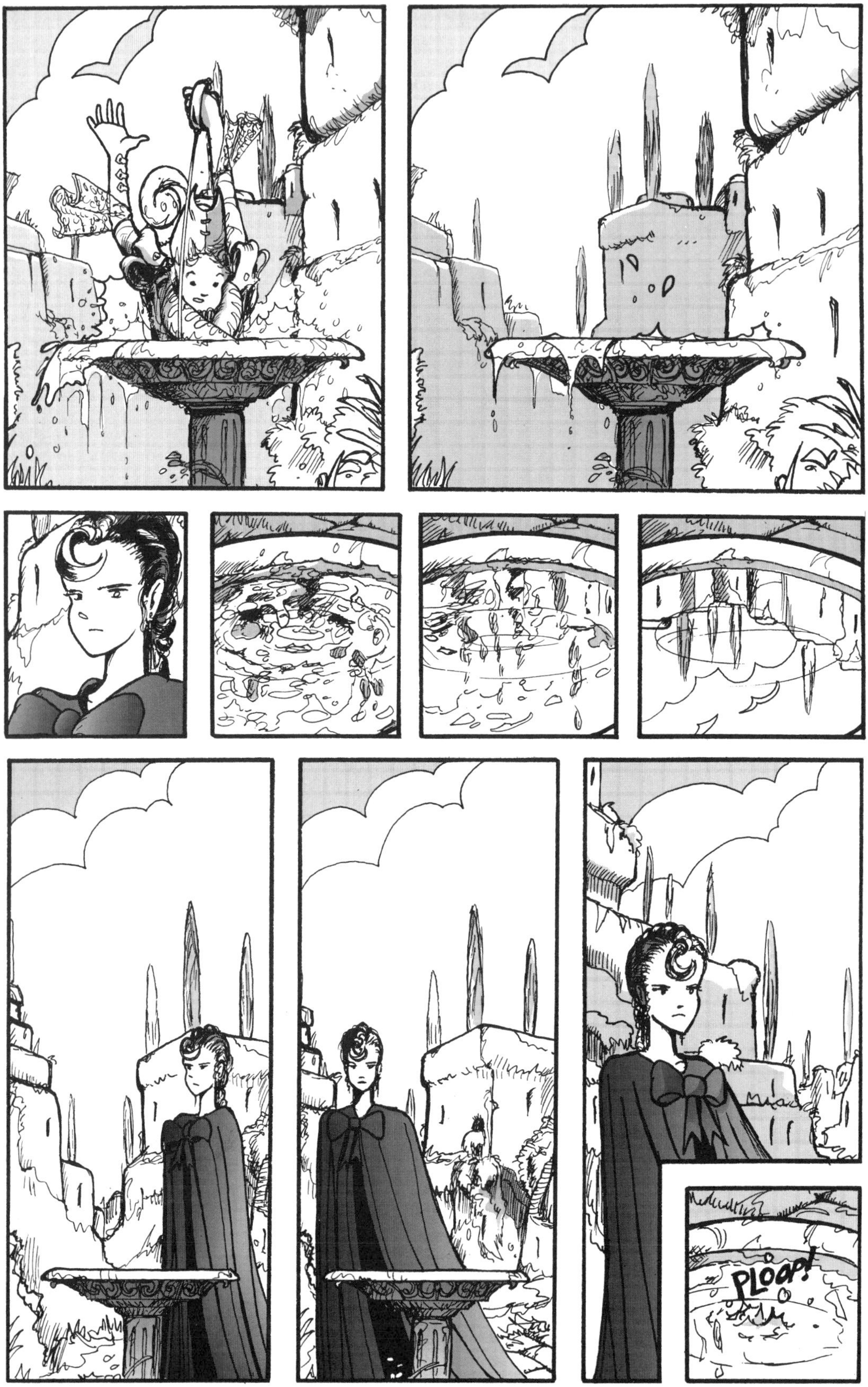
PLOOP!

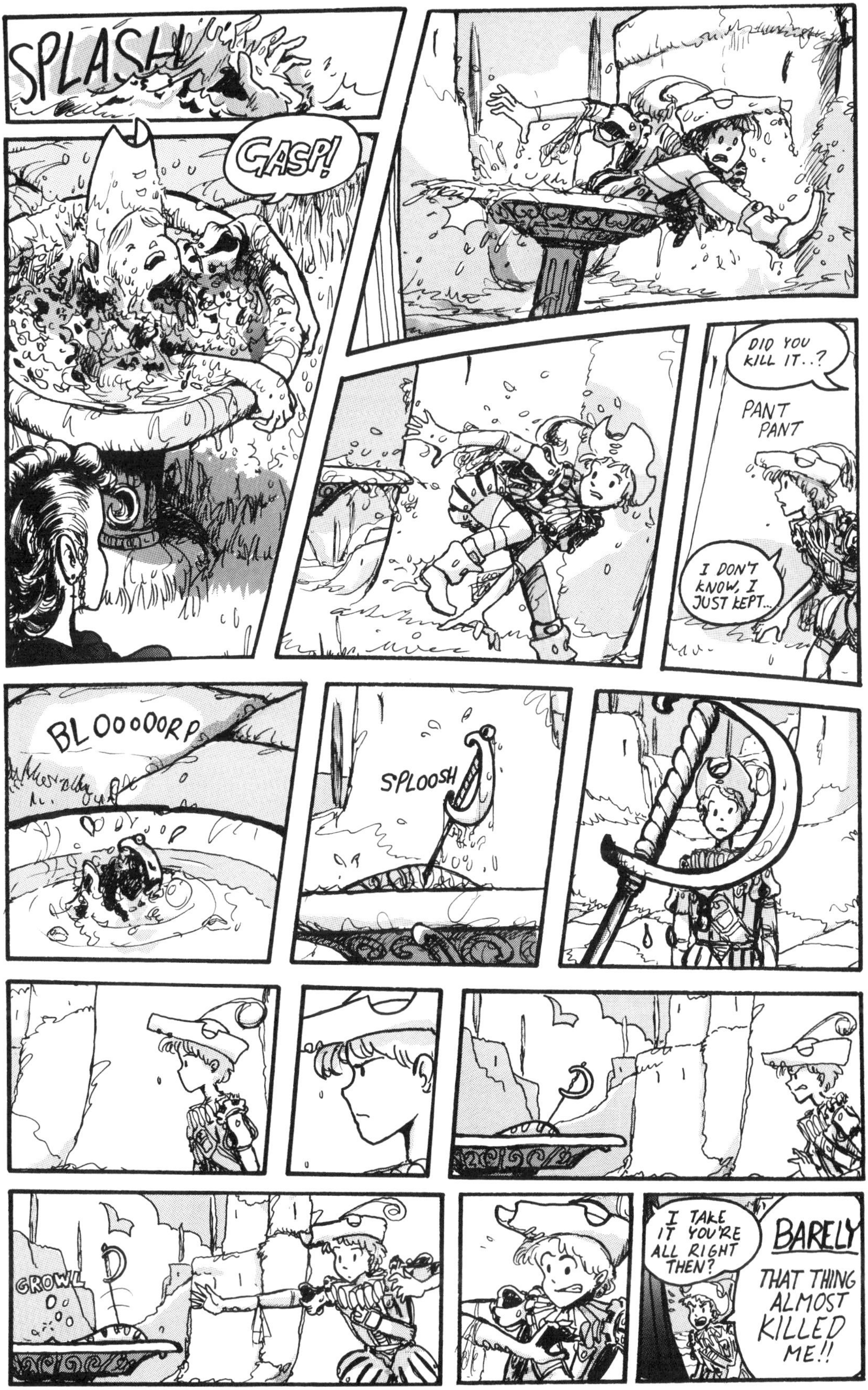
SPLASH
GASP!
DID YOU KILL IT..?
PANT PANT
I DON'T KNOW, I JUST KEPT...
BLOOOOORP
SPLOOSH
GROWL
I TAKE IT YOU'RE ALL RIGHT THEN?
BARELY
THAT THING ALMOST KILLED ME!!

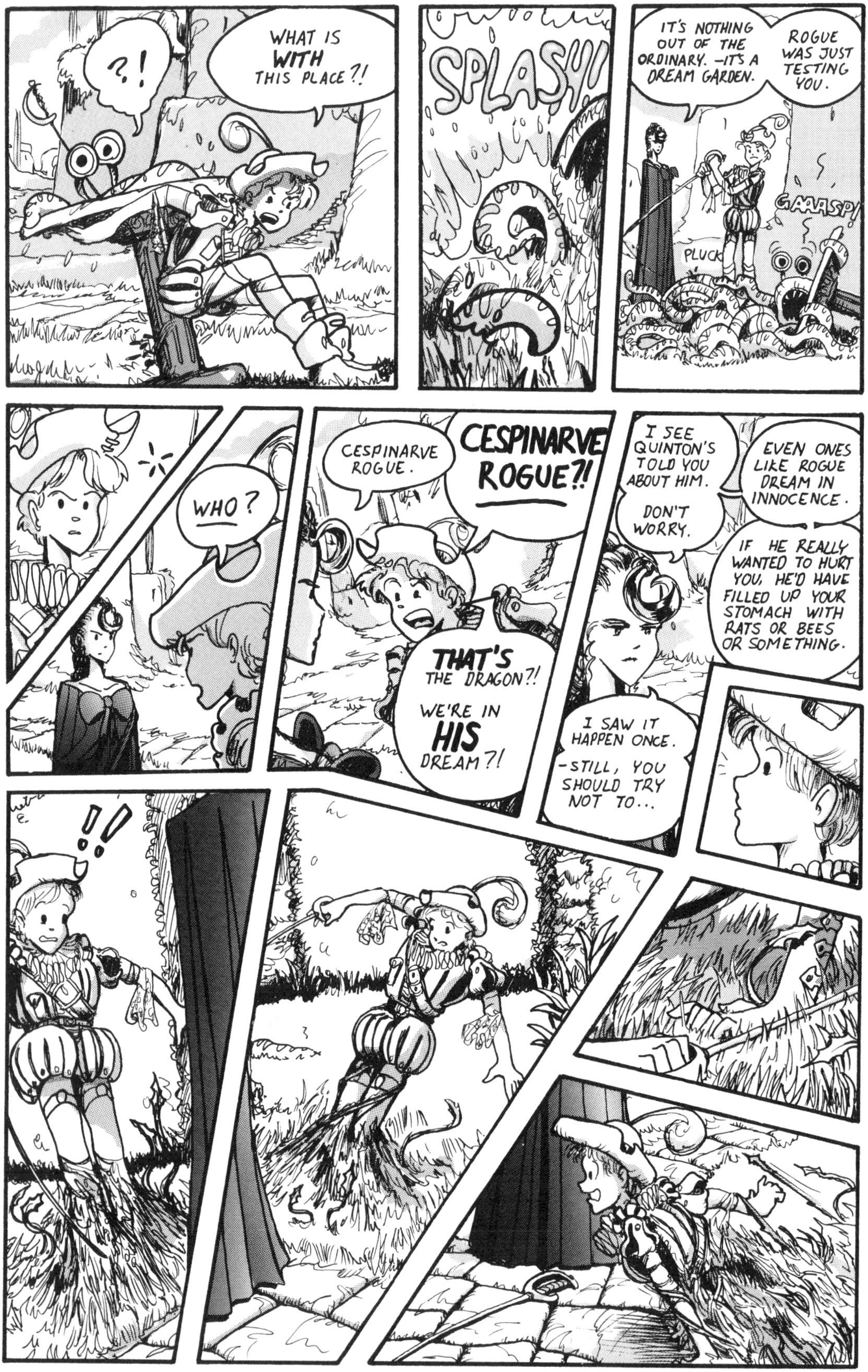

?!
WHAT IS WITH THIS PLACE?!
SPLASH!
IT'S NOTHING OUT OF THE ORDINARY. —IT'S A DREAM GARDEN.
ROGUE WAS JUST TESTING YOU.
PLUCK
GAAASP!
WHO?
CESPINARVE ROGUE.
CESPINARVE ROGUE?!
THAT'S THE DRAGON?!
WE'RE IN HIS DREAM?!
I SEE QUINTON'S TOLD YOU ABOUT HIM.
DON'T WORRY.
EVEN ONES LIKE ROGUE DREAM IN INNOCENCE.
IF HE REALLY WANTED TO HURT YOU, HE'D HAVE FILLED UP YOUR STOMACH WITH RATS OR BEES OR SOMETHING.
I SAW IT HAPPEN ONCE.
-STILL, YOU SHOULD TRY NOT TO...
!!

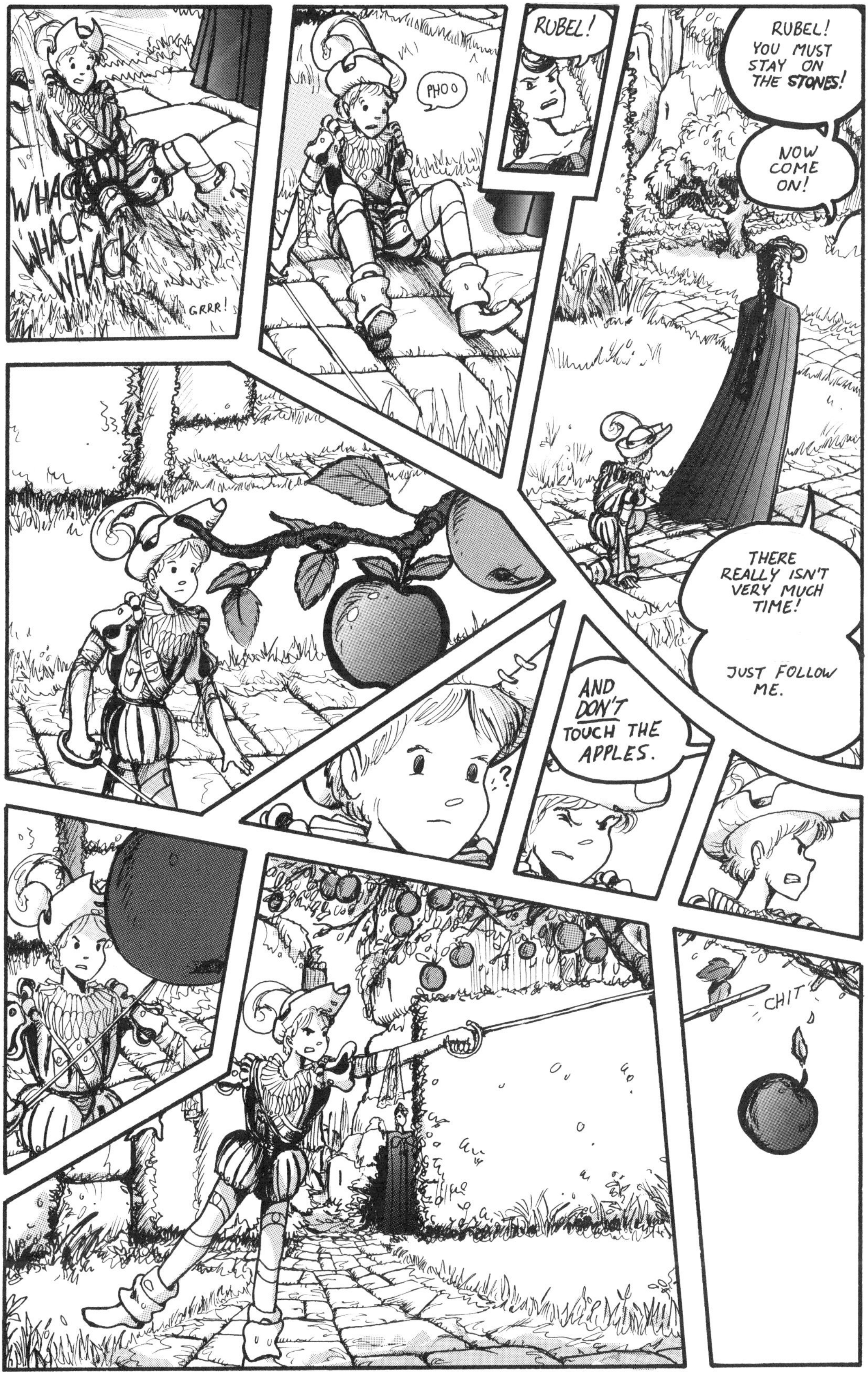
WHACK
WHACK
WHACK
GRRR!
PHOO
RUBEL!
RUBEL! YOU MUST STAY ON THE STONES!
NOW COME ON!
THERE REALLY ISN'T VERY MUCH TIME!
JUST FOLLOW ME.
AND DON'T TOUCH THE APPLES.
?
CHIT

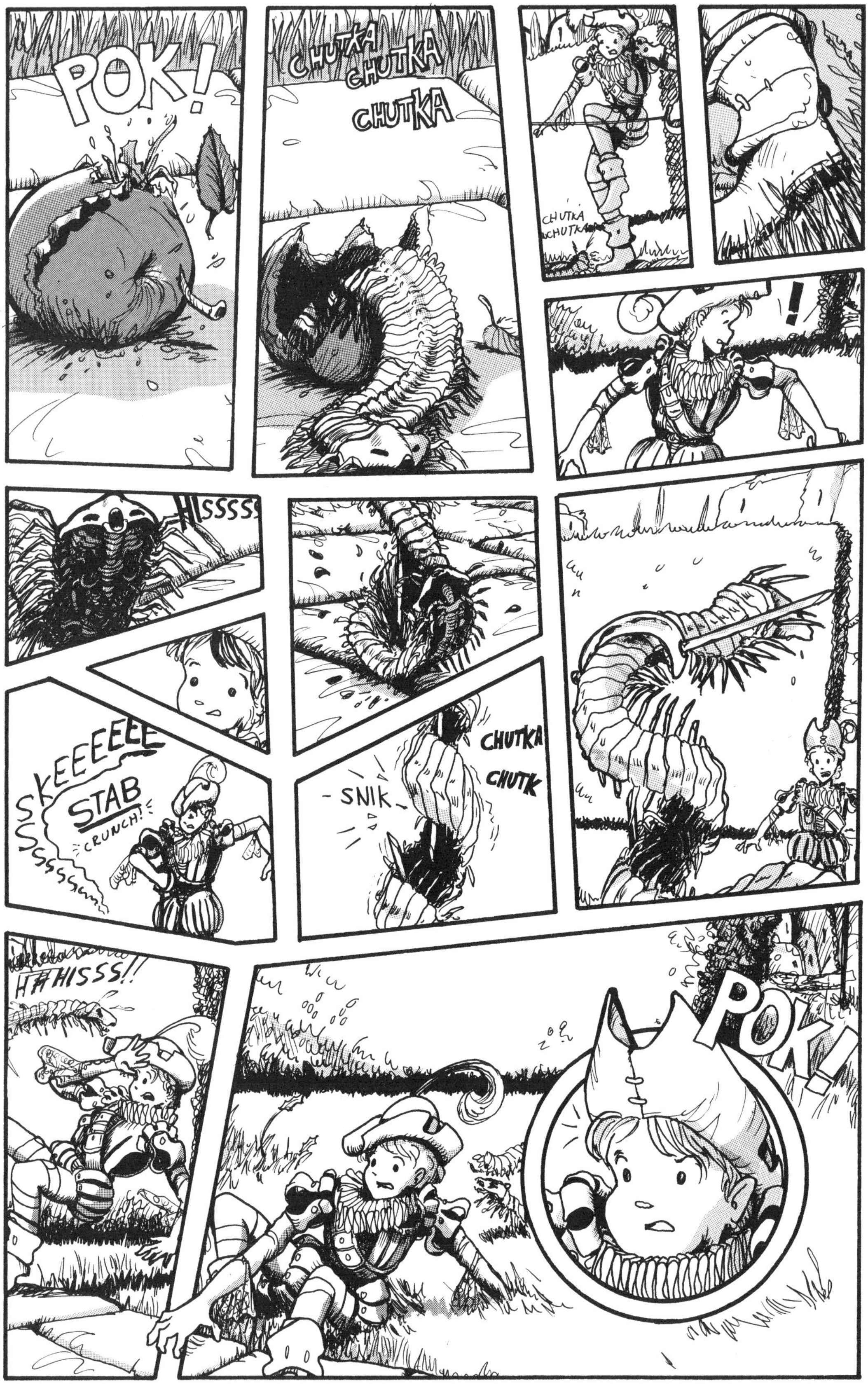
POK!
CHUTKA CHUTKA
CHUTKA
CHUTKA
CHUTKA
!
HISSSSS
CHUTKA
CHUTK
SNIK
SKEEEEEEE
STAB
CRUNCH!
SSSSSSS
HHHISSS!!
POK!

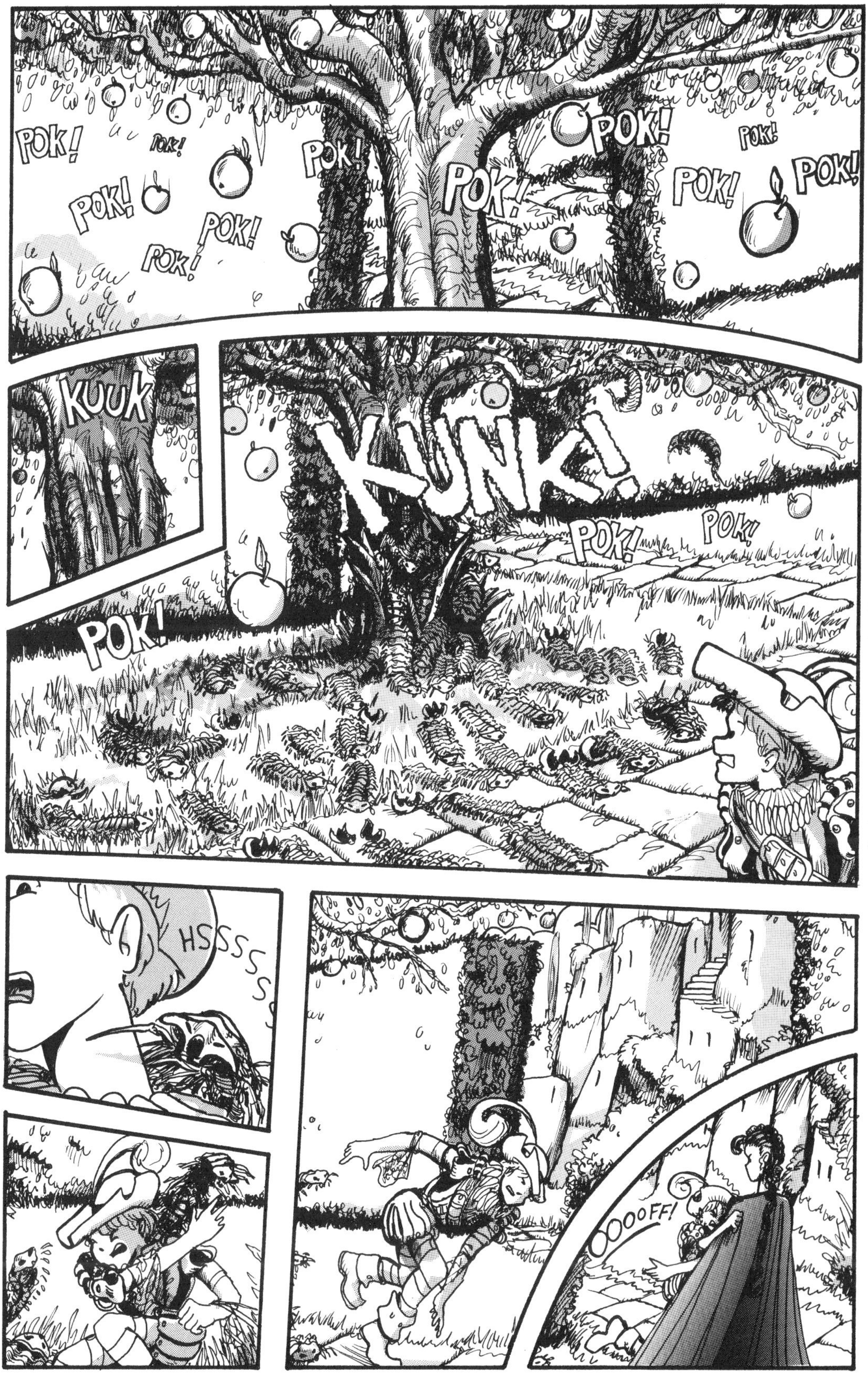
POK!
POK!
POK!
POK!
POK!
POK!
POK!
POK!
POK!
POK!
POK!
KUUK
KUNK!
POK!
POK!
POK!
HSSSSS
OOOOFF!

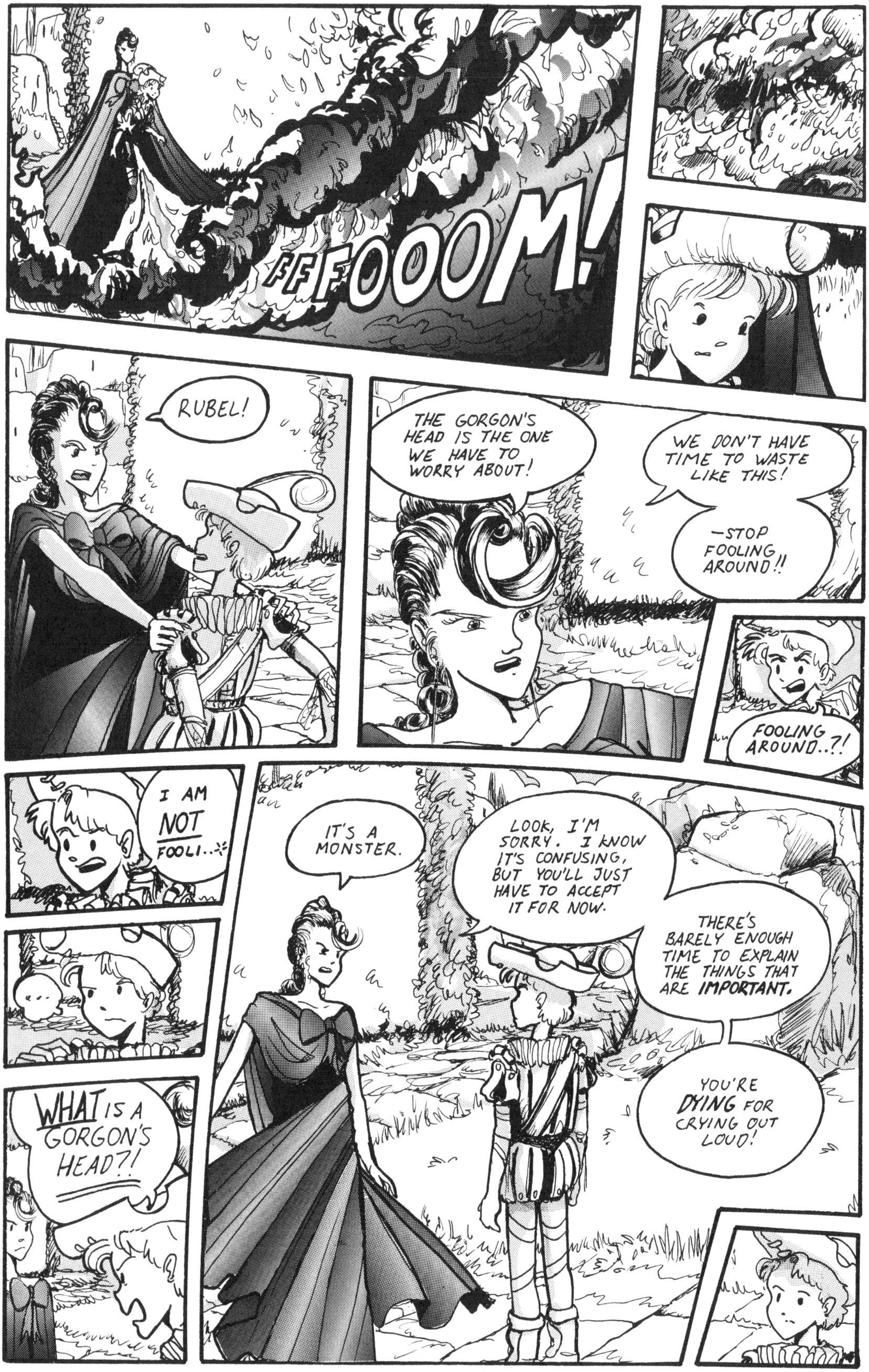
FFFOOOM!
RUBEL!
THE GORGON'S HEAD IS THE ONE WE HAVE TO WORRY ABOUT!
WE DON'T HAVE TIME TO WASTE LIKE THIS!
—STOP FOOLING AROUND!!
FOOLING AROUND..?!
I AM NOT FOOLI..
WHAT IS A GORGON'S HEAD?!
IT'S A MONSTER.
LOOK, I'M SORRY. I KNOW IT'S CONFUSING, BUT YOU'LL JUST HAVE TO ACCEPT IT FOR NOW.
THERE'S BARELY ENOUGH TIME TO EXPLAIN THE THINGS THAT ARE IMPORTANT.
YOU'RE DYING FOR CRYING OUT LOUD!

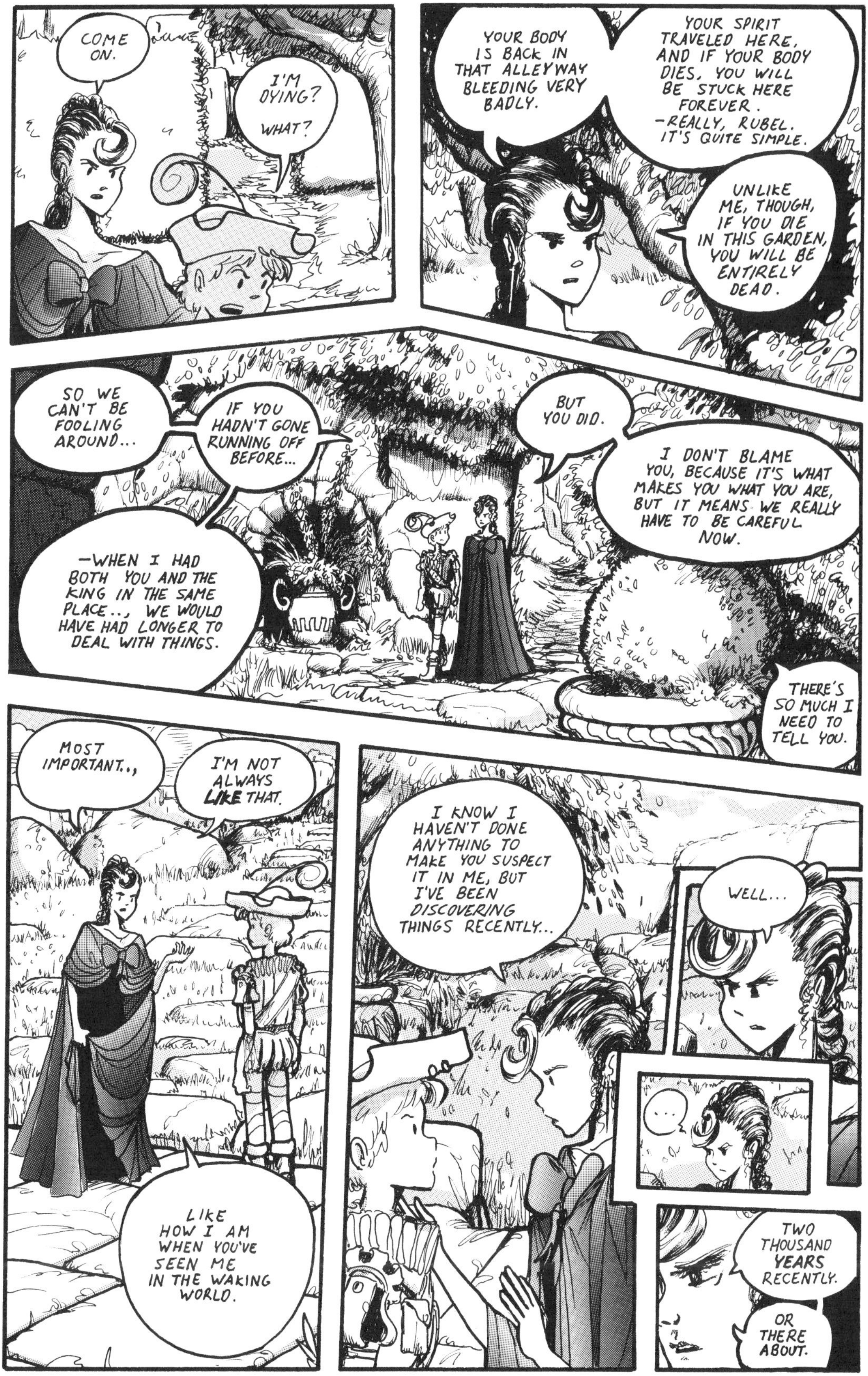
COME ON.
I'M DYING? WHAT?
YOUR BODY IS BACK IN THAT ALLEYWAY BLEEDING VERY BADLY.
YOUR SPIRIT TRAVELED HERE, AND IF YOUR BODY DIES, YOU WILL BE STUCK HERE FOREVER. —REALLY, RUBEL. IT'S QUITE SIMPLE.
UNLIKE ME, THOUGH, IF YOU DIE IN THIS GARDEN, YOU WILL BE ENTIRELY DEAD.
SO WE CAN'T BE FOOLING AROUND...
IF YOU HADN'T GONE RUNNING OFF BEFORE...
—WHEN I HAD BOTH YOU AND THE KING IN THE SAME PLACE.., WE WOULD HAVE HAD LONGER TO DEAL WITH THINGS.
BUT YOU DID.
I DON'T BLAME YOU, BECAUSE IT'S WHAT MAKES YOU WHAT YOU ARE, BUT IT MEANS WE REALLY HAVE TO BE CAREFUL NOW.
THERE'S SO MUCH I NEED TO TELL YOU.
MOST IMPORTANT..,
I'M NOT ALWAYS **LIKE** THAT.
LIKE HOW I AM WHEN YOU'VE SEEN ME IN THE WAKING WORLD.
I KNOW I HAVEN'T DONE ANYTHING TO MAKE YOU SUSPECT IT IN ME, BUT I'VE BEEN DISCOVERING THINGS RECENTLY...
WELL...
...
TWO THOUSAND **YEARS** RECENTLY.
OR THERE ABOUT.

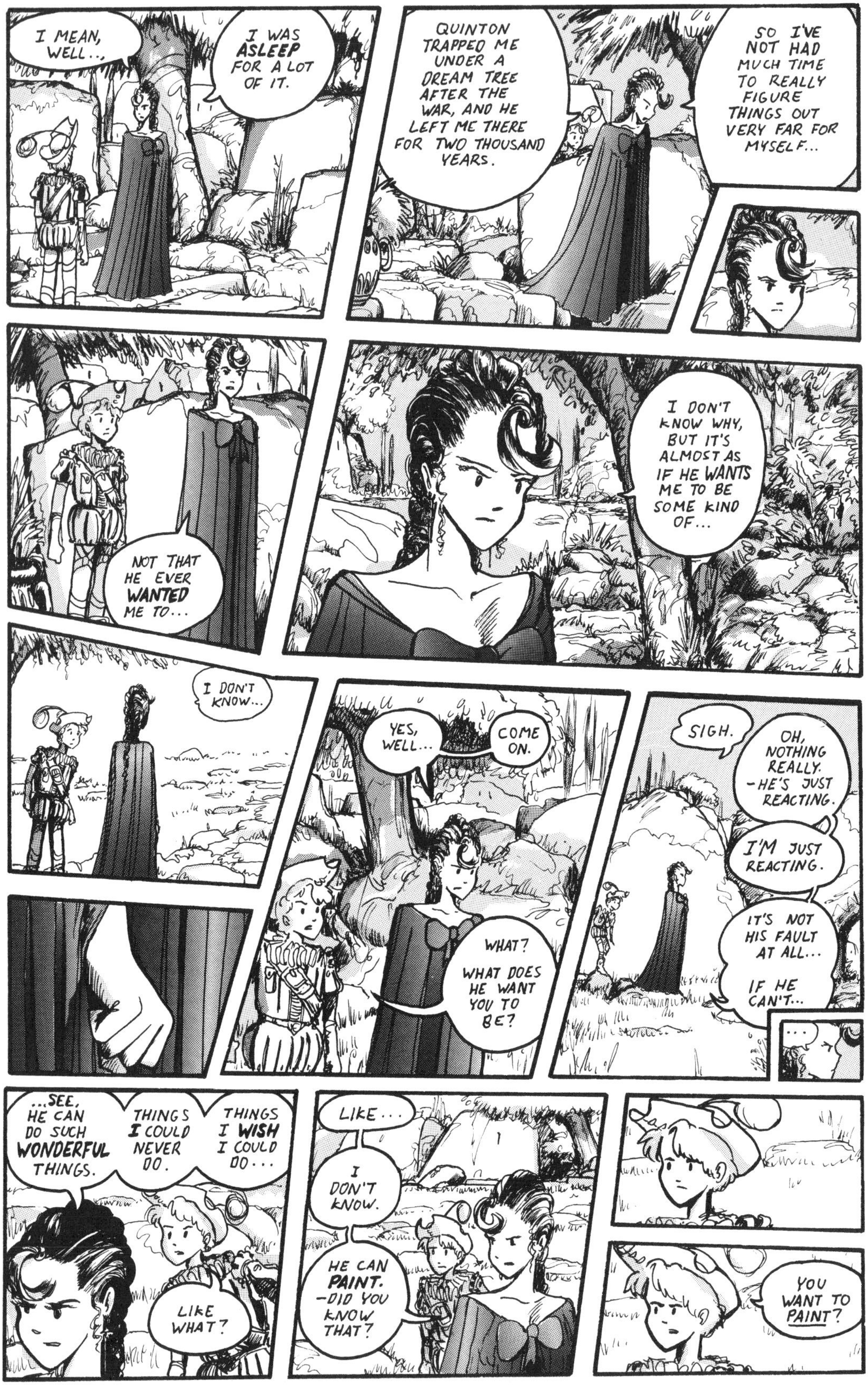
I MEAN, WELL...
I WAS ASLEEP FOR A LOT OF IT.
QUINTON TRAPPED ME UNDER A DREAM TREE AFTER THE WAR, AND HE LEFT ME THERE FOR TWO THOUSAND YEARS.
SO I'VE NOT HAD MUCH TIME TO REALLY FIGURE THINGS OUT VERY FAR FOR MYSELF...
NOT THAT HE EVER WANTED ME TO...
I DON'T KNOW WHY, BUT IT'S ALMOST AS IF HE WANTS ME TO BE SOME KIND OF...
I DON'T KNOW...
YES, WELL...
COME ON.
WHAT? WHAT DOES HE WANT YOU TO BE?
SIGH.
OH, NOTHING REALLY. -HE'S JUST REACTING.
I'M JUST REACTING.
IT'S NOT HIS FAULT AT ALL... IF HE CAN'T...
...
...SEE, HE CAN DO SUCH WONDERFUL THINGS.
THINGS I COULD NEVER DO.
THINGS I WISH I COULD DO...
LIKE WHAT?
LIKE...
I DON'T KNOW.
HE CAN PAINT. -DID YOU KNOW THAT?
YOU WANT TO PAINT?

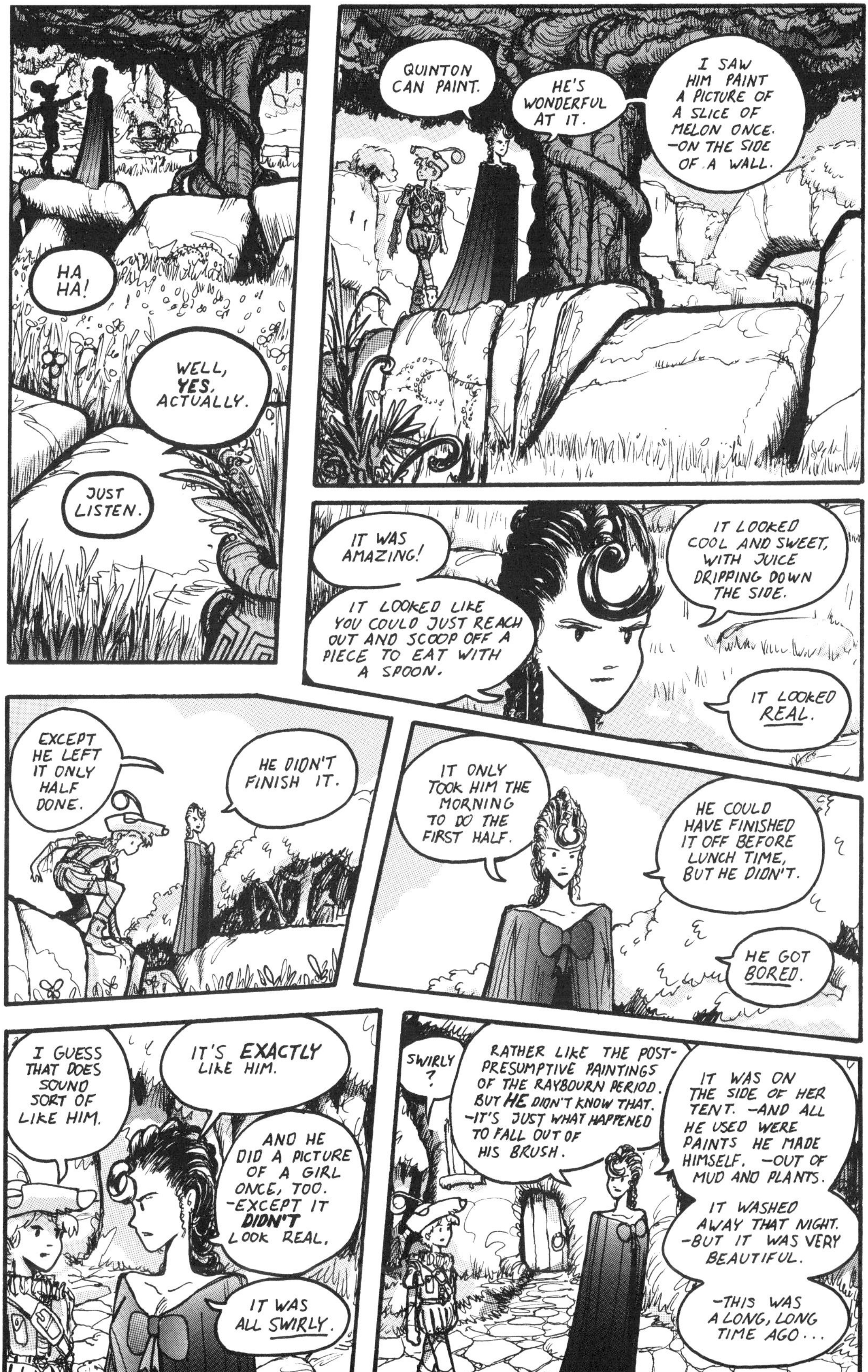
HA HA!
WELL, YES, ACTUALLY.
JUST LISTEN.
QUINTON CAN PAINT.
HE'S WONDERFUL AT IT.
I SAW HIM PAINT A PICTURE OF A SLICE OF MELON ONCE. —ON THE SIDE OF A WALL.
IT WAS AMAZING!
IT LOOKED LIKE YOU COULD JUST REACH OUT AND SCOOP OFF A PIECE TO EAT WITH A SPOON.
IT LOOKED COOL AND SWEET, WITH JUICE DRIPPING DOWN THE SIDE.
IT LOOKED REAL.
EXCEPT HE LEFT IT ONLY HALF DONE.
HE DIDN'T FINISH IT.
IT ONLY TOOK HIM THE MORNING TO DO THE FIRST HALF.
HE COULD HAVE FINISHED IT OFF BEFORE LUNCH TIME, BUT HE DIDN'T.
HE GOT BORED.
I GUESS THAT DOES SOUND SORT OF LIKE HIM.
IT'S EXACTLY LIKE HIM.
AND HE DID A PICTURE OF A GIRL ONCE, TOO. —EXCEPT IT DIDN'T LOOK REAL.
IT WAS ALL SWIRLY.
SWIRLY?
RATHER LIKE THE POST-PRESUMPTIVE PAINTINGS OF THE RAYBOURN PERIOD. BUT HE DIDN'T KNOW THAT. —IT'S JUST WHAT HAPPENED TO FALL OUT OF HIS BRUSH.
IT WAS ON THE SIDE OF HER TENT. —AND ALL HE USED WERE PAINTS HE MADE HIMSELF. —OUT OF MUD AND PLANTS.
IT WASHED AWAY THAT NIGHT. —BUT IT WAS VERY BEAUTIFUL.
—THIS WAS A LONG, LONG TIME AGO...

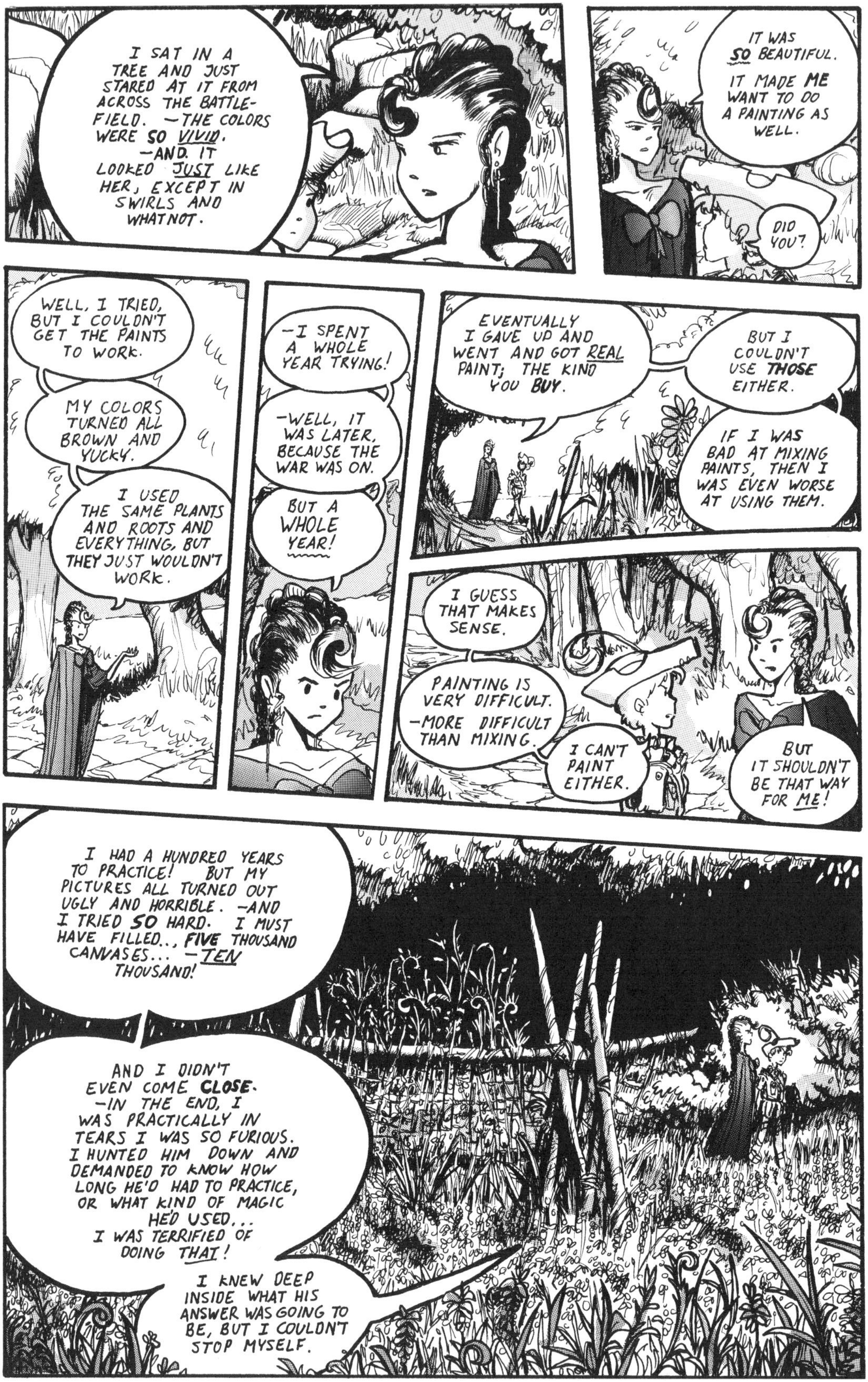
I SAT IN A TREE AND JUST STARED AT IT FROM ACROSS THE BATTLE-FIELD. —THE COLORS WERE SO VIVID. —AND. IT LOOKED JUST LIKE HER, EXCEPT IN SWIRLS AND WHATNOT.
IT WAS SO BEAUTIFUL.
IT MADE ME WANT TO DO A PAINTING AS WELL.
DID YOU?
WELL, I TRIED, BUT I COULDN'T GET THE PAINTS TO WORK.
MY COLORS TURNED ALL BROWN AND YUCKY.
I USED THE SAME PLANTS AND ROOTS AND EVERYTHING, BUT THEY JUST WOULDN'T WORK.
—I SPENT A WHOLE YEAR TRYING!
—WELL, IT WAS LATER, BECAUSE THE WAR WAS ON.
BUT A WHOLE YEAR!
EVENTUALLY I GAVE UP AND WENT AND GOT REAL PAINT; THE KIND YOU BUY.
BUT I COULDN'T USE THOSE EITHER.
IF I WAS BAD AT MIXING PAINTS, THEN I WAS EVEN WORSE AT USING THEM.
I GUESS THAT MAKES SENSE.
PAINTING IS VERY DIFFICULT. —MORE DIFFICULT THAN MIXING.
I CAN'T PAINT EITHER.
BUT IT SHOULDN'T BE THAT WAY FOR ME!
I HAD A HUNDRED YEARS TO PRACTICE! BUT MY PICTURES ALL TURNED OUT UGLY AND HORRIBLE. —AND I TRIED SO HARD. I MUST HAVE FILLED.., FIVE THOUSAND CANVASES... —TEN THOUSAND!
AND I DIDN'T EVEN COME CLOSE. —IN THE END, I WAS PRACTICALLY IN TEARS I WAS SO FURIOUS. I HUNTED HIM DOWN AND DEMANDED TO KNOW HOW LONG HE'D HAD TO PRACTICE, OR WHAT KIND OF MAGIC HE'D USED.. I WAS TERRIFIED OF DOING THAT!
I KNEW DEEP INSIDE WHAT HIS ANSWER WAS GOING TO BE, BUT I COULDN'T STOP MYSELF.

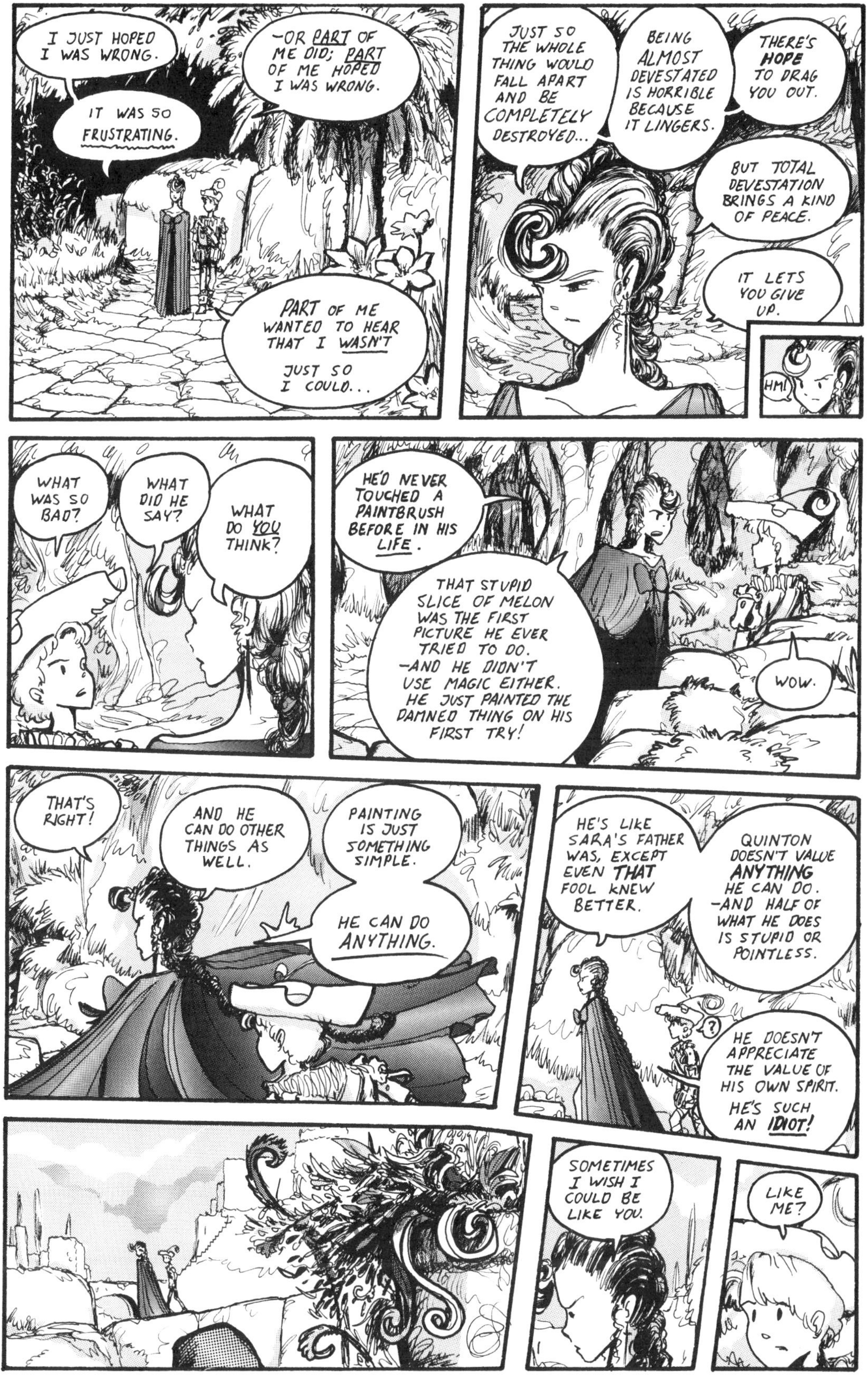
I JUST HOPED I WAS WRONG.
IT WAS SO FRUSTRATING.
-OR PART OF ME DID; PART OF ME HOPED I WAS WRONG.
PART OF ME WANTED TO HEAR THAT I WASN'T
JUST SO I COULD...
JUST SO THE WHOLE THING WOULD FALL APART AND BE COMPLETELY DESTROYED...
BEING ALMOST DEVESTATED IS HORRIBLE BECAUSE IT LINGERS.
THERE'S HOPE TO DRAG YOU OUT.
BUT TOTAL DEVESTATION BRINGS A KIND OF PEACE.
IT LETS YOU GIVE UP.
HM!
WHAT WAS SO BAD?
WHAT DID HE SAY?
WHAT DO YOU THINK?
HE'D NEVER TOUCHED A PAINTBRUSH BEFORE IN HIS LIFE.
THAT STUPID SLICE OF MELON WAS THE FIRST PICTURE HE EVER TRIED TO DO. -AND HE DIDN'T USE MAGIC EITHER. HE JUST PAINTED THE DAMNED THING ON HIS FIRST TRY!
WOW.
THAT'S RIGHT!
AND HE CAN DO OTHER THINGS AS WELL.
PAINTING IS JUST SOMETHING SIMPLE.
HE CAN DO ANYTHING.
HE'S LIKE SARA'S FATHER WAS, EXCEPT EVEN THAT FOOL KNEW BETTER.
QUINTON DOESN'T VALUE ANYTHING HE CAN DO. -AND HALF OF WHAT HE DOES IS STUPID OR POINTLESS.
?
HE DOESN'T APPRECIATE THE VALUE OF HIS OWN SPIRIT.
HE'S SUCH AN IDIOT!
SOMETIMES I WISH I COULD BE LIKE YOU.
LIKE ME?

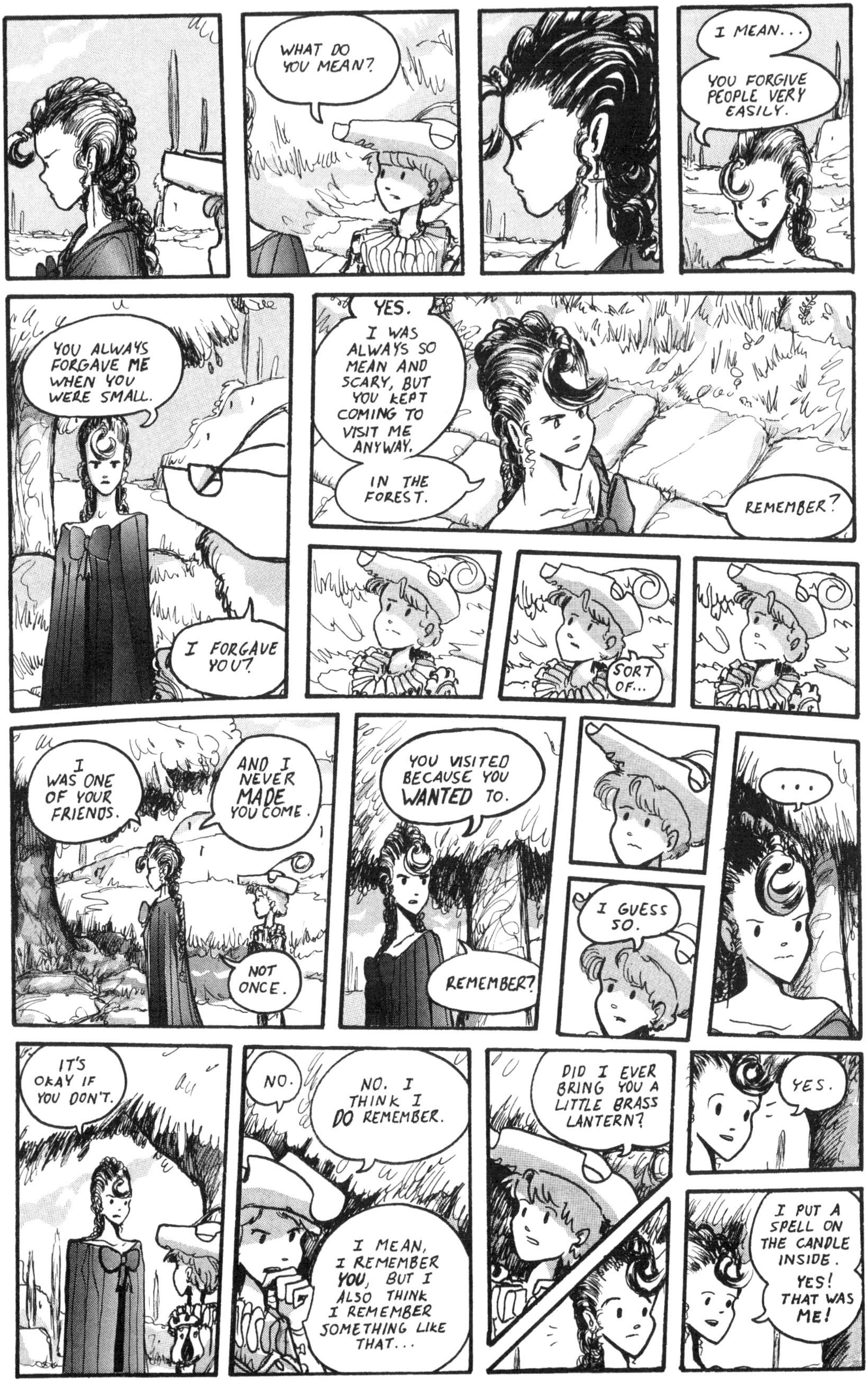
WHAT DO YOU MEAN?
I MEAN...
YOU FORGIVE PEOPLE VERY EASILY.
YOU ALWAYS FORGAVE ME WHEN YOU WERE SMALL.
I FORGAVE YOU?
YES.
I WAS ALWAYS SO MEAN AND SCARY, BUT YOU KEPT COMING TO VISIT ME ANYWAY.
IN THE FOREST.
REMEMBER?
SORT OF...
I WAS ONE OF YOUR FRIENDS.
AND I NEVER MADE YOU COME.
NOT ONCE.
YOU VISITED BECAUSE YOU WANTED TO.
REMEMBER?
I GUESS SO.
...
IT'S OKAY IF YOU DON'T.
NO.
NO. I THINK I DO REMEMBER.
I MEAN, I REMEMBER YOU, BUT I ALSO THINK I REMEMBER SOMETHING LIKE THAT...
DID I EVER BRING YOU A LITTLE BRASS LANTERN?
YES.
I PUT A SPELL ON THE CANDLE INSIDE.
YES! THAT WAS ME!

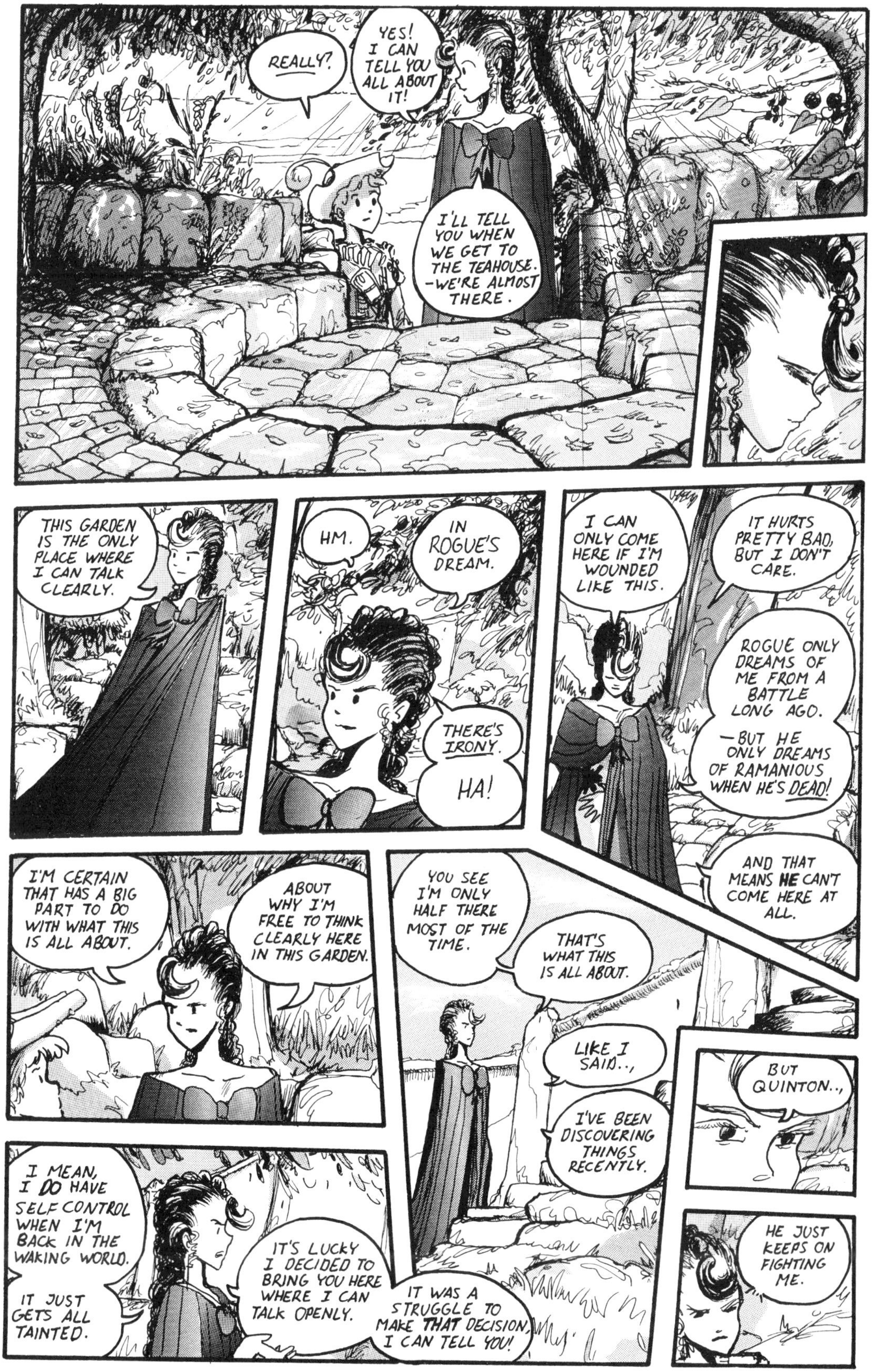
REALLY?
YES! I CAN TELL YOU ALL ABOUT IT!
I'LL TELL YOU WHEN WE GET TO THE TEAHOUSE. -WE'RE ALMOST THERE.
THIS GARDEN IS THE ONLY PLACE WHERE I CAN TALK CLEARLY.
HM.
IN ROGUE'S DREAM.
THERE'S IRONY.
HA!
I CAN ONLY COME HERE IF I'M WOUNDED LIKE THIS.
IT HURTS PRETTY BAD, BUT I DON'T CARE.
ROGUE ONLY DREAMS OF ME FROM A BATTLE LONG AGO.
-BUT HE ONLY DREAMS OF RAMANIOUS WHEN HE'S DEAD!
AND THAT MEANS HE CAN'T COME HERE AT ALL.
I'M CERTAIN THAT HAS A BIG PART TO DO WITH WHAT THIS IS ALL ABOUT.
ABOUT WHY I'M FREE TO THINK CLEARLY HERE IN THIS GARDEN.
YOU SEE I'M ONLY HALF THERE MOST OF THE TIME.
THAT'S WHAT THIS IS ALL ABOUT.
LIKE I SAID..,
I'VE BEEN DISCOVERING THINGS RECENTLY.
BUT QUINTON..,
HE JUST KEEPS ON FIGHTING ME.
I MEAN, I DO HAVE SELF CONTROL WHEN I'M BACK IN THE WAKING WORLD.
IT JUST GETS ALL TAINTED.
IT'S LUCKY I DECIDED TO BRING YOU HERE WHERE I CAN TALK OPENLY.
IT WAS A STRUGGLE TO MAKE THAT DECISION, I CAN TELL YOU!

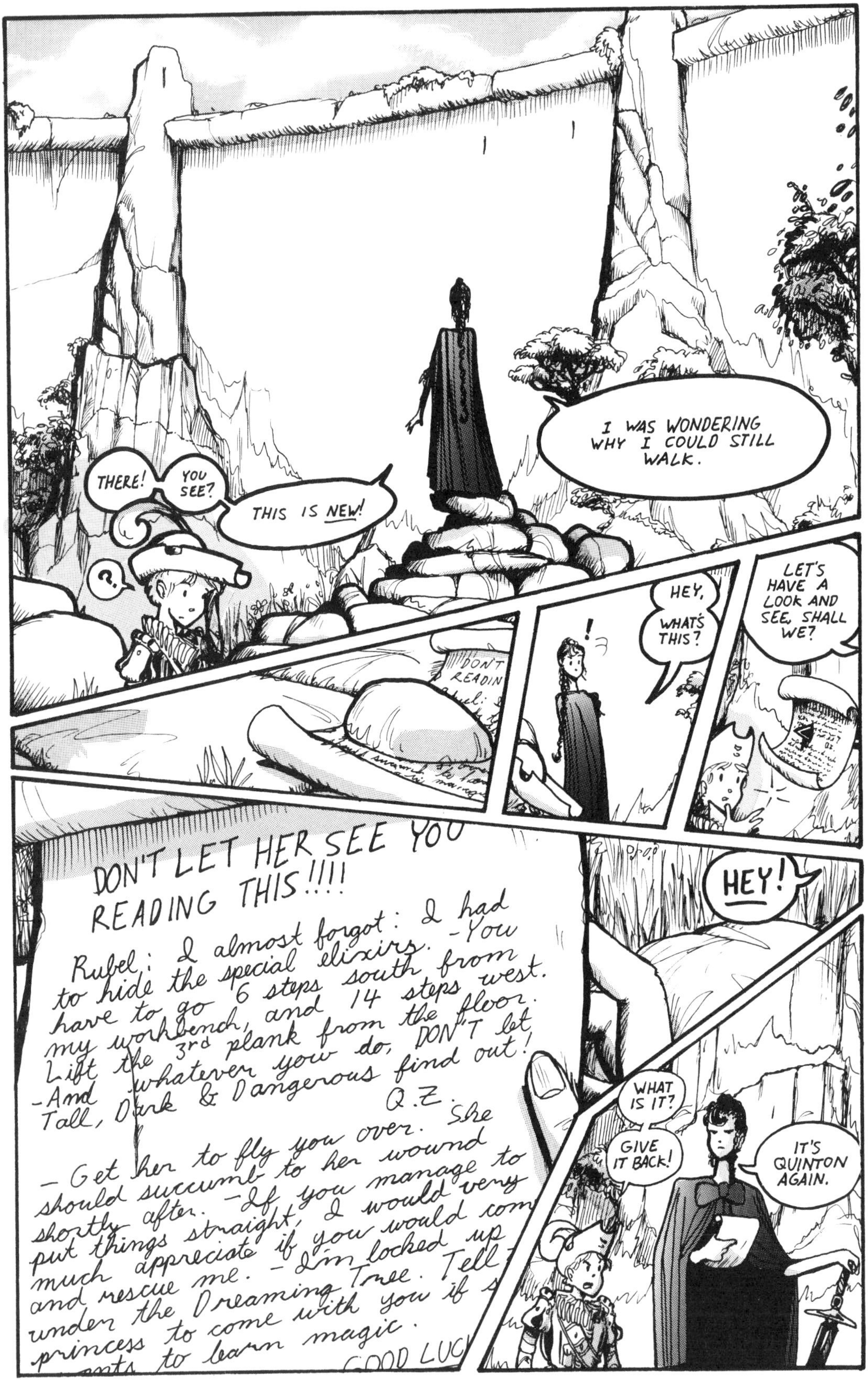
THERE!
YOU SEE?
THIS IS NEW!
?
I WAS WONDERING WHY I COULD STILL WALK.
DON'T
READIN
!
HEY, WHAT'S THIS?
LET'S HAVE A LOOK AND SEE, SHALL WE?
DON'T LET HER SEE YOU
READING THIS!!!!
Rubel: I almost forgot: I had
to hide the special elixirs. -You
have to go 6 steps south from
my workbench, and 14 steps west.
Lift the 3rd plank from the floor.
-And whatever you do, DON'T let
Tall, Dark & Dangerous find out!
Q.Z.
-Get her to fly you over. She
should succumb to her wound
shortly after. -If you manage to
put things straight, I would very
much appreciate if you would com
and rescue me. -I'm locked up
under the Dreaming Tree. Tell
princess to come with you if s
to learn magic.
GOOD LUC
HEY!
WHAT IS IT?
GIVE IT BACK!
IT'S QUINTON AGAIN.

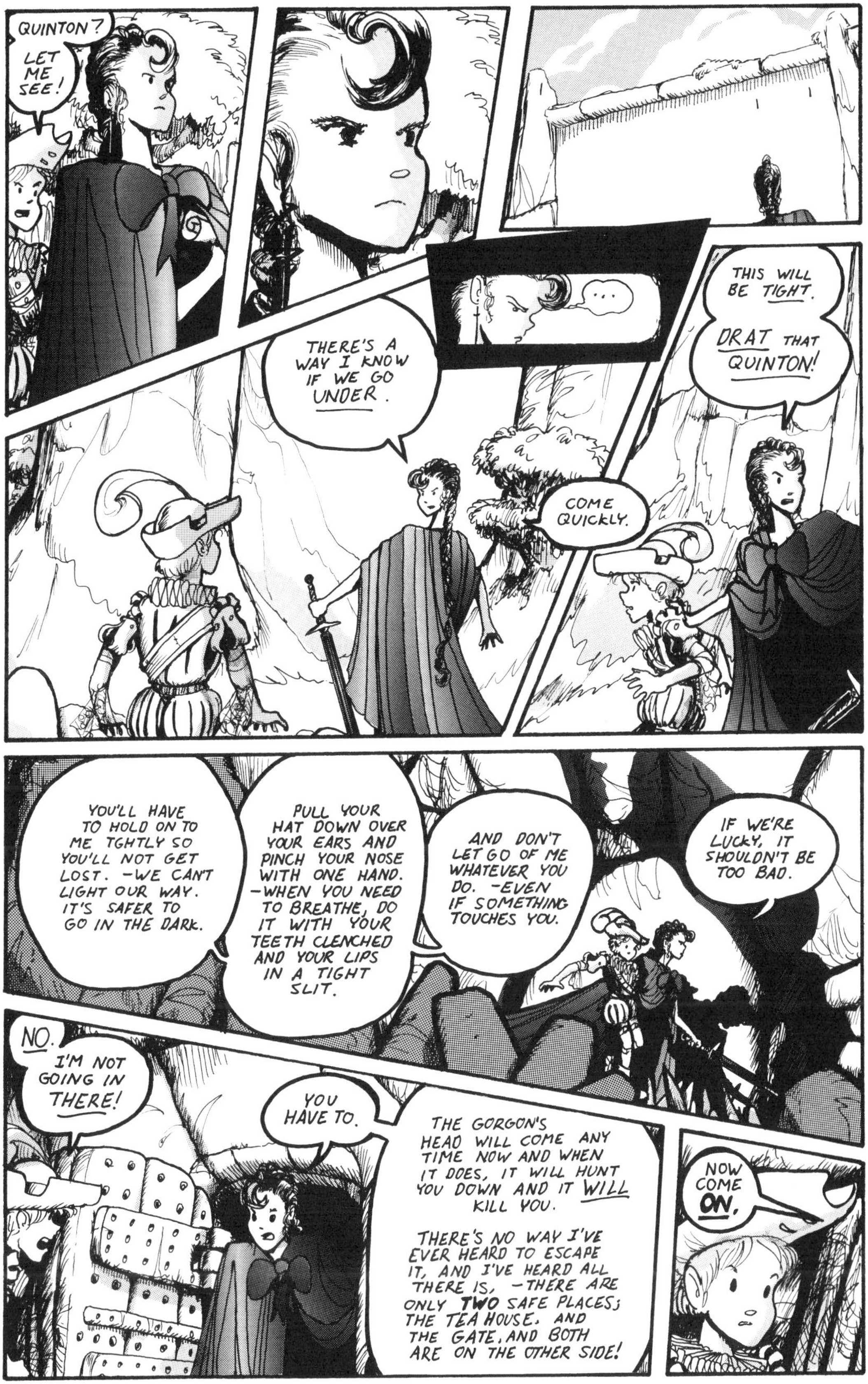
QUINTON?
LET ME SEE!
...
THIS WILL BE TIGHT.
DRAT THAT QUINTON!
THERE'S A WAY I KNOW IF WE GO UNDER.
COME QUICKLY.
YOU'LL HAVE TO HOLD ON TO ME TGHTLY SO YOU'LL NOT GET LOST. —WE CAN'T LIGHT OUR WAY. IT'S SAFER TO GO IN THE DARK.
PULL YOUR HAT DOWN OVER YOUR EARS AND PINCH YOUR NOSE WITH ONE HAND. —WHEN YOU NEED TO BREATHE, DO IT WITH YOUR TEETH CLENCHED AND YOUR LIPS IN A TIGHT SLIT.
AND DON'T LET GO OF ME WHATEVER YOU DO. —EVEN IF SOMETHING TOUCHES YOU.
IF WE'RE LUCKY, IT SHOULDN'T BE TOO BAD.
NO. I'M NOT GOING IN THERE!
YOU HAVE TO.
THE GORGON'S HEAD WILL COME ANY TIME NOW AND WHEN IT DOES, IT WILL HUNT YOU DOWN AND IT WILL KILL YOU.
THERE'S NO WAY I'VE EVER HEARD TO ESCAPE IT, AND I'VE HEARD ALL THERE IS, —THERE ARE ONLY TWO SAFE PLACES; THE TEA HOUSE. AND THE GATE. AND BOTH ARE ON THE OTHER SIDE!
NOW COME ON.

Chapter 14

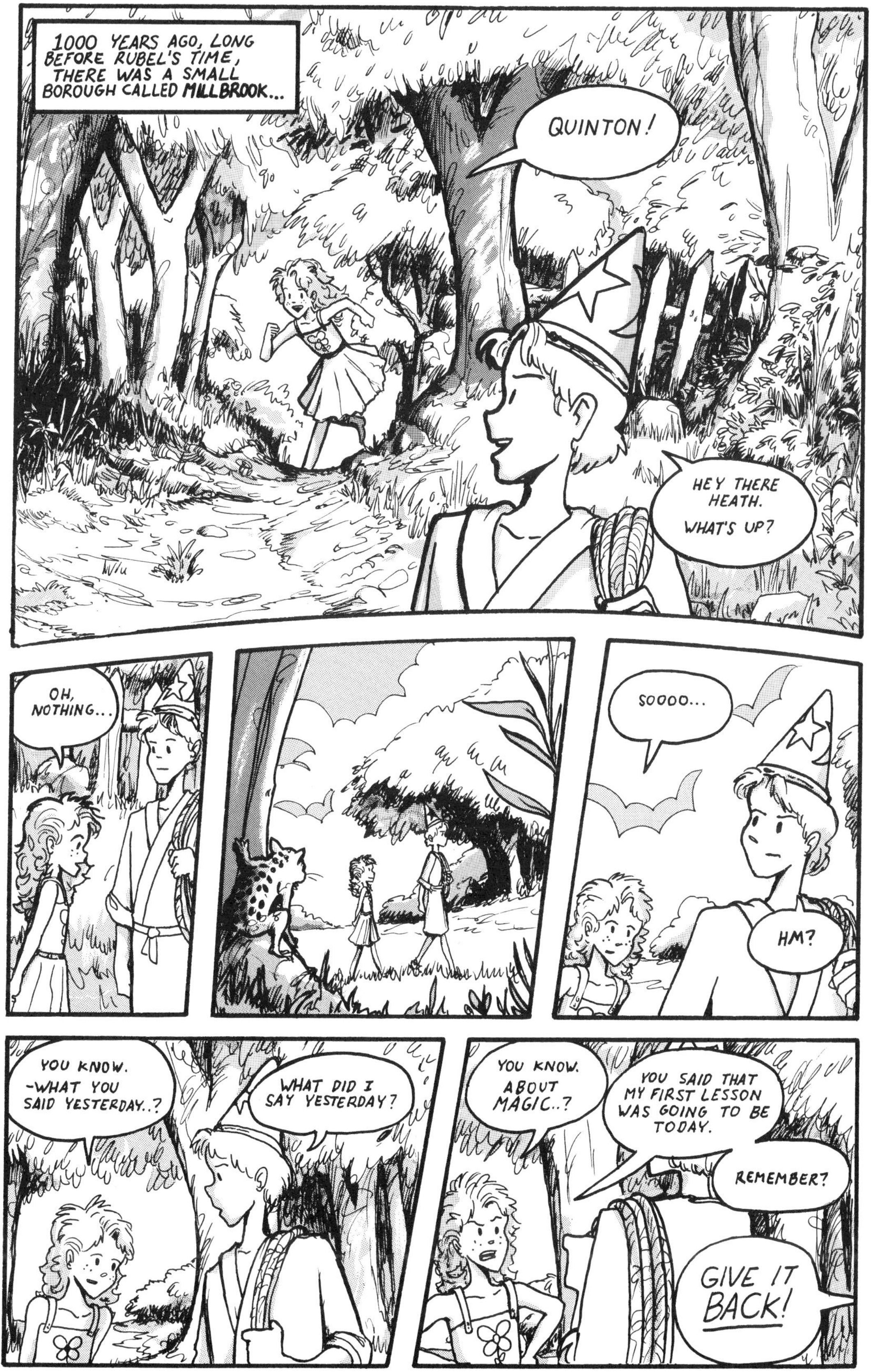
1000 YEARS AGO, LONG BEFORE RUBEL'S TIME, THERE WAS A SMALL BOROUGH CALLED MILLBROOK...
QUINTON!
HEY THERE HEATH.
WHAT'S UP?
OH, NOTHING...
SOOOO...
HM?
YOU KNOW. -WHAT YOU SAID YESTERDAY..?
WHAT DID I SAY YESTERDAY?
YOU KNOW. ABOUT MAGIC..?
YOU SAID THAT MY FIRST LESSON WAS GOING TO BE TODAY.
REMEMBER?
GIVE IT BACK!

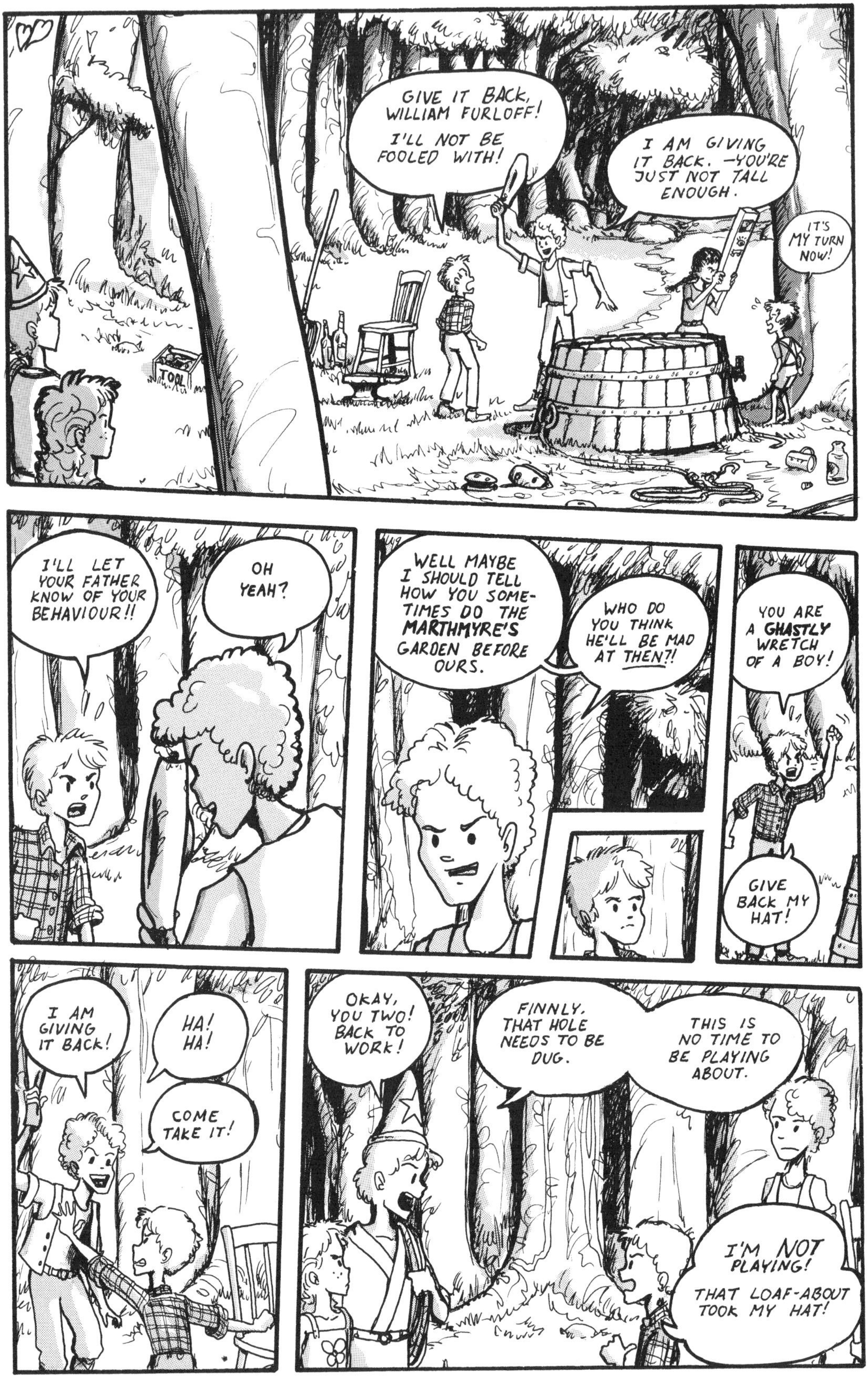
GIVE IT BACK, WILLIAM FURLOFF!
I'LL NOT BE FOOLED WITH!
I AM GIVING IT BACK. —YOU'RE JUST NOT TALL ENOUGH.
IT'S MY TURN NOW!
TOOL
I'LL LET YOUR FATHER KNOW OF YOUR BEHAVIOUR!!
OH YEAH?
WELL MAYBE I SHOULD TELL HOW YOU SOMETIMES DO THE MARTHMYRE'S GARDEN BEFORE OURS.
WHO DO YOU THINK HE'LL BE MAD AT THEN?!
YOU ARE A GHASTLY WRETCH OF A BOY!
GIVE BACK MY HAT!
I AM GIVING IT BACK!
HA! HA!
COME TAKE IT!
OKAY, YOU TWO! BACK TO WORK!
FINNLY. THAT HOLE NEEDS TO BE DUG.
THIS IS NO TIME TO BE PLAYING ABOUT.
I'M NOT PLAYING!
THAT LOAF-ABOUT TOOK MY HAT!

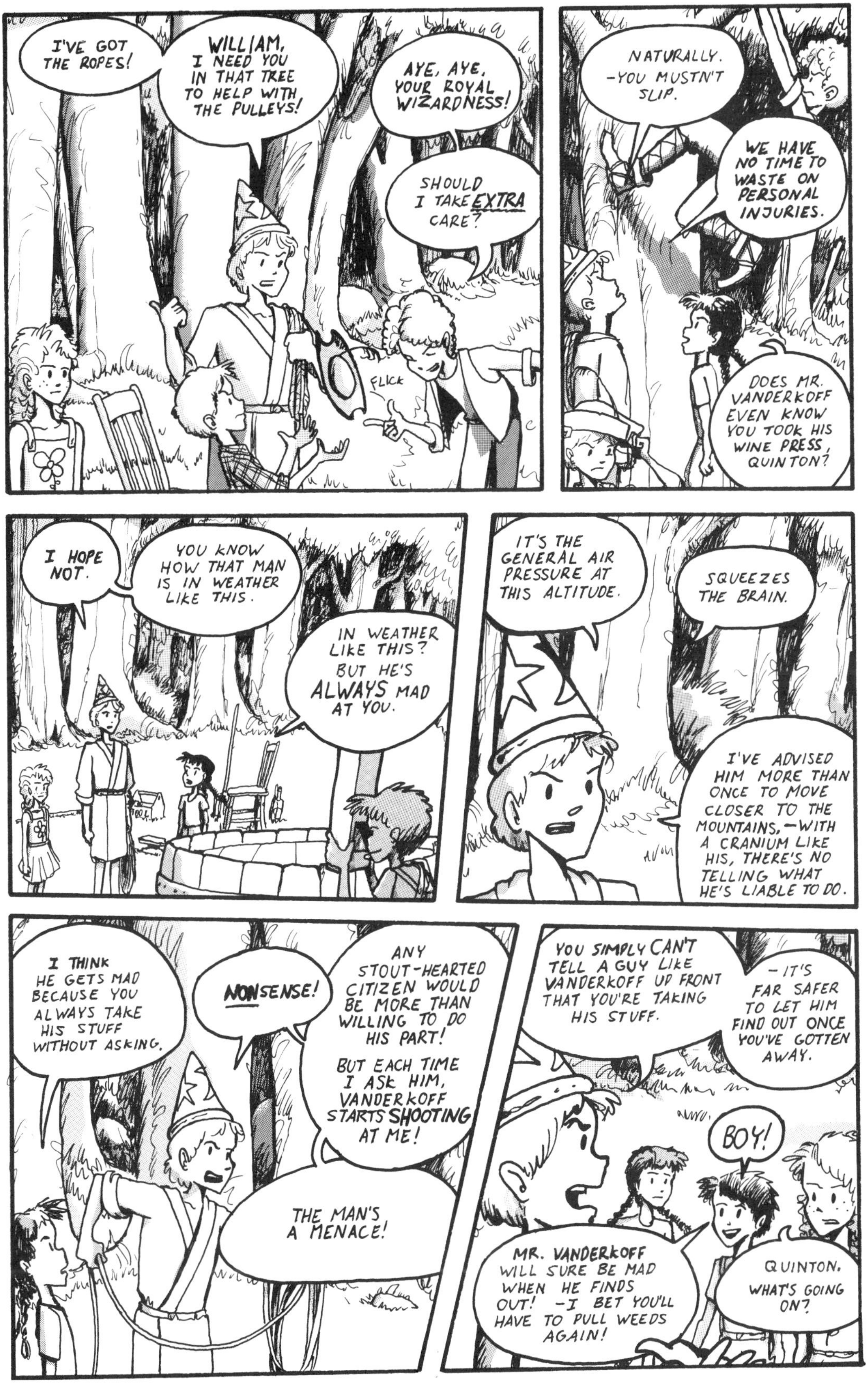

I'VE GOT THE ROPES!
WILLIAM, I NEED YOU IN THAT TREE TO HELP WITH THE PULLEYS!
AYE, AYE, YOUR ROYAL WIZARDNESS!
SHOULD I TAKE EXTRA CARE?
FLICK
NATURALLY. -YOU MUSTN'T SLIP.
WE HAVE NO TIME TO WASTE ON PERSONAL INJURIES.
DOES MR. VANDERKOFF EVEN KNOW YOU TOOK HIS WINE PRESS, QUINTON?
I HOPE NOT.
YOU KNOW HOW THAT MAN IS IN WEATHER LIKE THIS.
IN WEATHER LIKE THIS? BUT HE'S ALWAYS MAD AT YOU.
IT'S THE GENERAL AIR PRESSURE AT THIS ALTITUDE.
SQUEEZES THE BRAIN.
I'VE ADVISED HIM MORE THAN ONCE TO MOVE CLOSER TO THE MOUNTAINS, -WITH A CRANIUM LIKE HIS, THERE'S NO TELLING WHAT HE'S LIABLE TO DO.
I THINK HE GETS MAD BECAUSE YOU ALWAYS TAKE HIS STUFF WITHOUT ASKING.
NONSENSE!
ANY STOUT-HEARTED CITIZEN WOULD BE MORE THAN WILLING TO DO HIS PART!
BUT EACH TIME I ASK HIM, VANDERKOFF STARTS SHOOTING AT ME!
THE MAN'S A MENACE!
YOU SIMPLY CAN'T TELL A GUY LIKE VANDERKOFF UP FRONT THAT YOU'RE TAKING HIS STUFF.
-IT'S FAR SAFER TO LET HIM FIND OUT ONCE YOU'VE GOTTEN AWAY.
BOY!
MR. VANDERKOFF WILL SURE BE MAD WHEN HE FINDS OUT! -I BET YOU'LL HAVE TO PULL WEEDS AGAIN!
QUINTON. WHAT'S GOING ON?

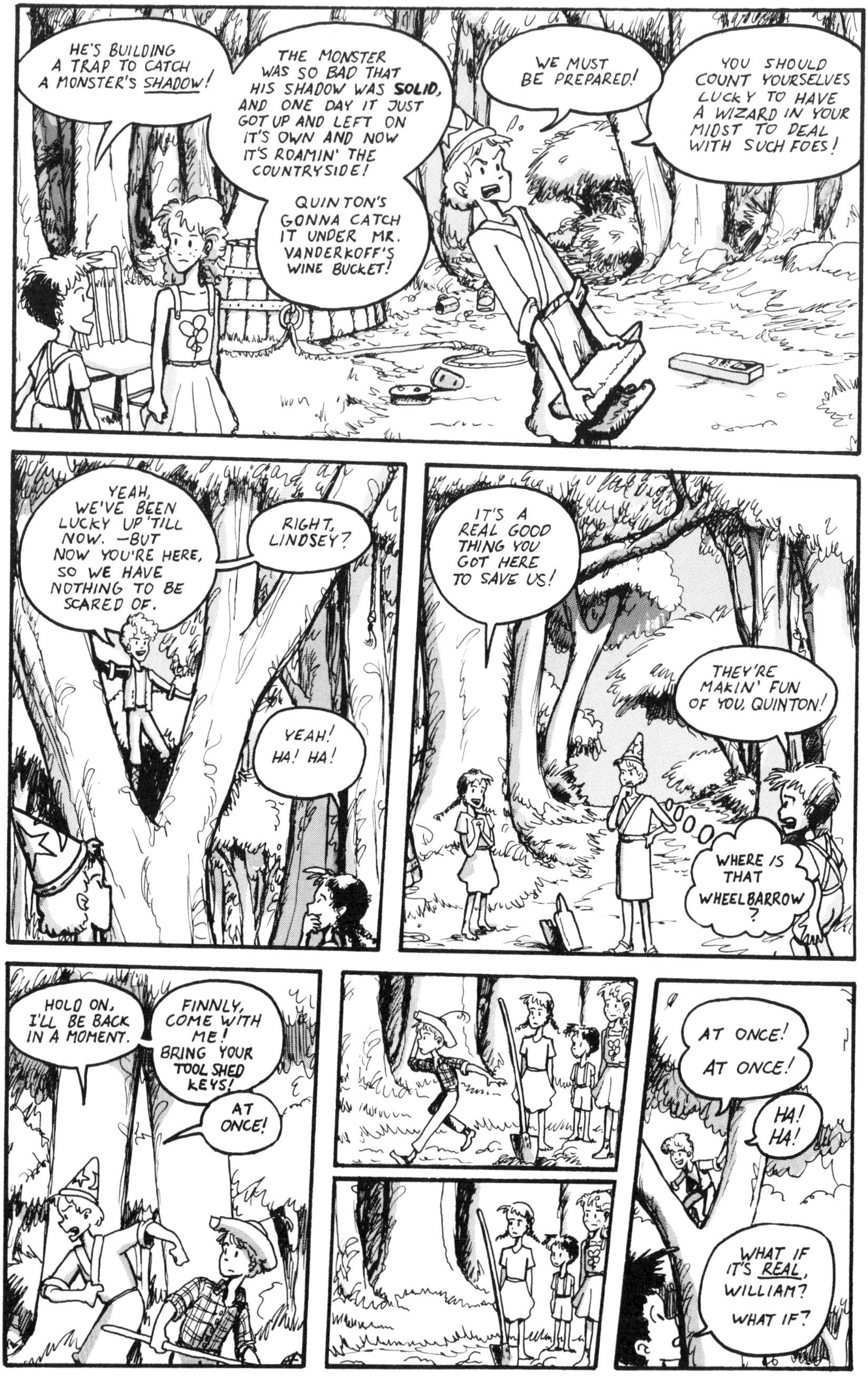

HE'S BUILDING A TRAP TO CATCH A MONSTER'S SHADOW!
THE MONSTER WAS SO BAD THAT HIS SHADOW WAS SOLID, AND ONE DAY IT JUST GOT UP AND LEFT ON IT'S OWN AND NOW IT'S ROAMIN' THE COUNTRYSIDE!
QUINTON'S GONNA CATCH IT UNDER MR. VANDERKOFF'S WINE BUCKET!
WE MUST BE PREPARED!
YOU SHOULD COUNT YOURSELVES LUCKY TO HAVE A WIZARD IN YOUR MIDST TO DEAL WITH SUCH FOES!
YEAH, WE'VE BEEN LUCKY UP 'TILL NOW. —BUT NOW YOU'RE HERE, SO WE HAVE NOTHING TO BE SCARED OF.
RIGHT, LINDSEY?
YEAH! HA! HA!
IT'S A REAL GOOD THING YOU GOT HERE TO SAVE US!
THEY'RE MAKIN' FUN OF YOU, QUINTON!
WHERE IS THAT WHEELBARROW?
HOLD ON, I'LL BE BACK IN A MOMENT.
FINNLY, COME WITH ME! BRING YOUR TOOL SHED KEYS!
AT ONCE!
AT ONCE! AT ONCE!
HA! HA!
WHAT IF IT'S REAL, WILLIAM? WHAT IF?

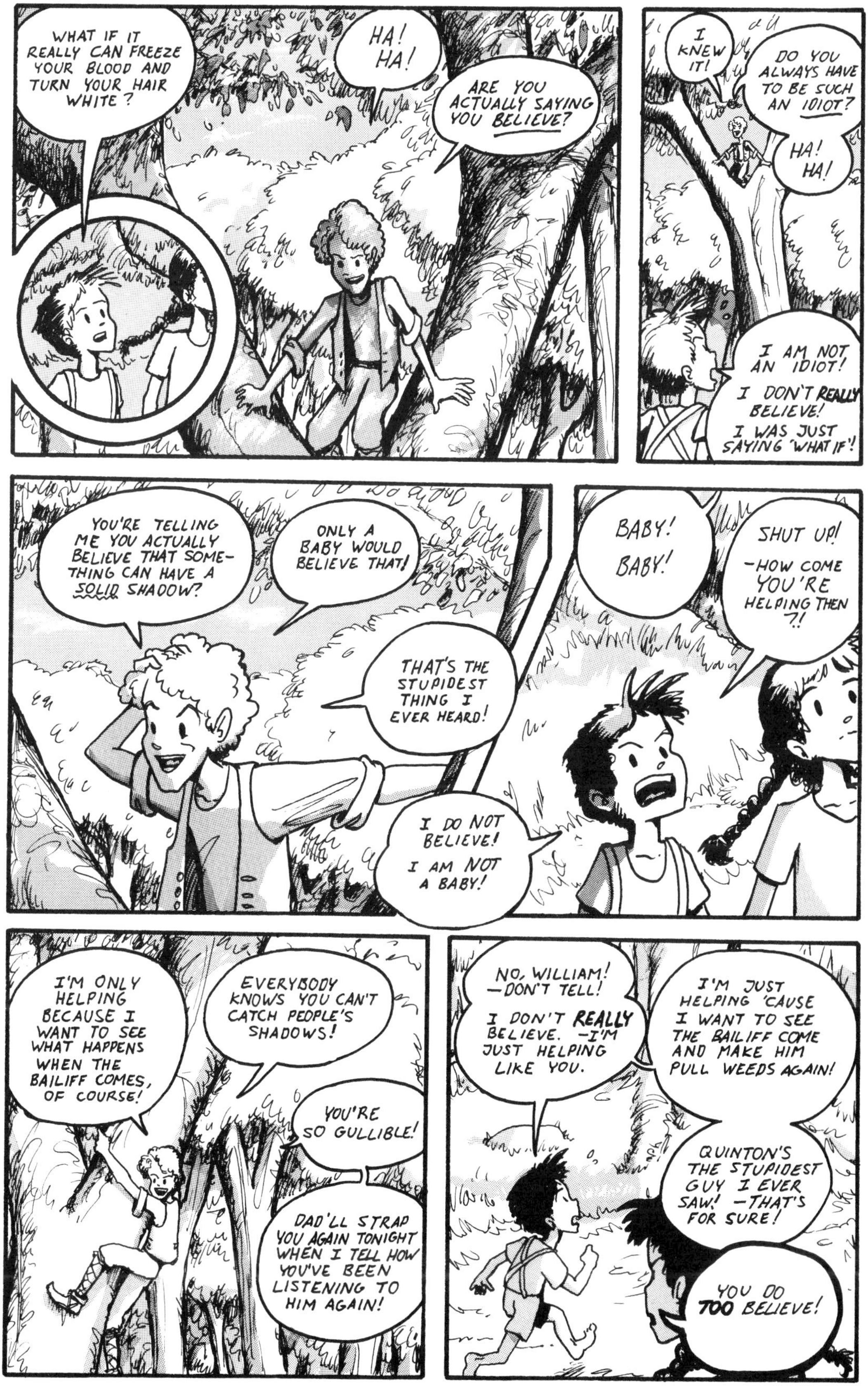
WHAT IF IT REALLY CAN FREEZE YOUR BLOOD AND TURN YOUR HAIR WHITE?
HA! HA!
ARE YOU ACTUALLY SAYING YOU BELIEVE?
I KNEW IT!
DO YOU ALWAYS HAVE TO BE SUCH AN IDIOT?
HA! HA!
I AM NOT AN IDIOT!
I DON'T REALLY BELIEVE!
I WAS JUST SAYING 'WHAT IF'!
YOU'RE TELLING ME YOU ACTUALLY BELIEVE THAT SOMETHING CAN HAVE A SOLID SHADOW?
ONLY A BABY WOULD BELIEVE THAT!
THAT'S THE STUPIDEST THING I EVER HEARD!
I DO NOT BELIEVE!
I AM NOT A BABY!
BABY! BABY!
SHUT UP!
-HOW COME YOU'RE HELPING THEN ?!
I'M ONLY HELPING BECAUSE I WANT TO SEE WHAT HAPPENS WHEN THE BAILIFF COMES, OF COURSE!
EVERYBODY KNOWS YOU CAN'T CATCH PEOPLE'S SHADOWS!
YOU'RE SO GULLIBLE!
DAD'LL STRAP YOU AGAIN TONIGHT WHEN I TELL HOW YOU'VE BEEN LISTENING TO HIM AGAIN!
NO, WILLIAM! -DON'T TELL!
I DON'T REALLY BELIEVE. -I'M JUST HELPING LIKE YOU.
I'M JUST HELPING 'CAUSE I WANT TO SEE THE BAILIFF COME AND MAKE HIM PULL WEEDS AGAIN!
QUINTON'S THE STUPIDEST GUY I EVER SAW! -THAT'S FOR SURE!
YOU DO TOO BELIEVE!

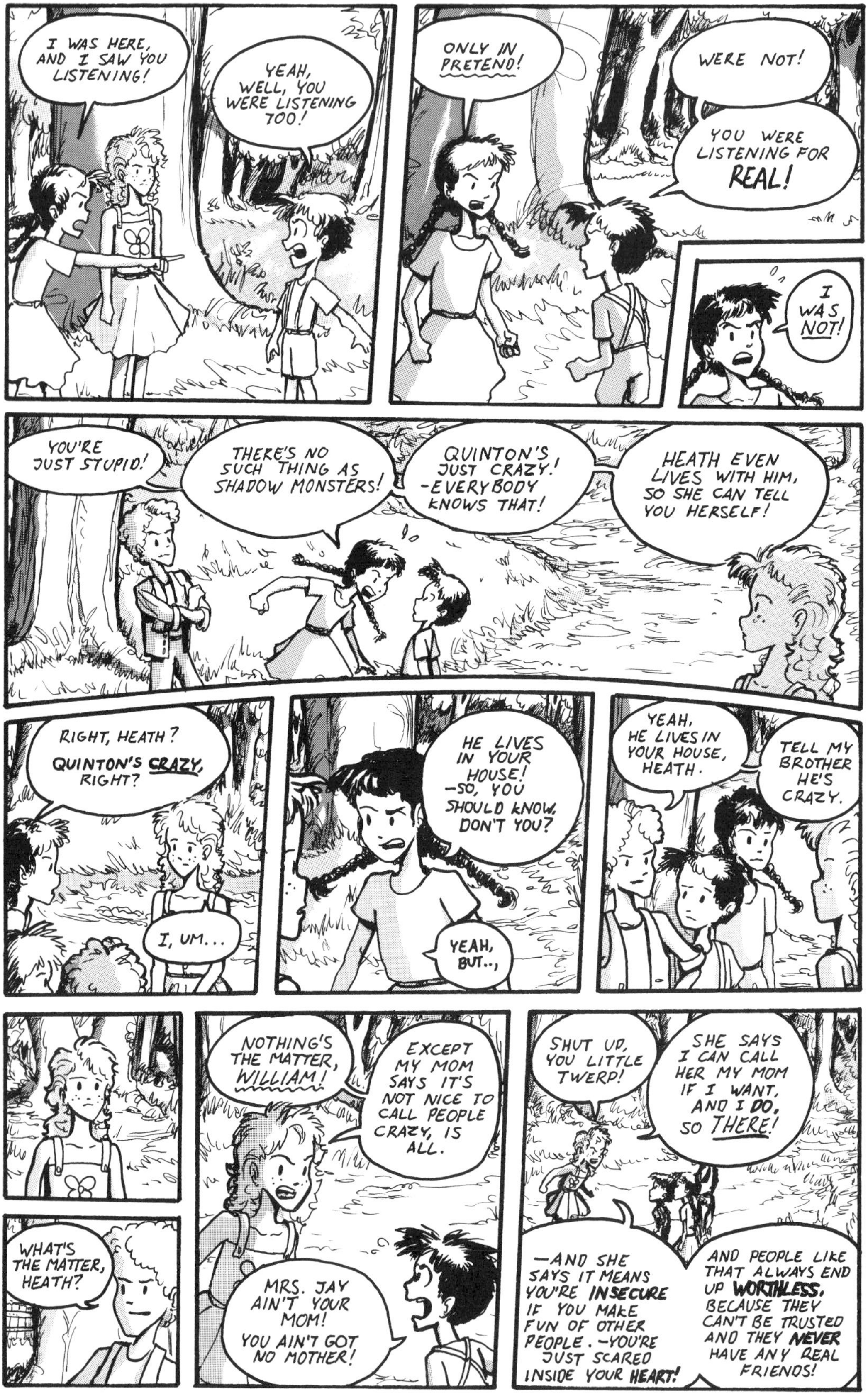
I WAS HERE, AND I SAW YOU LISTENING!
YEAH, WELL, YOU WERE LISTENING TOO!
ONLY IN PRETEND!
WERE NOT!
YOU WERE LISTENING FOR REAL!
I WAS NOT!
YOU'RE JUST STUPID!
THERE'S NO SUCH THING AS SHADOW MONSTERS!
QUINTON'S JUST CRAZY! -EVERYBODY KNOWS THAT!
HEATH EVEN LIVES WITH HIM, SO SHE CAN TELL YOU HERSELF!
RIGHT, HEATH? QUINTON'S CRAZY, RIGHT?
I, UM...
HE LIVES IN YOUR HOUSE! -SO, YOU SHOULD KNOW. DON'T YOU?
YEAH, BUT..,
YEAH, HE LIVES IN YOUR HOUSE, HEATH.
TELL MY BROTHER HE'S CRAZY.
WHAT'S THE MATTER, HEATH?
NOTHING'S THE MATTER, WILLIAM!
EXCEPT MY MOM SAYS IT'S NOT NICE TO CALL PEOPLE CRAZY, IS ALL.
MRS. JAY AIN'T YOUR MOM! YOU AIN'T GOT NO MOTHER!
SHUT UP, YOU LITTLE TWERP!
SHE SAYS I CAN CALL HER MY MOM IF I WANT, AND I DO, SO THERE!
—AND SHE SAYS IT MEANS YOU'RE INSECURE IF YOU MAKE FUN OF OTHER PEOPLE. —YOU'RE JUST SCARED INSIDE YOUR HEART!
AND PEOPLE LIKE THAT ALWAYS END UP WORTHLESS, BECAUSE THEY CAN'T BE TRUSTED AND THEY NEVER HAVE ANY REAL FRIENDS!

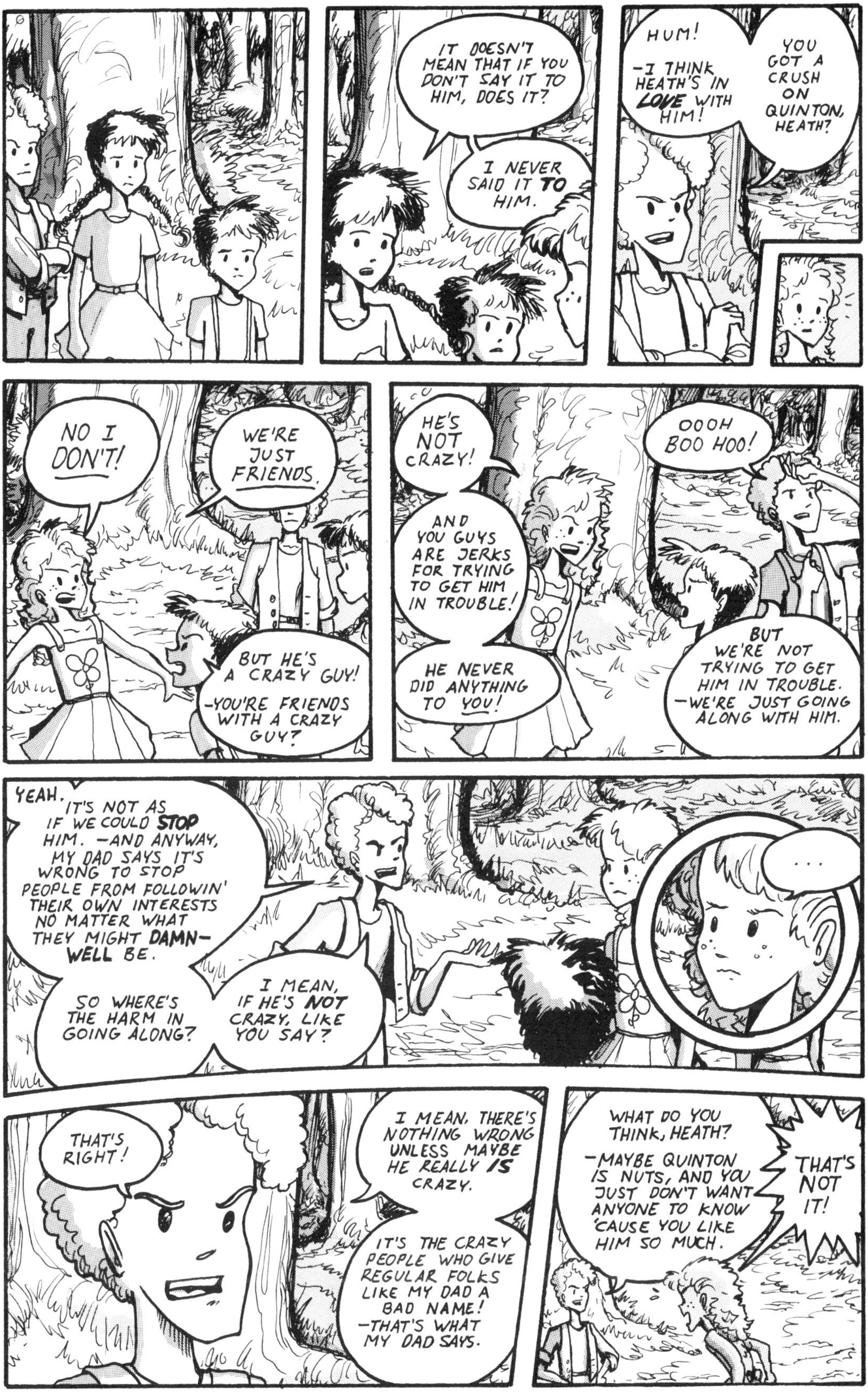
IT DOESN'T MEAN THAT IF YOU DON'T SAY IT TO HIM, DOES IT?
I NEVER SAID IT **TO** HIM.
HUM!
-I THINK HEATH'S IN **LOVE** WITH HIM!
YOU GOT A CRUSH ON QUINTON, HEATH?
NO I DON'T!
WE'RE JUST FRIENDS.
BUT HE'S A CRAZY GUY!
-YOU'RE FRIENDS WITH A CRAZY GUY?
HE'S NOT CRAZY!
AND YOU GUYS ARE JERKS FOR TRYING TO GET HIM IN TROUBLE!
HE NEVER DID ANYTHING TO YOU!
OOOH BOO HOO!
BUT WE'RE NOT TRYING TO GET HIM IN TROUBLE. -WE'RE JUST GOING ALONG WITH HIM.
YEAH. IT'S NOT AS IF WE COULD **STOP** HIM. -AND ANYWAY, MY DAD SAYS IT'S WRONG TO STOP PEOPLE FROM FOLLOWIN' THEIR OWN INTERESTS NO MATTER WHAT THEY MIGHT **DAMN-WELL** BE.
SO WHERE'S THE HARM IN GOING ALONG?
I MEAN, IF HE'S **NOT** CRAZY, LIKE YOU SAY?
...
THAT'S RIGHT!
I MEAN, THERE'S NOTHING WRONG UNLESS MAYBE HE REALLY **IS** CRAZY.
IT'S THE CRAZY PEOPLE WHO GIVE REGULAR FOLKS LIKE MY DAD A BAD NAME! -THAT'S WHAT MY DAD SAYS.
WHAT DO YOU THINK, HEATH?
-MAYBE QUINTON IS NUTS, AND YOU JUST DON'T WANT ANYONE TO KNOW 'CAUSE YOU LIKE HIM SO MUCH.
THAT'S NOT IT!

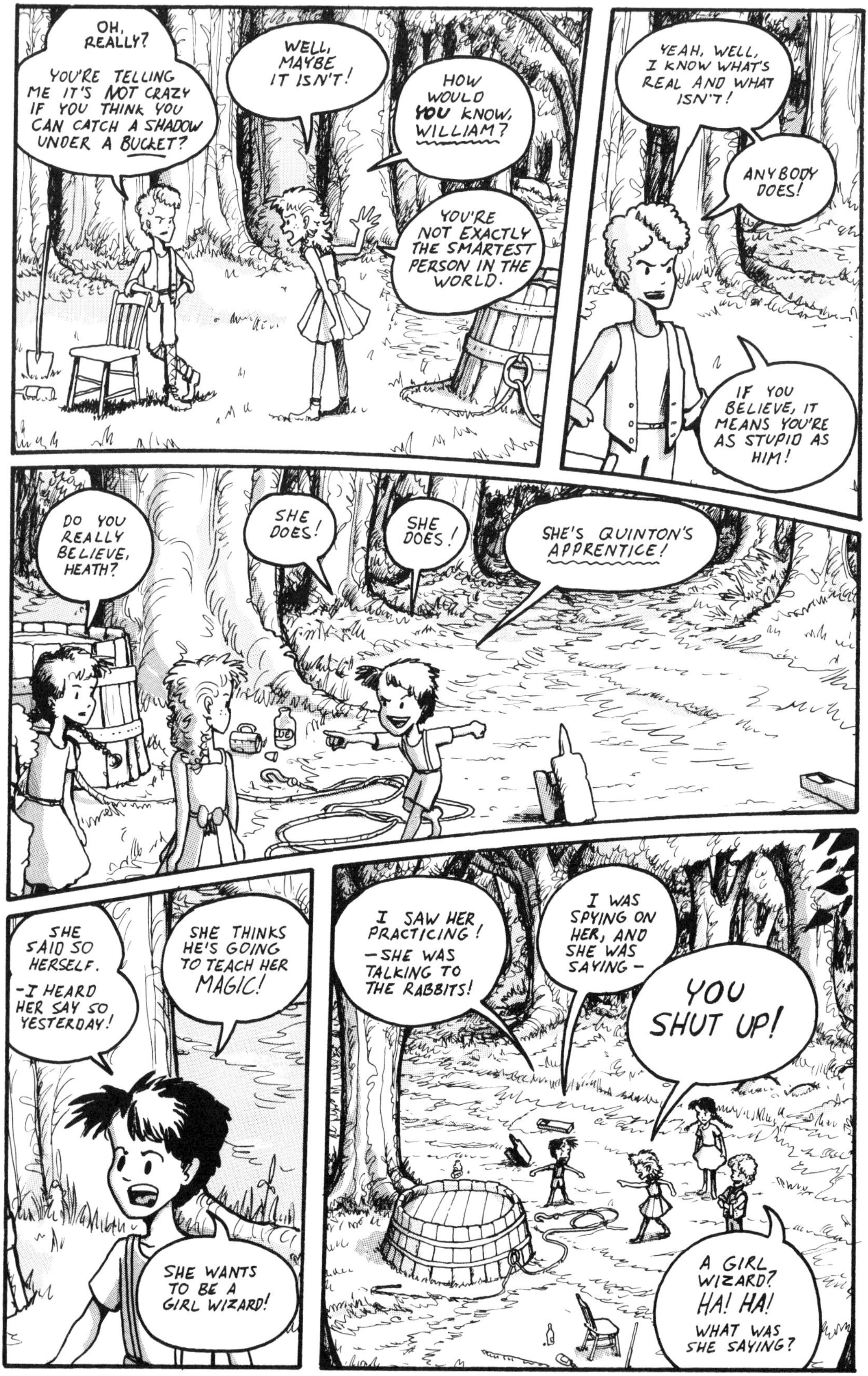
OH, REALLY?
YOU'RE TELLING ME IT'S NOT CRAZY IF YOU THINK YOU CAN CATCH A SHADOW UNDER A BUCKET?
WELL, MAYBE IT ISN'T!
HOW WOULD YOU KNOW, WILLIAM?
YOU'RE NOT EXACTLY THE SMARTEST PERSON IN THE WORLD.
YEAH, WELL, I KNOW WHAT'S REAL AND WHAT ISN'T!
ANYBODY DOES!
IF YOU BELIEVE, IT MEANS YOU'RE AS STUPID AS HIM!
DO YOU REALLY BELIEVE, HEATH?
SHE DOES!
SHE DOES!
SHE'S QUINTON'S APPRENTICE!
SHE SAID SO HERSELF.
-I HEARD HER SAY SO YESTERDAY!
SHE THINKS HE'S GOING TO TEACH HER MAGIC!
SHE WANTS TO BE A GIRL WIZARD!
I SAW HER PRACTICING!
-SHE WAS TALKING TO THE RABBITS!
I WAS SPYING ON HER, AND SHE WAS SAYING-
YOU SHUT UP!
A GIRL WIZARD? HA! HA!
WHAT WAS SHE SAYING?

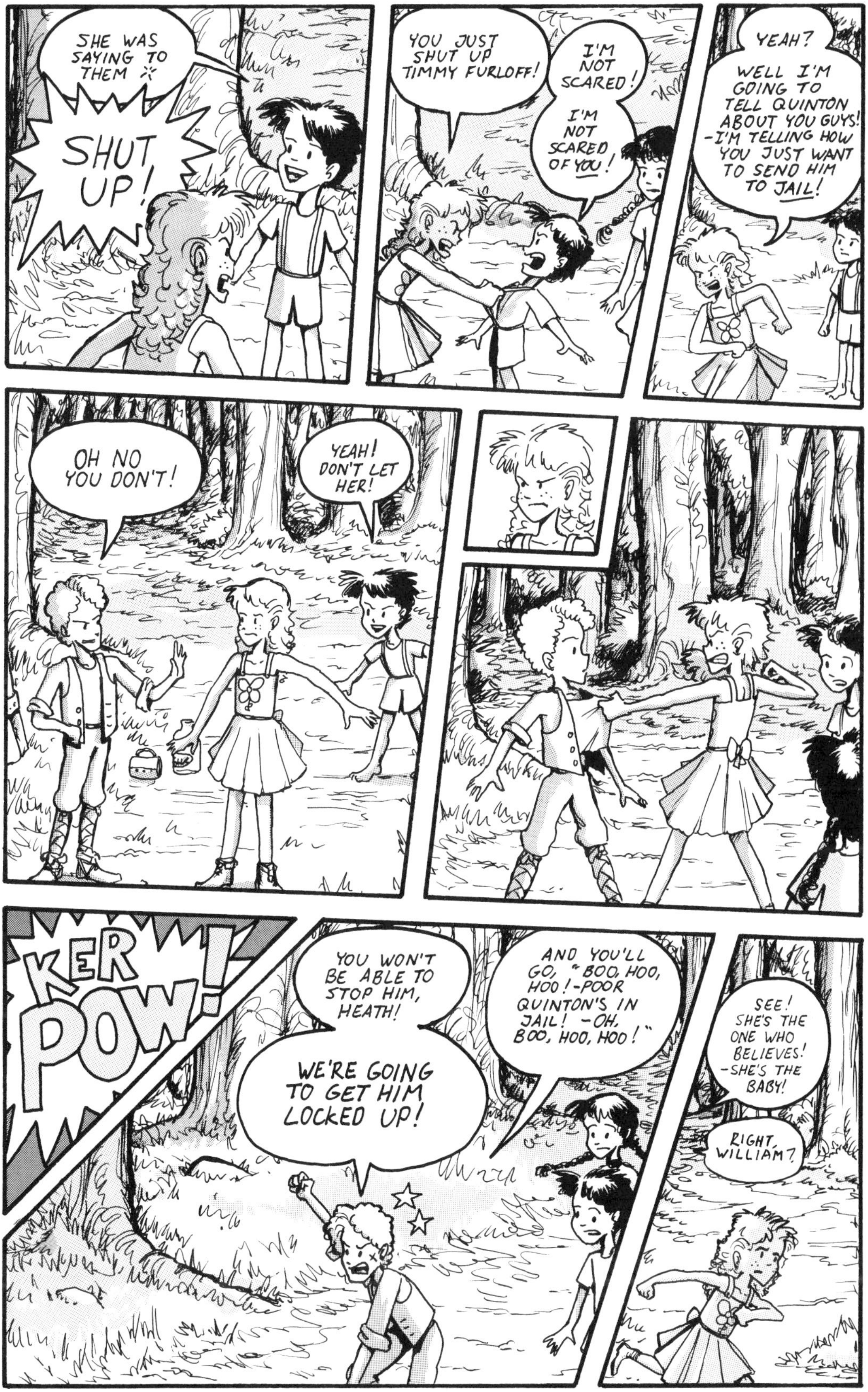

SHE WAS SAYING TO THEM ⁘
SHUT UP!
YOU JUST SHUT UP TIMMY FURLOFF!
I'M NOT SCARED!
I'M NOT SCARED OF YOU!
YEAH?
WELL I'M GOING TO TELL QUINTON ABOUT YOU GUYS! -I'M TELLING HOW YOU JUST WANT TO SEND HIM TO JAIL!
OH NO YOU DON'T!
YEAH! DON'T LET HER!
KER POW!
YOU WON'T BE ABLE TO STOP HIM, HEATH!
WE'RE GOING TO GET HIM LOCKED UP!
AND YOU'LL GO, "BOO, HOO, HOO! -POOR QUINTON'S IN JAIL! -OH, BOO, HOO, HOO!"
SEE! SHE'S THE ONE WHO BELIEVES! -SHE'S THE BABY!
RIGHT, WILLIAM?

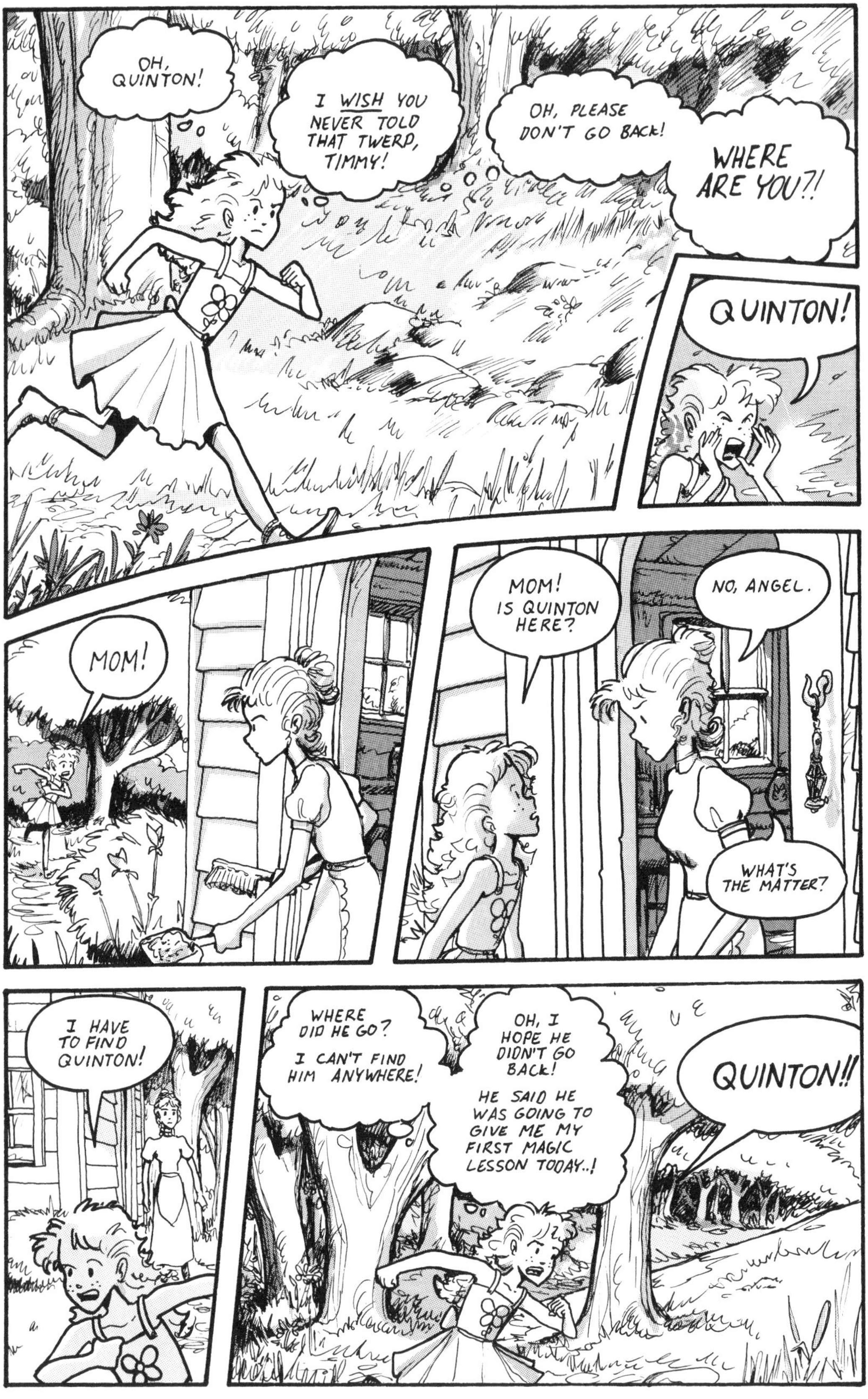

OH, QUINTON!
I WISH YOU NEVER TOLD THAT TWERP, TIMMY!
OH, PLEASE DON'T GO BACK!
WHERE ARE YOU?!
QUINTON!
MOM!
MOM! IS QUINTON HERE?
NO, ANGEL.
WHAT'S THE MATTER?
I HAVE TO FIND QUINTON!
WHERE DID HE GO?
I CAN'T FIND HIM ANYWHERE!
OH, I HOPE HE DIDN'T GO BACK!
HE SAID HE WAS GOING TO GIVE ME MY FIRST MAGIC LESSON TODAY..!
QUINTON!!

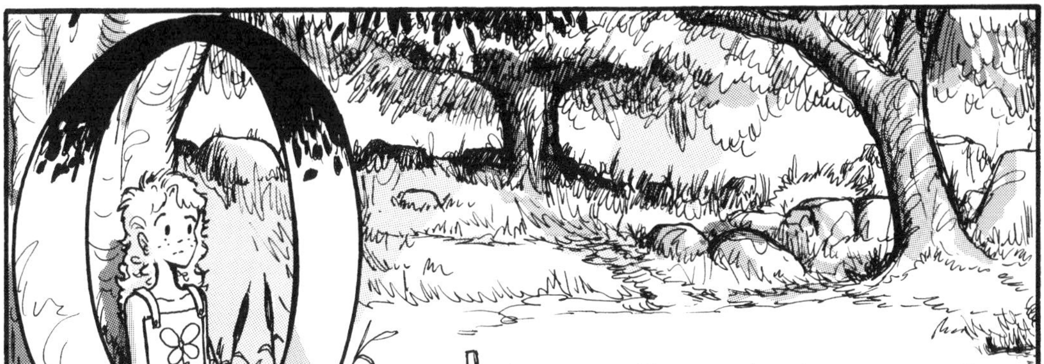

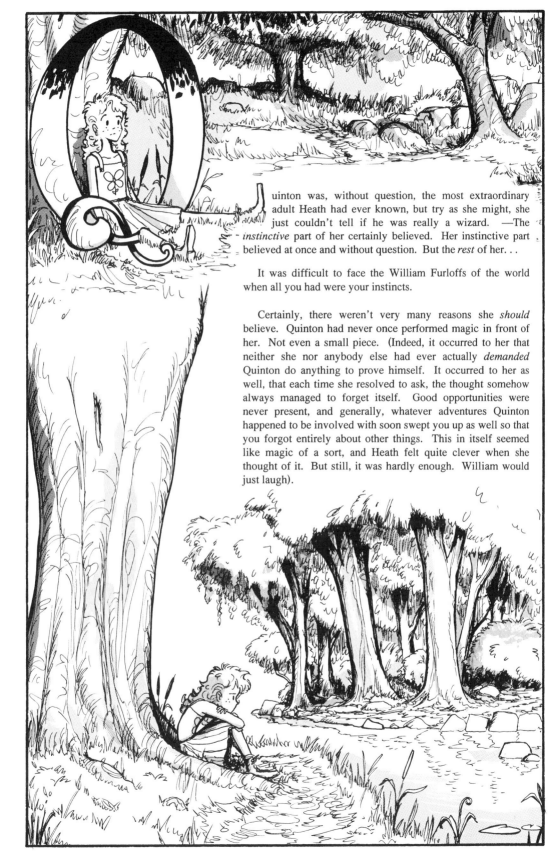

Quinton was, without question, the most extraordinary adult Heath had ever known, but try as she might, she just couldn't tell if he was really a wizard. —The *instinctive* part of her certainly believed. Her instinctive part believed at once and without question. But the *rest* of her. . .

It was difficult to face the William Furloffs of the world when all you had were your instincts.

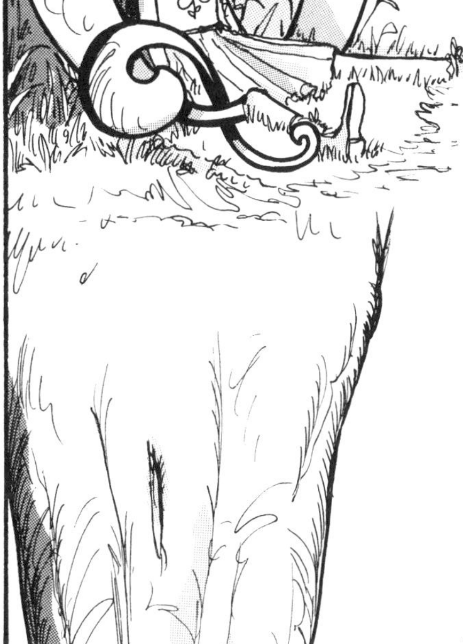

Certainly, there weren't very many reasons she *should* believe. Quinton had never once performed magic in front of her. Not even a small piece. (Indeed, it occurred to her that neither she nor anybody else had ever actually *demanded* Quinton do anything to prove himself. It occurred to her as well, that each time she resolved to ask, the thought somehow always managed to forget itself. Good opportunities were never present, and generally, whatever adventures Quinton happened to be involved with soon swept you up as well so that you forgot entirely about other things. This in itself seemed like magic of a sort, and Heath felt quite clever when she thought of it. But still, it was hardly enough. William would just laugh).

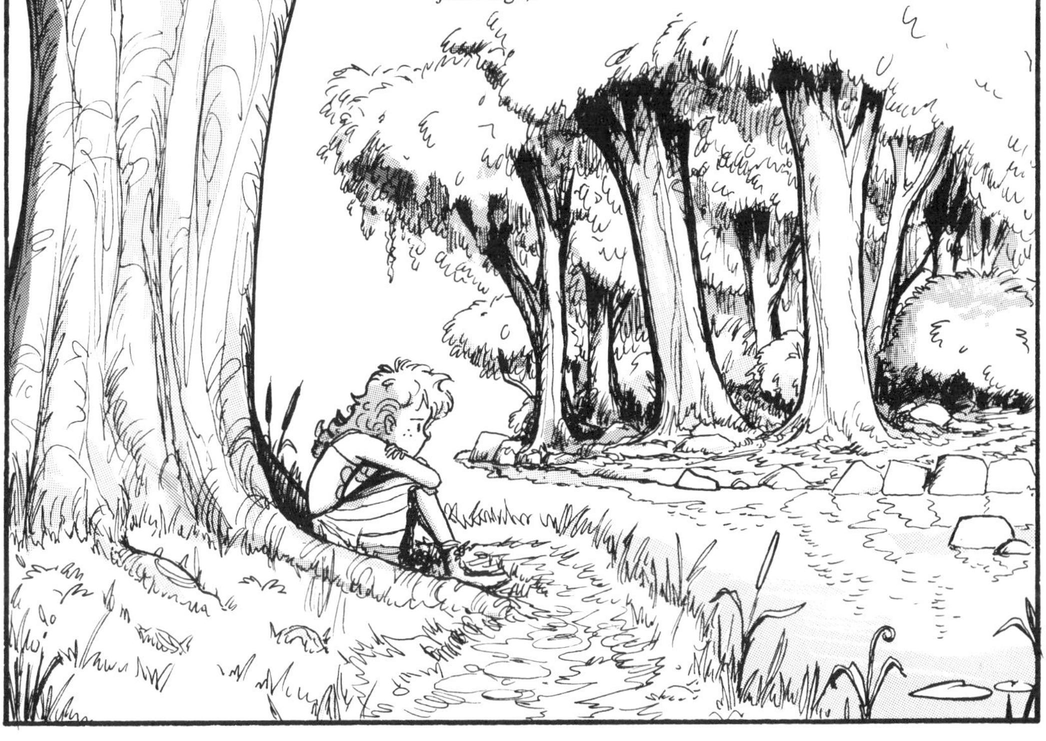

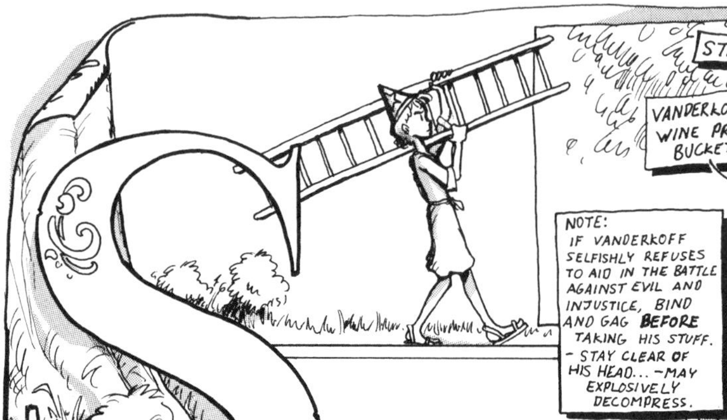
NOTE:
IF VANDERKOFF SELFISHLY REFUSES TO AID IN THE BATTLE AGAINST EVIL AND INJUSTICE, BIND AND GAG BEFORE TAKING HIS STUFF.
- STAY CLEAR OF HIS HEAD... -MAY EXPLOSIVELY DECOMPRESS.

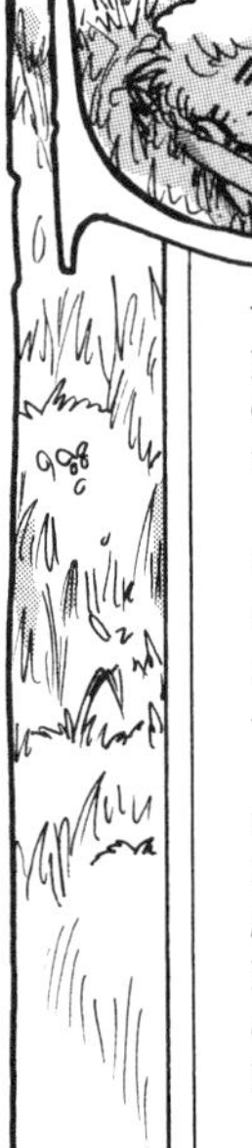

Still. . , it was clear to anybody that Quinton at least *thought* like a wizard. He said and did such remarkable things, —things that, surely, nobody but a real wizard could possible say or do. Unless, of course, he really *was* crazy. Though, Heath felt in her heart that this wasn't the case. Not for *real*.

Amelia from the Dales road; now *she* was crazy, and Quinton wasn't like that. Not at all. The things Quinton said made a wonderful sort of sense in their own way. And Quinton didn't scare her. Not like Amelia. — Amelia's eyes were wrong somehow.

Heath had heard somewhere that people's eyes were the windows into their souls, and Heath didn't like looking into Amelia's eyes. *Quinton's* eyes, however, *they* sparkled with intelligence and energy. Even when he was being serious about something important, his eyes sparkled and danced. Heath loved being around him.

She was certain that he would make a *splendid* wizard. —Not perhaps like the sort people often imagined; Quinton didn't have a long white beard or a deep and wise sounding voice. But, somehow, those things didn't matter. And how perfect it would be if it turned out he *was* real after all. How she hoped!

It was close to noon when Heath at last drifted off to sleep beneath the dark boughs of the riverside tree. It was close to noon when she began to dream. . .

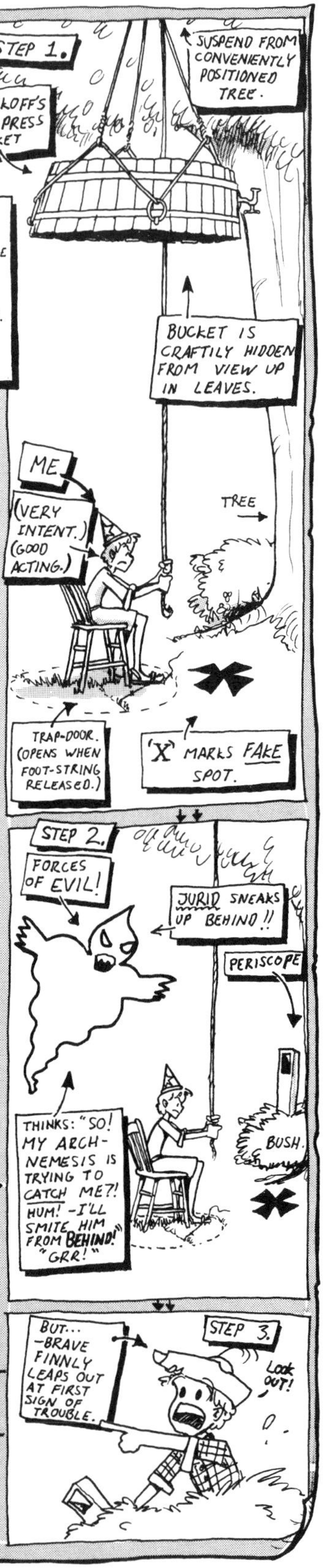
STEP 1.
SUSPEND FROM CONVENIENTLY POSITIONED TREE.
VANDERKOFF'S WINE PRESS BUCKET
BUCKET IS CRAFTILY HIDDEN FROM VIEW UP IN LEAVES.
ME.
(VERY INTENT.)
(GOOD ACTING.)
TREE
TRAP-DOOR. (OPENS WHEN FOOT-STRING RELEASED.)
'X' MARKS FAKE SPOT.
STEP 2.
FORCES OF EVIL!
JURID SNEAKS UP BEHIND!!
PERISCOPE
THINKS: "SO! MY ARCH-NEMESIS IS TRYING TO CATCH ME?! HUM! -I'LL SMITE HIM FROM BEHIND!" "GRR!"
BUSH.
STEP 3.
BUT... -BRAVE FINNLY LEAPS OUT AT FIRST SIGN OF TROUBLE.
Look OUT!

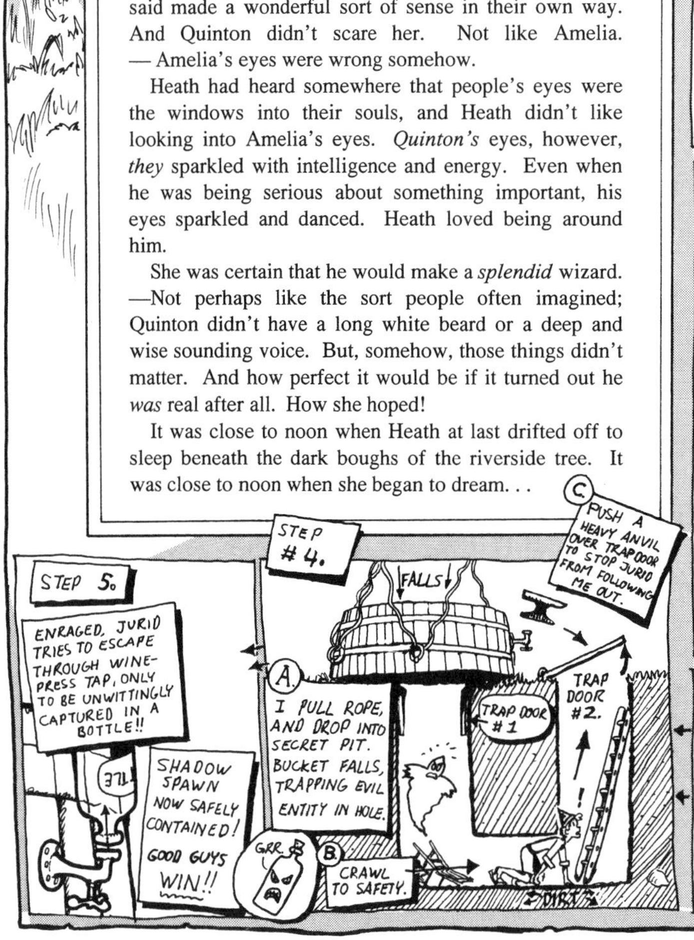
STEP #4.
C
PUSH A HEAVY ANVIL OVER TRAP DOOR TO STOP JURID FROM FOLLOWING ME OUT.
FALLS
A.
I PULL ROPE, AND DROP INTO SECRET PIT. BUCKET FALLS, TRAPPING EVIL ENTITY IN HOLE.
TRAP DOOR #1
TRAP DOOR #2.
B.
CRAWL TO SAFETY.
DIRT
STEP 5.
ENRAGED, JURID TRIES TO ESCAPE THROUGH WINE-PRESS TAP, ONLY TO BE UNWITTINGLY CAPTURED IN A BOTTLE!!
SHADOW SPAWN NOW SAFELY CONTAINED!
GOOD GUYS WIN!!
GRR.

She dreamed in the warm darkness which lay behind her eyelids. And in the cooler, moist darkness when she nudged sideways into the grass. The rich smell of earth surrounded her, and she sank further into the inky depths of sleep which lay beyond.

"Your eyes shut. Your mouth shut." a voice instructed. The words echoed from far, far off. Dire and hurried, but also very sure.

It was a woman's voice.

"Hm!" somebody answered through the darkness. "I don't like this. Not one bit!"

"Shut," the woman repeated.

Heath snapped alert to sound of the two voices, finding herself surrounded by a dark that was thicker than night. —Like the inside of a sealed closet, but somehow even darker than that.

'What is this now?' she asked in her mind, 'I heard somebody! I think I must be inside a cave!'

She took a step forward and her shoes scuffed and missed on the stone, very nearly pitching her into the blackness.

With arms flung out, she steadied herself. The earth seemed to spin ponderously beneath her, as though it were not quite sure of itself. Clutching and swallowing, she went ridged until the motion settled and stopped.

'This won't do!' she thought, straining her eyes into the darkness. 'I can't see a thing! What sort of dream is this? I've dreamed in all sorts of places before, but I've always been able to see at least *something!*'

Then, as though in silent answer, her surroundings quietly swam into view. The stones paused and shifted just beyond her perception, as though waiting for their forms to be fully decided before materializing through the shadows. She knew for certain then that she was in a dream.

"But this is still very different from anything I've ever dreamed before!" she said to herself, speaking aloud the way people sometimes do when they are trying not to be afraid.

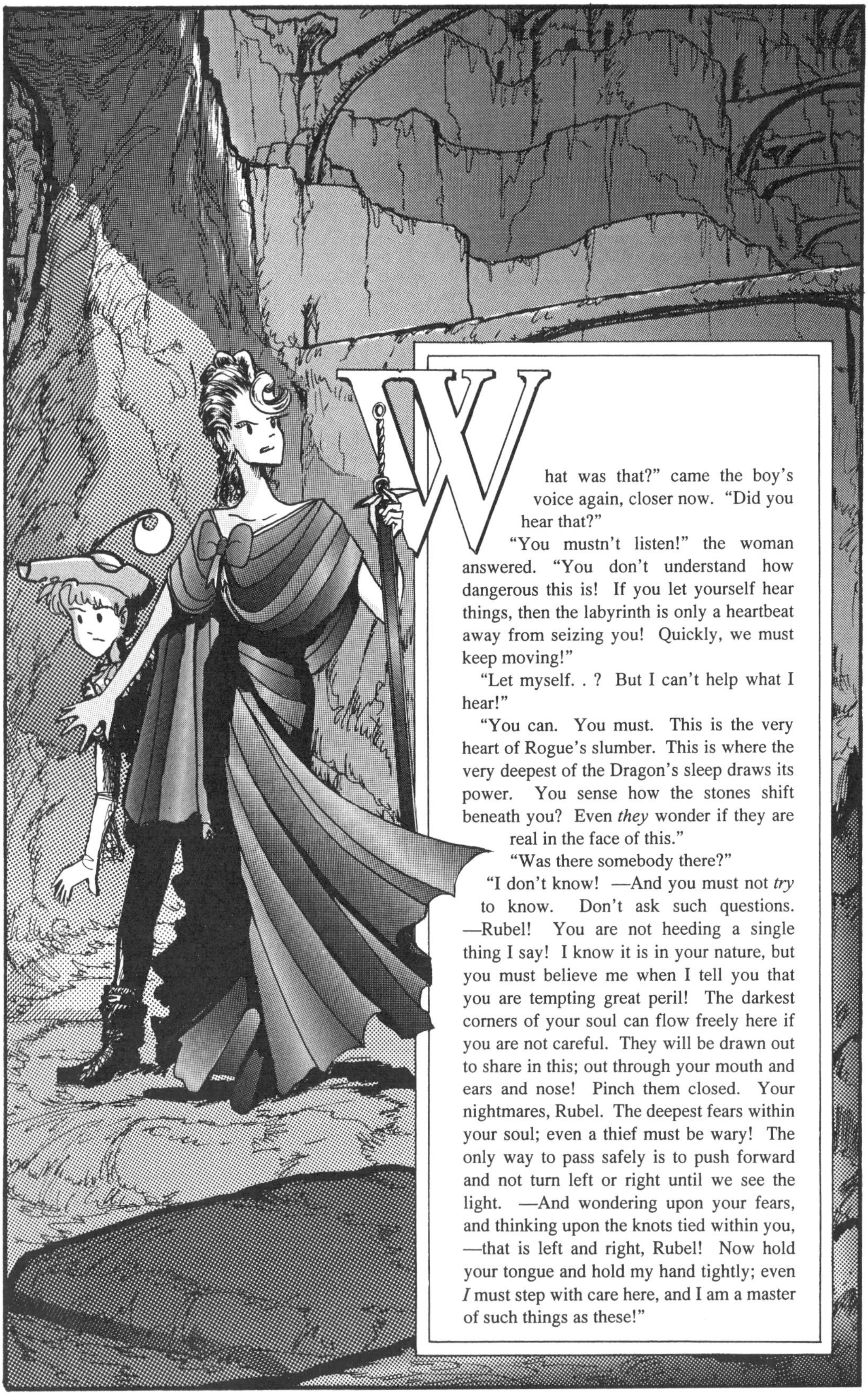

"What was that?" came the boy's voice again, closer now. "Did you hear that?"

"You mustn't listen!" the woman answered. "You don't understand how dangerous this is! If you let yourself hear things, then the labyrinth is only a heartbeat away from seizing you! Quickly, we must keep moving!"

"Let myself. . ? But I can't help what I hear!"

"You can. You must. This is the very heart of Rogue's slumber. This is where the very deepest of the Dragon's sleep draws its power. You sense how the stones shift beneath you? Even *they* wonder if they are real in the face of this."

"Was there somebody there?"

"I don't know! —And you must not *try* to know. Don't ask such questions. —Rubel! You are not heeding a single thing I say! I know it is in your nature, but you must believe me when I tell you that you are tempting great peril! The darkest corners of your soul can flow freely here if you are not careful. They will be drawn out to share in this; out through your mouth and ears and nose! Pinch them closed. Your nightmares, Rubel. The deepest fears within your soul; even a thief must be wary! The only way to pass safely is to push forward and not turn left or right until we see the light. —And wondering upon your fears, and thinking upon the knots tied within you, —that is left and right, Rubel! Now hold your tongue and hold my hand tightly; even *I* must step with care here, and I am a master of such things as these!"

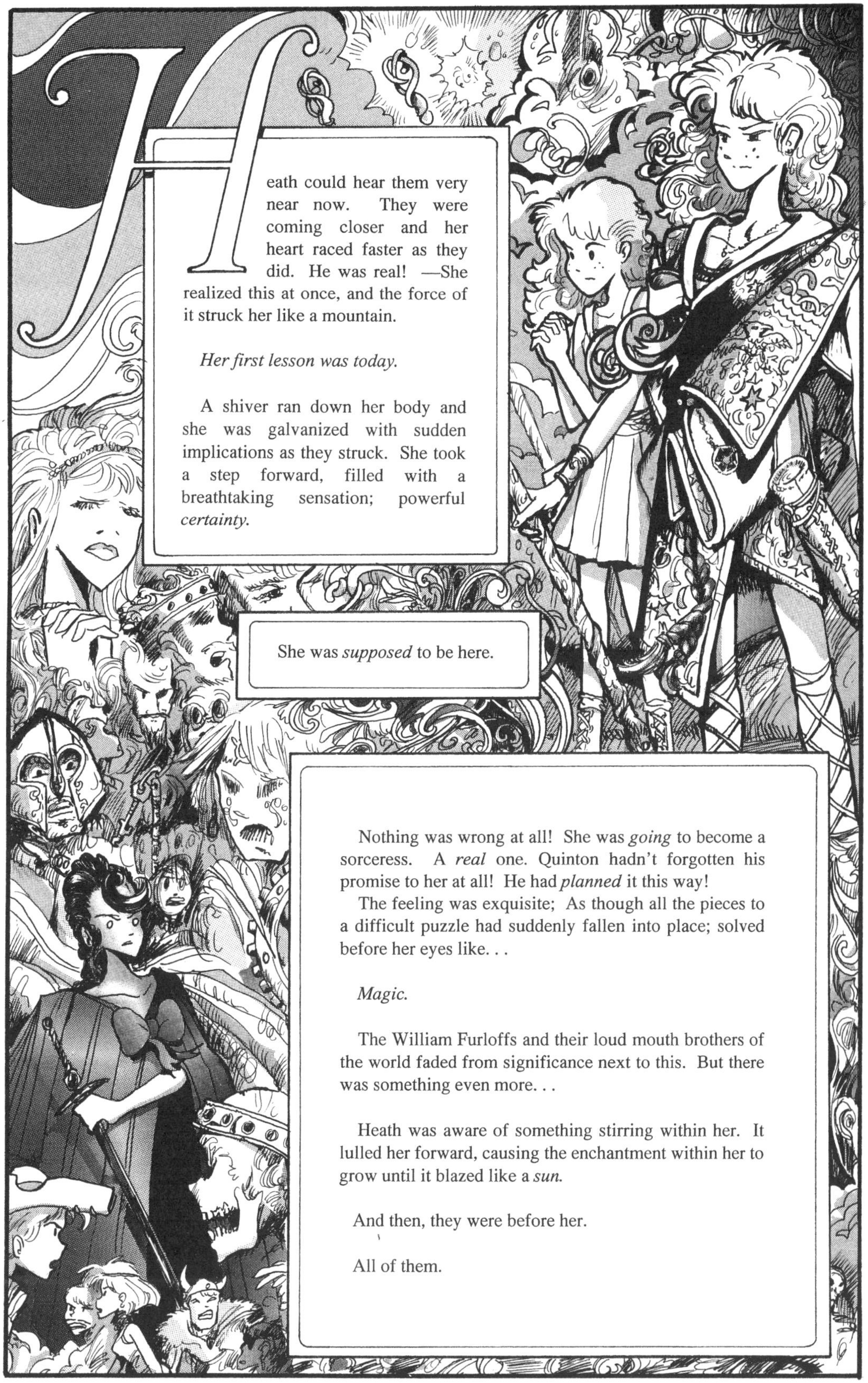

Heath could hear them very near now. They were coming closer and her heart raced faster as they did. He was real! —She realized this at once, and the force of it struck her like a mountain.

Her first lesson was today.

A shiver ran down her body and she was galvanized with sudden implications as they struck. She took a step forward, filled with a breathtaking sensation; powerful *certainty.*

She was *supposed* to be here.

Nothing was wrong at all! She was *going* to become a sorceress. A *real* one. Quinton hadn't forgotten his promise to her at all! He had *planned* it this way!

The feeling was exquisite; As though all the pieces to a difficult puzzle had suddenly fallen into place; solved before her eyes like. . .

Magic.

The William Furloffs and their loud mouth brothers of the world faded from significance next to this. But there was something even more. . .

Heath was aware of something stirring within her. It lulled her forward, causing the enchantment within her to grow until it blazed like a *sun.*

And then, they were before her.

All of them.

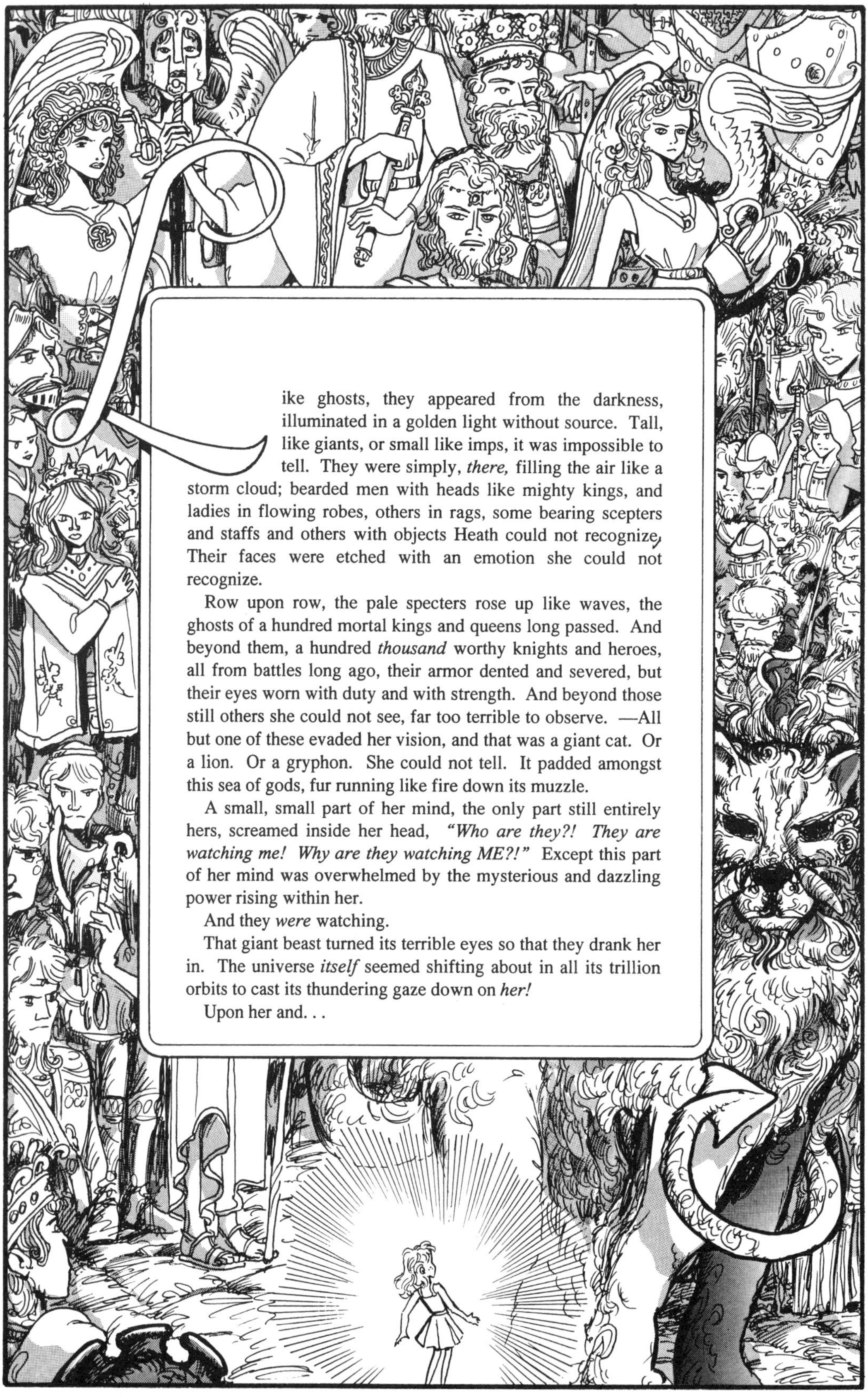

Like ghosts, they appeared from the darkness, illuminated in a golden light without source. Tall, like giants, or small like imps, it was impossible to tell. They were simply, *there,* filling the air like a storm cloud; bearded men with heads like mighty kings, and ladies in flowing robes, others in rags, some bearing scepters and staffs and others with objects Heath could not recognize, Their faces were etched with an emotion she could not recognize.

Row upon row, the pale specters rose up like waves, the ghosts of a hundred mortal kings and queens long passed. And beyond them, a hundred *thousand* worthy knights and heroes, all from battles long ago, their armor dented and severed, but their eyes worn with duty and with strength. And beyond those still others she could not see, far too terrible to observe. —All but one of these evaded her vision, and that was a giant cat. Or a lion. Or a gryphon. She could not tell. It padded amongst this sea of gods, fur running like fire down its muzzle.

A small, small part of her mind, the only part still entirely hers, screamed inside her head, *"Who are they?! They are watching me! Why are they watching ME?!"* Except this part of her mind was overwhelmed by the mysterious and dazzling power rising within her.

And they *were* watching.

That giant beast turned its terrible eyes so that they drank her in. The universe *itself* seemed shifting about in all its trillion orbits to cast its thundering gaze down on *her!*

Upon her and. . .

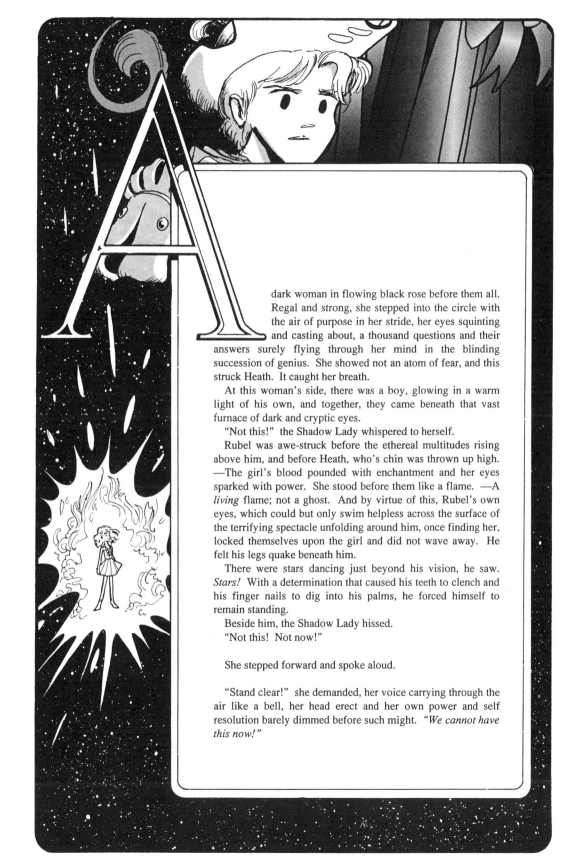

A dark woman in flowing black rose before them all. Regal and strong, she stepped into the circle with the air of purpose in her stride, her eyes squinting and casting about, a thousand questions and their answers surely flying through her mind in the blinding succession of genius. She showed not an atom of fear, and this struck Heath. It caught her breath.

At this woman's side, there was a boy, glowing in a warm light of his own, and together, they came beneath that vast furnace of dark and cryptic eyes.

"Not this!" the Shadow Lady whispered to herself.

Rubel was awe-struck before the ethereal multitudes rising above him, and before Heath, who's chin was thrown up high. —The girl's blood pounded with enchantment and her eyes sparked with power. She stood before them like a flame. —A *living* flame; not a ghost. And by virtue of this, Rubel's own eyes, which could but only swim helpless across the surface of the terrifying spectacle unfolding around him, once finding her, locked themselves upon the girl and did not wave away. He felt his legs quake beneath him.

There were stars dancing just beyond his vision, he saw. *Stars!* With a determination that caused his teeth to clench and his finger nails to dig into his palms, he forced himself to remain standing.

Beside him, the Shadow Lady hissed.

"Not this! Not now!"

She stepped forward and spoke aloud.

"Stand clear!" she demanded, her voice carrying through the air like a bell, her head erect and her own power and self resolution barely dimmed before such might. *"We cannot have this now!"*

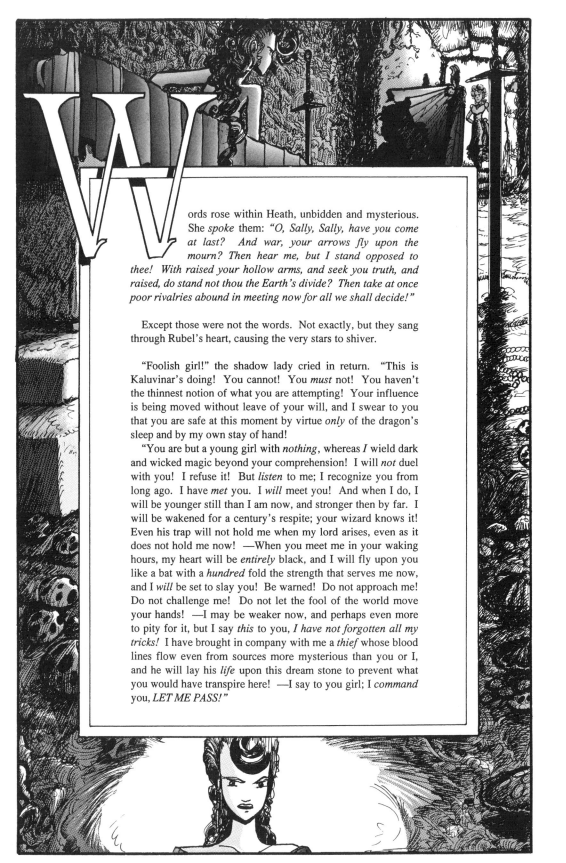

Words rose within Heath, unbidden and mysterious. She *spoke* them: *"O, Sally, Sally, have you come at last? And war, your arrows fly upon the mourn? Then hear me, but I stand opposed to thee! With raised your hollow arms, and seek you truth, and raised, do stand not thou the Earth's divide? Then take at once poor rivalries abound in meeting now for all we shall decide!"*

Except those were not the words. Not exactly, but they sang through Rubel's heart, causing the very stars to shiver.

"Foolish girl!" the shadow lady cried in return. "This is Kaluvinar's doing! You cannot! You *must* not! You haven't the thinnest notion of what you are attempting! Your influence is being moved without leave of your will, and I swear to you that you are safe at this moment by virtue *only* of the dragon's sleep and by my own stay of hand!

"You are but a young girl with *nothing*, whereas *I* wield dark and wicked magic beyond your comprehension! I will *not* duel with you! I refuse it! But *listen* to me; I recognize you from long ago. I have *met* you. I *will* meet you! And when I do, I will be younger still than I am now, and stronger then by far. I will be wakened for a century's respite; your wizard knows it! Even his trap will not hold me when my lord arises, even as it does not hold me now! —When you meet me in your waking hours, my heart will be *entirely* black, and I will fly upon you like a bat with a *hundred* fold the strength that serves me now, and I *will* be set to slay you! Be warned! Do not approach me! Do not challenge me! Do not let the fool of the world move your hands! —I may be weaker now, and perhaps even more to pity for it, but I say *this* to you, *I have not forgotten all my tricks!* I have brought in company with me a *thief* whose blood lines flow even from sources more mysterious than you or I, and he will lay his *life* upon this dream stone to prevent what you would have transpire here! —I say to you girl; I *command* you, *LET ME PASS!"*

Heath felt the power coursing through her body falter ever so slightly, and she realized at once that indeed she did not know what was going on. The thrilling knife edge of perfection she had been so effortlessly balancing on was, in that moment, lost. —And all the attention of the heavens was not such that it would hold itself upon something so faltering as that! It all began to unravel.

Heath cast her eyes about in confusion as the sea of ghosts began to fade, leaving her lost and shaky and frightened. The giant cat roiled its fiery pelt, and with a soft rumble from deep within its throat, slipped into the darkness and was gone. The Shadow Lady and thief faded last of all. Heath watched them as she was lifted up into the dizzy light and humid fragrance of the day.

The boy watched after her, his own chin turned up towards her, his gaze holding hers for one last instant. He stood at the shadow woman's side, his own light shining warm and strong about him. Vital. And then he was gone and the warm air of day filled her lungs sweetly, as though she had been holding her breath the whole time beneath her tree beside the river.

WE WERE EXTREMELY LUCKY, IS WHAT HAPPENED!

WHAT WAS THAT?! WHO WAS THAT GIRL? WHAT HAPPENED?!

I WAS A FOOL!

I CAN'T BELIEVE I JUST WALKED INTO THAT!

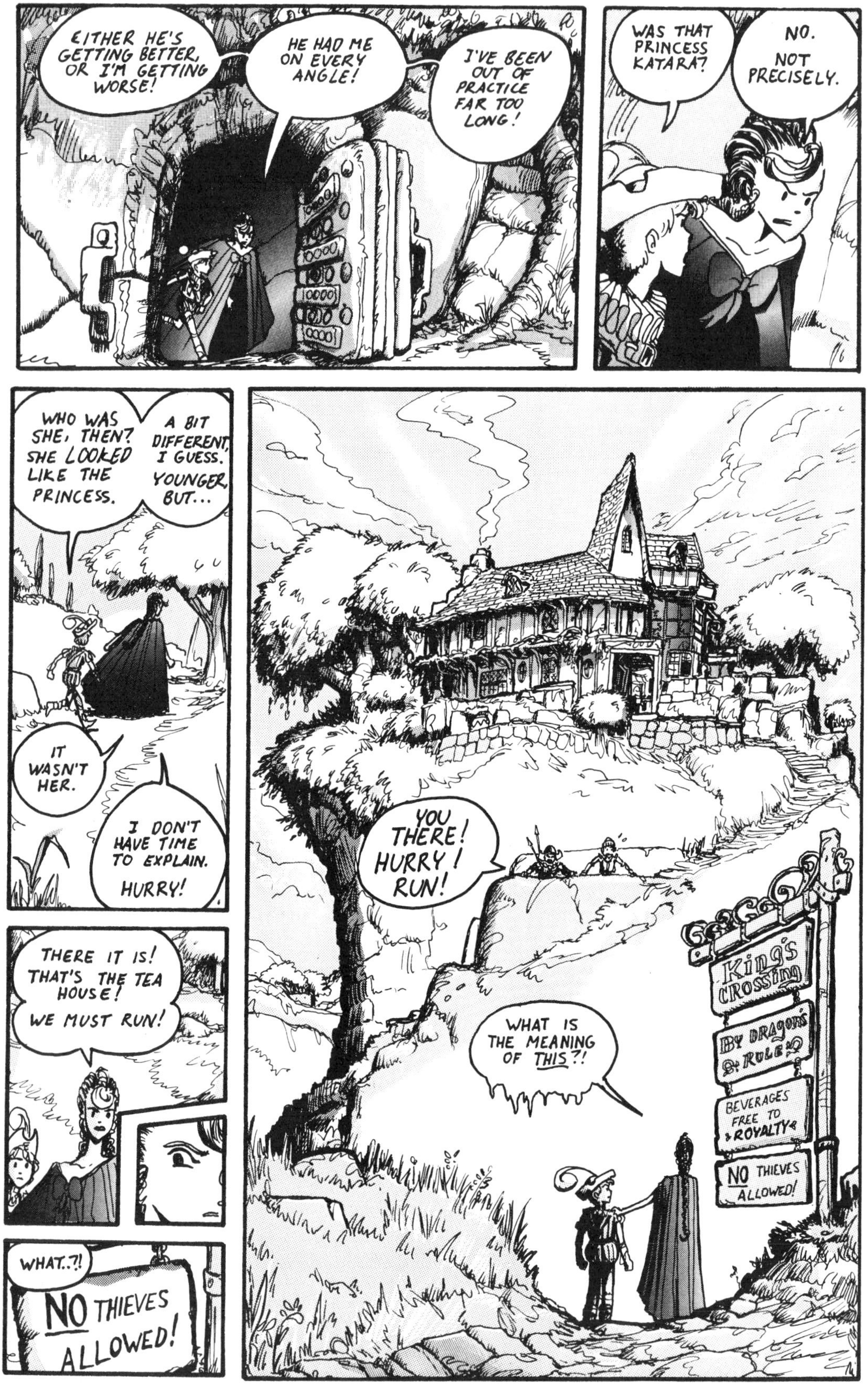
EITHER HE'S GETTING BETTER, OR I'M GETTING WORSE!
HE HAD ME ON EVERY ANGLE!
I'VE BEEN OUT OF PRACTICE FAR TOO LONG!
WAS THAT PRINCESS KATARA?
NO. NOT PRECISELY.
WHO WAS SHE, THEN? SHE LOOKED LIKE THE PRINCESS.
A BIT DIFFERENT, I GUESS. YOUNGER, BUT...
IT WASN'T HER.
I DON'T HAVE TIME TO EXPLAIN. HURRY!
THERE IT IS! THAT'S THE TEA HOUSE! WE MUST RUN!
WHAT..?!
NO THIEVES ALLOWED!
YOU THERE! HURRY! RUN!
King's CROSSING
BY DRAGON'S RULE
BEVERAGES FREE TO ROYALTY
NO THIEVES ALLOWED!
WHAT IS THE MEANING OF THIS?!

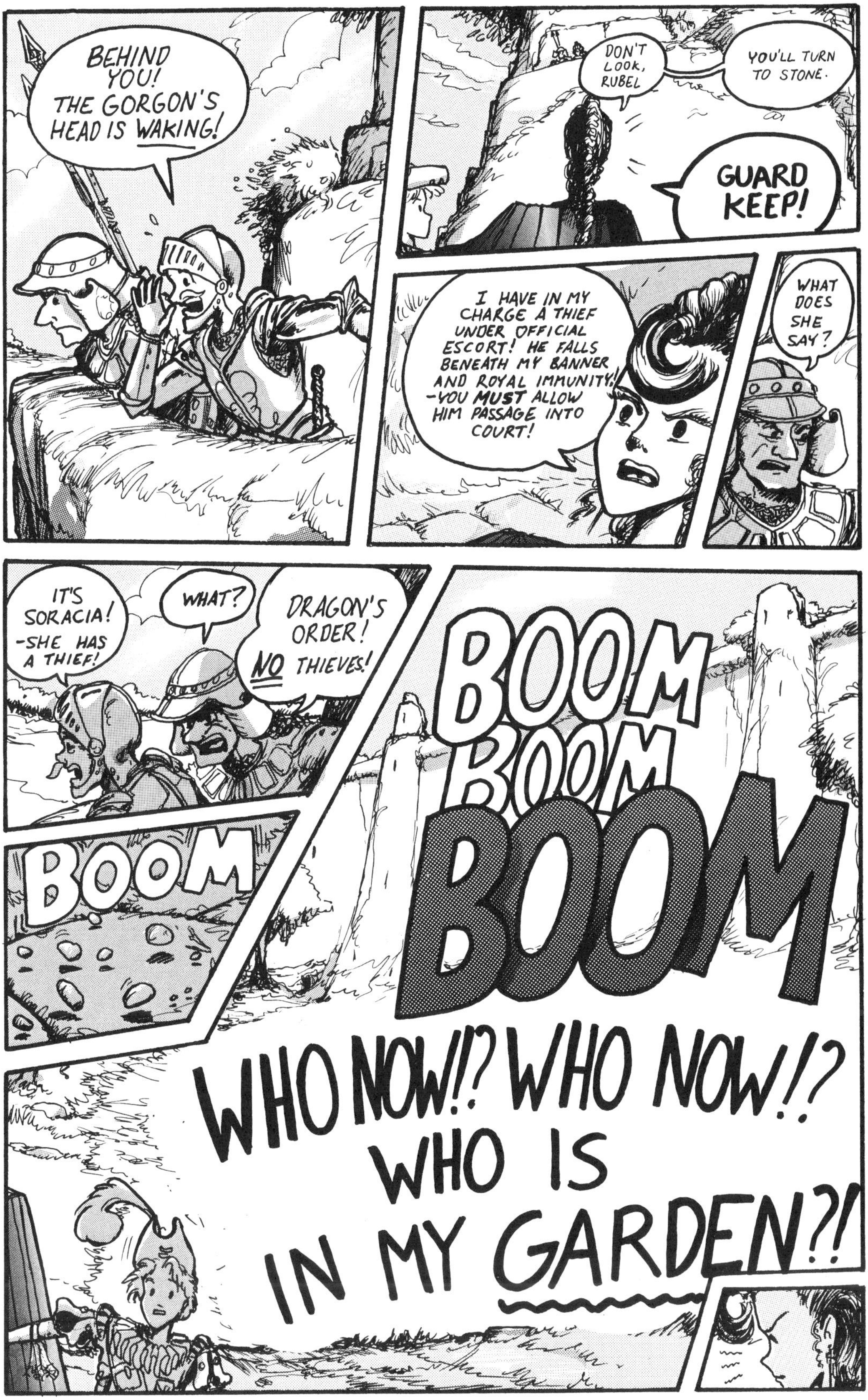
BEHIND YOU! THE GORGON'S HEAD IS WAKING!
DON'T LOOK, RUBEL
YOU'LL TURN TO STONE.
GUARD KEEP!
I HAVE IN MY CHARGE A THIEF UNDER OFFICIAL ESCORT! HE FALLS BENEATH MY BANNER AND ROYAL IMMUNITY! -YOU MUST ALLOW HIM PASSAGE INTO COURT!
WHAT DOES SHE SAY?
IT'S SORACIA! -SHE HAS A THIEF!
WHAT?
DRAGON'S ORDER! NO THIEVES!
BOOM
BOOM
BOOM
BOOM
WHO NOW!? WHO NOW!? WHO IS IN MY GARDEN?!

Chapter 15

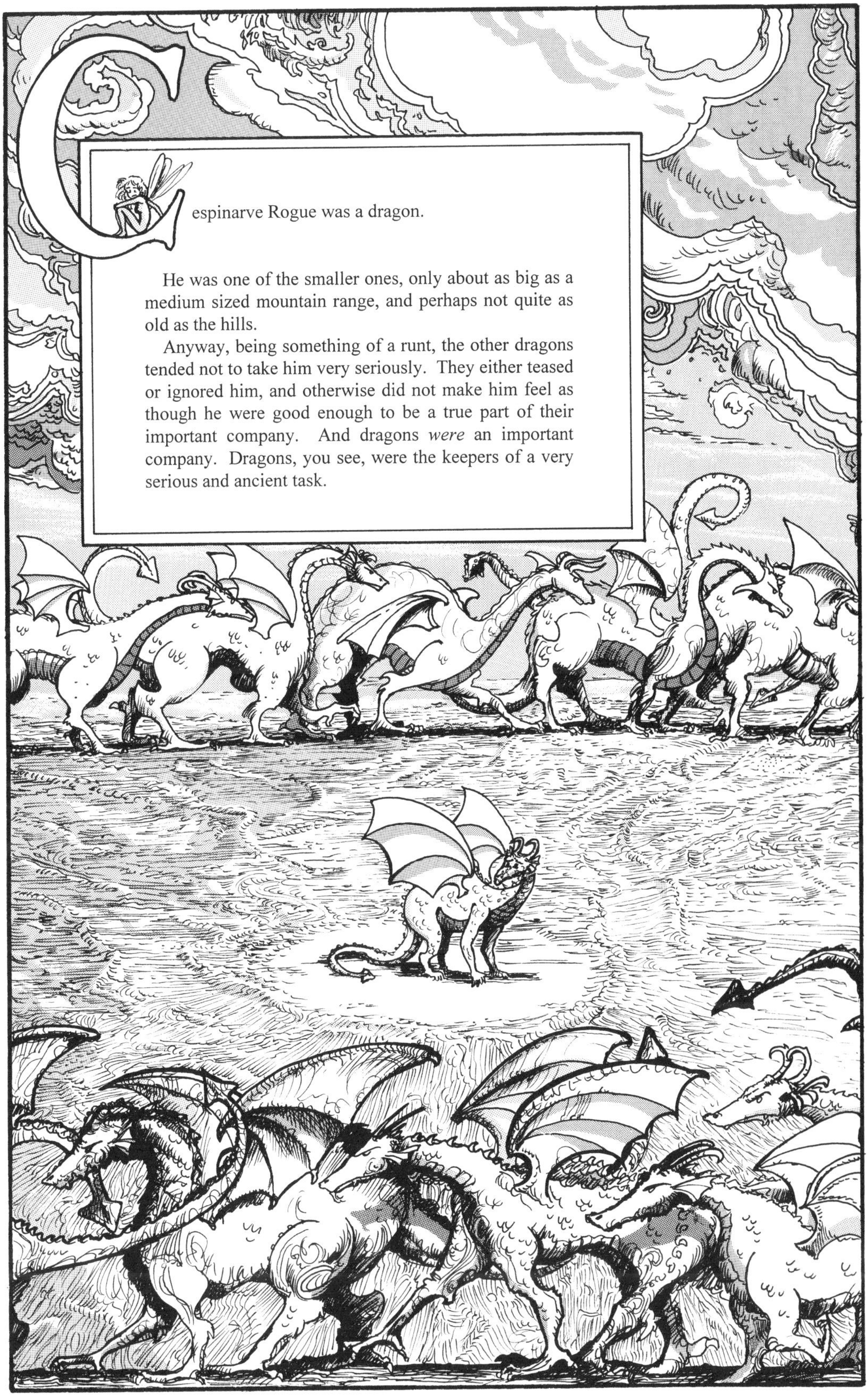

Cespinarve Rogue was a dragon.

He was one of the smaller ones, only about as big as a medium sized mountain range, and perhaps not quite as old as the hills.

Anyway, being something of a runt, the other dragons tended not to take him very seriously. They either teased or ignored him, and otherwise did not make him feel as though he were good enough to be a true part of their important company. And dragons *were* an important company. Dragons, you see, were the keepers of a very serious and ancient task.

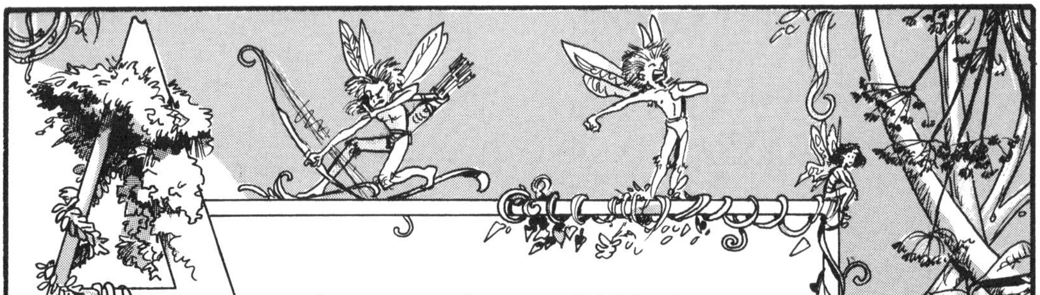

A long way away from where Rubel lived, there was an extraordinary land called *Nove.* —Although, it wasn't actually *called* Nove anymore. Not since everybody had forgotten the name. These days, the land was called by many other names. *Salisary*, *Amsil*, and *Troor* were a few of them, and as is the case with most lands, *Earth* was another. None of those names, however, was Nove. Not anymore. Not unless there were dragons around. The *dragons* called it Nove. Dragons were among the oldest living things, and so they remembered.

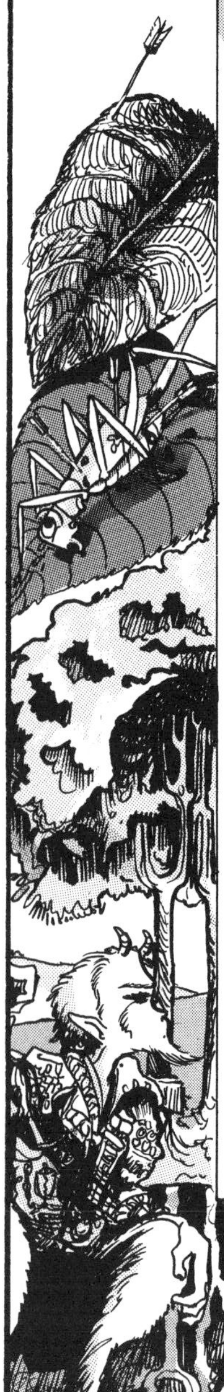

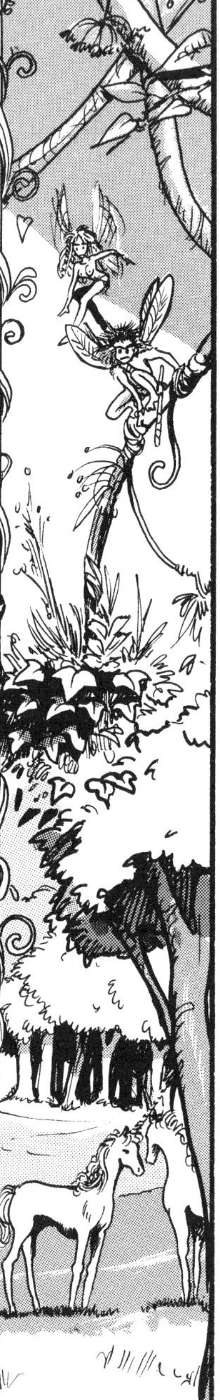

All the others came later; all the fairies and satyrs and unicorns, and all the other various creatures of myth and legend. —Nove was, in fact, where *most* of the fairy tale creatures, and indeed, where most fairy tales came from; where fairy tales were considered *history,* and not queer stories told to children.

Nove was a long, long way away, and very difficult to get to besides. In fact, so few ever went, that people hardly bothered even *believing* in Nove anymore. Small children, (though they hardly ever asked), were told that it was far off in the north. —You went north, all the way up to the north pole, and once you were there at the top of the world, you traveled north some more until you found it, spread out like a giant magic carpet at your feet. —Which was, of course, ridiculous, and why most people didn't believe anymore.

"After you get to the north pole, you can't go north anymore! The only direction you can go next is *south!* Doesn't matter which way you turn! It's like a ball, see," Adults would tell their children, and feel wise.

Anyway, they were wrong. About Nove being in the north, that is. It was in a much more easterly direction.

It was, in fact, through the sleeping wood. —The sleeping wood against which they had locked their city's eastern doors so long ago. (After the white stones had been broken all to bits.) And that's where the dragons lived. In Nove. Or rather, all around its edges, consuming it the way one might chew a bread crust.

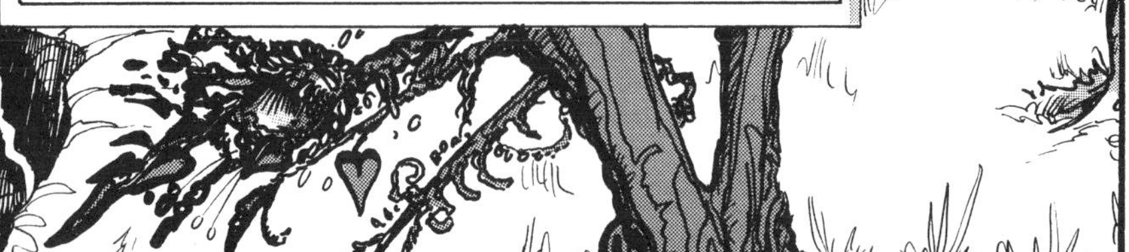

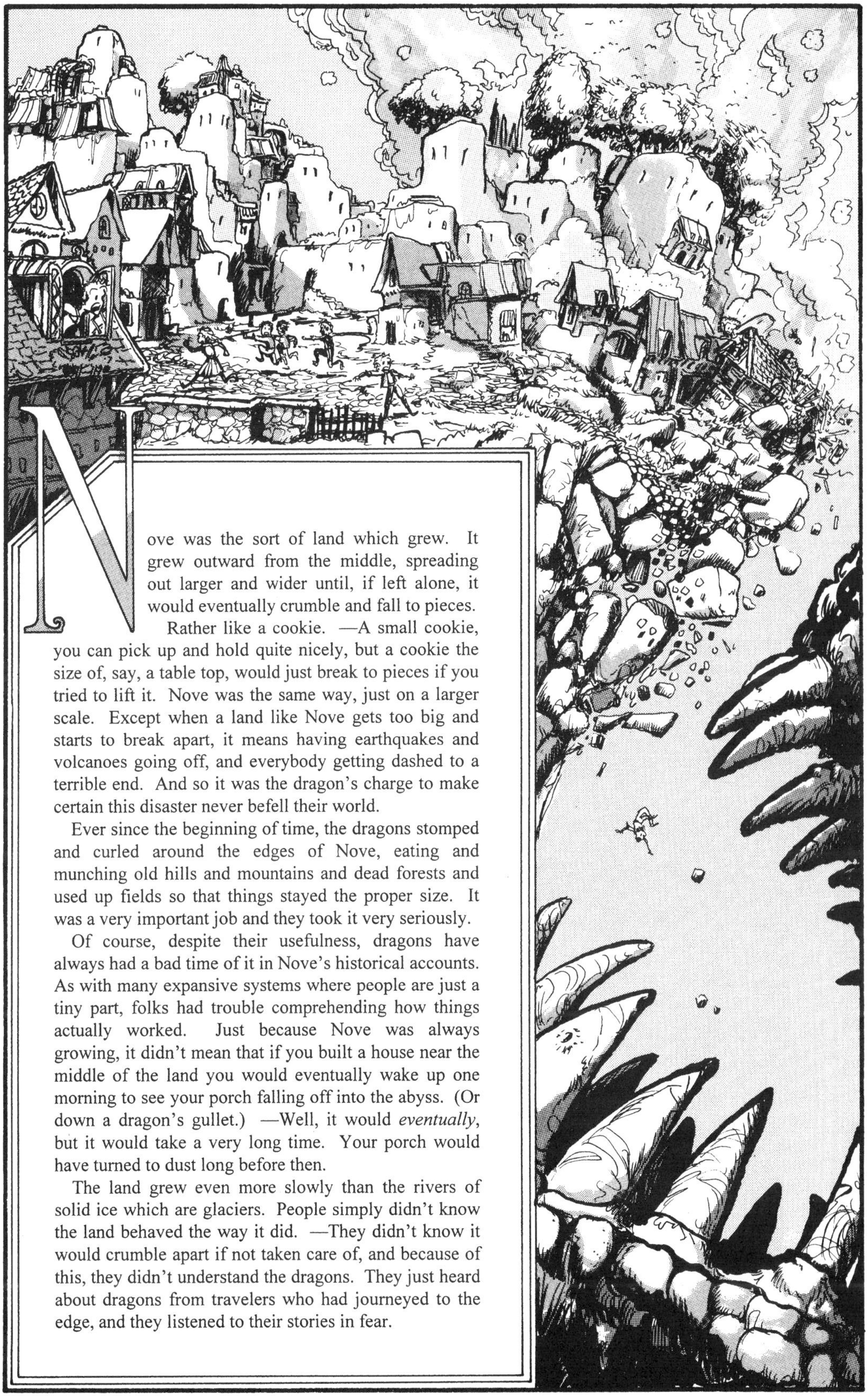

Nove was the sort of land which grew. It grew outward from the middle, spreading out larger and wider until, if left alone, it would eventually crumble and fall to pieces.

Rather like a cookie. —A small cookie, you can pick up and hold quite nicely, but a cookie the size of, say, a table top, would just break to pieces if you tried to lift it. Nove was the same way, just on a larger scale. Except when a land like Nove gets too big and starts to break apart, it means having earthquakes and volcanoes going off, and everybody getting dashed to a terrible end. And so it was the dragon's charge to make certain this disaster never befell their world.

Ever since the beginning of time, the dragons stomped and curled around the edges of Nove, eating and munching old hills and mountains and dead forests and used up fields so that things stayed the proper size. It was a very important job and they took it very seriously.

Of course, despite their usefulness, dragons have always had a bad time of it in Nove's historical accounts. As with many expansive systems where people are just a tiny part, folks had trouble comprehending how things actually worked. Just because Nove was always growing, it didn't mean that if you built a house near the middle of the land you would eventually wake up one morning to see your porch falling off into the abyss. (Or down a dragon's gullet.) —Well, it would *eventually*, but it would take a very long time. Your porch would have turned to dust long before then.

The land grew even more slowly than the rivers of solid ice which are glaciers. People simply didn't know the land behaved the way it did. —They didn't know it would crumble apart if not taken care of, and because of this, they didn't understand the dragons. They just heard about dragons from travelers who had journeyed to the edge, and they listened to their stories in fear.

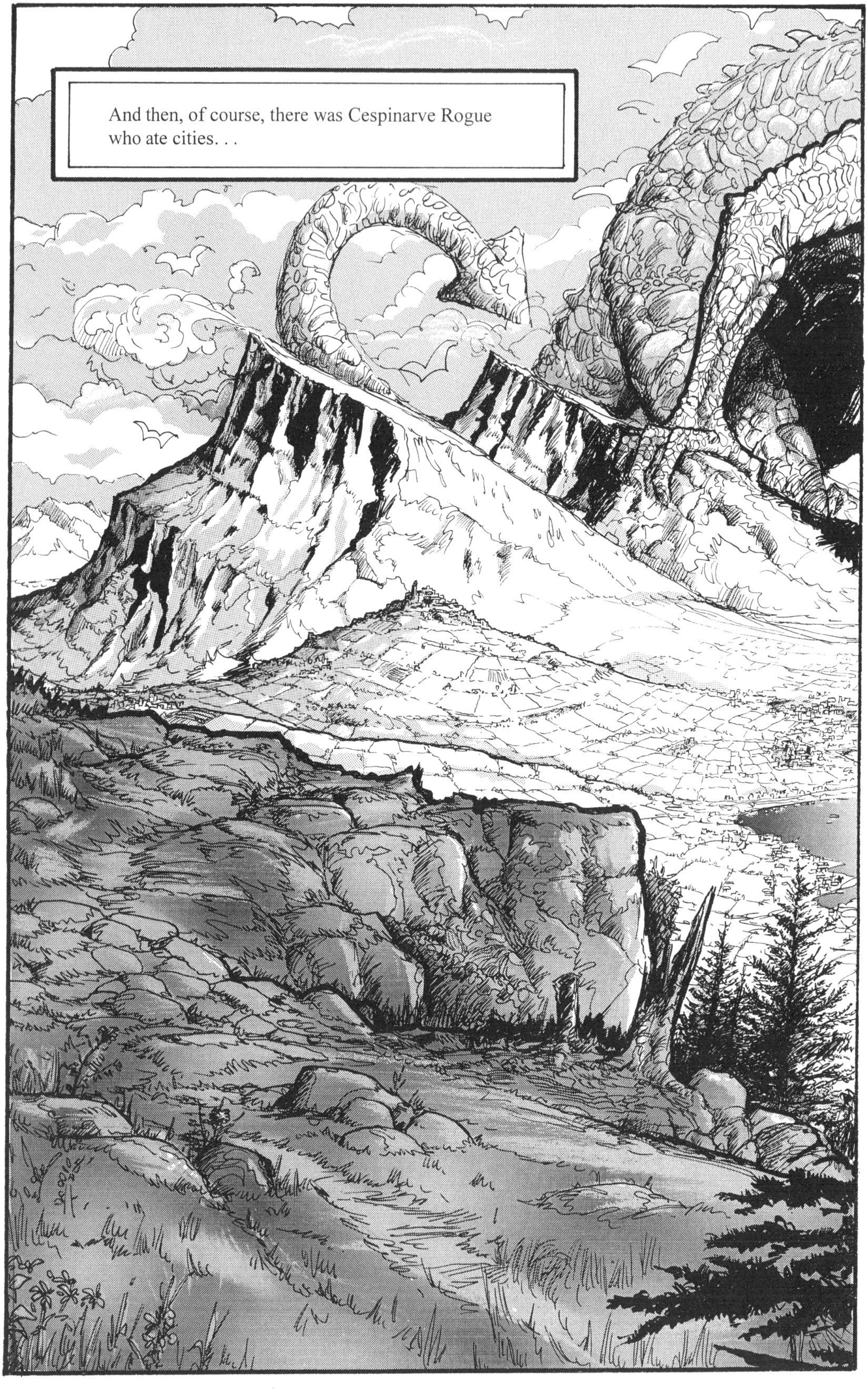
And then, of course, there was Cespinarve Rogue who ate cities. . .

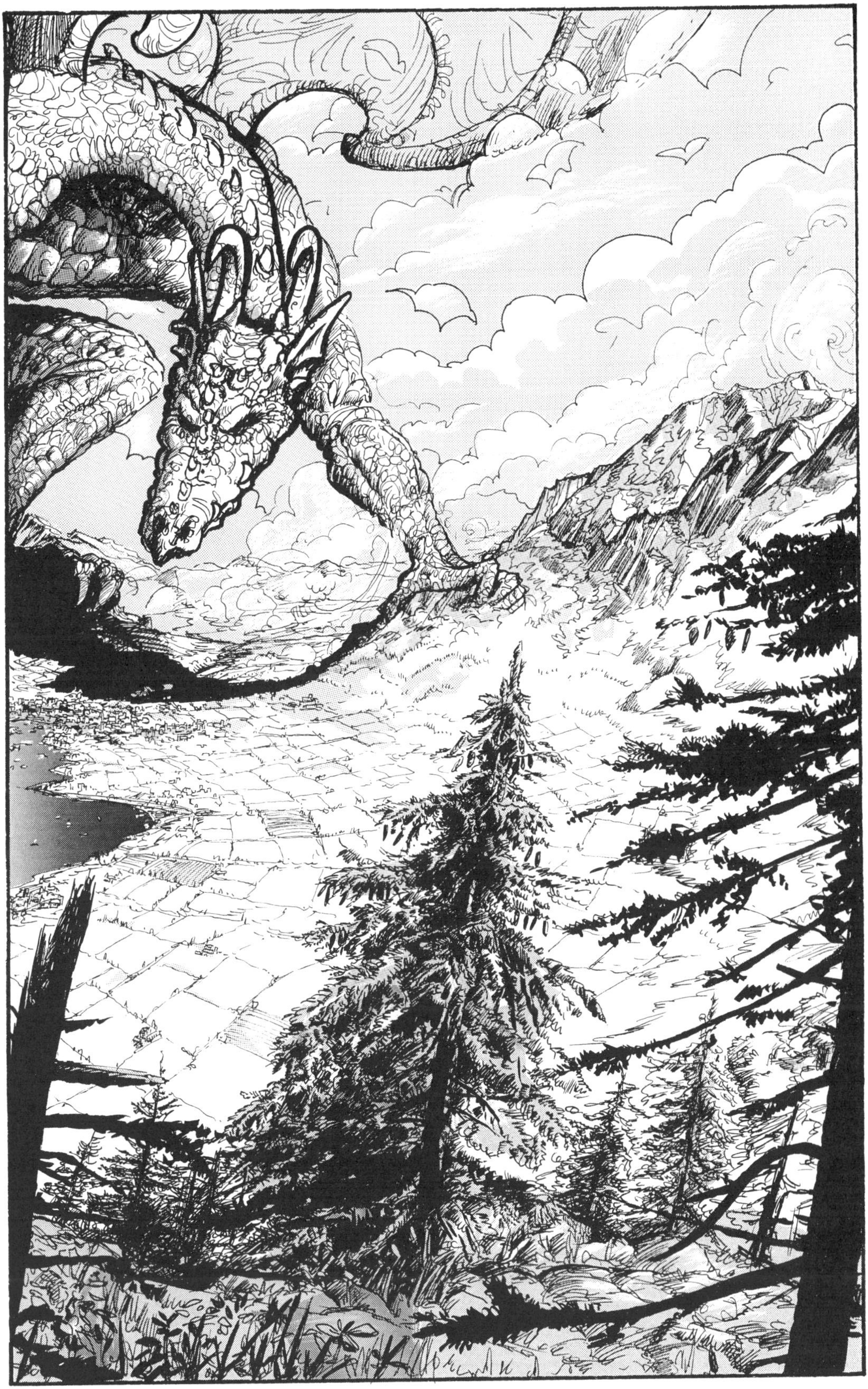

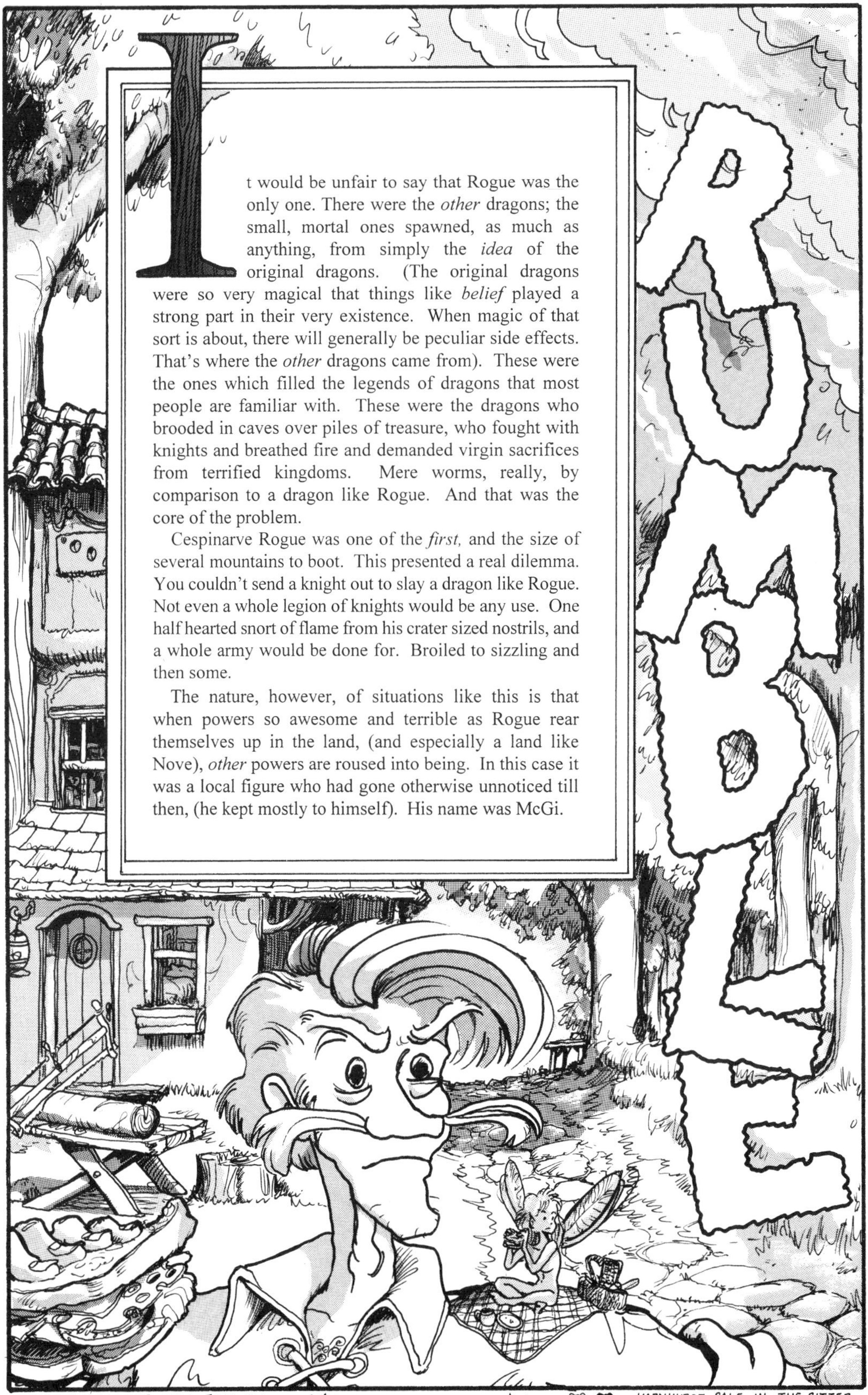
RUMBLE

It would be unfair to say that Rogue was the only one. There were the *other* dragons; the small, mortal ones spawned, as much as anything, from simply the *idea* of the original dragons. (The original dragons were so very magical that things like *belief* played a strong part in their very existence. When magic of that sort is about, there will generally be peculiar side effects. That's where the *other* dragons came from). These were the ones which filled the legends of dragons that most people are familiar with. These were the dragons who brooded in caves over piles of treasure, who fought with knights and breathed fire and demanded virgin sacrifices from terrified kingdoms. Mere worms, really, by comparison to a dragon like Rogue. And that was the core of the problem.

Cespinarve Rogue was one of the *first,* and the size of several mountains to boot. This presented a real dilemma. You couldn't send a knight out to slay a dragon like Rogue. Not even a whole legion of knights would be any use. One half hearted snort of flame from his crater sized nostrils, and a whole army would be done for. Broiled to sizzling and then some.

The nature, however, of situations like this is that when powers so awesome and terrible as Rogue rear themselves up in the land, (and especially a land like Nove), *other* powers are roused into being. In this case it was a local figure who had gone otherwise unnoticed till then, (he kept mostly to himself). His name was McGi.

MORTHALANVE AND JALE RODE ON ... YARNHURST PALE IN THE BITTER DAWN.

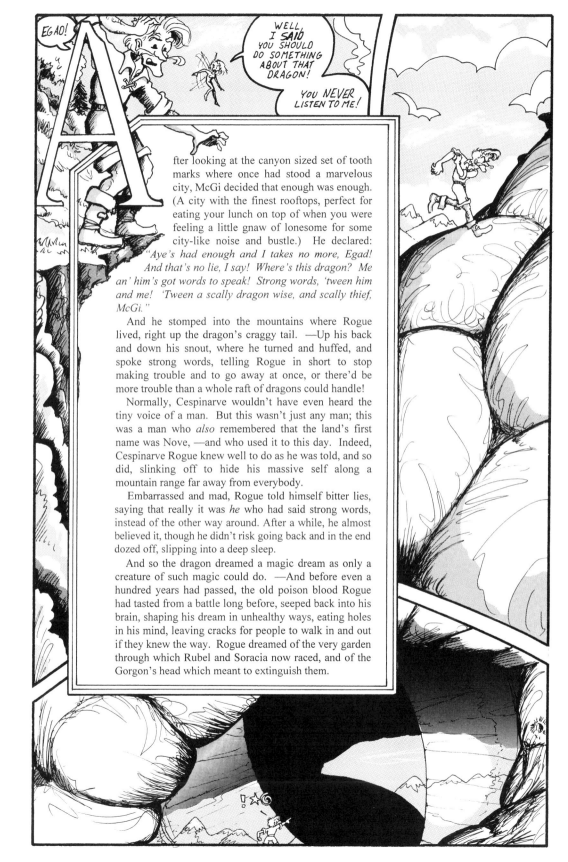

EGAO!

WELL, I **SAID** YOU SHOULD DO SOMETHING ABOUT THAT DRAGON!

YOU NEVER LISTEN TO ME!

After looking at the canyon sized set of tooth marks where once had stood a marvelous city, McGi decided that enough was enough. (A city with the finest rooftops, perfect for eating your lunch on top of when you were feeling a little gnaw of lonesome for some city-like noise and bustle.) He declared:

"Aye's had enough and I takes no more, Egad!
And that's no lie, I say! Where's this dragon? Me
an' him's got words to speak! Strong words, 'tween him
and me! 'Tween a scally dragon wise, and scally thief,
McGi."

And he stomped into the mountains where Rogue lived, right up the dragon's craggy tail. —Up his back and down his snout, where he turned and huffed, and spoke strong words, telling Rogue in short to stop making trouble and to go away at once, or there'd be more trouble than a whole raft of dragons could handle!

Normally, Cespinarve wouldn't have even heard the tiny voice of a man. But this wasn't just any man; this was a man who *also* remembered that the land's first name was Nove, —and who used it to this day. Indeed, Cespinarve Rogue knew well to do as he was told, and so did, slinking off to hide his massive self along a mountain range far away from everybody.

Embarrassed and mad, Rogue told himself bitter lies, saying that really it was *he* who had said strong words, instead of the other way around. After a while, he almost believed it, though he didn't risk going back and in the end dozed off, slipping into a deep sleep.

And so the dragon dreamed a magic dream as only a creature of such magic could do. —And before even a hundred years had passed, the old poison blood Rogue had tasted from a battle long before, seeped back into his brain, shaping his dream in unhealthy ways, eating holes in his mind, leaving cracks for people to walk in and out if they knew the way. Rogue dreamed of the very garden through which Rubel and Soracia now raced, and of the Gorgon's head which meant to extinguish them.

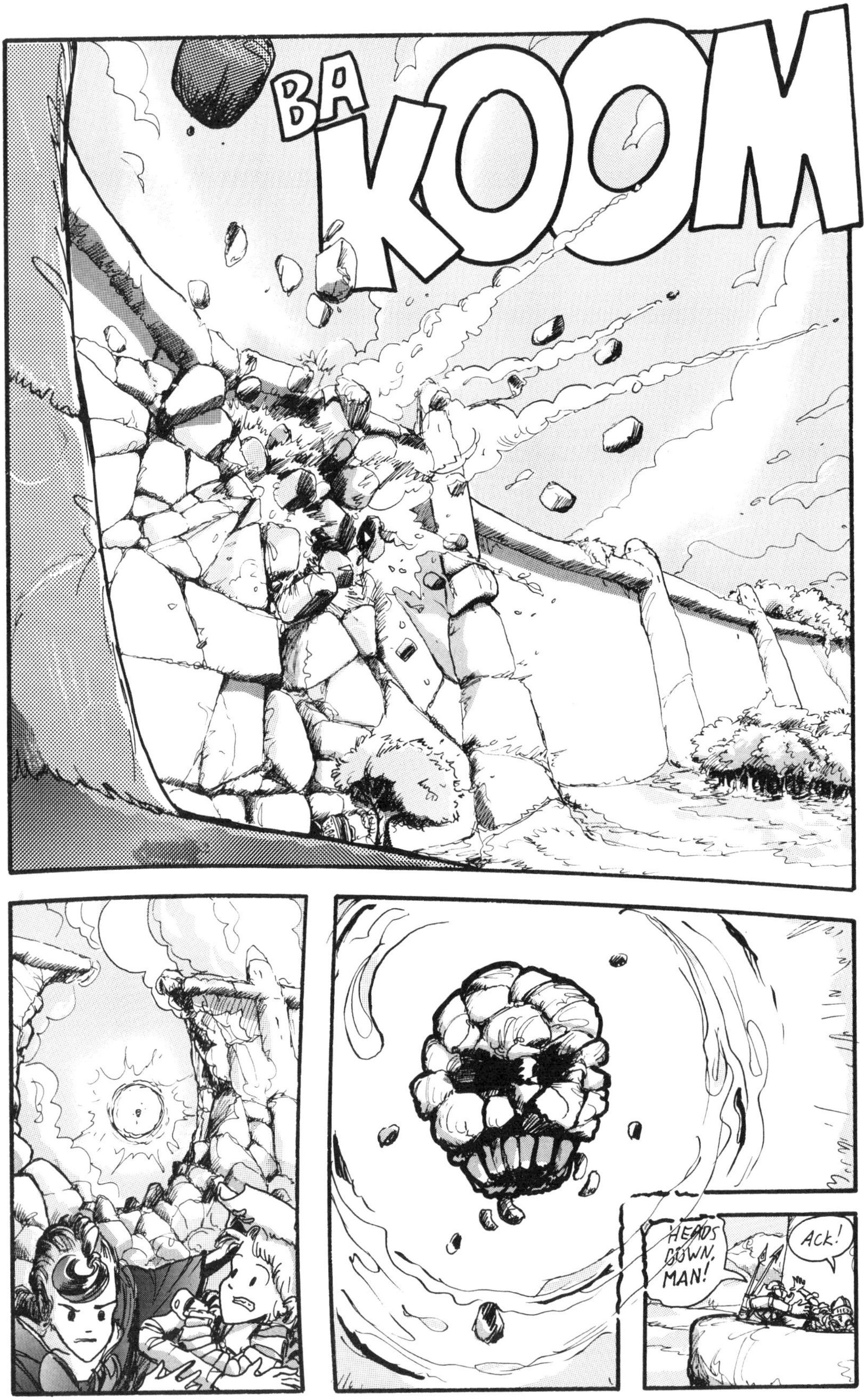
BA
KOOM
HEADS DOWN, MAN!
Ack!

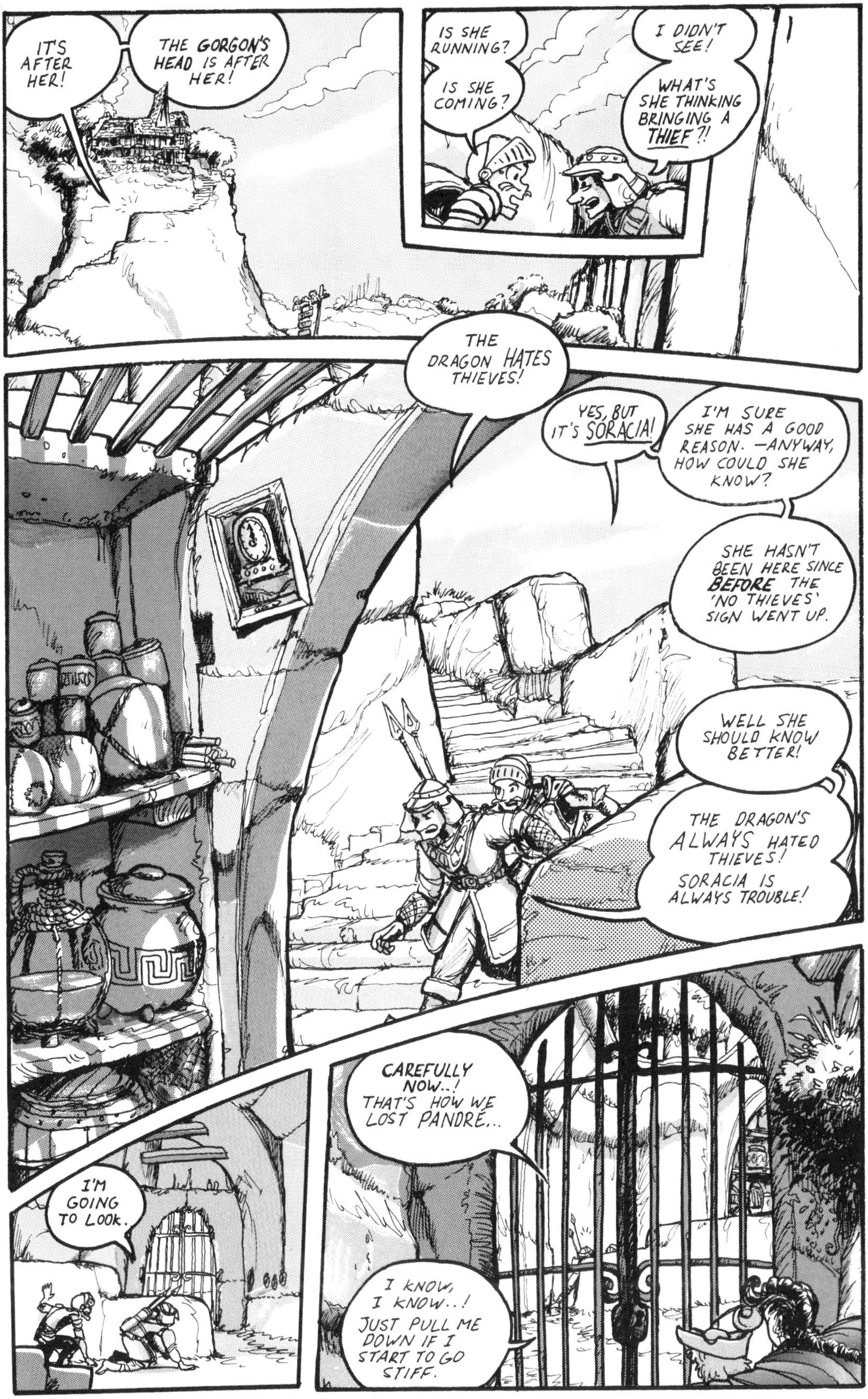
IT'S AFTER HER!
THE GORGON'S HEAD IS AFTER HER!
IS SHE RUNNING?
IS SHE COMING?
I DIDN'T SEE!
WHAT'S SHE THINKING BRINGING A THIEF?!
THE DRAGON HATES THIEVES!
YES, BUT IT'S SORACIA!
I'M SURE SHE HAS A GOOD REASON. —ANYWAY, HOW COULD SHE KNOW?
SHE HASN'T BEEN HERE SINCE BEFORE THE 'NO THIEVES' SIGN WENT UP.
WELL SHE SHOULD KNOW BETTER!
THE DRAGON'S ALWAYS HATED THIEVES!
SORACIA IS ALWAYS TROUBLE!
I'M GOING TO LOOK.
CAREFULLY NOW..! THAT'S HOW WE LOST PANDRE...
I KNOW, I KNOW..! JUST PULL ME DOWN IF I START TO GO STIFF.

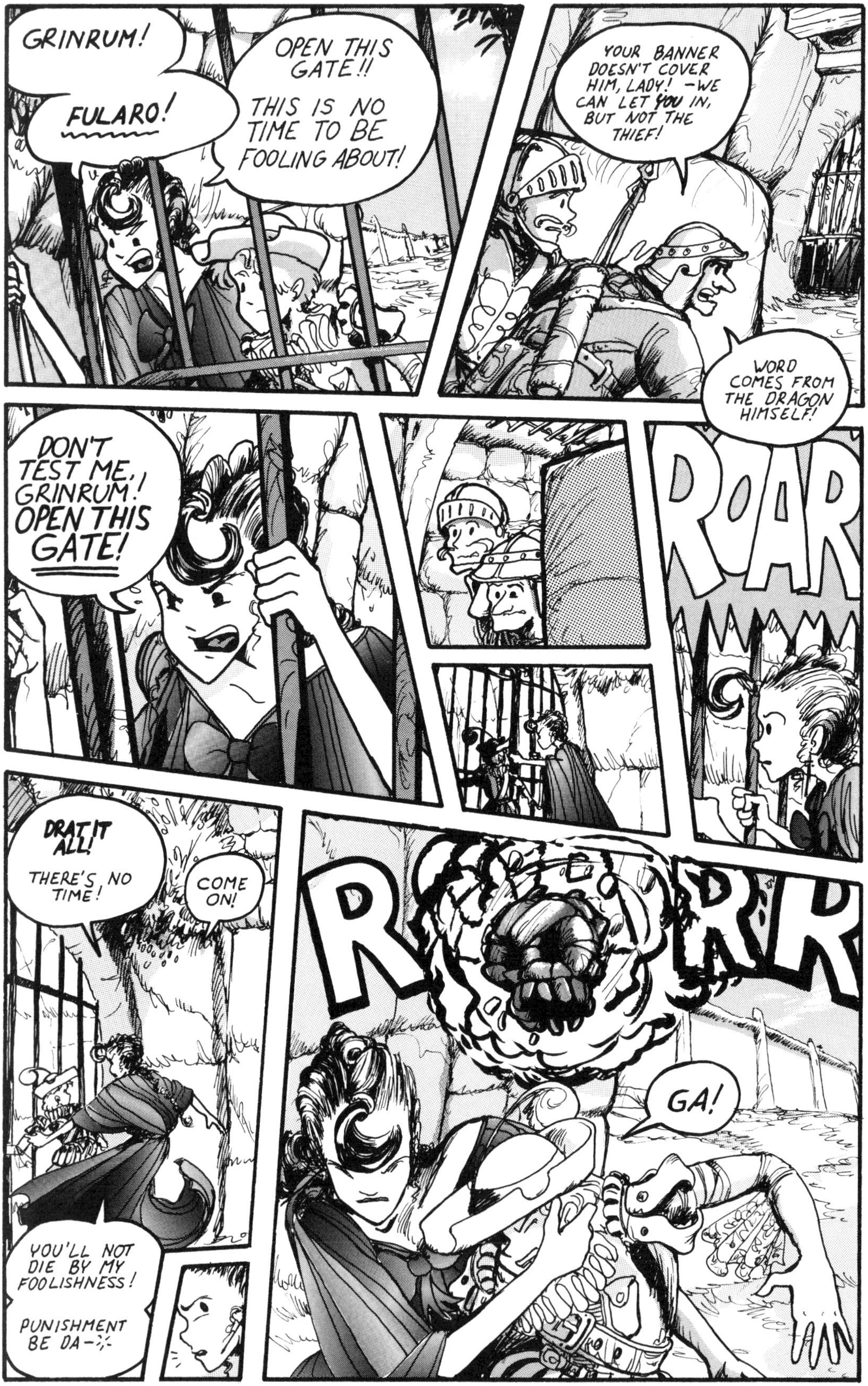

GRINRUM!
FULARO!
OPEN THIS GATE!!
THIS IS NO TIME TO BE FOOLING ABOUT!
YOUR BANNER DOESN'T COVER HIM, LADY! —WE CAN LET YOU IN, BUT NOT THE THIEF!
WORD COMES FROM THE DRAGON HIMSELF!
DON'T TEST ME, GRINRUM! OPEN THIS GATE!
ROAR
DRAT IT ALL!
THERE'S NO TIME!
COME ON!
YOU'LL NOT DIE BY MY FOOLISHNESS!
PUNISHMENT BE DA—
ROARR
GA!

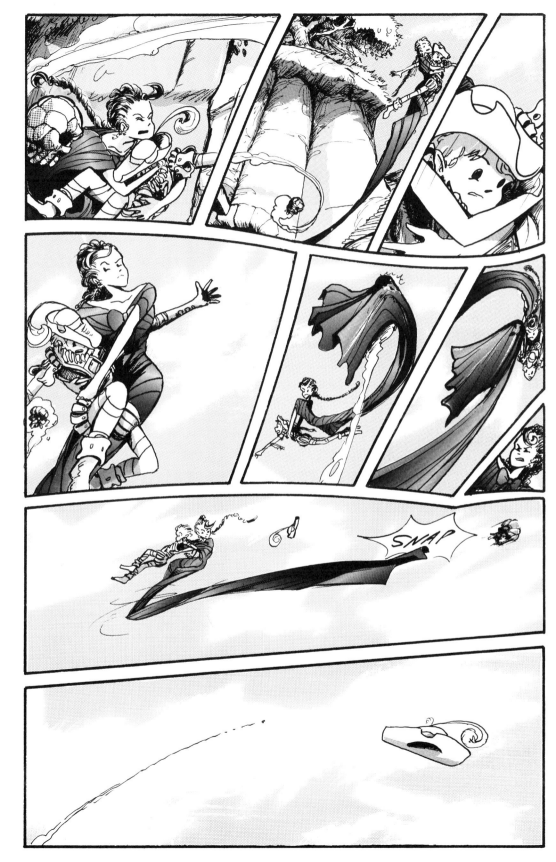

SNAP

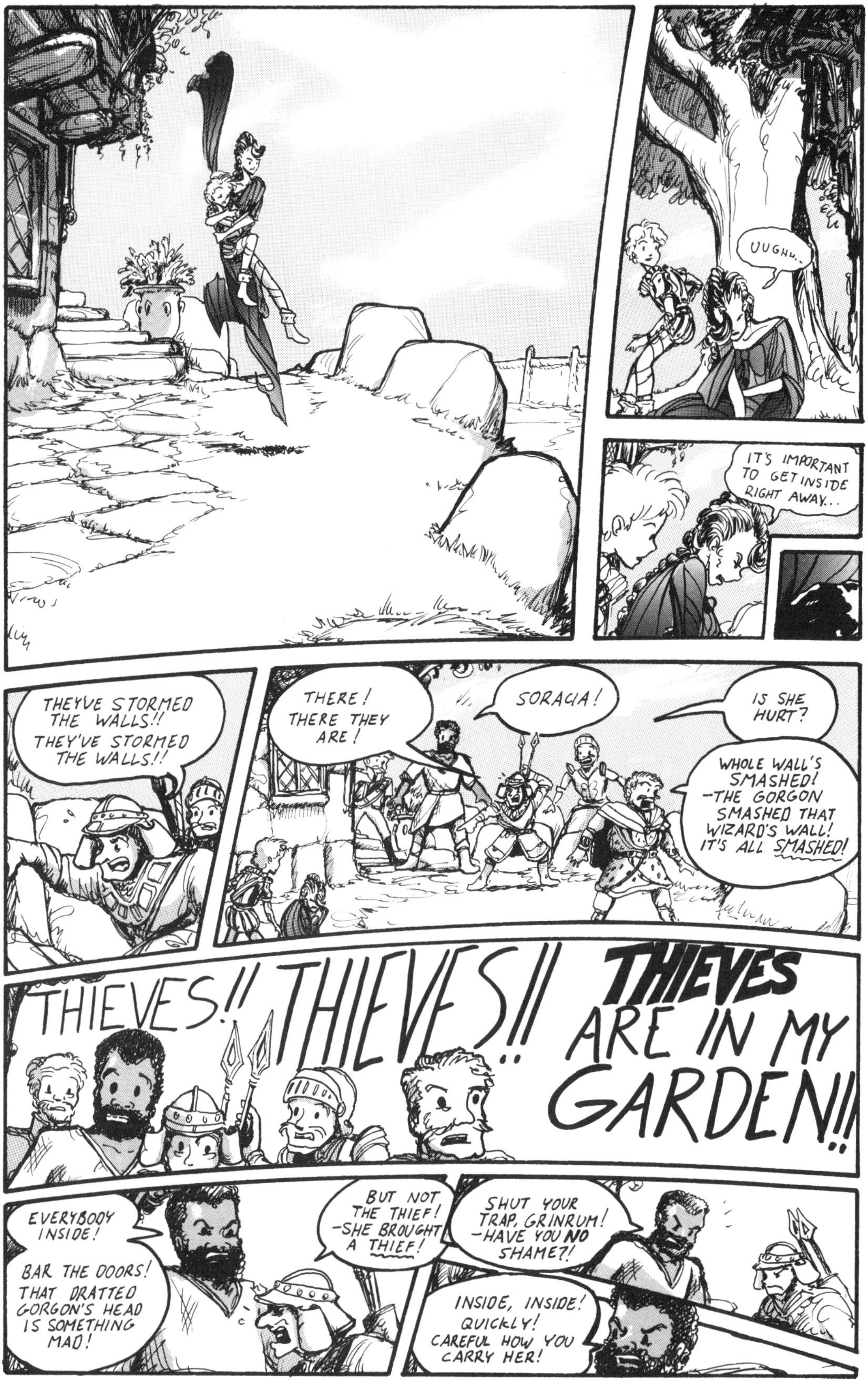
UUGHH..
IT'S IMPORTANT TO GET INSIDE RIGHT AWAY...
THEY'VE STORMED THE WALLS!! THEY'VE STORMED THE WALLS!!
THERE! THERE THEY ARE!
SORACIA!
IS SHE HURT?
WHOLE WALL'S SMASHED! -THE GORGON SMASHED THAT WIZARD'S WALL! IT'S ALL SMASHED!
THIEVES!! THIEVES!! THIEVES ARE IN MY GARDEN!!
EVERYBODY INSIDE!
BAR THE DOORS! THAT DRATTED GORGON'S HEAD IS SOMETHING MAD!
BUT NOT THE THIEF! -SHE BROUGHT A THIEF!
SHUT YOUR TRAP, GRINRUM! -HAVE YOU NO SHAME?!
INSIDE, INSIDE! QUICKLY! CAREFUL HOW YOU CARRY HER!

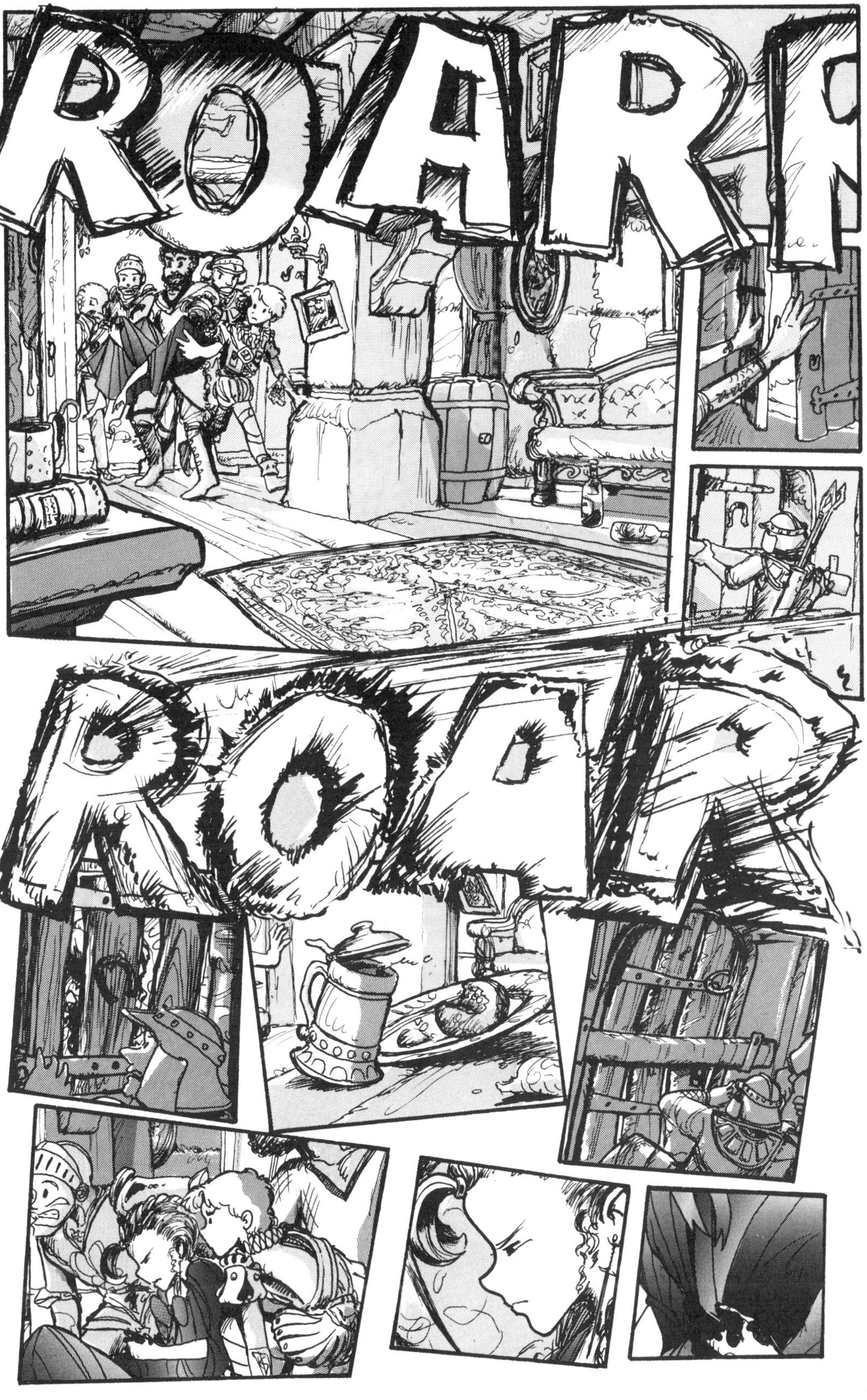
ROARR
ROAR

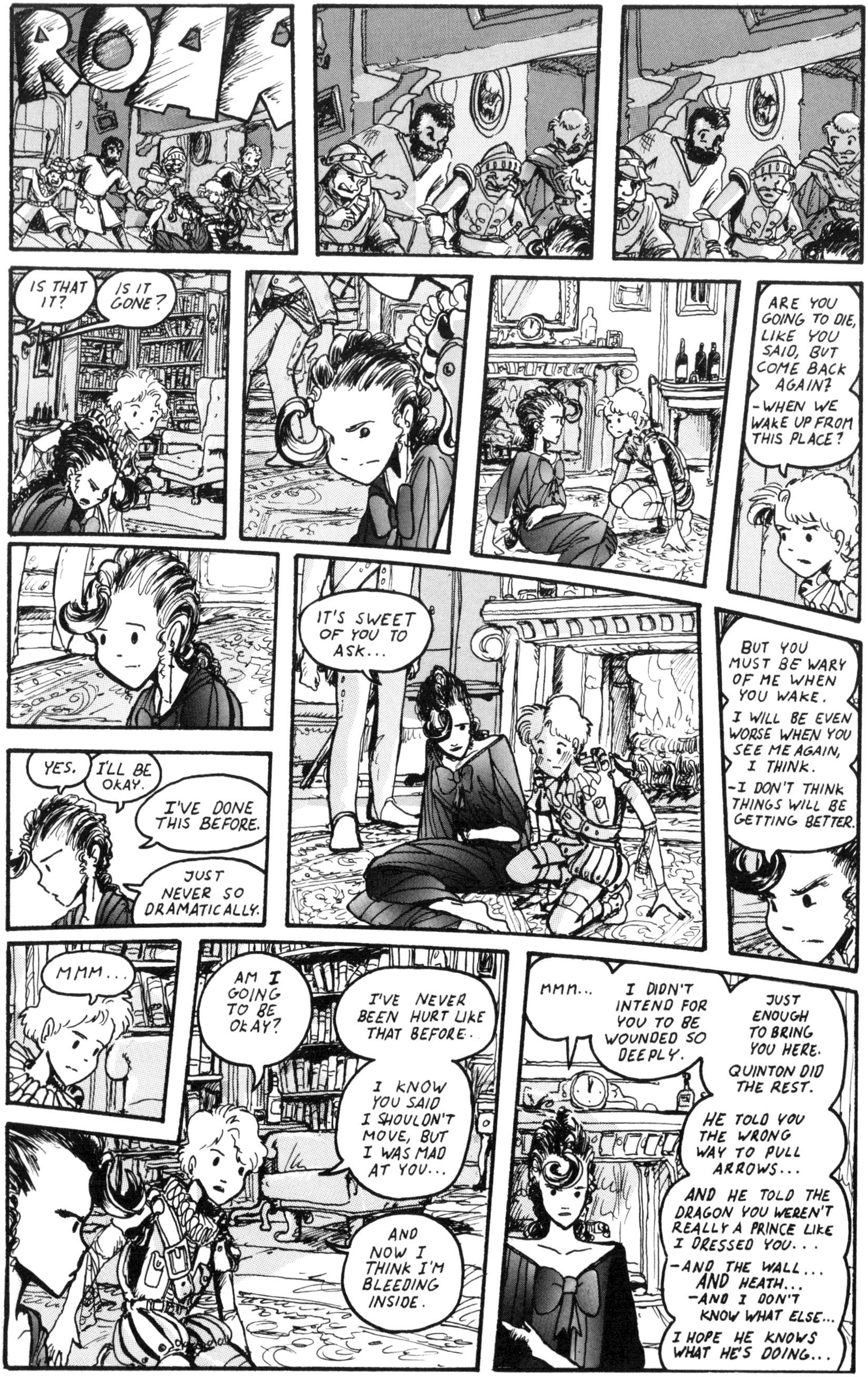
ROA
IS THAT IT?
IS IT GONE?
ARE YOU GOING TO DIE, LIKE YOU SAID, BUT COME BACK AGAIN?
-WHEN WE WAKE UP FROM THIS PLACE?
IT'S SWEET OF YOU TO ASK...
BUT YOU MUST BE WARY OF ME WHEN YOU WAKE.
I WILL BE EVEN WORSE WHEN YOU SEE ME AGAIN, I THINK.
-I DON'T THINK THINGS WILL BE GETTING BETTER.
YES.
I'LL BE OKAY.
I'VE DONE THIS BEFORE.
JUST NEVER SO DRAMATICALLY.
MMM...
AM I GOING TO BE OKAY?
I'VE NEVER BEEN HURT LIKE THAT BEFORE.
I KNOW YOU SAID I SHOULDN'T MOVE, BUT I WAS MAD AT YOU...
AND NOW I THINK I'M BLEEDING INSIDE.
MMM...
I DIDN'T INTEND FOR YOU TO BE WOUNDED SO DEEPLY.
JUST ENOUGH TO BRING YOU HERE.
QUINTON DID THE REST.
HE TOLD YOU THE WRONG WAY TO PULL ARROWS...
AND HE TOLD THE DRAGON YOU WEREN'T REALLY A PRINCE LIKE I DRESSED YOU...
-AND THE WALL...
AND HEATH...
-AND I DON'T KNOW WHAT ELSE...
I HOPE HE KNOWS WHAT HE'S DOING...

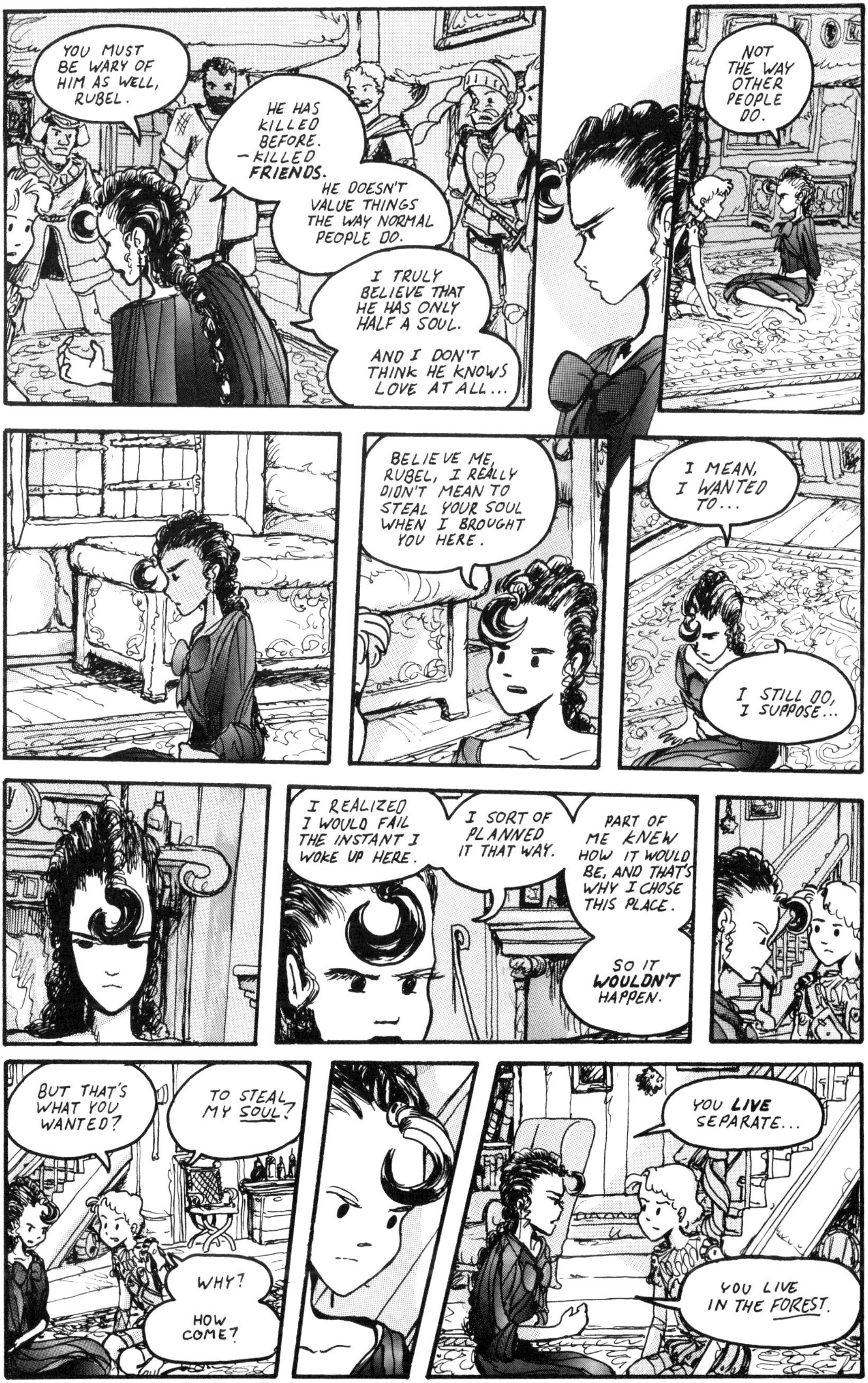
YOU MUST BE WARY OF HIM AS WELL, RUBEL.
HE HAS KILLED BEFORE. —KILLED **FRIENDS.**
HE DOESN'T VALUE THINGS THE WAY NORMAL PEOPLE DO.
I TRULY BELIEVE THAT HE HAS ONLY HALF A SOUL.
AND I DON'T THINK HE KNOWS LOVE AT ALL...
NOT THE WAY OTHER PEOPLE DO.
BELIEVE ME, RUBEL, I REALLY DIDN'T MEAN TO STEAL YOUR SOUL WHEN I BROUGHT YOU HERE.
I MEAN, I WANTED TO...
I STILL DO, I SUPPOSE...
I REALIZED I WOULD FAIL THE INSTANT I WOKE UP HERE.
I SORT OF PLANNED IT THAT WAY.
PART OF ME KNEW HOW IT WOULD BE, AND THAT'S WHY I CHOSE THIS PLACE.
SO IT **WOULDN'T** HAPPEN.
BUT THAT'S WHAT YOU WANTED?
TO STEAL MY SOUL?
WHY?
HOW COME?
YOU **LIVE** SEPARATE...
YOU LIVE IN THE FOREST.

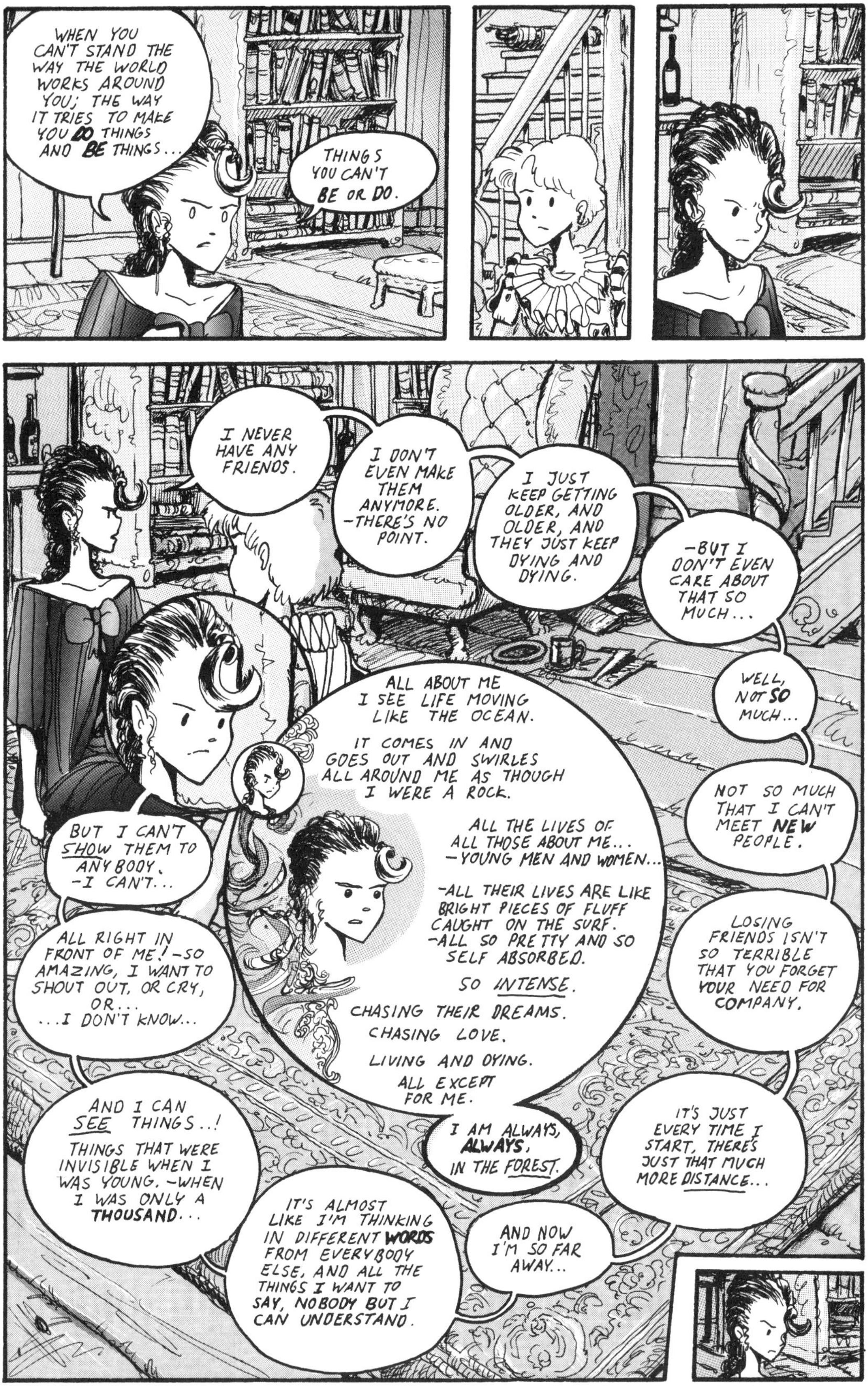
WHEN YOU CAN'T STAND THE WAY THE WORLD WORKS AROUND YOU; THE WAY IT TRIES TO MAKE YOU **DO** THINGS AND **BE** THINGS...
THINGS YOU CAN'T **BE** OR **DO**.
I NEVER HAVE ANY FRIENDS.
I DON'T EVEN MAKE THEM ANYMORE. -THERE'S NO POINT.
I JUST KEEP GETTING OLDER, AND OLDER, AND THEY JUST KEEP DYING AND DYING.
-BUT I DON'T EVEN CARE ABOUT THAT SO MUCH...
WELL, NOT **SO** MUCH...
NOT SO MUCH THAT I CAN'T MEET **NEW** PEOPLE.
LOSING FRIENDS ISN'T SO TERRIBLE THAT YOU FORGET **YOUR** NEED FOR **COMPANY**.
IT'S JUST EVERY TIME I START, THERE'S JUST THAT MUCH MORE DISTANCE...
AND NOW I'M SO FAR AWAY...
ALL ABOUT ME I SEE LIFE MOVING LIKE THE OCEAN.
IT COMES IN AND GOES OUT AND SWIRLES ALL AROUND ME AS THOUGH I WERE A ROCK.
ALL THE LIVES OF ALL THOSE ABOUT ME... -YOUNG MEN AND WOMEN...
-ALL THEIR LIVES ARE LIKE BRIGHT PIECES OF FLUFF CAUGHT ON THE SURF. -ALL SO PRETTY AND SO SELF ABSORBED.
SO INTENSE.
CHASING THEIR DREAMS.
CHASING LOVE.
LIVING AND DYING.
ALL EXCEPT FOR ME.
I AM ALWAYS, **ALWAYS**, IN THE FOREST.
BUT I CAN'T SHOW THEM TO ANYBODY. -I CAN'T...
ALL RIGHT IN FRONT OF ME! -SO AMAZING, I WANT TO SHOUT OUT, OR CRY, OR... ...I DON'T KNOW...
AND I CAN SEE THINGS..!
THINGS THAT WERE INVISIBLE WHEN I WAS YOUNG. -WHEN I WAS ONLY A **THOUSAND**...
IT'S ALMOST LIKE I'M THINKING IN DIFFERENT **WORDS** FROM EVERYBODY ELSE, AND ALL THE THINGS I WANT TO SAY, NOBODY BUT I CAN UNDERSTAND.

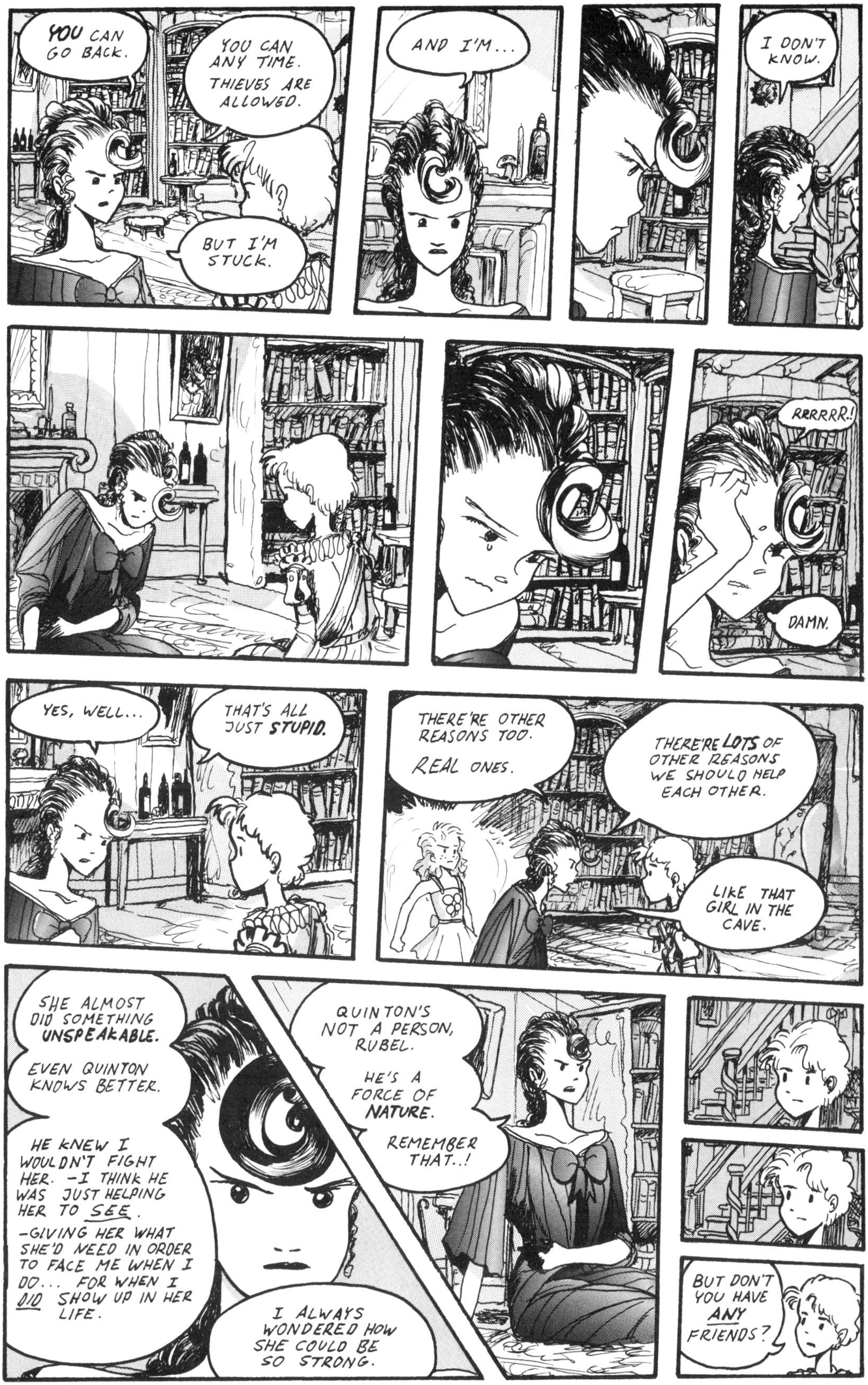

YOU CAN GO BACK.
YOU CAN ANY TIME. THIEVES ARE ALLOWED.
BUT I'M STUCK.
AND I'M...
I DON'T KNOW.
RRRRRR.!
DAMN.
YES, WELL...
THAT'S ALL JUST STUPID.
THERE'RE OTHER REASONS TOO. REAL ONES.
THERE'RE LOTS OF OTHER REASONS WE SHOULD HELP EACH OTHER.
LIKE THAT GIRL IN THE CAVE.
SHE ALMOST DID SOMETHING UNSPEAKABLE. EVEN QUINTON KNOWS BETTER.
HE KNEW I WOULDN'T FIGHT HER. -I THINK HE WAS JUST HELPING HER TO SEE. -GIVING HER WHAT SHE'D NEED IN ORDER TO FACE ME WHEN I DO... FOR WHEN I DID SHOW UP IN HER LIFE.
I ALWAYS WONDERED HOW SHE COULD BE SO STRONG.
QUINTON'S NOT A PERSON, RUBEL. HE'S A FORCE OF NATURE. REMEMBER THAT..!
BUT DON'T YOU HAVE ANY FRIENDS?

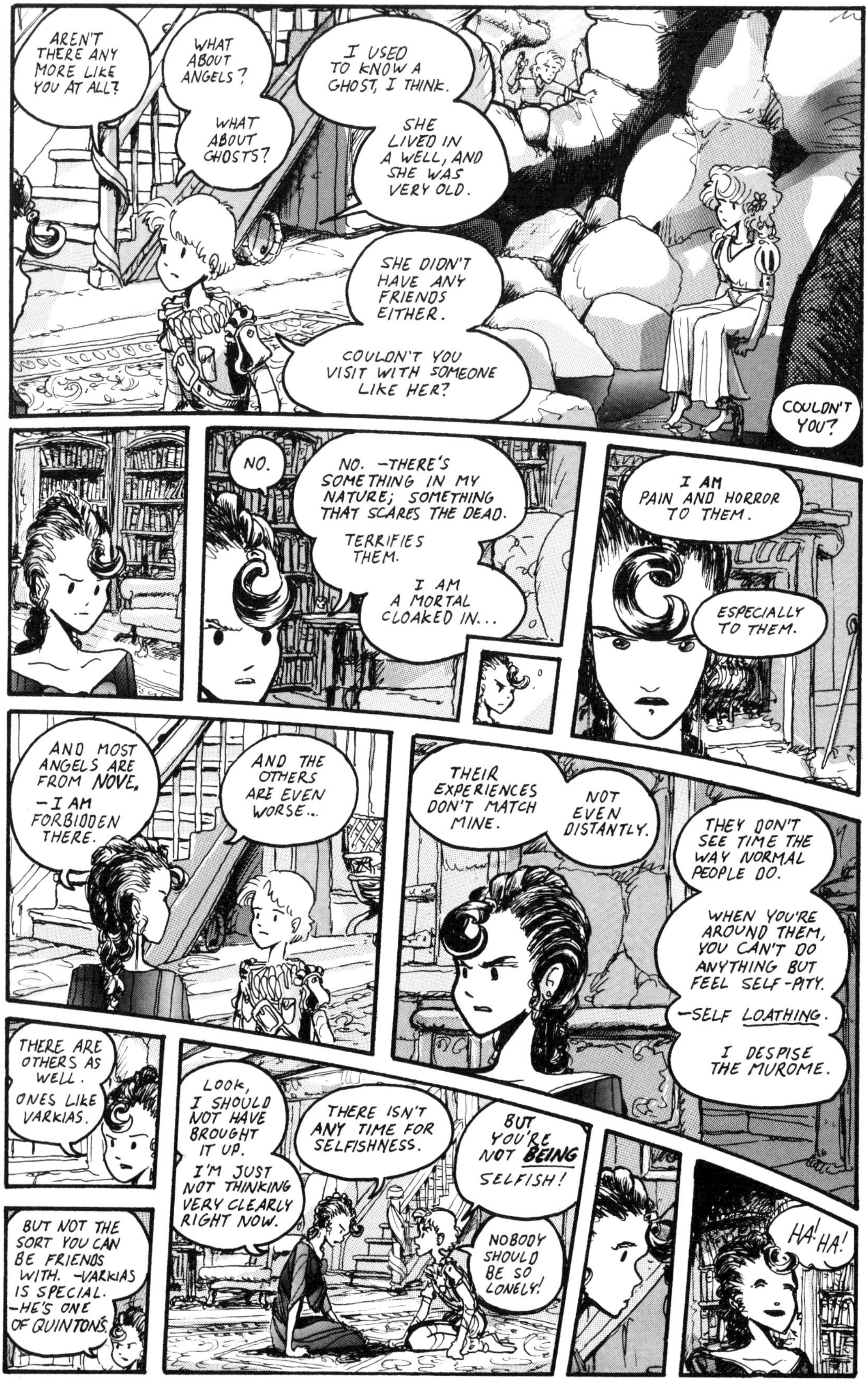
AREN'T THERE ANY MORE LIKE YOU AT ALL?
WHAT ABOUT ANGELS?
WHAT ABOUT GHOSTS?
I USED TO KNOW A GHOST, I THINK.
SHE LIVED IN A WELL, AND SHE WAS VERY OLD.
SHE DIDN'T HAVE ANY FRIENDS EITHER.
COULDN'T YOU VISIT WITH SOMEONE LIKE HER?
COULDN'T YOU?
NO.
NO. —THERE'S SOMETHING IN MY NATURE; SOMETHING THAT SCARES THE DEAD.
TERRIFIES THEM.
I AM A MORTAL CLOAKED IN...
I AM PAIN AND HORROR TO THEM.
ESPECIALLY TO THEM.
AND MOST ANGELS ARE FROM NOVE. —I AM FORBIDDEN THERE.
AND THE OTHERS ARE EVEN WORSE...
THEIR EXPERIENCES DON'T MATCH MINE.
NOT EVEN DISTANTLY.
THEY DON'T SEE TIME THE WAY NORMAL PEOPLE DO.
WHEN YOU'RE AROUND THEM, YOU CAN'T DO ANYTHING BUT FEEL SELF-PITY.
—SELF LOATHING.
I DESPISE THE MUROME.
THERE ARE OTHERS AS WELL.
ONES LIKE VARKIAS.
BUT NOT THE SORT YOU CAN BE FRIENDS WITH. —VARKIAS IS SPECIAL. —HE'S ONE OF QUINTON'S.
LOOK, I SHOULD NOT HAVE BROUGHT IT UP.
I'M JUST NOT THINKING VERY CLEARLY RIGHT NOW.
THERE ISN'T ANY TIME FOR SELFISHNESS.
BUT YOU'RE NOT BEING SELFISH!
NOBODY SHOULD BE SO LONELY!
HA! HA!

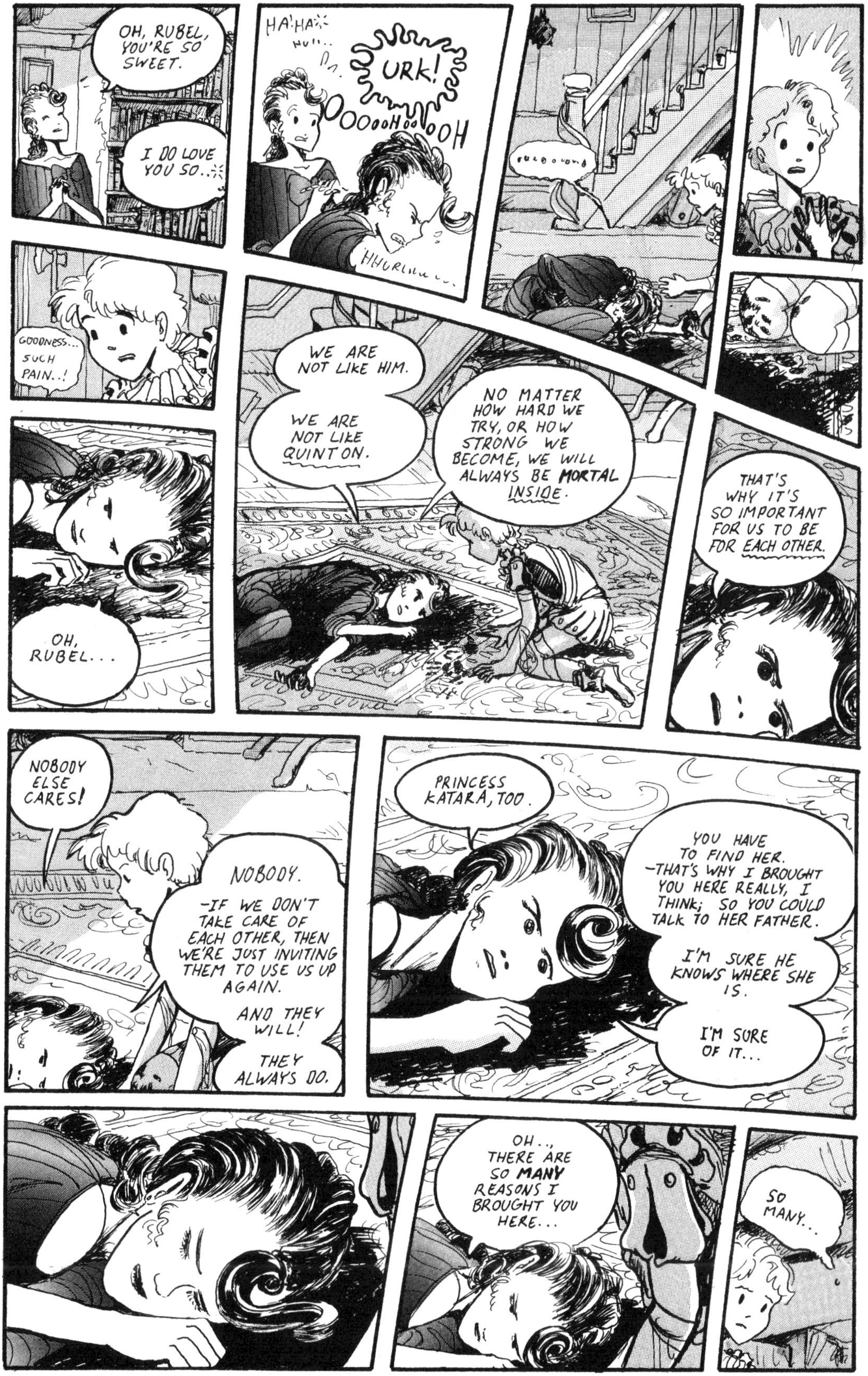

OH, RUBEL, YOU'RE SO SWEET.
I DO LOVE YOU SO..
HA HA
URK!
OOOOOHOOOOH
GOODNESS... SUCH PAIN..!
WE ARE NOT LIKE HIM.
WE ARE NOT LIKE QUINTON.
NO MATTER HOW HARD WE TRY, OR HOW STRONG WE BECOME, WE WILL ALWAYS BE MORTAL INSIDE.
OH, RUBEL...
THAT'S WHY IT'S SO IMPORTANT FOR US TO BE FOR EACH OTHER.
NOBODY ELSE CARES!
NOBODY.
-IF WE DON'T TAKE CARE OF EACH OTHER, THEN WE'RE JUST INVITING THEM TO USE US UP AGAIN.
AND THEY WILL!
THEY ALWAYS DO.
PRINCESS KATARA, TOO.
YOU HAVE TO FIND HER. -THAT'S WHY I BROUGHT YOU HERE REALLY, I THINK; SO YOU COULD TALK TO HER FATHER.
I'M SURE HE KNOWS WHERE SHE IS.
I'M SURE OF IT...
OH.., THERE ARE SO MANY REASONS I BROUGHT YOU HERE...
SO MANY...

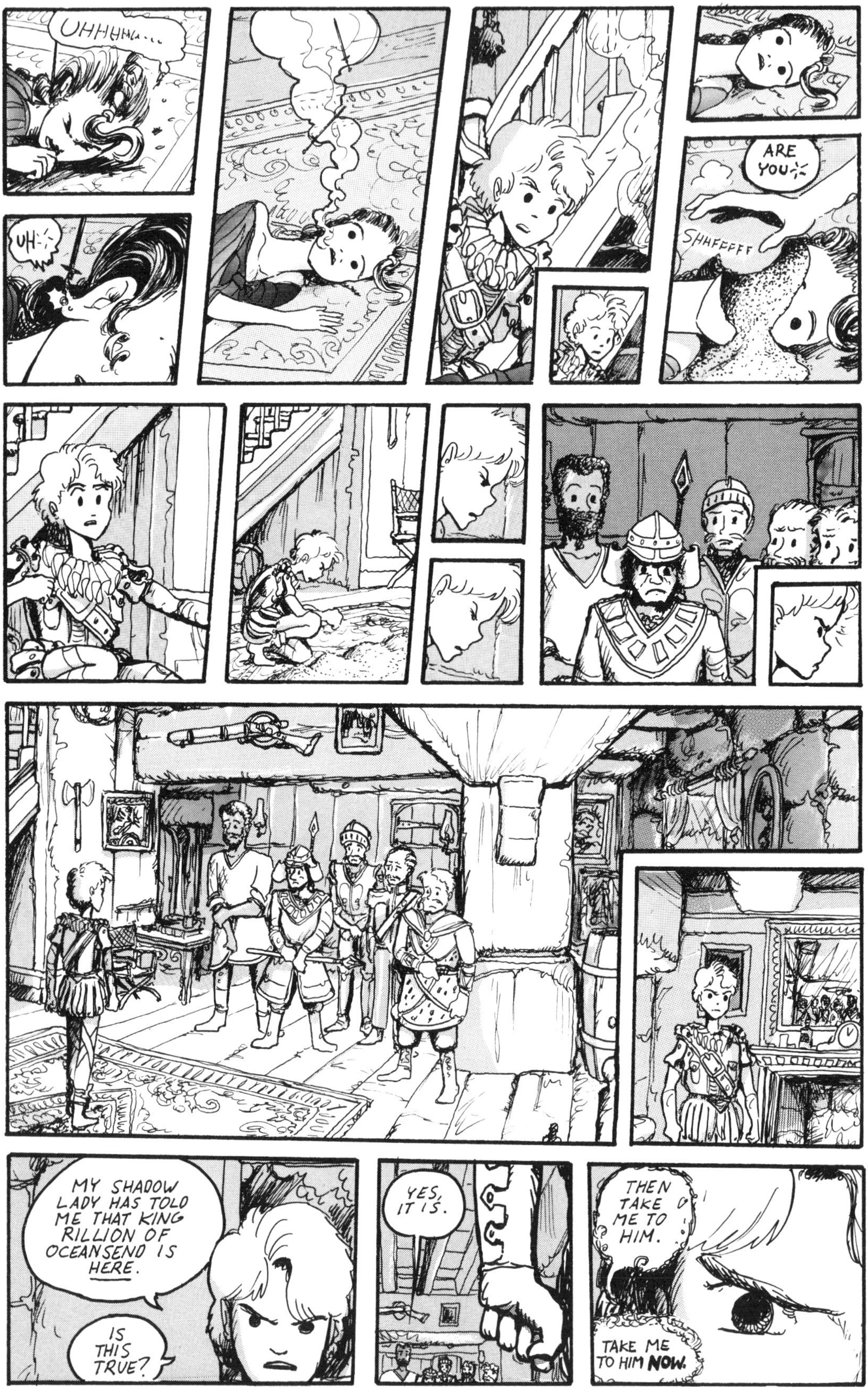
UHHHMM...
UH-!
ARE YOU-!
SHHFFFFF
MY SHADOW LADY HAS TOLD ME THAT KING RILLION OF OCEANSEND IS HERE.
IS THIS TRUE?
YES, IT IS.
THEN TAKE ME TO HIM.
TAKE ME TO HIM NOW.

Chapter 16

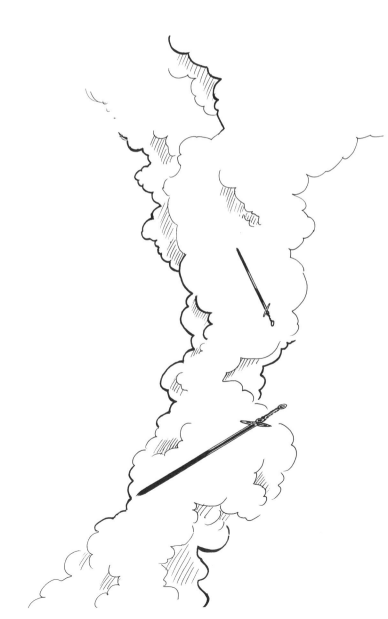

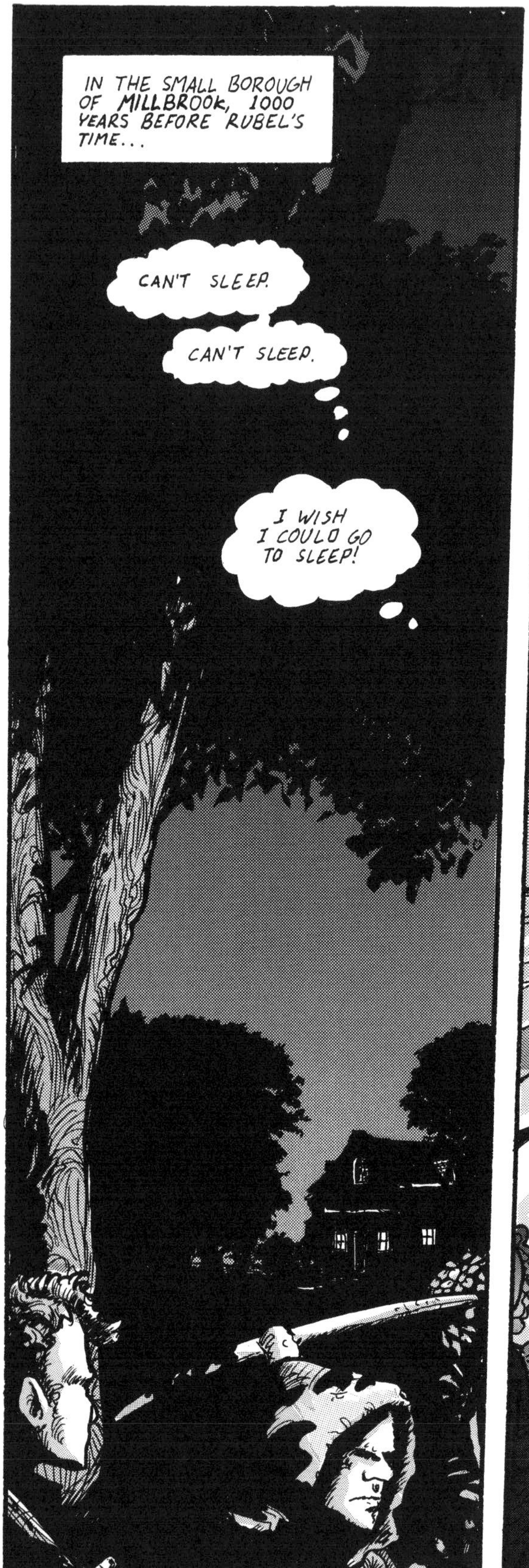
IN THE SMALL BOROUGH OF MILLBROOK, 1000 YEARS BEFORE RUBEL'S TIME...
CAN'T SLEEP.
CAN'T SLEEP.
I WISH I COULD GO TO SLEEP!

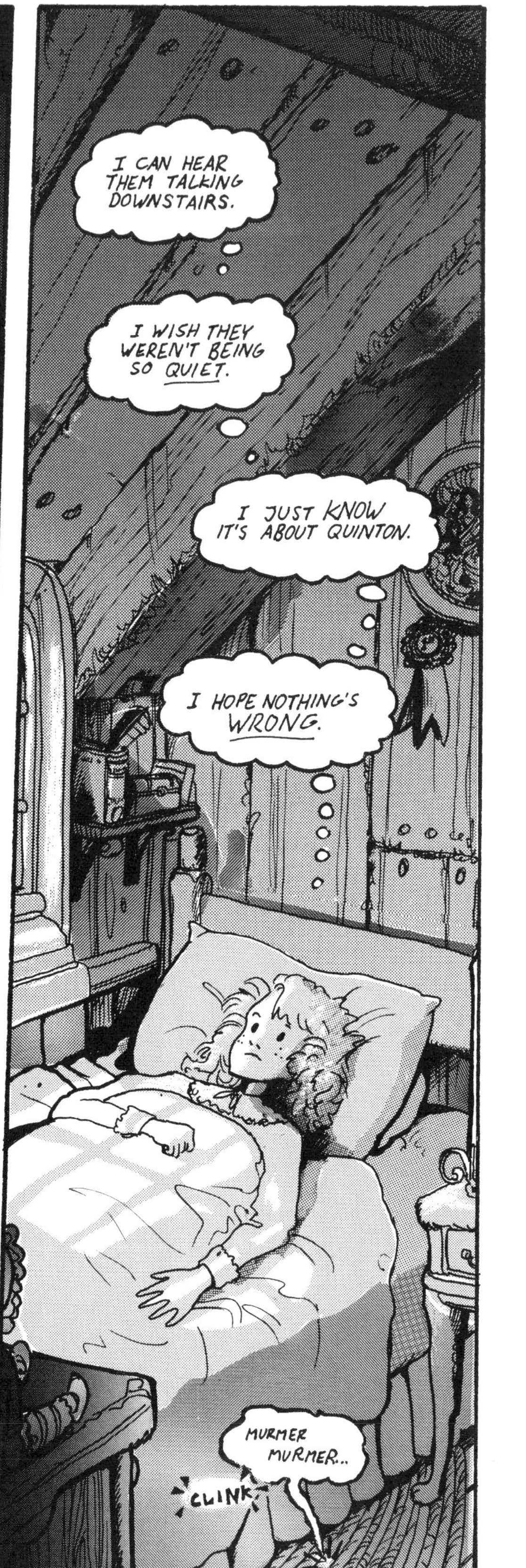
I CAN HEAR THEM TALKING DOWNSTAIRS.
I WISH THEY WEREN'T BEING SO QUIET.
I JUST KNOW IT'S ABOUT QUINTON.
I HOPE NOTHING'S WRONG.
MURMER MURMER..
CLINK

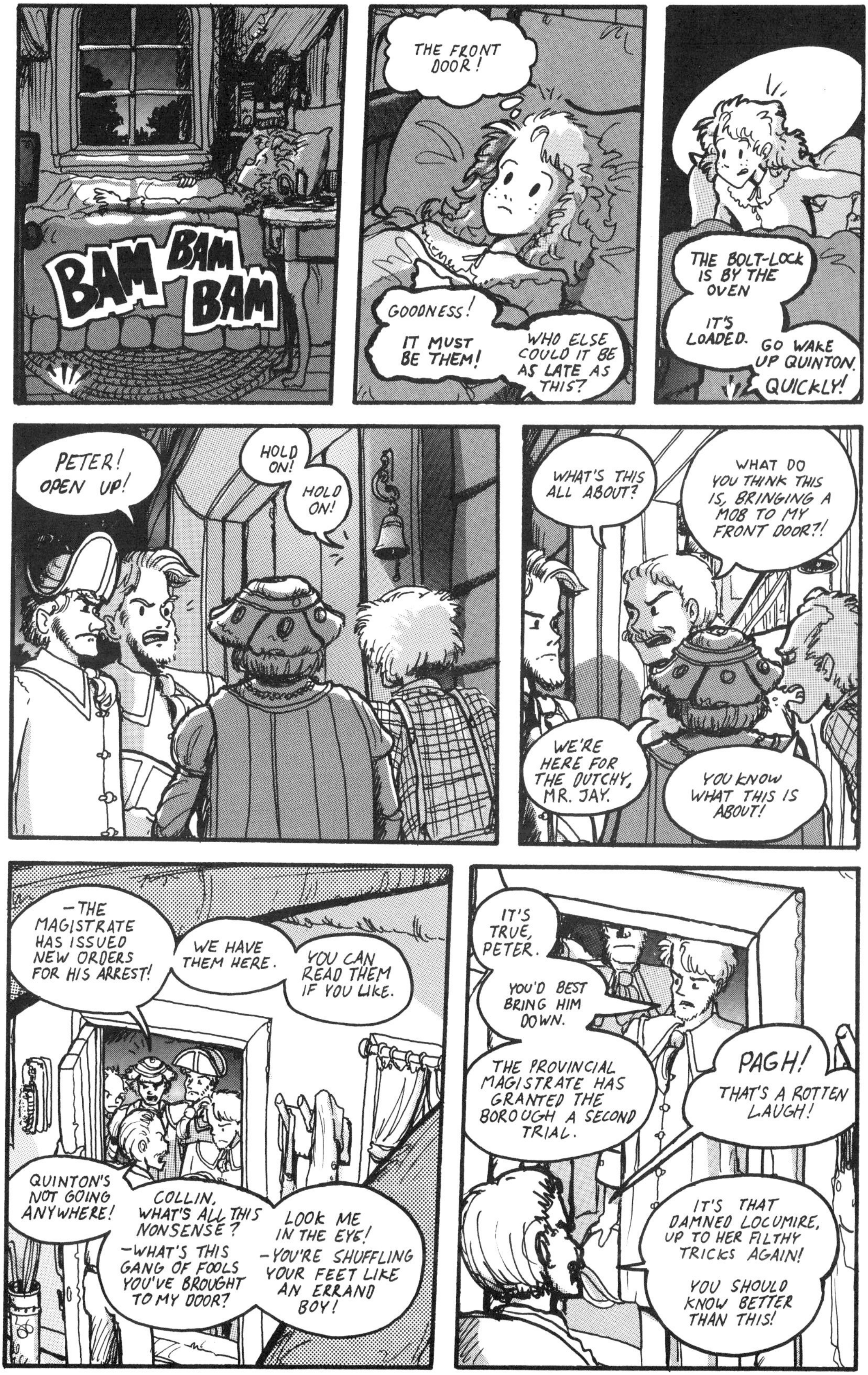
BAM BAM BAM BAM
THE FRONT DOOR!
GOODNESS! IT MUST BE THEM!
WHO ELSE COULD IT BE AS LATE AS THIS?
THE BOLT-LOCK IS BY THE OVEN
IT'S LOADED.
GO WAKE UP QUINTON. QUICKLY!
PETER! OPEN UP!
HOLD ON!
HOLD ON!
WHAT'S THIS ALL ABOUT?
WHAT DO YOU THINK THIS IS, BRINGING A MOB TO MY FRONT DOOR?!
WE'RE HERE FOR THE DUTCHY, MR. JAY.
YOU KNOW WHAT THIS IS ABOUT!
–THE MAGISTRATE HAS ISSUED NEW ORDERS FOR HIS ARREST!
WE HAVE THEM HERE.
YOU CAN READ THEM IF YOU LIKE.
QUINTON'S NOT GOING ANYWHERE!
COLLIN, WHAT'S ALL THIS NONSENSE? –WHAT'S THIS GANG OF FOOLS YOU'VE BROUGHT TO MY DOOR?
LOOK ME IN THE EYE! –YOU'RE SHUFFLING YOUR FEET LIKE AN ERRAND BOY!
IT'S TRUE, PETER.
YOU'D BEST BRING HIM DOWN.
THE PROVINCIAL MAGISTRATE HAS GRANTED THE BOROUGH A SECOND TRIAL.
PAGH! THAT'S A ROTTEN LAUGH!
IT'S THAT DAMNED LOCUMIRE, UP TO HER FILTHY TRICKS AGAIN!
YOU SHOULD KNOW BETTER THAN THIS!

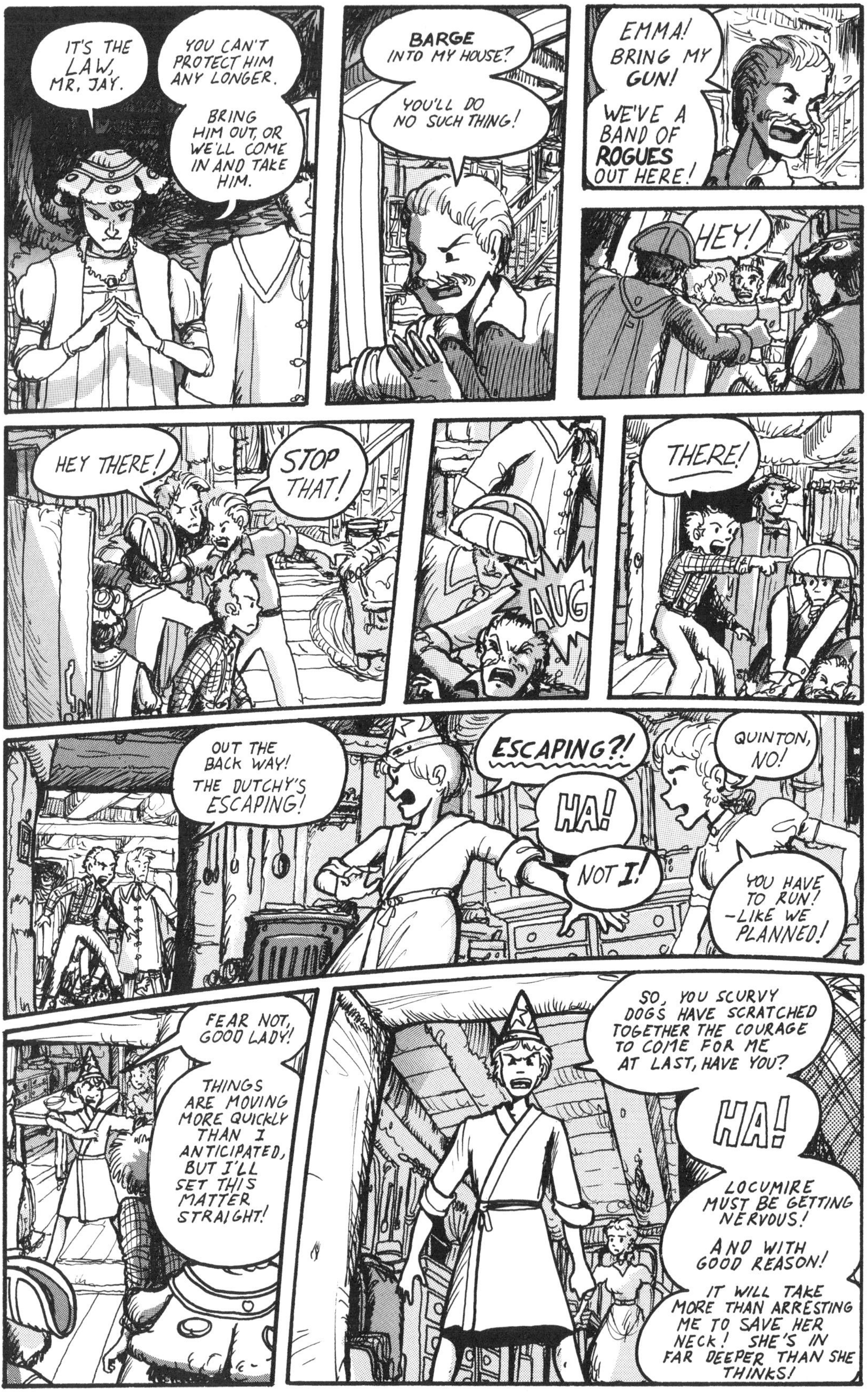
IT'S THE LAW, MR. JAY.
YOU CAN'T PROTECT HIM ANY LONGER.
BRING HIM OUT, OR WE'LL COME IN AND TAKE HIM.
BARGE INTO MY HOUSE?
YOU'LL DO NO SUCH THING!
EMMA! BRING MY GUN!
WE'VE A BAND OF ROGUES OUT HERE!
HEY!
HEY THERE!
STOP THAT!
AUG
THERE!
OUT THE BACK WAY!
THE DUTCHY'S ESCAPING!
ESCAPING?!
HA!
NOT I!
QUINTON, NO!
YOU HAVE TO RUN! -LIKE WE PLANNED!
FEAR NOT, GOOD LADY!
THINGS ARE MOVING MORE QUICKLY THAN I ANTICIPATED, BUT I'LL SET THIS MATTER STRAIGHT!
SO, YOU SCURVY DOGS HAVE SCRATCHED TOGETHER THE COURAGE TO COME FOR ME AT LAST, HAVE YOU?
HA!
LOCUMIRE MUST BE GETTING NERVOUS!
AND WITH GOOD REASON!
IT WILL TAKE MORE THAN ARRESTING ME TO SAVE HER NECK! SHE'S IN FAR DEEPER THAN SHE THINKS!

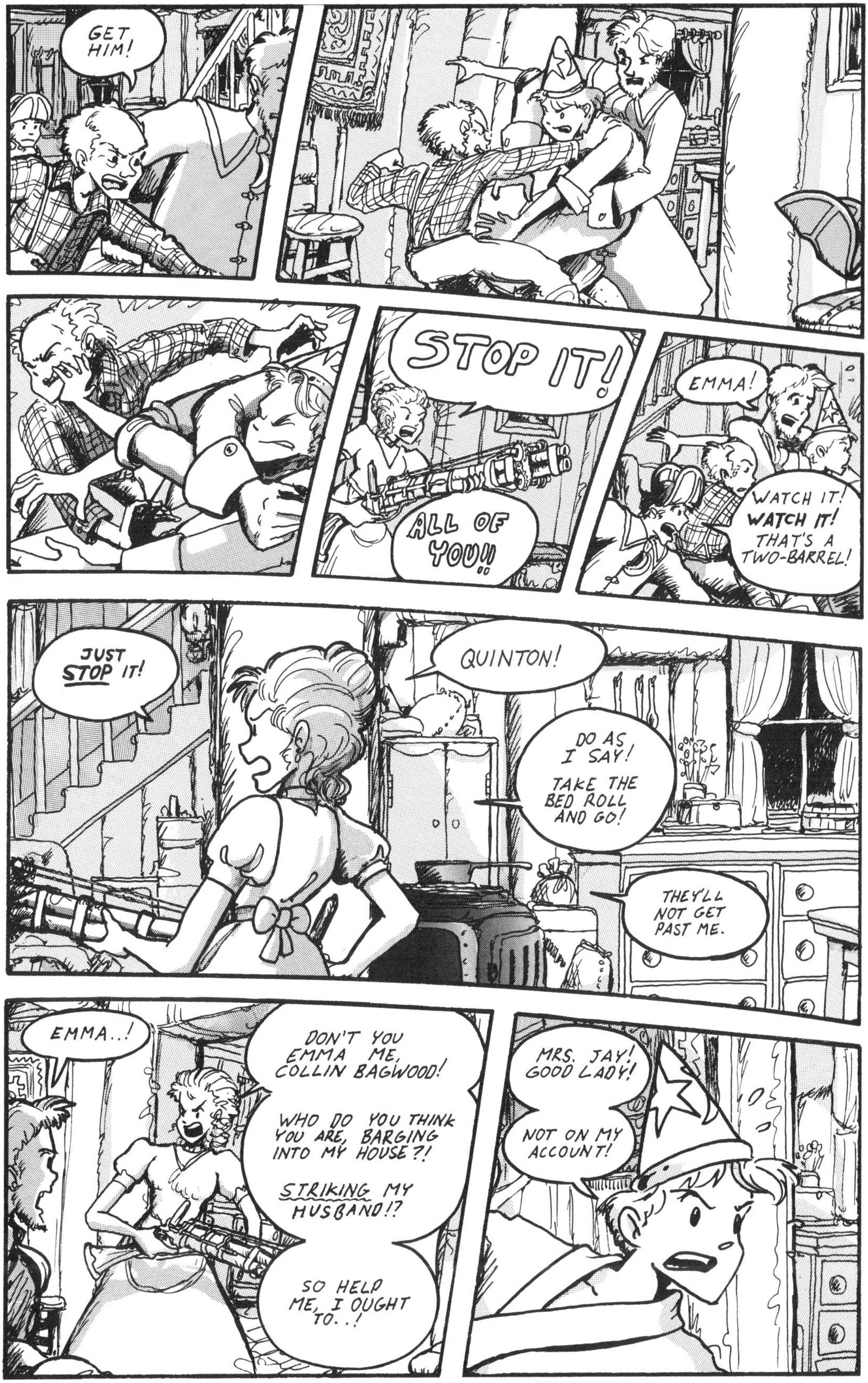

GET HIM!
STOP IT!
ALL OF YOU!!
EMMA!
WATCH IT! WATCH IT! THAT'S A TWO-BARREL!
JUST STOP IT!
QUINTON!
DO AS I SAY! TAKE THE BED ROLL AND GO!
THEY'LL NOT GET PAST ME.
EMMA..!
DON'T YOU EMMA ME, COLLIN BAGWOOD!
WHO DO YOU THINK YOU ARE, BARGING INTO MY HOUSE?!
STRIKING MY HUSBAND!?
SO HELP ME, I OUGHT TO..!
MRS. JAY! GOOD LADY!
NOT ON MY ACCOUNT!

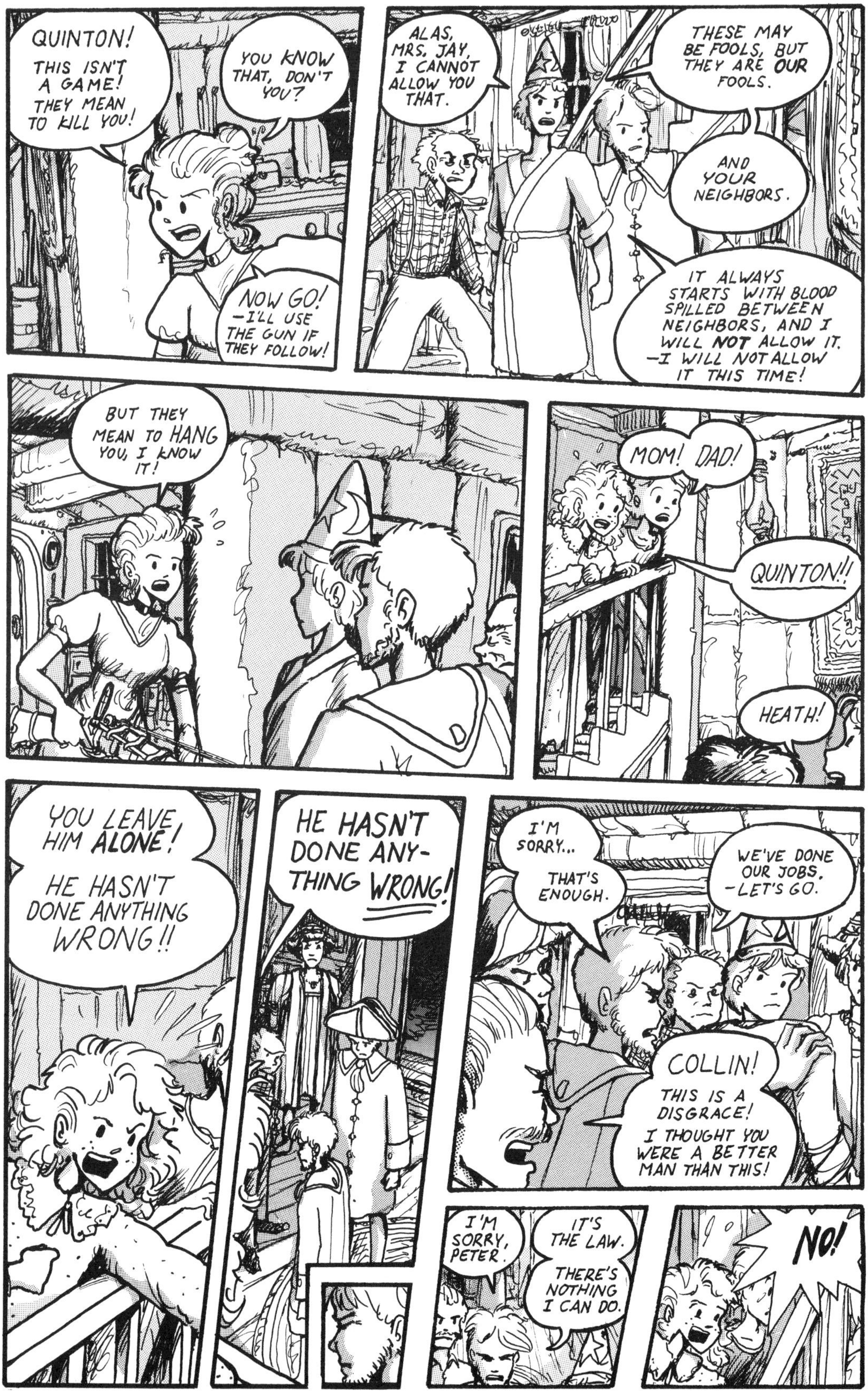
QUINTON! THIS ISN'T A GAME! THEY MEAN TO KILL YOU!
YOU KNOW THAT, DON'T YOU?
NOW GO! —I'LL USE THE GUN IF THEY FOLLOW!
ALAS, MRS. JAY, I CANNOT ALLOW YOU THAT.
THESE MAY BE FOOLS, BUT THEY ARE OUR FOOLS.
AND YOUR NEIGHBORS.
IT ALWAYS STARTS WITH BLOOD SPILLED BETWEEN NEIGHBORS, AND I WILL NOT ALLOW IT. —I WILL NOT ALLOW IT THIS TIME!
BUT THEY MEAN TO HANG YOU, I KNOW IT!
MOM! DAD!
QUINTON!!
HEATH!
YOU LEAVE HIM ALONE!
HE HASN'T DONE ANYTHING WRONG!!
HE HASN'T DONE ANY-THING WRONG!
I'M SORRY... THAT'S ENOUGH.
WE'VE DONE OUR JOBS. —LET'S GO.
COLLIN! THIS IS A DISGRACE! I THOUGHT YOU WERE A BETTER MAN THAN THIS!
I'M SORRY, PETER.
IT'S THE LAW.
THERE'S NOTHING I CAN DO.
NO!

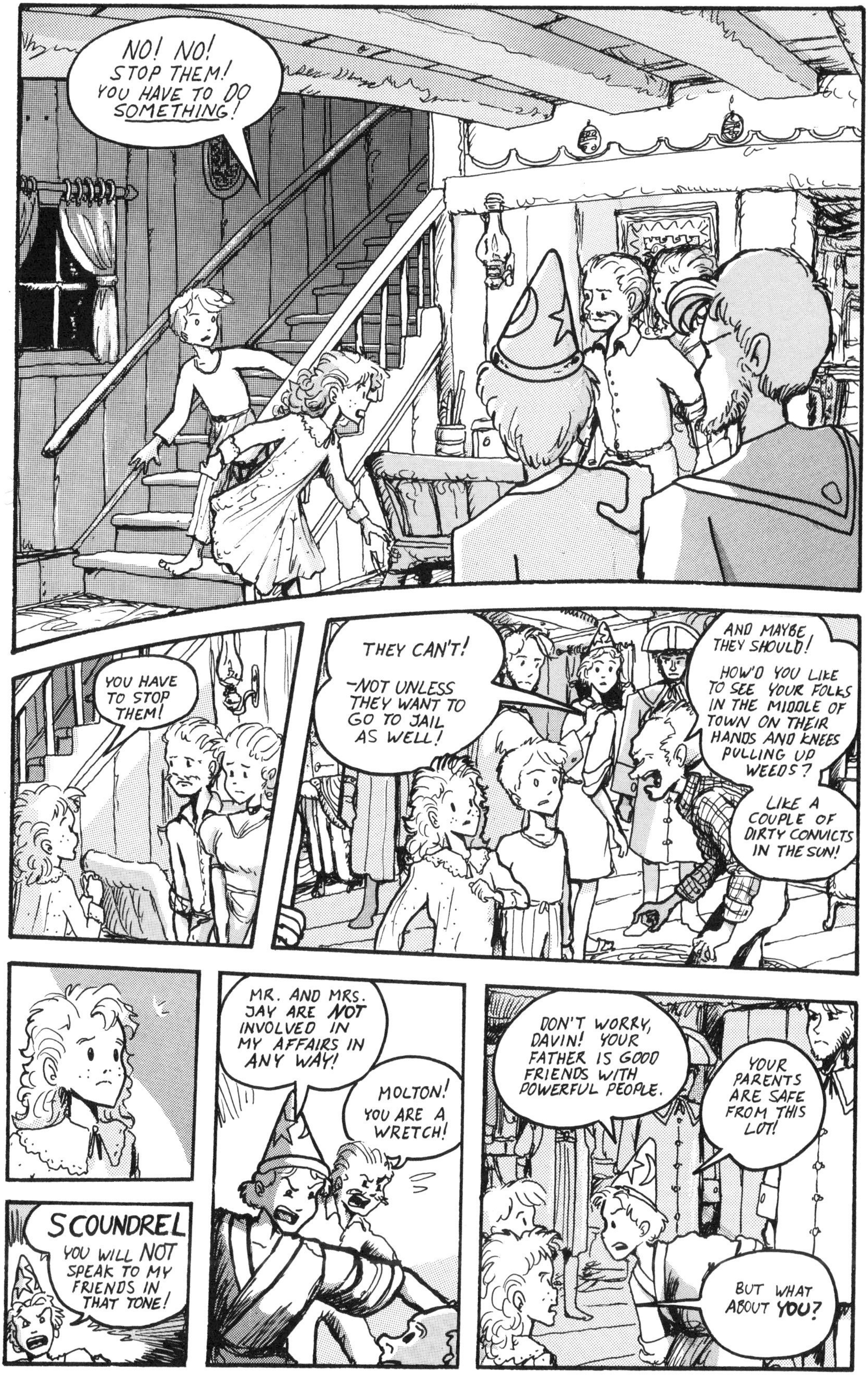

NO! NO! STOP THEM! YOU HAVE TO DO SOMETHING!
YOU HAVE TO STOP THEM!
THEY CAN'T!
-NOT UNLESS THEY WANT TO GO TO JAIL AS WELL!
AND MAYBE THEY SHOULD!
HOW'D YOU LIKE TO SEE YOUR FOLKS IN THE MIDDLE OF TOWN ON THEIR HANDS AND KNEES PULLING UP WEEDS?
LIKE A COUPLE OF DIRTY CONVICTS IN THE SUN!
SCOUNDREL
YOU WILL NOT SPEAK TO MY FRIENDS IN THAT TONE!
MR. AND MRS. JAY ARE NOT INVOLVED IN MY AFFAIRS IN ANY WAY!
MOLTON! YOU ARE A WRETCH!
DON'T WORRY, DAVIN! YOUR FATHER IS GOOD FRIENDS WITH POWERFUL PEOPLE.
YOUR PARENTS ARE SAFE FROM THIS LOT!
BUT WHAT ABOUT YOU?

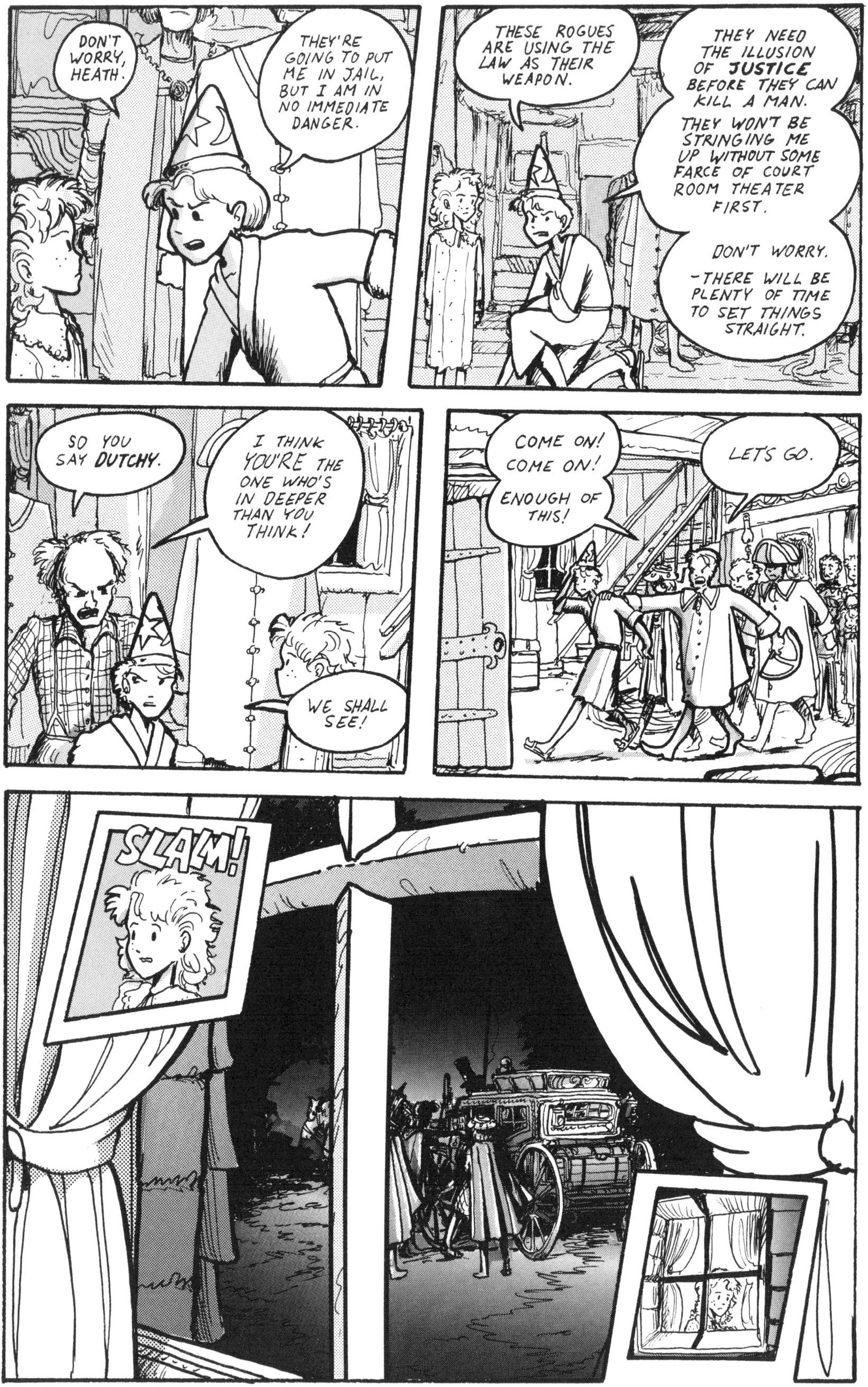
DON'T WORRY, HEATH.
THEY'RE GOING TO PUT ME IN JAIL, BUT I AM IN NO IMMEDIATE DANGER.
THESE ROGUES ARE USING THE LAW AS THEIR WEAPON.
THEY NEED THE ILLUSION OF JUSTICE BEFORE THEY CAN KILL A MAN.
THEY WON'T BE STRINGING ME UP WITHOUT SOME FARCE OF COURT ROOM THEATER FIRST.
DON'T WORRY.
-THERE WILL BE PLENTY OF TIME TO SET THINGS STRAIGHT.
SO YOU SAY DUTCHY.
I THINK YOU'RE THE ONE WHO'S IN DEEPER THAN YOU THINK!
WE SHALL SEE!
COME ON! COME ON!
ENOUGH OF THIS!
LET'S GO.
SLAM!

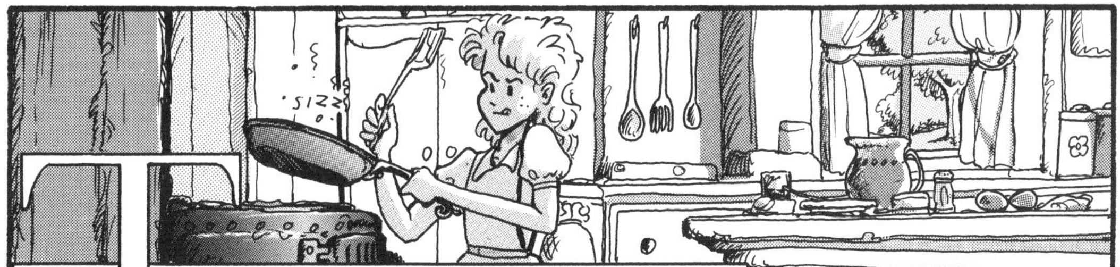
SIZZ

The night did not end quickly after Quinton's arrest. First of all, Mr. Jay sent his son off to fetch two other men who lived near by, and Mrs. Jay dressed the wound on her husband's chin. Davin returned red-faced from his mission with Mr. Spreigman and Mr. Donnel, and Mr. Donnel's eldest son, Jeremy. Mrs. Jay made hot drinks for everybody and Davin threw up from all the excitement and had to be washed up and put to bed. Heath, refusing to go to bed as well, stayed up quietly and listened to the men as they paced the house and discussed and looked both grave and excited.

Much of what they had to say went over her head, though she was under the impression that there were many dire events transpiring. Important sounding names and places were discussed; some of which she thought she had heard mentioned before, but which at the time had neither paid attention to nor understood. Even the king's name was spoken. It all seemed very big to her, and very far away.

Though, as thrilling as it all was, Heath chewed her lip and wondered when they would talk about *Quinton*, who it seemed to her was clearly the most wronged by the evening's events. His name, however, was hardly mentioned at all. In the end, all the discussing and pacing began to lull and swirl about her, making less and less sense as it did. The tumbly feeling of excitement inside her gave way to a warm, swimmy sleepiness which made her yawn and blink and nod. It was very late when Mrs. Jay took pity and led Heath to the little room where her bed was kept and tucked the girl in.

When morning came, Heath slept very late, and when she awoke, she scolded herself for it and got up immediately. Downstairs, Mrs. Jay had guests; Mrs. Spreigman and another woman Heath did not know. The three of them were deep in discussion, waving their hands and raising their eyebrows as they talked. Heath hurried through breakfast and raced past them on her way outside. Davin was already out, talking to Finnly.

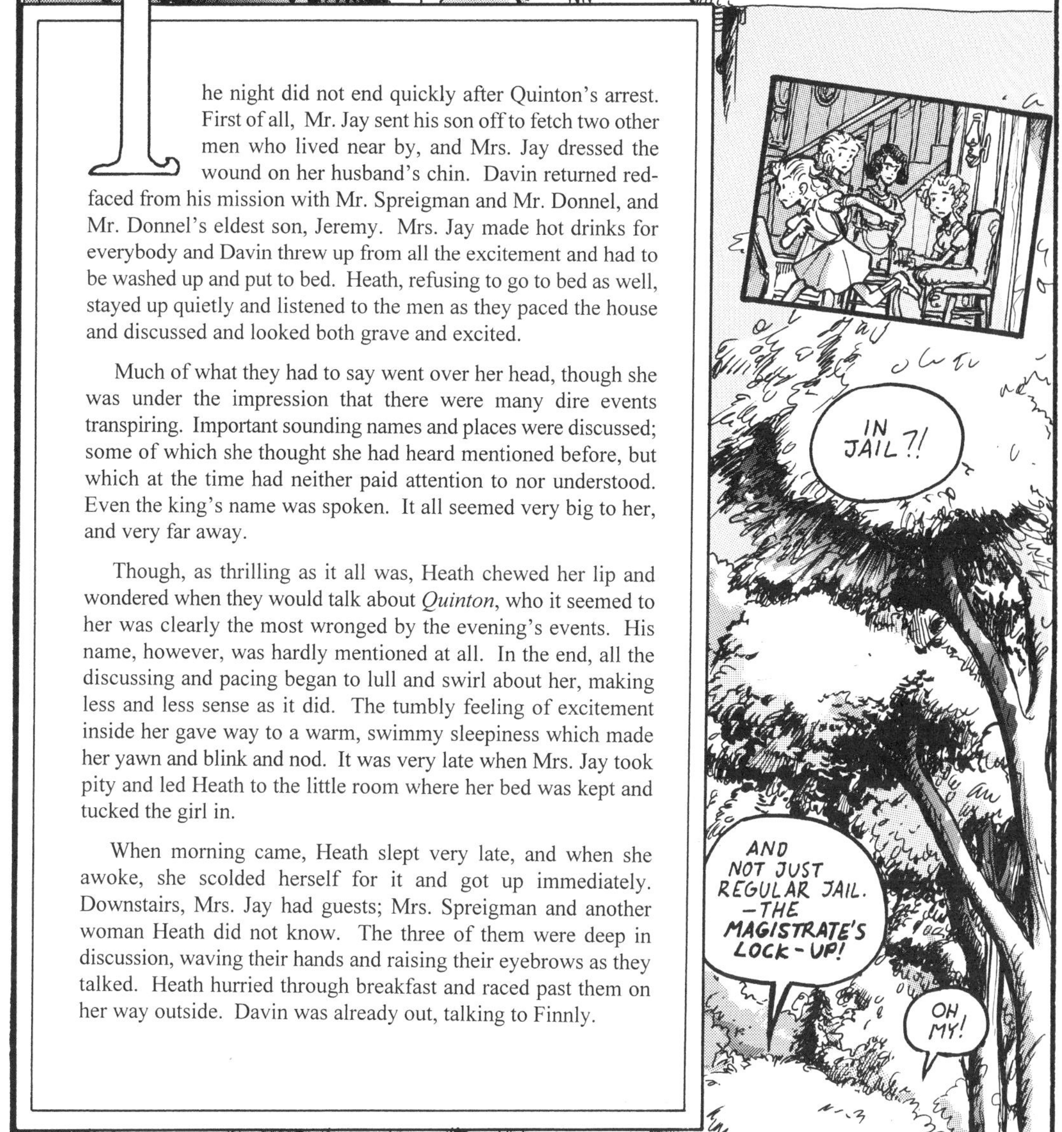
IN JAIL?!
AND NOT JUST REGULAR JAIL. —THE MAGISTRATE'S LOCK-UP!
OH MY!

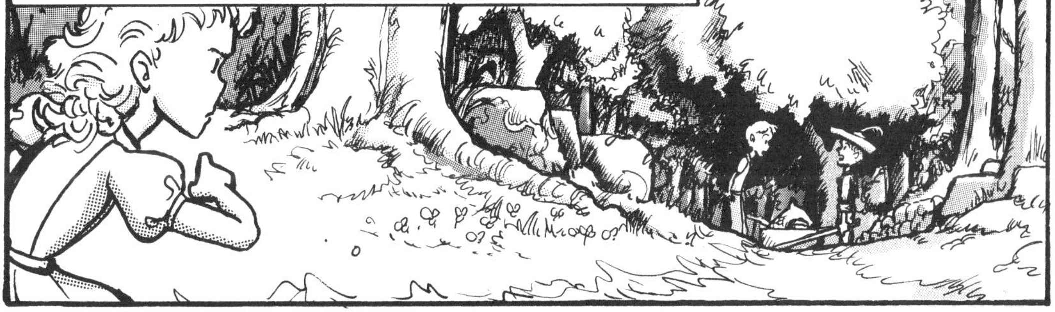

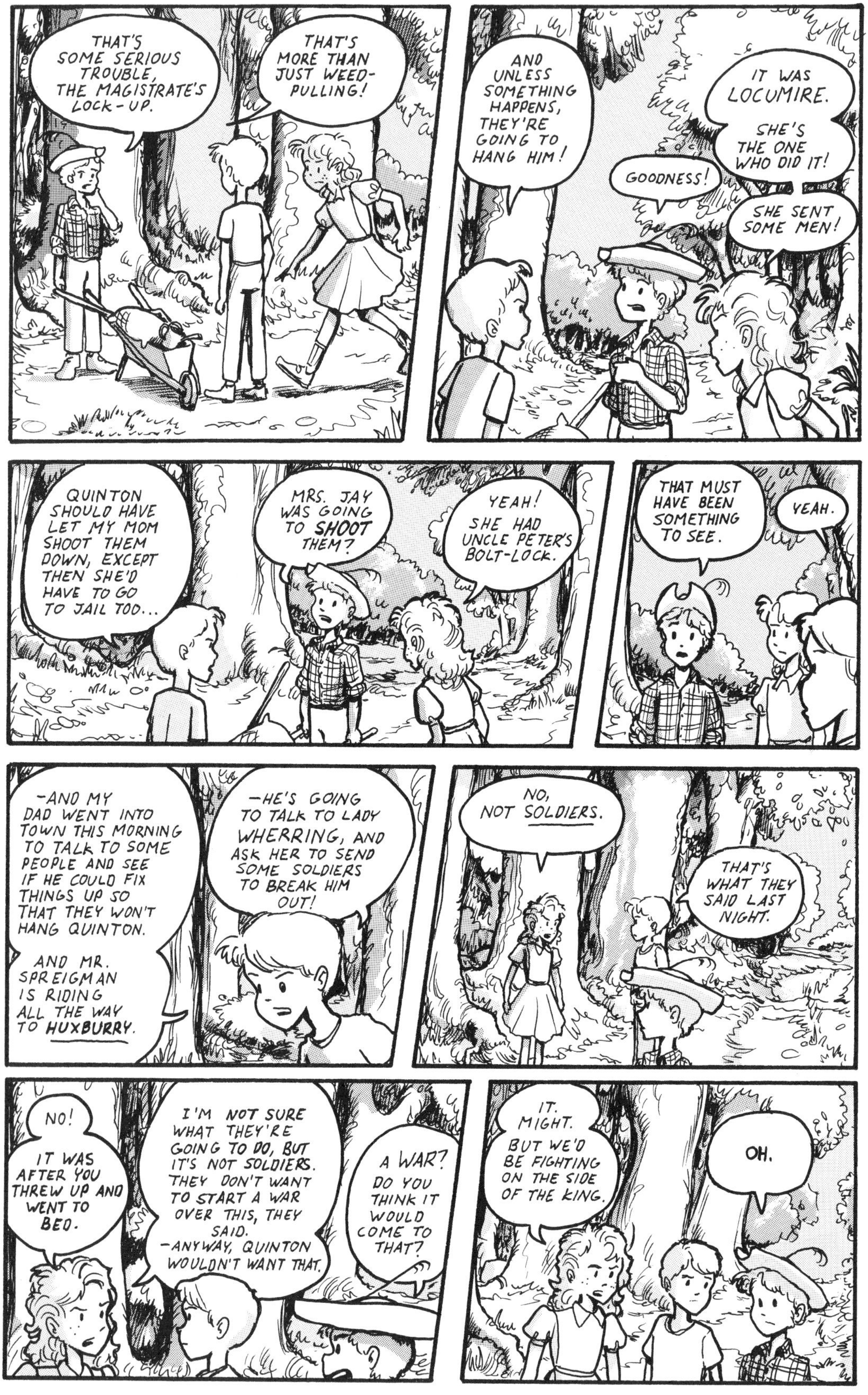
THAT'S SOME SERIOUS TROUBLE, THE MAGISTRATE'S LOCK-UP.
THAT'S MORE THAN JUST WEED-PULLING!
AND UNLESS SOMETHING HAPPENS, THEY'RE GOING TO HANG HIM!
IT WAS LOCUMIRE.
SHE'S THE ONE WHO DID IT!
GOODNESS!
SHE SENT SOME MEN!
QUINTON SHOULD HAVE LET MY MOM SHOOT THEM DOWN, EXCEPT THEN SHE'D HAVE TO GO TO JAIL TOO...
MRS. JAY WAS GOING TO SHOOT THEM?
YEAH! SHE HAD UNCLE PETER'S BOLT-LOCK.
THAT MUST HAVE BEEN SOMETHING TO SEE.
YEAH.
-AND MY DAD WENT INTO TOWN THIS MORNING TO TALK TO SOME PEOPLE AND SEE IF HE COULD FIX THINGS UP SO THAT THEY WON'T HANG QUINTON.
AND MR. SPREIGMAN IS RIDING ALL THE WAY TO HUXBURRY.
-HE'S GOING TO TALK TO LADY WHERRING, AND ASK HER TO SEND SOME SOLDIERS TO BREAK HIM OUT!
NO, NOT SOLDIERS.
THAT'S WHAT THEY SAID LAST NIGHT.
NO!
IT WAS AFTER YOU THREW UP AND WENT TO BED.
I'M NOT SURE WHAT THEY'RE GOING TO DO, BUT IT'S NOT SOLDIERS. THEY DON'T WANT TO START A WAR OVER THIS, THEY SAID.
-ANYWAY, QUINTON WOULDN'T WANT THAT.
A WAR? DO YOU THINK IT WOULD COME TO THAT?
IT. MIGHT.
BUT WE'D BE FIGHTING ON THE SIDE OF THE KING.
OH.

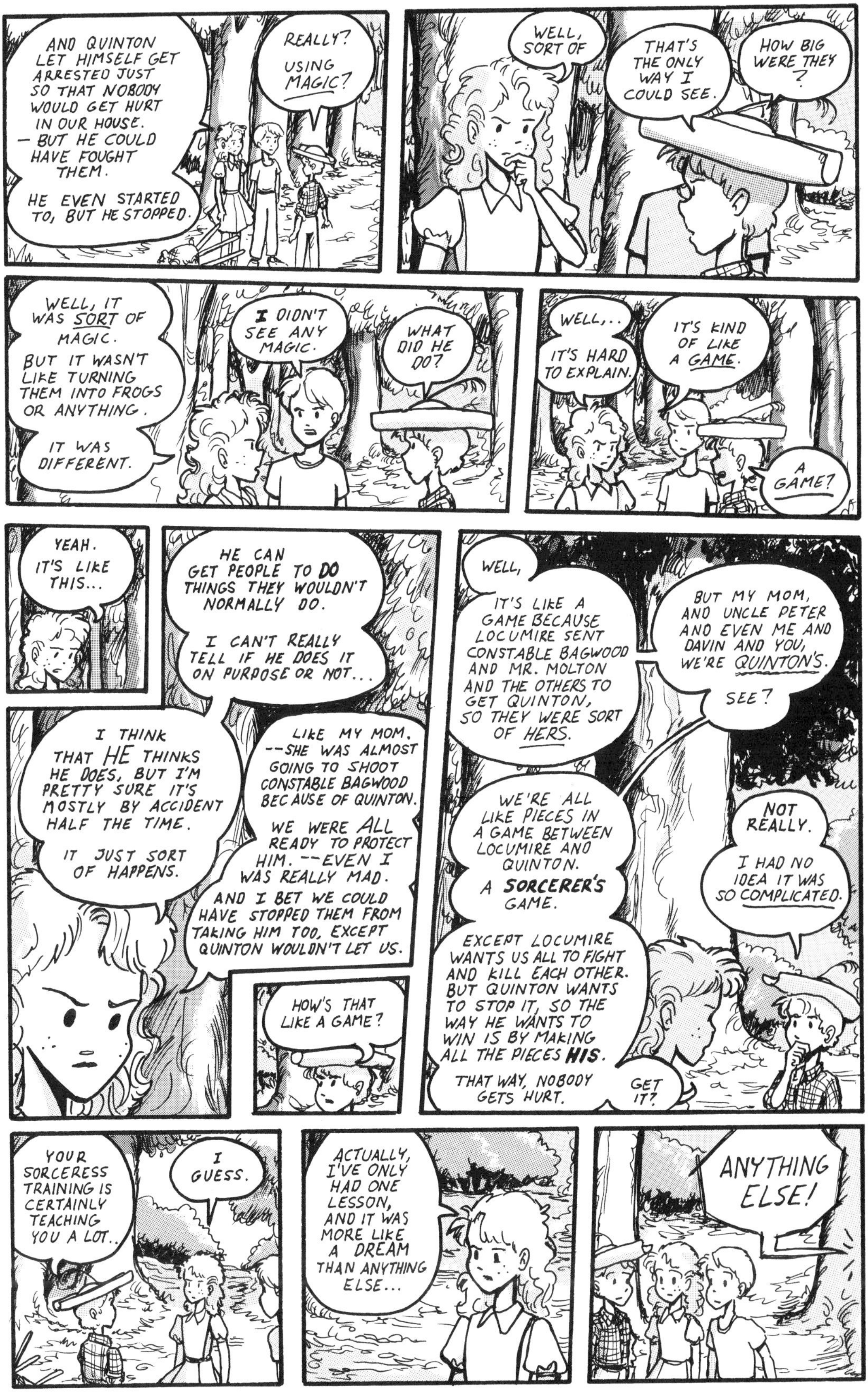
AND QUINTON LET HIMSELF GET ARRESTED JUST SO THAT NOBODY WOULD GET HURT IN OUR HOUSE. — BUT HE COULD HAVE FOUGHT THEM.
HE EVEN STARTED TO, BUT HE STOPPED.
REALLY? USING MAGIC?
WELL, SORT OF
THAT'S THE ONLY WAY I COULD SEE.
HOW BIG WERE THEY?
WELL, IT WAS SORT OF MAGIC.
BUT IT WASN'T LIKE TURNING THEM INTO FROGS OR ANYTHING.
IT WAS DIFFERENT.
I DIDN'T SEE ANY MAGIC.
WHAT DID HE DO?
WELL,..
IT'S HARD TO EXPLAIN.
IT'S KIND OF LIKE A GAME.
A GAME?
YEAH. IT'S LIKE THIS...
HE CAN GET PEOPLE TO DO THINGS THEY WOULDN'T NORMALLY DO.
I CAN'T REALLY TELL IF HE DOES IT ON PURPOSE OR NOT...
I THINK THAT HE THINKS HE DOES, BUT I'M PRETTY SURE IT'S MOSTLY BY ACCIDENT HALF THE TIME.
IT JUST SORT OF HAPPENS.
LIKE MY MOM. --SHE WAS ALMOST GOING TO SHOOT CONSTABLE BAGWOOD BECAUSE OF QUINTON.
WE WERE ALL READY TO PROTECT HIM. --EVEN I WAS REALLY MAD.
AND I BET WE COULD HAVE STOPPED THEM FROM TAKING HIM TOO, EXCEPT QUINTON WOULDN'T LET US.
HOW'S THAT LIKE A GAME?
WELL,
IT'S LIKE A GAME BECAUSE LOCUMIRE SENT CONSTABLE BAGWOOD AND MR. MOLTON AND THE OTHERS TO GET QUINTON, SO THEY WERE SORT OF HERS.
BUT MY MOM, AND UNCLE PETER AND EVEN ME AND DAVIN AND YOU, WE'RE QUINTON'S.
SEE?
WE'RE ALL LIKE PIECES IN A GAME BETWEEN LOCUMIRE AND QUINTON.
A SORCERER'S GAME.
EXCEPT LOCUMIRE WANTS US ALL TO FIGHT AND KILL EACH OTHER. BUT QUINTON WANTS TO STOP IT, SO THE WAY HE WANTS TO WIN IS BY MAKING ALL THE PIECES HIS.
THAT WAY, NOBODY GETS HURT.
GET IT?
NOT REALLY.
I HAD NO IDEA IT WAS SO COMPLICATED.
YOUR SORCERESS TRAINING IS CERTAINLY TEACHING YOU A LOT..
I GUESS.
ACTUALLY, I'VE ONLY HAD ONE LESSON, AND IT WAS MORE LIKE A DREAM THAN ANYTHING ELSE...
ANYTHING ELSE!

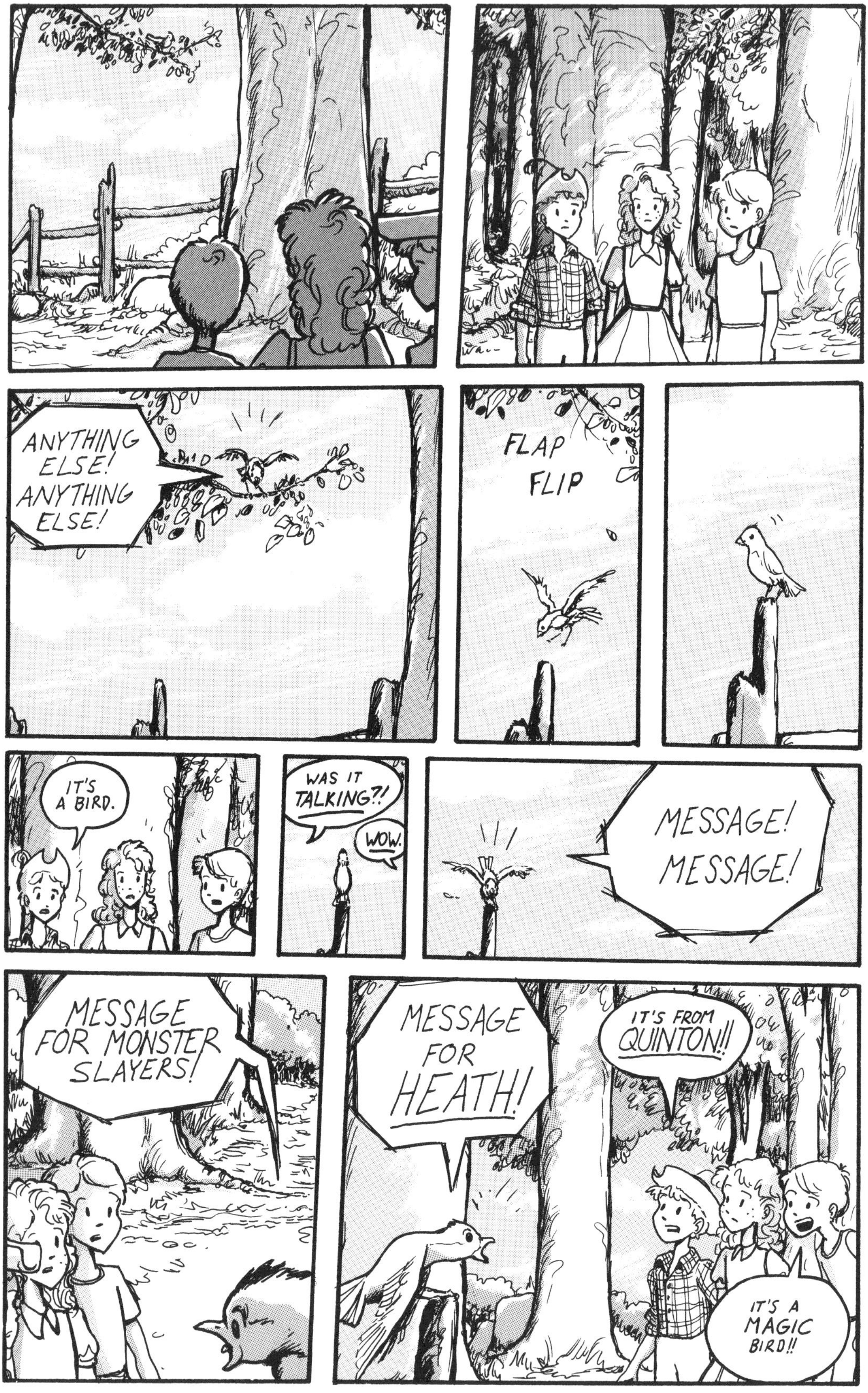
ANYTHING ELSE! ANYTHING ELSE!
FLAP
FLIP
IT'S A BIRD.
WAS IT TALKING?!
WOW.
MESSAGE! MESSAGE!
MESSAGE FOR MONSTER SLAYERS!
MESSAGE FOR HEATH!
IT'S FROM QUINTON!!
IT'S A MAGIC BIRD!!

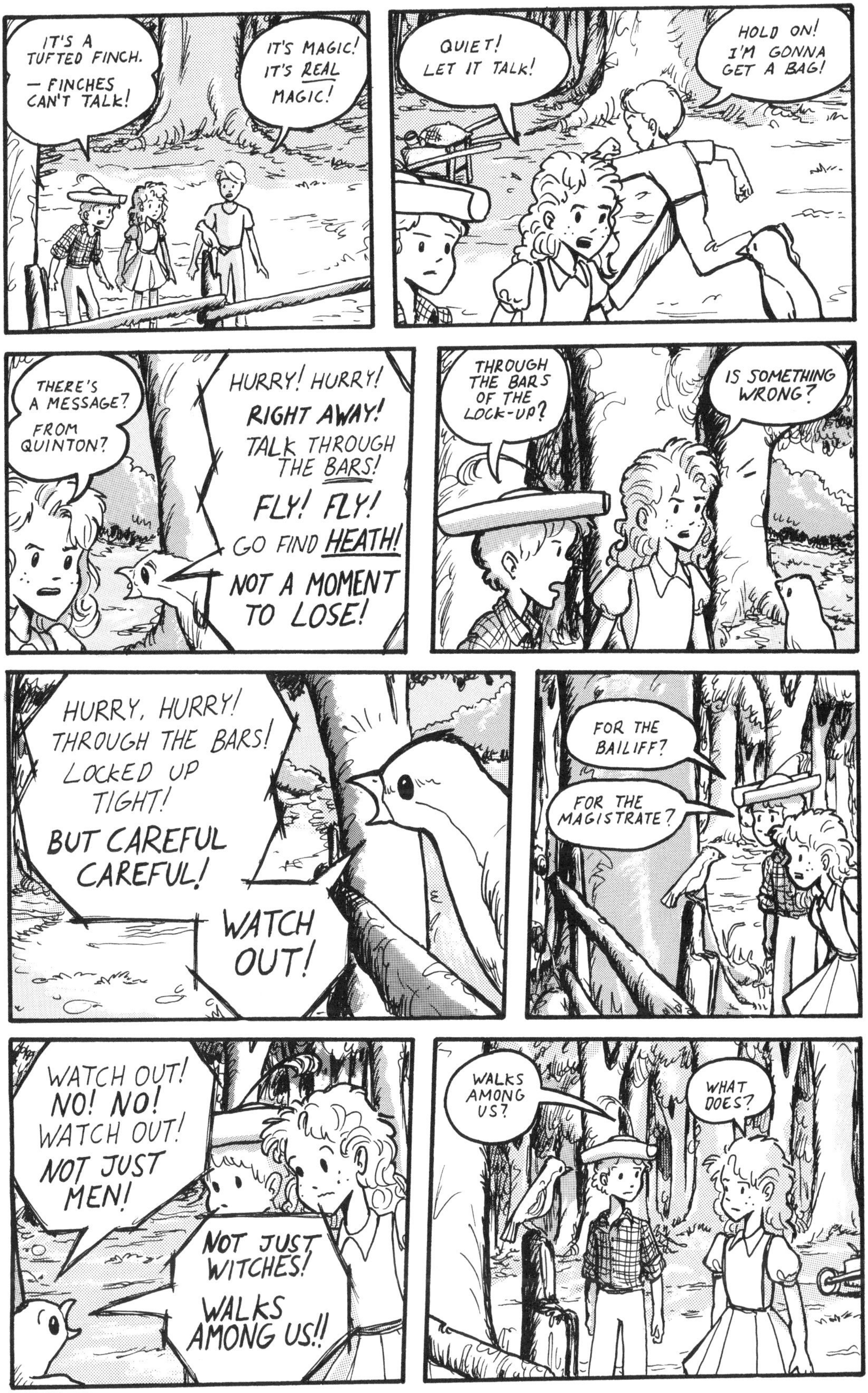
IT'S A TUFTED FINCH. — FINCHES CAN'T TALK!
IT'S MAGIC! IT'S REAL MAGIC!
QUIET! LET IT TALK!
HOLD ON! I'M GONNA GET A BAG!
THERE'S A MESSAGE? FROM QUINTON?
HURRY! HURRY! RIGHT AWAY! TALK THROUGH THE BARS! FLY! FLY! GO FIND HEATH! NOT A MOMENT TO LOSE!
THROUGH THE BARS OF THE LOCK-UP?
IS SOMETHING WRONG?
HURRY, HURRY! THROUGH THE BARS! LOCKED UP TIGHT! BUT CAREFUL CAREFUL!
WATCH OUT!
FOR THE BAILIFF?
FOR THE MAGISTRATE?
WATCH OUT! NO! NO! WATCH OUT! NOT JUST MEN!
NOT JUST WITCHES! WALKS AMONG US!!
WALKS AMONG US?
WHAT DOES?

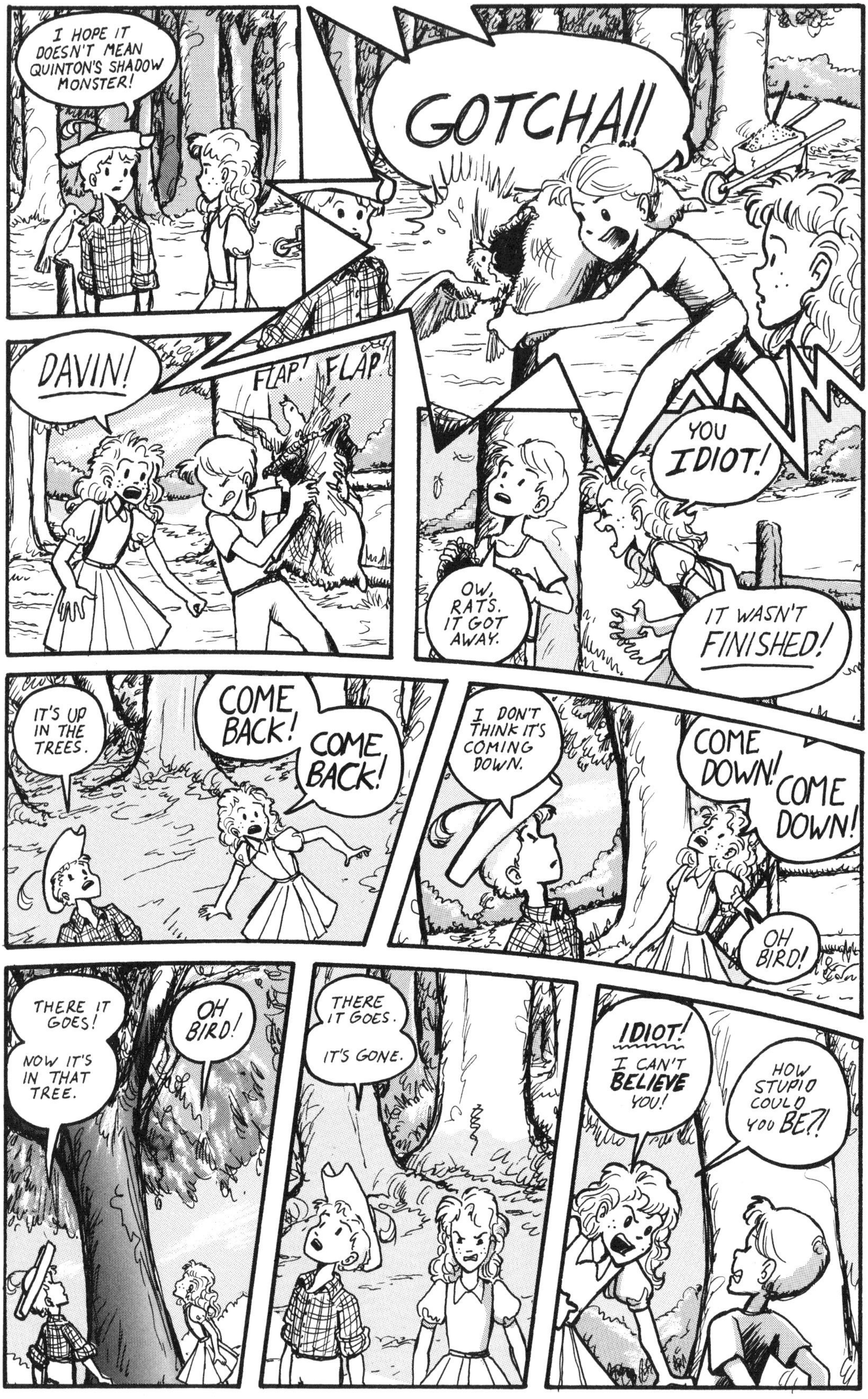
I HOPE IT DOESN'T MEAN QUINTON'S SHADOW MONSTER!
GOTCHA!!
DAVIN!
FLAP! FLAP!
YOU IDIOT!
OW, RATS. IT GOT AWAY.
IT WASN'T FINISHED!
IT'S UP IN THE TREES.
COME BACK!
COME BACK!
I DON'T THINK IT'S COMING DOWN.
COME DOWN!
COME DOWN!
OH BIRD!
THERE IT GOES!
NOW IT'S IN THAT TREE.
OH BIRD!
THERE IT GOES.
IT'S GONE.
IDIOT!
I CAN'T BELIEVE YOU!
HOW STUPID COULD YOU BE?!

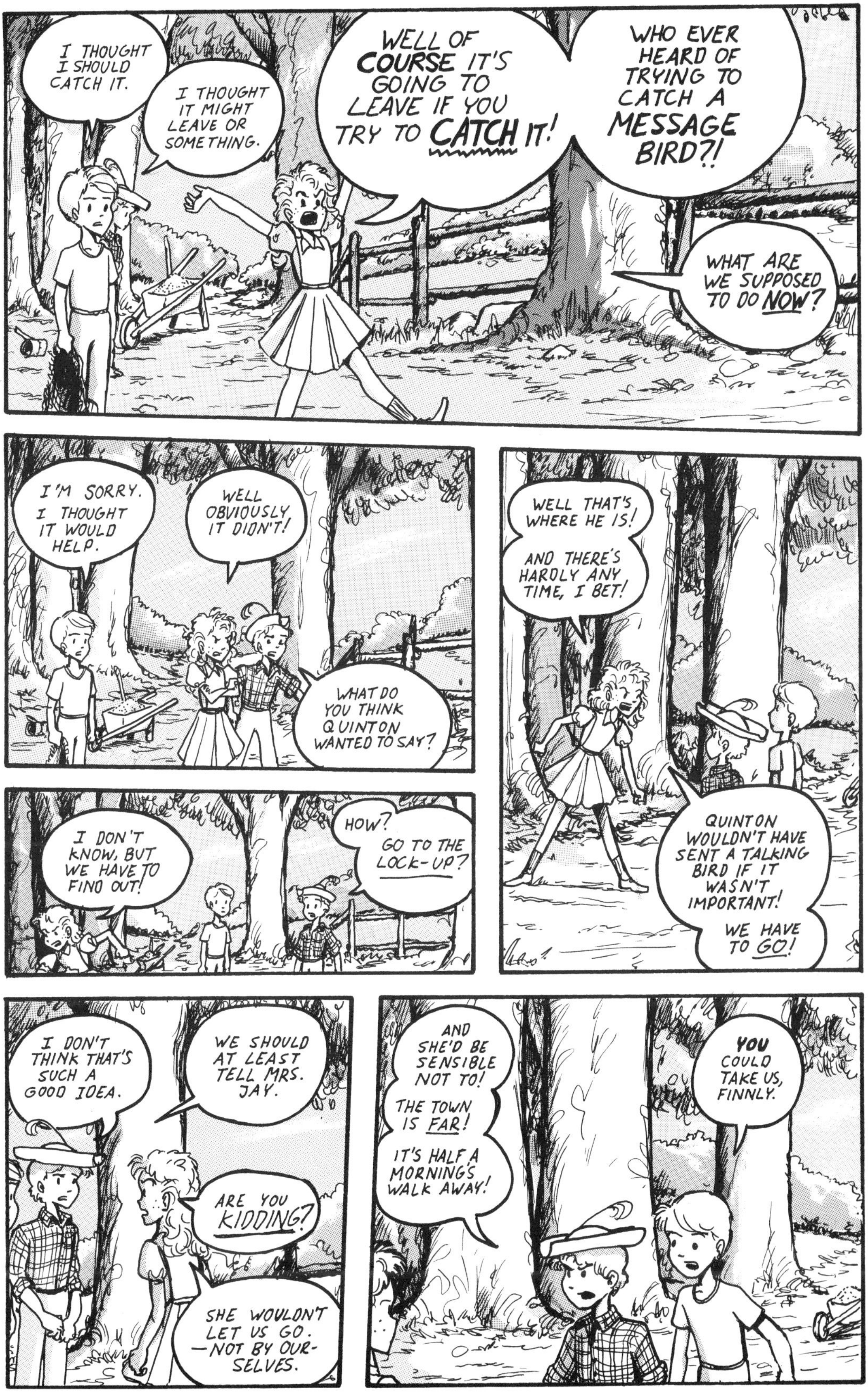

I THOUGHT I SHOULD CATCH IT.
I THOUGHT IT MIGHT LEAVE OR SOMETHING.
WELL OF COURSE IT'S GOING TO LEAVE IF YOU TRY TO CATCH IT!
WHO EVER HEARD OF TRYING TO CATCH A MESSAGE BIRD?!
WHAT ARE WE SUPPOSED TO DO NOW?
I'M SORRY. I THOUGHT IT WOULD HELP.
WELL OBVIOUSLY IT DIDN'T!
WHAT DO YOU THINK QUINTON WANTED TO SAY?
I DON'T KNOW, BUT WE HAVE TO FIND OUT!
HOW? GO TO THE LOCK-UP?
WELL THAT'S WHERE HE IS!
AND THERE'S HARDLY ANY TIME, I BET!
QUINTON WOULDN'T HAVE SENT A TALKING BIRD IF IT WASN'T IMPORTANT!
WE HAVE TO GO!
I DON'T THINK THAT'S SUCH A GOOD IDEA.
WE SHOULD AT LEAST TELL MRS. JAY.
ARE YOU KIDDING?
SHE WOULDN'T LET US GO. —NOT BY OURSELVES.
AND SHE'D BE SENSIBLE NOT TO!
THE TOWN IS FAR!
IT'S HALF A MORNING'S WALK AWAY!
YOU COULD TAKE US, FINNLY.

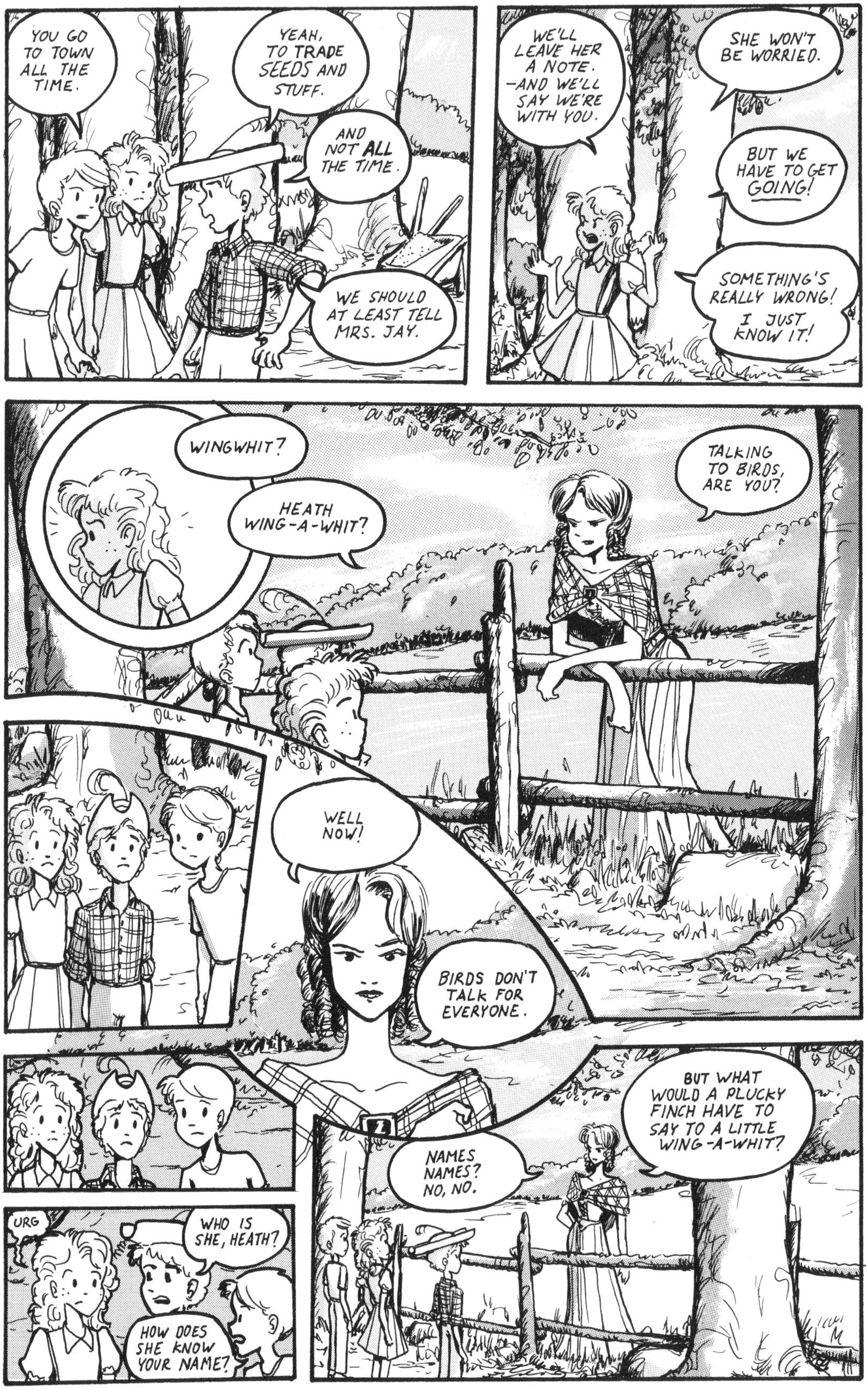
YOU GO TO TOWN ALL THE TIME.
YEAH, TO TRADE SEEDS AND STUFF.
AND NOT **ALL** THE TIME.
WE SHOULD AT LEAST TELL MRS. JAY.
WE'LL LEAVE HER A NOTE. -AND WE'LL SAY WE'RE WITH YOU.
SHE WON'T BE WORRIED.
BUT WE HAVE TO GET GOING!
SOMETHING'S REALLY WRONG! I JUST KNOW IT!
WINGWHIT?
HEATH WING-A-WHIT?
TALKING TO BIRDS, ARE YOU?
WELL NOW!
BIRDS DON'T TALK FOR EVERYONE.
BUT WHAT WOULD A PLUCKY FINCH HAVE TO SAY TO A LITTLE WING-A-WHIT?
NAMES NAMES? NO, NO.
URG
WHO IS SHE, HEATH?
HOW DOES SHE KNOW YOUR NAME?

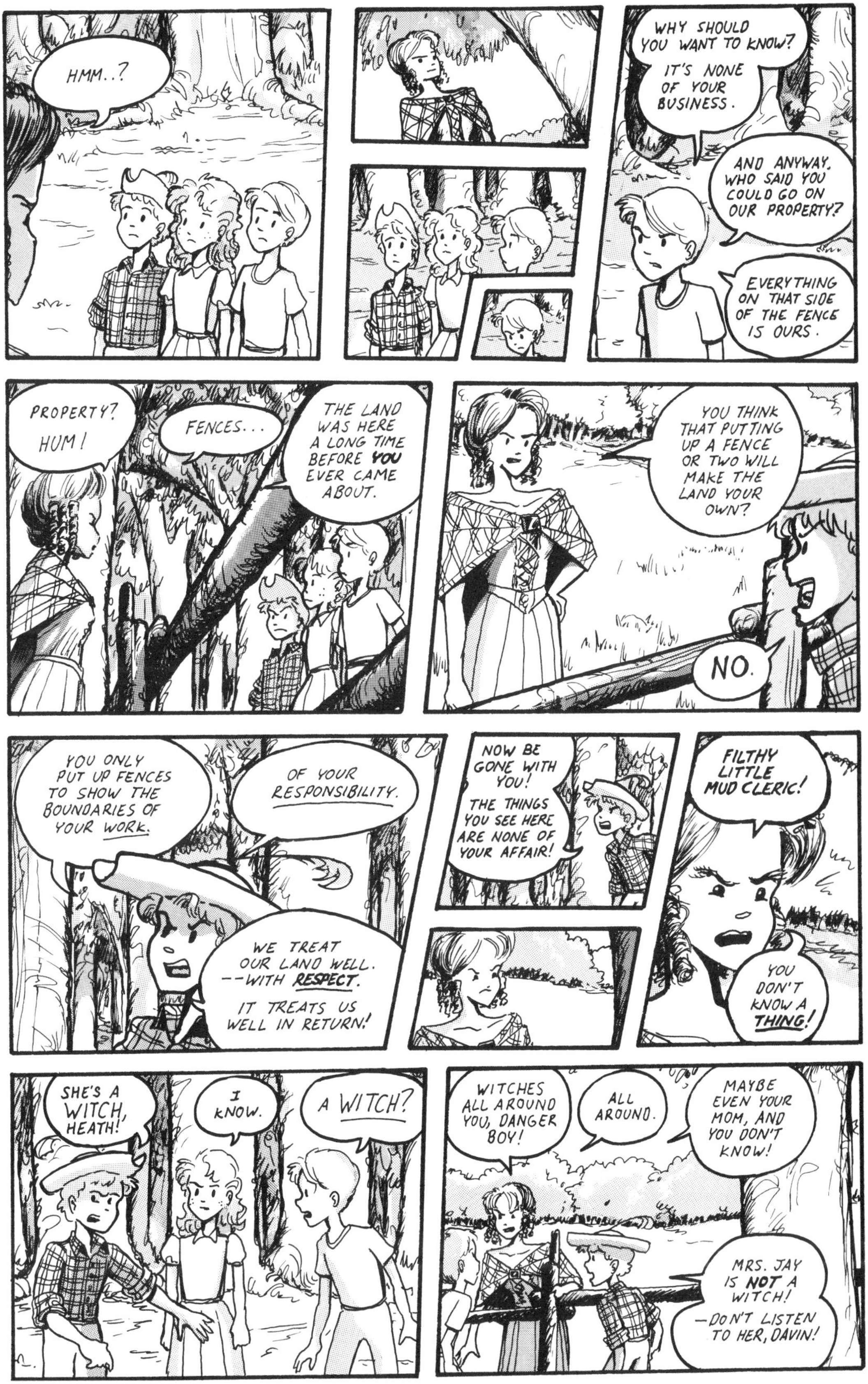
HMM..?
WHY SHOULD YOU WANT TO KNOW?
IT'S NONE OF YOUR BUSINESS.
AND ANYWAY. WHO SAID YOU COULD GO ON OUR PROPERTY?
EVERYTHING ON THAT SIDE OF THE FENCE IS OURS.
PROPERTY? HUM!
FENCES...
THE LAND WAS HERE A LONG TIME BEFORE YOU EVER CAME ABOUT.
YOU THINK THAT PUTTING UP A FENCE OR TWO WILL MAKE THE LAND YOUR OWN?
NO.
YOU ONLY PUT UP FENCES TO SHOW THE BOUNDARIES OF YOUR WORK.
OF YOUR RESPONSIBILITY.
WE TREAT OUR LAND WELL. --WITH RESPECT.
IT TREATS US WELL IN RETURN!
NOW BE GONE WITH YOU!
THE THINGS YOU SEE HERE ARE NONE OF YOUR AFFAIR!
FILTHY LITTLE MUD CLERIC!
YOU DON'T KNOW A THING!
SHE'S A WITCH, HEATH!
I KNOW.
A WITCH?
WITCHES ALL AROUND YOU, DANGER BOY!
ALL AROUND.
MAYBE EVEN YOUR MOM, AND YOU DON'T KNOW!
MRS. JAY IS NOT A WITCH!
—DON'T LISTEN TO HER, DAVIN!

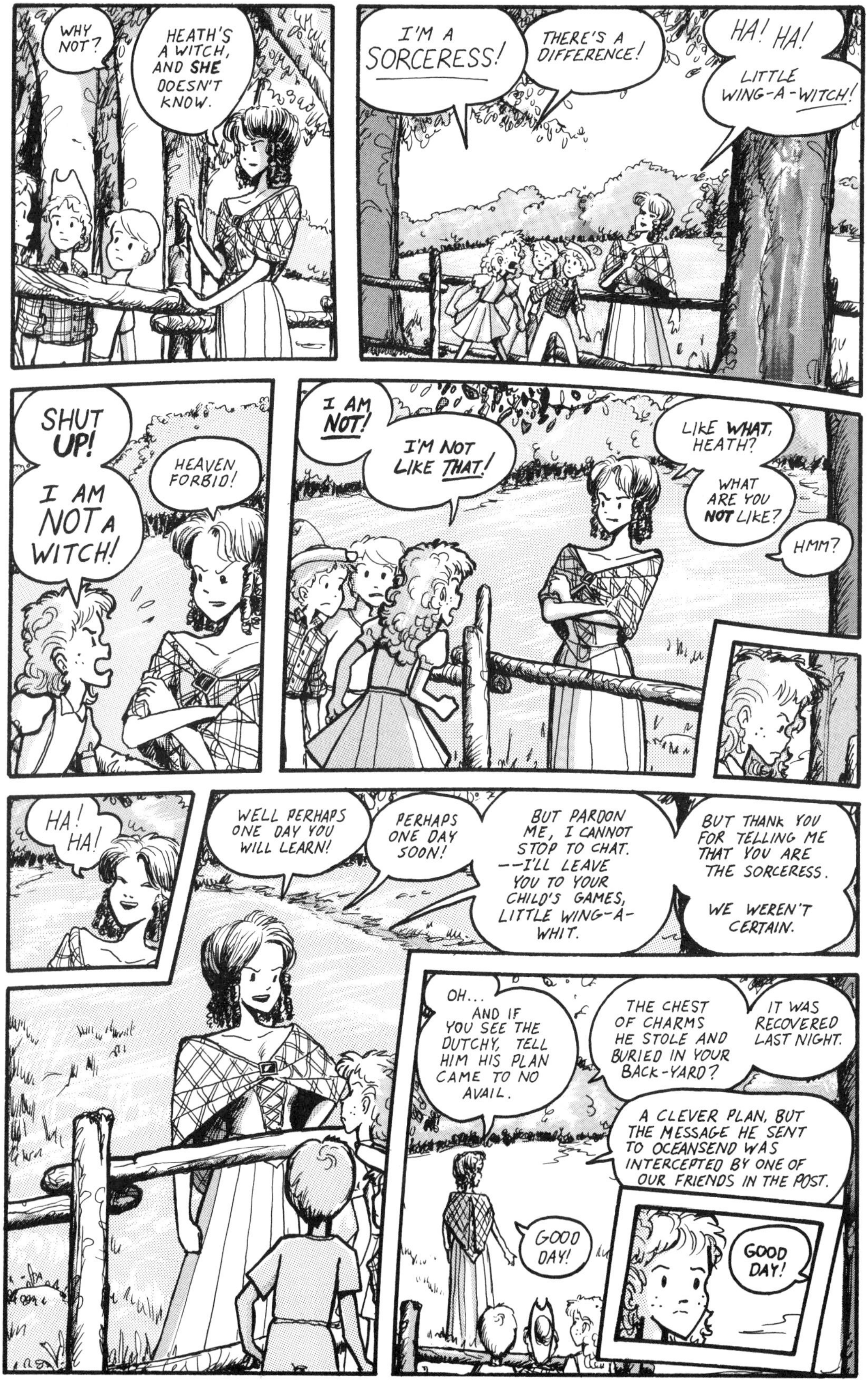
WHY NOT?
HEATH'S A WITCH, AND SHE DOESN'T KNOW.
I'M A SORCERESS!
THERE'S A DIFFERENCE!
HA! HA!
LITTLE WING-A-WITCH!
SHUT UP!
I AM NOT A WITCH!
HEAVEN FORBID!
I AM NOT!
I'M NOT LIKE THAT!
LIKE WHAT, HEATH?
WHAT ARE YOU NOT LIKE?
HMM?
HA! HA!
WELL PERHAPS ONE DAY YOU WILL LEARN!
PERHAPS ONE DAY SOON!
BUT PARDON ME, I CANNOT STOP TO CHAT. --I'LL LEAVE YOU TO YOUR CHILD'S GAMES, LITTLE WING-A-WHIT.
BUT THANK YOU FOR TELLING ME THAT YOU ARE THE SORCERESS.
WE WEREN'T CERTAIN.
OH... AND IF YOU SEE THE DUTCHY, TELL HIM HIS PLAN CAME TO NO AVAIL.
THE CHEST OF CHARMS HE STOLE AND BURIED IN YOUR BACK-YARD?
IT WAS RECOVERED LAST NIGHT.
A CLEVER PLAN, BUT THE MESSAGE HE SENT TO OCEANSEND WAS INTERCEPTED BY ONE OF OUR FRIENDS IN THE POST.
GOOD DAY!
GOOD DAY!

Chapter 17

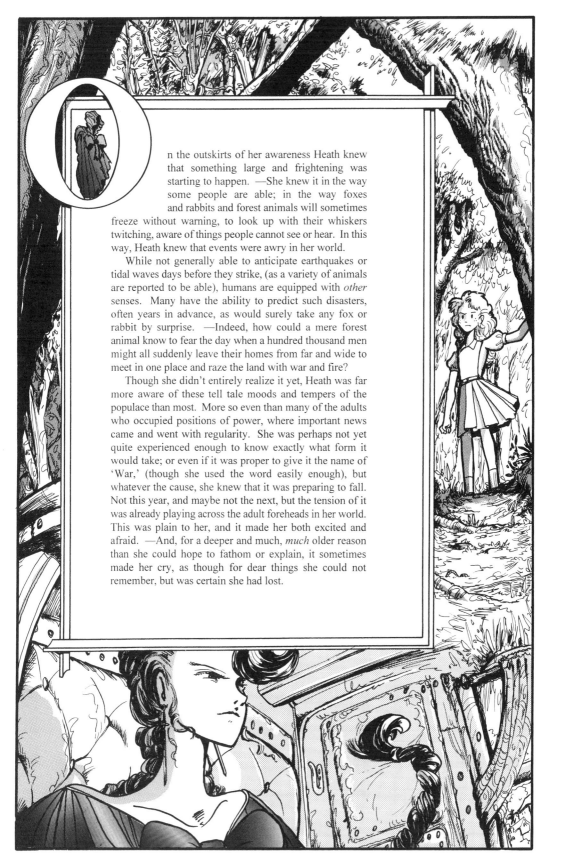

O n the outskirts of her awareness Heath knew that something large and frightening was starting to happen. —She knew it in the way some people are able; in the way foxes and rabbits and forest animals will sometimes freeze without warning, to look up with their whiskers twitching, aware of things people cannot see or hear. In this way, Heath knew that events were awry in her world.

While not generally able to anticipate earthquakes or tidal waves days before they strike, (as a variety of animals are reported to be able), humans are equipped with *other* senses. Many have the ability to predict such disasters, often years in advance, as would surely take any fox or rabbit by surprise. —Indeed, how could a mere forest animal know to fear the day when a hundred thousand men might all suddenly leave their homes from far and wide to meet in one place and raze the land with war and fire?

Though she didn't entirely realize it yet, Heath was far more aware of these tell tale moods and tempers of the populace than most. More so even than many of the adults who occupied positions of power, where important news came and went with regularity. She was perhaps not yet quite experienced enough to know exactly what form it would take; or even if it was proper to give it the name of 'War,' (though she used the word easily enough), but whatever the cause, she knew that it was preparing to fall. Not this year, and maybe not the next, but the tension of it was already playing across the adult foreheads in her world. This was plain to her, and it made her both excited and afraid. —And, for a deeper and much, *much* older reason than she could hope to fathom or explain, it sometimes made her cry, as though for dear things she could not remember, but was certain she had lost.

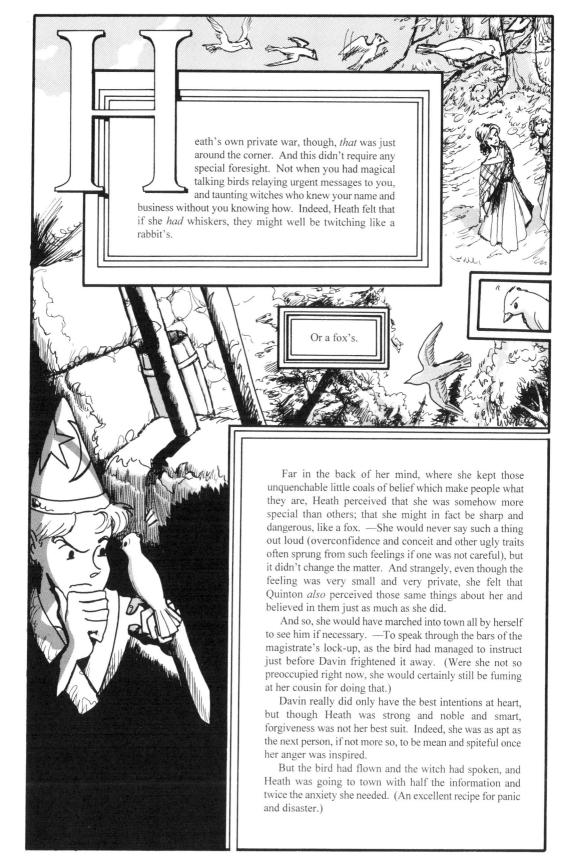

eath's own private war, though, *that* was just around the corner. And this didn't require any special foresight. Not when you had magical talking birds relaying urgent messages to you, and taunting witches who knew your name and business without you knowing how. Indeed, Heath felt that if she *had* whiskers, they might well be twitching like a rabbit's.

Or a fox's.

Far in the back of her mind, where she kept those unquenchable little coals of belief which make people what they are, Heath perceived that she was somehow more special than others; that she might in fact be sharp and dangerous, like a fox. —She would never say such a thing out loud (overconfidence and conceit and other ugly traits often sprung from such feelings if one was not careful), but it didn't change the matter. And strangely, even though the feeling was very small and very private, she felt that Quinton *also* perceived those same things about her and believed in them just as much as she did.

And so, she would have marched into town all by herself to see him if necessary. —To speak through the bars of the magistrate's lock-up, as the bird had managed to instruct just before Davin frightened it away. (Were she not so preoccupied right now, she would certainly still be fuming at her cousin for doing that.)

Davin really did only have the best intentions at heart, but though Heath was strong and noble and smart, forgiveness was not her best suit. Indeed, she was as apt as the next person, if not more so, to be mean and spiteful once her anger was inspired.

But the bird had flown and the witch had spoken, and Heath was going to town with half the information and twice the anxiety she needed. (An excellent recipe for panic and disaster.)

Luckily, she did not have to go alone. Quinton had seen to that. He had, after a fashion, provided her with companions who, as simple and unwilling as they perhaps sometimes were, would nonetheless be her knights. And though they didn't know it, Davin and Finnly were perhaps better able to serve her than anybody else in the world right then. In that time and place. They knew what she knew, and they believed without hesitation, and they both loved her very much. Often it is these intangible elements of a band which can make every difference in a fight.

Unfortunately, when Jurid struck, the difference was not quite enough.

Heath was too far up the path, leading her headstrong march, and Davin was too busy trying to quiet Finnly's concerns about the wheelbarrow of gardening tools (which Finnly did not want to take with him all the way into town). And so from the darkness of an old and rotted owl's nest, the Shadow flitted down, and unfolding itself, swooped upon the girl, intending to carry her away. —And perhaps bite off her hands and feet for good measure, so that she wouldn't be able to struggle and run if she found the chance.

But Heath had whiskers that day, and catching a flicker of movement from the corner of her eye, yelped and darted just in time. With its prey startled and run beyond its reach, the apparition let out a chilling howl and flew after her through the woods, leaving a startled Finnly and Davin gaping after them.

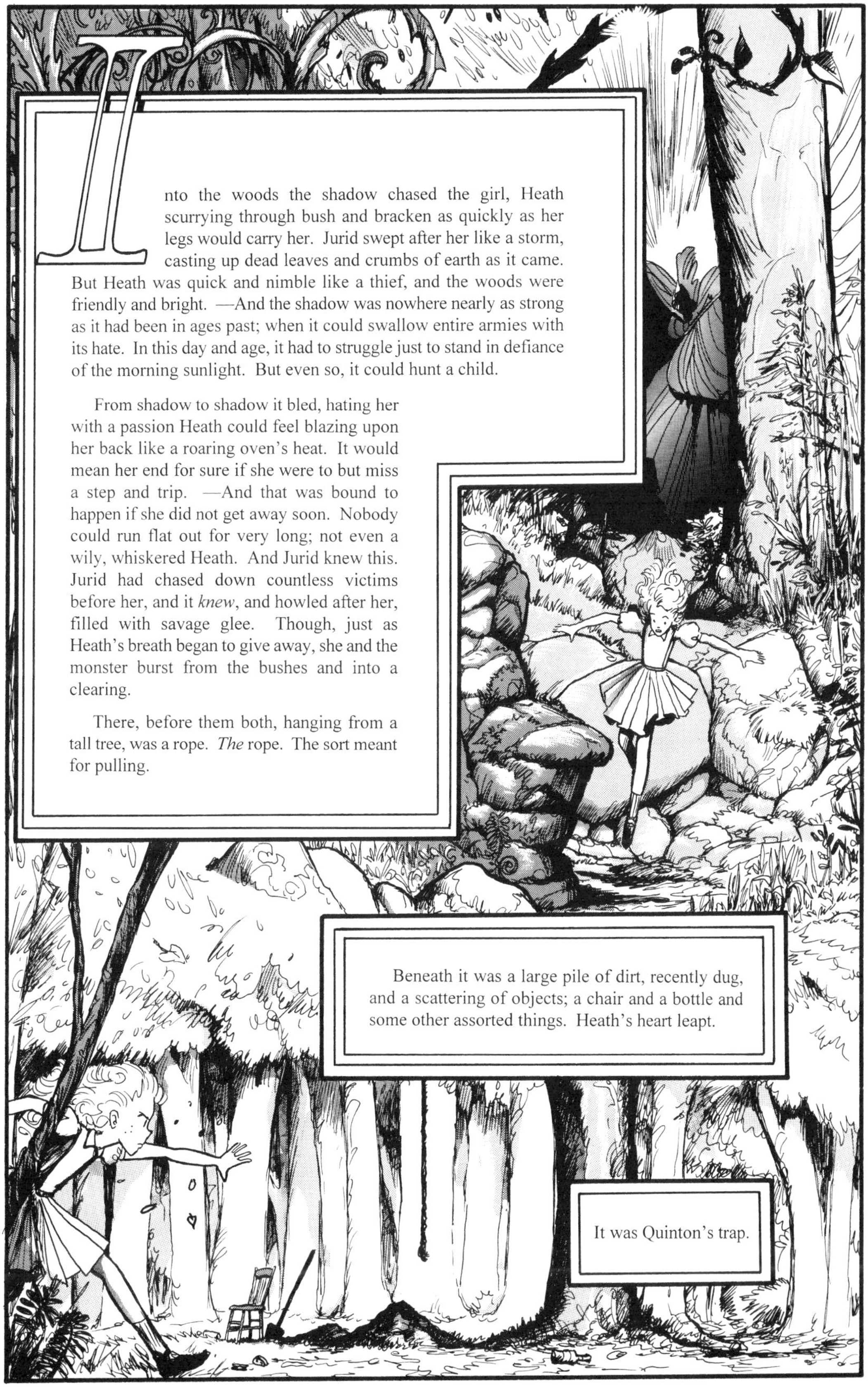

Into the woods the shadow chased the girl, Heath scurrying through bush and bracken as quickly as her legs would carry her. Jurid swept after her like a storm, casting up dead leaves and crumbs of earth as it came. But Heath was quick and nimble like a thief, and the woods were friendly and bright. —And the shadow was nowhere nearly as strong as it had been in ages past; when it could swallow entire armies with its hate. In this day and age, it had to struggle just to stand in defiance of the morning sunlight. But even so, it could hunt a child.

From shadow to shadow it bled, hating her with a passion Heath could feel blazing upon her back like a roaring oven's heat. It would mean her end for sure if she were to but miss a step and trip. —And that was bound to happen if she did not get away soon. Nobody could run flat out for very long; not even a wily, whiskered Heath. And Jurid knew this. Jurid had chased down countless victims before her, and it *knew*, and howled after her, filled with savage glee. Though, just as Heath's breath began to give away, she and the monster burst from the bushes and into a clearing.

There, before them both, hanging from a tall tree, was a rope. *The* rope. The sort meant for pulling.

Beneath it was a large pile of dirt, recently dug, and a scattering of objects; a chair and a bottle and some other assorted things. Heath's heart leapt.

It was Quinton's trap.

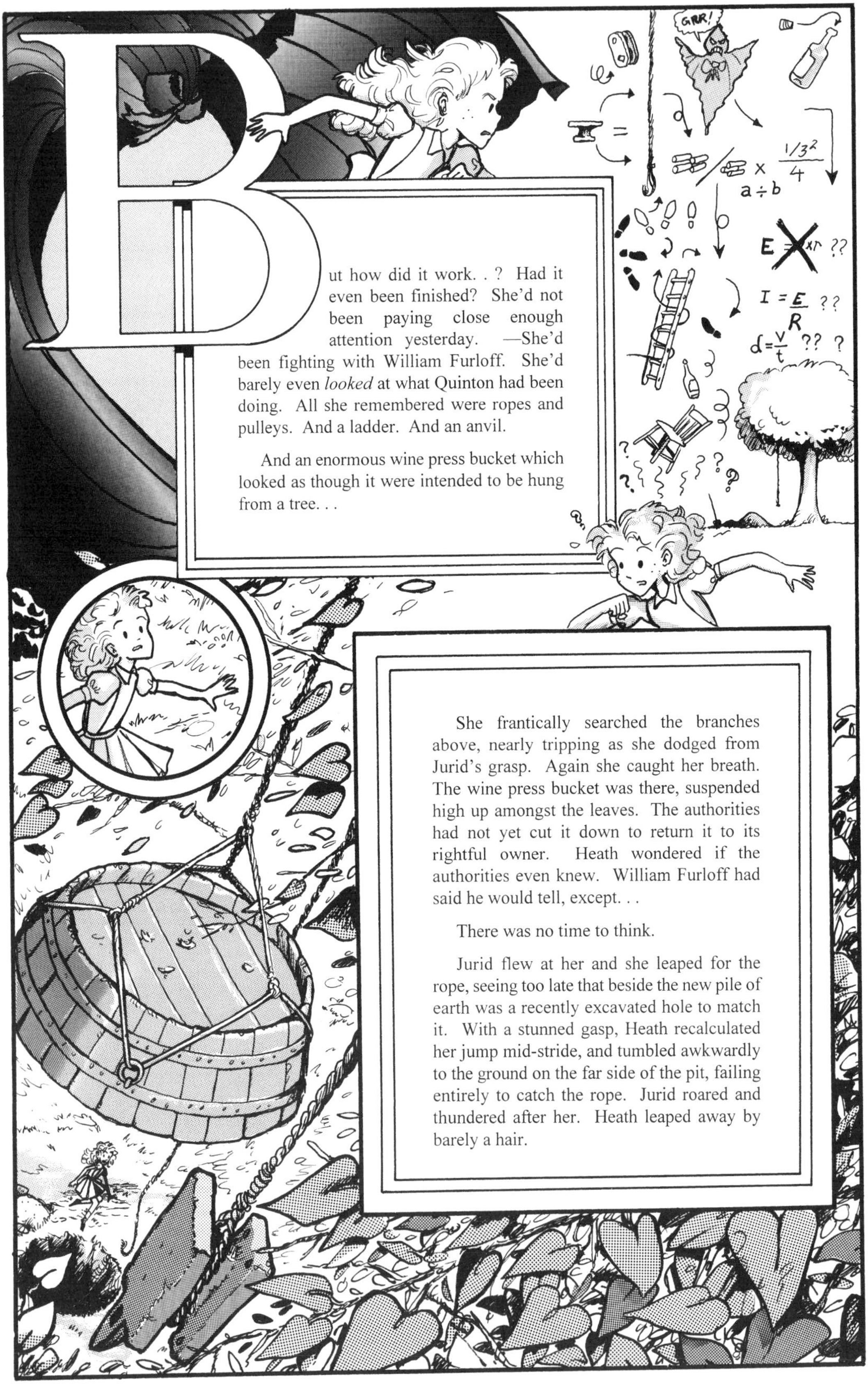
GRR!
=
$\frac{1/3^2}{4}$
x
a ÷ b
$I = \frac{E}{R}$??
$d = \frac{v}{t}$?? ?

But how did it work. . ? Had it even been finished? She'd not been paying close enough attention yesterday. —She'd been fighting with William Furloff. She'd barely even *looked* at what Quinton had been doing. All she remembered were ropes and pulleys. And a ladder. And an anvil.

And an enormous wine press bucket which looked as though it were intended to be hung from a tree. . .

She frantically searched the branches above, nearly tripping as she dodged from Jurid's grasp. Again she caught her breath. The wine press bucket was there, suspended high up amongst the leaves. The authorities had not yet cut it down to return it to its rightful owner. Heath wondered if the authorities even knew. William Furloff had said he would tell, except. . .

There was no time to think.

Jurid flew at her and she leaped for the rope, seeing too late that beside the new pile of earth was a recently excavated hole to match it. With a stunned gasp, Heath recalculated her jump mid-stride, and tumbled awkwardly to the ground on the far side of the pit, failing entirely to catch the rope. Jurid roared and thundered after her. Heath leaped away by barely a hair.

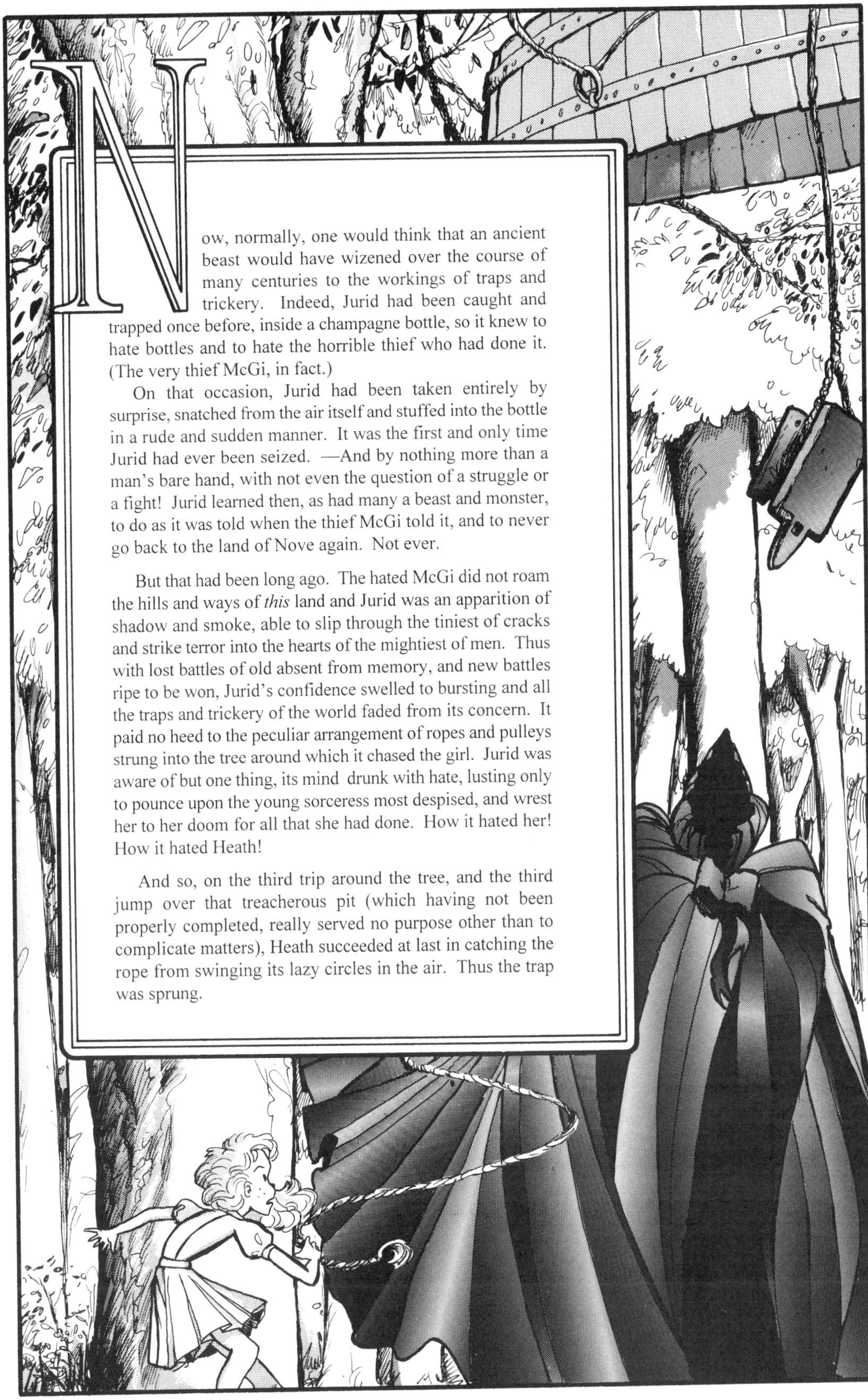

Now, normally, one would think that an ancient beast would have wizened over the course of many centuries to the workings of traps and trickery. Indeed, Jurid had been caught and trapped once before, inside a champagne bottle, so it knew to hate bottles and to hate the horrible thief who had done it. (The very thief McGi, in fact.)

On that occasion, Jurid had been taken entirely by surprise, snatched from the air itself and stuffed into the bottle in a rude and sudden manner. It was the first and only time Jurid had ever been seized. —And by nothing more than a man's bare hand, with not even the question of a struggle or a fight! Jurid learned then, as had many a beast and monster, to do as it was told when the thief McGi told it, and to never go back to the land of Nove again. Not ever.

But that had been long ago. The hated McGi did not roam the hills and ways of *this* land and Jurid was an apparition of shadow and smoke, able to slip through the tiniest of cracks and strike terror into the hearts of the mightiest of men. Thus with lost battles of old absent from memory, and new battles ripe to be won, Jurid's confidence swelled to bursting and all the traps and trickery of the world faded from its concern. It paid no heed to the peculiar arrangement of ropes and pulleys strung into the tree around which it chased the girl. Jurid was aware of but one thing, its mind drunk with hate, lusting only to pounce upon the young sorceress most despised, and wrest her to her doom for all that she had done. How it hated her! How it hated Heath!

And so, on the third trip around the tree, and the third jump over that treacherous pit (which having not been properly completed, really served no purpose other than to complicate matters), Heath succeeded at last in catching the rope from swinging its lazy circles in the air. Thus the trap was sprung.

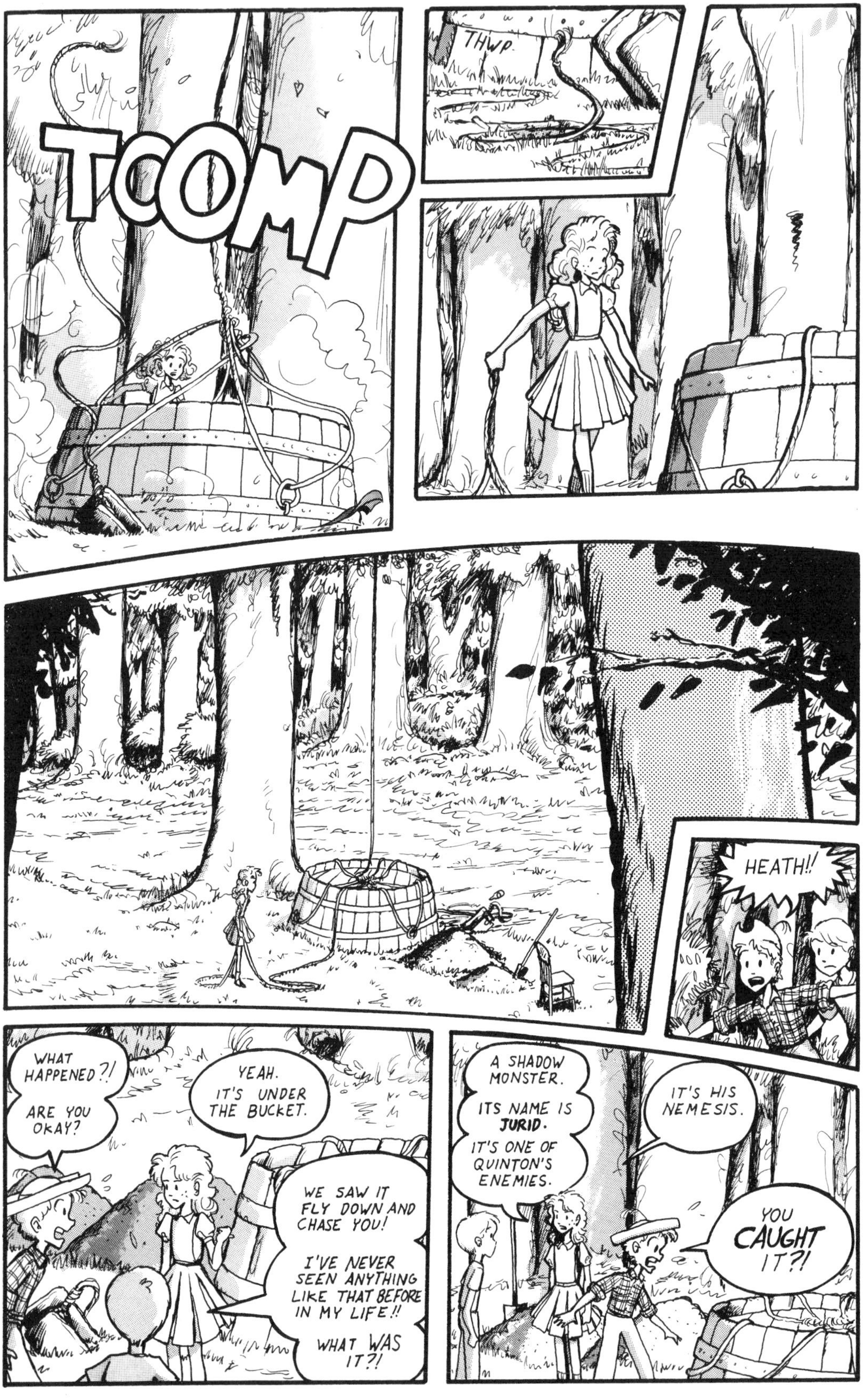
TCOMP
THWP
HEATH!!
WHAT HAPPENED?! ARE YOU OKAY?
YEAH. IT'S UNDER THE BUCKET.
WE SAW IT FLY DOWN AND CHASE YOU!
I'VE NEVER SEEN ANYTHING LIKE THAT BEFORE IN MY LIFE!!
WHAT WAS IT?!
A SHADOW MONSTER.
ITS NAME IS JURID.
IT'S ONE OF QUINTON'S ENEMIES.
IT'S HIS NEMESIS.
YOU CAUGHT IT?!

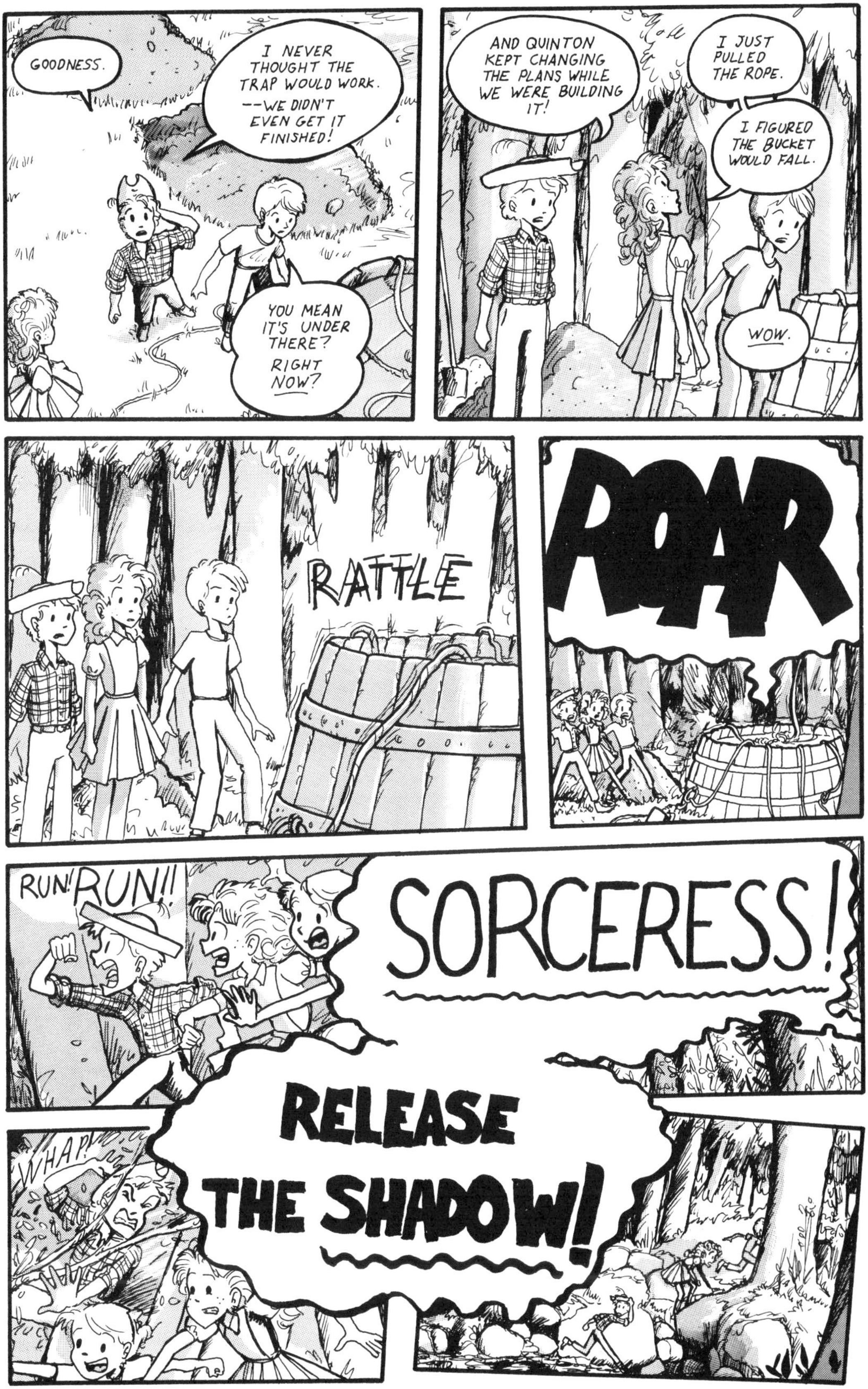
GOODNESS.
I NEVER THOUGHT THE TRAP WOULD WORK. --WE DIDN'T EVEN GET IT FINISHED!
YOU MEAN IT'S UNDER THERE? RIGHT NOW?
AND QUINTON KEPT CHANGING THE PLANS WHILE WE WERE BUILDING IT!
I JUST PULLED THE ROPE.
I FIGURED THE BUCKET WOULD FALL.
WOW.
RATTLE
ROAR
RUN! RUN!!
SORCERESS!
RELEASE THE SHADOW!
WHAP!

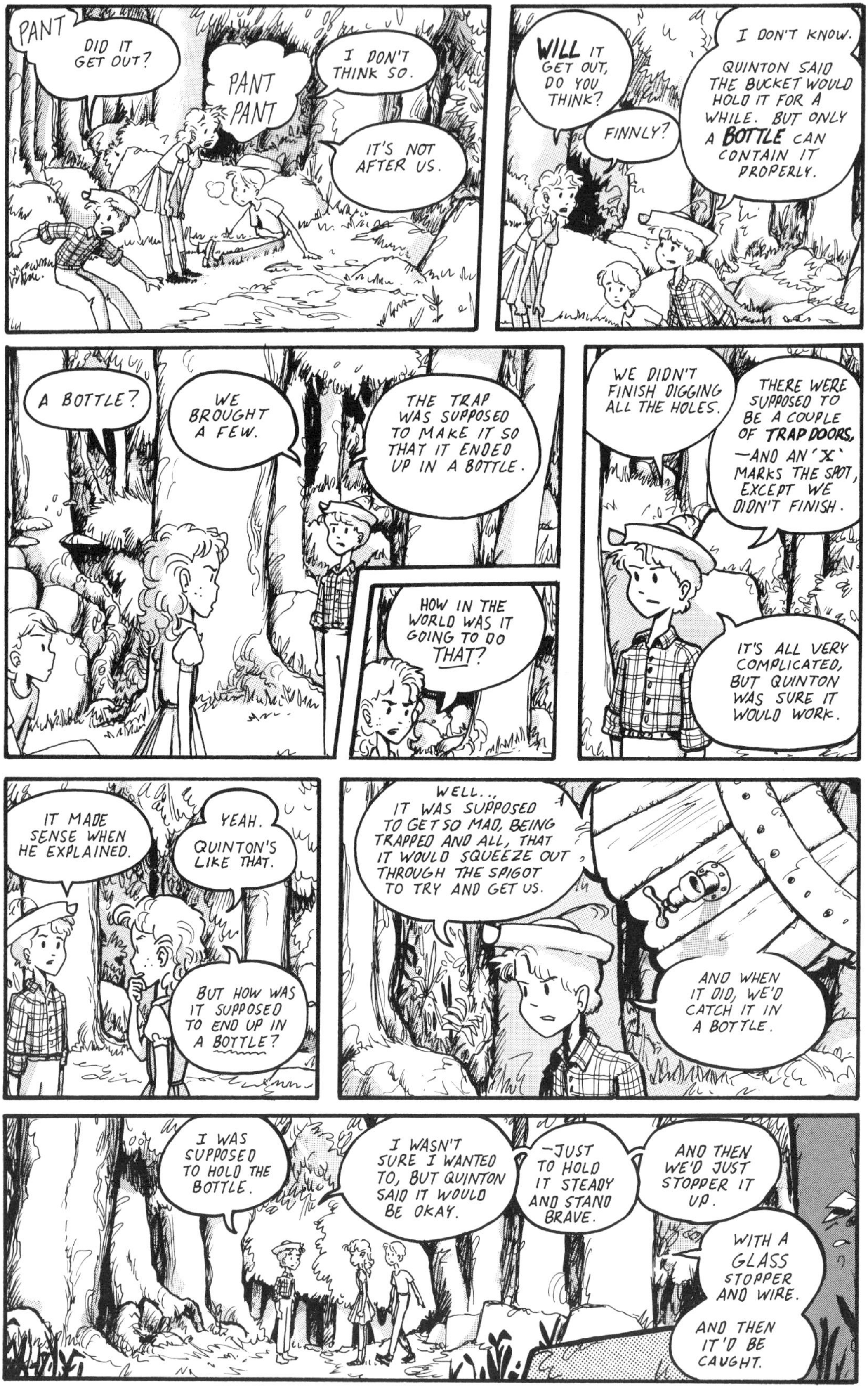
PANT
DID IT GET OUT?
PANT PANT
I DON'T THINK SO.
IT'S NOT AFTER US.
WILL IT GET OUT, DO YOU THINK?
FINNLY?
I DON'T KNOW.
QUINTON SAID THE BUCKET WOULD HOLD IT FOR A WHILE. BUT ONLY A BOTTLE CAN CONTAIN IT PROPERLY.
A BOTTLE?
WE BROUGHT A FEW.
THE TRAP WAS SUPPOSED TO MAKE IT SO THAT IT ENDED UP IN A BOTTLE.
HOW IN THE WORLD WAS IT GOING TO DO THAT?
WE DIDN'T FINISH DIGGING ALL THE HOLES.
THERE WERE SUPPOSED TO BE A COUPLE OF TRAP DOORS,
—AND AN 'X' MARKS THE SPOT, EXCEPT WE DIDN'T FINISH.
IT'S ALL VERY COMPLICATED, BUT QUINTON WAS SURE IT WOULD WORK.
IT MADE SENSE WHEN HE EXPLAINED.
YEAH.
QUINTON'S LIKE THAT.
BUT HOW WAS IT SUPPOSED TO END UP IN A BOTTLE?
WELL.. IT WAS SUPPOSED TO GET SO MAD, BEING TRAPPED AND ALL, THAT IT WOULD SQUEEZE OUT THROUGH THE SPIGOT TO TRY AND GET US.
AND WHEN IT DID, WE'D CATCH IT IN A BOTTLE.
I WAS SUPPOSED TO HOLD THE BOTTLE.
I WASN'T SURE I WANTED TO, BUT QUINTON SAID IT WOULD BE OKAY.
—JUST TO HOLD IT STEADY AND STAND BRAVE.
AND THEN WE'D JUST STOPPER IT UP.
WITH A GLASS STOPPER AND WIRE.
AND THEN IT'D BE CAUGHT.

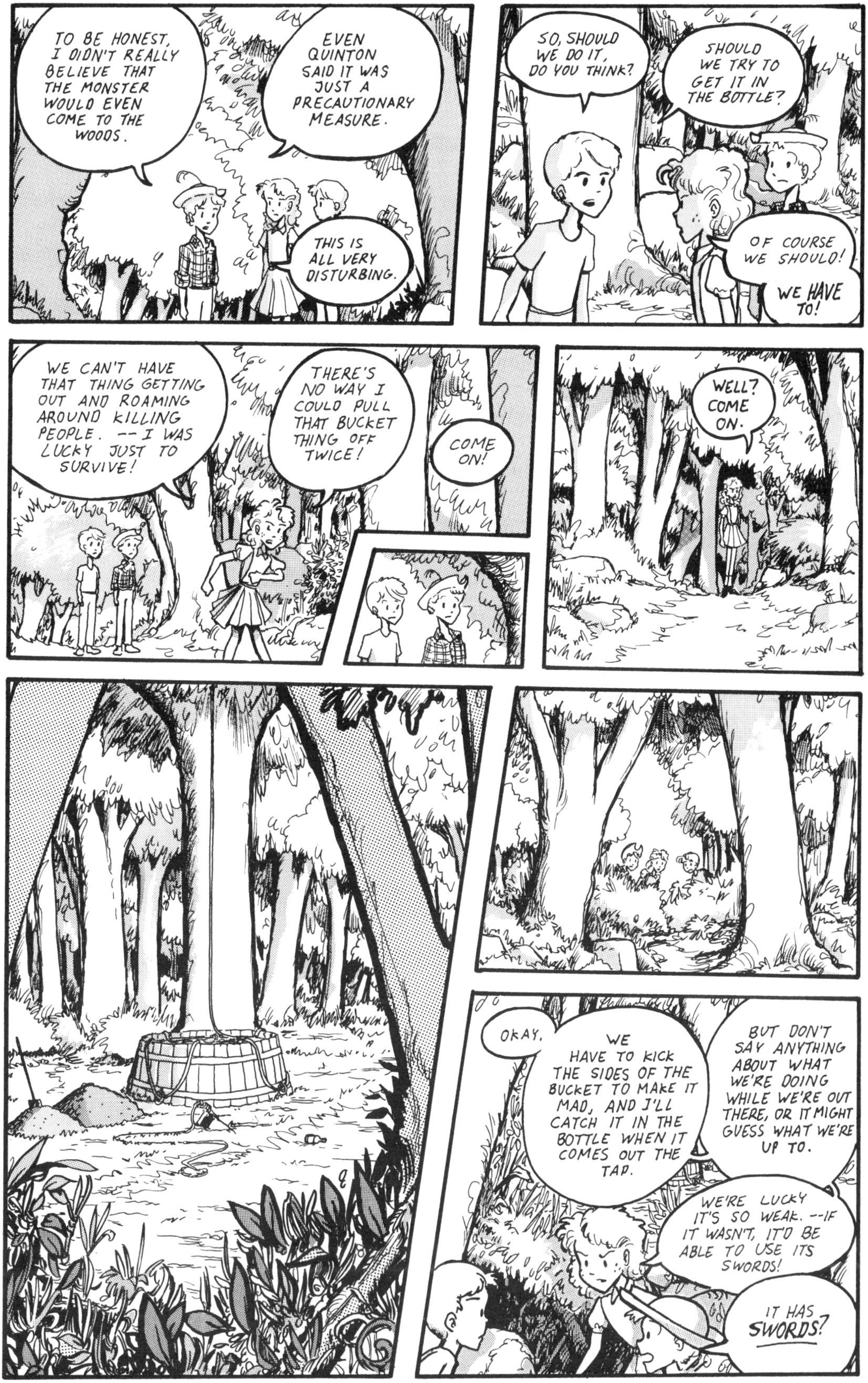
TO BE HONEST, I DIDN'T REALLY BELIEVE THAT THE MONSTER WOULD EVEN COME TO THE WOODS.
EVEN QUINTON SAID IT WAS JUST A PRECAUTIONARY MEASURE.
THIS IS ALL VERY DISTURBING.
SO, SHOULD WE DO IT, DO YOU THINK?
SHOULD WE TRY TO GET IT IN THE BOTTLE?
OF COURSE WE SHOULD!
WE HAVE TO!
WE CAN'T HAVE THAT THING GETTING OUT AND ROAMING AROUND KILLING PEOPLE. --I WAS LUCKY JUST TO SURVIVE!
THERE'S NO WAY I COULD PULL THAT BUCKET THING OFF TWICE!
COME ON!
WELL? COME ON.
OKAY.
WE HAVE TO KICK THE SIDES OF THE BUCKET TO MAKE IT MAD, AND I'LL CATCH IT IN THE BOTTLE WHEN IT COMES OUT THE TAP.
BUT DON'T SAY ANYTHING ABOUT WHAT WE'RE DOING WHILE WE'RE OUT THERE, OR IT MIGHT GUESS WHAT WE'RE UP TO.
WE'RE LUCKY IT'S SO WEAK. --IF IT WASN'T, IT'D BE ABLE TO USE ITS SWORDS!
IT HAS SWORDS?

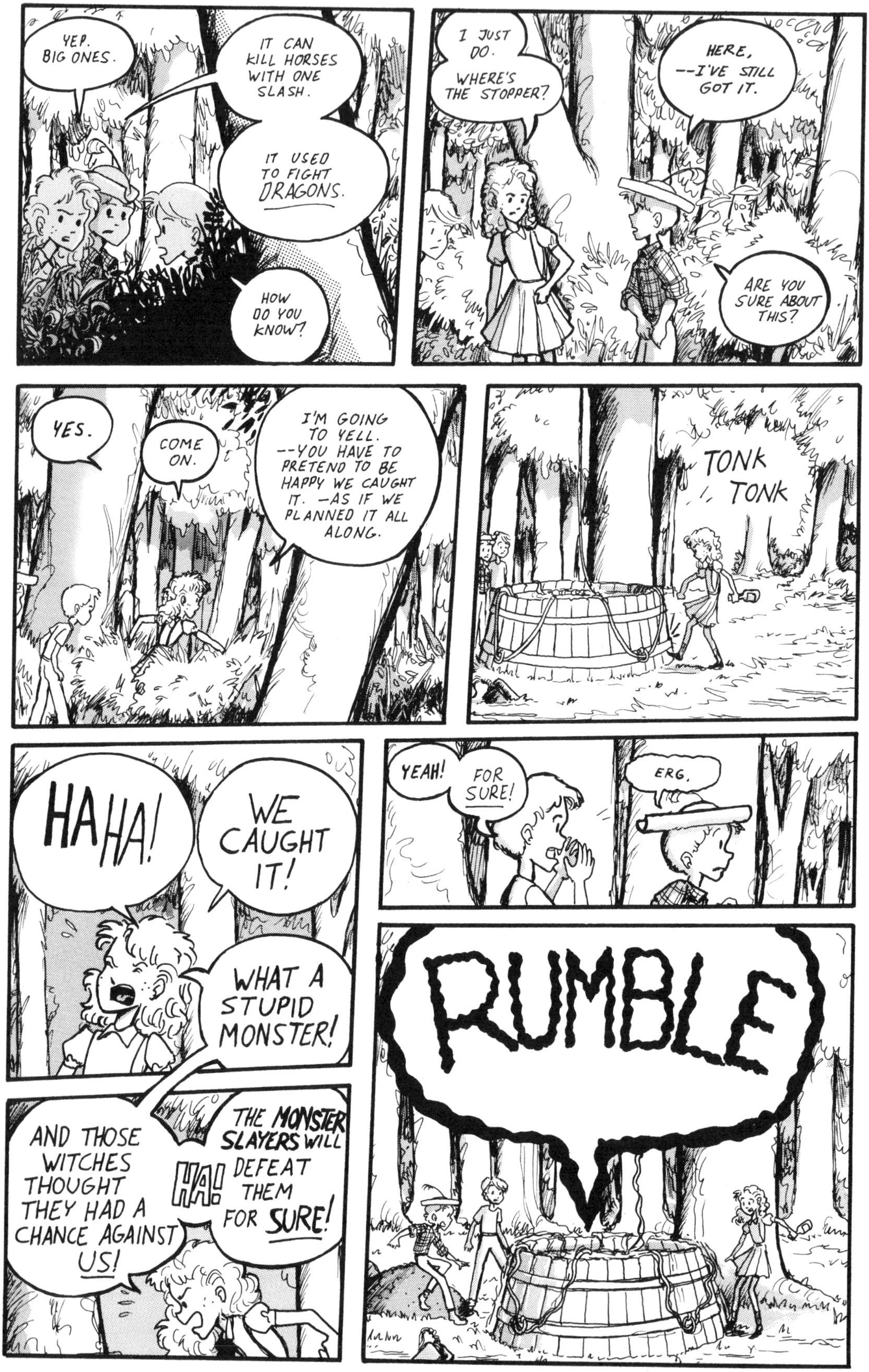
YEP. BIG ONES.
IT CAN KILL HORSES WITH ONE SLASH.
IT USED TO FIGHT DRAGONS.
HOW DO YOU KNOW?
I JUST DO.
WHERE'S THE STOPPER?
HERE, --I'VE STILL GOT IT.
ARE YOU SURE ABOUT THIS?
YES.
COME ON.
I'M GOING TO YELL. --YOU HAVE TO PRETEND TO BE HAPPY WE CAUGHT IT. —AS IF WE PLANNED IT ALL ALONG.
TONK TONK
HAHA!
WE CAUGHT IT!
WHAT A STUPID MONSTER!
AND THOSE WITCHES THOUGHT THEY HAD A CHANCE AGAINST US!
HA!
THE MONSTER SLAYERS WILL DEFEAT THEM FOR SURE!
YEAH!
FOR SURE!
ERG.
RUMBLE

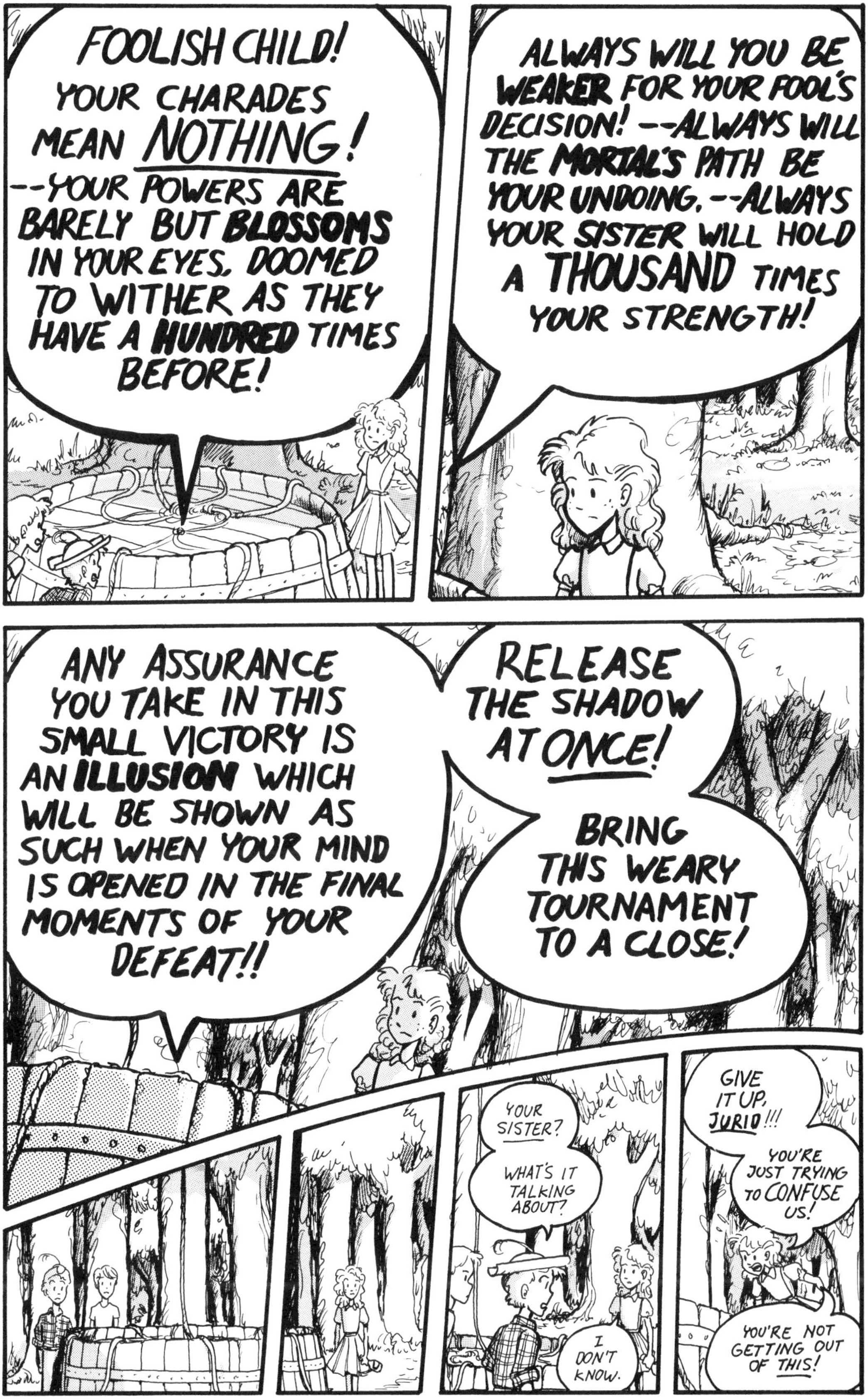
FOOLISH CHILD! YOUR CHARADES MEAN NOTHING! --YOUR POWERS ARE BARELY BUT BLOSSOMS IN YOUR EYES, DOOMED TO WITHER AS THEY HAVE A HUNDRED TIMES BEFORE!
ALWAYS WILL YOU BE WEAKER FOR YOUR FOOL'S DECISION! --ALWAYS WILL THE MORTAL'S PATH BE YOUR UNDOING. --ALWAYS YOUR SISTER WILL HOLD A THOUSAND TIMES YOUR STRENGTH!
ANY ASSURANCE YOU TAKE IN THIS SMALL VICTORY IS AN ILLUSION WHICH WILL BE SHOWN AS SUCH WHEN YOUR MIND IS OPENED IN THE FINAL MOMENTS OF YOUR DEFEAT!!
RELEASE THE SHADOW AT ONCE!
BRING THIS WEARY TOURNAMENT TO A CLOSE!
YOUR SISTER?
WHAT'S IT TALKING ABOUT?
I DON'T KNOW.
GIVE IT UP, JURIO!!!
YOU'RE JUST TRYING TO CONFUSE US!
YOU'RE NOT GETTING OUT OF THIS!

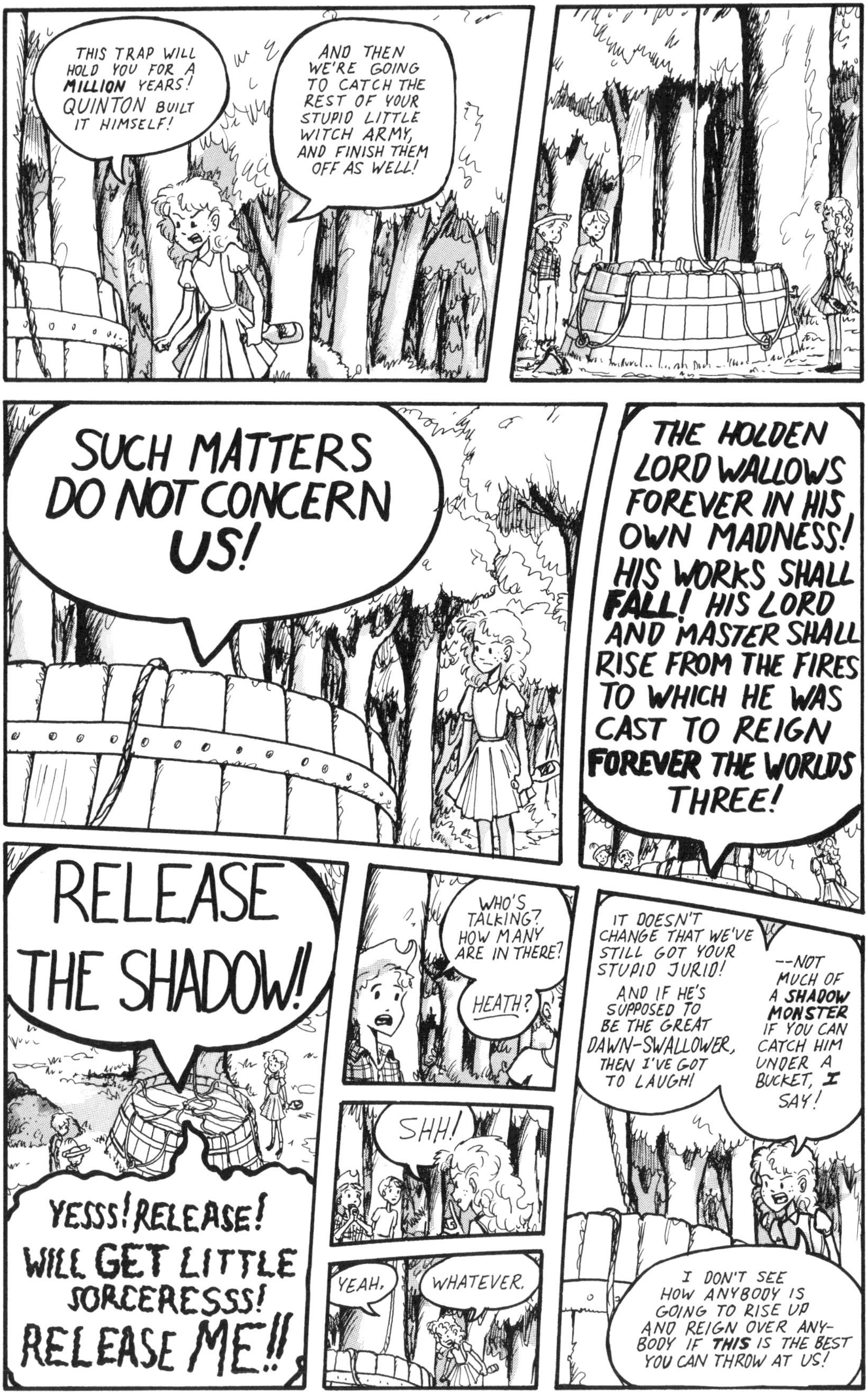
THIS TRAP WILL HOLD YOU FOR A MILLION YEARS! QUINTON BUILT IT HIMSELF!
AND THEN WE'RE GOING TO CATCH THE REST OF YOUR STUPID LITTLE WITCH ARMY, AND FINISH THEM OFF AS WELL!
SUCH MATTERS DO NOT CONCERN US!
THE HOLDEN LORD WALLOWS FOREVER IN HIS OWN MADNESS! HIS WORKS SHALL FALL! HIS LORD AND MASTER SHALL RISE FROM THE FIRES TO WHICH HE WAS CAST TO REIGN FOREVER THE WORLDS THREE!
RELEASE THE SHADOW!
YESSS! RELEASE! WILL GET LITTLE SORCERESSS! RELEASE ME!!
WHO'S TALKING? HOW MANY ARE IN THERE?
HEATH?
SHH!
YEAH,
WHATEVER.
IT DOESN'T CHANGE THAT WE'VE STILL GOT YOUR STUPID JURID!
AND IF HE'S SUPPOSED TO BE THE GREAT DAWN-SWALLOWER, THEN I'VE GOT TO LAUGH!
--NOT MUCH OF A SHADOW MONSTER IF YOU CAN CATCH HIM UNDER A BUCKET, I SAY!
I DON'T SEE HOW ANYBODY IS GOING TO RISE UP AND REIGN OVER ANYBODY IF THIS IS THE BEST YOU CAN THROW AT US!

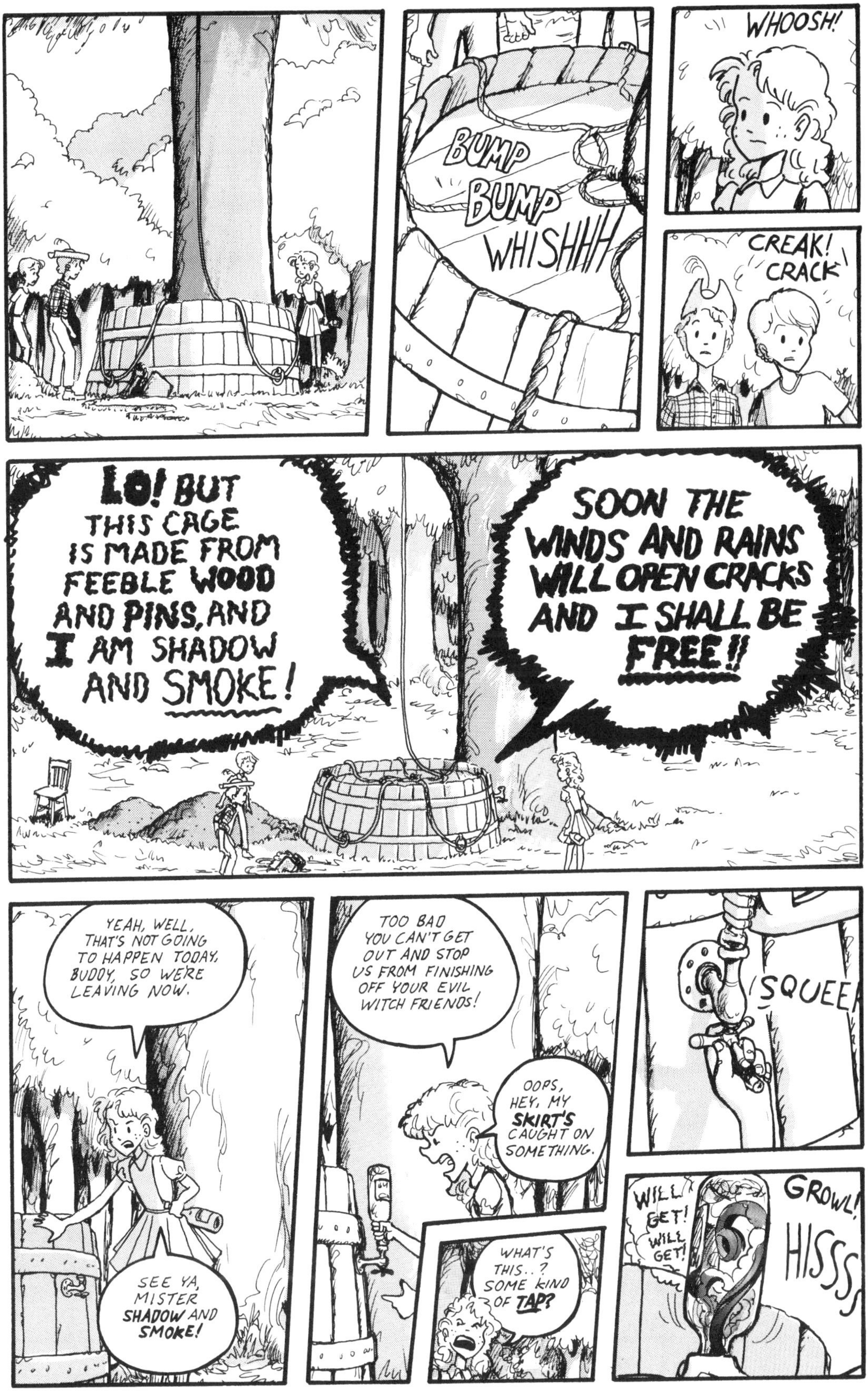

BUMP
BUMP
WHISHHH
WHOOSH!
CREAK! CRACK
LO! BUT THIS CAGE IS MADE FROM FEEBLE WOOD AND PINS, AND I AM SHADOW AND SMOKE!
SOON THE WINDS AND RAINS WILL OPEN CRACKS AND I SHALL BE FREE!!
YEAH, WELL, THAT'S NOT GOING TO HAPPEN TODAY, BUDDY, SO WE'RE LEAVING NOW.
SEE YA, MISTER SHADOW AND SMOKE!
TOO BAD YOU CAN'T GET OUT AND STOP US FROM FINISHING OFF YOUR EVIL WITCH FRIENDS!
OOPS, HEY, MY SKIRT'S CAUGHT ON SOMETHING.
WHAT'S THIS..? SOME KIND OF TAP?
SQUEE
WILL GET! WILL GET!
GROWL!
HISSS

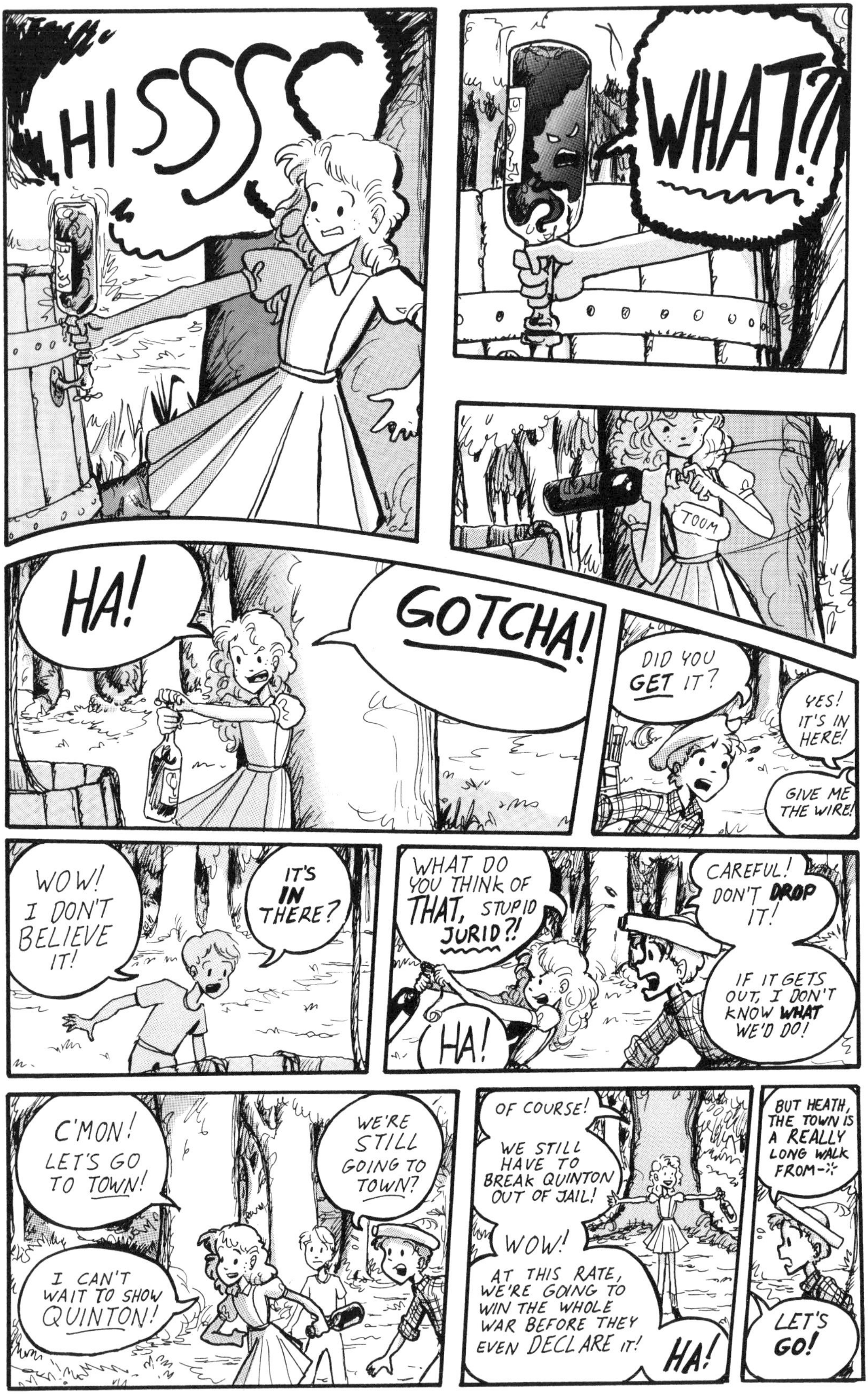
HISSSS
WHAT?!
TOOM
HA!
GOTCHA!
DID YOU GET IT?
YES! IT'S IN HERE!
GIVE ME THE WIRE!
WOW! I DON'T BELIEVE IT!
IT'S IN THERE?
WHAT DO YOU THINK OF THAT, STUPID JURID?!
HA!
CAREFUL! DON'T DROP IT!
IF IT GETS OUT, I DON'T KNOW WHAT WE'D DO!
C'MON! LET'S GO TO TOWN!
I CAN'T WAIT TO SHOW QUINTON!
WE'RE STILL GOING TO TOWN?
OF COURSE!
WE STILL HAVE TO BREAK QUINTON OUT OF JAIL!
WOW!
AT THIS RATE, WE'RE GOING TO WIN THE WHOLE WAR BEFORE THEY EVEN DECLARE IT!
HA!
BUT HEATH, THE TOWN IS A REALLY LONG WALK FROM--
LET'S GO!

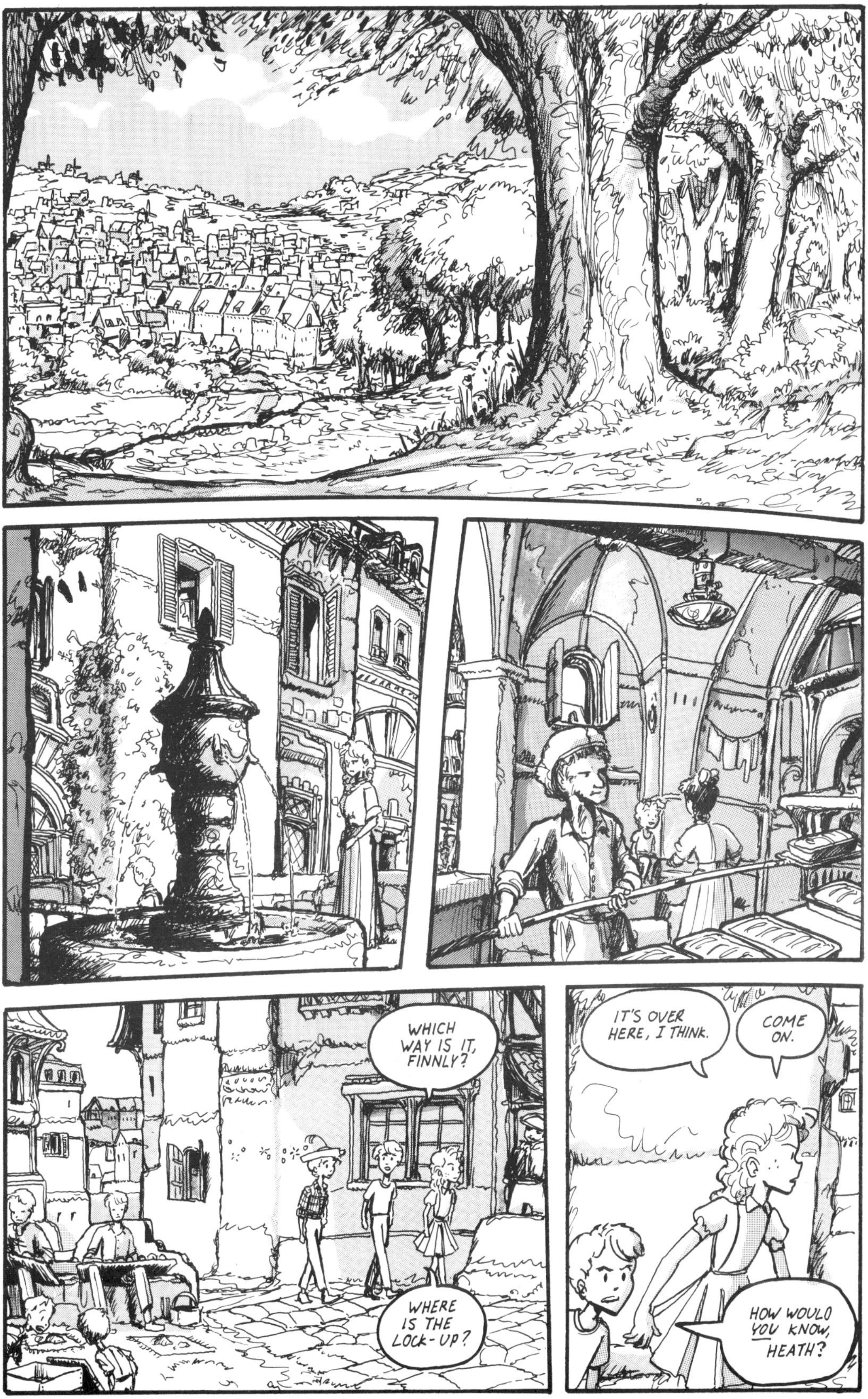
WHICH WAY IS IT, FINNLY?
WHERE IS THE LOCK-UP?
IT'S OVER HERE, I THINK.
COME ON.
HOW WOULD YOU KNOW, HEATH?

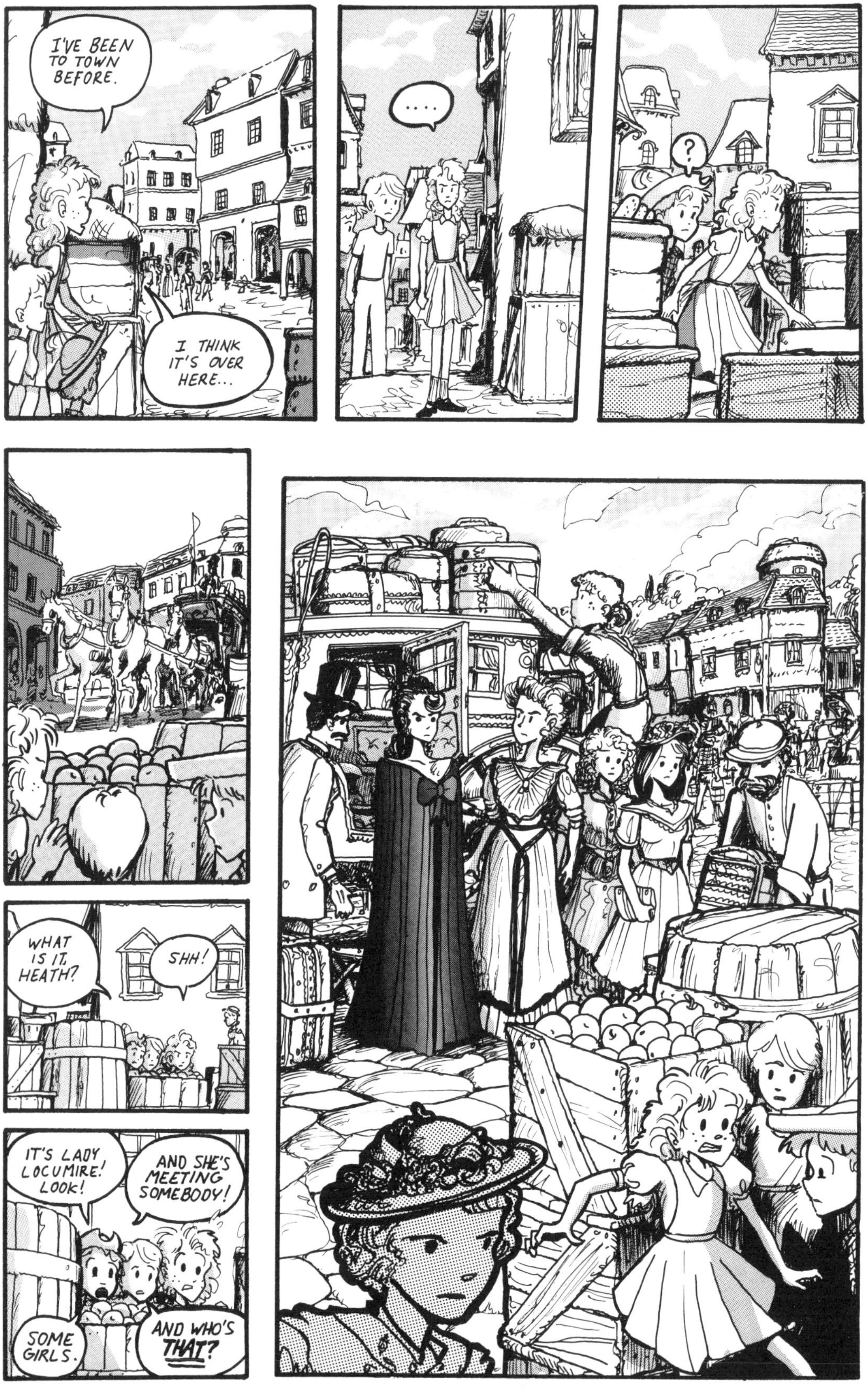

I'VE BEEN TO TOWN BEFORE.
I THINK IT'S OVER HERE...
....
?
WHAT IS IT, HEATH?
SHH!
IT'S LADY LOCUMIRE! LOOK!
AND SHE'S MEETING SOMEBODY!
SOME GIRLS.
AND WHO'S THAT?

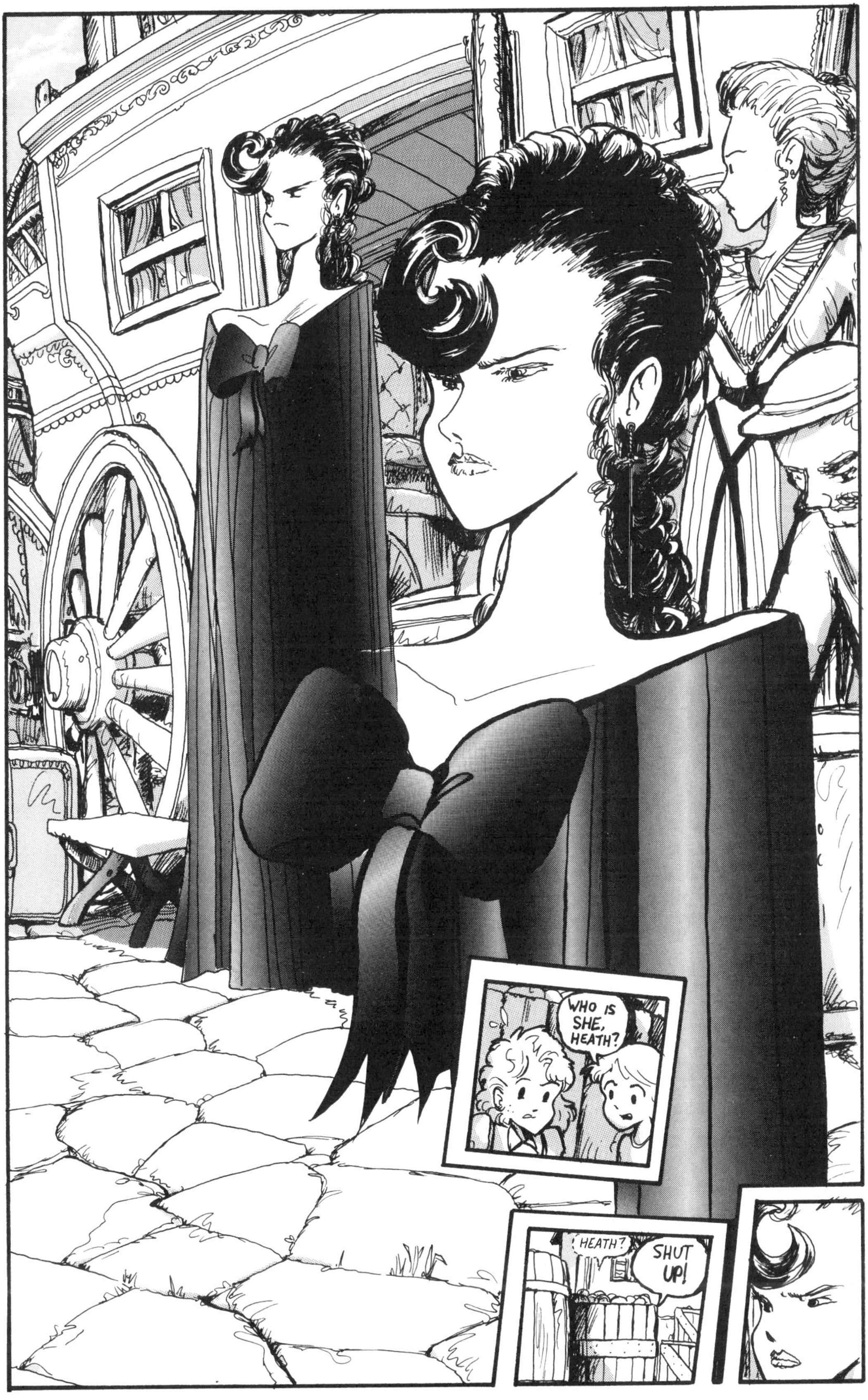
WHO IS SHE, HEATH?
HEATH?
SHUT UP!

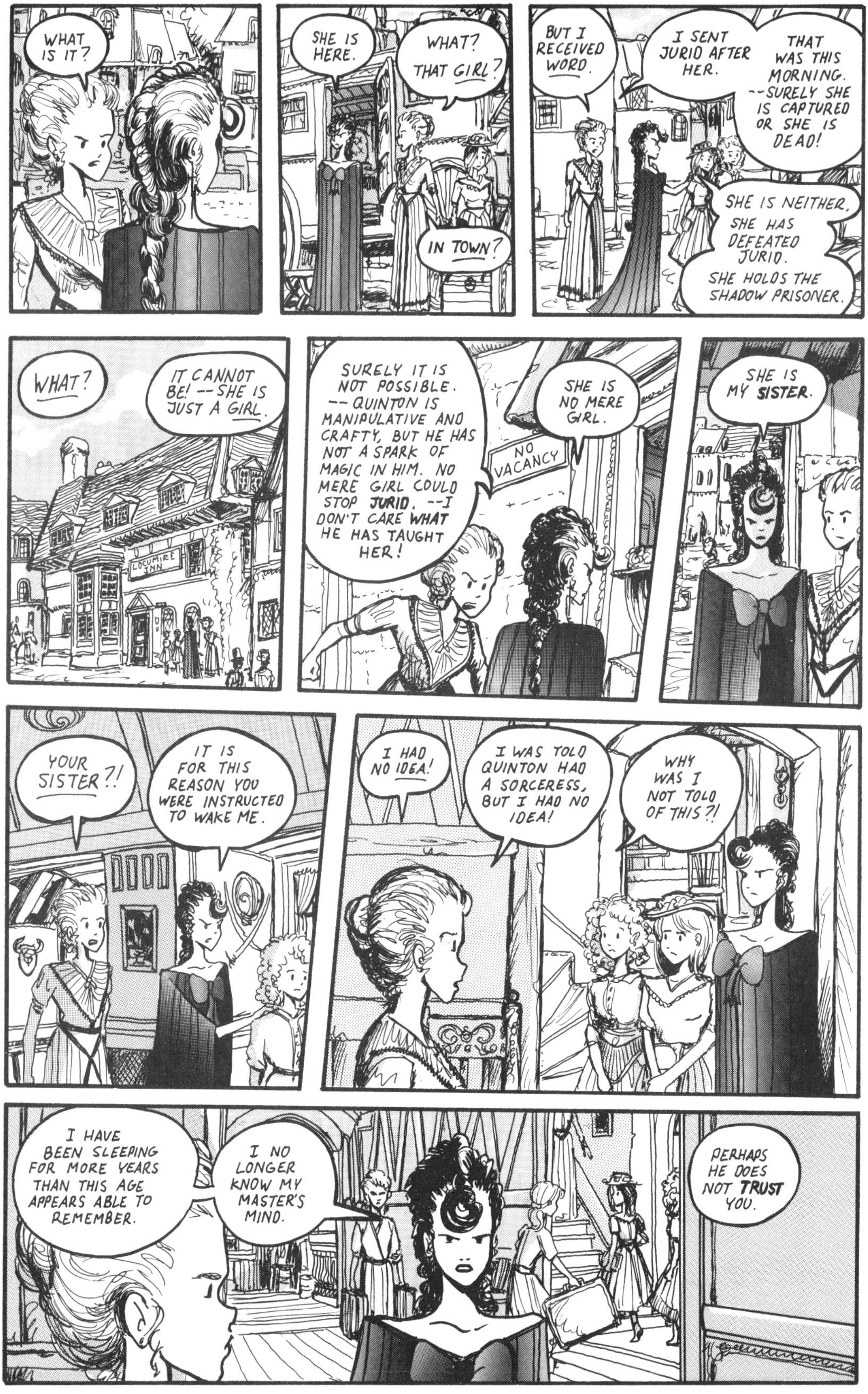
WHAT IS IT?
SHE IS HERE.
WHAT? THAT GIRL?
IN TOWN?
BUT I RECEIVED WORD.
I SENT JURID AFTER HER.
THAT WAS THIS MORNING. --SURELY SHE IS CAPTURED OR SHE IS DEAD!
SHE IS NEITHER. SHE HAS DEFEATED JURID.
SHE HOLDS THE SHADOW PRISONER.
WHAT?
IT CANNOT BE! --SHE IS JUST A GIRL.
LOCUMIRE INN
SURELY IT IS NOT POSSIBLE. --QUINTON IS MANIPULATIVE AND CRAFTY, BUT HE HAS NOT A SPARK OF MAGIC IN HIM. NO MERE GIRL COULD STOP **JURID**. --I DON'T CARE **WHAT** HE HAS TAUGHT HER!
NO VACANCY
SHE IS NO MERE GIRL.
SHE IS MY **SISTER**.
YOUR SISTER?!
IT IS FOR THIS REASON YOU WERE INSTRUCTED TO WAKE ME.
I HAD NO IDEA!
I WAS TOLD QUINTON HAD A SORCERESS, BUT I HAD NO IDEA!
WHY WAS I NOT TOLD OF THIS?!
I HAVE BEEN SLEEPING FOR MORE YEARS THAN THIS AGE APPEARS ABLE TO REMEMBER.
I NO LONGER KNOW MY MASTER'S MIND.
PERHAPS HE DOES NOT **TRUST** YOU.

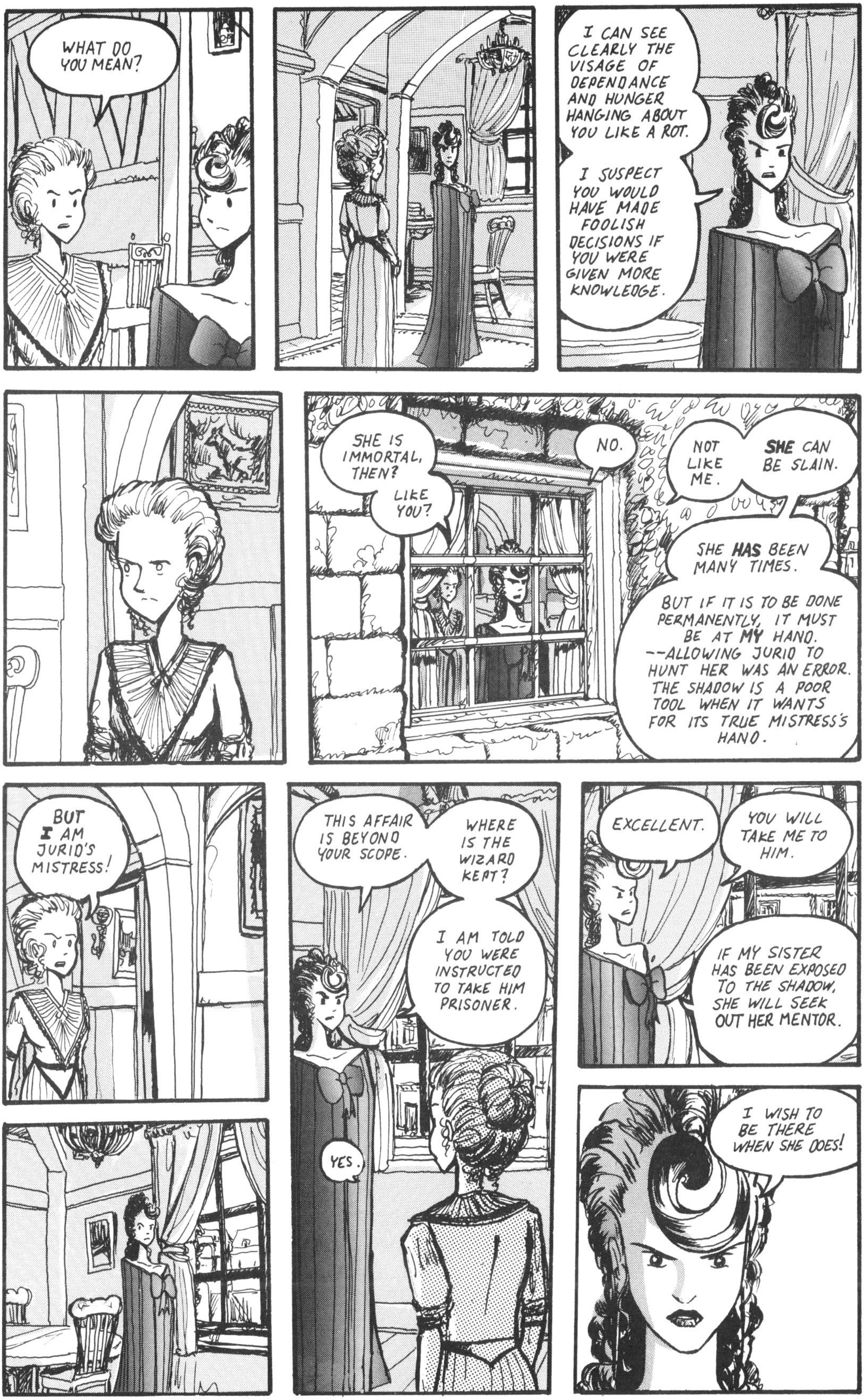
WHAT DO YOU MEAN?
I CAN SEE CLEARLY THE VISAGE OF DEPENDANCE AND HUNGER HANGING ABOUT YOU LIKE A ROT.
I SUSPECT YOU WOULD HAVE MADE FOOLISH DECISIONS IF YOU WERE GIVEN MORE KNOWLEDGE.
SHE IS IMMORTAL, THEN?
LIKE YOU?
NO.
NOT LIKE ME.
SHE CAN BE SLAIN.
SHE HAS BEEN MANY TIMES.
BUT IF IT IS TO BE DONE PERMANENTLY, IT MUST BE AT MY HAND. --ALLOWING JURID TO HUNT HER WAS AN ERROR. THE SHADOW IS A POOR TOOL WHEN IT WANTS FOR ITS TRUE MISTRESS'S HAND.
BUT I AM JURID'S MISTRESS!
THIS AFFAIR IS BEYOND YOUR SCOPE.
WHERE IS THE WIZARD KEPT?
I AM TOLD YOU WERE INSTRUCTED TO TAKE HIM PRISONER.
YES.
EXCELLENT.
YOU WILL TAKE ME TO HIM.
IF MY SISTER HAS BEEN EXPOSED TO THE SHADOW, SHE WILL SEEK OUT HER MENTOR.
I WISH TO BE THERE WHEN SHE DOES!

Chapter 18

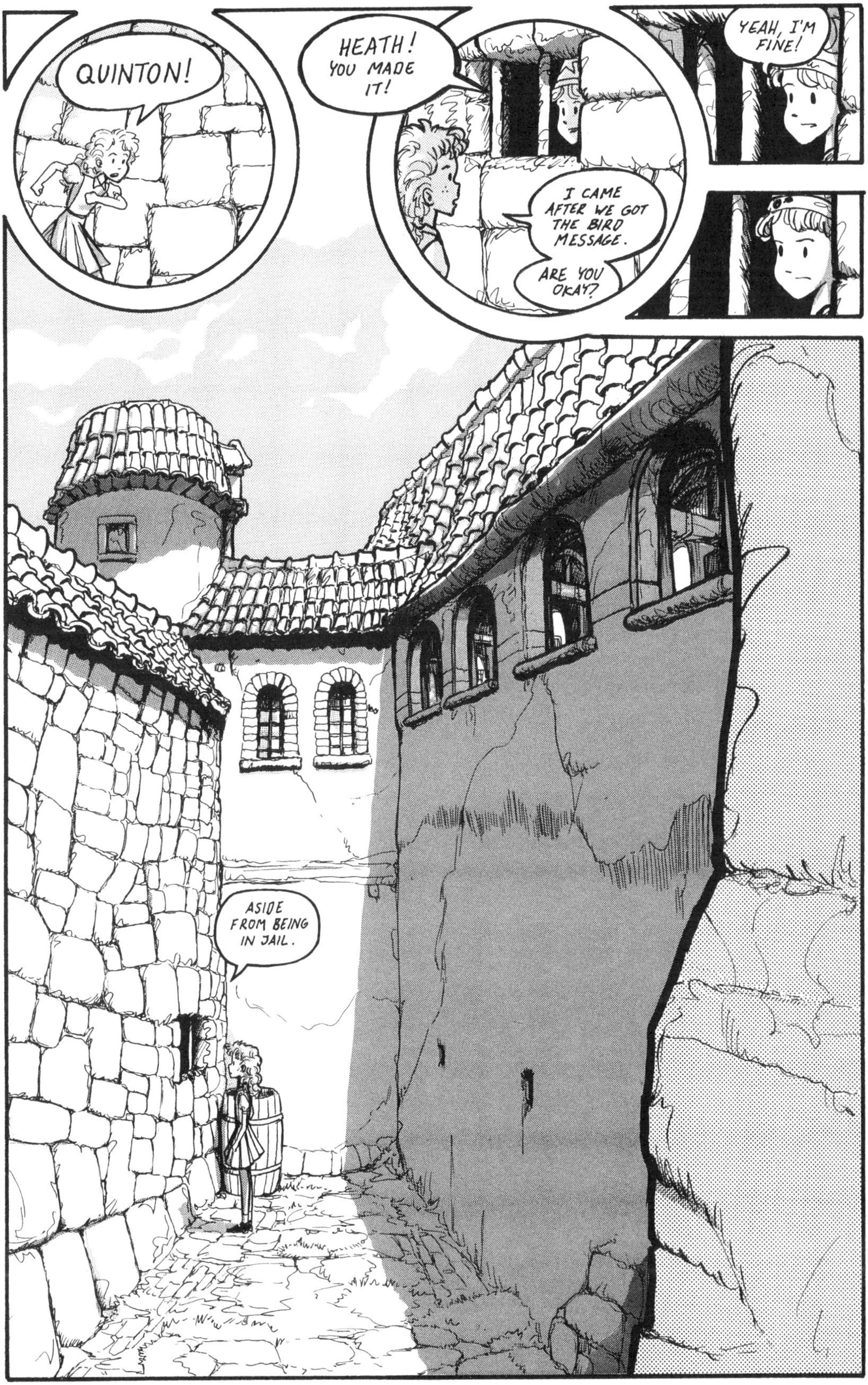
QUINTON!
HEATH! YOU MADE IT!
YEAH, I'M FINE!
I CAME AFTER WE GOT THE BIRD MESSAGE.
ARE YOU OKAY?
ASIDE FROM BEING IN JAIL.

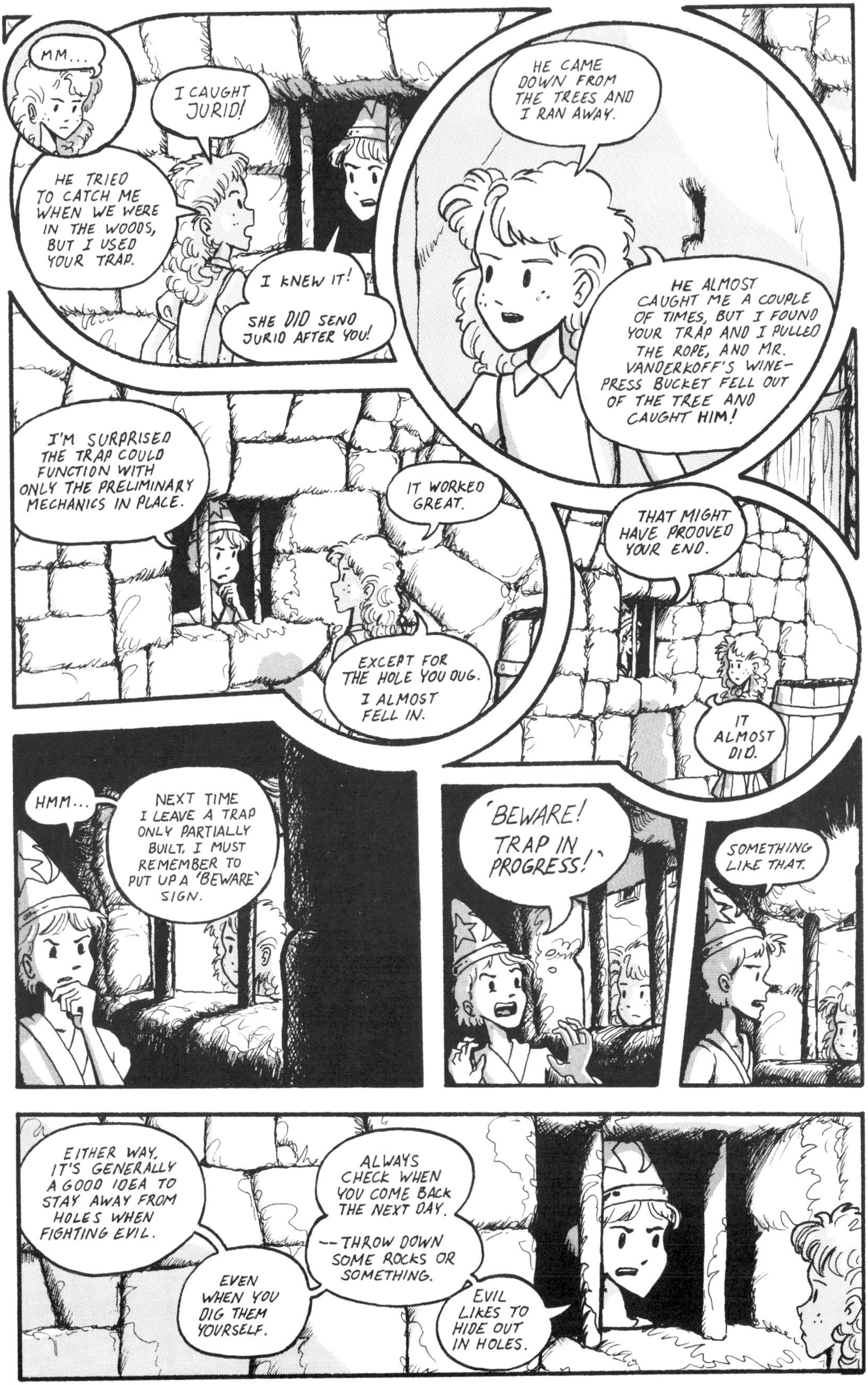
MM...
I CAUGHT JURID!
HE TRIED TO CATCH ME WHEN WE WERE IN THE WOODS, BUT I USED YOUR TRAP.
I KNEW IT!
SHE DID SEND JURID AFTER YOU!
HE CAME DOWN FROM THE TREES AND I RAN AWAY.
HE ALMOST CAUGHT ME A COUPLE OF TIMES, BUT I FOUND YOUR TRAP AND I PULLED THE ROPE, AND MR. VANDERKOFF'S WINE-PRESS BUCKET FELL OUT OF THE TREE AND CAUGHT HIM!
I'M SURPRISED THE TRAP COULD FUNCTION WITH ONLY THE PRELIMINARY MECHANICS IN PLACE.
IT WORKED GREAT.
EXCEPT FOR THE HOLE YOU DUG. I ALMOST FELL IN.
THAT MIGHT HAVE PROOVED YOUR END.
IT ALMOST DID.
HMM...
NEXT TIME I LEAVE A TRAP ONLY PARTIALLY BUILT, I MUST REMEMBER TO PUT UP A 'BEWARE' SIGN.
'BEWARE! TRAP IN PROGRESS!'
SOMETHING LIKE THAT.
EITHER WAY, IT'S GENERALLY A GOOD IDEA TO STAY AWAY FROM HOLES WHEN FIGHTING EVIL.
EVEN WHEN YOU DIG THEM YOURSELF.
ALWAYS CHECK WHEN YOU COME BACK THE NEXT DAY.
--THROW DOWN SOME ROCKS OR SOMETHING.
EVIL LIKES TO HIDE OUT IN HOLES.

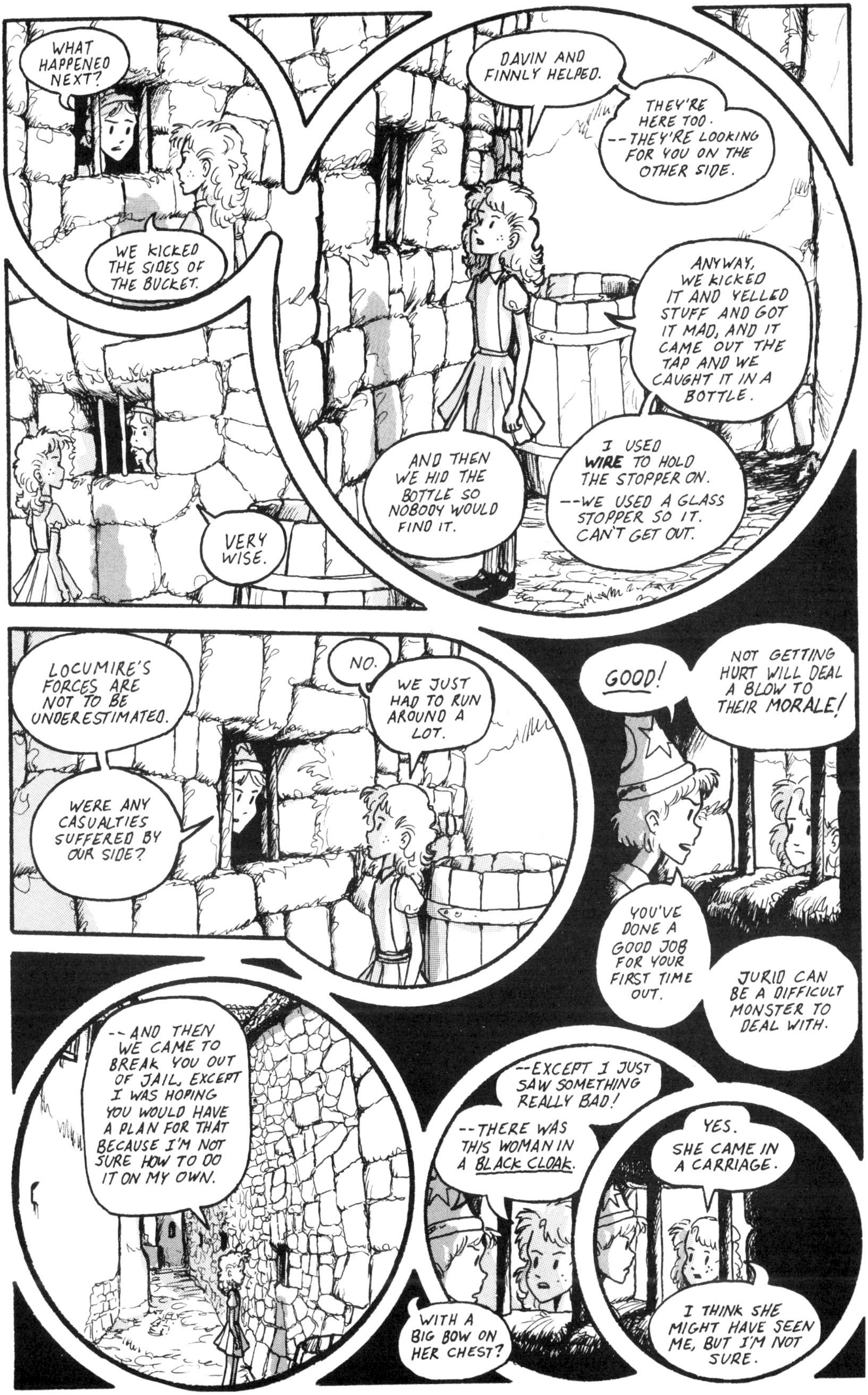
WHAT HAPPENED NEXT?
WE KICKED THE SIDES OF THE BUCKET.
DAVIN AND FINNLY HELPED.
THEY'RE HERE TOO. --THEY'RE LOOKING FOR YOU ON THE OTHER SIDE.
ANYWAY, WE KICKED IT AND YELLED STUFF AND GOT IT MAD, AND IT CAME OUT THE TAP AND WE CAUGHT IT IN A BOTTLE.
I USED WIRE TO HOLD THE STOPPER ON.
--WE USED A GLASS STOPPER SO IT CAN'T GET OUT.
AND THEN WE HID THE BOTTLE SO NOBODY WOULD FIND IT.
VERY WISE.
LOCUMIRE'S FORCES ARE NOT TO BE UNDERESTIMATED.
WERE ANY CASUALTIES SUFFERED BY OUR SIDE?
NO.
WE JUST HAD TO RUN AROUND A LOT.
GOOD!
NOT GETTING HURT WILL DEAL A BLOW TO THEIR MORALE!
YOU'VE DONE A GOOD JOB FOR YOUR FIRST TIME OUT.
JURID CAN BE A DIFFICULT MONSTER TO DEAL WITH.
--AND THEN WE CAME TO BREAK YOU OUT OF JAIL, EXCEPT I WAS HOPING YOU WOULD HAVE A PLAN FOR THAT BECAUSE I'M NOT SURE HOW TO DO IT ON MY OWN.
--EXCEPT I JUST SAW SOMETHING REALLY BAD!
--THERE WAS THIS WOMAN IN A BLACK CLOAK.
WITH A BIG BOW ON HER CHEST?
YES. SHE CAME IN A CARRIAGE.
I THINK SHE MIGHT HAVE SEEN ME, BUT I'M NOT SURE.

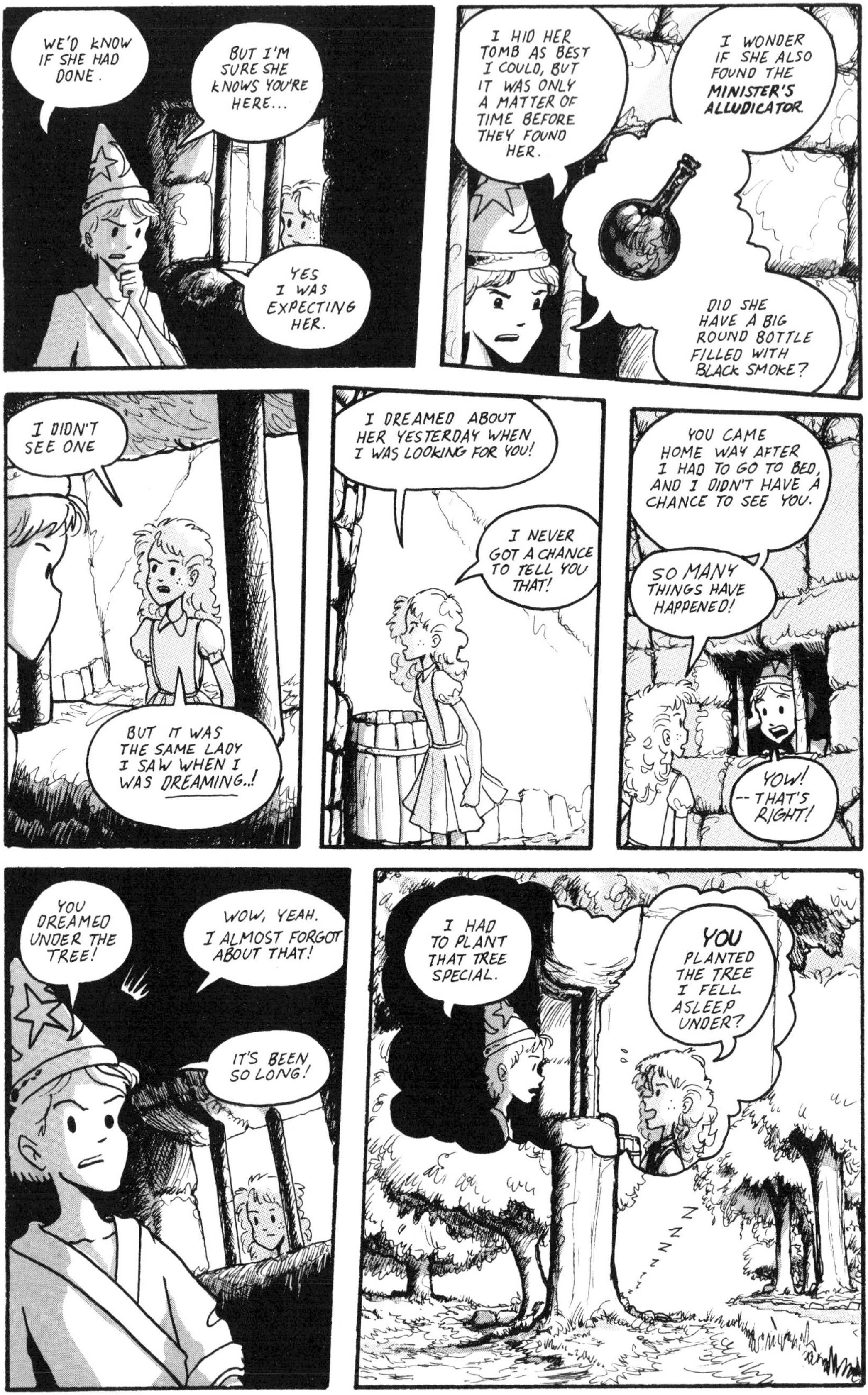
WE'D KNOW IF SHE HAD DONE.
BUT I'M SURE SHE KNOWS YOU'RE HERE...
YES I WAS EXPECTING HER.
I HID HER TOMB AS BEST I COULD, BUT IT WAS ONLY A MATTER OF TIME BEFORE THEY FOUND HER.
I WONDER IF SHE ALSO FOUND THE **MINISTER'S ALLUDICATOR**.
DID SHE HAVE A BIG ROUND BOTTLE FILLED WITH BLACK SMOKE?
I DIDN'T SEE ONE
BUT IT WAS THE SAME LADY I SAW WHEN I WAS DREAMING..!
I DREAMED ABOUT HER YESTERDAY WHEN I WAS LOOKING FOR YOU!
I NEVER GOT A CHANCE TO TELL YOU THAT!
YOU CAME HOME WAY AFTER I HAD TO GO TO BED, AND I DIDN'T HAVE A CHANCE TO SEE YOU.
SO MANY THINGS HAVE HAPPENED!
YOW! --THAT'S RIGHT!
YOU DREAMED UNDER THE TREE!
WOW, YEAH. I ALMOST FORGOT ABOUT THAT!
IT'S BEEN SO LONG!
I HAD TO PLANT THAT TREE SPECIAL.
YOU PLANTED THE TREE I FELL ASLEEP UNDER?
Z Z Z Z Z

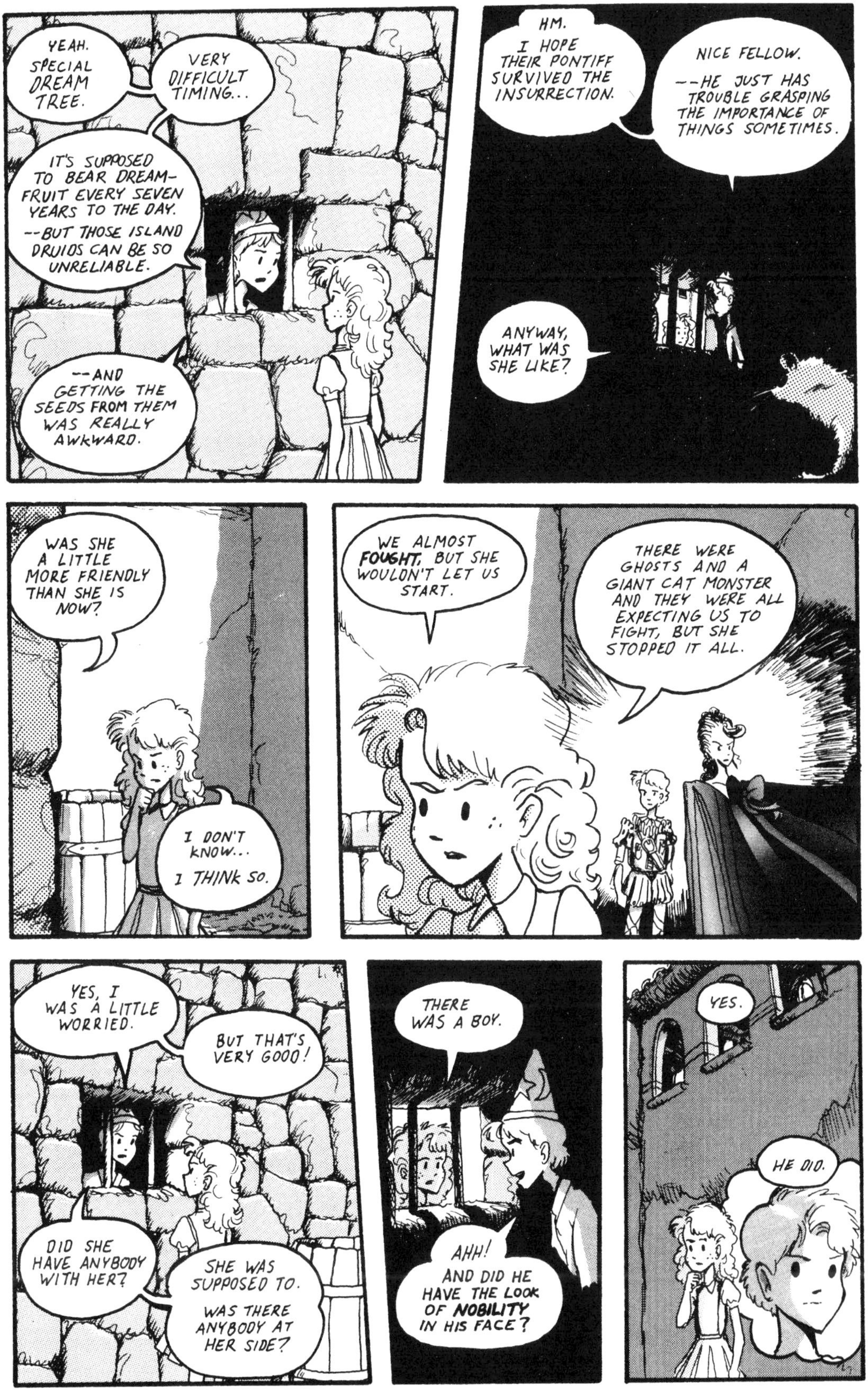
YEAH. SPECIAL DREAM TREE.
VERY DIFFICULT TIMING...
IT'S SUPPOSED TO BEAR DREAM-FRUIT EVERY SEVEN YEARS TO THE DAY.
--BUT THOSE ISLAND DRUIDS CAN BE SO UNRELIABLE.
--AND GETTING THE SEEDS FROM THEM WAS REALLY AWKWARD.
HM.
I HOPE THEIR PONTIFF SURVIVED THE INSURRECTION.
NICE FELLOW.
--HE JUST HAS TROUBLE GRASPING THE IMPORTANCE OF THINGS SOMETIMES.
ANYWAY, WHAT WAS SHE LIKE?
WAS SHE A LITTLE MORE FRIENDLY THAN SHE IS NOW?
I DON'T KNOW...
I THINK SO.
WE ALMOST FOUGHT, BUT SHE WOULDN'T LET US START.
THERE WERE GHOSTS AND A GIANT CAT MONSTER AND THEY WERE ALL EXPECTING US TO FIGHT, BUT SHE STOPPED IT ALL.
YES, I WAS A LITTLE WORRIED.
BUT THAT'S VERY GOOD!
DID SHE HAVE ANYBODY WITH HER?
SHE WAS SUPPOSED TO.
WAS THERE ANYBODY AT HER SIDE?
THERE WAS A BOY.
AHH!
AND DID HE HAVE THE LOOK OF NOBILITY IN HIS FACE?
YES.
HE DID.

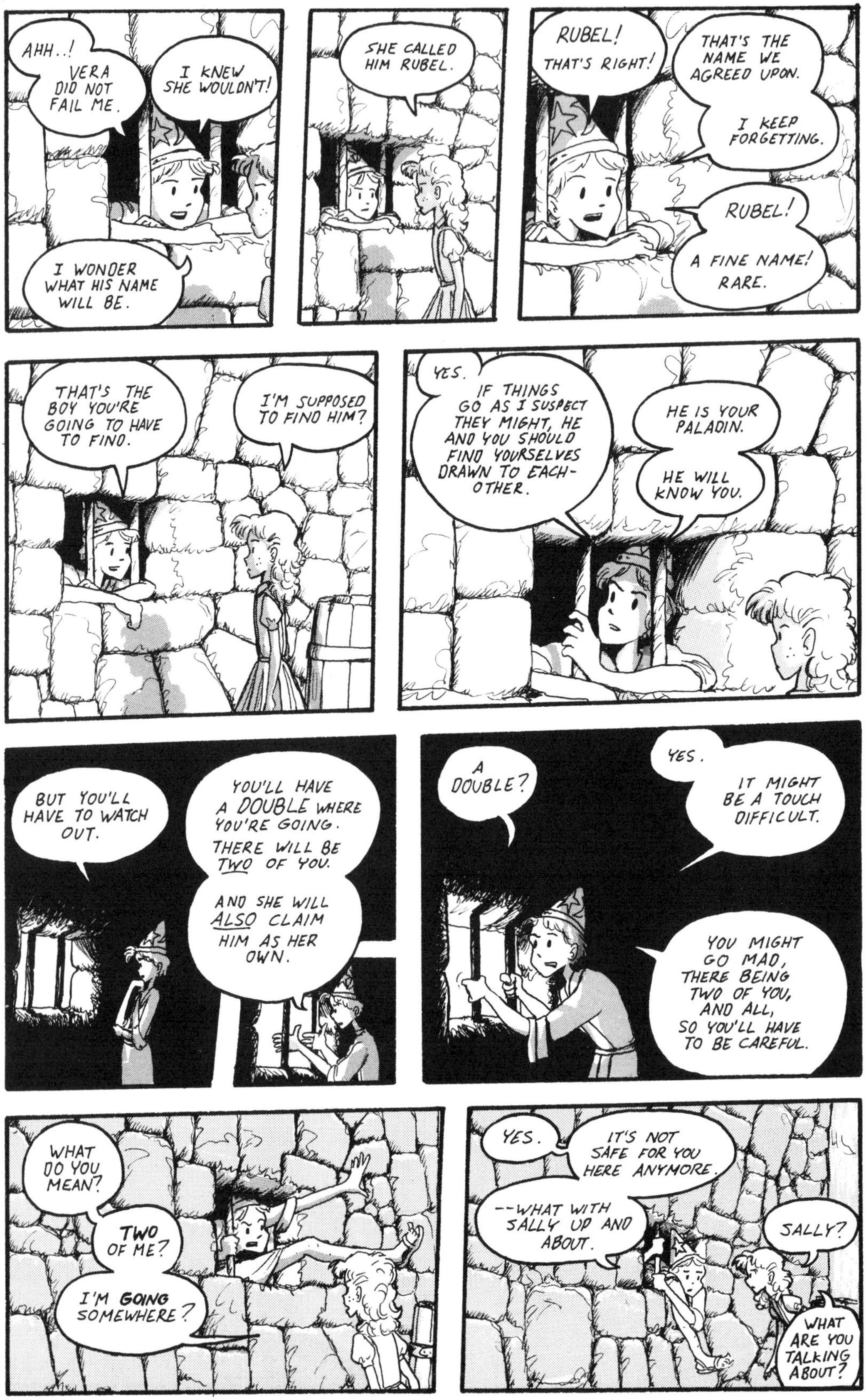

AHH..!
VERA DID NOT FAIL ME.
I KNEW SHE WOULDN'T!
I WONDER WHAT HIS NAME WILL BE.
SHE CALLED HIM RUBEL.
RUBEL! THAT'S RIGHT!
THAT'S THE NAME WE AGREED UPON.
I KEEP FORGETTING.
RUBEL!
A FINE NAME! RARE.
THAT'S THE BOY YOU'RE GOING TO HAVE TO FIND.
I'M SUPPOSED TO FIND HIM?
YES.
IF THINGS GO AS I SUSPECT THEY MIGHT, HE AND YOU SHOULD FIND YOURSELVES DRAWN TO EACH-OTHER.
HE IS YOUR PALADIN.
HE WILL KNOW YOU.
BUT YOU'LL HAVE TO WATCH OUT.
YOU'LL HAVE A DOUBLE WHERE YOU'RE GOING.
THERE WILL BE TWO OF YOU.
AND SHE WILL ALSO CLAIM HIM AS HER OWN.
A DOUBLE?
YES.
IT MIGHT BE A TOUCH DIFFICULT.
YOU MIGHT GO MAD, THERE BEING TWO OF YOU, AND ALL, SO YOU'LL HAVE TO BE CAREFUL.
WHAT DO YOU MEAN?
TWO OF ME?
I'M GOING SOMEWHERE?
YES.
IT'S NOT SAFE FOR YOU HERE ANYMORE.
--WHAT WITH SALLY UP AND ABOUT.
SALLY?
WHAT ARE YOU TALKING ABOUT?

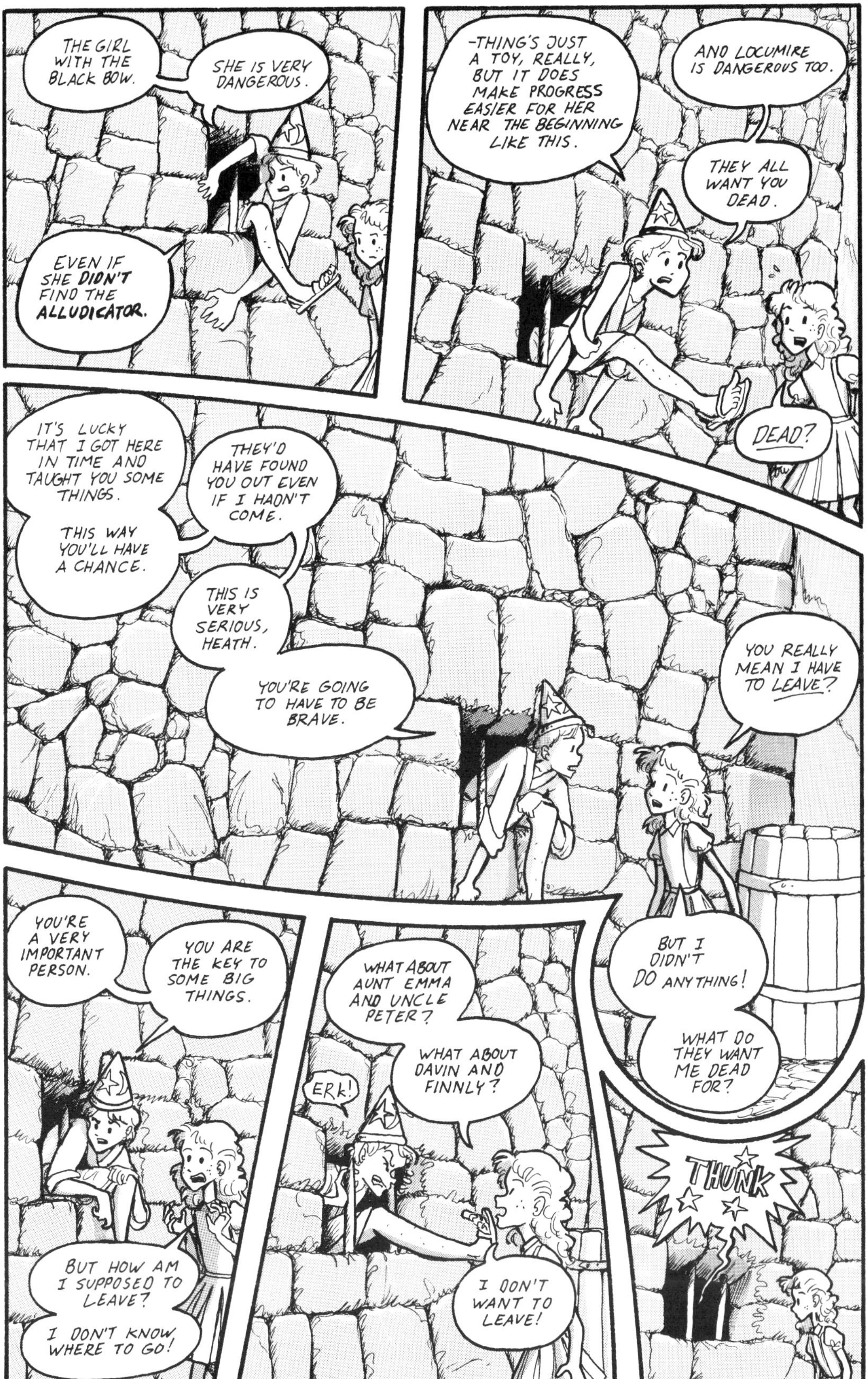
THE GIRL WITH THE BLACK BOW.
SHE IS VERY DANGEROUS.
EVEN IF SHE DIDN'T FIND THE ALLUDICATOR.
-THING'S JUST A TOY, REALLY, BUT IT DOES MAKE PROGRESS EASIER FOR HER NEAR THE BEGINNING LIKE THIS.
AND LOCUMIRE IS DANGEROUS TOO.
THEY ALL WANT YOU DEAD.
DEAD?
IT'S LUCKY THAT I GOT HERE IN TIME AND TAUGHT YOU SOME THINGS.
THIS WAY YOU'LL HAVE A CHANCE.
THEY'D HAVE FOUND YOU OUT EVEN IF I HADN'T COME.
THIS IS VERY SERIOUS, HEATH.
YOU'RE GOING TO HAVE TO BE BRAVE.
YOU REALLY MEAN I HAVE TO LEAVE?
BUT I DIDN'T DO ANYTHING!
WHAT DO THEY WANT ME DEAD FOR?
YOU'RE A VERY IMPORTANT PERSON.
YOU ARE THE KEY TO SOME BIG THINGS.
BUT HOW AM I SUPPOSED TO LEAVE?
I DON'T KNOW WHERE TO GO!
WHAT ABOUT AUNT EMMA AND UNCLE PETER?
WHAT ABOUT DAVIN AND FINNLY?
ERK!
I DON'T WANT TO LEAVE!
THUNK

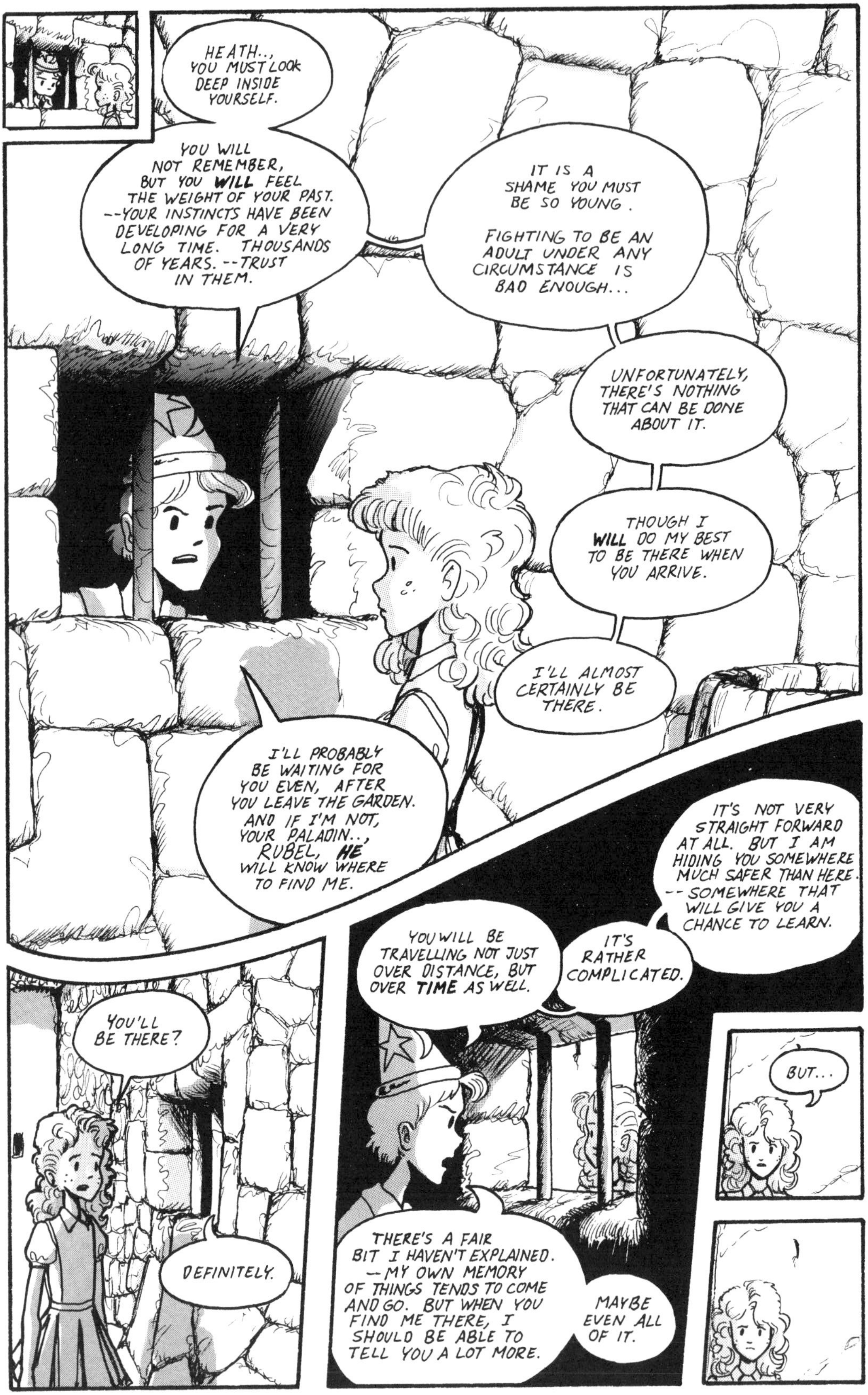
HEATH.., YOU MUST LOOK DEEP INSIDE YOURSELF.
YOU WILL NOT REMEMBER, BUT YOU **WILL** FEEL THE WEIGHT OF YOUR PAST. --YOUR INSTINCTS HAVE BEEN DEVELOPING FOR A VERY LONG TIME. THOUSANDS OF YEARS. --TRUST IN THEM.
IT IS A SHAME YOU MUST BE SO YOUNG.
FIGHTING TO BE AN ADULT UNDER ANY CIRCUMSTANCE IS BAD ENOUGH...
UNFORTUNATELY, THERE'S NOTHING THAT CAN BE DONE ABOUT IT.
THOUGH I **WILL** DO MY BEST TO BE THERE WHEN YOU ARRIVE.
I'LL ALMOST CERTAINLY BE THERE.
I'LL PROBABLY BE WAITING FOR YOU EVEN, AFTER YOU LEAVE THE GARDEN. AND IF I'M NOT, YOUR PALADIN.., RUBEL, **HE** WILL KNOW WHERE TO FIND ME.
YOU'LL BE THERE?
DEFINITELY.
YOU WILL BE TRAVELLING NOT JUST OVER DISTANCE, BUT OVER **TIME** AS WELL.
IT'S RATHER COMPLICATED.
IT'S NOT VERY STRAIGHT FORWARD AT ALL. BUT I AM HIDING YOU SOMEWHERE MUCH SAFER THAN HERE. --SOMEWHERE THAT WILL GIVE YOU A CHANCE TO LEARN.
THERE'S A FAIR BIT I HAVEN'T EXPLAINED. --MY OWN MEMORY OF THINGS TENDS TO COME AND GO. BUT WHEN YOU FIND ME THERE, I SHOULD BE ABLE TO TELL YOU A LOT MORE.
MAYBE EVEN ALL OF IT.
BUT...

BUT I DON'T UNDERSTAND.

I'VE ONLY BEEN HERE TWO YEARS.

AND AUNT EMMA SAYS IT'S OKAY TO CALL HER 'MOM'.

I KEEP ON GETTING MOVED AROUND. AND I JUST... HRK

I KNOW...

SOB

BUT THERE ISN'T ENOUGH TIME.

YOU SEE THAT RAIN BARREL?

SNIFF UH HUH.

THAT'S THE GATE. --IT'LL TAKE YOU THERE... TO A GARDEN.

NO BOTTOM?

IT SHOULD BE QUITE SIMPLE FOR YOU. YOU JUST HAVE TO GET IN AND SWIM DOWN. THERE'S NO BOTTOM IN THE BARREL. IT JUST GOES DOWN AND DOWN.

NOT FOR YOU. HOLD YOUR BREATH AND SWIM DOWN AND DOWN, AND THEN HALF WAY THERE, YOU'LL FIND YOURSELF SWIMMING UP INSTEAD. -- SO IT'S BETTER IF YOU GO IN HEAD-FIRST.

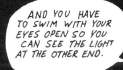

AND YOU HAVE TO SWIM WITH YOUR EYES OPEN SO YOU CAN SEE THE LIGHT AT THE OTHER END.

GO ONLY TOWARDS THE WHITE LIGHT.

THERE ARE OTHER PLACES YOU CAN GO DOWN THERE, AND I DON'T WANT YOU GOING TO ANY OF THEM.

-- JUST SWIM TO THE CLOSEST OPENING.

IT'LL BE THE BRIGHTEST.

CAN YOU KEEP YOUR EYES OPEN UNDER WATER?

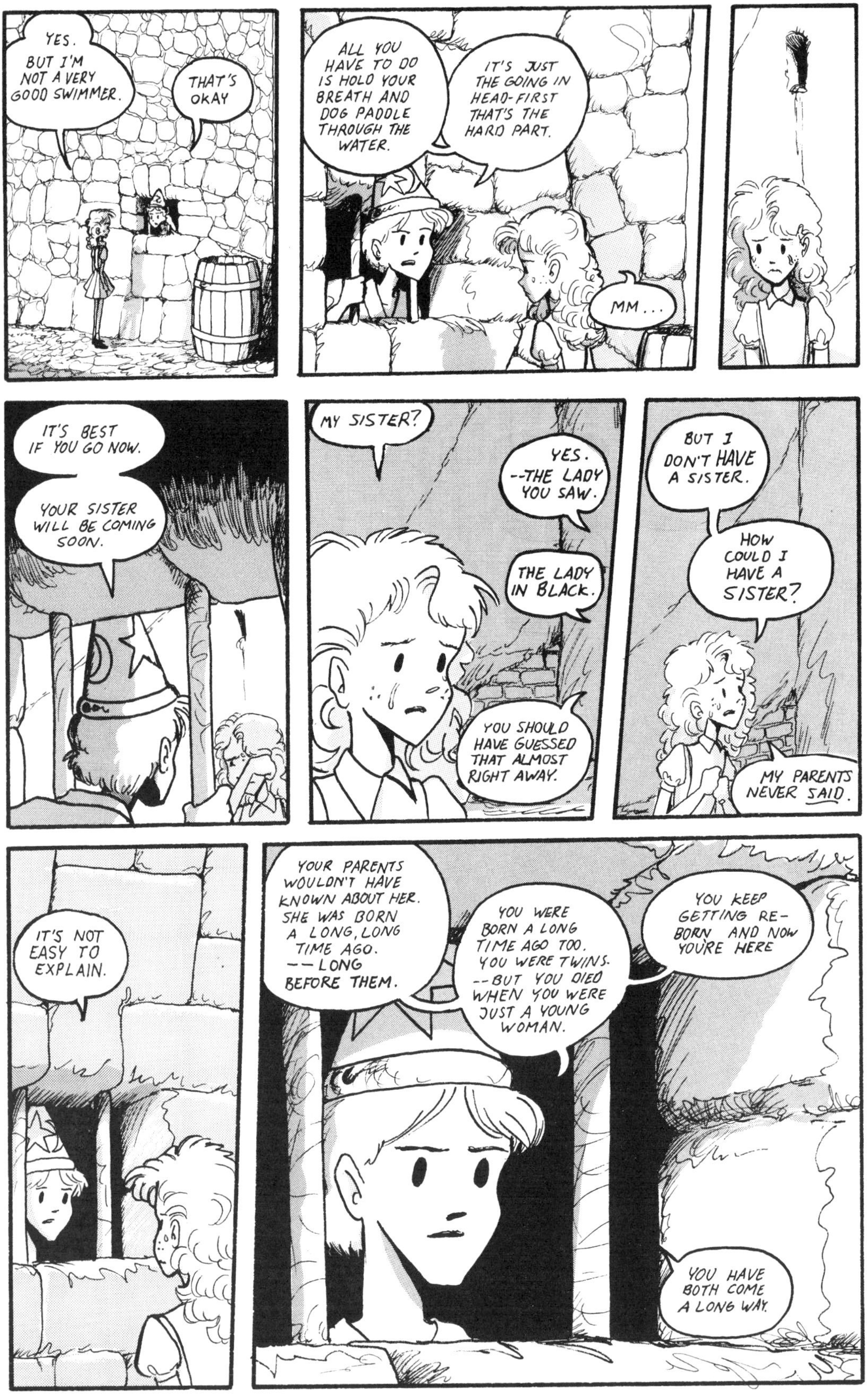
YES. BUT I'M NOT A VERY GOOD SWIMMER.
THAT'S OKAY
ALL YOU HAVE TO DO IS HOLD YOUR BREATH AND DOG PADDLE THROUGH THE WATER.
IT'S JUST THE GOING IN HEAD-FIRST THAT'S THE HARD PART.
MM...
IT'S BEST IF YOU GO NOW.
YOUR SISTER WILL BE COMING SOON.
MY SISTER?
YES. --THE LADY YOU SAW.
THE LADY IN BLACK.
YOU SHOULD HAVE GUESSED THAT ALMOST RIGHT AWAY.
BUT I DON'T HAVE A SISTER.
HOW COULD I HAVE A SISTER?
MY PARENTS NEVER SAID.
IT'S NOT EASY TO EXPLAIN.
YOUR PARENTS WOULDN'T HAVE KNOWN ABOUT HER. SHE WAS BORN A LONG, LONG TIME AGO. --LONG BEFORE THEM.
YOU WERE BORN A LONG TIME AGO TOO. YOU WERE TWINS. --BUT YOU DIED WHEN YOU WERE JUST A YOUNG WOMAN.
YOU KEEP GETTING RE-BORN AND NOW YOU'RE HERE
YOU HAVE BOTH COME A LONG WAY.

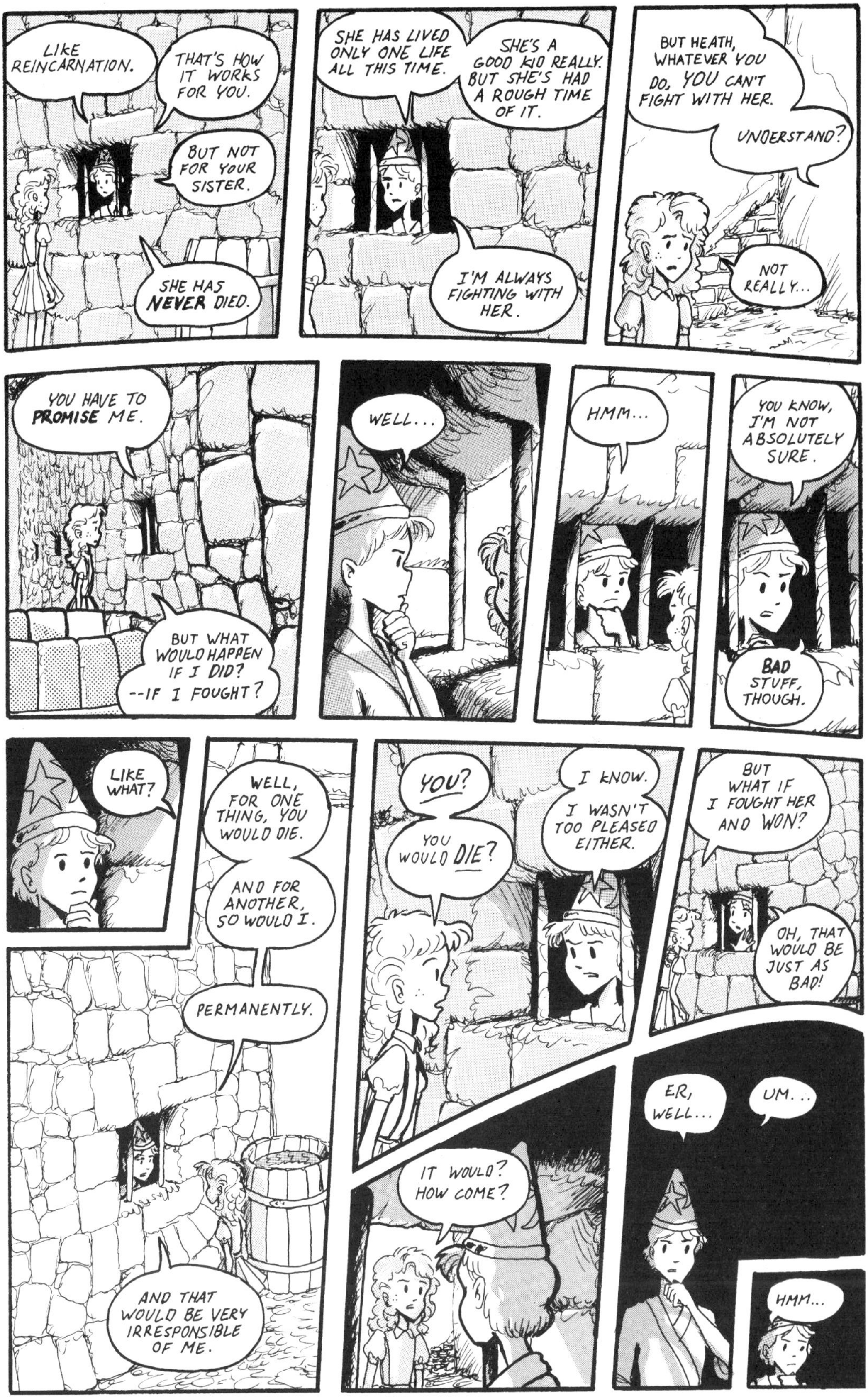
LIKE REINCARNATION.
THAT'S HOW IT WORKS FOR YOU.
BUT NOT FOR YOUR SISTER.
SHE HAS NEVER DIED.
SHE HAS LIVED ONLY ONE LIFE ALL THIS TIME.
SHE'S A GOOD KID REALLY. BUT SHE'S HAD A ROUGH TIME OF IT.
I'M ALWAYS FIGHTING WITH HER.
BUT HEATH, WHATEVER YOU DO, YOU CAN'T FIGHT WITH HER.
UNDERSTAND?
NOT REALLY...
YOU HAVE TO PROMISE ME.
BUT WHAT WOULD HAPPEN IF I DID? --IF I FOUGHT?
WELL...
HMM...
YOU KNOW, I'M NOT ABSOLUTELY SURE.
BAD STUFF, THOUGH.
LIKE WHAT?
WELL, FOR ONE THING, YOU WOULD DIE.
AND FOR ANOTHER, SO WOULD I.
PERMANENTLY.
AND THAT WOULD BE VERY IRRESPONSIBLE OF ME.
YOU?
YOU WOULD DIE?
I KNOW.
I WASN'T TOO PLEASED EITHER.
BUT WHAT IF I FOUGHT HER AND WON?
OH, THAT WOULD BE JUST AS BAD!
IT WOULD? HOW COME?
ER, WELL...
UM...
HMM...

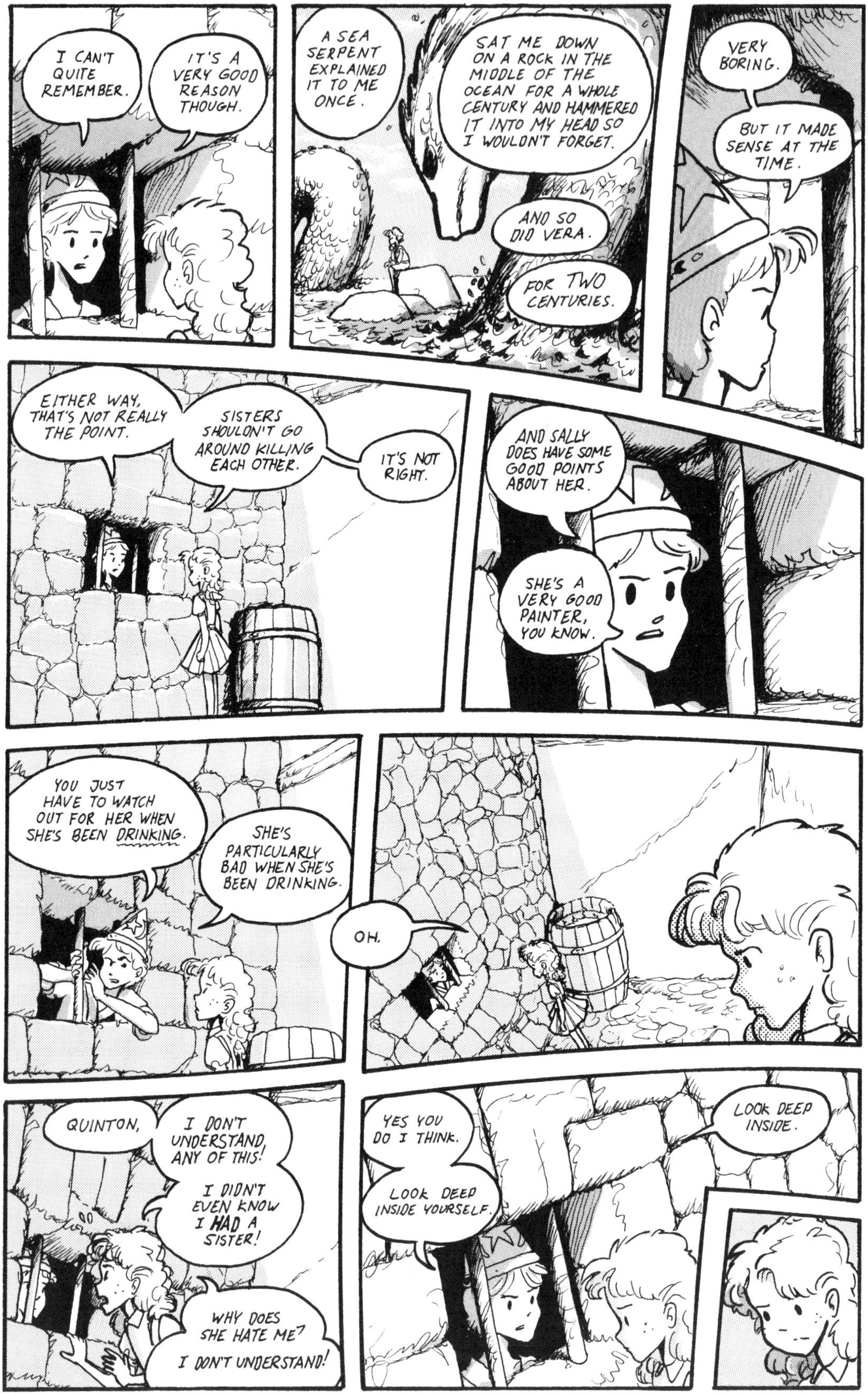
I CAN'T QUITE REMEMBER.
IT'S A VERY GOOD REASON THOUGH.
A SEA SERPENT EXPLAINED IT TO ME ONCE.
SAT ME DOWN ON A ROCK IN THE MIDDLE OF THE OCEAN FOR A WHOLE CENTURY AND HAMMERED IT INTO MY HEAD SO I WOULDN'T FORGET.
AND SO DID VERA.
FOR TWO CENTURIES.
VERY BORING.
BUT IT MADE SENSE AT THE TIME.
EITHER WAY, THAT'S NOT REALLY THE POINT.
SISTERS SHOULDN'T GO AROUND KILLING EACH OTHER.
IT'S NOT RIGHT.
AND SALLY DOES HAVE SOME GOOD POINTS ABOUT HER.
SHE'S A VERY GOOD PAINTER, YOU KNOW.
YOU JUST HAVE TO WATCH OUT FOR HER WHEN SHE'S BEEN DRINKING.
SHE'S PARTICULARLY BAD WHEN SHE'S BEEN DRINKING.
OH.
QUINTON,
I DON'T UNDERSTAND ANY OF THIS!
I DIDN'T EVEN KNOW I HAD A SISTER!
WHY DOES SHE HATE ME?
I DON'T UNDERSTAND!
YES YOU DO I THINK.
LOOK DEEP INSIDE YOURSELF.
LOOK DEEP INSIDE.

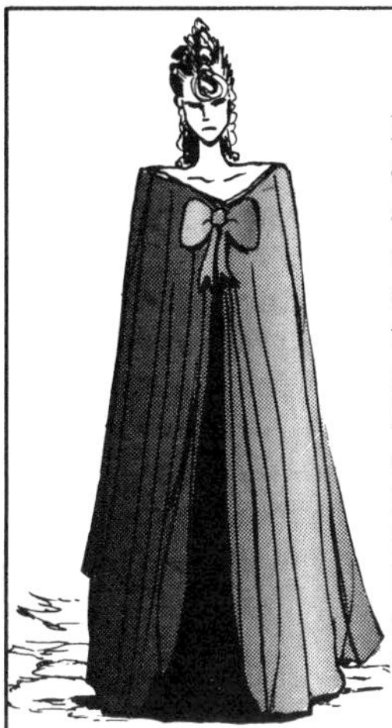

Heath looked deep, but could see nothing out of the ordinary, except that she was not at all happy about any of this. It had been fun and exciting just before she got here. It had been serious too, but somehow she believed that everything was going to be okay and that she and Davin and Finnly and Quinton were going to save the day together. Falling into this dizzy kind of thinking had been easy enough after the capture of Jurid, which really *was* a remarkable feat; far more than Heath knew or had been given credit for. Long ago, Jurid really *had* been called the Dawn Swallower, and though the beast was much weaker now, Heath by all rights should not have survived. She was very lucky.

She did not, however, have long to contemplate this because all at once, Soracia arrived.

Soracia. Sally. The Shadow Lady. Queen of Halves. Heath's dark sister. . . And the woman who would one day seek the company of a boy thief for comfort and relief, and perhaps friendship and love. All the same person, she strode down the alley-way with a countenance of ice and hatred and swirls of black magic which seemed to cause all the world to crash loose.

Heath and Soracia locked eyes, and for a moment the dark queen felt triumph pawing at her heart, knowing that Heath would be drawn into battle by forces which had grown nearly irresistible with the passing of the ages. —Especially irresistible for an inexperienced mortal child. But Heath, with an effort that made her gasp and clench her teeth, turned away and leaped toward the barrel. Soracia squinted at her sister, momentarily confused, and then realizing at once the danger, flew like a bat upon the barrel into which the girl was struggling.

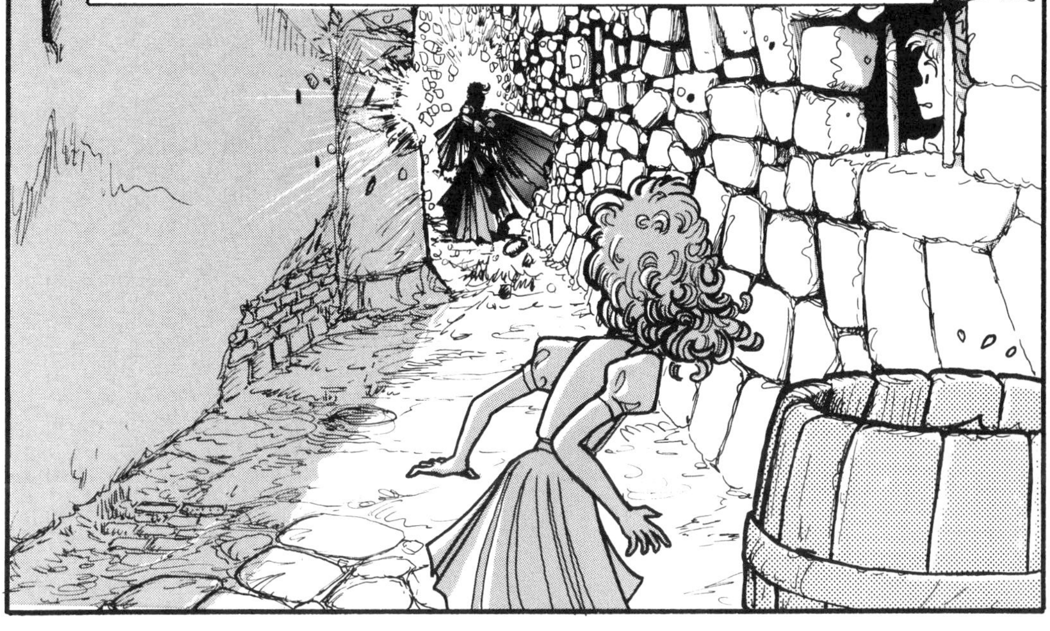

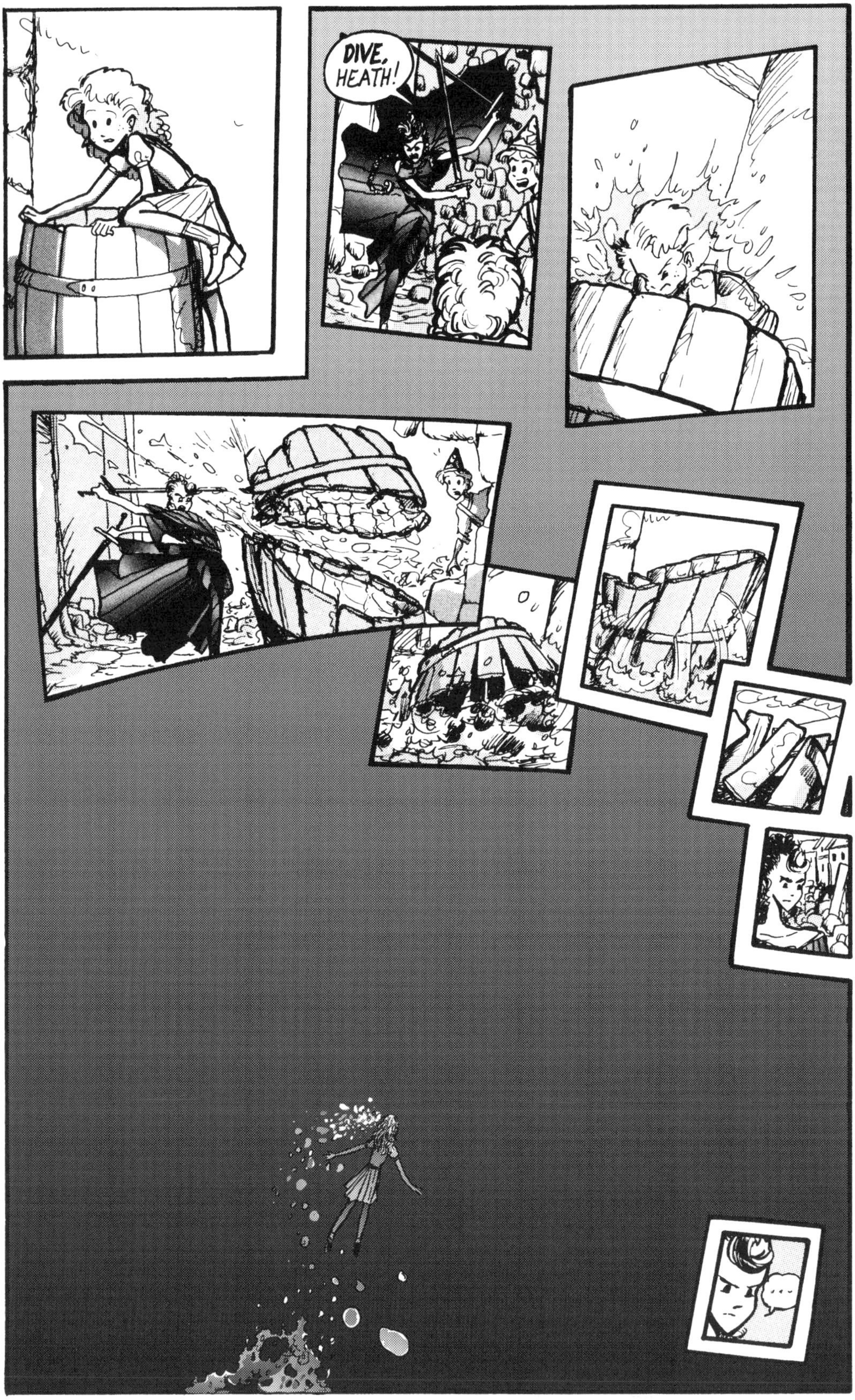
DIVE, HEATH!
...

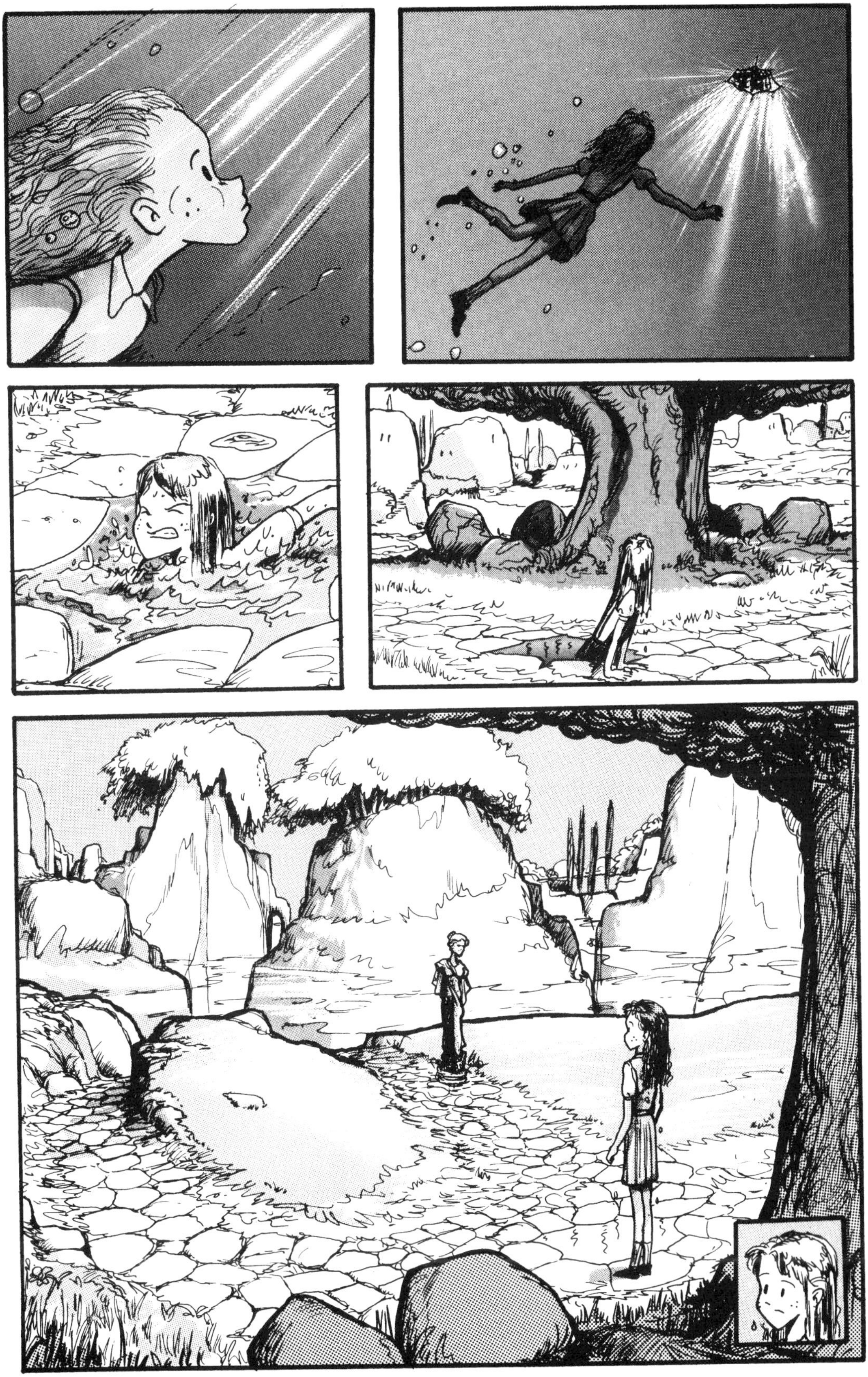